Music's Modern Muse

Eastman Studies in Music

Ralph P. Locke, Senior Editor
Eastman School of Music

(ISSN 1071–9989)

Music's Modern Muse:

A Life of Winnaretta Singer, Princesse de Polignac

Sylvia Kahan

®R University of Rochester Press

First published 2003
by the University of Rochester Press

The University of Rochester Press
668 Mt. Hope Avenue, Rochester, NY 14620, USA
Boydell & Brewer, Ltd.
P.O. Box 9, Woodbridge, Suffolk IP12 3DF, UK
www.urpress.com

ISBN 1–58046–133–6
ISSN 1071–9989

Library of Congress Cataloging-in-Publication Data
Kahan, Sylvia.
    Music's modern muse : a life of Winnaretta Singer, princesse de Polignac / Sylvia Kahan.
        p. cm. — (Eastman studies in music; ISSN 1071-9989 ; v. 22)
    Includes bibliographical references (p.) and index.
    ISBN 1-58046-133-6 (acid-free paper)
    1. Polignac, Winnaretta, princesse de, 1865–1943. 2. Music patrons—France—Biography. I. Title. II. Series.

    ML429.P645K34 2003
    780'.92–dc21   2003007785

British Library Cataloguing-in-Publication Data
A catalogue record for this book is available from the British Library

Designed and typeset by Straight Creek Bookmakers
Printed in the United States of America
This publication is printed on acid-free paper

To Prince Edmond de Polignac,
spiritual heir to his Tante Winnie's legacy

and to Princesse Edmond de Polignac, née Valéria Bohringer,
une très noble dame

Contents

Illustrations

Acknowledgments

This biography is an expansion of my doctoral dissertation, "The Princesse Edmond de Polignac (1865–1943): A Documentary Chronicle of Her Life and Artistic Circle" (City University of New York, 1993). I am indebted to my mentors from the CUNY Graduate Center, Joel Lester, Arbie Orenstein, and the late Barry Brook, for their guidance during my initial period of research.

The dissertation—and this subsequent book—could never have been realized without the help of three wonderful Frenchmen, all of whom have passed away in the decade since I completed my doctoral studies. The great grand-nephew of Winnaretta Singer-Polignac (WSP), the charming and delightful Prince Louis de Polignac, gave wings to my project by permitting me access to the combined music libraries of Edmond de Polignac, WSP, and Comtesse Jean (Marie-Blanche) de Polignac, a collection that includes the manuscripts of the works commissioned by WSP. The library (including the musical autographs) is now in a private collection. Prince Louis's staff in Monaco, Paris, and Brittany facilitated my research in many ways; for their kindness, I am grateful to Agnès Briffe, Janine Garrigue, Marie-Odile Maciotta, Colette Millo, and Françoise Penverne. Alain Ollivier, WSP's great-grandnephew on the Singer side, a man of exceptional warmth, generosity, and courage, gave me access to an important collection of letters addressed to WSP from composers, writers, scientists, and political and cultural figures. Finally, Doda Conrad, musician, impresario, and *raconteur extraordinaire,* provided marvelous information and insight into the behind-the-scenes relationships and workings of the Polignac circle. All three of these remarkable men, each of whom became cherished friends, are sorely missed.

After the death of Alain Ollivier, the collection of letters from public figures in his possession was donated to the Fondation Singer-Polignac in Paris. I am deeply indebted to the Fondation and its President, Édouard Bonnefous, for their encouragement and financial support; I am grateful as well to the Fondation's staff past and present, especially Mesdames Andrade, André, and Lemoine.

More than anyone else, Prince Edmond de Polignac, great-grandnephew and godson of WSP, and his wife Princesse Edmond, facilitated the successful completion of the work. They gave me unfettered access to family letters, diaries, and other primary documents, all of which make up a substantial portion of the text; additionally, they fed and sheltered me, and treated me as no less than an "honorary daughter." Their kindness, affection, and trust will never be forgotten.

I received no less "royal" treatment from various Singer descendants, especially the Duc and Duchesse Élie Decazes, who were my gracious hosts at the Palazzo Polignac in Venice, and Mrs. Gerald Selous, née Leeds, who provided me with invaluable information about the Singer family in England. Patrick and Joëlle Singer of Paris provided much-appreciated help, as did Singer descendants residing in New York: Édith de Montebello née Decazes and the late Georges de Montebello, and William Merritt Singer. It should be noted that there are more Polignac family letters and documents extant than there are on the Singer side. The fact, therefore, that the writings and anecdotes of more Polignac family members than Singer family members are included in this book is wholly circumstantial. I do not mean to slight the Singer side: the close and loving relationships that WSP maintained with her siblings and their offspring throughout her life were of vital importance to her.

I am grateful to the following institutions and people for granting permission to use material in the book: Armée du Salut, Paris; Archives départementales de la Nièvre, France; Artists' Rights Society, U.S.A.; Mme Claude Baugnies de Saint-Marceaux; Mme Nicole Berckmans; Lady Berkeley and The Lennox Berkeley Estate; Bibliothèque nationale de France; Mme Martine Boivin-Champeaux; Mme Denise Bouchet-Kervella; Princesse Eugénie de Brancovan; Marquise Séverine de Breteuil; The Britten-Pears Library, Aldeburgh, UK; Calvin Coolidge Foundation; Casalini Libri, Italy; Ms. Lisbeth Castelnuovo-Tedesco; Centre d'archives diplomatiques de Nantes, France; Mme Allegra Chapuis; Prince Philippe de Chimay; Dr. Myriam Chimènes; Cole Porter Trusts; David Higham Associates, UK; Éditions Fayard, Paris; Fondation Internationale Nadia et Lili Boulanger, Paris; Fondation Le Corbusier, Paris; Fondation Paul Sacher, Basel; Fondation Singer-Polignac, Paris; Mme Jean Françaix; Fundación Manuel de Falla, Grenada, Spain; G. Ray Hawkins Gallery, Los Angeles; Duc Antoine de Gramont; Comtesse Jacques d'Indy; Mme Hélène Joliot-Langevin; Kurt Weill Foundation, New York; M. Fritz Lehnhoff; Librairie Arthème-Fayard, Paris; Mariam Coffin Canaday Library, Bryn Mawr College, U.S.A.; M. Vaslav Markevitch; Mme Nathalie Mauriac-Dyer; New Directions Publishing Corporation, New York; The New York Public Library; John Phillips, Esq.; Prince Edmond de Polignac; Princeton University Library, U.S.A.; Princesse Mary de Rachewiltz; Royal Society of Literature Archives, Cambridge University Library, UK; Mme Judith Robinson-Valéry; Rutgers University, U.S.A.; Dr. Natalie de Saint-Marceaux-Guisset; M. André Schmidt; Commander and Mrs. Gerald Selous; Serge Prokofiev Archive, Goldsmiths College, London; Mme Rosine Seringe; Society of Authors, UK, Literary Representative of the Estates of Rosamond Lehmann and James Stephens; Maître Antoine Valéry; M. Eric Van Lauwe; M. Daniel de Vengohechea; Comtesse Bernard de Villele; Comte Patrice de Vogüé. Any errors or omissions in this list will be rectified in future editions.

Other family documents and anecdotal information vital to my research were generously provided by Sir Michael Berkeley, M. Hugues Cuénod, Sir

Charles Duff, Mme Rosamond Fellowes, Comte Gilles de Gastines, M. Bernard Gorgeu, Mr. Robert A. Letcher, M. Jacques Marsick, M. Benoît Maury, Mme Madeleine Milhaud, Prince Christian de Polignac, Mme Anne de Rambuteau, Mme Pierre-Henri Rigaud, Comte François Rozan, Comtesse Alix de Saxcé, Prince François de Scey-Montbéliard, Mr. William Merritt Singer, Sir Robert C. Synge, M. Yan-Pascal Tortelier, Mrs. Maureen Willson, Comtesse Jean de Vogüé, and Mme Carmen de Zayas d'Harcourt.

Librarians, curators, and archivists from many universities and other institutions were extremely helpful during my ten years of research. Chief among them was the incomparable Catherine Massip, director of the Music Department of the Bibliothèque nationale de France, to whom I owe an immeasurable debt of gratitude. No less helpful were her able staff members and colleagues at the BnF: Liliane Basque, Claudie Cabon, and Josiane Limousin-Corlay, as well as Pierre Vidal of the Bibliothèque de l'Opéra. Additionally, I wish to thank Kathleen Cann (Cambridge University Library, UK), Maggie Castellani (Kent State University Libraries, Ohio), Keiron Cooke and Jennifer Doctor (Britten-Pears Library, UK), Kendall Crilly (Yale University Music Library), Arnaud Dercelle (Fondation Le Corbusier, Paris), Joy Eldridge (University of Sussex Library, UK), Philip Errington (The John Masefield Society, London), Isabel de Falla (Fundación Manuel de Falla, Granada), Vincent Giroud (Beinecke Library, Yale University), Jane E. H. Hamilton (Agnew's of London), Dell Hollingsworth (Harry Ransom Humanities Research Center, University of Texas-Austin), Isobel Hunter (National Gallery, London), Kim Kowalke and David Stein (Kurt Weill Foundation, NY), Alexandra Laederich (Fondation International Nadia et Lili Boulanger, Paris), Régis Lecuyer (Archives du Palais Princier, Monaco), Jackie Lewis (Brighton Local Studies, UK), Noëlle Mann (Serge Prokofiev Archive, Goldsmiths College, University of London), Claire McKendrick (Glasgow University Library, UK), Harold L. Miller (State Historical Society of Wisconsin), Ulrich Mosch, Felix Meyer, Robert Piencikowski, and Johanna Blask (Paul Sacher Stiftung, Basel), John Shepard and David Chan (New York Public Library), Amélie Simier (Musée du Petit Palais, Paris), Julia Abel Smith (Royal Society of Literature, London), Caroline Szylowicz (Kolb-Proust Library, Champaign, IL), and Ornella Volta (Fondation Erik Satie, Paris). I also wish to thank Julia Mann, who assisted me with research in the Serge Prokofiev Archive, as well as C. Robert Spooler (St. John's Episcopal Church, NY), M. Pierre-Henri Guignard of the French Foreign Service, and Paul B. Williams of the Salvation Army (France).

A large number of musicologists, scholars, authors, and creative and performing artists, many of whom I am honored to call friends, shared with me not only other documents, but the fruits of their own research, as well as invaluable insights into the world of late nineteenth- and twentieth-century French music and culture. They are: Alexandra Anderson-Spivy, David Austin, Gabriel Badea-Päun, Bruno Berenguer, Barry Bergdoll,

Michael Bloch, Adrienne Fried Block, Ruth Brandon, the late Philip Brett, Myriam Chimènes, Michael Christoforidis, Margaret Cobb, Anne Conover, Blanche Wiesen Cook, Marcia Ewing Current, Mimi Daitz, Walter Frisch, Lynn Garafola, Jay Gottlieb, William Harris, Selina Hastings, Roy Howat, Phillip J. Kass, Nicole Labelle, the late R. W. B. Lewis, Cho Liang Lin, Christopher Lyndon-Gee, Claude Mignot-Ogliastri, Nesta Macdonald, Bernard Minoret, Edgar Munhall, Jean-Michel Nectoux, David Nice, Robert Orledge, Jann Pasler, Catherine Perry, Sabina Teller Ratner, Ned Rorem, Jan-Christoph Rößler, Philippe Rougier, Frédéric and Chantal Saffar, Carolyn Shuster-Fournier, Cécile Tardif, Richard Taruskin, Andrew Thomson, Charles Timbrell, J. Rigby Turner, Basil Twist, Stephen Walsh, and John R. A. Wilson.

Micheline Weisbroadt was an exemplary translator; Sylviane Louzoun was no less helpful with last-minute translations. Certain individuals offered help far above and beyond the call of duty. Dr. Linda de Cossart very kindly allowed me full access to the research materials and source notes used by her late husband Michael de Cossart in his book *The Food of Love*. Fritz Lehnhoff, an incomparable gentleman and friend, was an invaluable source of Singer family history and information about artistic and aristocratic culture. And genealogist Duncan Bray, director of Sovereign Ancestry, found key documents for me, unearthed in places where no one has gone before.

Conductor Bernard Tétu, pianist Noël Lee, and violist Karine Lethiec enabled me to hear and become familiar with the magnificent compositions of Prince Edmond de Polignac. Pascaline Maugat and Christine Taberlet, administrators of the Solistes de Lyon–Bernard Tétu, made these musical encounters possible.

Many friends on both sides of the Atlantic assisted me in incalculable ways, providing translations, interpretations, computer assistance, personal contacts, housing, transportation, and general moral support. For these and a hundred other kindnesses, I am grateful to Jean-Pierre and Marie-Hélène Babinot, Gisèle Bellew, Stéphane Birmant, Catherine Bréhier, Barbara Brooks, Christopher Bruhn, Michael-Thomas Gilman, Joshua Gordon, Anne Grenard, Charles-Efflam Heidsieck, Eric and Tanya Heidsieck, Richard Hundley, Alice Jaffe and Bernard Rose, Geraldine and John Kunstadter, Jeannette and Sylviane Louzoun, Ron and Linda Mayer, the late Ted McIrvine, Daniel Popesco, Michael Recchiuti, Karine Sansot, Joan Sapinsley and Richard Lewis, Morty Schiff, Arthur Reis e Sousa, Ruth Waterman, and Alethea Worden. Special thanks and affection are due to my Parisian friends Claudine Cibrélus, Marie-Michèle Banaletti, and Hugues Gavrel, who bore with Herculean fortitude, patience, and good humor my indefatigable approach to research and the frequent importunities that came with it.

My family has been an unflagging source of support ever since the day I uttered the improbable words: "I must go to Paris to meet a Prince." All my love and gratitude are due to my parents, Norman and Shirley Kahan, and to my siblings and their spouses, Eric Kahan and Elizabeth Goldfeder, and Judith and Michael Rowland.

I am more grateful than can be expressed for the wisdom and unfailing encouragement of Ralph Locke, Professor of Musicology at the Eastman School of Music and Senior Editor of Eastman Studies in Music, who helped me through some dark days. For their guidance and support, I am grateful to the staff of the University of Rochester Press, especially Mark Klemens, Tim Madigan, Molly Cort, and Susan Dykstra-Poel; and to John Blanpied and Louise Goldberg. They have all been wonderful every step of the way.

Finally, this book could never have come to fruition without the complicity and precious friendship of Peter Kurth, who understood Winnie as I did and indispensably helped bring her to life.

A Note on Translation

All translations into English, from both original and secondary sources, are my own unless otherwise noted.

Introduction

This book is first and foremost a study of a remarkable life in music. The daughter of sewing machine industrialist Isaac Merritt Singer, Winnaretta Singer-Polignac (WSP) used her colossal fortune to champion the cause of musical modernism. She commissioned over twenty pieces of new music, providing important opportunities to composers such as Chabrier, Fauré, Stravinsky, Satie, Falla, and Poulenc at critical junctures in their careers. Many works commissioned by and dedicated to her received their first performances in her salon, which also showcased any number of world-class instrumentalists and singers. No less important are the great number of good works done on behalf of art, literature, and the sciences, to say nothing of her underwriting of public housing and other social service projects.

WSP's prescience in her choice of musical and artistic projects was re-markable: she always seemed to be one step ahead of musical trends. She was an ardent Wagnerite before idolatry of the German and his music swept through the French artistic community, and she championed Debussy's music at a time when it was still considered to be "unhealthy." Her commissions of works for chamber ensembles came from her insight, first articulated in 1912, "that, after Richard Wagner and Richard Strauss, the days of big orchestras were over and that it would be delightful to return to a small orchestra of well chosen players and instruments."[1]

In the present work, WSP's long-lasting influence on twentieth-century music will be examined at length, but I would like to point out two seminal ways in which she changed the course of the art of her time. First, two of her artistic preferences—a love of the music of J. S. Bach, and her fascina-tion with Hellenic language and culture—led directly to the rise of what is broadly called "neoclassicism" in music. Maurice Ravel's popular 1899 piano work, *Pavane pour une infante défunte*, a model of Apollonian cool-ness and calm, foreshadowed this trend. More important still was Erik Satie's *Socrate*, with texts by Plato, commissioned by WSP in 1918, a sig-nificant marker in modernist music; this influential piece would lead other composers directly along the path towards a compositional style that would inform musical composition for the next two decades. Stravinsky's Piano Sonata (a work dedicated to WSP) and Germaine Tailleferre's Piano Con-certo (a commissioned work) would each manifest fully this new direction.

Second, the music that WSP helped bring into being bears almost no resemblance to the conventional definition of "salon music" today: forget-table, superficial *bonbons* of a faded era. On the contrary, WSP had it in mind to develop a new genre: great music for a small space by up-and-coming composers. The term "small space" is relative: some of the music rooms in the homes of the aristocracy and the *haute bourgeoisie* were actually the size of small concert halls. Winnaretta's *atelier* held one hundred people comfortably; her larger music salon seated two hundred. Yet, the fact that these composers were asked to write music for performance in intimate—non-public—surroundings influenced both the scope and the substance of their scores. In numerous instances, the constraints imposed by the patron inspired the composers to seek out new creative solutions that, in some cases, had a major impact both on their artistic development and on public perceptions of their music. A good case in point is Manuel de Falla's *El Retablo de Maese Pedro* (1923). Based on a text from Cervantes's *Don Quixote,* the work was long in its gestation, the composer struggling with the need to balance musical-theatrical flamboyance with the small dimensions of the space in which the work would be presented. Considered one of the composer's masterworks, the *Retablo* positions archaic elements (the harpsichord) alongside modernist elements (placement of the "voices" of the life-sized marionettes amidst the instruments of the chamber orchestra, disembodied from the figures). The "chamber" dimensions of the work and their impact on the finished product elicited this reaction from eminent critic Boris de Schloezer after its Paris public debut:

> [Falla's *Retablo* is] a veritable masterpiece of taste, grace, and feeling, where the rigor and the exactitude of the musical realization are allied with a diversity and a vigor of expression made all the more remarkable because the means put in play are extremely modest: a small orchestra (winds and brass), harpsichord, harp-lute and three soloists. But these elements are treated with such tact and ease that, without ever forcing the voice and by always giving the impression that he remains beneath the limits he has imposed upon himself and could do still more, Falla arrives at this elegantly equilibrated plenitude—this vigorous grace, which is, in art, one of the most precious and rare things that exists.[2]

The path of great art, however, like that of true love, never did run smooth. The trials and tribulations of bringing commissions into being were many. WSP was a determined, indomitable woman. In many cases, it was only because of her energy and indefatigability that the commissions were ever fulfilled at all. Those traits had their costs, of course: WSP's energy often became relentlessness; her indefatigability often caused her to ride roughshod over the feelings and capabilities of the artists under her "protection." A challenge to present and future WSP biographers is to find a way of understanding the motivations and actions of an enigmatic and difficult woman, a woman who made little effort to be understood, and made even less effort to be likeable. But it is this very complexity, this "warts-and-all" fearlessness, coupled with an astonishing ability to take advantage of and play within the social systems in effect during her lifetime that make WSP such a unique, fascinating character to contemplate.

Another intriguing aspect of WSP's life and legacy is the wide chasm between her renown as a *grande mécène*—a great patron—and her reputation as a "famous lesbian." Partly because of her wealth, partly because of her problematic personality, WSP's personal and sexual history has generated as much story-telling as her patronage activities. Because she is so inscrutable, she is exactly the sort of biographical subject that lends itself easily to becoming a mirror of the writer's desires: that which is laudable is magnified; that which causes discomfort is either excised or gossiped about with cruelty and malice; that which appears larger than life is raised to the level of legend. In the absence of hard information, her wealth, her willful independence, and especially her sexuality have made WSP's life an easy target for rumor and gossip, even up to the present day.

And hard information, on these as on other crucial aspects of WSP's life and activities, was essentially not available to scholars until recently. Winnaretta Singer-Polignac's own "Memoirs," published posthumously in 1945 in *Horizon* magazine, while often enlightening and always fascinating, are full of factual and temporal errors—not surprising, since many of the events therein were recalled at a remove of more than fifty years. Until now, the only full-length biography of the Princesse de Polignac was Michael de Cossart's *The Food of Love: Princesse Edmond de Polignac (1865–1943) and Her Salon* (London: Hamish Hamilton, 1978), subsequently translated into French as *Une Américaine à Paris* (Paris: Plon, 1979). Mr. Cossart's research and large bibliography provided a helpful starting point for my own research. However, though considered in its day a laudable effort to recount a complicated life, and widely cited as a reliable source ever since, *The Food of Love* suffers both from its author's lack of access to vital primary documents and also from his willingness to report, uncritically, rumors and outlandish stories—particularly those related to its subject's sexuality. Those kinds of stories are better taken as testimony to the aura of WSP than as a carefully sifted account of her likely activities, thoughts, and feelings.

The stance of the present biography is that WSP's lesbianism was a fact of her life. No theorizing is offered beyond that. While there may exist a "queer reading" to be gleaned from this material, it must be left to a future author. I do, however, address some of the issues related to WSP's sexuality that directly affected her patronage activities. My jumping-off point is Philip Brett's article, "Musicality, Essentialism, and the Closet," in the collection of essays on gay musicology, *Queering the Pitch*. As Brett suggests, music for the young Winnaretta Singer became a means to channel her feelings and at the same time gain the approbation of a revered father and an emotionally distant mother. Music has long been considered as an agent of moral ambiguity, a conduit for feelings that are "different, irrational, unaccountable."[3] It is not a stretch, then, for society to regard a musical person as being in some way "deviant." Musicality may function as a symbol for, or a displacement of those feelings.

> For the musician in general, and particularly for the gay or lesbian musician, there is an involvement in a social contract that allows comforting deviance only at the sometimes bitter price of sacrificing self-determination. . . . Music is a perfect field for the display of emotion. It is particularly accommodating to those who have difficulty in expressing feelings in day-to-day life, because the emotion is unspecified and unattached. The piano, let us say for example, will thus become an important means for the attempt at expression, disclosure, or communication on the part of those children who have difficulties of various kinds with one or both parents. To gay children, who often experience a shutdown of all feeling as the result of sensing their parents' and society's disapproval of a basic part of their sentient life, music appears as a veritable lifeline.[4]

WSP epitomized this concept, and it is in this context that her homosexuality is discussed.

The concept of the homosexual closet may in fact be extended within this context to be applicable to the Polignac salon itself. In an era predating gay identity (a late twentieth-century construct), the musical salon may have provided a means for homosexuals to interact with other homosexuals in sensually pleasing *and* socially acceptable circumstances. One could even assert that, given the erotic nature of much of the music of that era, attendance at private musical gatherings served as a sublimation of, or substitute for, sexual activity. In WSP's case, given the extent to which music served as a psychological refuge, the notion can be advanced that her salon was her closet, a place of safety, of mediation within the rigidly structured world of Parisian aristocracy. WSP's salon/closet was not a confined or confining interior space; rather, it was a haven, a warm, opulent studio (with all the creative and experimental connotations attached to the word), the favored room in a Paris mansion. WSP's salon was completely under her control, where she could hide in plain sight, and which offered a "comfort zone" not only to her, but to the other homosexual friends in her milieu.

A second area of inquiry is the putative homosexual "inner circle" of the Princesse de Polignac. The scholar and writer Elizabeth Wood, author of the article "Sapphonics" in *Queering the Pitch*, presents the following idea: "The princess . . . was central to a well-financed urban artistic community, a homosexual subculture in Paris . . . whose members actively promoted and performed one another's work."[5] Wood implies that WSP championed the work of certain homosexual composers and performers, not only on the intrinsic merits of the works, but because of the artists' sexual preferences and proclivities. But was there in fact an inner circle whose homosexual members were given preferential treatment over composers and performing artists who were not homosexual? The answer appears to be "no." The notion that WSP showed any bias, overt or covert, towards gay artists, in terms of who received financial help or other support (introductions to conductors, impresarios, or theater directors, for example) cannot be substantiated by the evidence. Examination of programs, newspapers reports, collections of letters, and diaries does not reveal any favoritism towards homosexuals or their art. Of the seventeen composers who received one or more commissions to create new works for the salon, four were gay, bisexual, or "queer": Igor Markevitch, Erik Satie, Francis Poulenc, and Henri Sauguet. A commission offered to Karol Szymanowski did not come to fruition, nor did one offered to Maurice Ravel, whose sexual inclination remains uncertain. If there was any methodology at all to WSP's choices of composers from whom to commission music, it remains elusive. Why Fauré and not Debussy? Why Sauguet and not Auric? Why Tailleferre and not Smyth?

Of course, gay, lesbian, and bisexual composers were fixtures in the Polignac salon—among them Pierre de Bréville, Reynaldo Hahn, Camille Saint-Saëns, and Ethel Smyth—as were many of the numerous performing artists heard there, including Pierre Bernac, Renata Borgatti, Doda Conrad, Léon Delafosse, Jacques Février, Reynaldo Hahn, Clara Haskil, Vladimir Horowitz, and Wanda Landowska. The great impresario Serge Diaghilev and the choreographers, dancers, and scenic and costume artists of the Ballets Russes were frequent beneficiaries of the Princesse de Polignac's largesse, as were numerous librettists, poets, and journalists associated with music, including Jean Cocteau, Colette, Marcel Proust, and Paul Verlaine. But the presence of many gay composers and performers in WSP's salon does not appear to have an overarching meaning: the same musicians and other artists were the ones sought after in *all* the important salons, as sought after as the many heterosexual composers and performers whom WSP also hired (and whom Wood does not mention).[6] It was the artistic gifts of the individuals, and nothing else—not their sexuality, not the influence of friends and associates (even the much-beloved Nadia Boulanger could not always influence the Princesse to support her protégés), not even their financial need—that inspired WSP to favor this or that composer or performer.

If the theory of the homosexual salon cannot readily be substantiated, it is, on the other hand, much easier to make the case for WSP's proto-feminist leanings. While WSP would probably never have considered herself or called herself a feminist, the aggregate of her activities on behalf of women speaks clearly. WSP championed, and financially underwrote, the creative undertakings of numerous women, including, among others, the composers Adela Maddison, Marcelle de Manziarly, Ethel Smyth, Germaine Tailleferre, and Armande de Polignac; the performing musicians Renata Borgatti, Marya Freund, Clara Haskil, Olga Rudge, Marie-Blanche de Polignac, Blanche Selva, and, most especially, Nadia Boulanger; the dancers Isadora Duncan and Loïe Fuller; the scientist Marie Curie; and the writers Augustine Bulteau, Anna de Noailles, and Colette. While not officially supporting the British suffragette movement, she gave discreet aid to its members, including Emmeline Pankhurst and Ethyl Smyth. WSP made special efforts to insure the financial well-being and security of her nieces; her estate and the disposition of her legacy was left entirely in the hands of the next generation of Singer women.

A final important area to be examined is WSP's marriage to Edmond de Polignac. Extant love letters from husband to wife, and letters from the widowed Princesse de Polignac to her relatives and friends, leave no doubt as to the profound attachment that existed between the two. Given that the marriage did not include a physical component, music became the symbol, the actualization, of their love. Here, too, the salon served as a substitute for sex. In his wife, Edmond found a loving friend who genuinely admired and championed his compositions. WSP put all of her formidable energy and passion into the development of her salon, with the express purpose of promoting her husband's music. The emotional fulfillment her marriage to the Prince brought her thus becomes a central issue in the examination of her lesbian relationships. It is possible that these relationships with women included companionship, artistic communion, and good friendship, as well as just plain sex. Regardless of her own erotic hungers and the manifestation of them, the overarching engine of her psyche was the love of her father and her husband. Her life's legacy—especially through the medium of music—was the celebration of that love.

Prelude

The woman sat in front of the fireplace on that chilly October day, watching the hungry flames lick the stone walls. Her son was at her side, the piles and piles of letters stacked at their feet. She was about to carry out the dictates of her aunt's last will and testament.

> All personal papers and documents which I possess in my town house, Avenue Henri-Martin and Rue Cortambert, shall be handed to my niece . . . who shall have free disposition thereof. My Testamentary Executor shall particularly see to this. . . .
>
> I ask my Testamentary Executor to destroy all my letters and papers. . . .

The will had authorized "the autograph letters of celebrated persons" to be spared. These were separated out first. But then the woman started to read what she had promised to destroy. It was heartrending: so many testimonials to such a full, rich, complicated life, destined for the fire.

Her aunt had been one of the most famous women in Europe, lauded in her adopted country of France for the generosity with which she supported charitable causes, for her efforts on behalf of the arts, sciences, and letters, and most especially for her initiatives on behalf of music from all ages, on behalf of modern music in particular, initiatives that had earned her the title of *la Grande Mécène,* the Great Patron of modern music.

But her aunt had also been inscrutable, sphinx-like. No one really knew her. And not everyone in her family or her husband's family had liked her. Some had been jealous; some had found her private life scandalous; not a few had wished for her social downfall. One nephew had described the aunt that he called *la silencieuse*—the silent one—in the most uncomplimentary of terms.

> When I'm there, she shuts herself up "in the silence of the infinite spaces."
> . . . I offer her a newspaper, in which she takes refuge; I pick up mine. I don't speak to her, she says nothing to me, and this is how our charming conversation is pursued.

And yet that same nephew's wife had understood her aunt better, and had seen through the impenetrable, glacial gaze, an unhappy side effect of her terrible shyness.

> Tante Winnie! What a wound to our hearts, this death of our great friend. Great was the word that applied to her remarkable personality. She was great in intelligence and in heart, which the initiated discov-

ered, behind her cold expression, was so rich in tenderness. You remember when her steely eyes became blue, such a soft blue. . . .

Winnaretta Singer, the Princesse de Polignac, wished to be remembered not for who she was, but for what she had accomplished. She wished for the buildings that she had built, the studies and research that she had underwritten, and most especially the music that she had commissioned to be her lasting legacy. For the world of sound that she loved and that protected her, her energy had been positive, determined, indefatigable.

But to allow others to see through the fears behind her strength, the cracks in her courage—no, that the Princesse de Polignac could not allow, not in life, not in death.

And so with compassion and regret, the woman consigned the documentary vestiges of her aunt's life, those that Winnaretta herself had kept tucked away, to the flames.

But Winnaretta Singer-Polignac had been too famous, too loved, too hated—too *memorable*—to be able to will herself out of memory. Innumerable people—from family members to famous musicians, writers, and artists—had kept her letters, written down her dryly humorous anecdotes, kept the rapid and insightful little drawings that she had sketched one day on a hillside, another day in a gondola, in a hotel, on a concert program. . . .

The following history has been constructed from the pages the fires did not consume.

1

An International Child

Winnaretta Singer-Polignac, as befitted a future princess, was born in The Castle, a sumptous mansion situated on a hundred acres of parkland perched above a river. The Castle boasted room after room filled with the most elegant and costly furnishings that money could buy. A battalion of servants bustled through the house, attending to the needs of family members and guests. The large stable contained, in addition to horses and sleighs, a canary-yellow carriage that could transport thirty-one people.

What was unusual about the Singer Castle was its location: not in Sussex, or the Loire Valley, or in Bavaria, but in Yonkers, a northern suburb of New York City. Winnaretta's parents were not royalty, and in fact both came from humble backgrounds. And yet both father and mother came to be known in every corner of the globe—he for his family name, which was seen in millions of households, emblazoned on the machine that he had perfected and manufactured, the Singer sewing machine; she because of her beautiful face, which was rumored to have inspired sculptor Frédéric Bartholdi in creating the Statue of Liberty, the world's most visible woman. How could a child grow to equal—or surpass—such parents?

Winnaretta Singer was her father's twentieth child. In all, Isaac Merritt Singer would father twenty-four children from two legal and three common-law marriages. Although he would disavow all liaisons prior to his marriage with Winnaretta's mother, Singer acknowledged every single one of his children by name in his will and left each of them a handsome bequest. Like Paul Bunyan of American folklore, Isaac Singer lived a life of fantastic, even mythic proportions. His life bespoke big dreams, outsized curiosity, bold actions, enormous wealth, and huge appetites.

Winnaretta's godfather was Edward Harrison May, the English-born, French-trained American artist, best known at that time for his contribution to the 1851 "Grand Moving Panorama of the Pilgrim's Progress." Moving panoramas were paintings hundreds of feet long, unrolled across a stage in "scenes." Their stories, travelogues or epic tales, were accompanied by narration and music. These mid-nineteenth century "blockbusters" of visual art toured from city to city, attracting thousands of paying spectators, earning May over $100,000. He and Singer had been friends for years. They had much in common: both were purveyors of modernism for the masses. May was a fitting choice of godfather to a little girl who would eventually devote her life to the patronage of modernist music and art, and who found perpetual delight in being surrounded by talented non-conformists. "Everywhere I go," she would write to one friend, "I continue to meet remarkable and sublime beings created especially for me."[1]

Isaac Singer was born in Schagticoke, in Rensselaer County, New York, on 27 October 1811, to Adam Singer, a German immigrant, and his American wife. The young boy spent his earliest years in the most wretched poverty. When his mother died, his father remarried, and Isaac, who disliked his stepmother, left home at the age of twelve, never to return.[2] As a young man he was unusually handsome, of imposing physical appearance, well over six feet tall, brawny, with bright red hair and a penetrating gaze. These attractive traits were offset by a loud and often exceedingly foul mouth. However, he was intellectually quick, and from a young age manifested a predilection for experimentation and invention with simple elements— wood, wire, pieces of sheet-iron, whatever was available. His real love, however, was the theater, and he dreamed of a career on the stage. His mechanical abilities gave him an opportunity to earn a living until such time as he could realize his dreams of fame.

After leaving home, Isaac maintained himself doing mechanical work, spending his free time studying to be an actor. He joined a theatrical road company, quickly graduating from small walk-on parts to the title role in *Richard III*. Later he formed his own troupe, the Merritt Players, and toured—as the starring actor—throughout the Eastern and Midwestern States. For twenty years he lived a dirt-poor existence, traveling with all of his possessions in a wagon; more than once he was reduced to skipping town in the middle of the night without paying his local production and hotel costs. It was only a dearth of theatrical engagements—and dire indigence—that forced Singer to return to work as a mechanic. Yet he did not regard this occupation as drudgery: intellectually curious and optimistic, he continued to sharpen his mental and mechanical skills by making improvements on the machines he maintained and mended. In the process, he invented two new devices, a steam-driven rock drill, and a machine for carving wood, metals, or marble. He patented his inventions, but neither achieved much success. He continued to live hand-to-mouth, often pawning his few possessions to obtain the money for food and lodging.

In 1850, now living in Boston, Isaac began to tinker with the sewing machine. Although several sewing devices had been patented, the machine was still primitive and impractical. Seeing an opportunity, Isaac made a preliminary design for a new, improved machine, scrounged a loan of forty dollars to buy materials, and built a prototype in a borrowed workshop. He would later claim that he worked for eleven straight days, taking almost no time for food or sleep. At first the machine device produced a row of slack stitches. Isaac was ready to give up in despair, when he suddenly realized the flaw in his mechanical calibrations that had prevented the device from running smoothly. He rushed back to the workshop, corrected the error, and retested the machine. This time the stitches came out strong and smooth.

Subsequent improvements were made, and in 1851 Isaac patented his invention. That same year, the Singer sewing machine earned a gold medal award at the Fair of the American Institute. The public clamored to purchase such a timesaving device. Isaac had given little thought as to how to secure capital to manufacture the device, and, despite the public interest in his machine, his initial attempts at finding investors to back production were unsuccessful. The difficulties multiplied when inventor Elias Howe initiated a $25,000 claim against him, claiming patent infringement. Although the Singer and Howe machines operated with completely different mechanisms, and despite the fact that Isaac's design and engineering was much the more effective, Howe continued his litigation until 1854, ultimately winning a settlement entitling him to a share in the royalties on all Singer sewing machines produced. This would have created an insurmountable financial burden for Isaac, and once again he almost gave up in despair.

Luck intervened in the person of Edward Clark, a wealthy lawyer and investor who became Isaac's business partner. The levelheaded Clark took charge of the manufacturing end of the company, allowing the imaginative, impractical Singer to concentrate on further improvements of his invention and applications for new patents. The consequent financial rewards came quickly. In Isaac's case, it was the stuff of American mythology: a poor immigrant's son, who in 1850 could barely scrape together enough for food and lodgings, had by 1855, through enterprise and the sweat of his brow, become wealthy beyond his wildest dreams. In his larger-than-life style, he rose to his new circumstances admirably. He moved into a large house at 14 Fifth Avenue, in New York's most fashionable district. To travel around the city, he designed and had built a canary-yellow carriage that could seat thirty-one people.[3] By 1860, Singer's company was the largest producer of sewing machines in the world, and his perfection of the device had helped launch nothing less than a socio-economic revolution. Indeed Isaac was one of the key figures in the brave new world of industrialism, which brought in its wake the introduction of interchangeable parts, licensed factories, and multinational sales outlets. And he had inadvertently played a key role in the liberation of women, who were, thanks to the sewing machine, freed from the endless stultifying hours spent making garments by hand in their homes and in sweatshops.

It is not a little ironic that this charismatic folk hero-liberator of modern women was such a Lothario in his personal relations. Rich or poor, Isaac seemed to inhabit his own moral universe, one in which rules and conventions simply didn't exist. In 1830, at the age of nineteen, Isaac married fifteen-year-old Catherine Maria Haley, with whom he had two children. While on tour with his theater troupe, he took up with eighteen-year-old Mary Ann Sponsler, who subsequently joined the troupe. Although still legally married, Isaac lived with Mary Ann for long periods of time over the next twenty-four years; it was an itinerant, impoverished existence, and the two frequently lived out of a wagon. Ten children were born of this liaison, eight of whom survived to adulthood. When Isaac's fortunes rose, he moved Mary Ann and the children into the house at 14 Fifth Avenue, but continued to enjoy the company of other women. These dalliances invariably yielded tangible results. An 1850 affair with Mary Walters of New York produced a daughter, who was given the family name of "Merritt." Mary McGonigal of San Francisco had five children with Singer between the years 1852 and 1857, under the family name "Matthews." Perhaps the use of aliases appealed to Isaac's theatrical bent. In any event, he enjoyed being surrounded by the children of all his mistresses, past and present. Like a biblical patriarch, the freewheeling, pleasure-loving industrialist was happy to claim them all.

On 23 January 1860, Singer obtained a decree of divorce from Catherine Haley. Mary Ann, who for some time had been introduced by Isaac as "Mrs. Singer," felt confident that at long last he would propose marriage. But one day, she saw her handsome lover riding down Fifth Avenue with Mary McGonigal. When she confronted him, he struck her. The police arrested him for assault, and Mary Ann moved out. She took her grievances to the press, claiming that Isaac had "[given] himself up to riotous living."[4] Edward Clark was put in the position of cleaning up the public relations messes caused by Singer's misadventures. Worried about the future litigation that might be directed towards the company by any number of his partner's disgruntled former "companions" and children, Clark tried to convince Singer to convert the company into a joint stock corporation. This arrangement would enable the inventor to retain a financial interest in the company, but would absolve him from active management responsibilities.

Isaac could not be bothered with such mundane matters. He took an extended trip to Europe with Mary McGonigal's sister Kate, just as American Civil War hostilities began. Before he left, he made a donation of one thousand sewing machines to the Union army. Isaac remained in Europe for the better part of 1861–62. He lived in high style, enjoying the fruits of the company's success, while making no contribution to its creative or administrative health. His travels eventually brought him to Paris, where, as a wealthy industrialist, he was able to circulate comfortably in monied social circles. Not much time elapsed before he began another romantic adventure, with a beautiful young woman thirty years his junior.

Isaac's new love interest, Isabella Eugénie Boyer, was born in Paris on 17 December 1841, the daughter of a Frenchman, Louis Noël Boyer, and his

English-Scottish wife, Pamela Lockwood Boyer. Louis Boyer may have come from a monied background, for in official family documents he is listed under the column of "rank or profession" as "gentleman";[5] Singer biographers, however, have given his profession as a tavern-keeper.[6] Isabella grew up along with five siblings in a comfortable bourgeois household at 13 rue Monceau, in the 8th *arrondissement* (district). The children were raised speaking both French and English. During Isabella's teenage years her parents separated amicably, apparently due to religious differences: Louis Boyer, a Catholic, could never completely reconcile himself with his wife's Protestantism or the fact that she had raised her children in that faith.[7] Mme. Boyer subsequently opened a *pension* to support her family.[8] Isabella was required to go to work as well. The young woman was pretty and high-spirited. Although she was considered by her family to be a "tomboy,"[9] she had a fine eye and ear, and a lovely singing voice. Through her self-education, she developed sophisticated tastes in the arts, especially music. And, if family anecdotes are to be believed, the pretty Isabella was also vain and narcissistic.[10] She had a fiercely independent temperament, and yearned to rise above her middle-class existence, longing for a life of luxury, adventure and travel. For the present, however, she was obliged to work as a baker's assistant.

The circumstances—and consequences—of the meeting of Isabella Boyer and Isaac Singer remain muddied by family and popular legend. Singer biographer Ruth Brandon asserts that Isaac's first attentions were paid to Isabella's mother, Pamela Boyer, during a period when he was a lodger at the *pension,* but that, upon meeting the pretty young Isabella, he transferred his affections to her.[11] A contemporary newspaper report claimed that Isaac and Isabella met when the industrialist walked into the bakery where the young woman was working. Singer was smitten by her beauty; they became lovers and traveled throughout Europe.[12] Isabella's past, however, seems to have been more complicated than these romantic legends imply. Unpublished letters to her mother indicate that, before meeting Isaac, Isabella had lived with a man—never named in letters, but possibly called Summerville—and, with him, had a daughter named Emily.[13] It is not clear what the relations were between Isabella and her lover at the time that Isaac came to Europe. These facts can be substantiated: by autumn 1862 Isabella and Isaac had become romantically involved; by November of that year Isabella was pregnant. Isaac Singer returned to New York City in early 1863. In March of that year, Isabella left Emily in the care of her mother and crossed the Atlantic under the name of "Mrs. Summerville."[14] By June she had moved into Isaac's five-story mansion at 14 Fifth Avenue. She was impressed, but by no means intimidated, by its "splendid parlors and bedrooms . . . all carpeted and elegantly furnished."[15] Finally, she was getting the life to which she felt entitled. Isaac, perhaps truly in love for the first time, showered his pretty young mistress with elegant clothing and diamond jewelry.[16] As Isabella approached her sixth month of pregnancy, Isaac proposed marriage, taking steps to divest himself completely of his complicated prior entanglements. He forced Catherine Haley and Mary Ann Sponsler, both of whom claimed to be "Mrs. Singer," to sign documents renouncing all claims to his estate.

On 13 June 1863, Isabella Eugénie "Summerville" married Isaac Merritt Singer in his Fifth Avenue mansion. Two of the witnesses were Isaac's eldest son and daughter from his union with Mary Ann—"more like brothers and sisters to me than anything else," wrote Isabella to her mother.[17] The ceremony was performed by the Reverend Edwin Cook, Rector of St. John's Episcopal Church in New York.[18] Neither Isaac nor Isabella was a member of the parish; moreover, according to St. John's rules and regulations, it was expressly forbidden for a minister of the church to perform a marriage between two individuals when one or both of them was divorced. Singer's amorous adventures had received much publicity in the press, and Isabella was clearly in an advanced state of pregnancy. Apparently Singer found a way to make it worthwhile for Reverend Cook to officiate. Remarkably, no marriage license was ever filed with the City of New York. Nonetheless, Isabella wrote to her mother, "I am *married,* married in the law in the eyes of God and man. . . . You should see my great thick wedding ring, it will never wear out."[19] On 25 July 1863, six weeks after the couple was united, a son, Adam Mortimer, was born. When the baby's birth was registered in the New York City Hall of Records, the names of the two parents were listed as Isabella and *Eugene* Singer. Clearly Isaac was still indulging his penchant for aliases.[20] Isabella was happy with her handsome, rich "Pappy"—and with the material success that her marriage brought her. She wrote to her mother, "I have at last arrived in the place to accomplish all that I used to dream about and tell you when I was a child. I have the most elegant house in New York. . . . I have a Dear honorable, kind, clever, and loving Father, and husband. . . . How happy it ought to make you to tell every boddy that your Isabelle is married, is rich. . . ."[21]

Even with a multimillionaire husband, Isabella could not shake her bourgeois sense of economy: "Every thing is an horrible price here, why I have to paye for a decent pare of slippers 25 frs or 5 dollars and for a summer bonnet 125 francs [or] 25 dollars . . . we paye 300 frs a week for the house we live in."[22] A planned visit to Europe with baby Mortimer was postponed because "Gold is so very high . . . it would be folly to come under such circumstances, and run the risk of ruining my husband."[23] Isabella worried for naught: Isaac's already impressive wealth was about to increase. In 1862, Edward Clark had hammered out a proposal for the conversion of Singer Sewing Machine into an incorporated company; a year later, the Singer Manufacturing Company was formed. The company absolved Singer of the responsibilities of active management, although he remained on the board of trustees. Singer and Clark each retained a forty percent share of the public offering. The financial rewards of this arrangement were reaped almost immediately: a share bought at twenty dollars in 1863 had quadrupled in value less than two years later. At the age of fifty-two, Isaac Singer was assured of living out the rest of his days a wealthy man.

In the spring of 1864, Isaac abruptly decided to break from urban living and, with it, his tumultuous past. He purchased several hundred acres of land on the outskirts of Yonkers, a semi-rural town north of New York City. On this land he built an enormous house of solid granite. The house and property cost $50,000, an unheard-of sum at that time.[24] In July the family (including two of Singer's daughters from a previous liaison) moved into their new home, which Isaac named "The Castle." The Singers invited hundreds of townspeople to a get-acquainted party. But Isaac's reputation for "riotous living" had caught up with him. One newspaper reported, "Great preparations were made for a house warming. Hundreds were invited. Few went. Singer's previous life had been the topic in nearly every circle. Residents in Yonkers ignored him, and few of his old associates clung to him."[25]

Isabella had hoped that she and her husband and child would travel to Europe that summer, but the move to The Castle interrupted these plans. Isaac was preoccupied with his business, which had only continued to improve, despite the fact that the Civil War had plunged the American currency into a state of crisis.[26] Isabella was keenly disappointed, as she wrote to her mother, "I had hoped, at least, to have you near me when I should be confined, for, dearest mother, I unluckily am again in the family way."[27]

The baby girl born to the Singers on 8 January 1865 was christened Winnaretta Eugénie. Late in life, Winnaretta, joining in the tradition of embellishing the family mythology, would tell her friends, with a perfectly straight face, that her name derived from "Red Indian" origin.[28] More likely, however, "Winnaretta" was an invention entirely of her father's making. Isaac had always had a penchant for giving his children fanciful names: Lillian Cleopatra, Jasper Hamet, Voulettie Theresa.

At the time of Winnaretta's birth, her father was busy renovating The Castle, intent on filling his house with the most up-to-date appliances and sumptuous furnishings that money could buy. A new coal furnace was installed to stave off the winter cold. The rooms were filled with costly and elegant furniture. Behind the main house, a hothouse was constructed in the form of a palace, with four separate wings for the different varieties of exotic flowers and plants. "We have just picked a bushel of oranges," Isabella wrote to her mother, "and we have the most rare flowers all winter."[29] But oranges in winter could not replace the lively bustle of New York City. Twenty-three-year-old Isabella keenly felt the solitude of country life. The Singers' home on Fifth Avenue had always been filled with Isaac's business associates and friends, but in Yonkers the Singers were isolated, ignored by the local population. The only people her own age that Isabella saw were Isaac's older children. In addition to caring for two infants, she had to minister to the needs of a fifty-three-year-old husband who was beginning to suffer from rheumatism and the other encroaching discomforts of middle age.[30] Isaac's ailments had no effect on his virility, however: only a few months after Winnaretta's birth, Isabella found, to her dismay, that she was pregnant once more. She suffered a miscarriage in June,[31] but was pregnant again by September.

Finally, Isabella insisted that she could no longer endure the rural existence: if she must continue to bear children, she wished them to be born in Europe. This time her husband acceded. In November 1865, Singer sold The Castle and its possessions—including the canary-yellow carriage—to a hat manufacturer, and sailed for London with his growing brood. By February 1866 the family had settled in Isabella's hometown of Paris, where Washington Merritt Grant Singer was born in June. The Singer family moved into a large apartment at 89*bis* boulevard Malesherbes in the 8th *arrondissement*, not far from Isabella's childhood home on the rue Monceau. A fourth child, Paris Eugene, was born in November 1867, and named for the city of his birth. Two more children, Isabelle-Blanche and Franklin Morse were born in 1869 and 1870, respectively. As her new family grew, Isabella definitively abandoned her old one: little Emily Summerville was left in the care of her grandmother Pamela Boyer, and Isabella's maternal role was reduced to the sending of monthly child support funds.[32]

Early photographs of Winnaretta posed with her mother and three brothers when she was about three years old show a very serious-looking little girl. In these family portraits, Winnaretta's chin juts out and the corners of her mouth turn downward, taking the shape of an upside-down "U." This unfortunate configuration of features became a cause for comment by contemporary chroniclers in her adult life; one wonders therefore what sort of reaction Winnaretta's seemingly "negative" demeanor may have evoked in those close to her during her formative years. The pretty and vain Isabella may have rejected a daughter who was not fashioned sufficiently in her own lovely image. The extant letters from Isabella to her own mother, which extend through Winnaretta's fifteenth year, lend credence to this theory: after writing in March 1865 that her two-month-old daughter "is getting on very well," Winnaretta is never again mentioned in her mother's letters.

The Singers settled into Paris's animated daily life, indulging to their hearts' content their passion for music and theater. In 1869, Winnaretta's godfather Edward May painted Isaac's portrait.[33] With his confident pose and penetrating gaze, dressed in a white satin vest and a red velvet dressing-gown lined with gold fabric, and sporting a long distinguished beard, Isaac looked like an odd cross between a Gilded Age industrial magnate and a beneficent Father Christmas. But he and his family were not destined to remain on the Continent. In July 1870, political tensions between Napoleon III's French Empire and Wilhelm I's Kingdom of Prussia reached a breaking point; on 19 July, France declared war. By August, Bismarck's superior armies had penetrated deep into France. Isaac realized that Paris was no place for foreigners who had no need to be there, and he made plans to move his family to a safer location. Two weeks before the Prussian invaders reached Paris, the Singers and their six young children, including the infant Franklin, caught a train to the Channel coast, and boarded a boat to England.

Winnaretta's first significant experience in what was to become her new country was a memorable one. Upon arriving in London, the family took lodging at Brown's Hotel. Soon after they settled in, Winnaretta found herself alone in her hotel room. She began to hear strange noises, and, to her horror, watched a film of smoke slowly creep beneath her door. Before she could react, the door was suddenly flung open and a very tall man rushed in, grabbed her, set her on his shoulders, and raced downstairs with her towards the street. Only later did Winnaretta discover what an illustrious person had come to her aid: her rescuer was the writer Ivan Turgenev, living in England before his permanent move to Paris the following year.[34]

Winnaretta's memoirs, written late in her life and published posthumously in 1945, make no mention of this dramatic experience; in fact, in her recollections of childhood, there is a total absence of any event or feeling that could be described as even remotely tragic or traumatic. She begins the narration of her childhood years in England with a vague memory of her family's first London house, at 32 Grosvenor Gardens, virtually adjacent to Buckingham Palace.[35] The nomadic Singer family did not stay there more than a year, however. Isabella was still weak after the birth of Franklin. Isaac's health was beginning to fail; nearing his sixtieth year, he wanted nothing other than rest and quiet. Finding the London winter too harsh, the Singers moved to Devonshire, about 150 miles southwest of London. Six-year-old Winnaretta was enchanted by the beauty of the region, "with the coloured, rolling countryside that leads up to Dartmoor as far as Tavistock. . . . [T]he surrounding counties seem grey compared to the rich red of the Devon rocks and fields, against which the ilex trees, with their dark green foliage, make even in winter so rich a contrast."[36]

In 1873, having decided to settle permanently in England, Isaac sought to purchase property in the fashionable beach resort of Torquay, where the international aristocracy summered. To his astonishment, he was spurned once again by the local populace, just as he had been in Yonkers: an uncultured, uncouth American tradesman, millionaire or not, was not considered welcome in rigidly stratified British society. Undeterred, Isaac traveled five miles south, to the unprepossessing village of Paignton. There he purchased a twenty-acre estate overlooking the sea. Not satisfied with the house already on the property, he contracted for the building of a new mansion, a structure that he intended to outrival the baronial castles of Devonshire, but one that would embrace all the most up-to-date improvements for comfortable living. A local architect, George Bridgman, and a hundred twenty workers were hired to renovate the property. In America Isaac had named his home "The Castle." Castles being commonplace in England, Isaac chose for his new abode an American name. "I want a big wigwam," he told Bridgman, "and I shall call it the Wigwam."[37]

When completed, Isaac's new abode was a wigwam in name only. The new house bore a greater likeness to a luxurious continental villa. Its four stories comprised one hundred rooms, including ballrooms and banquet halls, immense wine vaults and conservatories. Isaac's love of modern technology and gadgetry resulted in the installation of a kitchen and bathrooms equipped with the newest appliances on the market. On 10 May 1873 Isaac and Isabella threw a huge housewarming party to celebrate the laying of the Wigwam's foundation stone. Family and local townspeople—including the one hundred twenty workmen—were present as Isabella laid the cornerstone, in which oldest son Mortimer had placed with a bottle containing copies of local newspapers, English, French, and American coins, and photographs of the family. Winnaretta, then eight years old, solemnly added a brass plate, which was fixed to the foundation stone as a record of the proceedings.[38]

One of the most unusual new constructions on the estate was a large circular brick building facing the main house, called the Arena. In winter the space was used for exercising horses; in the clement seasons it was used as a private theater, where circuses, children's parties, and other boisterous entertainments could be accommodated. Isaac Singer had lived the first forty years of his life in the most desperate poverty; the subsequent twenty years had brought the unexpected creation and development of a colossal industrial empire. Now, in his golden years, wealthy beyond his wildest dreams, all Isaac wanted to do was to live comfortably, surrounded by his family, and have fun. The freewheeling, flamboyant environment that he created at the Wigwam enabled him to return, if only vicariously, to his first love: theater. The Singer children grew up in a splendid, fantastic world, in which performances and entertainments were part and parcel of their daily lives. In his exuberant fashion, Isaac spared no expense in mounting the most colorful, dazzling productions that Singer money could buy. Winnaretta was especially enchanted by the puppet shows and pantomimes presented in the Arena; her passionate interest in these genre of entertainment would have far-reaching consequences in her adult life.

In contrast to her husband's tastes for theatrical entertainments, Isabella made her own particular, more refined, contribution to the family's regular artistic fare. Home music-making was a standard feature of French bourgeois life, and within the context of her childhood milieu, Isabella had managed to form remarkably sophisticated musical tastes. At the Wigwam she continued the tradition, hosting musicales in the mansion's capacious salons, performed by family members and local musicians, where she herself sang songs and operatic arias.

Despite the variety of entertainments offered at the Wigwam, the Devonshire elite rarely deigned to attend the balls, concerts, and holiday parties thrown by the Singers. The local paper reported on Isaac's eccentricities: "He actually tried driving six horses—three abreast—in Devonshire lanes; but as the outside wheelers and leaders used to get pushed up into the adjoining fields, he abandoned the practice, and contented himself with dressing each of his five men-servants in a different livery."[39] The local tradespeople, however, did not suffer from the same social scruples, and were more than happy to partake of the Singers' munificent hospitality. The Arena was the scene of numerous celebrations of "special days": the Fourth of July, Christmas, and Isaac's birthday. On these occasions, Torquay's "Italian Band" would play inside the carriage stand, while the adults and children danced and played in the Arena's circular floorspace.[40] For Isaac's sixty-second birthday party, held on 27 October 1873, two daughters from his previous "marriages" joined the younger children in providing the entertainment, which included a scene from Shakespeare, popular songs, and a comic opera. Winnaretta participated by singing a song called *Spooning in the Sands*.[41] Two months later Isaac dressed up as Father Christmas, and, after distributing meat and other provisions to the poor of the region, invited all the Paignton townspeople to the Wigwam to celebrate the holiday, giving toys to the children, and various other forms of seasonal cheer to the adults.

For Winnaretta, her childhood home must have seemed like some kind of fairyland, with her adored father the chief magician. She had developed into an introspective girl, not conventionally pretty but sweet looking, with penetrating blue-gray eyes that contained a hint of perpetual melancholy; this, coupled with her natural sense of reserve, made her seem distant and somewhat odd. Those who might have assumed that this serious, shy girl was a soft, pliant creature, however, were astonished to learn that beneath her quiet demeanor lay a will of steel. Like all other young girls of her class, Winnaretta received her education from governesses. Painting and piano lessons were standard in the curriculum of well-brought-up young ladies; Winnaretta took to these activities eagerly. Living in the country with four boisterous brothers, and freed from the restraints imposed upon young girls in urban society, Winnaretta and her sister Isabelle-Blanche could and did participate in sports and roughhouse outdoor play. Yet, despite her poise and athleticism, Winnaretta was terrified by thunder, lightning, and loud noises. These fears would plague her throughout her life.

Her love for her father bordered on worship. The irresistible magnetism and charisma that had captivated scores of women had no less a powerful effect on Isaac's adoring daughter. She cherished the times they spent to-

gether. Isaac introduced her while she was still young to American authors
such as Harriet Beecher Stowe and Mark Twain, and encouraged her to
give free rein to her imagination. She was fascinated as well by her father's
adeptness with tools and gadgets. She loved his sense of theater and the
sensational. The fact that he encouraged her to perform in the family entertainments may have helped her to surmount her shyness.

Not only did Winnaretta participate in the plays and musicales written
and produced with her siblings, she was already proficient enough as a
musician to be able to hold her own in the more serious entertainments
hosted by the family. Like her mother, she had a keen and refined aesthetic
sense, and her sensitive eyes and ears were alert to every form of beauty,
especially music. These qualities were not sufficient, however, to endear
her to her mother, who favored primarily her sons, and secondarily her
younger, prettier, and more malleable daughter and namesake, Isabelle,
known as Belle-Blanche. Winnaretta was fortunate enough, however, to
find a mother-substitute within her own family circle, when Isabella's sister
Jane Boyer came to live with them. Winnaretta turned to her aunt for the
maternal love that was lacking elsewhere. A strong bond of trust and affection developed between Jane and her niece; as an adult, Winnaretta would
assert that it was actually her aunt who raised her.[42] Isabella seemed perfectly content with this arrangement, just as she had been content to abandon her first daughter, Emily, to the care of her mother a dozen years earlier. She seemed to prefer spending time with Isaac's elder children from his
previous alliances, many of who came to live at the Wigwam at various
periods.

The carefree life of the Singer family was soon to change. Since his arrival in England, Isaac had been afflicted with heart ailments, and in the
spring of 1875 his condition became acute. By June he was in constant
pain and told his wife that he prayed for death.[43] He died soon after, on 24
July 1875. The townspeople of Paignton turned out in force to pay homage
to the extraordinary man who, in the three years that he had lived among
them, had won their admiration and respect. The funeral procession was
nearly three-quarters of a mile long: when the first of the carriages following Isaac's casket arrived at the Torquay cemetery, the last were just leaving
Paignton.[44] After the resplendent procession, the industrialist's remains were
interred in an enormous mausoleum overlooking the town. In death, Isaac
Singer was finally allowed to mingle with the polite society that had snubbed
him.

In September Singer's will was read. The industrialist had left a colossal
fortune, estimated at thirteen million dollars. Much of it was in Singer
stock, of which Isaac held forty percent, and which was held and administered by a Canadian trust. The estate had been divided into sixty equal
parts, left in varying portions to Isabella and twenty-two of Isaac's twenty-
four children. At this point, Isaac's past came back to haunt him, when

Mary Ann Sponsler filed a suit claiming that it was she, not Isabella, who was Isaac's legal widow. A protracted battle over the will ensued, and the court proceedings were reported in newspapers all over the world.[45] The suit was decided in Isabella's favor in January 1876, but she and the children were forced to endure the ignominy resulting from the dredging up of the patriarch's past. When the dust finally settled, Isabella and her children had all inherited sizable fortunes.

Eleven-year-old Winnaretta's portion of the estate was worth approximately $900,000.[46] If she had any idea that she was an heiress, it was surely small comfort to her. The loss of her father was devastating, and from that point, the feeling that she was completely alone in the world never ceased. She withdrew even more deeply into herself, creating what she would later refer to as "a cult" around the idealized memory of her father. The 24th of July, the day of Isaac's death, became a sacred day, an annual reminder of the magnitude of her loss. Commemorating the anniversary of Isaac's death some sixty years later, she wrote to a niece, "I don't talk of my sorrow any more, but not one instant has it grown easier to bear. The one thing I had, I lost then—and there is not a day that dawns on which I don't say, like Brontë, 'How can I face the empty world again!'"[47]

There is no indication that Isabella ever understood the depth of her daughter's grief. Soon after Isaac Singer's will was settled in 1876, his widow's restiveness with British country life rose to the surface; the lack of opportunities in Devonshire for her own social advancement became a pressing issue. Isabella began to make more frequent trips to Paris, ostensibly to visit her mother, leaving the children in the care of their aunt. She did, however, see to it that her children received proper educations. Whatever maternal warmth she may have lacked, Isabella understood that if her sons and daughters were to advance in life, they would need a solid intellectual formation to complement their vast wealth: such a fortuitous combination should ensure a brilliant place in the wide world beyond Devon. Mortimer was sent off to boarding school in London, while Winnaretta and her younger siblings received private tutelage at the Wigwam. The children were also given athletic "drilling lessons" in the Arena, to "improve [their] muscles."[48]

As she entered adolescence, Winnaretta's natural tendency towards introversion became even more pronounced. She would go for long rides alone over the green Devonshire hills on her new pony, Coruba.[49] She also found comfort in creating her own new "family"—an aviary. "Auntie gave me a present . . . [of] six little quails," she reported to her grandmother. "I expect a young brood of Pheasants out in a day or two, as I have put twenty-one eggs under a large hen. . . . The Peacock and the Peahen are quite fine now. . . . The Peacock's tail *has grown very handsome*."[50] Her willful independence would often put her at odds with her mother. She became a self-appointed "protector" of her younger sister, Belle-Blanche,

who had become increasingly prone to bouts of "melancholy"—what today would be called depression.[51]

A photograph taken during this period shows Isabella and Winnaretta
in the garden of the Wigwam. The Widow Singer is seated, dressed in great
finery, and looking off into the distance, past her daughter. The teenage
Winnaretta, perhaps twelve or thirteen years old, is dressed in what appears to be a costume in Russian style. She is looking directly into the
camera, her eyes dark and somber.

Life with Mother

In mid-1878 Isabella Singer announced her decision to move herself and her children back to the Continent. She returned to Paris with her children just as the city was preparing for the 1878 World's Fair. A long-awaited attraction was the head of the Statue of Liberty, recently completed by sculptor Frédéric Bartholdi and installed on 28 June in the Champs de Mars. Crowds thronged to view the face of the illustrious woman, whose features evoked both classicism and tragedy. Rumors flew as to the identity of Bartholdi's model, a secret never disclosed by the sculptor. Was it Bartholdi's mother, his wife . . . or Isabella Boyer Singer?

That Isabella inspired the features of Lady Liberty is now firmly ensconced in Singer family mythology. Bartholdi may have met her while the Singers lived at Boulevard Malesherbes in the late 1860s, or possibly in New York in 1876, when Isabella was settling Isaac's will, and when Bartholdi was making his first studies for the statue. As Bartholdi's biographers point out, a "proper" woman of the 1870s would never have posed for a sculptor, except for a project resulting in a bust that could sit unobtrusively in the parlor.[1] Whatever Isabella's—and Isaac's—sense of propriety, it probably would not have been enough to stand in the way of a project that paid such tribute to her vanity. What is remarkable is the resemblance between Miss Liberty and the young Winnaretta Singer.

As she approached her fortieth year, Isabella had every expectation of rising to an estimable social level in the wealthy bourgeoisie. A photograph of her taken around 1880 reveals her to be a beautiful, albeit haughty-looking woman. Endowed with good looks, charm, and a multimillion-dollar legacy, the Widow Singer had probably been pursued by potential suitors from the moment that her official mourning period ended.

She made her choice too soon, and not wisely. Victor-Nicolas Reubsaet was a handsome violinist and tenor, born on 26 April 1843 near Maastricht, Holland, the son of a Dutch shoemaker. He was said to have made something of a concert career in Brussels and Antwerp.[2] For years he had claimed that a ducal title had lain dormant somewhere in Italy; he told the story so often that his friends took to calling him "the little Duke."[3] According to one account, "he wanted that title and could not get it because he lacked the golden key which alone could unlock the doors of the Royal Chancellery, where, mildewed and musty, lay the necessary documents."[4] While awaiting his dukedom, Reubsaet managed to conjure up an uncle whose convenient death conferred upon him the title of Vicomte d'Estenburgh. That questionable title earned him small credibility in European aristocratic circles, however, and he was forced to seek his fortune elsewhere. He went to New York, where his good looks, gentlemanly manners, and good humor—in addition to his alluring title, which worked like a charm with the more credulous Americans—gained him entry into the homes of the wealthy.[5]

Perhaps Isabella met Victor in 1876 in New York, while she was seeing to the last details in the settlement of Isaac's will. Or perhaps these two attractive social climbers met in Paris, at a musical soiree, where Victor dazzled Mme. Singer with his violinistic prowess. Isabella, no doubt, was equally dazzled by the idea of becoming a viscountess, perhaps even a duchess, just as Reubsaet would have been seduced by the idea of becoming a beneficiary-by-marriage of all that Singer money. Whatever the circumstances of their meeting, it was said to be love at first sight. By early 1878, the Singer children were making references to their mother's new friend "the Vicount" [sic] in letters to their grandmother.[6] That spring, Isabella hired a private yacht to take her children and her new companion on sailing excursions. Winnaretta did not join them, "for," as she wrote to Pamela Boyer, "I am not a good sailor as you know."[7] It was true: although she loved the sea, she was terrified of storms and easily prone to seasickness. In this instance, however, her "mal de mer" may only have been an excuse to avoid joining her mother and her suitor, whom she had decided that she did not like, even if she thought him a good violinist.

Isabella Singer married Victor Reubsaet shortly before moving back to Paris; by the spring of 1879, she was using the name Vicomtesse d'Estenburgh. In remarrying, she lost a sizable portion of her estate, her life-interest in the Wigwam, which now was divided and reverted to her children. But the remainder of her inheritance, the cash and Singer stock, was still considerable. Isabella bought a large townhouse (known in French as an *hôtel particulier*) at 27 avenue Kléber, in the fashionable 16th *arrondissement*.[8] The house, which had been built some years earlier by an American couple, had many reception rooms, decorated in Louis XVI, Empire, and "Sarah Bernhardt" style, the centerpiece of which was the *grand salon*, a center for musical and artistic gatherings.[9] It was in her mother's salon that Winnaretta was introduced to the great works of the chamber music and vocal repertoires.

The Parisian "salon" was born during the Age of Enlightenment, when nobles and intellectuals began to invite scientists, writers, and wits to their home to discuss literature or philosophy—or to "converse," for at that time conversation was considered an art form. After the Revolution of 1848, Parisians continued to assemble to discuss art, literature, and politics—but also to attend parties and balls. The salons allowed the wealthy hostesses to display their financial and social prestige. Each of these women

had a particular "day" upon which she received. Even after the fall of the
Second Empire, the aristocratic salons continued to flourish under the new
Republic. At the same time, the rising wealthy bourgeois class began to
create their own salons in opulent mansions erected in the newly constructed
neighborhoods to the north of the Champs-Élysées. New to all these gatherings was the special place accorded to music. Earlier in the century, in the
elegant mansion of Napoleon's niece Princesse Mathilde, or in the more
"artistic" homes of Marie d'Agoult or George Sand, music served as a
backdrop to amusing conversation, or to literary, philosophical, or political discussions. But in the expansive age of Napoleon III, music became the
express object of the meetings.[10]

Winnaretta's new stepfather used the salon to his own good advantage.
Armed with Isabella's fortune and his newfound nobility, he began to entertain in lavish style, hosting numerous balls and musical soirees. The
couple did not long ornament society under the name of Estenburgh, however. The title of Vicomte began to seem too paltry for the ambitious Victor. Thwarted for so long in his quest for a title by his lack of a "golden
key," he found in his marriage not only the missing key, but also the lively
determination to turn it more than once. In 1881, after taking the precau-
tion of becoming a naturalized Italian subject, the recently minted nobleman suddenly "discovered" the papers verifying the long-buried ducal title
held by his ancestors in that country. Soon thereafter Victor re-emerged as
the Duca de Camposelice, the title having been restored to him by no less
an eminence than King Umberto of Italy.[11]

One of the first to pay tribute to the new duke was acclaimed violin
virtuoso and composer Henri Vieuxtemps. Vieuxtemps, who had known
Reubsaet in Brussels, was in the midst of writing a set of thirty-six etudes
for violin and piano during the period that Victor received his title; he
honored his friend by subtitling the fifteenth etude "Dédiée à Mr le Duc de
Camposelice." For the first performance of the work at avenue Kléber,
Victor decided that he needed a violin as important as the music, and bought
a 1731 Joseph Guarnerius violin for 7500 francs. From that first purchase
sprang the notion, apparently embraced by Isabella, to assemble an important collection of stringed instruments.[12] Over the next five years Victor
would use his wife's fortune to amass an extraordinary group of Stradivarius
and Guarnerius violins, violas, and cellos, eventually assembling a double
quartet of Stradivarius instruments.[13] These included Vieuxtemps' own violins, sold after the virtuoso's death in June 1881. The papers reported that
"the prices which [the Duc de Camposelice] paid for the French Paganini's
Stradivarius and Guarnerius startled French amateurs."[14] Winnaretta never
forgot the weekly chamber music recitals in the grand salon, "played by
the finest performers in Paris on instruments which were then unique and
are now, I suppose, unobtainable."[15] The great string quartets of Beethoven,
Mozart, and Schubert were regularly featured at these gatherings; this rep-

ertoire, including the late quartets of Beethoven, considered bewildering
even to enlightened music-lovers, formed the basis for Winnaretta's musical education and preferences. She would sit quietly among the listeners,
drinking in the beauty of the music that filled her parents' salon.

On 27 June, more than four hundred guests attended a ball at avenue
Kléber celebrating Victor's new title. The particulars of the music recital
that began the festivities were recounted in detail by the press.

> Not withstanding the lateness of the season, some of the most distinguished
> of Parisian society were present. Among those who added greatly to the
> enjoyment of the evening we may name M. van der Heyden, whose talent
> on the violoncello is unrivalled; Mlle. Mariani, who sang the grand "Air de
> Bijoux" from *Faust,* and *La Manola,* composed by M. Émile Bourgeois,
> a melody not easily forgotten. M. Bourgeois played with his exquisite
> taste several new pieces, accompanied by M. Loret on the harmonium
> organ, the effect of which was quite charming and created a sensation.
>   Perhaps, however, we have left the most effective performance to the
> last—the charming singing of the Duchesse de Camposelice, who is gifted
> with a lovely voice, and delighted her friends by singing both Italian and
> English songs. The Duca also allowed his splendid tenor voice to be
> heard, and played in great style *La Légende* de Wieniaski [*sic*] on one of
> the finest Stradivarius violins, enough to make any artist jealous. The
> Duca was accompanied on the piano by the eldest daughter of the
> Duchesse, who is an excellent pianist and pupil of M. Bourgeois. The
> evenings are far too short passed in such society, where all the arts—
> music, painting, and sculpture—are cultivated.[16]

Winnaretta may have been willing to put a good face on things by serving as her stepfather's accompanist, but she disliked him thoroughly, as did
her siblings. This did not help the already strained relations between her
and her mother. At heart they were too much alike. Isabella probably saw
her own independence mirrored in her daughter, and she didn't like it,
because she couldn't control her. And it may be imagined that Winnaretta
made no effort to hide her dismissive attitude towards her mother's frivol-
ity. There was strength of purpose in Winnaretta's independence, and she
simply could not take Isabella seriously.

Winnaretta distanced herself from the family situation by immersing
herself in two newfound loves: museum-going and painting lessons. In her
memoirs, she recalled:

> As was usual in large families, the parents decided very early which
> child should become a musician, a painter, an architect, or a diplomat;
> and it was decided that I was not to study music but to learn painting at
> an *atelier* in the Rue de Bruxelles, conducted by a Monsieur Félix Barrias.

Although I secretly loved music most, painting attracted me almost equally, and I spent all the time possible at the Musée du Louvre, without understanding much of what I saw there, but forming the strongest likes and dislikes.[17]

Winnaretta flourished under the tutelage of Barrias, a Prix de Rome winner.[18] Barrias's paintings, while not innovative, were well made, and appealed to a broad public. Although academic in his approach to technique, he was able to give effective guidance and encouragement to the impressionable young girl, just as he had encouraged the young Edgar Degas some twenty years earlier. His instruction stressed the discipline of drawing, a thorough study of the human figure, and the need to build up a composition from numerous preparatory studies of its different parts.

Winnaretta eagerly soaked up her teacher's ideas, but she was also open to influences outside of his studio. She attended the annual exhibitions of modern French painting in Paris, which opened up the world of the visual arts to her, and taught her quickly that the officially sanctioned painting of the Academy were not to her taste.[19] But she was able to find other outlets to satisfy her curiosity about artistic trends. One of her colleagues in Barrias's class was a young woman named Madeleine Fleury, whose portrait was being painted by none other than Degas. Winnaretta asked to accompany Madeleine to one of the sittings.

With a beating heart I climbed up the dark steep staircase that led to his *atelier,* for I admired his works more than I can say. . . . I sat in a corner. At that time my great admiration for Claude Monet and the Impressionists made me feel certain that only painting from nature was admissible, so it was a shock to see that Degas was painting from drawings and that the whole color scheme of his portraits was chosen from the Persian rug that was near at hand, from which he had composed a palette.

I remember that in speaking of some landscapes that Madeleine Fleury was then painting, he said, to my great surprise: "To paint a landscape of the sort you describe, the best way would be . . . to paint the sky emerald green, and then put the canvas in a corner, prepare a good lunch (he was a great gourmet of the old French school) and leave the picture alone for several days."

Before my dazzled eyes, he brought out over a hundred pictures, sketches, and sepia drawings and I was overwhelmed with admiration, and of course much too terrified to say a word. When the sitting was over and we parted, and Degas (as I afterwards heard) said to my friend: "Who was that half-wit you brought with you? She never said a word about my pictures, nor about any of my drawings," and I understood from that moment that, however humble one may be, any great artist expects some praise when showing his work even to the most ignorant visitor.[20]

Winnaretta was especially attracted to the movement of painting called
L'École de plein air, which featured the bright colors and violet-hued shad-
ings of the outdoors. This fresh approach to color, in marked contrast to
the dull browns and greys favored by the conservative members of the
Académie des Beaux-Arts, excited the young girl's imagination. She loved
the works of Monet, Sisley, and Boudin, thrilled by "the beauty of this art
which seemed to give me a new insight and throw a fresh light and meaning on all that surrounded me in the visual world."[21] Her favorite artist in
this new school was Édouard Manet, who, in showing the true images of
modern existence, scandalized the French public, and earned him the rejection of the official Salon and vituperative attacks by the press. Winnaretta's
espousal of Manet was met with derision: "My enthusiasm was at once put
down as eccentric, promoted by a wish to excite attention, and deserving
only of discouragement."[22] Her godfather, Edward May, was particularly
critical of Manet. The two artists had been students together in the studio
of conservative painter Thomas Couture; May referred to Manet as a
"crank" who had been considered the laughing-stock of the Couture studio, the *"Michel-ange du mauvais* [the bad artist's Michaelangelo]."[23]
Winnaretta recalled, "At the painting class I attended every day, my admiration of Manet was a standing joke, most of the pupils having decided
that he did not know how to draw, that his colors were ridiculous and his
subjects beneath contempt. . . . I took no notice."[24]

However, as Winnaretta would confide to her posthumous readers, she
"secretly loved music most." The depth of her passion for music was hardly
guessed at by her family, but they learned soon enough. Shortly after the
family's move to Paris, Isabella asked her daughter what she wanted as a
present for her fourteenth birthday. Suggestions were offered: a little
watch from Boucheron's or a fan painted by Chaplin, a well-known
portrait painter. To Isabella's astonishment, Winnaretta chose as her
"birthday surprise" a performance of her favorite work by Beethoven—
the Fourteenth Quartet in C-sharp Minor, Op. 131.[25] Fifty-odd years
after their composition, the late quartets of Beethoven were considered
incomprehensible to all but the most sensitive and sophisticated musical palates. The C-sharp Minor quartet is particularly otherworldly; its
opening fugue, ethereal and mournful, requires its listeners to enter a rarefied emotional world where sorrow and exaltation are mysteriously merged.
Those who gathered for Winnaretta's command birthday concert in the
salon in January 1879 must have wondered at the strangeness of this birthday request. But already, for the lonely, taciturn young woman, music had
become a lifeline.[26]

Winnaretta's initiation into the richness of Parisian musical life no doubt
took take place shortly after her arrival in the city. Beginning in August
1878, organist Alexandre Guilmant inaugurated the newly built Trocadéro
Palace's magnificent Cavaillé-Coll organ with a landmark series of fifteen

concerts, featuring the music of J. S. Bach.[27] Winnaretta fell in love simultaneously with Bach's music and with the sound of the organ. She may have asked for organ lessons at this time, but apparently her request was not granted. Like any young woman being groomed for a place in society, she studied the piano. Her teacher was Émile Bourgeois, a respected Parisian freelance musician and rehearsal accompanist at the Opéra-Comique. Bourgeois was well-known in his day for numerous piano-vocal reductions of opera scores by contemporary composers;[28] his creative output of approximately one hundred technically brilliant, if musically vapid, salon pieces enjoyed considerable popularity.[29] Bourgeois's talents as a pedagogue have not been documented, but one can imagine that Winnaretta was an eager and gifted pupil.

The young woman's musical growth was greatly enriched in the summer of 1880, when she met the composer Gabriel Fauré. Isabella had recently purchased the Château de Blosseville in Pennedepie, a picturesque village on the coast of Normandy, just east of fashionable Deauville. It did not take long for the château's elegant parlors to be given over to musical activity, inspiring the admiration and curiosity of the region's music-lovers.[30] Fauré was one of those in attendance in the salon of the Singer-Camposelices that summer: he was their neighbor, staying in the nearby town of Villerville amongst a colony of artistic and musical friends that included painter Ernest Duez and composer Roger Jourdain. Often Fauré would entertain the group with his latest compositions—the Piano Quartet, Op. 15, as well as his beautiful songs and short pieces for piano. Winnaretta was enchanted with Fauré's subtle and expressive harmonies; his works seemed to her "worthy to rank with those of Chopin or Schumann."[31] She admired him personally as well: "he had a keen sense of humour and was intensely alive to the absurdity of the pretentious."[32] The easy rapport that sprang up between the thirty-five-year-old composer and the fifteen-year-old Winnaretta may have seemed odd to some, but it was a significant relationship for both of them. Fauré, recognizing Winnaretta's intelligence and artistic sensibilities, may have had feelings for her similar to those of Schumann for the young Clara Wieck before the blossoming of their romance. As for her, the dashing, ardent composer was the young woman's first musical mentor, and an important friend.[33]

A second landmark in Winnaretta's musical growth occurred during the summer of 1882, when, at age seventeen, she accompanied her mother to the Bayreuth Festival for the first performances of Wagner's *Parsifal*. Winnaretta instantly fell under the spell of the rich, complex music that magnifies and illuminates the legend of the Holy Grail and the theme of redemption from human suffering. It would still be some years before Wagner idolatry reached its full flower in the French musical community, but Winnaretta Singer was already a confirmed devotee, and henceforth made a pilgrimage to Bayreuth an annual event.

Winnaretta's artistic life flourished on multiple fronts during the early 1880s. Among the regulars in the Camposelice salon were the lithographer and etcher Jean-Louis Forain[34] and his wife. Often Winnaretta accompanied Forain to the Louvre, where the artist was engaged in restoration work. He was so impressed with the young woman's knowledge of art and art history that he secured a position for her as a translator of the museum's English language catalogue.[35] Sometimes Winnaretta joined Forain in his studio, where, while she painted, he would sketch the ironic visual and verbal commentaries on French political and social life that made him famous. While they worked, he would tell her stories about his younger years in Paris's artistic community. Forain's tales of poets Verlaine and Rimbaud, with whom he burned the midnight oil in the cafes during his student years, were particularly memorable. "He had for some time shared rooms with them," wrote Winnaretta. "He had been present at many scenes between them, but in no way confirmed the general view of the friendship that bound these two great men."[36] It is not surprising that Forain engaged in autobiographical revisionism in recounting to a teenage girl the destructively orgiastic lives of these two great poets, but his omission of their homosexual affair is curious. Did he sanitize the story out of deference to the age and sex of his protégée, or was it an insight into Winnaretta's own sexual preferences that held him back?

Spending time with Forain and other artists may have enabled Winnaretta to avoid being at home, where the situation was becoming increasingly ugly. Having already used a hefty chunk of his wife's fortune in procuring his ducal title, Victor continued to plunder his way through her Singer inheritance with breathtaking speed. Isabella, not wishing to jeopardize her social standing, was complicit in this life of matrimonial extravagance. "I warned Madam and begged her not to marry that man," wailed George Woodruff, the English administrator of the Singer Sewing Machine Company.[37] When Isabella finally realized the extent to which her estate was depleted, she tried to object, but Victor responded with violent fits of temper. Winnaretta's younger brother Paris wrote Woodruff that "they [Victor and Isabella] go for weeks without speaking to each other and he has heard the Duke tell his Mother that he got all the property in his own name and if she did not mind what she done he would turn her out."[38]

Not satisfied with exhausting his wife's income, Victor turned an avaricious eye towards the inheritances of his stepchildren. Winnaretta and her brothers knew of the danger, as did the estate's executors, who had been mandated by Isaac Singer to protect the interests of his minor offspring. Yard Eastley, Isaac's solicitor in Paignton, came up with an idea to shelter the fortunes of the four boys: each of them, upon reaching the age of sixteen, was to run away to England and become a ward of the court.[39] Winnaretta's brother Mortimer had already done so, and Washington would soon follow suit. But the girls did not have that option, and Winnaretta and her sister Belle-Blanche were still trapped in the role of pawns in their mother's social machinations. Although not quite as wealthy by inheritance as their brothers, the girls had an extraordinary net worth, which they could not touch until they reached major age.[40] Victor plotted ways in which he could avail himself of his stepdaughters's fortunes. In the meantime, appearances were maintained: the balls continued, with guest lists up to a thousand. Relations between Isabella and her husband were at that point quite frosty, and the newspaper reporters noted the Duke's absences from his own festivities.[41] The two girls, however, were obliged to appear at their mother's side, greeting the guests, taking part in the newly fashionable dance figures, and staying up for the concluding supper, served at four o'clock in the morning.[42]

In February 1883, Richard Wagner died. Winnaretta's grief at the death of her musical hero was compounded when Édouard Manet died two months later. Winnaretta yearned for some kind of talisman commemorating her late artistic idol. Summoning up all her courage, she went to Manet's studio at 77, rue d'Amsterdam, to ask the concierge to make her a gift of the visiting card that had been nailed to the artist's door. Winnaretta got her wish, and she guarded the treasured card for many years.[43] As fate would have it, she would make many more visits to that studio: her painting teacher, Félix Barrias, subsequently took over the space. For years Winnaretta produced her own paintings in the very room where Manet had created his masterpieces. She struck up a friendship with the building's concierge, who loved to regale the young woman with stories about the master. Once he showed her a pencil drawing that Henri Fantin-Latour had done of Manet, the first sketch of a well-known portrait. Winnaretta convinced the concierge to sell her the precious drawing. This first purchase of a work of art gave her the desire to start a real art collection, which, she decided, must begin with the purchase of a Manet canvas.[44]

If the beginning of her eighteenth year was marked with the death of her artistic heroes, its end marked another symbolic end of her childhood. Her beloved aunt Jane Boyer, now forty-four, had divided her time between Paris and Paignton, her son Frederick having become a rancher in California.[45] During one of her stays at the Wigwam, Jane had attracted the attention of an elderly Irish baronet and retired Naval officer, Sir Robert Synge, who lived on a neighboring Paignton estate. Twice widowed, his children grown, Sir Robert may have seen in the sweet-natured Jane Boyer an ideal companion for his golden years. The two were wed in 1884 and settled in Paignton. Shortly thereafter, Winnaretta's grandmother, Pamela Boyer, decided that it would be wiser for her to live out *her* golden years in closer proximity to the least self-centered of her daughters. She too moved to Paignton, leaving Winnaretta stranded in her mother's care, bereft of the two most stable feminine influences in her life.

Nineteen years old, Winnaretta began to push the boundaries of what a young woman could do in society. Without ever crossing over into what might be considered scandalous behavior, she made her first tentative forays into the salons and the cafes, the hubs of Parisian artistic and musical life. She was obliged to find a way to negotiate the conflict between her terrible shyness and her equally pressing desire to be part of interesting artistic and intellectual discussions. She developed the modus operandi—one which she employed until the end of her life—of sitting quietly amongst a group of people, listening with an intensity that made itself felt, despite her lack of verbal participation. On the rare occasions that she would speak, it would be in slowly delivered words uttered between clenched teeth, giving a low, gravelly sound to her carefully expressed opinions. Often, to the surprise of the surrounding crowd, she would come out with some scathingly funny remark, delivered in a deadpan style, her French marked by a British accent. She continued to circulate alone during her summer travels as well. In 1884, the young French composer Vincent d'Indy was in Munich to attend dress rehearsals of Wagner's *Ring* cycle. After the *générale*, he accompanied two friends, poet Robert de Bonnières and conductor-impresario Charles Lamoureux, to the Café Maximillian, a popular post-concert meeting place across from the Opera House. There, seated among the singers and writers, was nineteen-year-old Winnaretta, unchaperoned, quietly taking in the impassioned discussion of Wagner's music already in lively progress.[46]

If she was timid about expressing her opinions in public, Winnaretta was beginning to hit her stride as a painter. She continued her studies with Barrias, who captured her iron resolve in an 1885 portrait entitled *Winnaretta Buonaparte,* in which his student is depicted in Empire battle regalia.[47] Winnaretta also sought out the occasional advice of another respected painter, Paul Mathey.[48] The artistic guidance of these two mentors, as well as the encouragement of her godfather Edward May, yielded fortunate results. In 1885, one of her paintings, *Les Graves à Villerville,* was accepted by the Salon de Beaux-Arts.[49] The following year, a striking life-size portrait of her sister Belle-Blanche, clearly inspired by Manet, was not only accepted by the Salon, but also given wall space at the exhibition.[50]

Events at home overshadowed her artistic accomplishments. Victor's machinations to seize his stepdaughters' fortunes continued. The danger became more acute as Winnaretta approached majority age. Through the years of her minority, David Hawley, the executor of the Singer will, had capably managed her inheritance, as well as those of her brothers and sister, carefully investing and reinvesting her liquid assets with profitable results.[51] In 1886, without calculating in her share of the Oldway estate, her net worth totaled over a million dollars, a truly enormous figure for that period, and worth approximately ten times that in today's currency.[52]

On 8 January 1886, Winnaretta turned twenty-one. And before anyone had time to realize what she was doing, the young Miss Singer took charge of her destiny. In February she left Paris for Hyères, in southern France, to stay with friends. Once out of her mother and stepfather's purview, she empowered her French lawyers to arrange for her stocks, bonds, and cash to be put in her name.[53] On 12 March 1886 Winnaretta formally came into legal control of her inheritance, and had her assets transferred to a Rothschild-owned bank.[54]

Before returning to her mother's house, Winnaretta decided to satisfy her long-nurtured desire to buy a painting by Manet. She prevailed upon her artist friend, Ernest Duez, to act as her intermediary. Duez went to visit Manet's widow, who agreed to sell the canvas for 3500 francs.[55] The 1868 work, entitled *La Lecture* (Reading), dated from a period when Manet was inspired by the light *plein air* style of his colleague Berthe Morisot. The artist created a "symphony in white," a blending of traditional tonal painting with his own revolutionary sense of perspective. From the center of the canvas, a woman stares out at the viewer with a look at once tranquil and defiant—a new representation of modern life. When Winnaretta brought the painting home, everyone thought her quite mad to have frittered away so much money on a picture so devoid of interest: a woman dressed all in white, sitting on a white couch.[56] Winnaretta ignored the disparaging comments. Shortly thereafter, she bought a second canvas, Monet's recently painted *Champs de tulipes en Hollande,* which she purchased from Monet himself, thus beginning a new friendship with an important artist.[57]

Upon her return to Paris, Winnaretta began investigating the possibility of buying her own house. Her mother and stepfather were furious. Victor was still spending his wife's fortune without restraint, and Winnaretta's unexpected financial independence deprived him of another potential source of funds. He had just purchased another Stradivarius violin dated 1722 for the astronomical price of 30,000 francs.[58] By now the Camposelices' attempts to buy their way into society had made them the laughing-stock of the very people they were trying to impress. The press had a wonderful time exposing Victor's foppish affectations.

> The Duke of Camposelice . . . like most of the wearers of newly acquired titles . . . was intensely Duke, far more so than those of Norfolk or de Luynes or Medina-Coert. I remember once meeting him at the house of a charming English lady on whom he was making an afternoon call, it being her reception day. He talked a good deal about his wife, whom he invariably mentioned by her title. "The Duchess," quoth he, "was not altogether pleased with our new ballroom, but now that the decorations are finished the Duchess is quite delighted with it. The Duchess, indeed, suggested that we should give a ball immediately, but I prefer closing the entertainments of the Parisian season with a grand affair at our house, so I decided to put it off till the end of May. At least that was my advice to the Duchess."

The ball came off, and a very magnificent affair it was. The invitations were handed about Paris like ices upon trays for at least two months

beforehand. Then the ducal pair gave several magnificent private concerts, at which the company never quite came up to the aspirations of
the Duke and Duchess or to the quality of the entertainment, and some
of the titled gentlemen who condescended to become their guests indulged in strange liberties.[59]

Foppishness is one thing, a violent and dangerous temper another. The
legitimate newspapers, which reported the routine goings-on in society,
were not averse to having a bit of fun at the expense of the aristocracy and
the newly rich: if a member of society had the misfortune to become involved in a public scandal, the press did its utmost to keep readers informed. When it came to private family matters, however, the newspapers,
for the most part, kept their polite distance. It is therefore noteworthy that
the Camposelice furor made the papers: if the altercation taking place in
the family house was publicly reported, it suggests that the noise emanating from within its walls was simply too loud to be ignored.

> Now the Duchess, formerly Mrs. Singer, is the mother of several chil-
> dren by her first husband. Among these there is a daughter, Miss
> Winnaretta Singer, . . . an amateur artist of some note, painting pictures
> occasionally that are accepted at the Salon. Between this young lady and
> her titled stepfather a feud of gigantic dimensions has appeared to rage
> of late. The quarrel has reached such a pitch that Miss Singer has left her
> home and has gone to board at a convent. Lawyers have been engaged,
> members of the damsel's family have been summoned, and while the
> cause of the dissention continues to be a mystery to the world at large,
> the noise of the conflict has become distinctly discernible.[60]

The conflict at issue can only be guessed at. Victor had long been reputed
to be a man of "extremely uncertain temper."[61] The story, repeated up until
this day, began to circulate that Winnaretta had been raped by her stepfather.[62] The tenacity of this rumor would have the unfortunate consequence
of attempts by future biographers to "prove" or "justify," in a cause-and-
effect way, Winnaretta's future choices of sexual partners and lifestyle.

Whatever violence, sexual or otherwise, was suffered at Victor's hands,
Winnaretta characteristically kept her secret to herself—but she also hired
a lawyer. To ensure her safety, she left Paris and went to stay with some
friends in Cannes. Upon her return, she wasted no time in finding a house
of her own. Winnaretta's decision to buy property upon coming of age
reflected what would become a lifelong interest in real estate, as well as an
economic sagacity that would serve her well until the end of her days.

The property that Winnaretta acquired on 8 May 1887 was of a size
and splendor befitting the daughter of a dreamer of grandiose dreams, Isaac
Singer. Located not far from avenue Kléber, it was situated in the neighbor-

hood of Passy, a fashionable distance from central Paris, on the corner of avenue Henri-Martin and rue des Sablons (renamed rue Cortambert in 1891). The property was just a short distance from the Place du Trocadéro, from whose heights one could see the beginnings of the construction of the Tour Eiffel across the Seine. The almost two thousand square meters of property included two houses: a large imposing mansion that ran along avenue Henri-Martin, and alongside it, a smaller house in the form of a chalet that faced the rue des Sablons.[63] Yet merely owning a house was not enough to make Winnaretta secure or independent: no matter how wealthy she was, she could not, as a young woman in polite Parisian society, expect to live alone without doing irreparable harm to her reputation. Winnaretta's espousal of the avant-garde was fine as far as her artistic propensities were concerned, but in terms of society's expectations of propriety, she had neither the desire nor the power to challenge the status quo.

Only one solution was available to her: she had to marry, and soon. Finding a husband would pose no problem, for surely any number of young men with impressive family names would be happy to ally themselves with the Singer fortune. The real difficulties had to do with the lack of any trustworthy adult female in her life whom Winnaretta could ask to act as intermediary in the delicate arena of matrimonial negotiation. There was no one with whom to discuss the more personal, intimate aspects of marital obligations, either. She could not solicit her mother's advice or intervention on her behalf; indeed, she had no desire to contact Isabella, whom she regarded as one of the agents of her betrayal and current peril. Ordinarily she would have turned to her Aunt Jane, but it is quite possible that Lady Synge, having herself found social and financial security in middle age, would have counseled her niece to make a "sensible" decision—to marry, and to marry rich and titled. Winnaretta was completely alone.

She made the best choice that she could. Prince Louis-Vilfred de Scey-Montbéliard had been among the thousand guests at one of the glittering balls at rue Kléber in 1883. He was a pleasant-looking young man of twenty-nine, from an old and well-respected Protestant aristocratic family of the Franche-Comté region.[64] He was in no way remarkable: like other men of his class, his life revolved around hunting and his men's club. As the third son of the Marquis de Scey-Montbéliard, Prince Louis's prospects were not brilliant, for the family fortune and property were destined to pass to his oldest brother. But Winnaretta was not looking to make a brilliant match. Scey-Montbéliard had sufficient social standing to suit her, and besides, she had her own fortune. Indeed, there was a term for young American industrial heiresses who allied their wealth with a title—they were called "dollar princesses," and Winnaretta was about to join their ranks.[65] A wedding was planned for the month of July.

It was French law that a woman, upon marrying, ceded her estate, both money and property, to her new husband. Winnaretta, however, was not willing to put her new house into her intended's name. George Woodruff, her financial advisor, tried to convince her to put off the marriage. On 24 June, he wrote:

> Your letter shows some anxiety, and a most prudent forethought as to the propriety of a brief postponement in consequence of . . . the many unhappy incidents that have disturbed the harmony and happiness of your family. . . . If you were my own child I should not only advise but insist so far as I could that you settle in the most clear and definite way your Estate for your own personal use, before you ever enter upon marriage, no matter how much you love, respect and trust your intended.[66]

Winnaretta took Woodruff's financial advice to heart: she established a Trust Deed, vesting her Paris property in two trustees—her brothers Mortimer and Washington—for her personal benefit.[67] Events would prove the wisdom of her actions soon enough.

Dressed in a cream-colored satin gown, Miss Winnaretta Singer married the Prince de Scey-Montbéliard at the Église St. Pierre de Chaillot on Thursday, 28 July 1887. One newspaper, which described the bride as "tall, lithe and delicate in form, with sweet blue eyes and an abundance of wavy brown hair," could not resist adding some ugly gossip.

> There has been a great deal of scandal circulated recently as to the cause of the separation of Miss Singer from her mother, the Duchess de Camposelice. The only true reason for Miss Singer's leaving her mother's home was her utter inability to get along with her stepfather, the Duke, whom his best friends admit to be a man of extremely uncertain temper. The Duchess does not lead the happiest of lives. . . . Neither the Duke nor the Duchess of Camposelice attended the ceremony.[68]

Washington Singer, assuming the requisite paternal role, walked his sister down the aisle, but, sadly, Winnaretta was deprived of the presence of a mother-substitute: her Aunt Jane, who should have acted as surrogate for Isabella, had just received the tragic news of the death in California of her son Frederick; her bereavement prevented her attendance. The circumstances cast a pall over the wedding dinner, which was attended by only a small number of family members and close friends, including Gabriel Fauré, composer Déodat de Sévérac[69] and his wife, Félix Barrias, and Ernest and Amélie Duez.[70] After the somewhat subdued celebration, the couple left for Prince Louis's family's château in the Franche-Comté region.

The poor bride, the poor groom, it is hard to know for whom to feel sorrier. Winnaretta, in her haste to achieve independence, clearly had not thought through all the ramifications of the married state. There would have been no way to explain to her new husband that, given both her nascent attraction to women and the trauma of her recent (alleged) sexual abuse, she was not at all interested in a conventional relationship. The unsuspecting Prince Louis could not have imagined the reception he would receive when he entered the honeymoon chamber on his wedding night. According to family legend, he found Winnaretta atop a large wardrobe, brandishing an umbrella, and yelling, "If you touch me, I'll kill you!"[71]

If Winnaretta was unprepared for her husband's sexual expectations, it was nothing compared to the news that came only one month later: Victor Reubsaet was dead. The predatory Duke had suffered a sudden heart attack while staying at the Château de Blosseville, and died on 1 September 1887.[72] It was rumored that his end was hastened by a cruel trick of one of his enemies, who, in the style of Mozart's mysterious visitor requesting a Requiem, sent an employee of the funeral parlor to the château to take measurements for Victor's coffin. The funeral was held at St. Pierre de Chaillot, which had been, ironically enough, the scene of Winnaretta's wedding only five weeks earlier. The church was handsomely draped in black and silver hangings, and in the center of the church, four silver torches threw green flickering lights around the room. Isabella was not there: the papers reported that she was "too prostrate with grief to attend the funeral ceremony."[73] Franklin Singer was the chief mourner, and a handful of Victor's musical colleagues came to pay their last respects. But, noted one reporter, "few of those who were so prompt to respond to invitations to the dead man's fêtes and concerts thought it worth while to attend his funeral."[74]

The irony of Winnaretta's situation was not lost on the press. "Her marriage to Prince Louis [was] supposed to have been the result of her desire to possess a home of her own and protection from the importunities of her mother's impecunious but enterprising husband. Now death has relieved her of the old Duke's presence, and she may have occasion to regret her haste."[75] No doubt Winnaretta was entertaining similar thoughts.

Figure 1. Isaac Singer, Paris, ca. 1868. Collection of the author.

Figure 2. Isabella Boyer Singer, after her marriage to the Duc de Camposelice, ca. 1880. Collection of the author.

Figure 3. Winnaretta as a child, Paris, 1868. Private collection. Used by permission.

Figure 4. Singer family in the garden of Little Oldway, Paignton, ca. 1873. Left: Isabella and Isaac Singer; children, left to right: Winnaretta, Franklin, Paris or Washington seated, right foreground: Alice Eastwood "Merritt" Singer, Caroline Virginia Singer. Private collection. Used by permission.

Figure 5. Isabella and Winnaretta in the garden of the Wigwam, 1878. Collection of the author.

Figure 6. Winnaretta as a young woman. Private collection. Used by permission.

Figure 7. Winnaretta in a romantic pose. Private collection. Used by permission.

Figure 8. *Portrait of Princesse Louis de Scey-Montbéliard* (Winnaretta Singer), by John Singer Sargent, 1889. Private collection. Used by permission.

A Woman of the World

It was clear from the start that the marriage of Winnaretta Singer and Prince Louis de Scey-Montbéliard could not bring happiness to either party. Therefore, both sought out what could be gleaned from a marriage of convenience. The Prince, in wedding a wealthy "dollar princess," was now the symbolic—if not legal— "master" of a large and elegant *hôtel* and his wife's even larger fortune. As for Winnaretta, she was now a titled woman. She knew that there were obligations as well as privileges that came with her new identity. That she intended to make patronage a focal point of her life is affirmed in an 1888 letter from Paris Singer. "I wish you every happiness that this world can offer. There are many noble and charitable works to be done in Paris and I am sure you will occupy your leisure moments in relieving the wants of those whom God has not blessed with name, beauty and riches as he has you."[1] Winnaretta would spend a lifetime fulfilling this charge.

For the moment, however, being able to add the title of "princess" to her calling cards was satisfaction enough. She was now welcomed into the aristocratic salons, including the celebrated gatherings at the homes of the Baronne de Poilly and Madame Lydie d'Aubernon, whose literary salons were unparalleled in their prestige.[2] Winnaretta was stimulated by the intellectual atmosphere at these gatherings, which welcomed artists, musicians, and dramatists, but also amused by the foppish behavior of some members of the nobility. Comte Barbey d'Aurevilly, for example, had sartorial tastes dating back to the era of Louis XV: he would come dressed in waistcoats of silk and lace, buttons of amethyst and rhinestone. Once novelist Paul Bourget made an admiring comment about his choice of clothing: "How handsome you are tonight, Monsieur d'Aurevilly," to which the gentleman replied, "I am simply being polite."[3]

Winnaretta hoped that, having "settled down" with a prince husband, there might be a détente in her relations with her mother, but events soon focused all of Isabella's attentions on her younger daughter. Belle-Blanche had recently captured the affections of a young nobleman, Duc Élie Decazes; by January 1888 they were engaged. The Decazes family had long ties to French politics and international affairs: the young Duke's grandfather had been minister to Restoration monarch Louis XVIII, who conferred upon him his ducal title; his father had been a deputy and an ambassador. Any reservations that the Decazes family might have had about their son's marriage to an industrialist's daughter were allayed by Belle-Blanche's beauty and charm—and by the prospect of an alliance with the Singer millions. The press, whose fascination with the Singer family had not abated since Isaac's death, made much of the story. While the French papers reported the engagement with the respectful tone accorded the aristocracy, the American papers felt no such constraints. *The World* reported: "What the original cost of the Duke was does not appear, but it is evident already that French noblemen properly married, decorated, appointed, housed and fed are very costly commodities for an American heiress to deal in."[4] *The New York Herald* led its article with the headline "She Pays All The Bills—He Thinks Himself Cheap At The Price."[5] On 28 April 1888, three thousand guests representing the worlds of the aristocracy, diplomacy, and high finance squeezed into the Église St. Pierre de Chaillot to celebrate the marriage. Illustrations of the bridal party appeared in fashion magazines, where Winnaretta was depicted looking lovely in a gold-trimmed silk frock coat.[6]

Under the circumstances, Winnaretta could not discuss her unhappiness with Belle-Blanche. As in her younger years, she buried her feelings by escaping into art and music. The role of women in French society was highly circumscribed; repressive laws dating back to the Napoleonic code allowed very limited means of self-expression outside the home sphere. But in the salon, a woman could reign, albeit within a strict code of rules ordained by her milieu. She could define herself according to the great minds or talents with whom she surrounded herself. She could aid in her own elevation in society according to the prestige of her guests. And if she had her own artistic talents, she could display them in her own home domain. In fact, a certain degree of artistic talent was well looked upon by society. The ability to paint and draw was admirable (although sculpture was considered to be an eccentric means of expression). And it was practically obligatory for young women to know how to play the piano; having a pretty voice was even more of an asset.

The music salons were at the height of their popularity; it seemed that all of Paris had become a metropolis of *mélomanes*, or music-lovers. The prevailing notion that salon repertoire and performances had little to do with "real music" and "real concerts" does not hold up under scrutiny. Major works from the standard repertoire by major composers—Schumann, Wagner, Mozart, Beethoven, and J. S. Bach, among others—formed the basis of most of the salon recital programs. Among contemporary French composers, the most popular works were those of Saint-Saëns, Massenet, Fauré, and Ambroise Thomas, director of the Conservatoire and author of the celebrated opera *Mignon*.[7] The artists who performed these works were often of great renown, as many of the greatest artists of the capital devoted a significant amount of their professional lives to performances in the salons: these venues were perceived as important stepping-stones to greater visibility in the public sphere. Composers, too, aspired to have their pieces performed in private gatherings, as important contacts could be made: conductors, critics, directors of theaters were frequently in attendance. Saint-Saëns, Fauré, Debussy, and Ravel were among those who came to the public's attention in part because of their participation in salon culture at the beginning of their careers. There were potential benefits for the hosts and hostesses as well: the more interesting the music presented, the more renowned the performers, the greater the likelihood of an attentive audience; if the audience members were part of the nobility or the upper bourgeoisie, the greater the likelihood of the ascent in reputation of the hostess in the fiercely competitive arena of salon culture.[8]

Since most members of the aristocracy did not work, it was possible to spend entire afternoons and evenings moving from salon to salon, mixing music and conviviality. Every hostess had her "day" upon which she received. Paris socialites, dressed in their finest splendor, would be driven down the long boulevards in their carriages, alighting at one or another of the magnificent mansions, where they would be treated to a musical program of the highest quality, performed by a renowned diva or tenor, or an acclaimed virtuoso pianist or violinist; these artists might on occasion be accompanied by a full orchestra. These musical feasts were an integral part of a schedule that included art openings, evenings at the Opéra, and, in pleasant weather, long rides in a carriage to the Bois de Boulogne, including a stop at the Bois's restaurant, the Pré Catalan, to sip a cool lemonade or a glass of cognac.

Many matinees and soirees featured the mistress—or master—of the house as star performers. Aristocrats might not be gainfully employed, but in the artistic realm they did not rest idle. The Comtesse de Fontenailles sang the original compositions of her husband, who accompanied her on the piano; the Princesse de Broglie hosted a soiree where she sang Spanish songs, accompanied by mandolins, harps, and guitars, all played by her titled friends. While most of these performers were dilettantes, some were true artists. The Comtesse de Guerne was one of Fauré's favorite interpreters of his music. The Princesse Rachel de Brancovan, despite her extremely nervous disposition, was a virtuoso pianist; she would entertain her guests with magnificent performances of Chopin ballades, Paderewski etudes, and Mozart concertos. The pianistic prowess of the Marquise de Saint-Paul (who was equally renowned for her biting tongue) was so formidable that it earned her the nickname *"serpent à sonates"*—a pun on *"serpent à sonnettes,"* or rattlesnake.[9]

Salon culture was not just limited to the aristocracy. There were highly renowned salons in the *haute bourgeoisie,* the most prestigious of which were those of Mme. Émile Straus (daughter of Fromental Halévy, widow of Georges Bizet) and Mme. Édouard André, who was also an important art collector.[10] Still other salons, such as that of novelist Alphonse Daudet[11] and his wife, were strictly "artistic" in nature.[12] One of Winnaretta's favorite salons was that of Madeleine Lemaire. An amateur painter from the bourgeoisie, particularly well known for her watercolor depictions of flowers, Lemaire presented Saint-Saëns, Massenet, and Fauré at weekly musical gatherings. Composer-singer-pianist Reynaldo Hahn and pianist Édouard Risler played at her "Tuesdays" for nearly two decades. Both young men were doing their military service at the time Winnaretta met them, in the early 1890s. They would arrive at Lemaire's house in uniform and entertain the guests until the wee hours of the morning.[13] Winnaretta struck up a friendship with the Argentinean-born Hahn, a former student (and possibly a former lover) of Saint-Saëns. She was enthralled when the handsome composer would sit at the piano, accompanying himself in performances of his own *mélodies*; she recalled that he "sang in the perfect way composers have . . . always exactly as one imagined the song should be sung." The two saw each other frequently, discussing and playing "every sort of music,"[14] and Hahn's compositions in all genres became staples of Winnaretta's own musical gatherings.

The hostess who proved to be Winnaretta's most important mentor was Marguerite ("Meg") Baugnies, half-sister of composer Roger Jourdain and wife of painter Eugène Baugnies. On Friday nights, Meg would open up her house at 100 boulevard Malesherbes to "friends coming from work, tired after a full day, neighbors who decided at the last minute to leave their fireside corner to come sit at mine, painters still wearing their smocks."[15] Meg's guests comprised a wide circle of artists, composers, performing musicians, and writers, including those of the avant-garde. Winnaretta recalled those evenings in her memoirs. "Nobody who had not exhibited a piece of sculpture or a picture, or who was not a composer, a scientist or an inventor would ever be invited to these gatherings, to which no simple '*mondain*' or mere social star was admitted. I could fill pages with the names of all the remarkable people I met in this Salon." The atmosphere was much more casual than that found in the homes of the aristocracy: the artists would be off in a corner engaged in a friendly "painter's quarrel"; Fauré or pianist Édouard Risler would sit at the piano, playing for no one in particular; tenor Maurice Bagès would launch into the songs of Schumann or Pierre de Bréville with whatever accompanist was available; Emma Calvé would give a powerful performance of an aria without ever leaving her chair.[16]

Claude Debussy, whom Winnaretta met for the first time at Meg's house, made an unforgettable first impression. "Debussy's appearance was most striking; his short nose and deep-set eyes, his faunlike features and rather curly black hair and slight beard gave the impression of an Italian model, especially as his complexion was very dark and he sometimes wore small plain gold hooped earrings." Winnaretta had always assumed that all modern composers shared her adoration of **Wagner**. It therefore came as an enormous surprise to her to hear Debussy assert that Wagner's music "did not stir him in the least" and that he preferred the Russian composers Musorgsky, Borodin, and Balakirev, finding their music "clearer, more delicate and simple."[17] Sometimes he and his composer colleagues—Messager, Chabrier, Schmitt, and Chausson—would engage in musical "duels": in various four-hand duos, they would challenge each other to improvisational feats of prowess: "Try to top that . . . keep coming, I'll get you back."[18] Not all the music performed at Meg's was modern, however. Sometimes the evening was devoted to an impromptu performance of a Bach cantata, with the guests serving as soloists and choir.[19] From these readings, Winnaretta developed a lifelong love of Bach's sacred choral music.

Winnaretta established her own salon shortly after her marriage. Her predilection for the avant-garde manifested itself early on. What constituted the avant-garde in 1888 may seem surprising now, but the songs of Claude Debussy and the sparkling piano pieces of Emmanuel Chabrier were considered by the conservative musical mainstream—represented by Saint-Saëns, Massenet, and Ambroise Thomas—to be incomprehensible. Along with Fauré, Emmanuel Chabrier was one of the first major composers to become a regular member of Winnaretta's musical circle. Short and stout, he had abandoned a functionary post in the Ministry of the Interior to devote himself to composition. He wrote in a light and brilliant style, quite different from the overripe romanticism of contemporaries such as Franck, Chausson, and Lalo. At Winnaretta's table, Chabrier's humor and ebullience were as irrepressible as his passionately—often violently—expressed views on music, delivered "in a rich flow of language, full of fantasy and wit . . . often irresistibly comic."[20] Winnaretta recalled:

> Emmanuel Chabrier was a remarkable pianist. He was most enthusiastic and energetic, and very often after playing the whole act of an Opera before dinner, he had hardly swallowed the last mouthful and smoked a cigarette, when he would suddenly remark, "*Il y a longtemps qu'on n'a fait de la musique* [It's been a long time since anybody made music]," would fly to the piano and play again for an hour or two, singing every part of the score: tenor, bass or soprano, at the top of his voice, and rendering on the piano the sonority and tone of a full orchestra.[21]

Like most of his contemporaries, Chabrier had been seduced by Wagner's music, and attempted to incorporate the German's system of leitmotifs into his own stage works of a serious nature, perhaps to the detriment of his natural lyrical gifts and comic instincts. One such work from 1883, *Gwendoline,* was infused with this Wagnerian sense of drama. For years Chabrier had been trying to interest the Paris Opéra in the work, but to no avail, even though it had a successful first performance in Brussels in 1886.

The composer became bitter and discouraged. Perhaps it was the Wagnerian qualities that made Winnaretta take a particular interest in the opera. She stepped in to help, offering to give a concert version of the work in her salon, complete with soloists, chorus, and orchestra.[22]

It was frowned upon for a woman in society to undertake personally the organization of musical or artistic manifestations. There were two broad exceptions: she could lend her name as a *dame patronnesse* to help the success of a concert or theatrical presentation whose proceeds would benefit a charitable organization, or she could organize an artistic gathering of a specifically *mondain* character.[23] In either case she could not take an *active* role in the organization or production of the event; she could not have direct contact with a conductor, a musician, or a theater manager, for it was a generally accepted belief that show people led dissolute lives (although the occasional exception could be made for well-known composers).[24] Therefore, when Winnaretta offered to host the presentation of *Gwendoline,* it was undestood that Chabrier himself would have to see to the details of organization. The composer secured the aid of his composer friends in realizing the project. To Ernest Van Dyke, principal tenor in Bayreuth, Chabrier outlined the plan.

> A complete performance of *Gwendoline* will be given, 8 and 15 May, at the home of a very rich lady, with Madame Lureau-Escalaïs, Melchissedec, twenty-four choristers, double quartet, harp, harmonium (Fauré), piano (me), conductor (Gabriel Marie), on percussion, d'Indy and Messager. This should be *très chic,* and a *big secret, keep quiet, only you know about it,* as I'm in very serious negotiations with the Opéra, I've chosen on the advice of this woman (the Princesse de Scey-Montbéliard, née Singer) the lads of the Opéra who could then sing the roles on a moment's notice.[25]

Behind the scenes, Winnaretta marshaled her own forces as well. She put off the performance for one more week in order to insure a better performance. Although some of the artistic personnel changed between the planning stage and the evening of the soiree, the composer was still able to secure some of the best lyric and orchestral musicians for the salon execution. In addition to *Gwendoline,*[26] Winnaretta added Fauré's song *Clair de lune* (orchestrated for the occasion) to the program, along with works by d'Indy and Chausson.[27] *Le Figaro,* which acted as the mouthpiece for high society, customarily reported the goings-on in the most elite salons on its front page. If the Scey-Montbéliard soiree were to appear there, it would be a sure signal that Winnaretta achieved the recognition she desired among the musical hostesses. On 16 May 1888 she got her wish, when *Le Figaro* announced that "next Tuesday, a most interesting musical soiree will be given at the home of the Princesse de Scey-Montbéliard, where works of

MM. Emmanuel Chabrier and Gabriel Fauré will be performed."[28] Two days later, *Le Figaro* reported that "the soiree given . . . by the Princesse de Scey-Montbéliard was very brilliant," and went on to give full details of the guest list.[29] "It was a great success," remarked Winnaretta, "although the public thought the music extraordinarily modern and advanced."[30] The Paris Opéra must have concurred with the guests, for they could not be convinced to produced *Gwendoline* until 1893. But the occasion marked a turning point for Winnaretta in two ways: she had received the public recognition that she desired in high society, and she had begun what would become a lifetime career as a patron of composers and new music.

In French, acts of patronage—commissions, financial support, often coupled with social influence—are given the collective appellation of *mécénat*. French arts patrons were known as *mécènes,*[31] and the Princesse de Scey, whose Singer millions were being put to use to bring new music before the public, certainly deserved the designation. From the time of the *Gwendoline* soiree onward, both the salon hostesses and the musicians of Paris sought her out. Taking her cue from Meg Baugnies, Winnaretta hosted increasingly numerous performances of modern music, offering her home for performances of new works by young French composers, many of whom were members of the Société Nationale de Musique, an organization founded in the aftermath of the Franco-Prussian War by Camille Saint-Saëns and Romaine Bussine to promote contemporary French music.[32]

Meanwhile, she continued to keep up appearances with her husband. The Prince de Scey-Montbéliard had served as one of the witnesses in Belle-Blanche's wedding party. That summer, the Scey-Montbéliards made the round of *villégiatures,* or country house visits, an obligatory part of the aristocratic calendar. They traveled with Winnaretta's brothers down to the Château de Tencin, the Grenoble estate of the Marquise Joséphine ("Mina") de Monteynard, where Winnaretta and the Marquise spent their days painting and playing through the latest songs by Fauré.[33] From there the Sceys continued on to Bayreuth to attend performances of *Parsifal* and *Die Meistersinger von Nürnberg.*[34] That summer Meg Baugnies had arranged a mysterious "lottery," whose proceeds allowed the impoverished Fauré and fellow composer André Messager to fulfill their unrealized dream of traveling to Bayreuth. Fauré was ecstatic to be in attendance, but he was puzzled by some unspecified behavior of Winnaretta's, which prompted him to write to Meg, "Madame de Scey-Montbéliard is three parts mad!!!"[35] It was a madness that clearly appealed to the composer, however. Upon his return to Paris he gave Winnaretta a gift of a little piece of music, a one-page manuscript in his own hand bearing the comical title *Pensée fugitive mais définitive*—"Fugitive but Definitive Thought, by Roger Jourdain, transcribed for three hands and one foot by G. Fauré."[36]

In November 1888 the Scey-Montbéliards traveled to Paignton for a series of balls and festivities held at the Wigwam, given in honor of the coming-of-age of Paris Singer, who had married in 1887, and was now a family man and the new proprietor of the family estate.[37] Other than brief mentions in newspaper articles, there is not much indication of how the Prince de Scey spent his time during his marriage. But it is clear that while Winnaretta may have paid obeisance to social convention on the surface, privately she did what pleased her, with or without her husband. She continued to entertain her avant-garde friends. An anecdote concerning Chabrier recounted by Francis Poulenc, who had had the story confirmed by Winnaretta herself, reveals the extent to which the composer felt free to speak "in the vernacular" in front of his hostess. One evening after the performance of *Gwendoline*, Chabrier dined with the Princesse de Scey. When his hostess had passed him asparagus, he leaned over to her, and said in an easily audible stage whisper, "You eat that, Madame, and it will make your urine stink!"[38]

What did the Prince de Scey-Montbéliard think of his wife's eccentric guest? One wonders if he was present at the dinner table at all. But by now, Winnaretta had ceased caring what her husband thought. She had kept up the pretense of the marriage for two years, but that had now become untenable. Her troubles were further compounded in December 1888, when her oldest brother, Mortimer, brought suit against the Singer executor, David Hawley, charging that Hawley had paid himself too much money in commissions. The international press picked up the story, and there soon appeared a new series of articles rehashing the scandals around Isaac's will, and recounting the details of the fabulous inheritances of the Singer children. "[They] draw upon Mr. Hawley as they need money," reported one of the New York papers. "They have their own houses and carriages, and tutors and servants. They are worth $1,500,000 each."[39]

The Prince de Scey-Montbéliard may have decided that he was entitled to some of that inheritance just at the moment that Winnaretta was coming to the realization that she had had enough of being married. She had lived, unhappily, under one roof with her husband for almost exactly the length of time—twenty-one months—that it took to assemble the metal pieces of the Eiffel Tower, and in the Spring of 1889, just about the time when Gustave Eiffel was mounting a platform at the top of his creation to accept the Legion of Honor award, Winnaretta was serving her husband with separation papers. She eventually secured freedom from her marriage, although not without a struggle with her husband's family. This is attested to in an 1889 letter from Winnaretta's mother to Hawley, in which Isabella can barely conceal her gloating sense of triumph. "You will be surprised to hear that Winnaretta is suing for a separation from her husband—it seems they have bothered her so much for money that she won't stand it any longer and he married her with false papers he is no more a Prince than I am so she is paying for her bad behavior to me and getting punished for it—however I do not think she cares one bit about it."[40]

Isabella had assessed her daughter accurately. Winnaretta's separation from Louis de Scey-Montbéliard was due only in part to their incompatible sexual preferences. It was more likely that the constraints associated with being an aristocratic wife, both within her own home, and as perceived by the wider society of the nobility, slowed her down too much. Winnaretta picked up the pieces of her life with astonishing speed. No sooner had her husband packed his bags than she initiated a complete reconstruction of the rue Cortambert part of the property. While the house was being gutted she went to live at 12 rue de Lübeck, the home of her sister Belle-Blanche and brother-in-law Duc Élie Decazes. This stay lasted almost the full two years between her separation and her divorce.[41] During that period she also began the arduous process of applications and interviews that she hoped would lead to the Vatican's annulment of her marriage. Divorce in those days was a rarity, and Winnaretta was surely aware of the social stigma that would be attached to the act. But she perceived it as a necessary first step in a process leading to her spiritual freedom.

The separation, giving her a legal definition of her new identity, was the first of three stages in the remaking of Winnaretta's life. The second stage was the reconstruction of her house, the domain that would become the center of her universe. The idea of a woman having the freedom to move, to act constructively in the outside world, was not one that could have ever been imagined even by someone as willful as Winnaretta. Therefore, if she sought to create, and to foster creation, that activity would have to take place in her home. Consequently, plans for a complete overhaul of her property were drawn up. The heart of the house was to be a new *atelier,* a space to be used for daily work on her art and her music, and a center for the most up-to-date manifestations of art and music, brilliant enough to attract the elite of Parisian aristocratic and cultural circles.

The third stage had to do with deciding on a personal mission in the world beyond her home. Paris Singer had alluded to the "many noble and charitable works to be done in Paris," and Winnaretta must have instinctively known that her best contribution could be made on behalf of the contemporary arts. Giving money to existing institutions, however, would not be enough to satisfy her needs for intellectual stimulation: Winnaretta envisioned a life in which her Singer fortune and her own personal drive could be put to active use in the perpetuation of and influence on new music and art.

In that spirit, she participated in many aspects of musical life. She studied organ, taking lessons with the greatest organists in the capital, Alexandre Guilmant and Eugène Gigout.[42] She became a regular at Marguerite Baugnies's "Fridays," savoring the musical feasts offered every week in Meg's comfortable and unpretentious salon. On 6 April 1889 (still using the name of Princesse de Scey-Montbéliard) she sponsored a concert of new works under the auspices of the Société Nationale de Musique.[43] In a

thank-you letter, Fauré wrote that the general consensus of those in attendance (including Tchaikovsky) was that "Saturday's concert was the most
interesting and the most successful that we've had in a long time."[44] Even
while the rue Cortambert music room was in the process of being rebuilt,
Winnaretta still continued to host salon gatherings there. A letter of gratitude from Vincent d'Indy, received after she had hosted a performance of
his new Piano Trio in July 1889, is typical: "I was able, thanks to you, to
hear my work in the performance conditions of good acoustics and public
exposure for which it was written. . . . I have never had the occasion to hear
this trio in a fashion that so fully satisfied me, and I am happy, Princesse, to
owe this impression, rare in one's artistic career, to you."[45] Shortly thereafter, Winnaretta made the pilgrimage to Bayreuth, in the company of her
mother (no doubt imposing herself upon her daughter as chaperone) and
Chabrier.[46] His usual irrepressible self, Chabrier thought nothing of clam-
bering into the car with Winnaretta and the Duchesse de Camposelice after
the performance, and when invited to dine with them, managed, even at
the advanced hour, to "eat enough for four people."[47]

Winnaretta maintained her involvement with the art world as well. She
continued to make paintings, using the ground floor rooms of the rue de
Sablons house as a studio. The progressive growth of her talent enabled
her to enter two canvasses, *Printemps* and *Portrait de Madame la Marquise de M. . .*[48] in the Salon de Beaux-Arts in 1889, and another one, a
portrait of her teacher Félix Barrias, in the 1890 exhibition.[49] She sought to
broaden her contacts and friendships with young artists, at the same time
building her own personal art collection. In 1889, she purchased Claude
Monet's *En Norvégienne* from the Galeries Georges Petit.[50] That same year,
when Monet was soliciting donations from Manet's admirers for a project
to buy his famous *Olympia* and donate it to the Louvre, Winnaretta helped
him to organize the fund. She contributed 2000 francs, the single largest
contribution, so that her childhood idol could posthumously "receive the
place that he deserves" in the pantheon of great French artists.[51] She was
aided in her organization of the fund by the American painter John Singer
Sargent, who was in Paris to visit the Exposition Universelle. The elegant
portraitist and landscape painter had scandalized the Paris establishment
in 1884 with his exhibition of the bare-shouldered, haughty "Madame X";
since moving to London, however, he had become one of the most sought-
after portrait painters in England and the United States. Winnaretta had
met Sargent years earlier through her friends Ernest and Amélie Duez. She
admired his work, as well as his ardent devotion to music and championship of modern composers—especially Fauré.[52] She commissioned him to
execute a full-length portrait of her. The resulting *Portrait of the Princesse
Louis de Scey-Montbéliard* was executed during the summer of 1889—at
the same moment of her separation. The painting depicts its subject as a
commanding, regal, and aloof personnage, dressed in a resplendent white

embroidered gown and fur stole. The dark wood panelling, Louis XVI chairs, and Aubusson carpet in the background amply identify her as a woman of means.[53]

Meanwhile, during the same period, the American city of Chicago was preparing to host the 1892 World's Fair, which would coincide with the 400th anniversary of the arrival of Christopher Columbus in the New World. Paris's 1889 Exposition Universelle had signaled the advent of a new spirit of industrial and technological modernism in Europe, and the most exuberant symbol of this spirit was the Eiffel Tower that now towered over the urban landscape. The Chicago fair, officially titled the World's Columbian Exposition, intended to go its European predecessor one better: not only would it display the most up-to-date manifestations of American commerce and technology, but would give equal place to the value of education and culture. The United States looked to Europe to set the standard. In 1890, architectural plans were drawn up and construction begun on a domed Beaux-Arts Palace of Fine Arts, designed to be large enough to hold eight thousand artworks of all genres from countries around the globe.

It was probably Sargent who alerted Winnaretta to the imminent visit to Paris of the Exposition's Committee of Fine Arts, which would begin the process of selecting works by European artists, and works by American artists living in Europe, to be exhibited in the Palace. Sargent had entered a number of his works, and surely counseled Winnaretta to do the same. Not surprisingly, nine of Sargent's canvasses were accepted—he was already a famous painter. Winnaretta, to her astonishment and delight, had a painting accepted as well, a work from 1890 entitled *Spring Study.*[54] There must have been a particular satisfaction for this expatriate daughter of one of American's great industrialists to have her artwork exhibited in the land of her birth; equally satisfying must have been the knowledge that her work would be joining that of other French artists in her circle: her teachers Barrias and Mathey, and her friends Roger Jourdain, Jacques-Émile Blanche, Madeleine Lemaire, Ernest Duez, Georges Clairin, and Paul Helleu.

The acceptance of Winnaretta's piece into the World's Fair coincided with ongoing construction of her new *atelier.* Towards the end of 1890 she decided that she should commission some new works of music and visual art for the official "opening" of the salon, works that would attract the attention of society, the cultural community, and the ever-important press. In extending her largesse towards talented French composers and artists, she could bring renown to her salon by the association of the new works with the space in which they would be performed and exhibited. Her motives were not altogether altruistic: she was a materialist. Satisfaction as a patron would come not just by providing funds for these new works, but also, because she had paid for them, the works would, in her words, "belong completely to her."[55]

Here begins the true career of Winnaretta Singer, who sometime during the year 1890 decided definitively to consecrate part of her fortune to the patronage of the modernist arts, especially modernist music. She would become a *commandatrice,* which traditionally meant a woman who commissioned a portrait or some other work of art. In Winnaretta's case, the commissioning of new works, financed by dividends from Singer sewing machine stock, became an activity that would preoccupy her for the next fifty years. In her role as *commandatrice* Winnaretta would prove herself a complicated figure, alternatively forward-thinking and autocratic, flexible and rigid, open-handed and penny-pinching. Happily, an extensive correspondence concerning the genesis and progress of her first two projects is still extant. These letters provide a fascinating portrait of the woman as a young patron.

Interestingly, Winnaretta's first commission was not for a piece of music, but for a piece of art, and it was John Singer Sargent who inspired her interest in the artist. During the period that he was executing her portrait, Sargent attended the Paris exhibitions of an innovative sculptor and ceramicist, Jean Carriès. One of the first exponents in his genre of Symbolist design, Carriès had been experimenting with new methods of covering sandstone objects with enamel glazes. Seeking to integrate artisanry with artistry, Carriès infused his objects with a mystical strangeness, strongly influenced by Gothic style. His strange figures seemed to inhabit some kind of fantastic bestiary from Celtic or Germanic legends; yet, instead of repelling, the figures attracted the viewer because of the way the artist had combined bizarre forms with beautiful execution. Seeking to incorporate into the objects of everyday the fantastical world of the imagination, Carriès was an important precursor of the Art Nouveau movement, then just at its beginning; in subsequent years major figures of the Art Nouveau style, including Gallé and Guimard, would adapt his innovations into their own work.

Still relatively unknown, Carriès was invited to present his work in 1888 in the home of two well-known "free thinkers," Paul and Aline Ménard-Dorian. The couple hosted an unusual salon that combined discussions of radical socialist politics with fine musical performances.[56] Their influence in a number of cultural circles, as well as the intelligent presentation of Carriès's work, created a sensation with those who came to see his curious pieces. John Singer Sargent was among them, and at his behest Winnaretta went to see Carriès's work for herself in November 1889.[57] She was still under the thrall of the magnificent performances of Wagner's *Parsifal* that she had heard in Bayreuth a few months earlier, and perhaps the startling ceramic figures in the artist's studio recalled to her the magical paganism of Klingsor's castle. It seems that at this time she unveiled to Carriès an extraordinary project: she intended to purchase a manuscript of *Parsifal,* and wanted to create a room in her house that, like a tabernacle, would house nothing but the manuscript.

Did Winnaretta actually ever carry through with her plans to purchase the *Parsifal* manuscript? It remains one of the tantalizing unsolved myster-

ies of this story. Her name does not appear in the list of sources for the
extant manuscripts of Wagner's works;[58] moreover, there are no letters from
Winnaretta or other documents alluding to this matter in the Wagner archives housed at Bayreuth.[59] This does not preclude the possibility that
Winnaretta really intended to buy either a full score or an extract of Wagner's
great religious music-drama, but whether her intentions or requests ever
reached the Wagner family at all cannot be proved one way or the other.
What is known is that the name of the opera became immediately attached
to the project, and that Winnaretta apparently did nothing to disabuse the
public of the notion that she in fact possessed the manuscript. From the
inception of the project with Carriès, the work became known as *La Porte
de Parsifal*. The title has survived until the present day, and is still used in
current art history scholarship.[60]

Let us give Winnaretta the benefit of the doubt about her intention to
purchase the manuscript in 1889. It would have been on her mind when
she was first introduced to Jean Carriès's original and alluring work. She
was apparently equally impressed by the artist himself, who spoke on the
day of their meeting with passion and eloquence about his creative ideas
for monumental pieces in enameled ceramic, works that would be, in the
words of art critic Arsène Alexandre, "at once harmonious and fantastic,
refined and barbaric."[61] All the while, he spoke in a spirit of "absolute
disinterestedness"—that is, he was not terribly concerned about remuneration for these great projects.[62] Winnaretta was intrigued, and a proposition
was made: would Carriès be interested in designing and realizing an ornamental door that would become the entryway to this manuscript, a work
of art unique on its own terms, and worthy of protecting the precious object contained within?

It was an irresistible proposition. With the help of his colleague Eugène
Grasset, Carriès submitted a rendering in pencil of the projected door to
Winnaretta on 16 January 1890. The design was a monumental three-
pronged arch in the shape of a gracefully bowed "M" in Art Nouveau
style, with Gothic-style figures—monks, knights, magicians, maidens—
embedded within its form. From the looks of the drawing, it appears that
the Wagner manuscript was to be housed in a portion of the new *atelier*,
still under construction, underneath the organ loft. At the top of the central prong, acting as a sort of strange guardian angel, was the figure of a
young woman with a long face, a disconcertingly intense expression, and a
downturned mouth—an ethereal rendering of his patron? The individual
design elements were intricately interwoven, and the overall plan was extremely complex. Yet it was, the artist proclaimed to Winnaretta, a work
that would integrate his daring new ideas about art: it would create the
synthesis between artisanry and artistry that he had long hoped to achieve.
Winnaretta was dazzled by the design conception, but as Carriès had not
thought through the practical considerations of the project—the time needed

to realize it, and the issue of what a reasonable fee might be for the work—it took some time to reach a contractual arrangement. Finally, on 22 March Winnaretta sent the artist a letter spelling out the terms: Carriès would be paid 60,000 francs for a work that should be completed in eighteen months, or two years at the most. Roughly two-thirds of this sum would be put into a bank account in installments as needed to cover the material costs of realizing the project; final payment would be made upon completion and installation of the work.[63] It was understood that the sum was sufficiently large that Carriès would undertake no other commissions or independent projects until the work for Winnaretta was completed.

The project began with good will on all sides. Winnaretta put an initial 10,000 francs on account for the artist's use. The assemblage of a full-size plaster model of the doorframe was completed in the summer of 1890.[64] In his Burgundy studio[65] Carriès began to mold and fire the individual small figures that eventually would be fitted into the larger design of the doorframe. With money in his pocket and the deadline seemingly far in the future, the artist gave free reign to his imagination. His style began to undergo subtle changes. Unlike the gently curving pre-Raphaelite figures that had predominated the 1889 exhibition, the newly molded figures had begun to take on more and more grotesque shapes. The expressions of the figurines manifested gaping mouths, grimaces, or mocking smiles bordering on the monstrous. Behind every human face lurked the spirit of a diabolical gargoyle from an ancient cathedral. It seemed that Carriès's inner demons were finding their way into his art. These conceptual changes necessitated a rethinking of the larger design concept, for all the figures were interwoven with each other and with the shape of the door. Each change in the overall design conception required remolding, recasting, and refiring of the figures, as well as the help of workmen to fashion the molds and fire the kilns. Sometimes the final product would be too large or too small to fit into its projected place in the doorframe. And each miscalculation required another remolding and refiring, which resulted in another expense to be born by the artist. As his artistic and practical anxieties mounted, his morale and progress lagged.

Winnaretta traveled down to Burgundy in December 1890 to see the artist's studio and the work in progress. She was shocked that Carriès would soon require another advance to pay his workmen. More shocking still, however, was the visible stylistic change that was manifested in the newest figurines. Her letter says much about her reactions, and her patronage style.

Your work is really beautiful, and the work that you have accomplished in these last months is marvelous. I was at first a bit worried faced with all these large and terrible masks, and I almost regretted that there were not here and there a few more consoling figures. I'm telling you my impression, but I have the greatest confidence in you, and I'm aware of the charm that your beautiful enamel pieces will add to the work, so I don't want to influence you.

You should have warned me *in advance* that you needed such a large amount of money in only a few days, especially at the end of the year. It is impossible to put 15,000 francs at your disposal right away. . . . I will send you a check for 7,500 francs [now] and another 2,500 francs in the month of January. . . .

Since we are speaking of money matters, I have to tell you that I can't change the conditions agreed upon between us. . . . I speak to you [so frankly] only because, thinking you so disinterested and so impractical for the ordinary things of life, I'm afraid that you will completely forget the question of interests, very annoying, but unfortunately very real also.

I reiterate my admiration for your superb work; you *alone* perhaps are capable of following it through to the end.[66]

With the *Porte de Parsifal* undertaken, Winnaretta now turned her attention to commissioning a piece of music with which to inaugurate her *atelier.* She decided to offer the commission to her first musical friend, Fauré, who was still an important part of her musical and emotional life. In late 1888, at the moment of the death of Pamela Boyer and the period of greatest difficulty in her marriage, he had dedicated a song, *Larmes* [Tears], Op. 51, to her. The song is written in the traditionally dramatic key of C Minor. It is one of the composer's most turbulent compositions: the harmony is densely chromatic, and the text, a poem by Jean Richepin, is marked by ferocious accents. One might well speculate that it was Fauré's comprehension of his friend's unhappiness that inspired the almost violent emotionalism evoked in the song. The composer's own life was not particularly happy during this period either. He was still laboring in relative obscurity, making his living primarily as an organist and choir director at the Madeleine, and as a suburban piano teacher. His name was frequently confused with that of Jean-Baptiste Faure, a baritone whose sentimentally pious compositions enjoyed great popularity among the less sophisticated musical public. At this point the composer was frightfully overburdened by an impossible work schedule and financial worries; insecure by nature, he fretted that his music would never be received by a larger public.[67] But Gabriel Fauré *did* have a shadow career of some renown—in the salons. His works were among those most frequently played in the musical matinees and soirees of the aristocracy and of the Paris musicians themselves.[68] Works like the Sonata for Violin and Piano, Op. 13, and the Piano Quartet, Op. 15, now staples of the chamber music repertoire, as well as any number of the songs, first came to the attention of the larger musical public as a result of their championship in the private homes of the cultured wealthy class.

Winnaretta decided that she could be of service to Fauré. Their friendship had deepened over the year, and they were regularly together at Meg

Baugnies's Friday evening salon. The depth of the composer's attachment to the younger woman can be measured by a letter written to her in mid-January 1891, after Winnaretta left for England to attend the marriage of her youngest brother Franklin: "I can't tell you how greatly you are missed here, how painful a process it is to get out of the habit of seeing you at frequent intervals. Talking about you amongst ourselves is but poor consolation! . . . *Fridays* are not the same without you."[69]

From Paignton, Winnaretta wrote to Fauré, offering to pay him 25,000 francs for a short musical work with a mutually agreed-upon libretto or poetic text.[70] For the composer, the proposed fee represented a truly enormous sum;[71] he accepted the commission with "gratitude and enthusiasm."[72] Upon Winnaretta's return to Paris, the two met to decide on a poet to write the text; together they decided that Paul Verlaine should be approached. A member of a group of "decadent" poets that also included Rimbaud and Mallarmé, Verlaine espoused a philosophy of moral freedom, creative self-expression, and the principle of art for art's sake. His poetry, constructed from simple, musical language, was a celebration of sensation and moment-to-moment impressions. Winnaretta was a reader of *Le Décadent,* a review founded by Verlaine and his colleagues in 1886, and she was interested in the group's aesthetic values as well as its creative fruits. She contacted the poet to solicit his participation in the project, and offered him a handsome fee.[73] Verlaine's response was charmingly whimsical: he didn't want money, he declared, but would be happy if the princesse would open a credit for him at his tailors or his bootmakers.[74] Eager to put the project in motion, Fauré contacted Verlaine to square away the details of "length, type of subject, approximate period, type of verse. . . ."[75] But the poet chose this moment to drop out of sight. A longtime alcoholic, his life had become an "endless to-and-fro between the pub and the poorhouse,"[76] as Fauré himself described it. Verlaine finally surfaced in mid-January 1891—at the Hôpital Saint-Antoine, undergoing treatment for his addiction to absinthe (*he* claimed it was treatment for rheumatism).[77]

Winnaretta was not going to let the poet's alcoholism stand in the way of her plans. She promised Verlaine that she would make the payments for his hospital room; she further agreed to give him complete latitude in choosing the subject matter of the poem.[78] All efforts were made on behalf of the poet with one goal in mind: to get the besotted genius working on the project—and it was poor Fauré who was charged with the Herculean effort of keeping him on task.[79] The composer made several visits to the dismal room at the Hôpital Saint-Antoine, on one occasion making a little sketch of this "unique, strange, incomprehensible character"[80] in his miserable bed.[81] Finally in April, Verlaine was released from the hospital; assuring Fauré that he had begun work "on *our* project," he asked if the composer could secure a cash advance for the work from the Princesse.[82] Each day Fauré would meet the poet in a café, hoping to see some results, each day he returned disappointed. "I won't conceal from you," he wrote to Winnaretta, "that this man, with all his extraordinary gifts, seems to me to have become incapable of the kind of effort, the kind of sustained application that a work of any importance would require. . . . Nothing counts for him, nothing matters to him, as long as he has something to drink!"[83]

Winnaretta removed herself from the situation entirely. In the spring, awaiting word from Rome on the progress of her annulment proceedings, she suddenly was seized by the notion of staying for an extended time in Venice. She had first experienced the seductive delights of that city as a teenager, when she made a visit with her painting teacher Félix Barrias. This time Winnaretta and her brother Franklin and his new wife rented a small palace on the Grand Canal. The fifteenth-century house was nicknamed the Casa Wolkoff after its current owner, a Russian count who had been a longtime resident of Venice, and who had known Richard Wagner.[84] She set off for Italy in April, inviting Fauré, as well as their mutual friends, the Jourdains and the Duezes, to join her there in the latter part of May. Fauré's daily stresses had recently taken the form of chronic headaches, and the invitation to go on holiday offered a much-needed respite from the daily grind—not to mention an escape from the stalled Verlaine project. He arrived in Venice on 18 May, and the almost six weeks that he spent there turned out to be one of the happiest periods in his life. Winnaretta recalled in her memoirs: "I carefully prepared a quiet room with a piano as a study for Fauré to work in, but I had forgotten how fond he was of cafés; and I am obliged to say that he wrote his *Cinq Mélodies de Venise* at a little marble table at the Café Florian on the Piazza, in the midst of the noise and turmoil of a busy Venetian crowd, rather than in the peaceful room I had arranged for him."[85]

In this vibrant atmosphere, Fauré began to reacquaint himself with Verlaine's previous work, and discovered the lyrical power of the poet whose creative genius had so sadly foundered as a result of his addiction. It was the musicality of the poems that particularly struck Fauré. Within a few weeks he had written two exquisite new *mélodies* on two of Verlaine's early poems, *Mandoline* and *En Sourdine*. Three more were written upon Fauré's return to Paris; together the songs on Verlaine's celebrated poems became known as the *Cinq Mélodies de Venise*. In fact, the last three songs of the cycle, *Green*, *A Clymène*, and *C'est l'extase*, were composed some months later, between late June and September 1891. Naturally, Fauré dedicated the songs to his hostess.[86] The two songs completed that summer had their first performance by Amélie Duez, a fine singer, accompanied by the composer who played a little "yacht piano," a gift to Winnaretta by one of her brothers, whose keyboard was approximately the same range as a harpsichord. The instruments, the musicians, and the guests were often taken out at night on a *peata*, or fishing boat, as evening entertainment. It was thus that, on one of those evenings, while the boat sailed slowly down the lagoons, the haunting strains of *En Sourdine* blended with the enchantment of the warm peaceful Venetian evenings.[87]

The lively days and sultry nights spent in Winnaretta's company had as intense an effect on Fauré's emotions as it did on his creative powers. Was Fauré in love with Winnaretta? His 1883 marriage to artist Marie Fremiet, while not loveless, was not particularly emotionally satisfying either. Throughout his life the intensely passionate composer sought out relationships, both sexual and platonic, with women with whom he felt more temperamentally compatible. Implausible as a liaison with Winnaretta may have seemed from a sexual point of view, it is apparent that the composer regarded her as someone more than "just" a friend. Her obvious adoration of his music, dating from her teenage years, must have touched the struggling composer, whose insecurities and lack of good luck had thus far hobbled his career. Fauré's perception that Winnaretta understood him, that she held him in high esteem, had always inspired him to open up to her in a unique way.[88] During this period, manuscripts and autographed copies of Fauré's works dating from 1890—*La Passion,* for chorus and piano reduction, and the songs *Nocturne, La Rose,* and *Shylock,* in a version for voice and harp[89]—found their way into Winnaretta's music library, although it is not clear whether Fauré presented them as gifts, or whether Winnaretta bought them in an effort to ease her friend's financial woes. That summer, whatever latent feelings of romantic love he had suppressed over their decade-long friendship apparently came to a head during his stay in Venice. He poured out his conflicted emotions to Meg Baugnies:

> Nor is there a word to express the extent of the admiration and almost something more (ouch) that I feel for our adorable hostess! A parenthesis at this point! BUT YOU MUST SWEAR NOT TO GIVE ME AWAY! Not that it makes any difference since we are going home soon and it will all be over! . . . But this, I repeat, is a crisis, the last one of course and I have a feeling that as soon as I step into the train to go home it will all blow over and I shall be left with nothing but a great amazement! . . . And I love Marie, I promise you, and I know no one to equal her! Don't worry, it's nothing! But it's true what you told me: our princess is exquisite on closer acquaintance. She's so original in everything she does, with a real aptitude for so many intelligent things, and so charmingly good-humored and so kind![90]

At the same time that Fauré was struggling with his amorous feelings for Winnaretta, he was attempting to resolve the problem of a librettist for her commissioned work. The object of his affection, influenced by the rage for Orientalism that permeated late nineteenth-century French culture,[91] had conceived of a different subject for a libretto: the life of the Buddha. Having despaired of Verlaine's participation, Fauré thought of poet Maurice

Bouchor, who had written a book on ancient religions, as a potential collaborator;[92] in late May, the composer approached Bouchor about the "Buddha" project.[93] At the very moment that Bouchor agreed "in principle" to
a collaboration,[94] Verlaine wrote to say that had finally decided on an idea
for a project: it would be of a comic nature, and would have as a title
L'Hôpital Watteau.[95] The text was based on one of the last scenes from the
Comoedia dell'Arte, in which Pierrot, Columbine, and Harlequin, confined
to a hospital ward, waxed philosophical from their beds about the nature
of life and love.[96] Winnaretta was delighted with Verlaine's idea. Fauré,
however, was not attracted to the idea of creating music for this subject.[97]
The "Buddha" idea appealed to him even less: the earthy, sensual composer had never evinced the slightest interest in the spiritualism and occult-
ism that fascinated *fin-de-siècle* Parisians. "I am a long way from the divine
Buddha and his goodness!" he confessed in one letter to his patron.[98]
Throughout his career Fauré would always have difficulty composing music for texts that did not suit his temperament and rejected a number of
money-making projects on this basis.[99]

On this occasion, however, he was reluctant to oppose the wishes of
either of his friends, poet or patron. To avoid confronting the issue, he
simply lost touch with Verlaine, accidentally on purpose, so to speak.
Winnaretta, however, equally anxious about the health of the poet and the
health of the project, pressed Fauré to find him. She sent several advances
intended to stave off Verlaine's degradation and illness and to motivate
him to write.[100] Both she and Fauré may have hoped that the prospect of
the commission would be an incentive to the poet to assist himself, physically and psychologically, in his own recovery. But Verlaine continued to
deteriorate, and the entire project was put on hold. Fauré, meanwhile, tried
to divert Winnaretta's attention by discussing his other, more current compositions that could be performed in Winnaretta's salon. "My quintet . . .
simply *must* be finished by [October] in order that the *first* performance
may take place at your house as your '*welcome home*'![101] If you would like
that, you would give me such pleasure!"[102] At the same time Fauré was
plunged in the composition of the last three of the *Mélodies de Venise.* In
late July, sending the manuscript of *Green* to avenue Henri-Martin, he wrote
to his friend, "The song has come back to me at last and I enclose it here-
with in fear and trembling! Have I adequately expressed this marvelous
hymn of adoration? I don't know. Do not tear it up with your two white
hands."[103]

As pleased as she may have been by the dedication of the song cycle,
Winnaretta was nonetheless growing impatient. She feared that the Verlaine-
Fauré collaboration would never bear fruit. To make matters worse, Carriès
was not even close to completing the *Porte de Parsifal* by the originally
agreed-upon deadline. Later that summer Winnaretta informed the artist
of her wish to have the project finished by June or July 1892, adding "You

understand my impatience to see the work in place, and also to see finished the decoration of my *atelier,* which will not be very habitable without the Door having been put in place."[104]

Carriès had become consumed with his anxieties, artistic and financial. As the summer deadline neared, the basic technical problems of the piece had yet to be resolved, and more funds were needed immediately for yet another round of modeling and firing of the figurines. He asked his patron for what remained of the 60,000 francs, but Winnaretta, unaware of the complexities of Carriès's situation, reiterated that final payment would be made only *"when the door was in place and everything finished."*[105] Overwhelmed by the project's scope, worried about the expense of each new firing, frustrated by the endless series of unsuccessful results, and terrified by the monsters and gargoyles that peopled his creative universe,[106] Carriès shifted the blame for his anguish and impoverishment to his patron. "My work has taken everything, I'm walking around in a painful dream, and this woman (Madame la Princesse de Scey) will really have the flesh of my flesh when she receives my work."[107] It was thus that Winnaretta's next letter, inquiring as to the progress of the project, provoked the following shocking response from the artist:

For the commissioned work, I have worked non-stop for thirty-four months for the modest sum of 46,000 francs, which doesn't even represent the cost of materials, not counting my time and my costly ceramic experiments. My error in this whole business was undertaking this enormous work, without precedent in the ceramic arts, for the sum of 60,000 francs, of which 46,000 have been received, and two times more spent by me for my expenses.

But let's not dwell on that. For the moment, what interests you is when the job will be finished. It is impossible to say. The difficulties in attempting a work of new art are too great and impossible to anticipate.

But what is always possible and easy is gross banality. I could do that for you rapidly for your money. I'd rather give [you your money] back.[108]

Winnaretta responded in the bluntest terms.

I can't let you continue the role of "martyr" that you are playing with me. . . . Since you began my work, I absolutely paid . . . *all your expenses* without exception. . . .

I gave you, in all respects, the greatest freedom. Since I was interested in you, I commissioned a very important work from you, and I gave you considerable sums of money.

Whatever you might think, I don't think that you would often find similar conditions. And it's after having acted thus, after having also given you the occasion to develop your ideas, and having shown you a

generosity and a trust quite out of the ordinary, that you allow yourself
to take towards me an attitude of victim. . . .

I am surprised and pained by your attitude. You use the expression
"practical business woman" [to describe me]. I hardly need to add that
if it were justified, I would not have had the pleasure of knowing you.[109]

The dispute with Carriès dragged on, ultimately with unhappy results.
Winnaretta's first experience of feeling that she had been treated unjustly
by an artist whom she had supported with the best intentions would be a
recurrent theme throughout her career.

She had other worries. She was aware of her tenuous standing in society,
amidst the very members of cultural and aristocratic Paris that she hoped
to draw into her home. The 1888 *avant-première* of Chabrier's *Gwendoline*
that she had hosted as the Princesse de Scey-Montbéliard had drawn the
desired attention from influential members of society, as well as the notice
of the press, but it was the fact that she was the newly married young
Princesse de Scey as much as the music that had generated the interest.
Now that she was a divorced woman (her civil divorce had been granted
on 25 March 1891), it was not certain that the aristocracy would continue
to socialize with someone who was merely Madame Singer.[110]

With impeccably poor timing, Madame the Duchesse de Camposelice
chose that same period to announce an important decision about her own
social standing. At the age of fifty she had decided to marry again. She was
still an attractive woman, but her finances had been severely depleted by
the impecunious Victor Rubsaet. Aiming her sights considerably lower, she
found a husband nine years younger than she, Paul Sohège, who had nothing to recommend him but his youthful good looks. Remarriage did nothing to cure Isabella of her profligate habits: to maintain her opulent lifestyle,
she began to sell off her collection of Stradivarius and Guarnerius stringed
instruments.[111] If the Singer children were disgusted by their mother's latest
lack of judgment in her choice of husbands, at least by this time they were
all of major age, and could rest easy in the knowledge that Monsieur Sohège
could not touch their fortunes.

To succeed in society, Winnaretta was going to need assistance from
someone with the requisite clout and influential contacts in the rarefied
and socially mystifying world of the nobility. To that end, in 1891 she
sought out the reigning queen of Paris society, Comtesse Élisabeth Greffulhe.

Born in 1860, the beautiful countess was the daughter of Prince Joseph
de Caraman-Chimay, a Belgian-born diplomat of modest means, and his
wife, née Marie de Montesquiou, a talented pianist who had studied with
Clara Schumann and played chamber music with Franz Liszt.[112] Élisabeth
de Caraman-Chimay grew up in a loving family circle, where literature,
music, and art were an integral part of daily life. She lived a good deal of
her early life in the public eye, attending diplomatic social functions with

her father. At age eighteen, her parents arranged for her to wed Vicomte (later Comte) Henry Greffulhe, eleven years her senior and sole heir to a substantial fortune. A staunch materialist of immature character, Greffulhe disparaged his young wife's artistic interests, and demanded that she adhere to the rigid mores of his extended family, who lived in the same *hôtel* as the couple. Élisabeth submitted to this limiting and stultifying existence for the first few years of her marriage, but as her husband's temper became more volatile and his infidelities more flagrant, she began to carve out a new life in the society from which she had unwittingly been obliged to retreat. Starved for intellectual and artistic stimulation, she established a salon in her palatial *hôtel* on the rue d'Astorg, surrounding herself with the most brilliant and talented representatives of the worlds of music, art, literature, and politics. Although she became a champion of Republican causes, her social values remained elitist: she received only those select few deemed worthy of her consideration. As a consequence the Greffulhe salon became all the more sought after because of its inacessibility. The Comtesse, always exquisitely dressed in Worth and Fortuny gowns, played on her physical allure, intelligence, and haughtiness to carve out a prominent place for herself in society. She worked constantly to improve her general culture: she studied photography with Paul Nadar and contemporary literature with her cousin, the effete dandy Comte Robert de Montesquiou.

In 1889, on the advice of Montesquiou, Greffulhe undertook the organization of a performance of excerpts from Handel's *Messiah*, held under the auspices of the Société Philanthropique. The performance of the oratorio, a work unknown to French audiences, was one of the great events of the season, both an artistic and financial triumph. Empowered by her success as an organizer (a role strictly forbidden to aristocratic women), she turned her attention to the promotion of living French composers. Through her patronage of, and friendship with, Gabriel Fauré, she became aware of how difficult it was for young French composers to have their works heard and promoted in public venues. The existing concert organizations of the period were extremely conservative, and their programs Teutonically inclined (the works of Mozart, Beethoven, and Weber occupying the primary places of honor). In 1890 Greffulhe founded a new musical organization, the Société des Grandes Auditions Musicales de France, whose goal was "to assure in our country the primacy of French works, a honor too often reserved for foreigners."[113] The idea, which appealed to both patriotic and artistic sentiments, was lauded by the press and the public. The advisory board consisted of Franck, Chausson, Fauré, and d'Indy; the fundraising committee included, besides the Comtesse and some of her family members, a certain Prince Edmond de Polignac. If Élisabeth Greffulhe did not have her own money to contribute to the project (her husband kept her on a tight leash with regard to her own personal expenses), she was by this time highly skilled in charming her wealthy friends into opening their pocketbooks to contribute to her worthy causes. Thus, the Société's first grand concert, a presentation of Berlioz's *Béatrice et Bénédict,* was financed by a few very rich patrons and a large number of subscribers from high society. With the receipts from this event, young composers were able to receive subventions for compositions that might be heard during future events. The success of the Société des Grands Auditions cemented the Comtesse's already estimable reputation; eventually she came to be known as one of the principal exemplars of cultural taste and discrimination in Paris.

It was Fauré, a beneficiary of Greffulhe's patronage and friendship, who called Winnaretta's attention to the Société des Grandes Auditions, and, no doubt, to the particular influence that its founder held in Paris musical society.[114] Knowing that she needed the approbation of women like Greffulhe to establish her own place in that world, Winnaretta sought an introduction to the Comtesse. In her memoirs, Élisabeth Greffulhe recounted their meeting, which probably took place in the spring of 1891. The tone of the text suggests that the Comtesse felt herself to be descending socially in receiving the divorced former princess, the daughter of a lowly industrial magnate.

> A woman who called herself Madame Singer asked one of my friends to question me, to find out if I would be willing to receive her at my home, and if this friend would consent to present me to her. I accepted because of my dear friend, who told me that this woman was someone who loved music very much, and that she would be an interesting person to meet. We talked music and she told me how happy she would be to attend all the performances of the Société des Grandes Auditions Musicales de France. . . .[115]

Winnaretta and Mme. Greffulhe had much in common, especially the desire to take an active role in the promotion of modern music, and the exceptional drive that would enable them to accomplish their goals despite the obstructive machinations of husbands, family, and society. But these two intelligent and artistically inclined women could never really become friends. In late nineteenth-century culture, it was generally sisters or other close female relatives who filled the role of confidante. In this case, the dramatic differences in ancestries alone would have made any true friendship nearly impossible. The Comtesse Greffulhe confined her social relations to those "of the race"—that is, of the old aristocracy. Nonetheless, she would soon enough play an important role in Winnaretta's personal life.

Greffulhe's particular brand of patronage and influence on musical modernism would form a sort of counterpoint to the Princesse de Polignac's in later years. The differences in their roles stemmed from important differences in their substance and in their style. The money that Winnaretta would spend to foster musical creation and performance was her own; Greffulhe had no personal fortune. Winnaretta would devote her energies during her first thirty years as a patron to creating repertoire "that would belong to her," and that would magnify and embellish the private world of her salon; Greffulhe used her salon, and her interactions with the musicians and artists that frequented it, as a stepping-stone into the larger arena of Parisian cultural life—and, in the process, became a skillful fundraiser for grand, very public projects. In short, Winnaretta devoted her energies to a *mécénat* that would draw the world to her salon; Greffulhe devoted her energies to *mécénat* that would get her out of the house, away from the stifling milieu of her husband and his family.

It may have been Greffulhe who introduced Winnaretta to painter and engraver Paul Helleu. Helleu's glamorous portraits of society women had brought him considerable success of late; his drypoints and etchings of female faces and body language, at once flattering and insightful, made him an artist much in demand. That spring, Winnaretta told Helleu that she wanted him to execute an album of portraits of all her women friends[116]—on the condition that, after the initial rendering, he would destroy the plates, so that each image in the album would be "unique in the world." Helleu was an inveterate gossip, and it took little time for the news of Winnaretta's unusual request to make the rounds. Before long, the newspaper *La Vie Parisienne* had taken up the story, noting (without mentioning Winnaretta by name) that the society woman in question "would have to have a princely fortune to carry out this caprice."[117] Ultimately, Winnaretta decided that the caprice was too expensive, even for her, and she cancelled the commission. But the story about Winnaretta's album—and her motivations for initiating it—lingered long afterwards.

Despite this curious incident (or perhaps because of it), the Comtesse Greffulhe evidently found "Madame Singer" sufficiently interesting to be socially acceptable. She invited Winnaretta to attend the ball she was giving on the island in the Bois de Boulogne on 21 July 1891. One of the highlights of the evening was a performance of Fauré's *Pavane* for chorus and orchestra, with a text by Robert de Montesquiou, a work dedicated to Greffulhe and choreographed for the occasion. Winnaretta described the event to Meg Baugnies as "very mysterious and refined," and was impressed by "the pretty green lights in the trees, and Madame Greffulhe's floating white draperies, under the pouring rain. I had great fun."[118] Fun, perhaps, but in the course of that evening, a young man, identified by Winnaretta in her letters only as "Monsieur de D.," became infatuated with her. In her haste to escape the young man's advances, Winnaretta clambered into a rowboat with the intention of paddling her own way back across the river. She slipped upon entering the boat too hastily, and fell into the Seine.[119]

This mishap notwithstanding, Winnaretta seems to have adjusted to single life quite well. Awaiting an appointment with the curate in Rome to apply for the annulment of her marriage, she spent six weeks in London. Thanks to her brother Paris's favorable standing at the Royal Court, she was able to circulate in the highest echelons of society, even attending the royal wedding of Queen Victoria's granddaughter, Princess Marie-Louise of Schleswig-Holstein, to Prince Joseph of Anhalt at Windsor Castle.[120] "[As I was] very well placed," she reported to Meg Baugnies, "I was able to watch the good old Queen and her ugly little coffee-colored horses, the fat Prince, the beautiful Princess of Wales, the whole wedding party, very amusing."[121] The breezy tone of her letter suggests both that Winnaretta moved very comfortably in such lofty company, and that she was easily accepted in these royal circles. "I [studied] the Londoners that I only knew as a tourist. . . . [I did] a lot of horseback riding, attended an alarming number of tea parties, garden parties, concerts, and dances. I even gave a very successful ball. As far as intelligent things are concerned, I went to a superb performance of *Tristan* in German—*Tannhauser* [sic] etc."[122] After attending the annual regatta at Cowes in late July, she returned to France to spend several weeks with her mother and siblings at the family's Normandy château, with the idea of continuing on alone to the summer home of Meg Baugnies at Cuy-St-Fiacre. Despite a series of "horrible" anti-Wagner letters from her painter friend Georges Clairin ("he finds *Parsifal dirty, nasty,* the work of an impotent old man, full of flashy tricks," she wrote to Meg, "he acts as if our emotional admiration of Wagner's works can only come from the most terrible lack of moral sense"[123]), she looked forward to a quiet summer of long walks, music-making, and painting.

But unforeseen complications arose in the midst of this bucolic setting, for Monsieur de D., the "flirt" from the Ile du Bois, had discovered Winnaretta's whereabouts in Normandy and followed her to the region, settling in near the château.[124] Winnaretta wrote to Meg, "I can't go out without seeing him, and he absolutely doesn't want me to leave . . . it's just too terrific!"[125] Escape was made impossible when Winnaretta's mother insisted that she remain until 15 August to play the organ for a memorial mass for the Duc de Camposelice. Perhaps Isabella had cottoned to her daughter's ardent pursuer (his name had a particle, after all), and was eyeing him as a possible second husband for Winnaretta, for as late as the month of September he could still be found in the region, singing with Mme. Sohège in church and lunching at Blosseville. "I learned along the way," wrote Winnaretta to Meg, "that . . . we are having two picnics together, that there are dinners and parties being organized—in short, that we were never going to be apart from each other."[126]

Even more disconcerting was the sudden pressure brought to bear by Gabriel Fauré, who continued to write Winnaretta long, impassioned letters after his return to Paris. The ardent tone with which he discussed his newest works and his state of mind during their composition bespoke a sense of artistic and emotional intimacy surpassing that of a composer to his patron.[127] "Write, write, write, I beseech you: your every word becomes *a note of music!*"[128] The imminent annulment of Winnaretta's marriage may have caused Fauré to reveal more of his emotional attachment than he had intended. He began to show a proprietary interest in Winnaretta's travel plans, intimating that he would welcome an invitation to join her in Normandy. On 14 August, still "in captivity" at the chateau, Winnaretta wrote to Meg, "Oh, everything is so complicated! Fauré *sulked* for a full week, and wrote me some annoyingly upsetting letters, because he thought that I was at Cuy with Clairin. . . . If I were to spend a few hours with you tomorrow night as I would *really* like to do, Fauré's whining would start all over again. It's not worth going to the trouble of annulling my marriage to get stuck in these kinds of complications!"[129]

Winnaretta was finally rescued by the long-awaited communication from the Vatican, summoning her to leave immediately to plead the cause of her annulment.[130] In Rome, she endured the sweltering 90° heat, as well as the meticulous scrutiny of the most intimate details of her connubial relations, with stoicism and humor. A letter sent to Meg reveals her plucky state of mind:

I protest against all the violent names that you are using against me! What! I am deprived of finding my quasi-flirt, obliged to come to this dirty country, and now I still have to put up with your reproaches! It's too much. . . .

If you could see me here, all dressed in black, making the required visits to all the Cardinals (four obligatory grand salutes for each one) you would feel sorry for me.

When I arrived, they were just about to put off the whole business until the month of November, all because of an absolutely insignificant little piece of information that was needed from Paris. Fortunately by great dint of will I got everything arranged, and the result will be known in a few days.

I should say that I found some of the Cardinals very interesting and charming, and the greeting that they gave me delighted me. I launched into some political discussions and I gave Cardinal Rampolla, the Secretary of State, some advice on the attitude of the Vatican on the Socialist movement.

Self-confidence is a very good thing to have on a trip![131]

Upon her return from Rome, Winnaretta was shocked to discover that her "flirt" was still hot on her trail: he was at a neighboring table in a Paris restaurant; a week later he followed her back to Normandy. "Impossible to escape this new tête-à-tête," Winnaretta wrote to Meg. "Yesterday we had a big party—lunch at Dives, dinner at Trouville etc. You see that not a second is lost—the flirt starts at nine in the morning and finishes at midnight."[132]

Finally, Winnaretta seems to have rid herself of the unwanted suitor; in September, the stories about him cease. That month, Fauré notified her that he had submitted *Mandoline,* the first of the five *Mélodies de Venise,* to *Le Figaro,* for publication on their weekly "Page musicale."[133] Winnaretta was more concerned about the progress of her "Buddha." She had ultimately rejected Maurice Bouchor, who wanted to turn the story of the life of Buddha into a play for marionettes.[134] Fauré finally turned to poet Albert Samain, who enthusiastically agreed to write the libretto. The composer still had serious doubts about being able to find a musical equivalent for the proposed subject matter; he wrote to Winnaretta, "Are you sure you haven't set your sights too high *for me* and have you really taken stock of the magnitude and grandeur of such a subject? . . . never mind, I have *pulled myself together* and am quite ready to come to grips with the *sublime*!!!"[135]

Winnaretta invited Fauré and Samain to lunch on 2 January 1892, at which time she showed the men the progress of the remodeling of her two houses. An oval reception area had just been added to the first floor of the avenue Henri-Martin *hôtel.* The room opened out onto a garden that faced the side street, recently renamed rue Cortambert. The construction of the *atelier* that would link the mansion with the smaller house—"a hall of gigantic proportions," according to Samain—was still in progress.[136] On the day of Fauré and Samain's visit, the room's organ chamber was being built to house the fine new instrument that Winnaretta had commissioned from Paris's premier organ-maker, Aristide Cavaillé-Coll.

Samain described his hostess in a letter to his sister:

> Tall, slender, svelte, about twenty-five or twenty-six years old, a fine-featured and intelligent face with an element of determination, it would appear, about the forehead and chin. Her mouth is serious, the slightly protruding lower lip giving a touch of arrogance to her smile. She speaks slowly with a slight English accent. . . . I can see that she follows contemporary artistic trends very closely; she reads the progressive reviews, knows about unusual exhibitions, is a Bayreuth enthusiast, and seems genuinely interested in experiments that may lead to a new conception of art.[137]

The music that Winnaretta offered her guests for the opening of her salon may not have been the large-scale work that she had hoped for, but in terms of quality and importance, was no less auspicious. On 6 January 1892 a small group of friends gathered in the *atelier* to hear the first performance as a cycle of Fauré's *Cinq Mélodies de Venise,* five musical jewels whose autograph scores bore her name. The performers were tenor Maurice Bagès, with the composer at the piano. Fauré would become only the first of a long list of composers whose music, first introduced in the Polignac salon, was inspired by—and perfectly suited to—the proportions and the acoustics of the *atelier.* Three months later, after the first public performance under the auspices of the Société Nationale de Musique, one critic perceptively pointed out the need for an appropriate space to show the intimate quality of Fauré's songs to best advantage. After praising the composer's ability to produce in his music "the same impression of vague and evanescent fluidity, of delicate and fleeting nuances" as Verlaine's poems, the critic went on to note that "the [music's] charm is too discreet for a big hall like the Salle Érard; it requires, to reach the audience, a tranquil hearing in a salon, around a piano."[138]

The tone of the thank-you letter sent by Fauré to Winnaretta after the salon performance of the *Cinq Mélodies* commingles the respectful gratitude of an artist due his patron with a barely suppressed ardor.

Dear Princesse, I can't thank you enough for yesterday's wonderful soirée! No one knows as well as you how to bring out the best in me, and to share that part of me with others, through all the friendship that you have had the kindness to show me. Be assured that I am always minutely appreciative of all the testimonies of your dear friendship, and that I am grateful for them right down to the smallest corners of my being! It's been too long a time since I've been able to see you often, and this makes the life that I'm leading very lugubrious![139]

Winnaretta's response has not surfaced. Immediately after the recital, she headed back to Rome to await the verdict of her annulment proceedings. On the eve of her newfound independence, little did she realize that the standing she sought in society would arrive in the form of a new husband, and a new life among the nobility.

4

The Sewing Machine and the Lyre

On the first of February 1892 Winnaretta received the news that her marriage to Prince Louis de Scey-Montbéliard had been officially annulled by the Curia in Rome. Now that the last impediments to her freedom were removed, she had only to wait for the completion of the newly constructed *atelier* and the composition by Fauré to make her official re-entry into the musical and aristocratic salon circles. But she was not able to celebrate her good news just yet. In addition to the financial problems with Carriès, and the consequent delay to the completion of the *atelier*, Winnaretta had another issue to confront: her social status. She had once again begun signing her letters Winnaretta Singer. Now merely an ex-princess, Winnaretta risked a descent from the upper crust back into the ranks of the social-climbing bourgeoisie. Could she still draw the great ladies of the Faubourg St.-Germain all the way out to her home in Passy? Would her association with the musical circles of the avant-garde help or hinder her quest for social ascendance?

Let us leave Winnaretta temporarily, sitting in her mansion in the 16th *arrondissement,* mulling over her problems with unfinished projects, artistic crises, home decoration, and social position, and travel a short distance to the 8th *arrondissement,* in the quarter behind the Champs-Élysées. There, on that same first of February 1892, in a small apartment at 39 rue Washington, Prince Edmond de Polignac was contemplating some of the same issues besetting Winnaretta. Fifty-seven years old, all he had ever yearned for was to be a composer, recognized for his original music and his iconoclastic musical ideas. An inveterate dreamer, chronically inept with money, the victim of charlatans who had preyed on his credulity by luring him into "get-rich-quick" schemes, Edmond has recently lost the last of his small inheritance in the stock market.[1] Earlier that week, his few remaining possessions had been seized by debt collectors, and he sat in the empty apartment, burrowed in the one remaining armchair, wrapped in a shawl, his head covered with a knitted cap.[2]

In fact, despite the wretchedness of his present circumstances, this curious gentleman was descended from one of the oldest and most important families in France, the youngest of a line of princes who had enjoyed great favor in the court of Louis XIV. His father, Prince Jules de Polignac had loyally served as Minister of State in the ultra-royalist, fervently religious Restoration government of King Charles X. In 1830, the king, flouting the will of his more moderate Chamber of Deputies, issued a series of decrees revoking the Constitution and suspending freedom of the press. These tracts, which were penned by Jules de Polignac and publicly displayed before an astonished electorate, came to be known, odiously, as the "Thirty Ordinances." The most egregious of the ordinances, Article 14, gave the king absolute power in the name of "insuring the safety of the state." But the citizenry, who had fought so hard in the Revolution against the excesses of the ancien régime, mounted an insurgence, provoking the "July Revolution" that ended the reign of the Bourbon monarchs. Charles X managed to flee the country, but his cabinet members, Jules de Polignac among them, were captured as they attempted to escape. Tried and convicted, the Ultra-Royalists were condemned in December 1830 to *mort civile*: a complete loss of civil rights and incarceration for life at the fortress at Ham, one hundred kilometers north of Paris on the Somme marshes.

Jules had lost his first wife a dozen years earlier. He met his second wife, London-born Charlotte-Maria Parkyns, while he was serving as French ambassador to England. During the two marriages, Jules fathered five children, including one born just as he began serving his prison sentence. Princesse Charlotte dutifully brought her family to live in the cold bleak village of Ham. Despite the hardships of fortress life, liberal visitation policies were permitted the prisoners, and it was thus that two more sons were born to Jules while he was incarcerated. Edmond, the last of the seven children, was born on 19 April 1834. Because of Jules's *mort civile,* Edmond was considered to be nonexistent, legally speaking: on his birth certificate, he was declared to be the "son of the Prince called Marquis de Chalençon, presently on a trip."[3]

In 1836, when public opinion softened towards the imprisoned cabinet members, King Louis-Philippe granted a petition requesting their release on the grounds of their worsening physical health. Jules was set free on the condition that he leave Paris permanently. Having gained the favor of King Ludwig I of Bavaria, he moved with his family into the region near Landau, between the Isar and Vils rivers. There, after having received a second princely title from the king,[4] he purchased a large piece of property, upon which he built a Tudor-style château, named Wildthurn, where he could house his large family and finish out his remaining years in quiet comfort. Although physically frail since his earliest years, Edmond grew up happily in the warm, close familial atmosphere. Like his older brothers, Alphonse, Ludovic, and Camille, Edmond received a classical education, which included instruction in Greek, Latin, modern languages, and later, dancing and horseback riding.[5] The intellectual environment in the Polignac household was stimulating for the children, all of whom were exceptionally gifted.

The older boys had inherited their father's interest in mathematics, and it was not uncommon for the brothers to entertain each other with mathematical challenges in the same way that other young boys might dare each other with feats of strength. Additionally, the household was tri-lingual: French, German, and English were all spoken regularly. Edmond had his own gifts: from a young age, he demonstrated an artistic and curious spirit, as well as a natural flair for performance. He began to write plays and comedies for presentation in the children's theater built by their father. Responding to his father's fanatical religiosity, he became, at the age of nine, the household "preacher," improvising sermons, to the great amusement of his family.[6]

Edmond's older brothers were alternately loving and thoughtless and cruel. While they were willing to include him in Latin word games and number puzzles, they teased him mercilessly for his physical frailness and his athletic deficiencies, calling him the "little skeleton."[7] At one point they made him so miserable that he told his parents he wanted to leave home to go live with a carpenter, "the only person who really understood him."[8] As compensation, his parents permitted the nine-year-old Edmond, who had always shown a keen interest in music, to take lessons in piano and the rudiments of music.[9] From that point on, he had a joyful outlet for his passionate, sensitive nature.

The Polignac family returned to France, settling in November 1845 in the suburb of St.-Germain-en-Laye. Prince Jules, whose health had been irrevocably compromised in prison, died on 30 March 1847, less than a year before the social revolutions of 1848 pounded more nails into the coffin of royalism. Charlotte and her children moved into the center of Paris and occupied a private house in the newly constructed rue de Berri, just off the avenue de Champs-Élysées. Edmond continued his general education with a preceptor in the Faubourg St.-Germain. Other than posts in the military or the clergy, the sons of the aristocracy were not permitted to have "careers," as such, but Edmond by this time had set his heart on becoming a composer. By his teenage years he was writing songs, choruses, and chamber music for the entertainment of his family. Alphonse Thys, a Prix de Rome winner, was engaged to teach Edmond counterpoint, composition, and *solfège*.[10] Although his family indulged Edmond's endeavors, they viewed his activity as merely the hobby of a cultured young aristocrat. That the young man should ever aspire to become a "professional" was never seriously considered.

But Edmond was serious, and made application to the Conservatoire de Paris. In 1855 he was accepted into the Harmony class of Henri Reber, a well-respected but strict pedagogue. The rigors of the conservatory curriculum came as a shock to the spoiled young aristocrat, and Edmond's grades ranged from only "good" to mediocre.[11] From early childhood, he had been *frileux*— feeling constantly chilled; this condition, coupled with a natural tendency toward indolence, caused him to abandon his studies, often for lengthy periods, during which time he would flee Paris to "take the waters" at southern spas. While pursuing his formal musical education, Edmond was beset by chronic gastrointestinal problems, a condition that would plague him for the rest of his life. It is easy to imagine that the internal pressures of a concealed and, no doubt, mistrusted homosexuality contributed significantly to this problem. Periods of great musical productivity alternated with lengthy stretches of illness and inactivity. In 1859 Princesse Charlotte wrote to her son Ludovic, "Edmond is at last I think quite well tho' *il se dorlote* [he coddles himself], which does not prevent his going to Balls & concerts."[12]

Although Polignac's compositions received sporadic performances in the salons and at charitable functions sponsored by the aristocracy, his music never reached a wider audience. But in 1860, the new director of the Opéra-Comique, Alfred de Beaumont, asked him to supply the music for a new libretto by Roger de Beauvoir, a writer of light comic works. The completed *opéra bouffe,* entitled *Un Baiser de Duchesse* (A Duchess's Kiss), reveals Polignac's natural gifts of lyricism and comic wit. Unfortunately, Beaumont lost his position at the Opéra-Comique less than a year later, and the project came to naught.

Edmond's ensuing depression alienated him further from his family, who had come to regard him as an impractical dreamer. He was the only family member who had not yet made a practical decision about the path of his future. His brothers had entered the military; his sister had made a successful marriage to the Vicomte de La Rochefoucauld. Edmond was subjected to unrelenting pressure from family and friends to find a wealthy woman to marry: after that he could spend all the time he pleased in composition, or whatever else struck his fancy. Edmond traveled the width and breadth of Europe, going through the motions of courting various young heiresses. His combination of dramatic flair and childlike wit made him the darling of social gatherings, especially when he would dash to the piano and improvise graceful waltzes and dreamy nocturnes. Tall, handsome, charming, and of an impeccable aristocratic pedigree, Edmond de Polignac endeared himself to many marriageable women.[13] But, although rumors circulated for years about imminent engagements, Edmond never managed to acquiesce to the imperative to join in holy wedlock. Eventually, he came to loathe the social demands of his class; progressively his outward gaiety masked a growing need for solitude, until the point came where he would arrive at a host's house and disappear into his room for the better part of his stay.

In 1861, Edmond became a founding member of the Cercle de l'Union Artistique, whose purpose was the promotion of good performances of great music in other venues than theaters, and stimulating interest in this cause in refined social circles. Besides the *mélomanes* of the aristocracy, members of the club included Gounod, Berlioz, Auber, and Catulle Mendès. The Cercle ardently supported Wagner, and rallied to the composer's defense after his *Tannhäuser* suffered a resounding failure at its 1861 Paris

Opéra debut. Edmond, completely in the thrall of the German master, sought out occasions to socialize with him. Wagner later wrote, "I lunched with [Edmond de Polignac] one morning, and here he revealed himself as a musical fantast. He insisted on trying to convince me of the correctness of his interpretation of Beethoven's Symphony in A Major, the final movement of which he contended described a shipwreck, phrase by phrase."[14] Yet, as much as he idolized Wagner's music, Edmond's own compositions remained remarkably free of Wagnerian characteristics; on the contrary, over the years, the harmony and texture of his works would become leaner and clearer. He once said that he wanted his music to sound as if it were being sung "in the prairie."[15] He would later declare that, in producing works written in a fresh, natural style, he was creating *musique de plein air,* a compositional equivalent to the art world's *École de Plein Air.*[16]

In the 1860s amateur male choruses called *orphéons* began to proliferate throughout France. Part cultural movement, part social movement, these groups served as outlets for people from all classes, including common laborers, to participate in an instructive and satisfying artistic endeavor.[17] Charles Gounod, who had served as a mentor to Polignac during his years at the Conservatoire,[18] set the standard as leader of the highly esteemed Orphéon de Paris. Edmond showed a marked gift for choral composition, and in 1865 and 1867 he carried off first prizes in competitions for orpheonic works sponsored by the City of Paris. During this period Edmond also began to write for chamber ensembles. An 1864 string quartet, clearly influenced by the early works of Beethoven in that genre, reveals Edmond's skillful handling of the classical forms, as well as an impressive sense of lyricism and harmonic invention.[19]

But in mid-nineteenth-century France, opera was the only venue through which a young composer could really hope to gain broad public recognition. Edmond's hopes for professional acclaim were raised once again in August 1867, when, in conjunction with the World's Fair, the Ministry of Fine Arts mounted a contest for a new opera on the libretto *La Coupe du Roi de Thulé.*[20] There would be only one prizewinner, whose reward included a performance of the winning score at the Opéra. Forty-two contestants submitted their scores, their names hidden from the jury. The winner, Eugène-Émile Diaz de la Péna, was a student of the jury's chairman. The "losers" included Jules Massenet (whose score ranked second) and Georges Bizet (whose score ranked seventh).[21] Edmond later found out that his own work, which ranked fifth, had ultimately been rejected for first prize because "his instrumentation was too complicated—it called for *two* bass clarinets, an unpardonable monstrosity in the eyes of the judges!"[22] Once again, hopes for public recognition and fame were dashed.

Social clubs were all the fashion in Paris at that time, and Edmond belonged to several of these. In addition to the Cercle de l'Union Artistique, he was a member of the Jockey Club, the most exclusive men's club of the nobility. In 1867, Edmond joined a third club, the Cercle de la rue Royale, which had no particular goal other than to provide young titled men another venue in which to sit around, smoke cigars, and discuss politics and the stock market. The indolent lifestyle of the group is captured in James Tissot's 1868 painting, *Le Balcon du Cercle de la rue Royale.* The enormous canvas depicts a group of ten young aristocratic and other society men, including Charles Haas, Proust's prototype for Swann. Edmond is portrayed as a long, lean, bearded figure, shown lounging in a chair, staring off into space. In truth, Edmond's association with these men was probably more a result of habit and boredom than shared interests. He was a true intellectual, a voracious reader; his interest in both the humanities and the sciences ran deep; he was constantly in search for a way to satisfy his inventive streak. Modern technological advancements fascinated him; new discoveries about the nature of the solar system caused great rejoicing in his "supra-lunar spirit."[23] Edmond de Polignac was an amalgam of his obsessions, his enthusiasms, his passions, his sensitivities—and no one in his milieu could comprehend him. At best he was regarded as a somewhat hyperactive charmer, at worst a crackpot. Edmond buried himself in music, dreams, and secrets, and his stomach ailments grew worse.

In 1875 a new friend entered his life, one who seemed to understand him and share his deeper affinities. That year, during a visit to Cannes, Edmond made the acquaintance of Comte Robert de Montesquiou, a beautiful young man, tall, dark, and twenty-one years his junior. It is possible that shortly thereafter the two began a sexual relationship. At the age of twenty, Montesquiou already exhibited an interest in the aestheticism that would become his trademark in later years. His perceptions were ultra-refined, his narcissistic discourses—on art, music, the landscape, colors, odors, clothing, poetry—were virtuosic manipulations of language, replete with double- and triple-entendres. His barbed witticisms about the inhabitants of the aristocratic milieu, particularly its women, were received in high society with amused delight—although he or she who laughed on one day might very well find himself or herself the victim of the Comte's latest malicious quip the next. Years later, in middle age, the ostentatiously costumed dandy became the quintessential aesthete: one who values the surface appearance, the loveliness of the description and the interpretation of the sensory, over and above the thing in itself. The more studied and refined the surface became, the more it shielded Robert de Montesquiou from the necessity of expressing a simple, honest human emotion. As Montesquiou's character hardened into monstrous caricature, it came to invite literary treatment; thus, he is now remembered as the model for Des Esseintes in Huysman's *A Rebours,* and most especially as the Baron de Charlus in Proust's *A la Recherche du temps perdu.*

The friendship of Montesquiou and Polignac was of crucial importance to both men, but for different reasons: Edmond, by nature ardent and sincere, finally had someone with whom he could share his deepest longings. And, as Edmond's confidant and sounding board, Montesquiou could approach, if not actually engage in, genuine emotional interaction. Both were highly intelligent and cultured connoisseurs of poetry, art, and music. They became traveling companions, arriving together at the country houses of mutual friends, where they traded maliciously witty observations of the assembled guests. In 1885 they sailed off to London, where their first stop was the Handel Festival at the Crystal Palace (it was this event that converted Montesquiou into a devotee of the baroque master). A few days later they were given a personal tour of the art studios of James Whistler, William Morris, and Edward Burne-Jones by no less impressive a guide than Henry James.[24] The next year, they made the pilgrimage together to the musical Mecca of Bayreuth.[25] In Paris, Montesquiou, related by marriage to practically every great aristocratic family in France, helped Edmond mount performances of his music in various aristocratic salons. The Comtesse Greffulhe was especially charmed by her cousin's new friend, and welcomed his music, as well as his agile facility at the piano. Through this circle, Edmond made the acquaintance of Gabriel Fauré, who became a faithful lifelong friend and colleague. Both men were members of the Société Nationale de Musique; under the auspices of that organization, Edmond's compositions were performed alongside those of Chausson, Debussy,[26] and his friend Fauré.[27]

A subset of Edmond's friends from the Société Nationale included composer Vincent d'Indy, Charles Bordes, choir director at Saint-Gervais, organist Alexandre Guilmant, and music historians Bourgault-Ducoudray and André Pirro. These men, who formed the organizational committee of the Société des Chanteurs de Saint-Gervais, had in common a profound love of medieval, Renaissance, and baroque music. After presenting the first performance in France of J. S. Bach's *Christmas Oratorio* in January 1892 under the auspices of Madame Greffulhe's Société des Grandes Auditions, Bordes resolved to mount an entire program of sixteenth-century *a cappella* music with his choir for Holy Week 1892. Joining forces with d'Indy, the conductor presented an extraordinary range of settings from the liturgy by Palestrina, Victoria, Josquin, Orlando di Lasso, as well as two more "modern" works by J. S. Bach.[28] Edmond used his aristocratic connections to stir up interest in these concerts. The objective was achieved: subscriptions to the series of *concerts spirituels* included the great names of the Paris nobility.[29]

As steeped as Edmond was in the musical past, he was equally preoccupied with musical modernism. Although as a young composer he had drawn on traditional models, a chance musical "discovery" made in 1879 altered his creative path. An inveterate searcher for new and modern means of expression, and perhaps influenced by the mathematical games played with his brothers in childhood, Polignac began to tinker with the asymmetrical arrangement of whole steps and half steps that form major and minor scales. In doing so, he devised what he believed to be a "new" scale of eight notes, alternating whole steps and half steps in a repeating pattern. This scale, known today as the "octatonic scale," had in fact been a cornerstone of Russian folk music for centuries. Rimsky-Korsakov had used it "officially" in art music for the first time in his opera *Sadko* in 1867. Polignac may have been acquainted to some extent with contemporary Russian music,[30] but clearly was not aware of the association of the eight-tone scale with that repertoire; living and laboring alone, he believed that he had come up with something unknown, unique, and important. In the next few years he wrote several works based on this new scale, all of which had Orientalist themes. A three-part Passion oratorio, *Échos de l'Orient judaïque,* contained two octatonic movements; one movement in particular, *Pilate livre le Christ,* was full of jarring harmonic effects. This was followed by a suite of incidental music for a projected lyric version of *Salammbô,* Gustave Flaubert's historical novel about warfare, idol worship, and erotic passion in ancient Carthage. Polignac also wrote a long treatise on his new scale, attempting to fashion a theoretical language to explain its workings and applications for composition. One of the *Salammbô* pieces, *La Danse du serpent,* was published in a musical album put out by the newspaper *Le Gaulois* in 1888; it was performed along with *Pilate* in various salons and concert halls during the same year. The gritty, dissonant quality of these works evoked puzzled reactions from contemporary listeners and from the musical press, who likened the music to the "hallucinatory intoxication that fills the work of Loti."[31] Edmond's "discovery" brought him no recognition, and he lapsed into depression.

On the first of February 1892, Edmond de Polignac was in a state of utter penury; his apartment had been stripped bare of all furnishings by the debt collectors. As he contemplated his desperation, there was a knock on the door, and Edmond's two younger nephews, Guy and Melchior de Polignac entered, shocked to find their uncle sitting in the dark, empty room, wrapped in a blanket trying to warm himself next to the hearth. "Upon gentle interrogation [about the absence of furniture]," Melchior would later recall, "Edmond made a circular gesture—'Gone!', followed by another gesture, curt and horizontal—'Seized!', then in a deep voice, with two fingers pressing into his neck, 'Strangled by the creditors!'"[32] Even though Guy de Polignac came to the rescue, offering his uncle a loan that would temporarily assure his security, it was clear that further action would have to be taken by Edmond himself.

The solution proposed so many years earlier by the Polignac family now surfaced again between Edmond and Montesquiou: why not marry a rich woman? Montesquiou discussed his friend's predicament with his cousin Élisabeth Greffulhe. In the course of these conversations the name of Winnaretta Singer came to be bruited about. In fact, as the cousins considered the idea more carefully, the newly divorced ex-Princesse de Scey seemed like an ideal candidate. She was wealthy, she was not sexually interested in men, and she adored music.

Winnaretta had already come to Edmond's attention in 1886, under circumstances that he would have preferred to forget. That year, Monet's new painting, *Champs de tulipes en Hollande,* was exhibited at the Galerie Georges Petit. Edmond coveted the canvas, and endeavored to scrape together the funds to purchase it, but his dream was crushed when he discovered that it had already been bought by a Miss Singer. Enraged, he "cursed the name" of the rich American woman who had carried off "his" painting.[33] Their paths would cross again, in musical circumstances: both were at Bayreuth in 1888, when Winnaretta was still the Princesse de Scey-Montbéliard; both had attended the concerts of the Société des Grandes Auditions; both had been in attendance at the Comtesse Greffulhe's party on the island of the Bois de Boulogne in July 1891. In short, they had surely been thrown together in various musical and social settings long before the idea of an alliance between them was raised.

The advantages of the match were not lost on Edmond. The Comtesse Greffulhe recounted the day that he came to discuss the matter with her:

> He came to my house and, turning his back to the fireplace, he said to me: "I have something very important to say to you. Could you present my marriage proposal to Madame Singer, whom you know? It's clearly understood that, in this plan, she doesn't have to expect anything but a '*mariage blanc*' [an unconsummated marriage], that is to say that I will keep my room, she will have hers; but our artistic interests will mutually benefit each other, and I hope to be able to make her very happy with the admiration that we both have for art." I accepted this delicate mission with all the affection that I had for our dear Prince Edmond de Polignac, one of the most well-bred and intelligent men that I know.[34]

Montesquiou and Élisabeth Greffulhe devised the following strategy: Winnaretta would be attending the first public performance of the *Cinq Mélodies de Venise* to be given by the Société Nationale de Musique on 2 April. Edmond, who would also be in the audience to applaud his friend Fauré, should try to find a moment when he could speak to Madame Singer alone. He should then find out what musical salons she might be visiting that week: a meeting in a private home could provide a convenient situation for him to speak with her privately, in order to make at least some tentative forays into the subject of matrimony. Edmond, who had still not completely come to grips with the idea, was dubious about his own ability to bring about the desired conclusion. He wrote to Montesquiou,

I've taken note of your advice on the planned strategic campaign, and thank you for the intervention offered. All depends on a salon occasion favorable to the posing of the question, but up 'til now not even the shadow of an outstretched pole. Now, to make the hare come out, one must still go to the woods, and up until now the meetings have no longer been offered except in open view. . . . And then, crossing the bar, an old helmsman such as myself begins to tire. One arrives at an age when, in feminine questions, it is wise to say to myself "*quieta non movere* [don't upset the tranquility]."[35]

As it turned out, the prince-composer found an approach that, unbeknownst to him, was the surest way to this particular woman's heart: he engaged her intellectually and musically. A performance of his *Lamento*[36] was scheduled for 5 April 1892, and Edmond sent Winnaretta an invitation to the performance,[37] as well as a copy of the score, accompanied by a note:

Very happy that you are willing to honor me with your benevolent presence. . . . I take the liberty of sending you the piece that you will hear, sung by Mme. Caron.[38] It's a primitive version that I had to ornament with embroidery, in the accompaniment, according to the spirit of the day. There is, notably, in the third stanza: "Les belles de nuit demicloses," an artifice that I believe almost unique in the Musical Literature, in which one hears, under the vocal line, the initial motive, in the chorus (bouche fermée[39]) and in the orchestra simultaneously, in . . . four different note values.[40]

As it lends itself to suggestive and simple words, the musical color is established in the Oriental Latin diatonic scale,[41] rather that the Romantic German chromatic scale, which is perhaps too exclusively practiced today. . . . Excuse me, Madame, for this very pedantic digression, I risk passing myself off to you as a "Professional," as I know you avoid them.[42]

How could Winnaretta have failed to be moved by the beauty of this song, whose haunting melody by Edmond so perfectly matched Théophile Gautier's mysterious text? Perhaps the connection between the two was established from that moment. They were surely brought together again the following evening, when Winnaretta sponsored a concert for orchestra and choir under the auspices of the Société Nationale de Musique, which featured, among other works, the first public performance of the Fauré/ Montesquiou *Pavane*.[43] And Edmond was certainly impressed by Winnaretta's talent as an artist when a print of one of her paintings was included that spring in *La Revue indépendante*, Paris's prestigious symbolist periodical.[44]

As it turned out, it was Winnaretta who, by a subsequent action, unknowingly moved the Montesquiou-Greffulhe plot forward. She had met

Comte Robert in the company of Carriès the previous summer, and had been re-introduced to him at the Greffulhe *fête*. Since the mid-1870s Montesquiou had carefully decorated his apartment in exotic Decadent style, filling its rooms with Oriental artifacts and his collection of signature icons: decorative bats and blue hydrangeas—the winged nocturnal creatures perhaps because of their associations with melancholy and with "impure" and androgynous sexuality, the flowers because of Montesquiou's attraction to their "abnormal azure blue."[45] Winnaretta did not particularly share the count's taste, but she admired his originality. When she mentioned to him that she was renovating her house, he gallantly offered to advise her about its décor. The year elapsed without their meeting again, but seeing Montesquiou at the Société Nationale concert, she was reminded of his offer. She sent him a flattering letter, combining coquetry and politeness. "If I am now being indiscreet by reminding you of your kind promise," she wrote, "it's because the hope of being guided by your sure taste is so precious that I am easily willing to abandon discretion."[46] Montesquiou responded with an equally deft display of mincing prose, as ornamental as a baroque ballet. "You graciously anticipated the wish that I was forming myself, that our lovely meeting of last year not just be left at that. . . . I would very much like to come to see you, or to receive you myself, in accordance with whatever rendezvous it would please you to arrange with me, to follow up on some aesthetic suggestions, in the positive sense of a word much profaned."[47]

The following week, Montesquiou came to dine at rue Cortambert; his companions at table were Carriès, who came bearing "new and marvelous bits of his great decoration," and painter and engraver Paul Helleu, whose talents had also been solicited for the decoration of the *atelier*.[48] Over the next several weeks, Montesquiou spent many hours with Winnaretta, enjoying his role as her "aesthetic advisor." Not losing sight of his role as matchmaker for Edmond, the dapper count wrote to Winnaretta of his keen desire that she meet with the Comtesse Greffulhe, "whose intelligent interest is known to you"; he added, "I myself share with this lucid and discreet confidante the delicate responsibility of the ideas that she puts forward." He concluded, "May the future allow you to realize your serious and clear-headed enterprises, whose accomplishment would be a just price for your high aspirations."[49]

But Montesquiou lost touch with Winnaretta during the summer, when she celebrated her newfound independence with trips to London, Scandinavia, and Bayreuth. When she returned to Paris, Montesquiou requested the use of Winnaretta's *atelier* for a marvelous artistic project. The "Divine" Sarah Bernhardt had been a longtime friend of Comte Robert's; indeed, she was the only woman he had ever made love to (although this diversion from his true preferences resulted in a week of uncontrolled vomiting).[50] But the great actress was still devoted to the count, and it was in her name that Montesquiou made his application to Winnaretta:

My illustrious friend Sarah Bernhardt having expressed the desire to recite some of my poems in front of a select gathering, composed of names strictly designated by her and myself, and on a terrain at once neutral and brilliant, your magnificent hall came to me as being the ideal location for the realization of this dream, and I imagined asking you to let me have it for one evening, in the name of the gracious friendship that you have shown me and your well-established high regard for every dignified manifestation of art.[51]

Winnaretta had envisioned her *atelier* serving primarily musical purposes, but the prospect of presenting Sarah Bernhardt in her salon must have been too enticing to pass up. The *atelier* was still under construction, but Winnaretta suggested to Montesquiou that the absence of gas and electricity might allow for a lighting that was more "intelligent and appropriate" to the occasion.[52] However, her agreement to lend her *atelier* for the reading was predicated on the Count's agreeing to keep the event "absolutely secret"[53]: perhaps she was aware of the rumors of scandal surrounding Bernhardt's imminent presentation of the title character of Oscar Wilde's *Salome*.[54] In late September the *atelier* had its second "unofficial" inauguration, as "the Divine One" read Montesquiou's poems before a spellbound audience. The secrecy surrounding the event was apparently respected by all involved, as there are no eyewitness reports of the reading. One is left only to imagine the great actress declaiming Montesquiou's poems, illuminated by the glow of candlelight in the intimacy of Winnaretta's *atelier*.

Their collaboration having produced an unequivocal success, Montesquiou now renewed his request that Winnaretta speak with Madame Greffulhe. In November or December 1892 the Comte arranged for the meeting to take place at his home in the rue Franklin, but without revealing the purpose of the rendezvous. Winnaretta naturally was curious, and bemused by the secrecy. "Monsieur, I will come to your house Wednesday at 3 o'clock for this consultation which could *have very great consequences* for *me*."[55] No written account of that convocation remains, but one can imagine Winnaretta thunderstruck, and then listening, still dumbfounded, to all the reasonable arguments pressed upon her by Montesquiou and Greffulhe—her social position, compromised by her divorce, had to be considered; despite the thirty-one year difference in their ages, a marriage with Edmond would ally her with one of the oldest and most distinguished aristocratic families in France; and, the cousins discreetly hinted, Winnaretta could continue to lead her personal life as she wished, without the imposition of sexual demands that she had had to endure from the Prince de Scey.

To their shared amazement, a bond of friendship and affection grew between Winnaretta and Edmond. Their common musical tastes—Schubert, Wagner, Renaissance and baroque music, music of the avant-garde, such as that of Debussy—were only a point of departure. In Winnaretta, Edmond found an intellectual equal, a strong and levelheaded woman who could support him emotionally without smothering him. For Winnaretta, Edmond was a kinder, gentler version of her father. She loved his chimerical tendencies, his eccentricity, his inventiveness, but there was nothing to fear from his sexuality. And she genuinely loved his music. Here was finally a worthy goal for her careerist instincts and her nascent organizational skills: she could promote the art of her husband. In July 1893 she invited him to join her for the annual regatta at Cowes, England, where her boat-loving brothers gathered during the summers. Family pictures taken during the visit show Edmond smiling and happy, surrounded by a gaggle of grinning Singers.[56]

Meanwhile, Montesquiou was gloating over the near-accomplishment of his mission to arrange a conveniently asexual marriage for his friend. And yet he had no intention of letting Edmond forget his true nature. As 1892 drew to a close, he wrote a poem dedicated to Edmond called *Effusions,* featuring the most flagrant phallic imagery. The dedication was published in 1893 in Montesquiou's new collection, *Le Chef des odeurs suaves.* The title of the new volume was itself a paean to Edmond: the phrase "the chief of suave odors" came from Flaubert's erotically tinged *Salammbô,* set to octatonic music by Edmond seven years earlier. Edmond, for his part, waxed nostalgic, contemplating the change in the nature of his friendship with Montesquiou that marriage might bring: "Often, in recent days, I've thought back to our walks in Cannes, along roads between two low garden walls, by the sea, and you come back to me as you were then, in a checkered jacket: it was our first meeting, you read passages from 'Letters to a traveller' to me. You seemed to me lost in a foreign world, and also a bit like someone abandoned."[57]

But Edmond was already moving away emotionally from Montesquiou. He felt a sense of purity and communion with Winnaretta, whose musical and artistic sensibilties were so like his own. On one occasion Edmond played Schubert's song *Am See* for her, and she responded, "Here is a thought which has just been transmitted to us intact, as intense as the first day it was played."[58] In September, while Winnaretta was traveling (first to Bayreuth and then on to Mina de Monteynard's château near Grenoble), Edmond recalled this moment of shared musical and emotional intimacy in a moving letter.

> You flatter me beyond measure in awarding in me this exceptional Certificate of Goodness; I don't know if I deserve it. Perhaps I would prefer a spike of perversity, which is always less banal. It's perhaps you who inspires this goodness in me. In any case I fervently hope that you will always keep close to you (in the midst of torrents and ravines, blue lakes and society parties, over time and distance) the memory of an attachment (*rational* and irrational) that, I hope, nothing can ever destroy. . . .
> It is always good to feel that you are not alone, and . . . it is good, rare, and precious to know that someone understands you. . . . In my thoughts I call you the "blue-eyed Clairvoyant."[59]

In November 1893, Edmond de Polignac proposed marriage to Winnaretta Singer, and she accepted him, almost a year after the idea was first introduced to her. He was fifty-nine, she was twenty-eight. Winnaretta wrote to the Comtesse Greffulhe right away.

> I didn't want to wait to inform you of the news of my forthcoming marriage with Monsieur de Polignac. I know the great feeling of friendship that you have for him, and the memory of the kind interest that you showed me during some very sad days makes me hope that this solution will not displease you. . . . Today I am sure that it is the only reasonable, the only proper solution which will assure me the life of peace and work to which I aspire.[60]

Once the decision was made, events moved quickly. The wedding was arranged so hastily that even those nearest to the couple found out about the impending marriage only at the last minute. Winnaretta had guarded her secret well: Belle-Blanche, who was ordinarily her sister's closest confidant, was piqued to hear the news of the engagement secondhand. "*One* tells me," she wrote, "that you are going to marry. *One* tells me that the happy mortal is Edmond. My *musical soul* quivers with joy. But I'm at the point of being quite rankled that you have written nothing to me announcing this event. . . . I don't intend to be tossed aside for a brother-in-law, however charming he may be!!!"[61]

On 15 December 1893, Winnaretta and Edmond were married by the Abbé de Broglie in the Chapelle des Carmes. As the Polignac princely title had originally been granted by the Vatican, Pope Leo XIII extended the courtesy of sending his blessing to the couple. Only a small number of family members were invited to the ceremony.[62] The marriage produced mixed reactions on both sides of the family. Edmond's reputation for eccentricity and acerbity had preceded him. "I'm dying to get. . . to know him better," wrote Belle-Blanche, "but he intimidates me so much I shall never dare speak to him."[63]

The reaction of the Polignacs was even more guarded. Winnaretta Singer was certainly not one of "their people." She was the daughter of an American industrialist of questionable ancestry and a bourgeois mother (Isabella's former titles having been given no credence). But, on the positive side, there was . . . all that money. As Singer biographer Ruth Brandon put it, "All Americans were more or less equally unacceptable. One might therefore pick the richest without compunction."[64] This philosophy had motivated the 1890 nuptials of the debt-ridden Prince Joseph de Caraman-Chimay (Élisabeth Greffulhe's brother) and Detroit's Miss Clara Ward, badly dressed and socially unschooled, but already a millionairess at age sixteen. Comte Boni de Castellane would see things similarly in 1895 when he married Anna Gould, the homely, inelegant, but fabulously wealthy daughter of railroad magnate Jay Gould. The attitude of the Polignac family was perhaps best summed up by Edmond's niece Jane d'Oilliamson, in a letter to her uncle Ludovic: "Passing through Paris, I was able to attend the marriage of my Uncle Edmond. The woman seems to me to be very intelligent, pleasant, original in a way that has captivated my Uncle, and she has, in painting as well as music, a real talent. The *atelier* that she has built on avenue Henri-Martin is a real marvel. My Uncle seemed so truly happy that I think that we can only rejoice in this marriage."[65]

Paris society was fascinated by the notion of this match. Jacques-Émile Blanche recounted in his memoirs the reaction of his mother when Edmond came to announce his engagement. To prove to Madame Blanche that he was still in good enough shape to be considered "marriageable," Edmond began to gallop around the terrace in his checked trouser and Second Empire alpaca vest. With his feet together, he jumped over a chair, declaring, "Now you can say that you saw me jumping around like a race horse!" "So the sewing machine is going to marry the lyre," wryly commented Madame Blanche to her son.[66]

Robert de Montesquiou, in the meantime, was awaiting the effusive signs of gratitude that he felt were owed him by the beneficiaries of his matchmaking. In his mind, he had effected a marriage of convenience, a successful alliance of fortune and title—and nothing more. The fact that Winnaretta and Edmond actually appeared to feel affection for each other—and no longer needed him— put a crimp on his potential for social mischief-making. Although he had been one of the very few non-family members invited to the wedding, Montesquiou claimed to have never received the invitation, and fulminated to Élisabeth Greffulhe over the purported slight. The Comtesse reported her cousin's fit of pique to Edmond, who hastily wrote a letter assuring the Comte that he *had* checked the list, and yes, the invitation *had* been sent. "I write to inform you of this fact *right away,* so that you don't suppose any negligence on my part, and so that you will receive . . . the assurance of all my regrets."[67] Montesquiou was enraged by Edmond's impersonal, detached response. From that point on, he took every opportunity to cut down the Polignac couple as often and as publicly as possible. Winnaretta and Edmond paid no notice. Edmond joked that, now that he had married the American woman who had walked off with "his" Monet canvas, he could sit and look at the painting to his heart's content.[68]

And the society skeptics soon had reason to regret their words. What Montesquiou had conceived of as a marriage of convenience blossomed into a true love-match between two kindred spirits. During their short but happy marriage, the Prince and Princesse Edmond de Polignac transformed their home into a glorious ongoing musical feast. In Jacque-Émile Blanche's words, "the scoffers became the faithful of this Temple of Orpheus."[69]

5

Marriage and Music

Behind every successful man, as the old saying goes, one finds a woman. But in the story of the marriage of Edmond de Polignac and Winnaretta Singer, the formula worked well in both directions. For while Winnaretta provided support to her husband as a loving, devoted spouse and as the muse and promoter of his music, Edmond, by enabling her to become the Princesse de Polignac, allowed his wife to realize "the life and the work to which she aspired," as she had said to the Comtesse Greffulhe. What was so fascinating about the Polignac marriage, then as now, was the way that husband and wife transcended the elements of money, power, family prestige, and social ambition that factored into their union. That Edmond profited from the financial benefits of his wife's Singer millions cannot be ignored, nor the fact that Winnaretta Singer reaped the social benefits of becoming the Princesse de Polignac. If these advantages had been the most important factors in this marriage, the story could end here, for it would make this couple not particularly different from the numerous members of the nobility who had married American heiresses. But in Winnaretta and Edmond's case, a deep love of music and of each other also entered into the mix in a way that distinguished this marriage from others in Belle Époque Paris society.

If their union was a *mariage blanc*, with no sexual component, it nonetheless brought to each of the partners an unhoped-for degree of fulfillment. Much more than a marriage of convenience, the marriage was a celebration of respect and admiration, of intellectual growth and artistic activity, and of mutual understanding. In Edmond, Winnaretta found a man whose creativity, imagination, and childlike sense of wonderment had not been diminished by age; like her adored father, Isaac Singer, her husband energized and stimulated her intellectually. In Winnaretta, Edmond found a companion who not only tolerated but also affectionately accepted his fanciful eccentricities. She genuinely loved his music and truly understood him. She was his muse. And music was the symbol of their bond, their emotional lingua franca. In place of sex, they had a salon.

There appears to have been, nonetheless, a physical aspect to Edmond's feelings for his wife. His love spilled forth into poetry.

C'est toi qui reviens, ma fidèle inconnue
Qui m'apparaît sans cesse aux jours d'adversité.
Salut! j'ai bien souffert . . . sois donc la bienvenue
De mon vieux coeur brisé, je te rends la moitié . . .

Viens, fille au front rêveur, ma plus fidèle Amie,
Qui donc pourra jamais t'arracher de mes bras.
Je t'en délivrai, compagne de ma vie
Seule, au fond de mon coeur où tu vis, tu mourras![1]

[It's you who comes to me, my faithful unknown,
Who appears endlessly in days of adversity.
Greetings! I have suffered greatly. So you are welcomed
By my old broken heart, I'll share it with you.

Come, dreamy-faced girl, my most faithful Friend,
Who will never again be torn from my arms.
I will shelter you there, my life companion,
You alone: in the depths of my heart where you live, you will die!]

In a dozen or so extant letters addressed to his "dearest Winn" Edmond's declarations of love are as ardent as those of a young man. "I read the first pages, the very beautiful first pages of your letter; at the risk of seeming ridiculous to you, I was very moved by it, and, full of joy, I kissed the last word."[2] He closes one letter hoping that she will be willing to relate every last detail of a trip to "your old, loyal, devoted unique Leek. . . . I say unique because he is the only one to love you as he loves you."[3] Winnaretta, ordinarily as taciturn in letters as in speech, was only slightly less effusive. "I will be happy to chat with you, dearest Edmond. You were fabulously witty and delightful last Thursday. Billions of kisses from your W."[4]

Winnaretta's first challenge in her new marriage was to address the work of *being* the Princesse de Polignac. She had her work cut out for her in finding her niche in her husband's old, established, ultra-royalist family, which had for years looked disparagingly on Edmond's artistic endeavors. It took a while for the Polignacs to warm to her. The reaction of Edmond's sister-in-law, Amélie Rozan, confirming the details of a family dinner, was typical. "As Edmond and Winnaretta will be joining us tomorrow, and since they are very *mondain* [worldly], and since *mondains* [society people] dine late, I was obliged to move our meal to 7:45."[5] Public opinion was decidedly mixed as to the social acceptability of the Polignacs. The dyspeptic writer and aesthete Edmond de Goncourt, who received a visit from the couple some months after their marriage, noted in his diary that Edmond had "the air of a drowned dog," and that Winnaretta had "a cold beauty, sharp, cutting, the beauty of the daughter of the inventor of the sewing

machine." Goncourt continued archly, "It is said that the marriage between these two was concluded on the condition that the husband not
enter his wife's bedroom, in return for a sum of money that will permit him
to place his music, which the opera houses don't want."[6]

By far the greatest vitriol spewed forth from Robert de Montesquiou.
Outraged at Edmond and Winnaretta's lack of "gratitude" for his part in
arranging the marriage, the Comte circulated a story as extraordinary as it
was malicious. He claimed that he and his former friend had made a bet as
to whether Montesquiou could successfully arrange a match with Winnaretta
Singer. The loser would pay the sum of 100,000 francs "to the greatest
poet of our time, to Verlaine in his hour of need."[7] Upon "losing," that is,
marrying, Edmond paid Montesquiou the agreed-upon sum. "Naturally I
kept the 100,000 francs," boasted the Comte, "but I gave Verlaine a very
beautiful Charvet scarf."[8] After this, the Polignacs ceased to associate with
Montesquiou; in retaliation, the Comte attempted to turn public opinion
against them. The attempts of their common friends to keep the feuding
parties apart made for some very complicated social machinations.[9] But
the most fearsome weapon that Montesquiou wielded was his pen. The
women of the aristocracy were always afraid that they would be the next
subjects of one of Montesquiou's barbed, witty poems ridiculing the ladies
of his class. Winnaretta's turn came, in a scathing poem entitled
"Vinaigrette."

> Vinaigrette s'aigrit, qu'est ce donc qu'il lui faut?
> Une meilleure Amie, un mari sans défaut.
> Mais elle en prit, d'assaut, deux à ma connaissance
> Et d'autrui, à l'essai, qui prouvent leur puissance.
> Faut-elle une peinture? Un artiste la sert
> Et lui dit où se doit placer le bleu, le vert[10]. . .
> Elle signe, elle envoie au Salon, la médaille
> Est pour elle. Elle gagne, après mainte bataille,
> Une invitation par année, on la met
> Au bas bout de la table,[11] et d'autres au sommet
> Qui ne laisseront pas tomber les yeux sur elle
> De peur de mal dîner. Pourtant elle grommelle,
> Elle veut . . . Que veut-elle, à la fin, dîtes-moi?
> Etre considerée . . . Eh! Grand Dieu! comme quoi![12]

> [Vinaigrette is sour, so what does she need?
> A best Friend, a husband without faults.
> But she takes, by assault, two, to my knowledge,
> And others, just as experiments, to prove their potency.
> Does she need a painting? A artist serves her,
> Telling her where to place the blue, the green . . .

She signs the canvas, she sends it to the Salon, the medal
Is for her. She wins, after many a battle,
One invitation a year, and is seated
At the very end of the table, far from the others
So that they won't have to lay eyes on her
For fear of indigestion. And still she grumbles,
She wants . . . What does she want, in the end, tell me?
To be *considered* . . . Hmph! Great God! as what?]

But Winnaretta had little to fear from Montesquiou's bitter fulminations. Even though, at the beginning, she encountered a reserved reception
from some of her husband's relations, there was also a warm and welcoming group of family members and friends who took an instant liking to her,
and to her fresh, open "American" attitudes. Chief among these were
Edmond's brothers Ludovic and Camille, with whom Winnaretta formed
lifelong attachements.

Winnaretta developed a special rapport with Camille's daughter
Armande, who since childhood had manifested great talent as a pianist and
composer, and who would go on to study composition with Fauré and,
later, with d'Indy at the Schola Cantorum. Winnaretta and Armande shared
the same birth date, 8 January; this coincidence became a symbol for a
lifelong bond of affection. After Armande's 1895 marriage to Comte Alfred
de Chabannes-La Palice, the Polignacs made frequent visits to the couple's
estate in Fontainebleau, whose forested grounds served as the inspiration
for some of Edmond's *musique de plein air*. Armande enjoyed Winnaretta
and Edmond's similar sense of humor, quick and dry, which made for entertaining discussions around the dinner table. In witty verbal duels, where
music was often the main topic of "debate," each one took the opposite
view of the other—even though they generally shared the same opinion—
just for the pleasure of the riposte. One such humorous joust, on the subject of "codas," had Armande convulsed in laughter, as her aunt and uncle
launched into a verbal joust over the relative merits of Bach's efficient con-
clusions versus Beethoven's "slobbering exits." Often, the Polignacs and
the Chabannes were joined by Fauré for evenings of musical games, rhym-
ing contests, and the drawing of wickedly funny caricatures. On one such
occasion Winnaretta illustrated the score of Fauré's song *Après un Rêve*
(After a dream) with a depiction of an overturned bed, its occupant emerging in confusion from a chaotic pile of sheets and pillows.[13]

Common musical and artistic interests provided the basis as well for
Winnaretta's other new friendships. The widowed Romanian Princesse
Rachel de Brancovan, a virtuoso pianist and one of the finest musicians in
the aristocracy, had known Edmond for twenty years. Her estate in Amphion
on Lake Geneva was one of the few that he willingly visited (despite his
habitual complaint that there was "too much air" in the country), because

there was always interesting musicmaking going on there. The Princesse de Brancovan's beautiful and artistically inclined teenage daughters, Anna and Hélène, were fascinated with Edmond. They loved to follow him on his walks, when he would share with them his caustic and fantastical musings on philosophy, religion, art, and music. Winnaretta, a dozen years their senior, soon became like an older sister and artistic mentor to the young women. Painting in the *atelier* with Hélène and listening to Anna read her haunting, evocative poems became routine pleasures. Winnaretta would come to count the two sisters among her closest confidantes and emotional mainstays.

Another one of Edmond's friends helped Winnaretta give a public profile to her *mécénat*. Comte Eugène d'Harcourt, a composer and impresario, suffered none of the self-doubts that plagued his older colleague. Confident and tireless, in the 1880s he had organized a number of concerts featuring his and Edmond's works. In 1892, having decided to become a conductor, the Comte used his fortune to build a "Salle d'Harcourt," complete with a grand organ, at 40 rue Rochechouart. The following year he inaugurated several concert series at popular prices. One of these was a series of "Historical Concerts," a survey of musical masterworks from the sixteenth century to the present, launched in conjunction with Charles Bordes, the Chanteurs de Saint-Gervais, and organist Alexandre Guilmant. Winnaretta was interested in the first concerts in Harcourt's survey, featuring Renaissance and baroque repertoire. She was also learning about the value of music as a currency for gaining social power. She had taken good note of the way the Comtesse Greffulhe had negotiated the boundaries between private world of the musical salon, ruled by women, and the public musical world, dominated by men.[14] Following Greffulhe's example, Winnaretta approached Harcourt, offering to underwrite a three-concert series featuring the cantatas of J. S. Bach, to open the 1894 season of Historical Concerts. Harcourt accepted; the first cantata performance, featuring Bordes and Guilmant,[15] took place on Tuesday, 9 January 1894, only weeks after the Polignac wedding.[16] It was discreetly murmured that Winnaretta was the financial force behind the concerts.

While Winnaretta was testing her wings as a patron in public musical circles, Edmond was experiencing an upsetting revelation concerning his music. Reading the January issue of the magazine *La Nouvelle Revue*, he chanced upon an article by Hungarian musicologist and composer Alexandre de Bertha, who claimed to have invented a new series of "enharmonic scales" based on the alternation of half-steps and whole steps. Edmond, astonished, recognized these as being "his" octatonic scales. Infuriated, he wrote an excoriating letter to the editor of *Le Figaro*, publicly "asserting my rights of absolute priority over the invention and the naming of these same scales . . . whose reasoned invention and procedure of application are my exclusive artistic propriety."[17] The response of the nonplussed Bertha appeared in *Le Figaro*'s pages several days later. "Arranging whole steps and half steps . . . is a procedure that is in reach of the whole world. It's another thing to deduce a complete system, determining the resources that this new arrangement of intervals provides to melody, harmony and counterpoint. . . . This can only be done by special labor, not to be found within the framework of a society album, nor in a newspaper article."[18]

Winnaretta soothed her distraught husband in offering a pragmatic solution: why not let the public hear the octatonic compositions, and let the music speak for itself? And what better way to do it than to present Edmond's bold compositions in the context of a socially prestigious event, one that would draw an influential crowd from Paris society and cultural circles? Shortly thereafter, it was announced that the Princesse de Polignac would present a musical charity event at the Salle d'Harcourt, the proceeds of which would benefit a needy orphanage. The papers published articles listing in detail the names of the subscribers, who comprised the elite of the aristocracy (many of whom were Edmond's relatives) and the artistic community.[19] The concert, which took place on 15 May 1894, was a model of innovative programming. Edmond's octatonic *Pilate* opened the program; *Le Figaro* noted the "new scale" and the "striking effect" that it produced. The Comtesse de Guerne, a well-known *cantatrice mondaine* (society singer), was the soloist in Edmond's *Les Adieux de Deïdamia*; she was joined by artists from the Paris Opéra in the Trio from Gounod's *Faust*. Fauré's *Requiem*, Clément Janequin's *La Bataille de Marignan* (1550), and excerpts from Wagner's *Die Meistersinger* completed the program. "The concert's huge success was well deserved, both from the standpoint of its charitable goal and its superb program," raved *Le Figaro*. "The audience was quite brilliant."[20]

Winnaretta's chief desire, however, was building her musical influence within her home sphere. By the 1890s, salon culture had come to represent the height of elegance. The salon followed the social calendar: there was first a *petite saison* (short season), which lasted from Christmas until the middle of Lent, and a *grande saison* (long season) "from Easter until the Grand-Prix," that is to say from April to July.[21] The growth of salon culture coincided with an inspired marketing ploy by the newspapers to increase sales by satisfying its readership's insatiable curiosity about the goings-on in high society. To that end, in 1895, *Le Figaro* would create a special column called "Le Monde et la ville" (Society and the City); *Le Gaulois* followed suit with a counterpart called "Mondanités" (Society Life). The columns broke down into categories of *mondain* activity: "Social Information," "Clubs," "Charity Events," "Hunting," "Vacation Spots," "Marriages," "Deaths," and so forth. But by far the greatest amount of newsprint was devoted to the section entitled "Salons." The diversions offered by the various hostesses—whether literary, musical, or purely social—were reported in meticulous detail, as were the names of those in attendance. A reader could track the daily movements of the Duchesse de X or the Vicomte de Y by reading that the lady or gentleman in question had attended the Marquise de Saint-Paul's musical matinee on Monday, an elegant tea at the Princesse Murat's on Tuesday, a dinner followed by a vocal recital in honor of the Queen of Spain on Wednesday, the funeral of the Comte de Ganay on Thursday, and a *five o'clock* hosted by the Comtesse Greffulhe on Friday.

And music took pride of place in these reports, especially in *Le Figaro*: François Magnard, the paper's editor at the time of Winnaretta and Edmond's marriage, was particularly disposed to reporting musical events: he was a great *mélomane*, and his son, Albéric, was a gifted composer. After Magnard's death in November 1894, his successor, Gaston Calmette, gave even more space to the reportage of musical events in the salons: it was he who instituted "Le Monde et la ville," in which lengthy columns detailed the musical selections performed and the artists who performed them. On any given day, readers learned that pianist Alfred Cortot had played works by Chopin and Liszt in one salon, that Wagnerian soprano Félia Litvinne had sung excerpts from *Siegfried* in another, and that Gabriel Fauré had performed his newest piano works in yet another. An equal amount of space was devoted to performances by the hosts and hostesses. In the closed circle of the salon there were no failures; no talent was excluded. The aristocratic musicians who performed at home for their social peers could expect to receive unqualified approbation. And the society columnists did not disabuse them of their illusions: all the performances were "enormous successes," sung or played "with perfect taste." The "enthusiastic applause" came from "the most elegant" groups of "a select number of guests." It was an open secret that many of these "reports" were in fact written by the hostesses themselves.

Now, with Edmond at her side, Winnaretta began her second career as an aristocratic musical hostess in Paris. Despite the fact that the Carriès and Fauré commissions had not been completed, Winnaretta decided nonetheless to "open" her *atelier* in early 1894, albeit without the intended fanfare. By day, the newly renovated *atelier* was Winnaretta's painting studio; by night it became a recital hall. Measuring ten by twelve-and-a-half meters (roughly thirty-three by forty-one feet), the room was large enough to seat comfortably one hundred people. The vaulted ceiling was two stories high; a narrow balcony, built around the upper story's west and south walls, housed the magnificent Cavaillé-Coll organ, whose pipes rose impressively to ceiling height. Below, the room was decorated in Louis XVI style, with Winnaretta's favorite colors of blue and green predominating.[22] Two grand pianos dominated one wall. Despite the formal décor, the wood-panelled walls gave the room a warm, homey atmosphere. The "cozy corner" window seats, lining the north and east walls, provided a sense of intimacy. The leaded-glass windows, positioned to receive the optimum

light for painting by day, allowed visitors a view of the gardens that separated the avenue Henri-Martin mansion and the smaller rue Cortambert
house.

Many of the guests at those first gatherings, members of the great families of the aristocracy, were Edmond's relatives—a captive audience, so to
speak. Others came from the *haute bourgeoisie*. One frequent visitor to the
Polignac household was Madame Gaston Legrand, nicknamed "Cloton."
Well born and well known in society, Madame Legrand frequented everyone from Guy de Maupassant to Edward VII. She would become a lifelong
friend of Winnaretta's, although the two women spent the better part of
their time together bickering over trivial matters. The most interesting visitors, however, were the many talented individuals whose gifts—and peculiarities—would come to be protected and fostered in the Polignac salon.
That spring, the Polignacs welcomed to their home Oscar Wilde, already as
notorious for his affair with Lord Alfred Douglas as for his literary works.[23]
A typical gathering in June 1894 brought together a diverse group from the
literary, political, and artistic worlds: Edmond's brother Ludovic, a former
Army colonel, now living in Algeria; *Le Figaro*'s François Magnard and
Gaston Calmette; writer Maurice Barrès, who had recently abandoned
politics to direct the Republican newspaper *La Cocarde*; the pianist Princesse
de Brancovan; and the beautiful muse of the *art nouveau* movement, bisexual cross-dresser Baronne Deslandes.[24]

On Tuesday nights during that first winter of their marriage, the Polignacs
hosted a series of "organ soirees," where the great organists of the capital—Gigout, Widor, Vierne, Guilmant, Fauré—performed on the Cavaillé-
Coll. *Le Figaro* reported on Winnaretta's "organ evenings, so highly sought
after in Parisian high society,"[25] helping to add luster to her growing reputation as a musical hostess. On other evenings, chamber music was played.
Still other gatherings featured Edmond's music, often accompanied by
Winnaretta or Fauré. Not all those who frequented the Polignac salon were
there to hear the music, however, nor were they prepared to respect the
musical interests of those who were. Some of the guests were there simply
to see and be seen in the newest salon in the Parisian social landscape.
Many of them had no qualms about jostling their spoons against their
teacups, concentrating their attentions on their neighbors' garb, or, worse,
chattering to their neighbor through the course of the performance. Some
of the husbands, required to accompany their wives on their social rounds,
simply slept through the sonatas or the arias. But for the true *mélomanes* in
the crowd, those who had come expressly for the performances, the seriousness of purpose surrounding the execution of the music must have been
a welcome surprise.

Winnaretta's friend, Meg de Saint-Marceaux—the former Meg Baugnies,
widowed in 1891 and remarried in 1892 to sculptor René de Saint-

Marceaux—was frequently in attendance at the Polignac salon, and she noted her impressions in her diary. Her first visit to rue Cortambert took place on the evening of 21 May 1894; she found the *atelier* to be "a marvelous salon, where it is pleasant to make music."[26] That evening she and tenor Maurice Bagès sang some of Fauré's *mélodies* ("We shared the success").[27] The soiree provided Meg with her first opportunity to observe Winnaretta's new husband at close range, and her impressions were mixed: "The old prince happily tolerates his role of young husband. He was wearing a cardigan, a skullcap on his head. Seated beside his wife, young and in the pink of health, the contrast was quite unpleasant. But he's intelligent and very kind. He made us laugh by mimicking the sermons of the Protestant pastors in the London parks."[28] More unpleasant for Meg was the *mondain* atmosphere of the Polignac salon, so at odds with the relaxed ambiance of her own living room, where class distinctions did not exist, and where art alone ruled.

But Winnaretta thrived in this atmosphere. Indeed, she seemed to go from success to success in the first six months of her marriage. And yet her growing status as a salon hostess could not alleviate the frustration that she felt as a *mécène*-in-the-making: neither of the projects to which she had committed her patronage and her pocketbook had yet been completed. At the end of several years of alternately encouraging and harrassing Carriès and Fauré, she still had neither her Door nor her Buddha.

In the case of the latter, Fauré could no longer fall back on his old excuse about poet problems: Albert Samain, who had been engaged to write the "Buddha" text in 1892, had completed his libretto by the spring of that year. In truth, it was Fauré's undisguised ambivalence towards the subject matter that impeded his progress in completing the commissioned music. "To do the work of an artist one must get outside onself, and I'm going to try!" he wrote to his patron. "The notes are dancing before my eyes but will not let me catch them yet!"[29] Winnaretta had no patience for this. In June 1894, she wrote Fauré an imperious letter. It had been four years, she reminded him, since he had accepted her proposal to write a work "that would belong to [me] entirely."[30] Now she wanted to know what he intended to do.

> If you had not written other works since you gave me your formal promise, I would still understand, but that has not been the case. . . . Would you rather write a series of songs on some poems or other? Choose the form of the work that suits you, but decide something. . . .
>
> It's a great source of melancholy to feel how much our most sincere and seemingly worthy actions turn against us, and to know that what I believed to be a source of repose, a rare occasion to work freely, has only become a source of misunderstandings and discussion, is most particularly sad for me.[31]

A stupefied Fauré hastened to respond, "My dear Princesse, I am a simple human being, and I don't pretend to be worth either more or less than any other human being. However, I am quasi-certain that I am superior to what you seem to believe!"[32] He promised to fulfill the commission with the next large work that he composed. To her accusation that he had neglected their friendship, he responded, "It's rather *you* who have been, for the last two years, busier, more surrounded by others, and, if you'll permit yourself to remember, it's *you* who have had called on me much less."[33] Eventually all was forgiven, but privately, Winnaretta continued to hold a grudge—which she nursed until the end of her days—about the failure of the Verlaine-Fauré project. "I'm sure that [Verlaine's] libretto would have been wonderful," she wrote in her memoirs, "but I am sorry to say that Fauré refused to write the music, although it would have been a delightful theme that he could have treated marvelously." She believed too that Fauré had been disloyal on the personal level. "Although he was sensitive and sentimental, he was easily carried away by new affections, and was not always a faithful and perfect friend, being too much interested in new ties to trouble much about his old ones."[34]

She was even less forgiving of Carriès. Over the years, the problems surrounding the *Porte de Parsifal* had multiplied, as Carriès labored to assemble the six hundred enamel pieces that constituted the doorframe and its figurines. The artist was distraught because of his inability to surmount the technical problems of the piece; the pressures brought to bear by Winnaretta did not help: "She treats me like a common tradesman," he complained to a friend.[35] Desperate for money to live on, Carriès began to exhibit and sell the figurines rejected for use in the final product. The "Damoiselle" figurine had been presented in the annual Spring Salon of 1892, alongside "sad and laughing masks contracted by diabolique grimaces . . . madmen from the Mystery plays, and cathedral gargoyles."[36] These innovative pieces earned Carriès enthusiastic critical praise. "We await with curiosity the setting in place of these separate fragments [into the *Porte de Parsifal*], certain that the completed work will exude a strange perfume of mystic naturalism."[37] Winnaretta, however, was unhappy that pieces of "her" artistic property were being exhibited publicly before the Door was completed. Her displeasure escalated to fury when, in early 1894, Paul Helleu reported seeing seen the "Damoiselle" (or one of its copies) at the Ménard-Dorian house. Believing that Carriès had violated their agreement by making copies of "unique" work, Winnaretta threatened the artist with legal action.[38] His health ruined and his spirit broken, Carriès retreated to his Burgundy home, where he died on 1 July 1894 at the age of forty-nine. The unfinished *Porte de Parsifal,* the work that had consumed him for over four years, leading to his ultimate demise, would be considered by posterity to be his masterwork.

Winnaretta's reaction to Carriès's death is nowhere documented. At the time of his passing, she and Edmond were in England, visiting her brothers. Afterwards the couple traveled to Brittany to visit Edmond's nephew Comte—later Marquis—Guy de Polignac and his wife Louise (née Pommery, heiress to the champagne fortune). Conservative, traditional, religious, the "Breton" Polignacs were also family-oriented, fun-loving, and great *mélomanes*. Winnaretta was able to surmount her "outsider" status by playing guitar duets with Guy, and by ably acquitting herself as a boatswoman in the course of a family yacht trip.[39] In September Winnaretta and Edmond traveled down to the Princesse de Brancovan's villa on Lake Geneva, where they made music and came to dinner dressed *en travestis*.[40] Later that month Winnaretta introduced her husband to her favorite city: Venice. In the 1890s, Venice had not yet become an overcrowded tourist site. The summer denizens who occupied the palazzos were not only the wealthy, but also the many artists, composers, and writers who flocked to the city, attracted by the mysterious light along the water, the sultry climate, and the convivial atmosphere of the informal gatherings and fancy dress balls. Soon Edmond too was bewitched by the seductive calm of the lagoons; he would claim, "Venice is the only city where you can have conversations in front of the open windows without having to raise your voice."[41]

Upon returning to Paris, Winnaretta re-opened her salon. She commissioned a portrait of herself from society artist Antonio de La Gandara. In his lithograph, *Woman in a Black Dress,* La Gandara captures perfectly Winnaretta's duality. Dressed in a simple but elegant black velvet gown, she is attired for a formal occasion; her body is turned away from the viewer, her face in profile. A dignified young princess, a model of discretion, she is depicted as a public person—but one who is half-hiding.[42] A second—more impromptu, but equally ambiguous—rendering of Winnaretta was created during that same period by Paul Helleu in his drypoint, *Chez la Princesse de Polignac; Tissot et trois jeunes femmes.* This curious piece depicts painter James Tissot, and two women—friends? models? lovers?—gathered solicitously around Winnaretta, who is stretched out on a chaise longue, her expression hidden from view.[43]

Some imperceptible shift of stature seemed to have occurred since the previous year: in 1895, the papers suddenly began to take more frequent note of Winnaretta's activities, both in and out of the *atelier*. Winnaretta's talent as a painter was recognized in January, when some of her canvasses, signed with her maiden name, were shown in an "Exhibition of Women Artists" at the Galeries Georges Petit.[44] These works were singled out by the press, which remarked on her talents in both the artistic and musical domains.[45] On 4 February, *Le Figaro* announced, "the Princesse Edmond de Polignac will stay home next Wednesday to make music."[46] And, four days later, "A little music was made, two nights ago, at the Princesse Edmond de Polignac's, in her *hôtel* on rue Cortambert. A mere one hundred people were invited to this artistic feast."[47] This "small" group was treated to a delightful program, including two chamber music works by Edmond, accompanied by the Delsart Quartet,[48] the Schumann Piano Quartet, and songs by Fauré—including *Mandoline,* dedicated to Winnaretta—with the composer at the piano. Winnaretta served as organist for her husband's works and as pianist for the Schumann quartet.[49] That same week, scores of newspapers published advanced publicity for the forthcoming series of Bach-Schütz concerts by Charles Bordes, Alexandre Guilmant, and the Chanteurs de Saint-Gervais, to be mounted, "as in the previous year, at the Salle d'Harcourt . . . under the patronage of Madame the Princesse de Polignac."[50]

A formidable list of roles and accomplishments had been ascribed the mistress of the house: within just two months she had garnered praise as visual artist, society hostess, concert organizer, virtuoso pianist, and patron of music. But as much as the guests and the press may have lauded Winnaretta's manifold artistic gifts, it was nonetheless merely still part of the "woman's work" that made up the activity of the women of the aristocracy. This activity served not to open and broaden the world of culture, but to fill a self-referential private sphere of action and influence. In the eyes of the noble class, Winnaretta could aspire and even succeed mightily as a musician and patron within the invisible gilt walls of the Faubourg, but within its walls she and her accomplishments must remain. Within this limited sphere she surely received more approbation for her efforts than the courageous women who dared to dream of musical careers in the professional world. Operatic divas were in a class by themselves, of course: great prima donnas could drive audiences wild and command huge fees for their performances.[51] Women could aspire, if they wished, to careers as soloists, taking the full course of training at the Conservatoire, but upon receiving their diplomas they had to confront a disdainful battalion of (male) concert organizers, conductors, colleagues, competitors. And although some orchestras did admit women to their ranks, most were inaccessible as a professional venue even to the most talented women instrumentalists.

Women composers had the slightest chance of all to succeed, given, admittedly, how difficult it was for any composer to succeed. In 1890s Paris, the works of only two women composers were heard with any regularity outside of the salons: the Vicomtesse Marie de Grandval, whose numerous operas, written throughout the nineteenth century, were performed regularly,[52] and Augusta Holmès, whose bold and vital works were the most frequently played of any other woman composer of the late nineteenth century.[53] But even the renown and critical accolades garnered by Holmès since the 1880s were not enough to eradicate ambivalence—or sometimes, outright misogyny—concerning the creative achievements of women, even among her colleagues.[54] Vincent d'Indy, who advocated and fostered the training of young women composers and instrumentalists (including Armande de Polignac) at the Schola Cantorum, was ambivalent about Holmès. Despite her formal expertise in writing large works and her commitment to lofty artistic ideals, Holmès, according to d'Indy, had one insurmountable flaw: "Being a woman and lacking by nature [a penis], she is only preoccupied with acting as if *she had one*. The result: works which are big instead of great, with erections made from empty theory. . . . What I say is not intended to be mean-spirited . . . she's as artistic and high-minded as *a woman* can be, but despite that, there will always be something missing."[55]

Winnaretta chanced to see d'Indy's letter just before the first performance of Holmès's new opera, *La Montagne noire*. The work, which would receive a poor critical reception because of its "old-fashioned" style, was a topic of discussion between Winnaretta and Armande, who had also read her composition teacher's comments. The issue of women being taken seriously as composers must have continued to occupy Winnaretta's thoughts for some time afterwards. One day, traveling with her niece by train, she suddenly announced, "I'm going to write a piece." To Armande's astonishment, Winnaretta pulled out a piece of staff paper from her bag, spent the journey engaged in composition, and by the time the two women arrived at their destination, the piece was completed.[56] The work, for solo piano, was called *Halling*,[57] and was dedicated to Edmond de Polignac. Edmond's influence on his wife's creativity was clear: the melody heavily features the interval of the tritone, the backbone of the octatonic scale. "It was very interesting, and of a perfect originality,"[58] wrote Armande—and wrote truly, for in just a few short pages Winnaretta had created a work that balanced chromatic dissonance with lyrical melody, strange modulations with a lilting 6/4 meter, spare texture with passionate undercurrents. It was a unique creation: Winnaretta never wrote music again.

That year an unknown writer called Marcel Proust was invited for the first time to the Polignac salon. Winnaretta would remember him as "a handsome young man with melting brown eyes."[59] From a wealthy bourgeois family, Proust had made the acquaintance of Comte Robert de Montesquiou in 1893 at Madeleine Lemaire's salon. Years later, the count would reappear in Proust's world-renowned fiction as one of his most memorable characters, the malicious homosexual Baron de Charlus. But in the early days of their friendship, Proust admired the poet and dandy for his ancient lineage and impeccable manners. Keenly desirous of circulating in high society, he understood that the Count could pave the way to his ascent. Montesquiou fancied himself as some sort of latter-day Sophocles, destined to lead aesthetically minded young people towards the "beautiful Ideal."[60] Proust was happy to take advantage of the older man's patronage, and willingly became the fawning "disciple" of the vain aesthete. This calculating ploy paid off: soon Proust was frequenting the most elite of the Paris salons. He was introduced to Winnaretta and Edmond in the first months of their marriage. Edmond took a liking to the fragile young man—even if he had to bear what he dubbed "the terrible ordeal of [his] exaggerated kindness";[61] shortly thereafter, Proust was invited to join the Polignacs for an evening at the Théâtre Libre.[62] By the time Montesquiou became persona non grata at rue Cortambert, Proust was already receiving invitations on his own. His subsequent love affair with Reynaldo Hahn, among the best loved of Winnaretta's and Edmond's musical friends, cemented his position as a "regular" at their gatherings.

The Polignac salon provided Proust with a musical education of almost encyclopedic scope. The diversity of works performed there, spanning three centuries, was a revelation to the writer. This musical range, in fact, made for some heated post-concert arguments between Proust and Hahn, for, apart from their mutual admiration for Fauré, the two men had antithetical tastes: Hahn, an ardent Mozartian, despised the music of Wagner and Debussy, two composers whom the young writer adored.[63] It is quite possible that Proust was first exposed to the late quartets of Beethoven—works that figure prominently in *A la Recherche du temps perdu*[64]—in the rue Cortambert *atelier*. Proust's impressions of the activity and elegance of Belle Époque salon culture, which recur throughout the many volumes of his great novel, were surely formed in part by the memorable soirees at the Polignacs. A 1903 article, "The Salon of the Princesse Edmond de Polignac," would evoke the sense of wonderment that he experienced in these surroundings: "Often given during the day, these musical feasts would be illuminated by the glow that the sun's rays, filtered through the prisms of the windowpanes, would cast in the *atelier*." Proust recalled "the original and fervent interpretations of all the latest songs of Fauré, the Sonata of Fauré, the dances of Brahms."[65] He was also moved by the compositions of Edmond de Polignac. Generally, his thank-you letters to various salon hosts tended to be effusive and obsequious—a compensation, no doubt, for his insecurities in finding himself in such august company. But Proust's praise of Edmond's music, written after the soiree of 5 February 1895, was perfectly sincere. "It's music of princely elegance . . . the music of a rare musician, not of a musician-nobleman, but of a noble musician."[66]

The writer was present at a remarkable musical matinee given on 23 April, which comprised rarely performed masterworks of the Renaissance and baroque. The concert featured two works by Heinrich Schütz, including the magisterial *Dialogo per la Pasqua*.[67] The remainder of the matinee was devoted to large portions of Jean-Philippe Rameau's opera *Dardanus* (1739), a work that had not been presented in Paris in its entirety in over a century.[68] Charles Bordes conducted leading soloists from the Opéra; the instrumental accompaniment included a harpsichord (a complete rarity in those days) that had belonged to Edmond's father. Of the performance of *Dardanus,* "relatively unknown in our time, but of completely exceptional musical interest," *Le Figaro* reported a "colossal success for all these artists."[69]

On 16 June the Polignacs presented an even more unusual event, one that allowed Edmond to showcase both his compositions and his interest in technology. To accompany his works, performed by the Chanteurs de Saint-Gervais and Bordes, Edmond created a large panel showing the texts of the pieces and the musical motifs. The choir was hidden behind a screen, and the room was darkened. One moving light beam followed the inscribed text; a second beam followed the notated musical themes in such a way that the audience could refer to both during the course of the performance. In the program notes, Edmond made a valiant attempt to explain this strange, unprecedented sound and light show as "a sort of visual auditory experience [*une sorte d'audition visuelle*]."[70] At a century's remove, one can recognize the precursors of the illuminated "bouncing ball" of 1920s movie musicals and supertitles in modern opera houses. Behind the scenes, the financial arrangments for the event had proved even more daunting than the technological challenges. A letter from Charles Bordes to Edmond provides an interesting look into the financial tug-of-war engaged in by the Polignacs and the artists engaged to perform in their salon. For this concert, in place of the five francs per rehearsal and ten francs per performance customarily paid to Paris choristers (roughly ten and twenty dollars, in 2002 currency), Winnaretta instructed her husband to offer Bordes and his ensemble members one franc (two dollars) per chorister per service.[71] Bordes countered with an offer of four francs for the rehearsals and ten francs for the performance. "I would be surprised if you could find lower prices than those I offered you," he wrote. "No one has ever given less in a salon than 5 francs per rehearsal and 10 francs per performance to a chorister. I even know many salons where the choristers are paid 10 and 20 [francs]. . . . I cannot give you any bigger concessions than [these], and [I offer them] only because we are grateful to you for the kind interest that you have shown us."[72]

Winnaretta's niggardly compensation of musicians would follow through her long career as a salon hostess. Although publicly known by posterity as a "great patron," the multimillionaire Princesse de Polignac was notorious among the contemporary musicians who contributed so much to her salon as a *grippe-sou*, a penny-pincher. It seems likely, however, that during her husband's lifetime, Winnaretta was willing to make concessions that she would not make in later years. She wanted to insure Edmond's happiness, especially by promoting his music. Compensating the musicians with a reasonable fee was part of the price she had to pay, however reluctantly. The mutual affection between the couple was obvious. After one soiree, Meg de Saint-Marceaux noted, "Winni [*sic*] accompanied a chorus by Polignac on the organ. She was delightful and very kind in her manner of showing her husband to his best advantage."[73]

The couple was in demand everywhere in society; the newspaper columns recorded their attendance at music salons, balls, concerts, and grand dinners.[74] On 14 June 1895, the rue Cortambert *atelier* was the setting for an elegant cotillion, where a "mere" eighty people waltzed the evening away.[75] Edmond was not among the dancers: he was too frail. He could never get warm enough, despite the balmy air. Even in June, guests found him bundled up in plaid shawls and blankets.[76] "What do you want?" he would say to those who teased him about his outerwear. "As Anaxagorus said, 'life is a voyage'!"[77] Many years later, Proust would put these words in the mouth of the dying Bergotte in *A la Recherche du temps perdu*.

Summer was the period of voyages. A thoroughly modern couple, Winnaretta and Edmond often traveled apart, respecting each other's independence when the need for solitude arose. The trips that separated husband and wife for several months a year allowed Winnaretta to attend to her own intimate needs. In high society, women frequently traveled together without their husbands or other family members, and Winnaretta was able to carry on a discreet sexual life thanks to this convenient social device. Edmond encouraged and supported his wife's independence. During his solitary periods, he nursed his chronic physical ailments with trips to thermal spas.[78] In Paris he kept busy with a hobby that had fascinated him since childhood—furniture-making. Inspired by Art Nouveau design and the designs of William Morris,[79] he engaged a cabinet-maker to realize some of his drawings. Winnaretta was the recipient of one of these imaginative pieces, a little lemonwood side table.[80]

In 1895 the Polignacs met up at the end of the summer in Venice. In November they went to London to hear a private performance of recent works by Fauré in the opulent townhouse of impresario Leo Frank Schuster, one of Fauré's most ardent champions and financial supporters.[81] A marvelous program of the composer's works was performed that evening by a quartet of singers and a twenty-piece orchestra for an audience that included Lady Randolph Churchill, writer Henry James, actress Mrs. Patrick Campbell,[82] and painter John Singer Sargent.[83] That night the Polignacs also made the acquaintance of Adela Maddison, the wife of a wealthy lawyer and music publisher.[84] An aspiring composer herself, Maddison had studied her craft with Fauré; eventually she became his lover. Knowing of the Princesse de Polignac's support for composers, the Englishwoman did not hesitate to promote her own work: she presented Winnaretta with an autographed copy of a collection of her own songs.[85] The following year she dedicated a duo for women's voices, *Soleil couchant*, "to the Princesse Edmond de Polignac." It was surely intentional that Maddison chose to set to music a poem by Verlaine, given his association with both Winnaretta and Fauré. Sadly, the poet himself would never hear Maddison's lovely musical rendition of his work: Verlaine died on 8 January 1896, Winnaretta's thirty-first birthday.

That season, Fauré's music was featured prominently in Winnaretta's salon recitals. Her paradoxically linked impulses of generosity and posses-

siveness were evident in her attitude towards the composer, who was finally rising to international prominence. In 1896, she engaged Fauré to
become, as it were, the official "house musician" of the Polignac salon.
Thus, when Madame Ménard-Dorian invited Fauré to one of her own gatherings, he was obliged to respond in the negative: "I have music to make at
the Polignacs every Sunday night until the middle of March."[86] The first of
these "Fauré" Sundays featured the composer's C-Minor Piano Quartet
and a group of *mélodies,* sung by the silvery-voiced Comtesse de Guerne.[87]
Often Fauré's works were alternated with pieces by Edmond. On one such
evening, Edmond's *Salve Regina* was sung by a choir directed by Romain
Bussine. The performance proved to be the most moving one of the evening
for composer Ernest Chausson, who wrote in his diary, "This is not a religious piece for a church, but a religious hymn chanted by the angels in
Dante's Purgatory. A pretty mixture of mysticism, poetry, and the picturesque."[88]

Edmond's activities as part of the founding committee of the Schola
Cantorum gave his wife another opportunity to expand her range of influence. To increase the school's visibility and raise funds for its new headquarters on rue Stanislas, Winnaretta suggested the mounting of a performance of J. S. Bach's *St. John Passion,* a work largely unknown in Paris,
and one that would signal to the public the Schola's interest in reintroduc-
ing the religious masterworks of the Renaissance and the baroque.
Winnaretta convinced Eugène d'Harcourt to lend his hall for the performance, and she personally contributed one thousand francs towards the
production costs.[89] Of course, Winnaretta must have intimated to d'Indy,
her largesse might be even greater if Edmond's sacred a cappella work,
Martha et Maria,[90] could be included on the program. D'Indy assured her
that, of course, Edmond's chorus could be performed between the two
parts of the Passion—and then proceeded to ask her to contribute an additional thousand francs.[91] Ultimately, the entire project seems not to have
come off. Whether Winnaretta finally found the entreprise to be too financially questionable, whether there was not enough time for the choristers
to learn Bach's monumental oratorio, or whether the ecclesiastical community raised the question (as it did every so often[92]) of whether the performance could be considered a "sacred" concert, the *St. John Passion* was
not heard in Paris during the 1896 season.[93]

Instead, Winnaretta hosted her own "sacred concert" in her *atelier:* a
matinee performance of Edmond's a cappella choruses on religious texts,
followed by a performance of Heinrich Schütz's masterwork, his
Auferstehungs-Historie (History of the Resurrection), by Charles Bordes
and the Chanteurs de Saint-Gervais. Meg de Saint-Marceaux, hearing this
"admirable" work for the first time, was irritated by the rudeness of the
large crowd: "A stall of dukes and princes. Chattering in each group." The
young people in the audience were less taken by Schütz's music than with

the presence of poet Pierre Louÿs, whose recent literary triumph, *Aphrodite,* evoked ancient Greece in sensuous language that bordered on the risqué.[94]

Despite the social standing that her marriage had brought her, for all her activity and accomplishments as a musical hostess and patron, Winnaretta was still regarded by many in the Faubourg as an outsider—partly because she was a rich American, partly because of her association with the artistic fringe, partly because of the rumors about her sexual predilections. At one Polignac gathering, Meg de Saint-Marceaux was introduced to Winnaretta's friend the Marquise Joséphine ("Mina") de Monteynard, whom Saint-Marceaux found to be delightful. She was therefore shocked to hear the gossip that flowed freely and maliciously behind the backs of the two friends, prompting Meg de Saint-Marceaux to write, "The Marquise de Monteynard is charming; everything they're saying about her and Winnie seems hard to believe."[95]

What were "they" saying about Winnaretta? The end of the nineteenth century had seen a rise in the power and influence of "Paris-Lesbos," a hidden and mysterious subculture, many of whose members came from the highest echelons of society. This group, which included the Baronne de Nyvelt, the Marquise de Morny, and the Baronne Deslandes, intersected with an extraordinary group of Left-Bank lesbians artists and writers, such as expatriate American Natalie, the writer Colette, the poets Lucie Delarue-Mardrus and Renée Vivien, and the painter Romaine Brooks.[96] It was generally assumed that Winnaretta was part of this circle. Rumors inevitably circulated; some families considered it bad form to allow their daughters to visit rue Cortambert.[97] What most irritated Winnaretta's detractors—like Montesquiou—was how unabashedly happy she seemed in her *mariage blanc*—and how smoothly she combined wifely devotion with a (reputedly) lesbian sexual life. Unwittingly, she inspired jealousy—of her money, of her title, and most of all, of her ability to make obeisance to the social mores of class and flout them at the same time.

If Winnaretta was aware of this gossip, she kept it to herself. Having finally won an estimable position in society, she took great pains to keep her private life private. She was a textbook example of someone who succeeded by working inside a system: she used the codes and mores of the nobility's rigidly circumscribed world, and was protected by them. She followed especially the cardinal rule of her milieu: in private life, everything was permitted, everything was possible, as long as the smooth veneer of public life was preserved. Winnaretta's social standing provided her with an opportunity to hide in plain sight: she shielded herself behind her title and her inscrutable expression; her perceived haughtiness added to her allure. As long as she tacitly agreed not to court scandal, it would not come to find her.

The remainder of the season was filled with dinners, receptions, salon gatherings, and charity functions. Winnaretta attended many of these events with her sister Belle-Blanche, the Duchesse Decazes, still her closest friend and confidante. In 1893 the Decazeses had moved into a large *hôtel* on the fashionable avenue du Bois de Boulogne. Subsequently Belle-Blanche began to co-host a salon with her mother, who, her own fortune nearly depleted, had moved into a separate wing of her daughter's mansion with husband number three.[98] On the surface, the life of the lovely Duchesse Decazes was a happy one: a brilliant marriage, three beautiful children, and the admiration of all who knew her. In recent years, however, her health had become a matter of concern. Since her childhood she had suffered from bouts of "melancholy."[99] No one spoke of depression in those days; on the contrary, Belle-Blanche's softly brooding expression conformed to the poetic vision of womanhood in the romantic nineteenth century. After her marriage, her depressive states became more acute. Recently, she had begun to suffer from shortness of breath and unspecified heart problems, which necessitated frequent trips to the South of France, ostensibly to escape the poor air of Paris.[100] In late May 1896, Belle-Blanche abruptly collapsed, and Winnaretta cancelled all her activities to stay by her side.[101]

In June, satisfied that her sister's crisis had passed, Winnaretta and Edmond left Paris for Tencin, the estate of the Marquise de Monteynard. There, Winnaretta, wearing a comfortable old cardigan, her thick chestnut hair gathered in a fat braid, spent her mornings walking with Edmond down long paths lined with orange trees, adjusting her brisk gait to her husband's more hesitant step.[102] Later that summer the Polignacs attended the Bayreuth Festival together for the first time.[103] For the many years of her Wagnerian sojourns, Winnaretta had rented "Schloss Fantasie," the former summer residence of the margraves of Bayreuth, an enormous estate on the outskirts of the town's limits. This year, she leased the palace as usual for the duration of the opera season. While Edmond took his annual cure at the Saint-Gervais spa, Winnaretta prepared the house for the arrival of her husband and their guests. Despite the historical prestige associated with this "fantasy" castle, it was exceedingly rustic: Winnaretta was shocked to discover upon her arrival that there were no towels, and that the running water had been turned off.[104] She managed somehow to put the castle in order, preparing a special room where her husband could retreat and compose.[105] From St.-Gervais, Edmond sent a touching letter.

> Thank you for thinking ahead about coming to get me at the station. We can be cited as a model household, to be, after almost three years of common bondage, barely careworn and still new for each other, while so many others, after only one year, [are] already repulsed by each other. When they bother to go to the station, they meet up in the car with sadness, disillusionment, and periods of long silence, often disgusted as a result of knowing each other too well, feeling diminished and ashamed, like people who have done something dirty together.[106]

In August, reunited in Bayreuth, the couple welcomed Gabriel Fauré, who, astounded by the grandeur of Schoss Fantasie, wrote to his wife, "Too bad that you're not here! What a room, what a view! . . . There is, beneath my eyes, a giant park, a real pine forest, with hills and dales, it's wonderful."[107] Together the three friends attended the performance of the *Ring* cycle, presented in its entirety that summer for the first time since 1876, conducted by noted Wagner conductor Felix Mottl.[108] The hours not spent listening to the *Ring* were devoted to home musicmaking, by Fauré, Meg de Saint-Marceaux, Paris pianist Édouard Risler, and members of the Bayreuth opera orchestra.[109]

After Bayreuth, Edmond and Winnaretta returned briefly to Paris, where Winnaretta bought her husband a birthday present, a new blue coupé automobile; Edmond promptly joined the newly created Automobile Club of France, one of whose founding members was his brother-in-law, Paris Singer.[110] The couple spent the fall months in Venice, and then continued on to Monaco to spend some quiet time alone. But the joy of their solitude was not to last. While in Monaco, Winnaretta received news of her sister's sudden death. The Polignacs rushed back to Paris for the funeral, which was attended by over a thousand mourners.[111] Only twenty-seven, Belle-Blanche was reported to have collapsed from cardiac arrest,[112] although troubling questions about the role that "melancholia" had played in her demise circulated among those close to her. Winnaretta, who had always been a source of strength for her husband, was now shattered with grief, and Edmond, who, as a young man, had also lost a beloved sister, could offer his wife all his compassion, a warm hand to grasp, a shoulder—albeit a fragile one—to cry on.

6

La Belle Époque

Winnaretta had more than the death of her sister to shoulder as 1896 came to an end. In addition to a grieving husband, Belle-Blanche had also left behind three young children, two boys and a girl. Soon after the funeral, Belle's widower, Élie Decazes, asked his sister-in-law if she would be willing to take charge of raising his six-year-old daughter. It was thus that Winnaretta became a surrogate mother to Marguerite "Daisy" Decazes. Winnaretta adored her niece; less clear is what kind of maternal figure she was capable of being to the little girl. Like her aunt, Daisy was the somewhat plain daughter of an extremely beautiful mother; like her aunt, she manifested her natural willfulness by lapsing into inscrutable silence. But for now, Winnaretta did what she could to act as an emotional mainstay for her niece. Daisy and her clothes and dolls were moved into the rue Cortambert house. For the next thirteen years, until her marriage in 1910, Daisy Decazes would spend a portion of every year living with her Tante Winnie, often accompanying her on her far-flung travels.

The presence of a child in the Polignac household in 1897 did not significantly affect Winnaretta's and Edmond's life. Children in the upper classes were traditionally cared for by governesses and servants. Edmond's involvement in Daisy's life was probably minimal. He was primarily concerned with assuaging his wife's grief. To lift her spirits, he bought her a special birthday present that year: an 1851 edition of the complete works of Bach.[1]

During this period the city of Paris was experiencing the dramatic changes of modernism brought about by industrialization. More cars were to be seen in the streets among the horse-drawn carriages and bicycles.[2] Households that could afford them installed their first telephones.[3] For the music-lovers who did not wish to brave the crowds at the theaters, another new and curious electronic device, the *théâtrophone,* allowed subscribers to hear live broadcasts of productions at the Opéra and the Comédie Française through a receiver connected directly to the various theaters.[4]

But if the standard of living was improving during this period of peace and prosperity, events leading to what would become "The Dreyfus Affair" were beginning to unfold. The 1894 conviction, denunciation, and imprisonment of Army Captain Alfred Dreyfus, a Jew who had allegedly committed acts of treason, became a rallying point for groups whose power had been weakened after the Franco-Prussian War: the clerics, the royalists, and other anti-Republican groups. The denunciation of Dreyfus as a traitor to the nation also served to bolster the diminished reputation of the Army, the most potent symbol of national honor and might. However, in the summer of 1896, the illegality of Dreyfus's trial was exposed. In response, the Army generals, who believed themselves above politics and the law, began an enormous coverup, forging and tampering with documents in order to "prove" incontestably Dreyfus's guilt. In their actions they had the implicit support of the nation—for how could the Army, representing all that was brave, noble, and patriotic, possibly be guilty of lies and deception? But each time the pro-Dreyfusards produced evidence that refuted the original documents, each time a retrial was demanded, the more hardened the generals became in their positions. On 10 November 1894, an "irrefutably" damning piece of evidence, the famous *bordereau,* was "leaked" to the newspaper *Le Matin.*

Winnaretta would recall this politically charged period as one which "developed hatred of every kind in Paris; families were split up, husbands and wives parted, and it was not unusual at a dinner to see guests leave the room if anyone appeared of an opposite opinion from their own."[5] As the Affair progressed, the two halves of the intellectual world split wider and wider apart; former friends passed each other in silence, and any words they might have said "would never have carried across the worlds that lay between them."[6] These tensions were mirrored in the famous cartoon by the anti-Semitic artist Caran-d'Ache, whose first panel showed a family sitting down to dinner over the caption "Above all, don't talk about the Dreyfus Affair," followed in a second frame by a sketch of overturned furniture and broken crockery, over the caption "They talked about it."[7]

Given the range of political points of view in this large family, it was no surprise that this kind of impassioned divergence of opinion took place among the Polignacs. Edmond and his brother Camille were staunch pro-Dreyfusards, but most of their circle of family members and friendly intimates did not share their views. The majority of the members of the extended Polignac family, staunch royalists, were anti-Dreyfusard, a viewpoint shared by composers Vincent d'Indy and Augusta Holmès, poets Pierre Louÿs, Frédéric Mistral, and the artist Jean-Louis Forain. Edmond's old friend Maurice Barrès went even further, advocating an extreme nationalistic platform that embraced pro-clericism and anti-Semitism.[8] The Dreyfusard side of Edmond and Winnaretta's friends included writers Marcel Proust, Anatole France, and Abel Hermant, painter Georges Clairin, the Bibesco and the Brancovan families, and, perhaps most surprisingly, Anna's de Brancovan's fiancé, Comte Mathieu de Noailles, a military man bearing the name of one of France's most illustrious (and royalist) families.

Winnaretta maintained neutral political positions throughout her life. In the case of the Affair, she was considered pro-Dreyfus because her husband was pro-Dreyfus, but it is not clear that she would have advocated one position or another on her own. During those uneasy years, she used her salon to maintain peaceful relations with the friends and families whose political views did not coincide with Edmond's. Guy de Polignac and his extended family made up the audience of a musical soiree held on 9 May 1897, Winnaretta's first gathering following the end of her mourning period.[9] The evening was subdued: all talk centered on the horrific Charity Bazaar Fire, which, on 4 May, had claimed the lives of one hundred forty men, women, and children, including many of the Polignacs' friends and acquaintances. Providentially, Winnaretta had been busy planning for her soiree, and had been unable to attend the ill-fated event that plunged all of Paris society into mourning.

On 17 May the Polignacs opened their home to host the first concert of the Schola Cantorum, which featured the works of the school's composition students.[10] That summer the couple, joined by Armande de Polignac, returned to Bayreuth, where, over the course of ten days, they heard the *Ring* cycle and *Parsifal*.[11] Years later Armande would recall "the unforgettable evenings when, returning from the performances, we threw ourselves at the piano in order to prolong the ecstasy by playing from the scores into the wee hours of the night."[12] On the way back to France the trio stopped at Wildthurn, the Bavarian estate where Edmond's family had lived after his father was released from prison. While Edmond basked in childhood memories, Winnaretta played croquet on the lawn.[13] From Germany, the threesome proceeded on to Amphion to attend the grand marriage, on 18 August, of Anna de Brancovan to Comte Mathieu de Noailles.[14] The celebration was marred somewhat by the many background conversations, spoken in hushed voices, that revolved around the recent developments in the Dreyfus Affair. In October, Winnaretta suffered another personal loss: her beloved aunt Jane Synge, the kind woman whom Winnaretta had cherished as a substitute mother, died in England.[15] The Singer family convened in Devonshire for Jane's funeral, making for a tense reunion between Isabella and her children. Lady Synge was buried in Torquay Cemetery, and Winnaretta entered her second mourning period in two years.

The year 1898 opened dramatically with the publication in the newspaper *L'Aurore* of Émile Zola's famous manifesto, *J'accuse*. This blistering letter to the President of the Republic decried the treachery of the Army colonels and generals who concealed the documents that gave certain proof of Dreyfus's innocence, as well as the complicity of the French citizenry who had contributed to the poisoned atmosphere of religious prejudice and "social malfeasance." On the day the article appeared, Winnaretta happened to dine at the home of Jean-Louis Forain and his wife. Now internationally renowned for his satirical sketches, the artist was also a virulent anti-Dreyfusard. In her memoirs, Winnaretta recalled that Forain "was greatly impressed by [Zola's] article, which he read out to me with admiration for the author and indignation at the story he was told."[16] His momentary sympathy did not, however, ultimately dissuade him from his chosen political stance, and he made light of his own hypocrisy: "I have drawn so many comic figures of Jews and it will be so easy for me to continue to do so, so that I cannot change my line now; I have no choice but to become an 'anti-Dreyfusard.'"[17] If Winnaretta was perplexed by her friend's ability to sustain viewpoints repugnant to her, she explained it by remembering that Forain was one of the few people she knew who believed in the existence of the devil.[18]

After six months of mourning for her aunt Jane, Winnaretta resumed musical gatherings in the *atelier*. The soiree of 26 April featured performances by the Chanteurs de Saint-Gervais of Renaissance and baroque repertoire.[19] One month later pianists Édouard Risler and Alfred Cortot took star turns as soloists in works by Mozart, Liszt, and Fauré, after which Risler accompanied a performance of Schumann's *Dichterliebe*, sung, in a break with tradition, by soprano Marcella Pregi.[20] Edmond's works were not ignored during this season. He had remained productive as a composer during his marriage. Within the last year he had produced several new works for a cappella chorus. The first of these, an *Ave Maris Stella* for men's voices, was written during a visit to Florence in April, and paid homage to the style of a sixteenth-century motet. Two other works, *Effet de lointain* and *Le Vallon* (on a text by Lamartine), were written in a modernist style. These pieces, which explored non-tonal harmonies, were featured in a Polignac salon on 12 June 1898, performed by the Chanteurs de St. Gervais, led by Charles Bordes. Once again, Edmond used the occasion as an exploration of his interest in mixed media, illuminating the *atelier* with visual images during the execution of the music. The highly dissonant *Effet de lointain* was illustrated with an immense projection of night falling on a Flemish village, *Le Vallon* with a Fontainebleau landscape (photographed by Armande), and *Ave Maris Stella* with Fra Angelico's *Annunciation*.[21] Proust, greatly moved, sent his appreciative thoughts in a letter to Edmond:

> Prince, I have the habit of bothering you with admiring letters just after concerts where I hear your music. But it seems to me that poets should be thanked, and the other night I felt more than ever what a serious, what a vast and sweet poet you are. These sonorous waves overlap like the waves of the streams of *Le Vallon*, these vast spaces measured by the music between these distant songs in the mountains, the differences of altitudes and distances rendered perceptible, and the great sad majesty of these places and of these choruses, all that touched me very much.[22]

In between salon gatherings the Polignacs made a trip to London, to cheer on their friend Fauré on the occasion of his next British success. The private performances of the composer's music in Schuster's living room in 1895 had resulted in more British performances of his music and an offer by Maurice Maeterlinck to write the incidental music for the first London presentation of his 1882 symbolist play *Pelléas et Mélisande*. Working closely with the eminent actress Mrs. Patrick Campbell, the production's Mélisande, Fauré wrote the beautiful and refined incidental music for Maeterlinck's dark and haunting love story. The Polignacs arrived for the premiere performance at the Prince of Wales Theatre on 21 June 1898; they were seated alongside John Singer Sargent, who sketched Fauré as he conducted.[23] At the reception, Fauré surprised Winnaretta by telling her that he had decided to dedicate *Pelléas et Mélisande*'s incidental music to her, thus fulfilling his promise, made in 1894, that she would be the dedicatee of his next major work. To commemorate the occasion, he presented her with the manuscript of *Pelléas*'s Prelude, arranged for piano four-hands.[24]

On 8 July the Polignacs finished their musical season with a concert performed by the faculty and students of the Schola Cantorum, directed by Charles Bordes and accompanied at the organ by Alexandre Guilmant. The program was a celebration of polyphonic music, featuring not only sacred music by Renaissance masters and by Johann Sebastian Bach, but also newly written sacred music by, among others, Edmond de Polignac.[25] It is interesting to note how successfully the relatively new Schola had managed to promote and instill the venerable ancient tradition of polyphonic sacred music—modest, simple, and linear—at the same moment that the idolatry of Wagner's music—lush, sensual, and excessive—had reached its zenith among the denizens of Paris's music-loving society. Winnaretta and Edmond were able to appreciate and champion both sides of the musical coin.

Following the Schola concert, Winnaretta left for Versailles to spend several days painting in the company of Madeleine Lemaire, while Edmond stayed in Paris to work on his compositions. "We are leading a very calm little life," Lemaire wrote to Edmond, "in the middle of all these beautiful things. In the evenings we read some Baudelaire; Winnie makes a little music and, at dusk, as the shadows are falling, plays the guitar, filling our souls with melancholy."[26] Edmond confessed his loneliness in a return letter to his wife. "I will be very happy, very thrilled, to find myself again with my *dear dear* Winn on Tuesday. Nothing is worth more than the reciprocal trust, the certainty of affection and the indestructible knowledge that we shall always belong to each other. These are the real blessings of life."[27]

In August the Polignacs went down to Amphion to celebrate the marriage of the second Brancovan daughter, Hélène, to Prince Alexandre de Caraman-Chimay. In an uncanny echo of the Brancovan-Noailles marriage the preceding summer, major events in the Dreyfus Affair coincided with the happy event, sobering the festivities, especially for the newlyweds (Hélène was a Dreyfusard, her new husband was anti-Dreyfus). The papers were filled with the shocking news: while browsing through office files, a French Intelligence officer, an ardent anti-Dreyfusard, happened to come upon some of the more damning forged documents that had been touted as "irrefutable proof" by the Army a year earlier. Within weeks the culpable officers most heavily involved in the cover-up were relieved of their duties.

Edmond and Winnaretta did their best to steer clear of the tempests that ushered in the year 1899—the death of president Félix Faure, the failed attempt to overthrow the République by Barrès, Guérin, and Déroulède, the installation of the Dreyfusard Émile Loubet as new president. Instead, they enjoyed visits from their new neighbors, the young Noailles and Caraman-Chimay couples, who, after their respective marriages, had both moved to avenue Henri-Martin, on either side of the Polignac *hôtel*. A new series of musical soirees took place in the *atelier*. On 20 January the Chanteurs de St-Gervais, directed by Bordes, with Guilmant at the organ, sang a cantata by Bach. On 9 February tenor Maurice Bagès sang Fauré's *La Bonne Chanson*, a cycle of songs on poems by Verlaine, with accompaniment of string quartet. The soiree of 22 March featured the music of the master of the house and his composer-niece. Edmond's 1864 String Quartet in F Major and Armande's Quartet in E Major were performed by a string ensemble whose violist was the young Pierre Monteux.[28] On the second half of the program Winnaretta performed a Bach organ concerto.[29] During these evenings, while Winnaretta was seeing to her other guests, Edmond would often be attended to by "the incomparable" Anna and Hélène, who, in the words of Proust, were delighted to be the recipients of the "joy and paternal tenderness" of the prince, whose animated face age belied his numerical age.[30]

At the same time that Proust was mentally noting the details of these musical evenings, he was feeling the stresses of the *Affaire* even more keenly than most of the Polignacs' intimates. His fervent championship of Dreyfus's cause resulted in the closing of many doors in the Faubourg St.-Germain whose opening he had courted so assiduously. The Polignac salon was one of the few among the aristocracy in which he felt himself among those sympathetic to his political stance, his artistic tastes, and his sexual predilections. Edmond was quite content to bask in the young writer's prodigious and extravagantly expressed admiration of his music (for example, after hearing Edmond's quartet on 22 March, Proust wrote, "I *had* to tell you how beautiful I found your quartet, where there is, after accents of celestial charm, an ardent spirit, and finally, in those last measures, the eloquence of a concise and grandiose response").[31] Winnaretta, however, felt less warmly towards Proust.[32] His emotional hypochondria—the constant falling in and out of love, and the melodramatic self-pity that inevitably followed—grated against Winnaretta's habitual stoicism. She was happy enough, however, to accept his recommendations on reading material— Gobineau's *Pléiades* and Baudelaire's *Poèmes en prose*, among others—but their literary affinities could not ameliorate a certain brittleness that would always exist between them.[33]

The fact that Proust maintained an ongoing friendship with Montesquiou did not help. For all the moral courage that he showed in supporting Dreyfus, Proust was incapable of standing up to Montesquiou, who, to a large extent, still supervised his protégé's social life. The younger man had recently taken to giving lavish dinner parties, intended to bolster his social standing among his rich bourgeois friends and the luminaries of the Faubourg St.-Germain—those that were still talking to him, that is. He had scheduled a dinner for 24 April, to honor the new works of three poets: Montesquiou, Anatole France, and Anna de Noailles. The vituperative count gave him a long list of couples that were to remain, according to his dictates, persona non grata: the Blanches, the Hérédias, the Régniers, and, of course, the Polignacs. Proust was thus reduced to having to ask permission of his mentor to include Edmond and Winnaretta: "You could do a *very* good thing . . . in giving me the right to invite . . . those ones whom I dare no longer name, this couple so full of affection and admiration for you."[34] Montesquiou refused to yield; the Polignacs were not invited.[35]

Winnaretta and Edmond survived this snub unscathed. They traveled to Italy, where they struck up a friendship with Dom Lorenzo Perosi, choirmaster at St. Mark's Cathedral.[36] Upon their return to Paris, Edmond's songs were performed in the salon of the Comte and Comtesse Henri de Saussine.[37] Old friendships deepened, new friendships bloomed. Adela Maddison, the Polignacs' London friend, recently separated from her wealthy lawyer husband, had moved to Paris to pursue both her compositional career and her love affair with Fauré.[38] It was in the Maddison salon on rue de la Pompe that Winnaretta and Edmond met another British composer, Frederick Delius, whose opera *Koanga* (1897) was played on that occasion by "a few of the best young French musicians."[39] According to Delius, the Polignacs were "quite enthusiastic" about his music,[40] and it seems to have been so, for they came back frequently to the Maddison salon to hear the music of this most poetic of composers.

In recent years the Polignacs had also made new friends in the salon of Meg de Saint-Marceaux, including reporter-satirist Henry Gauthier-Villars, known by all as "Willy." A cousin of Jacques-Émile Blanche, Willy enjoyed a reputation as the charming, celebrated, and dangerous darling of Parisian arts journalism. Although not a musician himself, Willy had an encyclopedic knowledge of music, and was an ardent champion of young French composers, and of his hero, Richard Wagner. Under the pen-name "L'Ouvreuse du Cirque d'été," he wrote brilliant and wickedly funny commentary on the Paris music scene. His articles and satires dominated Paris music criticism for over two decades. He could make or break reputations: composers and artists who did not find favor with the journalist feared his barbed critiques, which were as dangerously pointed as his pen.

In 1893, Willy had married a shy young woman from the provinces, Sidonie-Gabrielle Colette. As the wife of the best-known music critic in

Paris, the young Gabrielle would accompany him to the city's concert halls, salons, and literary and artistic cafés (she would later call these excursions her "apprenticeships"). A writer in the making, she would sit quietly beside her husband; sometimes she would take notes, as Willy exchanged humorous anecdotes with the men and played the seducer with the ladies. Gabrielle Gauthier-Villars's future and lasting fame as the author Colette would vastly eclipse the fleeting celebrity of her husband, whom she would eventually divorce. Colette's vivid first impressions of the Polignacs, noted as she sat quietly in the back of the room at the Saint-Marceaux salon, were gathered in a retrospective article, entitled "A Salon in 1900." Colette found Edmond to be charming and young at heart, like "a big ironic bird."[41] Once he had found the warmest corner of the room, he spent the evening ensconced in the sofa's cushions, sketching, his large vicuna shawl alternately warming his thin shoulders or his knees.[42] Winnaretta, on the other hand, seemed unapproachable. In contrast to the *décolletage* that was a standard feature of women's evening wear in that era, she always wore high-necked dresses. Although Colette was intimidated by the woman "whose character of indestructibility emanated down from her deep blue-eyed gaze to her conqueror's chin," she sensed at the same time that there was something admirable about her.[43] In subsequent years the two women would develop a friendship that would last a lifetime.

Another fairly recent addition to the Saint-Marceaux salon was one of Fauré's composition students at the Conservatoire, Maurice Ravel. Short and slim, nattily dressed, at once dynamic and inscrutable, Ravel quickly endeared himself to Meg's Friday night group. Winnaretta had apparently not yet formed an opinion of him, thinking him perhaps just one more young composer with potential. Suddenly, in 1899, the twenty-four-year-old composer performed an audacious feat of artistic social-climbing. The Princesse de Polignac was shocked to discover that Ravel had written a new piece for solo piano, entitled *Pavane pour une infante défunte*—and had dedicated the work to her. This violated every breach of etiquette: in principle, Ravel should have first asked if she would deign to accept the dedication. But before Winnaretta could object to Ravel's impertinence, she was preempted by the work's reception. For the *Pavane*, written in a cool, measured style that evoked the grace and poise of a bygone age, was an immediate success. Audiences took to the young composer's work instantaneously. Since the approbation of the Princesse de Polignac had already become a de facto guarantee of the excellence of its creator, Winnaretta would have been hard-pressed to disclaim her involvement. She was obliged thereafter simply to say, "I was much surprised and deeply touched that he should have attached my name to these lovely pages."[44] As Ravel's talent deepened over the years, producing works as diverse as the Lisztian *Jeux d'eau,* the modally tinged String Quartet, and the revolutionary *Histoires naturelles,* Winnaretta came to count herself among his enthusiastic champions. The two did not become close, however. That Ravel remained aloof from the Polignac circle can be affirmed by the fact that he never gave a manuscript of his famous *Pavane* to its dedicatee. The Polignac music archives contain only a published copy of the first edition of the work, bearing the terse autograph, "Respectful homage, Maurice Ravel."[45]

In September, Edmond and Winnaretta traveled to Amphion for an extended stay with the Princesse de Brancovan; they were joined by the Princesse's daughters and their husbands, the Bibescos, writer Abel Hermant, and pianist Léon Delafosse.[46] Proust, vacationing with his parents in nearby Évian, came often to visit. The only anti-Dreyfusards among the group, Prince Alexandre de Chimay and Arthur Meyer, editor of *Le Gaulois,* politely kept a low profile. Dreyfus's retrial had begun in Rennes a month earlier, and had given rise to demonstrations and an assassination attempt against Dreyfus's attorney. These events were followed closely by the inhabitants of Amphion. Even in the calm environs of Lake Geneva, it was impossible to avoid the vituperations spawned by the *Affaire*. Visiting the nearby historic chateau of Coppet, Edmond and Winnaretta were received by its ultra-royalist owner, Comtesse Pauline d'Haussonville. After claiming to be delighted upon hearing of Proust's presence in the region, she unwittingly revealed her true prejudices with the cutting remark to Winnaretta, "I understand *perfectly* well what foreigners like you think about all this."[47] The awful news was received that same night: despite the evidence of his innocence, Dreyfus was found guilty of high treason with extenuating circumstances, and condemned to ten years in solitary confinement. The verdict caused an uproar. At Amphion, Anna de Noailles collapsed, sobbing, "How could they do that, how could they dare to say that to him? And the foreigners, and the whole world, what will they think? How could they?"[48]

Edmond was ill for the better part of his stay at Amphion; by the end of his visit he was too weak to leave the little cottage (part of a guest complex known as the Farmhouse[49]) where he and Winnaretta were staying. Every day the other guests took the carriage that drove the guests around the various habitations of the estate to come and pay him visits. Abel Hermant admired Edmond's "originality of thought, the courteousness of another era. . . . His strength of opinion [in support of Dreyfus] would make the young jealous."[50] Edmond enjoyed gently teasing Proust about his Jewish identity, inquiring mischievously, "So this old Syndicate, what's it up to now?"[51] The next day, while Edmond rested, Winnaretta took a walk in the woods with the writer. The two lost their way, causing Proust to become exhausted as the trek was excessively prolonged; they finally found the path, where they encountered the Princesse de Brancovan, a combination of "nervous twitches and Oriental extravagances."[52] Finally, an amelioration of Edmond's health enabled him to leave his cottage and join his hosts and the other guests just as the happy news was announced: President Loubet had granted Dreyfus's pardon. Two days later, Galliffet proclaimed in a military order: "The incident is over! . . . Forget the past so that you may think only of the future."[53]

After the tumultuous events of the previous year, 1900 began in a subdued manner. The French were soul-weary, tired of national strife, tired of dissent with their neighbors. Within months a bill calling for amnesty of all matters related to the *Affaire* was introduced by the Senate. Former sinners repented their evil ways: even an inveterate old decadent like Joris-Karl Huysmans announced that he was committing to "a conversation of my values, [in order to lead] the life of a pious man who fears God."[54] And yet as incremental shifts in values were taking place, radical new technologies and scientific discoveries were underway that would change people's lives forever. The first line of the Paris Chemin de Fer Métropolitain, nicknamed the Métro, began running trains from Vincennes to Porte Maillot; the first electrified trains began departures from the Gare d'Orsay. Two great exhibition halls, the Grand and Petit Palais, were opened to the public. Belgium announced the establishment of the first radio station, and in Vienna, scientist Karl Landsteiner was on the verge of discovering the different blood groups. These advances would be represented, if only symbolically, by the next World's Fair, which was under construction. The Fair promised to represent the gleaming vision of modernism, paying homage to the newest technologies, the newest glories of the machine age.

Musically, Paris seemed to be spending as much time looking backwards as it was looking forwards. The first complete Paris performance of Handel's *Messiah* since 1873 was being prepared by Eugène d'Harcourt. In the first week of 1900 the newspapers reported the discovery of a manuscript of Offenbach's *La Belle Hélène* (first performed in 1865). Large portions of the music and text of the celebrated operetta—itself a spoof on operatic conventions—had been crossed out in red pencil, in order to comply with nineteenth-century censorship laws. "What will our contemporary young pornographers think of the Republican censors?"[55] And, incredibly, despite the fact that the French comprised the majority of attendees every summer at Bayreuth, the Opéra de Paris was presenting a series of the *first* Paris performances of Wagner's *Tristan und Isolde* (in French) that season.

The first manifestation of musical modernism at the turn of the century did not in fact take place in the concert halls, but in the salon. It was introduced in the most informal way possible, one Friday night in 1900, when André Messager walked into the salon of Meg de Saint-Marceaux with the score of Debussy's *Pelléas et Mélisande* under his arm. "He pressed it to his heart," recalled Colette, "as if he had stolen it."[56] Messager, the dedicatee of his friend's opera, sat down at the piano and began to read it immediately, passionately humming its tunes."[57] This was miraculous music, the future made audible. Its clear expression, its subtly colored, intangibly mysterious harmonic progressions, were unlike anything ever heard since the rapturous music of Wagner's *Tristan* was first brought before nine-teenth-century audiences. But Debussy's music was the antithesis of the Wagnerian aesthetic: in its restraint and indirection, it was the embodiment of modern *French* music. Winnaretta, sitting at Edmond's side during the soiree, was moved by "its passionate sincerity, undeniable beauty and dignity."[58]

As Edmond became more frail, Winnaretta was intent that he should never lose the hope that his music would become known. She devised a number of projects that would bring her husband's compositions before a larger public. First, she took steps to have his works republished; to that end Edmond began to look closely through his old manuscripts, making corrections, adding improvements.[59] The octatonic *Pilate livre le Christ* was reproduced in a private printing, and bore the dedication "to Madame la Princesse Edmond de Polignac."[60] In early 1900 two of Edmond's works, including a newly written piece, *Aubade,* for mixed voices a cappella, were chosen for inclusion in a multi-volume collection of works by three hundred composers being assembled on the occasion of the World's Fair.[61]

Meanwhile, Winnaretta began to explore performance venues for her husband's music. In 1900 she asked conductor Camille Chevillard to look at Edmond's scores. Having just succeeded his father-in-law Charles Lamoureux as director of the Concerts Lamoureux, Chevillard was now regarded as one of Paris's most esteemed conductors, hailed equally for his performances of Wagner[62] and his championship of modern French composers. Despite his current renown—or perhaps because of it—he too made the rounds in the salons of the aristocracy and the *haute bourgeoisie*, the concert-going audience that provided the financial base for the Concerts Lamoureux. It is indicative of the power of salon culture that, even in the midst of his Wagner season at the Opéra, Chevillard could be found conducting a group of wealthy bourgeois "singers" who had gathered at the home of a Madame Hellman to perform *Götterdämmerung* (the hostess was the evening's Brunnhilde).[63] That same week Chevillard led a performance of *Das Rheingold* in the home theater of French automobile industrialist Louis Mors;[64] the vocal artists for that occasion were a mixture of soloists from the Opéra-Comique and a group of *mondain* singers ("who," reported the papers, "delivered their characters in the most remarkable fashion"), accompanied by an orchestra of eighty musicians.[65]

The Polignacs once again used their salon as a means to bridge the private and public musical spheres. On 24 March 1900 they welcomed to their home Siegfried Wagner, son of the composer, to repay the hospitality that the Wagner family had shown them during their numerous trips to Bayreuth. It was a glittering evening: members of the diplomatic corps and luminaries of Paris musical and aristocratic circles sat in rapt attention, as great French artists interpreted great German music. Pianist Alfred Cortot played transcriptions of *The Death of Isolde* and the first and fourth scenes from *Das Rheingold*; Maurice Bagès sang *Lieder* by Schubert.[66] As one of Paris's foremost exponents of Wagner's music, it is likely that Chevillard was among the guests that evening. Subsequently the conductor agreed to present two of Edmond's works in concert: *Les Adieux de Deïdamia,* an 1870s work based on Alfred de Musset's poem, for soprano solo, women's voices, and orchestra, and *Pilate livre le Christ,* for baritone, mixed voices, and large orchestra. During the year Edmond completely rewrote the orchestral scores, working directly with Chevillard to produce a definitive version.

After hosting a pair of musical gatherings in March (an all-Fauré soiree[67] and a charity concert held "for the benefit of Paris's Poor Italians"[68]), the Polignacs departed for Venice. They left just in time to avoid the opening ceremonies of the 1900 World's Fair, which brought to Passy a swarm of humanity eager to see the Far East pavilions at the Place du Trocadéro.[69] The Polignacs were joined in Venice by many Parisian friends seeking to escape the overcrowded and overexcited Capital: Hélène de Caraman-Chimay, poet Henri de Régnier and his wife Marie (daughter of poet José-Maria de Hérédia), Reynaldo Hahn, and Marcel Proust, in the company of his mother. During the day, Edmond and Hélène would take gondola rides down the Grand Canal, admiring the facades of each palazzo, dreaming of owning one; both agreed that the most beautiful of all was the Palazzo Contarini, near the Accademia.[70] At night, Hahn entertained the Polignacs and their guests on their moonlit sails around the lagoon, singing his songs and accompanying himself on Winnaretta's small yacht piano, which had been brought aboard her gondola.[71]

The Polignacs' stay in Venice ultimately turned out to be much more exciting than they had anticipated. One day they were invited to lunch by a wealthy American couple, Mr. and Mrs. Daniel Curtis. Cousins of John Singer Sargent, the Curtises lived in the Palazzo Barbaro on the Grand Canal, near the Accademia Bridge. It was in the writing room of their magnificent apartment that Henry James had first conceived his story *The Aspern Papers.* Relaxing on the Curtis's balcony after the meal, Edmond realized that he was sitting directly across from his favorite among all the palaces that lined the Grand Canal. This fine Lombard edifice was reputed in legend to have at one time been the home of Othello's Desdemona. When he saw it from the Curtis's balcony, Edmond spontaneously exclaimed, "Ah! that is the place to live in, and we must manage it get it in one way or another!" Winnaretta was amazed: her husband so infrequently asked for anything at all. It was the week of his birthday, and she decided to buy him the present of a lifetime. The next day she went to see a real estate agent. After a few months of wrangling, Winnaretta was able to secure the purchase of the palace, which would henceforth be known as the Palazzo Contarini-Polignac.[72]

The couple returned to Paris in time to hear three of Edmond's choruses performed at the Meg de Saint-Marceaux's salon on 11 May.[73] Then, after a particularly festive spring season, the couple spent much of the summer apart—Edmond setting off for Amsterdam in early July, Winnaretta for the thermal baths in Bad Kreuznach, Germany, the museums of Basel, and the social whirl of St. Moritz. While traveling, Winnaretta wrote Edmond, asking him to look into the purchase of a painting to adorn the walls of the palazzo. It had always been a given in their marriage that the Singer heiress paid for everything, but this time Edmond insisted on dipping into his meager personal fortune to contribute two thousand francs to the purchase of the canvas. This represented "a minimal portion [of the price], it is true," he wrote, but the contribution would testify to "a communal effort . . . in honor of our future Palaces."[74] The couple was apart until mid-August, when they both visited the Princesse de Brancovan in Amphion. Winnaretta left shortly thereafter, meeting up with Adela Maddison, Leo Schuster, and other British friends in Beziers to attend the first performance of Fauré's new opera *Prométhée*.[75] Edmond was too frail to travel; he stayed in the region with Mina de Monteynard at her Château de Tencin, envious at not being able to accompany his wife in cheering on his friend Fauré. His envy was ultimately replaced with relief, however: the première at the Théâtre des Arènes, scheduled for 26 August, had to be postponed because of gale-force winds.[76]

The Polignacs left on 29 August for Venice to sign the final documents necessary to put the Palazzo Polignac in their possession. They made a new friend during this particular trip—the bisexual woman of letters Augustine Bulteau, who wrote novels under the pseudonym Jacques Vontade and articles and essays for *Le Gaulois* and *Le Figaro* under the pseudonym Foemina. In Paris, Bulteau hosted an important literary salon at avenue de Wagram; the other half of the year she lived in Venice with her friend and lover, Comtesse Gontraud de La Baume-Pluvinel,[77] who had bought the Palazzo Dario-Angarani on the Grand Canal. Bulteau was an extremely charismatic woman, a kind of "guru" who, while revealing little about herself, exerted a powerful and uplifting influence over her numerous *protégés* of both sexes. "Those who came to her for the first time were sounded out, seen through, translated, and, in a certain way, brought to life and put in order," wrote art critic Jean-Louis Vaudoyer. "After an hour of conversation, you had learned things about yourself that you didn't know you had in you. . . . [T]he brief and sagacious questions that she asked you were just those that you didn't have the courage or the intelligence to ask of yourself. The answers given to these questions burst forth from the unexplored or unenlightened parts of the conscience."[78] Hélène de Caraman-Chimay, completely under Bulteau's sway, addressed her in correspondence as "my adored mother."[79]

Winnaretta, introduced to Augustine Bulteau by Anna and Hélène, was fascinated by this quietly powerful woman, who seemed to be a fount of knowledge, not only of literature, culture, and politics, but of the human soul. In turn, Bulteau admired Winnaretta's taciturn style, which she attributed to an Anglo-Saxon "art of not telling all, [a talent] that adds a prodigious buffoonery to your stories."[80] Winnaretta and Edmond soon figured among the artists and intellectuals who gathered regularly at the Palazzo Dario, which was filled with magnificent artworks, rare books, and an impressive collection of Renaissance and baroque musical instruments.[81] Bulteau's "regulars" included journalist and writer Léon Daudet, future director of the ultra-nationalist newspaper *L'Action française,* painters John Singer Sargent and Maxime Dethomas, the Henri de Régniers, decorator Henri Gonse, and Jean-Louis Vaudoyer.[82] Normally Hélène and Anna were present at these gatherings, but Anna, in an advanced state of pregnancy, had remained in Paris during the summer. On 18 September the Polignacs received the news of the birth of Anna's baby son, Anne-Jules, and they rushed back to Paris to celebrate the event with their friends.

Two weeks later, the legalities of taking possession of the palazzo were finalized. Winnaretta wrote to Bulteau, "Finally everything is finished and Montecuccoli is ours. I'm thrilled, and I can't wait to get back to Venice to see to the moving-in process, since we don't own more than the few odd pieces of furniture that you've seen—six chairs and four mirrors!"[83] Soon after New Year's Day 1901 the Polignacs returned to Venice to furnish their new home and survey its restoration work. Winnaretta's first purchase for the palazzo was a pair of Giandomenico Tiepolo frescoes, *Un sacrificio pagano* and *Un trionfo romano,* dating from around 1760 and transferred to canvas.[84] Her elation at having made such an important acquisition was disrupted, however, by an unnerving discovery: the workers, digging up the pavement in the ground-level entryway, had unearthed the remains of a man's skeleton, perhaps the last vestige of a private vendetta from Venice's tempestuous and often bloody past. Henri de Régnier would later write that this macabre discovery didn't prevent this palace from being one of the most beautiful residences of Venice; "I never heard tell," he wrote, "that it was haunted by other shades than those of the great musicians of whom the mistress of the house was a fervent admirer."[85]

Winnaretta and Edmond took advantage of the unusually mild climate that winter to explore their new neighborhood, which abutted the Accademia Bridge. On some mornings they spent their time at the feast of paintings by Carpaccio and Tintoretto that were within steps of their front door in the Gallerie dell'Accademia. On other days, while Winnaretta painted, Edmond would visit the music library of San Marco, reveling in "the glorious works of Monteverdi, and of Rossi, the great Venetian."[86] In the afternoons the Polignacs would visit Santa Maria del Rosario, a short walk away from the palazzo, where Winnaretta practiced on the church's Nacchini organ.[87]

Paris society buzzed merrily with the news of the couple's new Venetian dwelling.[88] True to form, even after so many years, Robert de Montesquiou found a way to use the Polignacs' good news as a conduit for malicious gossip. Bastardizing the name of one of the palace's former owners,

Montecuccioli, he wrote, "Those awful Polignacs just bought a palace in
Venice which had belonged to the Montecucullis [*sic*]. . . . The twice-re-
peated syllable will bring happiness to the new owners, as it calls them by
their name.[89] And nobody's jealous: one for each."[90] With no lack of irony,
he appropriated a verse from Gautier's *Affinités secrètes*—formerly a code
phrase of sympathetic understanding and complicity between himself and
Edmond—and wrote in his journal, with a malicious new title, "Old Palaces, Old Salons (which should remain hidden)":

> Sur les coupoles de Venise
> Deux ramiers blancs aux pieds rosés,
> Au nid où l'amour s'éternise,
> Un soir de mai se sont posés.[91]

> [On top of Venice's domes,
> Two white wood-doves with pink feet,
> In the nest where love becomes eternal,
> Settled one night in May.]

The Polignacs returned to Paris in time to hear the first public performance of Fauré's three-movement Suite from *Pelléas et Mélisande,* dedicated to Winnaretta, played by the orchestra of the Concerts Lamoureux
on 2 February 1901. As pleased as Winnaretta was to have her name associated with this beautiful music, she was more preoccupied with her plans
to promote her husband's compositions. The first such event organized in
Edmond's honor was an "artistic feast" coinciding with his sixty-seventh
birthday. The program consisted of choral works by Handel, Fauré, Brahms,
and, of course, Edmond de Polignac. For reasons unknown, Bordes and
the Chanters de Saint-Gervais had not been hired for this occasion; a choral group called L'Euterpe, led by Duteil d'Ozanne, had been engaged instead. This caused some unpleasantness between Bordes and the Polignacs:
in the small world of Paris freelance musicians, many of whom did not
always look favorably on the success of the Schola Cantorum and its associates (including Bordes), the word quickly spread that "the Chanteurs
de Saint-Gervais were not wanted." Bordes wrote to Edmond, hastening to
assure him that "I strongly doubt this, knowing the friendship and good-
will that you have always shown us. . . . I find it despicable that [these
gentlemen] are using your name to promote their dirty work. . . . They're
gnashing their teeth because the Schola has gone from strength to strength.
I hope you won't forget about us."[92]
　　Despite the behind-the-scenes machinations, the recital apparently went
well, the Euterpe Chorus acquitting itself admirably. *Le Figaro*'s society
column gave the event its customary blanket praise.[93] For once, however, a
more insightful report of the music, as well as a less pandering assessment

of the setting and the audience, appeared in an article in *La Vie Parisienne*, describing Edmond's music at length.

> His music has a curious power to burst the walls and to create fresh air. In listening to it, one breathes this ardent and ambitious sensuality that comes, on summer nights, from a passionate will to taste all the aromas of the atmosphere. There was, among these choral works of the other night, a certain *Ave Maris Stella*. . . . It was beautiful, and it was infinitely strange. . . . [F]or a moment, [it] erased the decorations of the grand *atelier*, . . . the wall of camelias which hid the singers and . . . the audience also!
>
> . . . All around, princesses with pretty hats and distracted dukes made as much noise as a henhouse; they got up, they sat down, they clanged their spoons against their saucers, they asked about people for whom they cared nothing.[94]

In fact, this private concert was a prelude to a much grander event. For years, those of Edmond's family members and friends who appreciated and championed his music had tried to convince him to have his compositions heard outside the salon. Camille de Polignac had exhorted his brother, "Follow the advice of Rossini: always play your music in public. Fauré does it, everybody does it. Why don't you do it?"[95] But for Edmond, who had always been timid about self-promotion, the notion of having his music exposed to public scrutiny filled him with panic. Winnaretta took matters into her own hands: she convinced her husband to allow her to arrange a public all-Polignac concert, to be performed in May, at the height of the *grande saison*. To mitigate the impression of a "vanity" concert, she put the event under the aegis of a charitable institution, the Société Philanthropique, and announced it as a fundraiser.

The question was, where to give the concert? Edmond's music included organ parts, and there was no centrally located major concert hall with a grand organ. The Trocadéro was too far from central Paris, and too big. The Salle d'Harcourt had a fine organ, but had never achieved the requisite prestige in the eyes of Parisian high society: Harcourt was perceived to have overreached in building the "vanity hall" that bore his name. Winnaretta thought about the Conservatoire's concert hall: it was centrally located, with fine acoustics and a grand organ. The hall was generally not available for hire, however, by parties outside the institution; its directors would certainly reject its use for a "society concert." But Winnaretta decided that the Conservatoire's hall was exactly what was needed. She sought out the intervention of the Minister of Beaux-Arts, who was able to "borrow" the hall. Once this step was accomplished, a prestigious group of musicians were engaged as performers. Baritone Paul Daraux and soprano Jane Hatto, the Opéra's latest rising star,[96] were engaged as featured soloists; the great Camille Chevillard would conduct the Lamoureux Orchestra and the Euterpe Chorus. Winnaretta solicited every influential contact she had in the press to promote the concert, and succeeded: both *Le Figaro* and *Le Gaulois* ran front-page articles on the upcoming event. "A Good Work and A Beautiful Work," was the caption in *Le Gaulois*.[97]

The concert took place on Ascension Thursday, 16 May 1901. There was very little rehearsal time to put the long and complicated program together—the choristers had been busy with their Easter services; for the soloists and orchestra, it was the height of the concert season. Nonetheless, the event was a triumph, and the hall was packed to bursting with the luminaries of both the aristocracy and the music world. "If I wanted to enumerate all the persons of noble company who attended this charming event, I'd need as much patience as Aeschylus counting the armies of Xerxes," quipped Willy, writing under his pen-name "L'Ouvreuse."[98] The ten compositions performed represented Edmond's work in many genres, from the pastoral *Robin m'aime* for orchestra to the brilliant "Queen Claribel's Aria," from the 1867 opera *La Coupe du Roi de Thulé*; from the mournful *Lamento* based on Gautier's poem—the song that first brought Winnaretta and Edmond together—to *Pilate livre le Christ*. Edmond himself conducted two of his sacred works for a cappella chorus, *Ave Maris Stella* and *Martha et Maria*.

The laudatory reports in both the daily papers and the musical press went beyond the mere conventional polite praise. Charles Joly, the critic of *Le Figaro*, ordinarily rather severe, wrote of the variety and wealth of ideas of the diverse works, admiring, while not completely understanding, Edmond's audacious modernism.[99] Appreciative letters from friends poured in,[100] but the most discerning assessment of Edmond's compositions came from someone who had not even been at the concert. Proust, in a long affectionate letter, expressed regrets that a severe asthma attack had impeded his attendance, joking that "It's fortunate that I couldn't leave my bed. For if I had gone to the Conservatoire, my rattling and coughing would have added some sounds to your orchestration that, no doubt, would not have been to the audience's taste."[101] His disappointment at not being able to hear many of Edmond's pieces in one sitting was keen.

It's through the juxtaposition of the works of one master that, in music, as in painting or literature, I'm able to grasp his personality. As objective as the works are, and as different are their subjects, they have . . . something in common, which is the essence of genius of their author. As different as two works like *Robin m'aime* and *Ave Maria* [sic] *Stella* are from each other, they have, even so, an air of being part of a family, which is the same resemblance to the soul of the Prince de Polignac. . . .

And then, Prince, . . . what would also have given me pleasure would have been to see the homage of the public, to listen to the attentiveness of its silence, to experience myself (and not through second-hand accounts) the applause, like the pulsations of a single and admiring heart, to see your beloved silhouette, as you conducted your works with a mysterious gesture, elegant and sure of success and glory.[102]

There was even a fitting "encore" to the event: two days after the concert, the "Literary Supplement" of *Le Figaro* published Edmond's most recent composition, *La Chanson de Barberine* (poem by Alfred de Musset) on its music page.[103]

But spring was still in full bloom, and the season held other pleasures in store. Earlier that year, the Polignacs had attended a recital in Meg de Saint-Marceaux's salon, introducing a new American transplant to Paris, the dancer Isadora Duncan. This striking woman, who danced in simple tunics and bare feet, sought to create a choreography that celebrated a naturalism and freedom of movement liberated from the artifices of classical ballet. The Comtesse Greffulhe was the next hostess to engage the dancer; she invited the cream of Paris society for the occasion, touting the young dancer's "renaissance of Greek Art." Duncan had indeed been inspired by her vision of the classical Greek arts, although, as she quipped in her autobiography, it seemed to her that her hostess "was rather under the influence of the *Aphrodite* of Pierre Louÿs . . . whereas I had the expression of a Doric column and the Parthenon pediments."[104] Winnaretta may have been impressed by the performance, but Edmond de Polignac was positively dazzled: something in the dancer's simple, athletic movements resonated with his own ideas about *musique de plein air.* Edmond attended her next recital at the home of painter Madeleine Lemaire; afterwards he could talk of nothing but forming a collaboration with the dancer. He implored his wife to act as emissary. One day, Isadora Duncan was surprised to find the Princesse de Polignac at her doorstep. The dancer's first impressions of her visitor were very similar to those of Colette at the Saint-Marceaux salon: she was struck by the imposing stature and powerful personality of the woman whose "entrance seemed to be announced by one of those Wagnerian motifs, deep and strong, and bearing portents of coming events."[105]

> She had a handsome face, somewhat marred by a too heavy and protruding lower jaw and a masterful chin. It might have been the face of a Roman Emperor, except that an expression of cold aloofness protected the otherwise voluptuous promise of her eyes and features. When she spoke her voice had also a hard, metallic twang. . . . I afterwards guessed that these cold looks and the tone of her voice were really a mask to hide, in spite of her princely position, a condition of extreme and sensitive shyness.[106]

Despite the intimidating physical demeanor of her unexpected guest, as well as the reputation of unapproachability that had preceded her, Duncan found herself surprisingly at ease with the Princesse. After glancing around the small, meagerly furnished apartment, Winnaretta listened attentively to the dancer, who explained the revolutionary ideas of aesthetics that inspired her dances and fired her professional aspirations. The Princesse offered to arrange a dance recital for Duncan in the rue Cortambert *atelier*, and asked her to visit the space the next afternoon. After she had left, Duncan discovered that the patron had left an envelope containing two thousand francs on the table.[107] The next day the dancer went to rue Cortambert, where she was greeted by Edmond, his delicate, chiseled face framed by a little velvet cap. After a demonstration of her dances in the music room, Duncan explained to the frail prince her theories of the relation of movement to sounds and her hopes for tracing dance back to its roots as a sacred art. Edmond, enraptured, hailed her as "a vision and a dream for which he had long waited,"[108] and played her some of his compositions on the family harpsichord. In an effusion of mutual admiration, the two affirmed their desire to collaborate, envisioning a program in which Duncan would create "religious dances" based on Edmond's music.[109]

Although her own opinions of Duncan's art are unknown, Winnaretta did not hesitate to support her husband's newest project. A program of "Danses-Idylles" was planned for the Polignacs's *atelier* the evening of Wednesday, 22 May 1901, barely a week after the concert at the Conservatoire.[110] In an effort to maximize the potential number of patrons for Duncan, Winnaretta invited not only the Polignacs' personal friends, but members of the greater artistic community as well.[111] To Augustine Bulteau she described Duncan as "a young American that you will find full of genius, who has reconstituted some dances according to the movements of the figures on the Etruscan vases."[112] The recital proved to be a grand event. Before the dances, Edmond gave a talk on the topic of "Greek Art." Duncan danced to a harp accompaniment played by Ada Sassoli, and a Monsieur Jancey recited poems by Leconte de Lisle in between each piece.[113] The interest generated by this program allowed Isadora Duncan to arrange a series of subscription concerts in her studio. Once again, to please Edmond, Winnaretta undertook promotion of the dancer among her friends, perhaps even underwriting the costs of the performances.[114]

Winnaretta hosted one last reception on 27 May, featuring an unpublished string quartet by Camille Chevillard.[115] The gathering provided the occasion for another celebration: the release on 8 May and the subsequent spectacular critical reception of Anna de Noailles's new collection of poems, *Le Coeur innombrable*.[116] On Tuesday, 18 June, the Polignacs attended an elegant dinner given by Marcel Proust at his new apartment on rue de Courcelles, organized in honor of the success of Anna's book.[117] Following the example of the Polignac salon, Proust audaciously invited entrenched political enemies to dine at the same table, forcing Dreyfusards and anti-

Dreyfusards to mingle against their will. The anti-Semitic Léon Daudet was astonished to discover that the beautiful young woman at his side was the daughter of a well-known Jewish banker; after his initial shock, he was obliged to admit that "the vibrations of understanding and good-will that emanated from Marcel spilled forth in whirlwinds and spirals across the dining room, and the most authentic cordiality reigned for two hours. . . . I don't think anybody else in Paris could have accomplished this feat."[118]

During this peaceable period, a charitable project was launched to re-pair damaged landmarks in the Park at Versailles. The fundraising fair took place on the palace grounds; the *dames patronnesses* who planned the event, seeking to evoke the lost era of Marie-Antoinette, dressed up in the white linen dresses of their great-grandmothers. Throughout the day they recreated the "activities" of the Queen: they pretended to be milk-maids churning butter, shepherdesses who adorned their goats and sheep with lace.[119] Winnaretta had agreed to organize a concert of period music at the Maison de la Reine.[120] She included one of Edmond's works that evoked the period: a *Romance pastorale*, written in 1852, composed in the pretty, delicate style of the eighteenth-century *romances* that Edmond had heard since the earliest days of his childhood. It was given a wonderful interpretation by the Comtesse de Guerne.

The Polignacs looked forward to the summer with happy anticipation. Edmond had plans to return to Amsterdam, having been so pleased with the salutary influence of the Dutch climate.[121] He had already booked the same rooms that he had taken the previous year, because, in his eccentric manner, when he liked a hotel room, he noted the number of the room and the direction of its exposure to be sure to have the same room for a subse-quent visit.[122] The couple planned to meet in Venice, where they would enjoy a prolonged stay in their beautiful palazzo. Bulteau had whetted Edmond's appetite by promising him free access to the Palazzo Dario's music library, filled with old and unpublished sixteenth- and seventeenth-century music.[123]

All plans were put aside, however, when Edmond fell ill in mid-July.[124] It was a hot summer, but he could not stop shivering under his covers. When it became clear that he could not make the trip to Amsterdam, Winnaretta wanted to telegraph the hotel to cancel his reservations. Edmond became upset, saying, "So that's it, you want to make me look like I'm skipping out." Despite his high fever and Winnaretta's protests, he exhausted him-self writing an eight-page letter to the director of the hotel.[125] His condition worsened, and Winnaretta hired an English nurse to ensure that he would have medical care around the clock. But in his delirium, Edmond confused the white-collared Englishwoman with the unpleasant British nannies who had tended him in childhood and sent her away, saying, "I have nothing to say to the Princess of Wales at three o'clock in the morning."[126] Finally Winnaretta undertook the care of her husband herself. She stayed by his side all night long, cherishing the hours spent talking about Mark Twain until dawn.[127]

On 9 August 1901, an article by Eugène d'Harcourt, on the front page of *Le Figaro,* began with the words: "My teacher and friend the Prince Edmond de Polignac has just died."[128]

Winnaretta was alone in the deserted city of Paris at the moment of her husband's passing, although Mathieu de Noailles and Hélène and Alexandre de Caraman-Chimay rushed back the next day to be with her.[129] Anna wrote sadly to Bulteau of the death of "our poor friend . . . who, under the guise of dryness and bitterness had an abundant soul, and the most touching delicacy of heart."[130] Her sister Hélène, at Winnie's side through the first days, was distraught over the death of the strange and gentle man whom she had known since childhood. "He was always in our lives," she wrote to Bulteau, "for us it's a deep loss."[131] Edmond's funeral services, which took place in the Church of the Madeleine on 12 August, brought together a large number of family members, friends, and members of the artistic community, many of whom returned from their vacations to be in attendance. The music, performed by the Chanteurs de Saint-Gervais and accompanied on the organ by Fauré, ranged from Gregorian plainchant to Ravel's *Pavane.*[132]

It was Edmond's wish to be buried in the Singer crypt in Torquay, so that he could spend eternity next to his wife upon her decease. Winnaretta borrowed the yacht of her brother-in-law Élie Decazes, and accompanied the body to the cemetery.[133] On the tomb she had inscribed a simple epitaph: "Edmond-Melchior-Jean-Marie, Prince de Polignac, Born 1834, Died 1901, Composer of Music." In tribute to the Polignacs' mutual love of music, the epitaph bore a line from Wagner's *Parsifal,* sung in the opera by a chorus of celestial voices: "Selig in Glaube, Selig in Liebe" (Happy in faith, Happy in love). And in honor of the loving, iconoclastic, and defiant nature of Edmond's and Winnaretta's marriage, the last line of the epitaph, taken from Corinthians II, alluded to the concept of the letter of the law versus the spirit of the law: "For the letter killeth, but the spirit giveth life."

Figure 9. Prince Edmond de Polignac, ca. 1893. Collection of Prince Edmond de Polignac. Used by permission.

Figure 10. Winnaretta, Prince Edmond, and Comte Robert de Montesquiou, ca. 1893. Private collection. Used by permission.

Figure 11. Costume party at Egypt House, Cowes, Isle of Wight, 1893. Top row, left to right: Louis Lalbé, Winnaretta, Prince Edmond, Mrs. Franklin Singer, née Blanche Marcelin, Franklin Singer. Bottom row, left to right: Henriette de La Brosse, Fred Marcelin, Mrs. Fred Marcelin. Private collection. Used by permission.

Figure 12. Winnaretta and friends at the Villa Bassaraba, Amphion, summer of 1899. Top row, left to right: Prince Edmond, Mme. Anatole Bartholoni, Marcel Proust, Prince Constantin de Brancovan, Mlle. Jeanne Bartholoni, and pianist Léon Delafosse. Second row, left to right: Marquise Joséphine de Monteynard, Winnaretta, and poet Comtesse Anna de Noailles. Bottom row, left to right: Princesse Hélène de Caraman-Chimay and writer Abel Hermant. Collection of the author.

Figure 13. Portrait of Princesse Armande de Polignac (Comtesse de Chabannes-La Palice), painted by Winnaretta, ca. 1900. Collection of Comtesse Bernard de Villele. Used by permission.

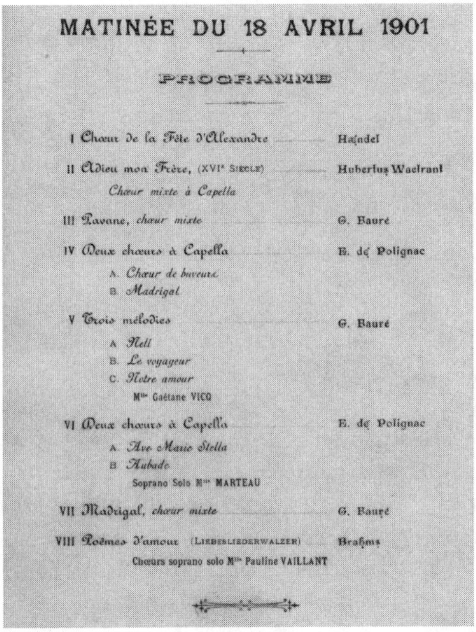

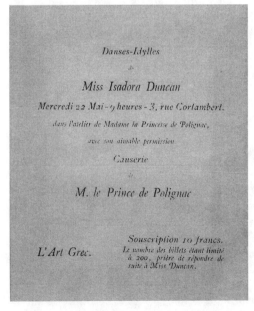

MATINÉE DU 18 AVRIL 1901

PROGRAMME

I Chœur de la Fête d'Alexandre — Hændel

II Adieu mon Frère, (XVIᵉ SIÈCLE) — Hubertus Waelrant
    Chœur mixte à Capella

III Pavane, *chœur mixte* — G. Bauré

IV Deux chœurs à Capella — E. de Polignac
    A. *Chœur de buveurs*
    B. *Madrigal*

V Trois mélodies — G. Bauré
    A. *Nell*
    B. *Le voyageur*
    C. *Notre amour*
        Mᵐᵉ Gaétane VICO

VI Deux chœurs à Capella — E. de Polignac
    A. *Ave Maria Stella*
    B. *Aubade*
        Soprano Solo Mᵐᵉ MARTEAU

VII Madrigal, *chœur mixte* — G. Bauré

VIII Poëmes d'amour (LIEBESLIEDERWALZER) — Brahms
    Chœurs soprano solo Mᵐᵉ Pauline VAILLANT

Figure 14. Music program from the Polignac salon, 18 April 1901. Collection of Prince Edmond de Polignac. Used by permission.

Danses-Idylles
de
Miss Isadora Duncan

Mercredi 22 Mai - 9 heures - 3, rue Cortambert.
dans l'atelier de Madame la Princesse de Polignac,
avec son aimable permission.

Causerie
de
M. le Prince de Polignac

L'Art Grec.

Souscription 10 francs.
Le nombre des billets étant limité
à 200, prière de répondre de
suite à Miss Duncan.

Figure 15. Invitation card to a program of "Danses-Idylles" by Isadora Duncan, performed in the Polignac salon, 22 May 1901. Isadora Duncan Collection, Robbins Dance Division, The New York Public Library for the Performing Arts. Used by permission.

Renovations

After Edmond's interment in the Singer crypt in Torquay, Winnaretta returned to Paris. On 31 August, she invited the most gifted of memory-
collectors, Marcel Proust, to come see her in the evening. Winnaretta reminisced at length, recalling her first meeting with Edmond's family members, whom he had nicknamed "the Big Reds" (*les gros rouges*).[1] They had
never understood him, and had told her that she was marrying an unbearable maniac. But to the contrary, she mused, she had never known someone so easy to live with, so fearful was he of being a bother to anyone.[2]
Proust was moved by the unusual emotional outpouring of this woman
who had always hidden herself so carefully behind a wall of unapproachable reserve.[3]

Just at that time a newly published novel sought to unmask the private
life that Winnaretta was purported to lead behind the circumspect public
image. Jean Lorrain's *Monsieur de Phocas* was a sensationalist tale of a
young man fascinated by and attracted to the world of Parisian sexual
subcultures. The open disgust with which the author treated his homosexual characters was, in fact, a veil for his own closeted homosexuality.[4]
Montesquiou, for example, becomes the perfumed Comte de Muzarett,
"the Narcissus of the inkpot," who has just completed a new book, entitled *Winged Rats*.[5] But Lorrain saves his particular venom for the character of the Princesse de Seiryman-Frileuse, a thinly disguised satirical portrait of Winnaretta de Polignac. The "ogress," as depicted by Lorrain, is
"interesting" and "very daring," having contracted an honorary marriage
with an elderly prince from an old and distinguished noble family.

> She has presented him with eighty thousand francs so that she should
> carry his name while parading before the world her depravity and her
> independence. Princess Seiryman is beautiful in her perverse fashion—
> look at the bitter willfulness of her hard profile, and look how those
> hard and mournful grey eyes, the color of melting ice, shelter the energy
> of thought and obstinacy.[6]

Whether or not she actually read it, Winnaretta surely knew about this
lurid new book. Its release so close to Edmond's death must have sharpened the sting of the portrait.

What was she going to do now? The thought of staying alone in the empty house was unbearable. She wrote to Madame Bulteau: "I know that you understood my pain. You know all that I lost. . . . You surely understood his unique nature, his piety and his enthusiasm for all that was beautiful and lasting, his astonishing vitality of mind. Having heard 'Martha et Marie' and 'Ave Maris Stella' you could intuit *all* the piety, the grandeur, the tender and deep beauty contained in his heart."[7] Winnaretta sought comfort in Switzerland with her sister's widower, Élie Decazes, and his three children, Louis, Daisy, and Jacques. The dependence of her nephews and niece on their Tante Winnie made her feel needed and gave her the illusion of being strong.[8] The October death of one of Winnaretta's favorite nephews, Marquis Guy de Polignac, necessitated a brief return to Paris for the funeral. "Paris is ugly, noisy, completely useless," she wrote to Bulteau. "I'm not doing well here."[9]

The joyful bustle of the Christmas season only served to aggravate Winnaretta's depression. She adopted a defensive mode of living, one that would become more pronounced in future years: she would spend days alone in her big house, the lights low, the heat off, eating little, consoling herself by sitting at the organ, playing Bach. A long-standing family rift added to her misery: for two years she had been estranged from her mother over a misunderstanding whose cause was long forgotten. Winnaretta longed for reconciliation, but Isabella did not extend herself to her daughter.[10] Others reached out: all four Singer brothers were in Paris to support their grieving sister. Friends offered their warmth as well, but the gaiety of the holiday season seemed almost an affront. An invitation to a Christmas Eve *réveillon* with Anna and Mathieu de Noailles and her friends Léon and Lucien Daudet was declined at the last minute. Exhausted, Winnaretta could not bear to leave her house, but proposed that her friends come over to listen to the organ's "mystical pleasures."[11]

February 1902 found Winnaretta once again in Venice. She spent the afternoon hours sitting on her balcony, painting the Church of the Santa Maria della Salute, whose dome took on the colors of the twilight. She sought a musical venue through which to honor Edmond; eventually, she asked the Duca della Grazia, the owner of the Palazzo Vendramin, Richard Wagner's former residence, if she could use his palace for a memorial concert. The Duke consented, and Winnaretta arranged to have the Venetian Municipal Band play *Siegfried's Funeral March* from Wagner's *Götterdämmerung,* in the courtyard underneath the windows of the room where the composer had died. Mathieu de Noailles came from Paris to lend his support. Winnaretta recalled the day in her memoirs:

It was a bright sunny day . . . and the Grand Canal looked its best; all the neighbouring houses had decked their balconies and windows with the brilliant hangings which were usually brought out on great occasions, and many of the best-turned-out gondolas in Venice (belonging to the great patrician families of Venice)—at least a hundred—guided beautiful ladies to the steps of the Vendramin Palace. The Banda Municipale played the Funeral March very creditably, the guests crowding round the windows that looked on to the Cortile, and after the concert there was a buffet in the big central room or sala.

I thanked the Duke profusely for all the trouble he had taken to have my wish carried out, and asked him how many years Liszt and Wagner had been his tenants. He replied: "Oh, quite a long time—for seven years, at least, off and on; they spent many months here." "And did you often see them?" I asked. "Oh, yes, they frequently came up to have coffee with us after dinner." I was much impressed, and added: "And what did they do, and what did they say?" "They sometimes talked about music, or played the piano." "Oh, how marvellous to have known these great men. What a wonderful experience!" The Duke replied, casually, "Oh yes, they were two characters."[12]

When Winnaretta returned to Paris in April, the musical world was buzzing with news about the approaching premiere of Claude Debussy's opera *Pelléas et Mélisande,* with a text by Maurice Maeterlinck. Even before the first performance, Debussy's work had already become the subject of virulent attacks in advance publicity from the conservative public and press, who ridiculed the composer's modernist musical ideas and Maeterlinck's symbolist text.[13] After *Pelleas et Mélisande* opened at the Opéra-Comique on 30 April 1902, public reaction was divided. Paris was still at the height of its Wagner idolatry, and Debussy's pointedly un-Wagnerian opera, with its fluid melodic lines, and its subtle, unpredictable harmonic progressions, was incomprehensible to all but the most sophisticated and forward-thinking of listeners.[14] Winnaretta loved the work: "Its passionate sincerity, undeniable beauty and dignity made it invulnerable, and . . . time has since made this opera seem even more wonderful, more human and more poetic."[15] The composers and professional musicians in the audience split into two diametrically opposed camps. Eugène d'Harcourt, now music critic for *Le Figaro,* wrote, "From the first day, I have deplored the esthetic of M. Debussy. . . . [H]is orchestration has a shimmering color, and all his works possess a poetry that captivates attention, but his music seems to me above all, if I may dare to express myself thus, antihygenic."[16] Winnaretta might have expected this reaction from the conservative Harcourt, but she was vastly more troubled to know that even Fauré found the work incomprehensible, declaring after the first performance, "If that is music, then I don't know what music is."[17]

The French customarily observe an *an de veuvage,* a "year of widowhood," during which the mourning process continues, and the social life of the mourner is curtailed. Even in her grief, Winnaretta felt the privation of that year, especially after attending the *Pelléas* performances: she missed being in the world, being with people, going to concerts and the opera. She missed the musical gatherings in her salon. She began to make plans for the future: she wanted to organize a concert of Edmond's works; she thought about reconstructing her home.[18]

The first of these endeavors was accomplished with the help of Élisabeth Greffulhe. In October 1902, the habitually aloof countess sent an unusually personal letter, evoking Edmond's "unique soul." Greffulhe offered her advice about programming his works in a public venue. "I am convinced," she wrote, "that with a judicious choice one could put together a very interesting program, perhaps in a church rather than in a concert hall. I find that there is in all his works a very deep *religious* and *sad* feeling."[19] The letter concluded, "I like you very much and feel for you a great affinity"; instead of the usual "Caraman-Chimay-Greffulhe" it was signed "Élisabeth."[20] The venue chosen for the concert was the Salle Humbert-des-Romans, a private thousand-seat concert hall in the 16th *arrondissement*.[21] On 13 May 1903 Winnaretta listened proudly to an afternoon concert of "modern music" by Vincent d'Indy, Eugène d'Harcourt, and Edmond de Polignac. Although Winnaretta's friends praised Edmond's compositions as being "the fruits of a powerful imagination,"[22] the papers barely mentioned the concert, paying more attention to the *mondain* aspects of the event and devoting the better part of the articles to the names and the elegant attires of the ladies in attendance. Winnaretta, who wore "a gown of black taffeta with a white lace collar, a black taffeta jacket, and a large hat in black crinolin and feathers," received more press attention for her apparent success in bringing a sense of fashion to the obligatory mourning attire than did her husband's music.[23]

Time would prove that, in addition to music-making, home renovation was one of Winnaretta's favorite antidotes to personal vicissitudes. She had built her *atelier* at the time of her divorce from Scey-Montbéliard. Reconstruction of her Venetian palazzo had begun before Edmond's death and had continued through her mourning period.[24] Now she began to think about completely remaking the *hôtel particulier* on avenue Henri-Martin. Her plans for musical activity required a venue larger and grander than the *atelier* could provide. She had recently seen the newly built home of Jean-Louis Forain and his wife on rue Spontini, near the Bois de Boulogne. Impressed by the beauty of the house's design, she engaged its architect, the young but already renowned Henri Grand'pierre, to do the renovation on her own home.[25] Her idea was to create a residence that would rival her father's Wigwam in opulence and modernity, but surpass it in taste and refinement. On 31 July 1903, the work permits were filed with the Prefecture of the Seine that would allow complete renovation of the old house to begin.

Winnaretta had succeeded in creating a multitude of projects to keep herself busy, but she had still not found the level of spiritual and emotional peace that would allow her to begin a new life without Edmond. She began to reread a book she had been introduced to as a young woman, Henry David Thoreau's *Walden, or Life in the Woods.* The American philosopher's plain, deep language consoled and inspired her; she took special comfort in Thoreau's words on solitude: "I experienced sometimes that the most sweet and tender, the most innocent and encouraging society may be found in any natural object, even for the poor misanthrope and most melancholy man. There can be no very black melancholy to him who lives in the midst of nature and has his senses still. There was never yet such a storm but it was Aeolian music to a healthy and innocent ear."[26]

Winnaretta decided to translate *Walden* into French. After ascertaining that no such translation had already been made, she began the project in Venice during the summer of 1902, and continued her work through early 1903, while staying with Ludovic de Polignac on his estate, the Bordj Polignac at Bouzareah, Algeria. There, perched on a mountaintop twelve hundred feet above Algiers, she shared her brother-in-law's odd and solitary lifestyle. Ludovic, nicknamed by Edmond "the dromedary of the Sahara,"[27] proved to be an ideal companion for his bereaved sister-in-law. Both of them were essentially introverted, and each seemed to understand instinctively the other's need for solitude. Winnaretta found Edmond's brother "good and thoughtful. . . . [He] did much to help me in days hard to live through."[28] It was fortunate that she felt that way, for their shared dwelling did not have much to offer. When Winnaretta arrived, Ludovic asked if there were anything lacking in the house that might make her stay more comfortable. Winnaretta was hard-pressed to give a tactful answer: not only was the house practically devoid of furniture, it also lacked even the most basic amenities for cooking. The old bachelor had taken to heating his food on a lamp heated with alcoholic spirits. Diplomatically, Winnaretta suggested that a rudimentary oil-heated cooking stove might be useful. "How practical! You Americans are astonishing," exclaimed Ludovic, "That's something I would have never thought of!"[29] At night Winnaretta retired to a hard bed in an otherwise empty room, where a family of cats had left numerous souvenirs. But the room had a terrace, which provided an incomparable view of both the sea and the distant snow-capped mountains of Kabylia.[30] And the living room was equipped with a piano and an organ. Winnaretta felt that she was actually living the kind of calm, self-sufficient life described by Thoreau. "There are neither neighbors nor visitors here, and we have been all by ourselves for two weeks," she wrote to Bulteau. "I am delighted by this solitude."[31] She immersed herself in her work, searching for French equivalents for the tranquil beauty of Thoreau's writing. At night she studied the scores of Beethoven's late string quartets, whose depth had never seemed to her so "gigantic and sublime—what a beautiful testament to sadness!"[32]

Winnaretta finished the translation in late April, and sent the manuscript to Bulteau for her professional blessing.[33] News of Winnaretta's latest project spread quickly among the serious readers of her social circle. Prince Constantin de Brancovan, Anna and Hélène's brother, who had recently assumed the editorship of the literary magazine *La Renaissance latine*, offered to publish excerpts of her work in two installments. The *Walden* translations appeared in December 1903 and January 1904. Their publication allowed the non-Anglophone literary public to enjoy for the first time the American philosopher's masterpiece, the elegant plainness of Thoreau's style successfully captured by Winnaretta in the French language.

Proud of her accomplishment and the approbation that it received, Winnaretta finally permitted herself to return to her life of friendships and social activity beyond the small circle of her intimate friends. For the first time since Edmond's death, she hosted several dinner parties followed by musical performances in the *atelier*. On 11 May 1903 the great Hungarian violinist-composer Georges Enesco performed the Fauré Violin Sonata with Fauré at the piano, and on 25 May the equally brilliant Belgian violinist-composer Eugène Ysaÿe, partnered by Paris piano virtuoso Raoul Pugno, performed works by J. S. Bach, Don Roffredo Caetani (a young Italian protégé of the Comtesse Greffulhe), and a transcription of Wagner's *Siegfried Idyll*.[34] In early June Winnaretta hosted a charity event combining dramatic readings by members of the Comédie Française and musical performances, during which composer Jules Massenet accompanied arias from his operas on the piano.[35]

Among the audience members at these events was Marcel Proust, in the company of composer Reynaldo Hahn. Proust had lost contact with his hostess for over a year after her unexpected epiphany following Edmond's death. When he encountered her at a dinner at Hélène and Alexandre de Caraman-Chimay's house in January 1903, he was delighted. His delight turned to dismay, however, when he heard about Winnaretta's nearly completed translation of *Walden*, for, as it happened, Proust had been planning to execute exactly the same project with Hélène's cousin, Prince Antoine Bibesco.[36]

In February 1903, Proust was engaged by *Le Figaro* to write a series of society pieces for the paper about the Paris salons. Over the next two years a half-dozen of his articles appeared, written under various pseudonyms, paying hommage to various hostesses, including Princesse Mathilde, Madeleine Lemaire, and the Comtesses Greffulhe, d'Haussonville, and Potocka. On 6 September 1903, the newspaper carried a piece, written under Proust's latest pen name, Horatio (taken from Shakespeare), entitled "The Salon of the Princesse Edmond de Polignac: Music of Today, Echoes of Yesteryear." Nominally, the article was an encomium to Winnaretta's musical activities. Proust praised the "supreme elegance" of the *atelier* as the sunlight filtered through the windowpanes, the "perfect performances of early music . . . the original and fervent interpretations of all the latest songs of Fauré, the dances of Brahms." [37]

However, much of the article was a source of profound embarrassment for Winnaretta. Edmond was the focus of a good portion of it. While Proust praised the Prince as "a great mind and a powerful musician," noting his progressive compositional tendencies and the innovative sound-and-light shows that accompanied the performances of his music, these laudable traits were deemed "miraculous," given the political transgressions of the father and the ignoble prison conception of the son. In the end, claimed the author, Edmond's individuality was a form of atavism, ultimately subsumed by the traits of his lineage. More troubling, Proust made subtle allusions to the Polignac couple's double life: the marriage of Edmond and Winnaretta had been a happy one, save one shortcoming: "she was always too hot, and he was extremely sensitive to the cold,"[38] which could easily be interpreted as a veiled reference to their sexual predilections. Proust's references to Winnaretta herself were ambivalent at best. Little was said about her own progressive tendencies in the programming of her musical gatherings. Instead, the writer spilled much ink on the familial connections among members of high society that the Princesse de Polignac had acquired through her marriage. Was she not the sister-in-law, the cousin, the aunt, of the La Rochefoucaulds, the Croÿs, the Lignes, the Gontaut-Birons, the Luynes, the Noailles . . . ?[39] This kind of name-dropping and social one-upmanship was thoroughly repugnant to Winnaretta. Her relations with Proust were to remain cool for a very long time after the release of the article. The chill had already set in when Winnaretta's translation of Thoreau appeared in *La Renaissance latine* in December: Proust wrote to Anna de Noailles of the "admirable pages of *Walden*"—but neglected to mention the translator.[40]

Winnaretta was far from Paris when the two installments were released. Her brother Paris, suffering from depression and insomnia, had received no relief from the doctors he consulted in England and France.[41] Despairing of finding a medical solution, he sought only a quiet refuge and asked Winnaretta to join him.[42] Having one year earlier healed her own spiritual malaise in the tranquil solitude of the Bordj Polignac, Winnaretta proposed to her brother that they stay in Kabylia, Algeria, not far from Ludovic's mountain retreat. Paris Singer felt the salutary effects of the warm, bright climate immediately, but Winnaretta was confronted with another crisis shortly after their arrival. Ludovic de Polignac, still living in isolation in his mountain aerie, was gravely ill; his sister-in-law found him frail and barely lucid. She was able to convince him to seek care at a military hospital in Algiers, but his tenuous state made her feel terribly abandoned. She opened her heart to Augustine Bulteau.

I have always needed the love of old people and some have loved me so much. But they are nearly all dead now and it gives me such a feeling of loneliness. Ludovic is the last who can give me that particular sort of affection I have always treasured so much—the tender, patient, unchanging, unselfish love the old alone can give. . . . When he leaves me he will take a great piece of my life. I shall have no home *"moralement."*[43] The hearts of those I speak of were really "homes" to me.[44]

Ludovic de Polignac died on 13 January 1904 with his sister-in-law at his side. In the midst of her grief, Winnaretta was still able to summon up a healthy appreciation of the absurd: with delight she took note of a sign written in English that she saw outside a café in Algiers—"Arabian coffee; dances by *unrestrained* ladies."[45]

Then, on 12 May, Winnaretta's mother passed away. In her last years Isabella had spent a good deal of her time at the casino at Le Touquet, where she would sit at the gaming tables wearing a green eye-shade, like the croupiers, gambling away what was left of her fortune.[46] She died in her opulent private apartment in the Decazes *hôtel* on the avenue du Bois de Boulogne. Although the papers wryly noted that she had been "one of the most most visible women of the American colony in Paris,"[47] the funeral was a quiet family affair. Mother and daughter had never reconciled, and whatever sorrow Winnaretta experienced at her passing was surely mixed with bitterness. In turn, Isabella's spitefulness towards her wayward child extended past the grave. In 1902 she had written a will leaving her estate, or what was left of it after her profligate life, to her third husband, Paul Sohège. The children were all bequeathed a small memento or a piece of jewelry, but Winnaretta was pointedly left out of the will.[48] The will further instructed that Isabella be buried in the Passy Cemetery, only steps from Winnaretta's house. She had purchased a sepulcher, and commissioned a bust of her image to be housed therein. Forever afterwards, when Winnaretta would walk from her home down avenue Henri-Martin towards the Trocadéro, she was obliged to pass directly beneath her mother's eternally youthful image.

But Winnaretta had had enough of mourning. On 16 July 1904, she attended the marriage of two Polignac cousins, Edmond's great-nephew Prince Henri, son of the Duc and Duchesse de Polignac, and Comtesse Diane, daughter of the late Marquis Guy de Polignac (the nephew who had rescued Edmond from indigence many years earlier) and his wife, née Louise Pommery, the bourgeois heiress of the Pommery champagne fortune. Winnaretta had a particular affection for Henri and Diane, both earthy, unpretentious young people, and she rejoiced in their union.

She rejoiced as well when, during the same period, Grand'pierre completed the exterior renovation of the avenue Henri-Martin *hôtel*. As the interior redecoration began, Winnaretta left for an extended stay at the Wigwam with her brother Paris, his family, and other Singer relatives gathered together from every corner of the globe. Her brother had just begun to rebuild the capacious if quirky mansion built by their father. More than any of the six children born to Isaac and Isabella, Paris Singer had inherited his father's manner of enthusiastic self-promotion. While the older Singer brothers, Mortimer and Washington, had settled into comfortable lives as English country gentlemen, tending their estates and breeding racehorses, Paris studied architecture in his early twenties at the École de Beaux-Arts in the city for which he was named. Back in England he put his skills to work on his own dwellings, as the sign "P. E. Singer, Architect" on the back door of his home at No. 3 Cadogan Gate attests.[49] In 1893 he bought out his siblings' interests in the family estate in Devonshire in order to take full control of its development; in 1904 he decided to put his architectural "training" to good use: Paris decided that nothing short of refashioning the family estate in the style of Versailles would do.

And in fact, when the renovation of the Wigwam was completed in 1907, the estate did in fact become known as "The Little Versailles."[50] The overhaul included the installation of a marble Grand Staircase in the style of Versailles's *Escalier des Ambassadeurs,* a raised terrace with Ionic colonnades, a gallery whose design was based on the famed *Galerie des glaces,* and formal gardens designed by French landscape architect Achille Duchesne.[51] The most visually arresting aspect of the interior of the house was the famous Jacques-Louis David painting, *The Crowning of Josephine* (1822), which hung over the landing of the Grand Staircase. The enormous canvas, measuring twenty-five by fifteen feet, had been purchased at auction in 1898 by Paris, who, at a time when the renovation of his dream home was still but an idea, nonetheless envisioned for its entrance hall no less a painting than one depicting the coronation of the wife of Napoleon. The one-hundred-room mansion, as much of an emblem of French pastiche as of the opulence of Edwardian England, certainly stands as a testament to the self-aggrandizing flamboyance of its designer. Winnaretta, whose tastes were more sober, makes no mention of this transformation of her childhood home in her memoirs.

In September 1904, Hélène de Caraman-Chimay and her mother, the Princesse de Brancovan, joined Winnaretta in Paignton. Hélène found the Singer family to be charming, but was unaccustomed to the casualness of English country life. She was especially astonished to discover a completely new side of Winnaretta, who, in the bosom of the boisterious Singer clan, was quick to shed her customary Gallic reserve, and to indulge in the distinctly un-aristocratic pleasures of her childhood, when, surrounded by brothers, she played freely in the countryside.

Every night at ten o'clock, every day regularly: a reunion . . . a family party in a swimming pool. The guests come too. Winnaretta swims— and all around her, splashing her, falling from the roof, launched by strange instruments, emerging from God knows where: nephews, brothers, young boys, men come in, leave, dive in feet first, dive in headfirst, huff, puff, shake off the water—to appear then quite correctly dressed in formal evening attire [*les smokings*] with a little air of sweet triumph on their faces. After dinner, there are other "games." Yesterday . . . we all ran after some potatoes, lined up on the carpet, and we had to gather them with a spoon. Mama was beaten black and blue by some robust young fellows, armed with utensils, who ran around the room blindfolded. We went to bed completely exhausted.[52]

After spending a few more days in the manic Singer household, where "I listen to music a lot, I go out a lot, I do everything a lot," Hélène and her mother left for Northern England, presumably to rest from their "vacation."

The Princesse de Caraman-Chimay was a sweet, quiet woman. As fond as she was of Winnaretta, it surely must have been taxing at times to be her friend. For Winnaretta, who undoubtedly found amusement in shocking the easily shockable Hélène, could not go long without subjecting her gentle companion to some new display of iconoclastic behavior. Hélène related one such incident to Bulteau.

Winnie came to see me. We were talking about the era of Pascal, about priests and pious people, when she revealed to me, audaciously, how much she had gained by going to confide some of her faults to an abbé, Abbé *What's-His-Name*, who, she said, had heatedly refused to give her a second appointment. I was scandalized: "What, Winn, *you* make confession?" To which she replied in a calm voice, "Why, yes, I rather like to have the opinion of someone who doesn't give a damn" [*Mais oui—j'aime assez avoir l'opinion de quelqu'un qui s'en fout*].[53]

It was her unique combination of intelligence, audaciousness, and dry Anglo-Saxon humor that endeared Winnaretta to her friends and shocked her detractors. But during this period the Princesse de Polignac met her match. Ethel Smyth was British, a composer, and a lesbian. Born in 1858, she rose to prominence with a Mass in D, performed in the Albert Hall in 1893. During the 1902–1903 season her opera *Der Wald* was presented by the Dresden, Covent Garden, and Metropolitan Opera companies. Winnaretta met Ethel in England in the first months of 1903, just before the composer's embarkation for New York and the American premiere of the opera. She may have attended a performance of *Der Wald* in London; if not, she had surely been aware of the work's success at Covent Garden.

From the moment of their introduction Ethel felt an immediate attraction to the Princesse: "As soon as she laid her hands on the piano, a friend, a friend!" wrote the composer in a letter to an unnamed correspondent. "Grave, natural, don't-care-ish, the soul of independence—in short all the things I like."[54] She was charmed by the Princesse's way of muttering terse statements through her teeth.[55] She sang Winnaretta's praises to all her friends, claiming she was "the most adorable human being in the world."[56] For her part, Winnaretta enjoyed the composer's talent as well as her insouciant frankness. No doubt she asked for a copy of *Der Wald* to add to her music library, for when Ethel came to Paris in the spring of 1903, she brought with her a copy of the opera score, bearing the inscription "to the patient Princess Polignac."[57] During this trip Ethel struck up friendships with Winnaretta's closest circle of women friends—Anna, Hélène, and Toche Bulteau. At first the Frenchwomen found Ethel overwhelming—"she burns up the air," observed Anna[58]—but soon came to appreciate the fiery musician's affection and devotion.[59] The women became a "fivesome," sharing a love of literature, music, and lively conversation, crossing the Continent and the Channel to visit one another's city and country homes. Winnaretta, Ethel, and Hélène were together at the Wigwam in September and at the Chimay estate in Belgium in October; Ethel was invited to stay at the Palazzo Polignac later in the month.

While at the Wigwam, Ethel, who had an impressively sonorous voice and loved to use it, sang and played excerpts from her new opera, *The Wreckers,* for Winnaretta's family and visiting friends. Hélène found Smyth's new composition to be "a very powerful thing, very poignant, quite magnificent."[60] She had no idea that it was in fact Winnaretta who had inspired much of the passion of the music. For Smyth had decided that Winnaretta was the woman of her dreams. The two women undoubtedly became lovers during their frequent sojourns together that year, but ultimately Winnaretta decided that she had no interest in anything other than friendship with the composer. They were too much alike—willful, indefatigable, and controlling—to sustain a romantic relationship. By contrast, Smyth was completely smitten. The object of her affection was shocked to receive an ardent declaration of love after the composer's return to England.

> It is difficult to stand up against my feeling for you. . . . It is because your personality has the inevitableness, the rare finality of nature itself. . . . There is one thing about you for instance, what I call your *pace,* unlike anyone else I ever saw. I think of a planet moving through space when I feel you moving along the road of your own life. . . . Other people seem to me so fussy, so personal, so conscious—or if they are on the calm lines, so dead—so bereft of possibilities. You are the only human being I ever saw who combines limitless serenity and limitless passion—and in all other things a quality & its opposite—comedy and tragedy—an instinct of balance and an instinct of excess—Bach & Fauré. . . . And so thro' everything—outside inexpansiveness & tendency to silence, within [lies] the stuff of which tempests are brewed. I am certain of one thing as death—I love you more in five minutes than anyone else ever did in five years.[61]

Winnaretta tried to extricate herself from this surfeit of unsolicited passion by asking Smyth to put off her visit to the Palazzo, but the composer was undaunted: she came to Venice anyway, and stayed with Augustine Bulteau, just in order to be in the same city as her beloved. Thus began a turbulent love-hate relationship that would last for the next forty years.

Meanwhile, Winnaretta had developed other romantic interests in England, women who traveled in a loftier social stratum than the composer. During her *an de veuvage,* the heretofore austere London court had become the height of fashion. This new trend was set by the ascent to the throne of Edward VII in 1901; with his tastes for luxury, gluttony, and mistresses, the new king turned Buckingham Palace into a new gathering-place for the European smart set. Among the frequent visitors was Paris Singer, who introduced his sister into court society.

There Winnaretta met the Baron and Baroness de Meyer.[62] Adolph de Meyer-Watson was born in 1868 into a family that supplied him with a title and a fortune large enough to enable him to pursue his avocation, photography, with passion and skill; his works still survive today as prototypes of great fashion photography.[63] Despite his Jewish heritage, his artistry and social grace enabled him to break into the most elegant London circles. His future wife was no less fascinating. Born Olga Alberta Caracciolo, she was reputed to be the illegitimate daughter of Edward VII, a rumor that neither of the parties in question made any effort to correct. Just before his ascent to the throne, the king helped engineer the marriage between Olga and the Baron de Meyer. Their union, apparently a happy one, lasted for more than thirty years, perhaps due to the fact that both partners preferred other partners of the same sex. In the pre-World War I years they held a preeminent place in British society, and turned their London salon into a lively gathering-place for their aristocratic and artistic and literary friends. At the Meyers, nobles such as Lord Alfred Douglas and Lady de Grey could rub elbows with the likes of Henry James, Percy Grainger, Auguste Rodin, John Singer Sargent, and Jacques-Émile Blanche.[64]

Winnaretta felt right at home in such an atmosphere. By the time she reached her fortieth birthday, in January 1905, she was ready to resume her social and amorous life. And it was with the salon's hostess, Olga de Meyer, that she began her first long-term affair since the death of Edmond. This pairing seemed altogether reasonable: the two women inhabited the same social milieu, and over the years they had frequented each other's homes in London and Venice. Winnaretta's taciturn demeanor, coupled with her intelligence and dry wit, proved a good balance to Olga's more passionate Italianate nature. Although the affair was discreetly carried out, it was Winnaretta's most public liaison to date, and the inevitable consequence was a good deal of gossip on both sides of the Channel.[65] Ethel Smyth was the source of much of the most virulent tattling, claiming that she was trying to rescue Winnaretta from the clutches of an unscrupulous couple. "By nature I detested and distrusted the M's," the composer wrote to Bulteau. "[T]hese people lie [about] all things, this I quite believe."[66] Nonetheless, the relationship lasted for almost a decade, thanks to the Baron's tacit approval and the willingness of the two lovers to undertake a good deal of international travel.

While she she was still involved with Olga, Winnaretta also began an affair in 1905 with another woman that she met in the de Meyer's salon, a young painter named Romaine Brooks. Born Beatrice Romaine Goddard,[67] she was tall, slim, with dark hair and a brooding sort of beauty. Romaine had lived a childhood of emotional upheaval with her powerful, aloof American mother, who lavished most of her attention on Romaine's mentally ill brother. When Mrs. Goddard took an extended trip to Europe to find a cure for her son, the young girl was left to live with a servant in New York. It was during this period that she began to draw. After her mother's death, Romaine inherited an immense fortune. Although independently wealthy, she was emotionally scarred by her abandonment in childhood. While living in an artists' colony on the isle of Capri, she met and married John Ellington Brooks, a pianist who had been a lover of W. Somerset Maugham. Although she hoped that marriage would provide her with a facade of propriety while she pursued an independent life, the alliance proved disastrous. Divorced in 1904, Romaine moved to London, where she was drawn into the de Meyer's social circle. She had brief love affairs with men such as Lord Alfred Douglas and poet Gabriele d'Annunzio, but, according to Brooks's biographer Meryle Secrest, her introduction to the Princesse de Polignac resulted in an attack of love at first sight—the proverbial *coup de foudre*.[68] Secrest posits the idea that Romaine was attracted to Winnaretta not only because she was intelligent and artistically sophisticated, but also she embodied the chilly demeanor and controlling sense of power of Romaine's mother.[69] In short order, Romaine relocated to Paris, moving into an apartment on avenue Henri-Martin just down the street from the Polignac *hôtel*.

It is not clear who initiated the idea of Romaine's painting Winnaretta's portrait, but the Princesse began to pose for the work shortly after their meeting. Brooks's style was attractive because it was so nonconformist. She eschewed the multiplicity of patterns so prevalent in the Victorian era aesthetic, preferring to flatten out her figures against a subdued light and an abstracted background, using the color gray as an artistic signature. Moreover, she defied the conventional wisdom of painting her subjects in a flattering way. Ignoring the tradition of placing them in the foreground, well-dressed, posed in an assured manner, Brooks willfully brought out their most inelegant features, enabling her to reveal, rather disconcertingly, the deeper aspects of their personalities.[70] Robert de Montesquiou, who was her ardent champion, called her the "thief of souls."[71] But the artist found Winnaretta singularly inscrutable, and painting her portrait presented her with a unique set of challenges. She noted her subject's features in her journal: "The head is bent forward with profile emerging from out of a profusion of dark hair. The lowered eye escapes detection. The nose is arched and noble, but the mouth with its protruding lower lip shows strong atavistic ruthlessness ever active in self-defence."[72]

Romaine was no fool, however. She was trying to build a career as a portraitist, and was aware of Winnaretta's position as the doyenne of new artistic trends in society: the Princesse de Polignac's approbation could mean many new commissions for portraits, while her displeasure could result in woefully opposite results. With these consequences in mind, Brooks broke with habit and altered her signature style. In this portrait, Winnaretta is posed in conventional profile; she is wearing a simple white flowing dress, one strap pulled off the shoulder, the other crossing her body—surely an evocation of the chiton of ancient Greek warrior women. The power of the Amazonian image is undermined, however, by the rendering of Winnaretta's face: the hooked nose and grim mouth have been softened, the angularity of the facial lines toned down; in short, the very features that manifest Winnaretta's complicated allure and steely strength have been all but eradicated.[73] While the completed portrait was not representative of the painter's best work, the calculated aesthetic strategy was entirely successful as far as the consequences for Romaine Brooks's career were concerned. Winnaretta, apparently pleased with the portrait, introduced her young protégée into her elegant social circle; suddenly Romaine became the darling of a coterie of titled and monied women, many of whom clamored to have their portraits painted by her. *Le Figaro* chronicled the unveilings of these new canvasses, as well as the numerous dinners, tea parties, and musical gatherings held at the artist's house.[74]

As for the love affair between Winnaretta and Romaine, documentation does not appear to exist that sheds light on their relationship. Throughout her career as a patron Winnaretta would exhibit a tendency to turn both friends and lovers into her "projects" whom she would "launch" in high society; there is no reason to think that she acted any differently with Romaine. But as willing as she may have been to serve as the younger woman's patron, she was not keen on becoming a mother figure to a chronically melancholy artist, even to one as beautiful, rich, and celebrated as Miss Brooks. As for Romaine, the inveterate nonconformist couldn't understand why a strong and intelligent woman such as Winnaretta was so attached to the narrow constraints and social *snobisme* of the French aristocracy, why she "valued this borrowed remnant of other days above all else . . . and willingly cramped herself to fit its form."[75] Romaine failed to realize that it was exactly through the agency of these time-honored forms that Winnaretta was able to negotiate the intricacies of Paris society, while maintaining her personal freedom. Even as a young woman, she had fully assimilated *the* crucial lesson during her formative years in Paris: pay attention to manners and to form, and then you can do anything. In adulthood, the forms were the smokescreens behind which all was possible, including her own particular brand of non-conformism and her lesbianism. Despite the frictions between the two women, Winnaretta continued to champion Romaine as an artist, attending her exhibitions and salon gatherings.[76]

During the period of the renovations on her house, Winnaretta moved into the home of her niece, Duchesse Yolande de Luynes on rue de Varennes, in the 7th *arrondissement*. There, Winnaretta maintained a "salon-in-exile" in the elegant Luynes reception rooms. Her programs featured repertoire ranging from the *Madrigal* and *Pavane* of Fauré to the *Liebeslieder Waltzes* of Brahms;[77] from French folksong arrangements[78] to arias from *Pagliacci,* sung by the tenor Rousselière.[79] On 15 February, the program featured the latest piano compositions of Debussy, played by the composer's renowned exponent, Spanish pianist Ricardo Viñes.[80] It was thus that a small group of ambassadors and aristocrats had the pleasure of hearing the *avant-première* of what would become one of Debussy's most beloved keyboard works, *L'Ile joyeuse.*[81]

Winnaretta continued to promote the works of her late husband, presenting his works at many of her musical gatherings, and prevailing upon her friends to have Edmond's compositions performed in their salons as well.[82] She arranged for his *Échos de l'Orient judaïque* to receive a public performance at a concert organized by pianist Alfred Cortot at the Nouveau Théâtre on 19 April 1905. Vincent d'Indy conducted the work, and Paul Daraux was the baritone soloist. Gabriel Fauré, who was working as a music critic for *Le Figaro,* wrote a long review, affectionately recalling his old friend.

> Here we are concerned with texts whose musical interpretations have already given rise to many masterworks. But no one yet has been as concerned with translating the spirit, with expressing the feelings, or with evoking at the same time the milieu in which the Prince de Polignac had such poetic vision. Here, the eloquence of the text and the emotion of the scenes have been enveloped in a truly far-away atmosphere, tinted with a truly Oriental color. In *Pilate livre le Christ,* it's truly the populace of Jerusalem that declaims ferociously "tolle, tolle"; it's truly, in *Christ à Gethsemani,* the nocturnal landscape of the Mount of Olives; and it's truly, after the anguished silence that follows the fall of the temple, the voice of the Christian bells that rises up, the hymn of the new era about to bloom. . . .
>
> Up until now the *Échos de l'Orient judaïque* has only been played in concerts of a private character and before a small audience. This utterly striking work deserves to be made known to a large public. For my part, I admire M. Alfred Cortot for having taken the initiative and for having brought to his realization a very artistic care.[83]

Just prior to the Cortot concert, Winnaretta was contacted by impresario Gabriel Astruc. Born in 1864, Astruc, a rabbi's son, was a man of extraordinary ambition and energy. At age forty, he began a career as an artists' manager and concert impresario. In 1904 he founded the Société Musicale Gabriel Astruc, a publishing house; at the same time, he launched a concert agency and production company, the "Grandes Saisons de Paris," under whose auspices he produced over one thousand performances by foreign artists, ensembles, and theatrical troupes. His roster included harpsichordist Wanda Landowska and pianist Arthur Rubinstein, an American blackface minstrel show, opera stars Enrico Caruso and Nellie Melba, and the Metropolitan Opera Company, conducted by Toscanini.[84] Astruc moved easily between the worlds of the aristocratic elite in the Faubourg St-Germain and the *nouveaux riches,* whose grandiose houses in the newer quarters of the 8th *arrondissement* testified to their "arrival." His colorful personality allowed him to become the darling of the *chers snobs* of Paris.

It was through the Comtesse Greffulhe, who used Astruc's agency for the adminstration of the Société des Grandes Auditions, that the introduction to Winnaretta took place.[85] Astruc hoped to add the Polignac salon to the list of prestigious private venues where he could secure engagements for his artists. The timing was fortuitous: Astruc's initial meeting with Winnaretta coincided with the permanent departure from Paris of Charles Bordes, Winnaretta's de facto contractor for almost a dozen years. Bordes's retirement to Montpensier not only ended the longtime association of the Chanteurs de Saint-Gervais with the Polignac salon, but it also deprived Winnaretta of someone who could attend to the practical organization of her concert programs. She may have been casting about for someone else to fill that role. Astruc found Winnaretta's soft spot right away—Edmond—and astutely played on it. First, he offered to re-release one of Edmond's songs, *Sur les Lagunes,*[86] under the auspices of his Société Musicale Gabriel Astruc.[87] The newly edited song appeared in the summer of 1905.[88] Subsequent publications included a number of Edmond's a cappella choruses.[89]

At this time all of musical Paris was talking about the scandalous exclusion of young Maurice Ravel from the Prix de Rome competition. Ravel was already celebrated in musical circles as the composer of *Jeux d'eau,* the String Quartet, and *Shéhérazade.* But in May 1905, the jury, composed primarily of faculty from the reactionary Conservatoire de Paris, rejected the work of the young composer, on the grounds that his music lacked sufficient technical accomplishment for it to be worthy of further consideration. The indignation of Ravel's supporters turned to outrage when it was revealed that the competition had been rigged. The "affaire Ravel," as the incident came to be known, had an unforeseen happy ending, for shortly afterward, Fauré was named new director of the Conservatoire. The notoriety that Ravel gained from the incident only enhanced his reputation as a new musical voice to be reckoned with.

The "affaire Ravel" cannot have failed to figure in Winnaretta's discussions with Astruc. She surely related the sense of injustice that Edmond felt in his rejection by the professional music community. Perhaps what was needed was a new competition for composers independent of any official body such as the Conservatoire. Astruc proposed the creation of an "Edmond de Polignac Foundation," which would sponsor a bi-annual competition for French composers or composers in permanent residence in France. Winnaretta was delighted with the idea, and a charter was drawn up. There would be no age limit on the contestants, and the winners would receive cash prizes, guarantees of publication and royalties, and performances of the prizewinning works by the Concerts Lamoureux and other prestigious ensembles. The founding committee was comprised of Winnaretta (President), Fauré (Vice-President) and Astruc (Treasurer), as well as composers Paul Dukas, Octave Maus,[90] and André Messager, conductor Camille Chevillard, and music critics Pierre Lalo and *Le Figaro*'s Robert Brussel.[91] While this worthy endeavor was never pursued beyond the planning stages, Astruc's efforts did not go unrewarded, for in 1906, he was able to add the name of the Princesse de Polignac to the list of aristocratic hostesses in his fold, and for the next several years he functioned as the contractor for the Polignac salon.

Winnaretta's abandonment of the new foundation may have had to do with a legal entanglement that preoccupied her throughout 1905. In January of that year, Paul Sohège, Isabella's widower, filed a lawsuit against Winnaretta and her siblings. The Sohèges had lived a profligate existence, and by the time Isabella died, there was little remaining of her Singer inheritance. Not content with the small amount of money left to him after his wife's debts had been settled, Sohège was now suing for a *part d'enfant,* a share of the Singer estate equal to those left to Isabella's five surviving children.[92] He had engaged a powerful lawyer, Jean Cruppi, a well-known political figure (and, ironically, a friend of Bulteau), to plead his case.[93] However, Winnaretta and her brothers had an equally formidable advocate: Raymond Poincaré, the future president of France. Although the case dragged on for many years, the Singer siblings eventually triumphed over their stepfather, thanks to Poincaré's talent and devotion to his clients' cause of action.[94]

The lawsuit necessitated Winnaretta's examination of old letters written by her mother. In reading these she relived happy memories of her Boyer grandparents and her beloved aunt Jane.[95] But she confronted difficult memories as well, in re-reading the financial terms of the contract that she signed just before her 1887 marriage to the Prince de Scey-Montbéliard.[96] Her Singer inheritance had afforded her a life of luxury, ease, and independence, but it had also resulted in an endless succession of familial disputes and legal tribulations, especially those generated by her mother's remarriages. Despite her closeness with her own and with Edmond's siblings,

Winnaretta wanted and sought a stronger, more positive connection with her extended Singer family.

Unforeseen circumstances gave her the opportunity for that connection. During the course of the trial, the name of William Alexander Singer, the oldest of Isaac's twenty-four children, came up. William was seventy-one years old, born the same year as Edmond. Having received a much smaller share of Isaac's estate than the rest of his half-siblings,[97] he was living in very modest circumstances in Brooklyn, New York. Winnaretta had never met her half-brother, and was curious to know about him. She was equally curious to know more about their father, and William, as the child who had known him the longest, was surely the one who could best answer her questions. Winnaretta wrote to him on 13 July 1905,[98] enclosing a check for twenty-five pounds sterling along with her letter.[99] She asked him to provide her with information about her father and her paternal grandparents, about whom she knew almost nothing. Some weeks later, she received a long, affectionate response from her American half-brother.

> *I am very sorry indeed that you cannot come to America this year,* but while there is life there is hope, and if we all live we may I dearly hope yet meet. I too, feel the deepest interest in all that concerns our dear Father, he was a wonderfull man, absolutely self-made. . . . It would deeply interest you to know *all* his wonderfull [*sic*] and very *unusual* history, but *it better not be on paper.* . . . In the winter of 1850 he invented his wonderfully successfull [*sic*] sewing Machine that led to his vast wealth and made many others also immensely wealthy. In 1863 he married his second wife, Isabella your dear lamented mother and my dear stepmother, and I loved her dearly for she was very kind to me at that time, and I never could forget it. In July 1875 dear father *died.* My God how I grieve and still do. . . . When we meet, if ever, I will be delighted to give you a vast deal more information of interest. No *romance* ever written is so absorbingly interesting as *that true full Singer history from Grandfather up to the present.*[100]

Winnaretta and her half-brother corresponded for another decade, but the two never met.[101] For the rest of his life she provided him with financial support, enabling him to spend the winter months in the warmer climes of Florida. It would be another two decades before Winnaretta traveled to America, and by that time William had died.

In October 1905 Winnaretta returned from Venice to her newly renovated Paris mansion. When Winnaretta purchased the house in 1887, it had been filled with the kind of bizarre decorations found in many homes of the Second Empire's newly rich. Above the central foyer, a sculptural piece had been adorned with a veritable menagerie of bronze elephants, rhinoceroses, and other wild animals, whose mouths spewed forth streams of water that ran down an elaborate series of staircases.[102] The architect Grand'pierre removed these excessive decorations, gutting the house and remaking it in late eighteenth-century classical French style. A long and elegant staircase led up to an oval reception room, whose windowed doors led out to the raised terrace garden. An enormous dining room, in floor-to-ceiling marble, was linked by a connecting passage to the rue Cortambert *atelier*. Winnaretta, ever her father's daughter, had authorized the purchase of the most technologically advanced conveniences of modern living. A gleaming new kitchen boasted the latest stoves and refrigeration units. The roof was equipped with a combination solarium-greenhouse. And in the basement, next to the wine cellar, a heated swimming pool was installed. But the spiritual heart of the house was the new music room, large enough to hold comfortably a chamber orchestra and two hundred guests. Banks of windows surrounded by mirrored glass shutters offset the dark hue of the walls. When the shutters were closed at night, they caught the sparkling reflections of two magnificent Venetian chandeliers.

Winnaretta continued to fill her home with important artwork, and a number of her acquisitions adorned the walls of her new salon. A 1905 Paris exhibition of the work of James McNeill Whistler, who had died two years earlier, rekindled her interest in the artist; she and Edmond had met Whistler on a number of occasions since the afternoon twenty years earlier when he had acted as Edmond's guide to Pre-Raphaelite London. When Whistler's paintings *Three Figures: Pink and Grey* and *Nocturne in Green and Gold* came up for auction at Agnew's Gallery in London in June 1905, she acquired the works.[103] A year later she bought four Monet paintings at auction at the Galeries Georges Petit, including *Pommiers en fleurs, Les Bords de la Seine, La Lecture sous les arbres,* and the extraordinary *Dindons,* in which Monet had placed a flock of strutting turkeys in the foreground.[104] She also made a purchase of a late eighteenth-century work: a boxed papier-mâché pastoral scene depicting Saint Agnes, patron saint of young girls and rape victims.[105]

Now that she was able to receive in her home again, she made a point of developing closer relationships with the younger members of the Singer and Polignac families. The difference in age between her and Edmond had, in the first years of her marriage, created a disconcerting situation whereby she was constantly addressed as "ma tante" by adults her own age or older. She got used to it: by time she reached middle age, the total number of Singers and Polignacs calling her "Tante Winnie" exceeded three dozen. In fact, she was called "Tante Winnie" so often in a typical family gathering that the appellation became an affectionate nickname used even by non-family members. The genial informality of the name did not, however, make her less intimidating to many of the children and young adults in her family circles. Her imposing stature, gravelly voice, steely expression, and domineering manner made her downright scary to some. And yet, the young Singers and Polignacs who made the effort to know their aunt discovered that she had a wicked sense of humor, and was willing to engage in the kind of spontaneous childlike romps not often enjoyed by other adults. Some of those nephews and nieces who found favor in their aunt's eyes were able to benefit from her broad cultural interests, as well as her interesting social gatherings in Paris and her frequent foreign trips. Winnaretta made her *atelier* available for the coming-out balls of her nieces, and sometimes she invited groups of her nieces and nephews to her palazzo. "I'll be in Venice the 9ᵗʰ for 10 days with 5 persons from the ages of 14 to 17," she wrote to Bulteau during one vacation period.[106] She threw a party at the palazzo for her young charges, during which the Venetian municipal musicians came to entertain them with the first Italian performance of Edmond de Polignac's *Tarantelle*.[107]

As Winnaretta prepared for a new season of soirees, a notable war of words was raging in the cultural journals. The Paris community of composers and critics of that time had divided into two factions, the "Scholists," those who supported the rigorous and more conservative "contrapuntalism" of the Schola Cantorum, and the "Debussyists," those who saw *Pelléas et Mélisande,* with its sensuous, moment-by-moment harmonies, as the harbinger of a new modernist ideal. It was, in fact, a false dichotomy, and d'Indy and Debussy themselves, who respected each other's work, were not involved in the passionate wrangling of their disciples. But the feud forced the taking of sides, and formerly amiable colleagues were soon pitted against each other.[108] Critic Émile Vuillermoz led a group of young "radical" composers (including Ravel, who was still enjoying the notoriety of the "affaire" that bore his name) in a heated polemic against the Schola and its fanatical Catholic and nationalist tendencies. On the other side of the fence, Albert Roussel headed the group of musicians who defended the traditionalism of the d'Indy school.[109] Only a few composers, such as Fauré, managed to remain neutral. This controversy continued until the outbreak of World War I.[110]

In at least one aspect, Winnaretta's interest in the Schola Cantorum was personal, for Armande de Polignac was one of the institution's longtime pupils. Armande had blossomed under the tutelage of Vincent d'Indy (his latent ambivalence towards women composers notwithstanding). She composed prolifically in all genres (signing her works with her maiden name), and excelled in her studies of orchestration and conducting.[111] In 1906 Winnaretta presented the *avant-première* of Armande's first opera, *La Petite Sirène* (The Little Mermaid), in her salon, a work praised later that year by *Le Figaro* for its expressiveness and clarity.[112] The work, based on Hans Christian Andersen's story, with a libretto by Henry Gauthier-Villars, was performed three years later under the composer's baton at the Opéra de Nice; it was the first of many performances of Armande's works by major opera companies, dance troupes, and symphonies throughout Europe up until World War II.[113]

Winnaretta's pride in Armande's accomplishments did not translate into a partisan attitude towards the Schola or its philosophies. She remained aloof from the squabbling going on among her musician friends on both sides of the Scholist-Debussyist dispute; her neutrality was manifested in her choice of repertoire for her salon programs during the 1905–6 season. The first soiree, on 10 December 1905, was an all-Bach concert, performed by the artist-professors of the Schola Cantorum.[114] Winnaretta joined the distinguished pianist Blanche Selva[115] and composer-conductor Marcel Labey in a performance of the Concerto for Three Pianos. D'Indy, the director of the Schola, was absent, being on tour in the United States, guest-conducting the Boston Symphony Orchestra in a program that included, ironically enough, the *Nocturnes* of Claude Debussy.[116]

An item about the Schola soiree appeared in the *Le Figaro*'s society column the next day.[117] Interested parties on both sides of the controversy must have been amused—or shocked—to read in the same article that Winnaretta's next concert would feature the compositions of the Debussyists. The program of 17 December, performed by a Madame Fourrier and pianist Ricardo Viñes, cannily mingled songs by Musorgsky and Balakirev with recent songs and piano works by Debussy and Ravel, who had drawn so much from those and other Russians. Ravel, the man of the hour since the "affaire," was represented by his celebrated Orientalist song cycle of 1903, *Shéhérazade,* and by his newly composed Sonatine for piano, receiving its brilliant first performance that evening.[118] It was not so long ago that Winnaretta had bristled at receiving the unsolicited dedication of Ravel's *Pavane*. She was now one of his staunchest admirers.

The first musical gatherings of 1906 continued the alternation of Scholist and Debussyist programs. The program of 14 January was devoted to Bach cantatas and sacred works by Schütz and Carissimi, accompanied by Fauré and Gigout.[119] Two weeks later the concert was comprised of three piano trios written by composers from the Schola, Albert Roussel and students Réné de Castéra and Pierre Coindreau.[120] Roussel wrote several days later, "I know what a sanctuary of Good Music your salon is, and I'm thus all the more flattered that my work was so warmly received there."[121] But Meg de Saint-Marceaux, in a brief diary entry, recorded a less flattering assessment of the evening's offerings: "Soiree Polignac. 3 Trios de Castéra, Coindreau, Roussel. Oof."[122] On 22 January the Debussyist program included songs by Balakirev and Ravel's newly written *Cinq Mélodies populaires grecques;* the second half of the program featured string quartets of Borodin and Debussy.[123] Finally, the "contrapuntalists" and "harmonists" were brought together in one program on 11 February, on which occasion choral works by Bach, Carissimi, Lully, and Edmond de Polignac were alternated with piano works by Chopin, Albéniz,[124] and Ravel, including Ravel's recently written *Alborado del Gracioso*. Ricardo Viñes joined forces with Winnaretta in a two-piano performance of Debussy's *Prélude à l'après-midi d'un faune*.[125]

Meanwhile, Astruc's role as organizer of the Polignac salon programs was growing steadily.[126] Over the course of the next year, Winnaretta's *atelier* became a standard venue for performances by Astruc's artists and the composers who were published by the impresario's Société Musicale. On 25 February Wanda Landowska, recently arrived in Paris from Poland, gave an extraordinarily diverse recital in the *atelier*. First playing harpsichord, then fortepiano, and finally a modern Steinway grand piano, Landowska performed a recital of keyboard works that began with works by the English virginalists and ended with Liszt transcriptions.[127] Some weeks later, Philippe Gaubert, the virtuoso principal flutist of the Opéra, played a recital of Bach flute sonatas.[128] Other evenings spotlighted new works by Henri Rabaud[129] and Déodat de Sévérac.[130]

The constant parade of new people passing through Winnaretta's life provided no end of stimulation and pleasure. "Everywhere I go," she wrote to Augustine Bulteau, "I continue to meet remarkable and sublime beings created especially for me."[131] A meeting with one such "remarkable being" took place on 22 February 1906, when Winnaretta attended an "at home" hosted by the de Meyers in London. That evening, the featured music was a group of British, Irish, and Welsh folksongs with new settings by Australian composer Percy Grainger.[132] Winnaretta and Grainger struck up a friendship, and he sent her home with a pile of folksong scores, each bearing a personal dedication.[133] Winnaretta did not, however, forget her old friends. She was always a willing participant whenever Anna de Noailles needed an audience for the recitation of her new verses.[134] In April 1907 a new collection of Anna's poems was released under the title *Les Éblouissements* (Resplendence); the volume sold, as Winnaretta told Jacques-Émile Blanche, "like little hotcakes."[135]

She continued to champion the work and activity of an old favorite, the charming and intelligent Reynaldo Hahn. Hahn, an unrepentant anti-modernist, was still writing operas, song cycles, and piano music in the romantic, sentimental style that bespoke the fading aesthetic of the Belle Époque. Despite her own progressive penchant, Winnaretta continued to include Hahn's music in her salon programs. On 11 April 1907 an audience of almost two hundred invited guests filled the large avenue Henri-Martin salon to hear a recital evoking the charms of the musical past. The program was comprised of works for wind ensemble by d'Indy and Mozart, songs by Saint-Saëns and Fauré, and choral works by Edmond de Polignac and Hahn (his *O Fons Bandusiae* [The Fountains of Bandusiae]).[136] After the intermission, the featured work, Hahn's *Le Bal de Béatrice d'Este*,[137] was performed by a ten-piece ensemble, conducted by the composer.[138] To evoke the court of the celebrated fifteenth-century duchess who was the *grande mécène* of her day, Winnaretta decorated her salon in "Renaissance" style: the stage was hung with damask and period tapestries; the room was illuminated by candlelight.

Hahn's performance brought Marcel Proust back to Winnaretta's house for the first time since the disaster of the *Figaro* article three years earlier. He sat mesmerized as Reynaldo conducted the other musicians from his seat at the piano. Every time a loud chord was sounded, the candles lighting Hahn's piano score quavered; Proust feared that they would fall and set fire to the paper roses on the dais. His sense of peril was forgotten, however, in watching Reynaldo's right hand, which seemed like "a magic baton that flew to the furthest corner of the orchestra, just in time to wake a little sleeping triangle. . . . I admired how you were able to force all these society people to stop and listen to a fountain weeping in silence and in solitude."[139] Some thoughts were melancholy: Proust's gaze drifted around the room to the faces of friends that he hadn't seen in several years. "All the people I used to know have aged so much! Only Polignac has finally attained the youth that is now joined with the sweetness of maturity."[140] The sweet atmosphere of the musical evening made a profound impression on Proust; he was able to return the favor on 1 July, when the Princesse de Polignac attended his "grand dinner" and recital at the Ritz, where a lively group paid tribute to Proust's longtime champion, Gaston Calmette.[141]

Shortly thereafter, a dispute flared up between Winnaretta and Adolph and Olga de Meyer. Winnaretta claimed that de Meyer had never repaid her a sum of fifteen hundred pounds that she had loaned him two years earlier and that he had refused to return the money; de Meyer retorted that he had not only repaid the debt—plus interest—but that he had a receipt signed by her to prove it. Winnaretta continued to accuse the Baron, vociferously, seemingly intent on destroying his and his wife's reputation in society.[142] Not surprisingly, the feud put an end to Winnaretta's love affair with Olga. Even though the women were together in Venice in July, by the end of the month their relationship had been irrevocably damaged by Winnaretta's allegations against de Meyer. Miserable, Winnaretta took refuge with Hélène at the Chimay family estate in Belgium. A period of reflection in those calm surroundings caused her to regret her actions. She entertained a hope of reconciliation, but a letter from Olga in August affirmed that the rupture was definitive.[143] Winnaretta became depressed and ill. Her low point occurred one afternoon when she and Hélène were caught in a sudden thunderstorm while walking in the woods. As the heavens opened, her lifelong fear of thunder and lightning sent her into a panic. Hélène was astonished to see her friend's imperturbable self-control abruptly vanish, as Winnaretta fled from the noise of the thunder in "a breathless gallop that pushed her forward, crossing the plains, jumping over ditches, her face contorted in silent terror, her skirt hoisted up right up to her thighs."[144]

Anna de Noailles was certain that her friend was "going to get better, [having] touched the bottom of your abyss"; she urged her to trust in a future "full of life, of hopes, of imagination, of tenderness."[145] And soon afterwards, Winnaretta's customary self-possession returned. She went back to Venice, and, ignoring the fact that Olga and her husband were in the city, she entertained houseguests and held grand dinners parties, where the likes of Prince Francis of Teck rubbed elbows with Isadora Duncan.[146] Reynaldo Hahn, one of the guests at the palazzo, was the musical master of ceremonies for these gatherings. The press noted the presence of the many "elegant personalities from the French aristocracy" who, on many an evening, came together at Winnaretta's house "where exquisite music was made."[147]

That month of September, suffused with Reynaldo Hahn's sweet and sentimental music, marked the end of an era in Winnaretta's life. The waning days of summer had much to do with reconciling with, and bidding farewell to, the past. From both a personal and artistic standpoint, Winnaretta's world was about to change. The Russians were coming.

Modern Times

In the years preceding World War I, roughly between 1906 and 1914, important changes began to penetrate the European cultural landscape, forming the basis of what is now called modernism. A wealth of new ideas—experimentalism, objectivism, classicism (new in that it was a reaction to romanticism), as well as influences as diverse as primitivism, exoticism, and folk and ancient cultures—began to permeate all the art forms. Artists from all over the world, seeking to question and reinvent their creative forms, converged in Paris, London, Vienna, and other great European capitals to join in the ferment of new ideas and movements. In the plastic arts, Fauvism replaced post-impressionism as the predominant style, only to be replaced by the cubism of Picasso and Braque a few years later. In 1907 Henri Bergson espoused a confident, optimistic philosophy of "Creative Evolution," defining the mind as pure energy, governed by a vital force. A new literary magazine, *La Nouvelle Revue française,* edited by André Gide, featured the work of a young group of writers and poets, including Paul Valéry, Marcel Proust, and Guillaume Apollinaire. These confident new voices toppled the rules of writing by infusing irony, burlesque, and unconventional syntax into their works. Maurice Ravel, the composer-*provocateur,* embraced these new stylistic trends in his 1906 settings of Jules Renard's *Histoires naturelles,* matching his musical declamation to the sounds and inflections of spoken French. The rebelliousness of Erik Satie's music lay in its tongue-in-cheek simplicity. The young, multi-talented gadfly Jean Cocteau had just arrived in Paris; his enormous output—poetry, scenarios, novels, and, later, films—would cement his reputation as the clarion voice of the avant-garde. And the century's newest medium, the motion picture, became more widely disseminated in 1907, as the Pathé brothers and industrialist Léon Gaumont built cinema theaters throughout Paris.

Le Figaro acknowledged the profound sense of change in the air when it published, on 20 February 1909, "The Futurist Manifesto," in which Filippo Marinetti declared that "We want to sing the love of danger, the habit of energy and rashness. The essential elements of our poetry will be courage, daring, and revolt. Beauty exists only in struggle. . . . We are on the extreme promontory of the centuries!"[1] Interest in these exciting new ideas attracted not only the art community, but the more adventurous members of high society as well: when Marinetti presented his "tragic satire," *Le Roi Bombance*, at the Théâtre de l'Oeuvre on 2 April 1909, his audience comprised not only a group of eminent writers, musicians, and artists (Proust, Ravel, Satie, Odilon Redon, Cocteau, Jacques-Émile Blanche, Feodor Chaliapin, José-Maria Sert, and Ida Rubinstein), but also Élisabeth Greffulhe, Anna de Noailles, and Winnaretta de Polignac.[2]

In the midst of the extraordinarily fertile atmosphere that reigned in 1906 Paris came a charismatic young Russian, Serge Diaghilev, who, within one short year, would embody the very conception of the new modernist art. Capitalizing on the fascination of Parisians with exoticism, primitivism, and "otherness," he would mount a series of exhibitions and productions in the pre-World War I years that would significantly alter and expand the vocabulary and the palette of the visual arts, dance, and music. It was, in particular, the performances of the dance troupe with which his name is forever linked—the Ballets Russes—that seized the imagination of the public, and opened wide the doors to modernism.[3]

Born in 1872 in a small village outside of Novgorod, Russia, Sergei Pavlovitch Diaghilev had first hoped for a career as a composer and a singer, but his wide-ranging interests—art, literature, and dance—inspired him to become an impresario. If he did not have a true creative imagination, he had the power to give concrete form to his prescient ideas by convincing others of the importance of his visions. Although he had no personal fortune, his passionate desire to promote the art he loved was matched by a flair for an organization, an oversized sense of self-confidence, and an irresistibly seductive charisma. This and his indefatigable energy had enabled him, in 1898, to launch a new monthly arts magazine, *Mir iskusstva* (The World of Art), which espoused an integration of the exciting new trends in Russian literature, theater, and scenic design. The name of the magazine was subsequently taken up by a number of aesthetes, mostly from aristocratic or intellectually refined backgrounds, who grouped around Diaghilev; The World of Art thus became a circle that mirrored the journal's viewpoints on art. In 1901, an offshoot group of musicians and music-lovers organized a series of "Evenings of Contemporary Music." The soirees united young Russian and French artists, creating new audiences for the music of Scriabin, Tcherepnin, and Rachmaninoff as well as the works of great contemporary French composers. It was at these concerts, which continued for over a decade, that the young Igor Stravinsky heard for the first time, in 1907, the music of Fauré, Debussy, and Ravel.

Despite the widely held perception of the group's modernist advocacy (and legacy), the philosophical tenets of The World of Art were not avant-garde. In essence, Diaghilev and his colleagues called for a return to the refined artistic world of the Russian eighteenth century, when the aristocratic, conservative values of enlightened individualism were the defining ideals of high art and culture.[4] The World of Art actually represented, according to musicologist Richard Taruskin, the conservative wing of the Russian avant-garde.[5] The aesthetic espoused by the group was fundamentally ornamental, a beautiful "refuge and repose from the modern world."[6] In February 1905, Diaghilev's "retrospective" vision was realized in his most ambitious project to date: in the shadow of the previous month's "Bloody Sunday," he opened an exhibition in St. Petersburg of two hundred years of Russian portrait art. The almost three thousand portraits, gathered from every corner of Russia, gave to the throngs of visitors a new understanding of the successive transformations of the country's artistic history, as seen through an astonishing visual patrimony spanning the Byzantine through the modern eras.

Even with the exhibition's success, Diaghilev knew that his prospects in his native country were limited.[7] Casting his sights further to the West, Diaghilev organized various artistic exhibitions in Greece, Italy, Spain, and Germany. He arrived in Paris in the spring of 1906 to organize a version of the Russian portrait exhibition in conjunction with the annual October *Salon d'automne*.[8] The show, which occupied twelve rooms of the Palais Royal, was no less impressive than its predecessor. Parisians, ignorant of Russia's rich artistic and cultural heritage, turned out in droves to view the portraits, and to attend a "Russian Historical Concert" at the Paris Opéra organized in tandem with the exhibition.[9] These events coincided fortuitously with an official visit by Russian ministers, who converted the events into gala convocations of political and society figures.[10] Prominent among the Russian nobles was Grand-Duke Vladimir, an ardent lover of art and music and one of the important sponsors of Diaghilev's October exhibition.

Winnaretta was not in attendance at the Russian portrait show: she seldom left Venice before the beginning of November, and this year had delayed her return to Paris even longer in order to hear the world premiere of Ethel Smyth's opera *The Wreckers* at the Leipzig Opera. But she may have attended the exhibitions organized by Diaghilev in Italy and Germany in 1905 during the course of her travels. The first known meeting of the two took place at the home of Winnaretta's friends, Grand-Duke Paul of Russia—brother of Alexander III and uncle of Tsar Nicolas II—and his wife, Countess Hohenfelsen. In late November or early December 1906 they introduced Winnaretta to Diaghilev, "a tall, energetic-looking young man with a white lock in the midst of his thick black hair."[11] Before the evening's end, the Princesse de Polignac too had fallen under the spell of the fascinating man "whose marvellous will-power, energy, and utter disinterestedness"[12] would soon introduce to the world the art, the dance, and the music of the future.

She was not responsible for his launching in Paris society, however. Diaghilev had already caught the attention of the Comtesse Greffulhe. In recent years, Élisabeth Greffulhe had spread her wings, artistically speaking, using her high position in society to promote modern music and musical artists. Under her directorship, the Société des Grandes Auditions had sponsored the Paris debuts of pianist Arthur Rubinstein and conductor-pianist Alfred Cortot and the presentations of two rarely performed operas, Berlioz's epic *Les Troyens* and Boito's *Mefistofele*. Greffulhe's silent partner in these enterprises was Gabriel Astruc, who, since 1904, had administered the practical and financial details of the performances through his production company. In the spring of 1907 the Société took the audacious step of sponsoring the first Paris performance of Richard Strauss's *Salome*, with its libretto by Oscar Wilde, whose reputation had not been softened by his death. Greffulhe's association with this work, undertaken in collaboration with Astruc, was noted by the right-wing press, which viewed her patronage of such a lascivious proto-Jewish and proto-homosexual "enterprise of puffism" as "a beautiful example of the decay of our mores."[13] Comte Greffulhe wrote to his wife, "If you continue to occupy yourself with music, I can't recommend strongly enough that you choose [works] that will not give rise to certain very painful discussions."[14] Despite Henry Greffulhe's protestations, the publicity around the work was enormous, and much of the audience at the *répétition générale* of *Salome* was comprised of the members of the wealthy *tout-Paris*. Élisabeth Greffulhe had the dual satisfaction of solidifying her reputation as a primary player in the public arena of Parisian musical culture and wreaking revenge on her philandering husband.

Greffulhe had been introduced to Diaghilev in the spring of 1906, during the planning stages of the Russian portrait exhibition. At first put off by Diaghilev's officious manner, she was finally won over by his ardor and remarkably wide culture. His charisma and powers of persuasion melted Greffulhe's customary haughtiness: by evening's end she had agreed to act as one of three honorary chairs of the organizational committee for the 1906 portrait show.[15] Following the exhibition's success, she lent her patronage to Diaghilev's "dream" scheme: the introduction of the masterworks of Russian opera and art music to Paris audiences. Two grand projects were sketched out: for 1907, a second season of "Russian Historical Concerts," and, for 1908, an even larger venture, the first Paris performances of Musorgsky's *Boris Godunov,* with the great Feodor Chaliapin in the title role, assisted by the musicians and dancers of the Russian Imperial Theaters. Astruc, a seasoned presenter of large and complicated enterprises, was called upon to both administrate and raise money for these events.

Much of the monumental work of securing funding was carried out in the musical salons themselves. Greffulhe played on her "snob appeal" to promote the Russian enterprises, while Astruc, who had his own influential contacts among the artistically inclined aristocracy, as well as the wealthy bourgeoisie, brought all of his talents to bear in convincing people to support the projects. For a full year, society luminaries, such as the Napoleonic

Princesse Murat and the Grand-Duke Paul, hosted gala soirees featuring full acts of *Boris Godunov* and other Russian operatic music. Stars from the major Russian theaters, including diva soprano Félia Litvinne,[16] tenor Dmitri Smirnov, and bass Vladimir Kastorsky,[17] were engaged to give appropriate panache to the performances.[18] By time the 1907 *grande saison* began, all of high society was eagerly anticipating Diaghilev's concerts. Winnaretta surely attended many of these events, and, her interest aroused, subsequently filled her music library with scores of Russian operas, art songs, and symphonies. She was in the audience for the five "Russian Historical Concerts" of May 1907, which introduced Parisians to the powerful music of Rimsky-Korsakov, Glazunov, Rachmaninoff, and Scriabin, all of whom came from Russia to conduct their works.[19]

While Winnaretta does not seem to have hosted any "Russian" soirees, she did introduce some important new Spanish musical repertoire to her salon audiences. On 2 January 1908, she hosted the first performances of a new set of piano works by the vibrant and iconoclastic Spanish composer Isaac Albéniz. Having settled in Paris as a pianist in 1893, Albéniz came under the influence of fine composers associated with the Schola Cantorum: Fauré, Dukas, and especially d'Indy. His studies at the Schola resulted in the composition of a set of twelve piano pieces in four books. These fiendishly difficult pieces, entitled *Iberia,* evoked various locales of Albéniz's native Spain. Young virtuoso pianist Blanche Selva, a professor at the Schola Cantorum and a regular presence in the Polignac salon,[20] was engaged to play the *avant-première* of these daunting works in Winnaretta's *atelier*[21] before the first public performance the following month under the auspices of the Société Nationale.[22] The pianist returned to the Polignac salon on 11 April 1908 to give a repeat performance of *Iberia*'s first three books.[23]

Winnaretta's association with new music and art began to attract the younger members of the avant-garde community, including eighteen-year-old poet Jean Cocteau. As Proust had done fifteen years earlier, Cocteau understood that an introduction into the prestigious salons, where the hostesses were always on the lookout for the next young "genius," would help smooth the path towards artistic renown. In 1908 he secured his first invitation to a luncheon at Winnaretta's house. He made a triumphal entry, declaring that "he had just come by foot from the Luxembourg gardens where he had awaited Spring, with whom he had a rendez-vous." Having greeted his hostess, "he executed a glissando across the polished floor" and seated himself at the table next to an astonished Princesse Marthe Bibesco.[24] Cocteau liked Winnaretta; he admired "her profile, which resembled a bust of Dante," and her way of "grinding out irrevocable judgments."[25] For the next thirty years, he would become a fixture in the Polignac salon.

That spring of 1908 all talk in musical circles was of Diaghilev and the upcoming performance of Musorgsky's *Boris Godunov.* Winnaretta joined the patronage committee assembled by Greffulhe, a group that united the

Russian and French aristocratic community with a broad range of important composers. When *Boris* opened on 19 May 1908,[26] Winnaretta's name appeared prominently in the printed program's list of patrons, just under that of the name of the Comtesse Greffulhe; it is reasonable to assume that her financial contribution was considerable.[27] Musorgsky's opera enjoyed fantastic popular reception and universal acclaim by the musical critics.[28] The audiences—high Tsarist officials, the literary intelligentsia, and Paris's throngs of opera-lovers—returned again and again not only to hear Musorgsky's music sung by the stars of the Russian operatic roster, but to feast on the visually lavish sets and costumes created by Diaghilev's old friends from The World of Art.[29]

While the performances of *Boris* were still in progress, Astruc asked Diaghilev if it would be possible to give a series of performances by the Ballets of the Russian Imperial Theaters.[30] Traditionally, the ballet had served as an adjunct to the opera, but Diaghilev had a novel idea: why not present a troupe that functioned as an independent artistic entity, and create a new repertoire involving the most innovative directors, choreographers, scenic designers, and composers before the public? The idea was received enthusiastically by Diaghilev's colleagues at the Imperial Theaters in St. Petersburg: designer Alexander Benois (one of the original World of Art partners), the adventurous young choreographer Michael Fokine, and composer Nicolas Tcherepnin, a recent graduate of the Conservatory and conductor of the Imperial Ballet orchestra. These young creative talents were all chafing under the conservative bureaucracy of the Theater's direction, and sought a new—an international—outlet for their works. The concept of exporting Russian ballet was exciting, but the problem, as usual, was money. *Boris Godunov* had been underwritten by the Russian government, after influence had been brought to bear by Alexander Nelidov, Russian ambassador to Paris, and French minister of state Aristide Briand. But the ballet project, a longer-term, more complicated endeavor, would require even more substantial funding. Diaghilev hoped to turn again to Grand-Duke Vladimir, uncle of the Tsar, who had headed the patronage committee of the Russian Historical Concerts.

By fortuitous happenstance, all three men—Astruc, Diaghilev, and the Grand Duke—were invited to a soiree that Winnaretta had scheduled following the penultimate performance of *Boris,* on 2 June 1908. The guest list for the Princesse de Polignac's "intimate" gathering of more than one hundred of Paris's society elite included, in addition to Grand-Duke Vladimir and his wife, many of Astruc's and Diaghilev's most faithful patrons. Grand-Duke Paul and his wife, Grand-Dukes Cyril and Andrei, as well as the usual cream of the aristocracy, were in attendance, in addition to a number of the wealthy bourgeois financiers.[31] On this occasion, Winnaretta had planned a special entertainment, even grander than her customary post-dinner musical offerings. During recent seasons the brothers Fernand and

Julien Ochsé, artist and writer respectively, had gained repute in staging entertainments of *tableaux vivants,* entitled *Eaux fortes,* stylized in the manner of Aubrey Beardsley. These spectacles had become so popular in Paris society[32] that Winnaretta decided to offer one for the delectation of her visitors. The garden behind her *hôtel* was illuminated by Venetian lanterns that, according to the papers, "cast a mysterious and poetic note on the tall trees."[33] After dinner, the guests were ushered into the grand salon facing avenue Henri-Martin. Accompanied by the music of an unseen orchestra, scenes with titles such as "The white fire that burns them is worse than the flames" and "A Pierrot whose white-face is almost funereally white," featured actors portraying the scenes in the Beardsley drawings, moving back and forth in fantastic fashion between the room's darkness and the eerie lighting designs.[34] Not all the guests were impressed: Mme. Henri de Régnier found the grandiose setting of the *hôtel,* with its dark-paneled walls and neobaroque ceilings, an inappropriate setting for such magical subject matter, and, punning on the title *L'Embarquement pour Cythère* (The Embarkation for Cythera), murmured to writer and critic Edmond Jaloux, "C'est l'enterrement pour Cythère" (It's the funeral procession for Cythera).[35] But a vastly more important success was realized that evening by Diaghilev and Astruc: they were able to amass enough pledges from Winnaretta's guests to be able to proceed with plans for a 1909 season of Russian opera and dance. From this moment the troupe ceased to function as an arm of the Imperial Theaters; it became an independent entity, henceforth known as the Ballets Russes.

The story of Diaghilev and the Ballets Russes, and their monumental impact on artistic modernism is one of the most exciting chapters in all of French cultural history. That Winnaretta's name figures in this story is not surprising; indeed, her role as powerbroker on 2 June 1908 is cited as one of the first of many examples of her largesse towards the Russians. But it is the aggrandizing and mythologizing of her patronage that is noteworthy—and questionable. Choreographer Serge Lifar, who wrote the first biography of Diaghilev shortly after the impresario's death, claimed that Winnaretta was nothing less than "Diaghilev's muse . . . the inspiration of practically all his creative activity."[36] Subsequent chroniclers of the era have portrayed Winnaretta as one of Diaghilev's main patrons and most dependable supporters.[37] This viewpoint has remained in force right up to the present day in the most current scholarship of the Ballets Russes.[38] Curiously, however, there is no documentary evidence whatsoever that provides a clear picture of Winnaretta's patronage of the Ballets Russes, or the extent of her participation. This is more than a little curious, given her general interest in trendsetting artistic enterprises, and the frequent—indeed, persistent—linking of her name with Diaghilev. The truth may very well be that, even though she contributed financially to the company during its first seasons, Winnaretta did not actually become one of the company's principal patrons until several years later, and then for reasons having to do with her admiration and patronage of Igor Stravinsky.

For the moment, most of her support of public artistic enterprises was carried out behind the scenes. Such was the case in her promotion of Ethel Smyth's music. Since 1904 Winnaretta had remained somewhat aloof from Smyth in the hopes of quelling the composer's unrequited ardor; in musical circles, however, she had continued to champion the Englishwoman's compositions, especially her opera *The Wreckers*, which Smyth had dedicated "to the memory of the great musician Prince Edmond de Polignac."[39] The 1906 debut of *The Wreckers* at the Leipzig Opera had been an unqualified success—the audience gave Smyth ten standing ovations[40]—but unfortunately, there were no subsequent offers from other houses to mount the work. Smyth's luck began to turn, however, when a number of her works were included in a concert of "Modern English Music" presented at the Salle Érard on 5 June 1908, only days after Winnaretta's post-*Boris* reception. As far as the public knew, the concert was presented under the patronage of Lady Bertie (wife of the Russian ambassador), Princesse Brancovan, and Fauré, but it is highly likely that Winnaretta helped to underwrite the event as well—in secret, not wanting Smyth to know of her involvement. Winnaretta was surely among those supporters who had sung the praises of Smyth's music, particularly *The Wreckers,* to *Le Figaro*'s music critic, Robert Brussel, and convinced him to attend the performance. Brussel's reaction to Smyth's compositions was one of unqualified enthusiasm.[41] The concert gave a much-needed boost to Smyth's reputation, and later that year *The Wreckers* was presented in concert form at London's Queen's Hall, once again to great critical acclaim.

If Winnaretta was content to show her affection for the composer by discreetly promoting her music, Smyth, on the other hand, still carrying a torch, continued to dwell on her conflicted feelings for her former lover. Upon learning that Winnaretta would attend the London concert, the composer wrote to Bulteau, "How glad I am. . . . I know I can never find anything for me, really, in that heart and I shall never hope for it. But to be separated from her, as I love her, kills me."[42] And instead of basking in the satisfaction of the success of the Salle Érard concert, Smyth afterwards fumed to Bulteau about her dissatisfaction with Winnaretta: "To feel you can never never uproot from your heart the person who you very deliberately think the worst human being you ever saw is distressing, bewildering. . . . And yet the dream of the fine character she might have been if the mask of words were the real person, possesses, and will I think forever possess my imagination."[43]

Winnaretta continued to bring *The Wreckers* to the attention of directors of other European opera theatres. She was unaware that the composer, acting as her own agent, was sabotaging her prospects of having the work produced because of her overzealousness. Winnaretta learned of Smyth's heavy-handed methods of self-promotion when, on 29 December 1908, the

Count Hans von Seebach, director of the Dresden Opera, came to lunch at rue Cortambert. The Princesse asked the *intendant* if he knew "a woman of genius, Miss Ethel Smyth," to which he responded, "Ach, Madame, don't talk to me about her! She's a very nice woman, but *impossible for a theater director*! I still get frightened when I think about the words 'Three Oaks,'[44] because it was from there that she sent me letters that were 1800 pages long!"[45]

Winnaretta saw von Seebach again in February, when she traveled to Dresden to hear one of the first performances of Richard Strauss's new opera, *Elektra*. Winnaretta was an admirer of Strauss; she and the composer enjoyed a cordial friendship, although, curiously, there is no evidence that any of Strauss's works were ever performed in the Polignac salon. In Dresden, *Elektra* startled audiences with its widely leaping vocal lines, its voluptuous orchestration, and its boldly atonal harmonic palate. Winnaretta was full of glowing reports of the new opera when she visited her composer friend Adela Maddison in Berlin a few days after the performance.[46]

Winnaretta's first salon gathering of 1909 took place on her forty-fourth birthday, 8 January, on which occasion she hosted a program of music of contemporary composers—many of whom would soon be enlisted by Diaghilev to provide music for the Ballets Russes. This soiree marked the first performance of the great mezzo-soprano Maggie Teyte in the Polignac salon. Teyte had been catapulted to fame when she replaced Mary Garden in the role of Mélisande in a 1908 production of Debussy's opera. From that point, in addition to her operatic career, Teyte became the most sought-after singer in the salon circuit. Often she was accompanied by Debussy himself, despite his great discomfort in, and contempt for, the aristocratic milieu. For the recital in the Polignac salon, however, Teyte was accompanied by Ricardo Viñes, who partnered her in works by Debussy, Fauré, and Duparc. Viñes then played solo piano music that included Armande de Polignac's *Miroitement* and, in its first performance, *Ondine* by Maurice Ravel.[47] *Le Figaro*, declaring the Ravel work to be "ingenious and picturesque," paid this tribute to the Princesse de Polignac: "Her salons, which are among the most sought-out in Paris, where art is cultivated with the greatest zeal and discernment, have many times opened their doors for exquisite diversions; last night's counted among the most delectable."[48]

During this period the dancer Isadora Duncan re-entered Winnaretta's life. By now Duncan was recognized as the prime force behind the new vocabulary of modern dance. Her 1909 Paris concerts, performed over five months in the two-thousand-seat Gaîté-Lyrique Theater, were sold out for the entire length of the run. The choreographers of the Ballets Russes readily acknowledged her influence.[49] What she had described as "The Dance of the Future" found its most ardent exponent in the work of Michel Fokine, who saw Duncan dance in St. Petersburg just as his own aesthetic ideas were taking concrete form. Fokine was smitten by the "sublime simplicity" of Duncan's choreographic vocabulary, as well as her innovative ways of linking movement with music. Duncan broke the mold, defying the out-moded conventions of dance; Fokine would use her creative platform to break new ground on his own terms.[50]

But, back in Paris, Isadora Duncan faced serious financial problems, and repeatedly voiced the solution, first as a joke, and then in earnest: "I must find a millionaire!"[51] Her prayers were answered. Paris Singer, on one of his trips to Paris, had chanced to see the dancer's concert. One day in February before a matinee performance he walked into Duncan's dressing room and offered her his patronage. Tall, blond, and handsome, Singer exuded the lofty good breeding of one who had spent much time in the milieu of the British court. He was, in the words of one chronicler, "the last of the universal men . . . an artist, athlete, scholar, scientist, art patron, sports patron, philanthropist, and amateur in architecture, medicine, and music."[52] In addition to the Wigwam, he had homes in London, Paris, and St. Jean-Cap-Ferrat, and an enormous yacht. Paris Singer was also a noto-rious lover of women; his compulsive need for new sexual conquests made him the heir to the less seemly side of his father's legacy. Isadora, for whom this last trait might not have been a detracting quality, was dazzled by this wealthy, charismatic man, whom she suddenly remembered meeting at the funeral of Edmond de Polignac in 1901. By the end of the conversation, Singer had offered to defray the total expenses of her dancing school, and to underwrite transporting Duncan and all her students into his villa on the Riviera. Within a week the dancer and her young charges were dancing on the veranda of the Singer mansion in the south of France.

For the next three years Isadora Duncan was indulged and pampered by the love-struck millionaire, whom she nicknamed "Lohengrin."[53] The couple lived an international life, interspersed with Duncan's dance tours; in 1910 the dancer would give birth to their son Patrick. Yet their affair was stormy from the beginning. Although in love with Singer, and perfectly happy to accept the millionaire's largesse, Duncan was disdainful of the very wealth that had made her life so comfortable. "This man, who had declared that he loved me for my courage and generosity, became more and more alarmed when he found what sort of red-hot revolutionary he had taken aboard his yacht. . . . It certainly is more difficult for rich people to accomplish any-thing serious in life."[54]

And indeed, Singer could not seem to rise above his dilettantism: all his grandiose schemes, whether related to architecture, art, or business, seemed to come to naught. Over the next several years he asked Isadora often to marry him, but she steadfastly refused, insisting on the freedom to pro-mote her artistic ideals, perform, teach, tour the world, and maintain her sexual independence. There were constant explosions and partings of ways. After one rupture with Duncan, Paris wrote to Winnaretta, "It is strange how life reserves knock-out blows when one thinks all is going well with a friend. It is a knock-out blow for me who had moved heaven and earth to marry her and thought her devoted to me."[55] Although his turbulent affair with Isadora Duncan would last for many more years, Paris Singer would never be able to rise above his feeling that she was more a beloved possession than a true partner. Dance was Duncan's entire life; Singer couldn't endorse this because it displaced him. One suspects that Winnaretta may have more sympathy for Duncan's point of view than she let on to her brother. While she often displayed a materialistic or acquisitive attitude in her patronage, she was also a true and talented artist, while her brother would never be more than a dilettante. Living a life apart for the sake of Art was a concept that Winnaretta could understand and support.

Whether she was willing to lend that support to the Ballets Russes in 1909 remains a mystery. Élisabeth Greffulhe had formed a "patronage committee," as well as a group of financial guarantors, for Diaghilev's 1909 "Russian season."[56] This year, Winnaretta's name figured on neither list. She had probably heard an earful from Astruc about the compromising professional and financial situations in which he had been placed during the last year due to Diaghilev's "unorthodox" management style.[57] Recent calamitous events may have added to her dubiouness about the viability of the Russian enterprise: on 17 February 1909, Grand-Duke Vladimir, the principle patron of Diaghilev's upcoming Paris season, died suddenly. His widow declined to honor her husband's promise of financial support to the company, and Diaghilev was left unexpectedly without a royal subsidy.[58]

The impresario was forced to rethink the programming of his forthcoming season, which was to have featured performances of full-length operas, interspersed with only a few short ballets. Now, because of the deep cutbacks in his budget, the only operatic offerings would be Rimsky-Korsakov's *Ivan the Terrible,* and single acts from Borodin's *Prince Igor* and Glinka's *Ruslan and Ludmilla.* These last two were to be presented in tandem with short, romantic ballets by Fokine and Benois: *Le Pavillon d'Armide,* on music by Tcherepnin, and *Les Sylphides,* choreographed to Chopin's re-orchestrated piano music. These ballet/opera bills still left a gap in the programming, and so Diaghilev quickly cobbled together a pastiche of nine "folkloric" dances from diverse operas and ballets, on music by Glinka, Rimsky-Korsakov, Glazunov, Tchaikovsky, and Musorgsky; this hodgepodge, bedecked with new costumes fashioned from sketches by young Russian painters, was called *Le Festin.* In short, a season that had been advertised as a serious successor to the 1908 *Boris Godunov* had now been unexpectedly transformed into a season of "colorful" ballet. The World of Art's fundamental emphasis on the synthetic, the decorative, and the retrospective, as opposed to the vocal, the musical, and the theatrical, would soon find its perfect expression in ballet. And what would amount to a seismic shift in modernist aesthetics would arise through the medium of the reconstituted "Russian" ballet.

When the curtain rose on the stage of the Théâtre du Châtelet on 19 May 1909, Paris had its first astonishing glimpse of the splendor of the

Ballets Russes, as the dancers made their entrance. Despite the setbacks of the preceding months, Diaghilev and his personnel, some two hundred fifty people in all, had pulled together to realize the impresario's dazzling vision: to bring a new vision, the color and splendor of "exotic" Russian art, before the Parisian public. The Châtelet, whose boxes and balconies had been swathed in forty tons of red velvet, was filled to capacity with luminaries from Paris's political, financial, social, and artistic worlds. Although none of the works performed was actually newly created for the Paris season, the public experienced these ballets as a revelation. *Le Pavillon d'Armide*, based on a Théophile Gautier story, seduced the audience through its inspired synthesis of Benois's elegant stage design and costumes, Fokine's animated choreography, and the virtuosic dancing of Karsavina and, in his Paris debut, the incomparable Nijinsky. The reaction of the public to the evening's other two offerings—the *Polovetsian Dances* from Borodin's *Prince Igor,* and the suite of dances grouped together as *Le Festin*—was no less enthusiastic. Here finally was the integrated approach to the creation of art that Diaghilev had espoused in *The World of Art* many years ago. Of this performance Anna de Noailles would write, "I didn't quite believe in the revelation I had been promised by certain initiates; but right away I understood that I was witnessing a miracle, that I was seeing something absolutely unique."[59]

The season's other productions also drew large crowds that cheered wildly after each performance.[60] These too were retrospective in nature, and owed their success primarily to the virtuosity of their interpreters: Rimsky-Korsakov's "exotic" opera *Ivan the Terrible* brought back to Paris Feodor Chaliapin, who sang the title role.[61] The one-act ballet *Les Sylphides* was given a brilliant realization of Fokine's choreography by the dancers (Pavlova, Karsavina, and Nijinsky). Finally, *Cléopâtre*, a one-act ballet by Fokine, appealed to the Parisian vogue for all things Oriental. This evocation of Egyptian antiquity, with its astonishing décors by Bakst, accompanied by a mélange of music by seven Russian composers, stunned audiences primarily because of the mesmerizing interpretation of the title role by Ida Rubinstein. The wealthy, androgynously beautiful Rubinstein had studied dance as an amateur in St. Petersburg with Fokine, who had cast her in the title role of his ballet *Salomé,* based on Wilde's play. Her performance had been so shocking that it was banned by Russian censors. At Fokine's urging, Diaghilev had agreed to cast her as the sultry Queen of Egypt for the Paris season. Surrounded by slaves in jewel-colored costumes who threw roses onto an Oriental carpet, the thin, angular Rubinstein assumed poses from Egyptian hieroglyphics. This sensational work proved to be the biggest box-office draw of the entire season. Astruc's publicity materials took pains to point up the fact that Rubinstein had abandoned her husband, her family, and her important position in Russian high society in order to "devote herself to choreographic art."[62] *Le Figaro* lampooned the reactions of the society women to Rubinstein.

"Aren't you tempted, dear friend, by her scintillating and encouraging example?"

"Oh, my dear! don't even mention it! . . . with our devilish prejudices, our cursed conventionality. . . . And my children! And my husband! And especially my in-laws! There are already enough stories when I sing in the charity matinees!"[63]

If society women failed to liberate themselves as a result of Rubinstein's example, the design values of the sexually charged *Cleopatra* had an immediate and powerful influence on fashion and interior design. Soon, many a grand house in the faubourgs included an "Oriental Room," and duchesses and marquises started to appear at the opera bedecked in sari-like dresses and brightly colored veils.[64]

The one component of the spectacles that came up lacking was the music. The music critics were dismissive of the coloristic aural effects in the Russian scores—curiously, the same kind of effects that had garnered such praise on the visual plane.[65] Michel Calvocoressi, writing for *Le Mercure de France,* penned a typical admonishment. "The young Russian composers had better get to work seriously and furnish some works of a more personal character, worthy of being shown here; otherwise the displays of Russian music abroad will be forced to maintain a retrospective character that will no longer interest anyone except historians."[66] It may have been concurrence with this point of view that explained Winnaretta's cautious involvement with the first seasons of the Ballets Russes. If so, that judgment would change one short year later.

While the "Russian season" continued to conquer Paris audiences, Winnaretta spent the month of June lending her name to charity events, and lending her *atelier* for coming-out parties for her many young relations. Her niece Daisy Decazes was now a marriageable nineteen years old; in June, a "Pink and White Ball" was given to introduce her to the eligible young men of the aristocracy.[67] And, within a year, Daisy was married, to Prince Jean de Broglie.

Later in the month Winnaretta traveled to England to spend time with the Singer clan and her London social circle. In recent years her trips across the Channel had become so frequent that she decided to buy property in England. After purchasing a little cottage in Surrey, she looked for a pied-à-terre in London as well, and ultimately bought a townhouse at 213 King's Road in Chelsea. Like a good Londoner, she planted an English-style garden in the backyard, "long, straight, and wild with geraniums."[68] Hélène de Caraman-Chimay, one of the first visitors, described Winnaretta's odd new home and garden to Augustine Bulteau: "It's mysterious, incredible, hallucinatory. . . . It's as if the dreams of the inhabitants of the house smoldered and created this gaudy, exultant flora, which speaks to their souls in a low voice. . . . For me, it's not Winnie who lives in [that house], but some singular heroine out of George Eliot, who, at night, sits by the fire, telling her story."[69]

Hélène had come to England to accompany Winnaretta to the first London performance of Ethel Smyth's *The Wreckers*. Despite their three-year feud, Winnaretta had continued to take an interest in Smyth's music. It was Thomas Beecham, a longtime friend of Winnaretta's, who had agreed to mount a fully staged production of the opera at Her Majesty's Theater. In June 1909, just before the first performance, Winnaretta wrote to Smyth and invited her to visit her Chelsea townhouse. Smyth, who apparently had no inkling of Winnaretta's behind-the-scenes efforts on her behalf, refused the invitation, on the pretext that she was too busy, coyly writing to Hélène, "Winnie showed her good intentions in wanting to see me . . . perhaps twenty years from now we will be good friends."[70] Winnaretta had no intention of waiting that long to repair their broken friendship: she attended the first performance of *The Wreckers* on 22 June, and was enthralled, as she wrote to Bulteau, by "the choral music . . . admirably well-written for the voice, the excellent orchestra, a beautiful sonority with great sobriety of means."[71] She was so swept away with admiration for the powerful music that she raced backstage after the final curtain and, to the consternation of all, planted a kiss on the astonished Ethel's mouth.[72] Eventually Ethel Smyth did overcome her unrequited love, and she and Winnaretta formed a friendship that lasted for forty years. There is an interesting postlude, however to the story of the opera. When the score of *The Wreckers* was published in 1909, the stormy and passionate Prelude to Act II, entitled *On the Cliffs of Cornwall,* bore the dedication "to the Princesse Edmond de Polignac." But apparently Winnaretta had influenced much more of the opera than just the prelude. "I began that opera in the beginning of my friendship with W," recalled the composer to Bulteau. "The first act bore on it 'in nomine W'; the second, nothing; the third, on page 1 (for I had some experience in those six months) 'in spite of W.'"[73]

Back in Paris that winter, Winnaretta recommenced her musical gatherings. Debussy's music had been given a noticeably more prominent place in Winnaretta's salon in recent years. The composer's *Poissons d'or* for piano and his *Chansons de Bilitis* were the featured works on an "hour of music" on 19 January 1910.[74] More of his songs were performed by Maggie Teyte at the musical reception of 23 February 1910. The program also included three of Edmond's a cappella choruses, followed by Debussy's recent work for the same formation, *Trois Chansons de Charles d'Orléans*. Winnaretta had been particularly drawn to Debussy's choruses when she first heard them performed the previous spring at the Concerts Colonne.[75] Written as conflation of modern harmony with polyphonic texture, the *Chansons* evoked the style of the Renaissance masters whom Winnaretta so revered.[76] Winnaretta invited the composer to come to conduct his own choruses, as well as to accompany Teyte. Was she thinking of grooming Debussy as her new "house musician"? Fauré had been obliged to abdicate that de facto position when he assumed the directorship of the Conservatoire. It is unlikely that Debussy, who abhorred the *mondanités* of the aristocratic salons—as well as organizational work of any kind—would have ever accepted such a role; in any case, it was not to be. Though the composer had agreed to conduct his *Trois Chansons* at the Polignac salon, he was forced to cancel because of a lingering illness, "which," he averred, "is absolutely not my fault."[77] Désiré-Émile Inghelbrecht, a friend of Astruc, was called in as a substitute conductor.[78] Sadly, the year 1910 also marked the beginning of Debussy's slow physical deterioration, which ended with the composer's death in 1918 from a late-diagnosed cancer.

Later in the season Winnaretta paid homage to Gabriel Fauré, who had recently been elected president of a new musical organization, the Société Musicale Indépendente. The SMI was launched as a breakaway group, an aesthetic antidote to the increasing conservatism of the Société Nationale de Musique, whose president, d'Indy, had turned the older group into a bastion of "Franckism" and a de facto offshoot of the Schola. The SMI's aims, codified by Fauré and his colleague Charles Koechlin, were to produce eclectic programs of "all works worthy of interest," selected independently of "cliques, dogmas and theories."[79] Winnaretta followed the development of this new organization with interest, but continued to maintain her anti-partisan stance: as she had done five years earlier at the inception of the "Debussyist vs. Scholist" controversy (which continued to rage on), she signalled her neutrality by programming vocal works by Franck and Koechlin side by side in a January salon program.[80]

She was appreciative, however, of Fauré's unique place in modern music. His recent works combined an increasingly exploratory approach to harmony, even as he stayed the course of tradition with his aesthetic reserve and use of classical forms. Winnaretta was struck anew by the combination of power and discretion in her old friend's music when she heard his new song cycle, *La Chanson d'Eve,* in its premiere at the SMI's first concert, on 20 April 1910.[81] Wishing to do something to show her appreciation, she joined with writer Robert d'Humières in organizing an all-Fauré soiree at Versailles in June 1910. Seated next to her composer friend along the Grand Canal of the palace gardens, Winnaretta listened as an invisible orchestra, hidden in the trees, played the *Sicilienne* from "her" *Pelléas.* Fauré then accompanied a group of his own songs, sung by Reynaldo Hahn, including *Clair de lune,* set to Verlaine's beautiful poem. Suddenly, as Hahn sang the well-known line "Au calme clair de lune, triste et beau," the moon rose above the trees and bathed the shimmering water in light. The listeners sat in stunned silence.[82]

During the same period, Winnaretta sought to bring her influence to bear on behalf of Fauré's former lover, composer Adela Maddison, who had left Paris to live in Berlin.[83] To her already substantial body of songs set to English and French texts, Maddison now added a large number of newly composed *Lieder* on poems by Goethe and other German poets. Soon thereafter she completed an opera in German, *Der Talisman*. At the same time, she organized concerts of modern French music in Berlin's Choralia Saal and in the embassies.[84] To help the valiant composer gain more recognition, Winnaretta asked Augustine Bulteau to intercede in securing for Maddison the "Palmes académiques," a prestigious decoration given to those who advance the cause of French culture, education, and the arts.[85] "I know she deserves them," she wrote to Bulteau, "because I saw the work she's been doing there and am aware of the difficulties she's had to overcome. All those ministers that fill your cupboards, can't one of them help her obtain something?"[86] While this request met with no success, another of Winnaretta's intercessions bore fruit: she seems to have been instrumental, as she had been on behalf of Ethel Smyth, in convincing the directors of the Leipzig Opera to mount *Der Talisman*. The work received its premiere on 19 November 1910—almost exactly four years after the premiere of Smyth's *The Wreckers* in that city—and ran for eight performances. Winnaretta was in the audience for the first performance, and reported to Bulteau that *Der Talisman* had enjoyed "a very great and very well-deserved success."[87]

If Winnaretta performed good deeds to promote art, her old nemesis, Robert de Montesquiou used art to promote malicious deeds. Thwarted in his attemps to bring Winnaretta down through gossip and innuendo, he had used his position as occasional art journalist for *Le Figaro* more than once to vent his malevolence towards her. In a 1905 essay on the work of John Singer Sargent, Montesquiou had cast aspersions on the artist's *Venetian Interior,* attributing the drabness of the room and the ugliness of its furnishings to the fact that "perhaps it's just the Palazzo Montecuculli" (once again, intentionally misspelled) "as reconstituted by the Princesse de Polignac."[88] Another occasion for malice was provided by the first solo exhibition by Winnaretta's former lover, Romaine Brooks, at the Galeries Durand-Ruel in May 1910. Montesquiou's putative review of the exhibition included scathing comments on portraits (not all of which were included in the exhibition) of four society women painted by Brooks shortly after her arrival in Paris: Anna de Noailles (Montesquiou's cousin),[89] Eugenia Errazuriz (a future patron of Picasso and Stravinsky), "Cloton" Legrand[90]— and, of course, the Princesse de Polignac, for whose portrait Montesquiou reserved his most virulent comments. As previously noted, Brooks had softened Winnaretta's features so as not to dissatisfy her powerful patron and (then) lover; she had also portrayed her in garb evoking antiquity. These flattering "improvements" gave Montesquiou the artillery to launch new attacks on Winnaretta: although he claimed that he did not "have the honor of knowing Madame de Polignac," he wondered "why Madame Brooks saw her and portrayed her . . . with the look of Nero—but a Nero a thousand times more cruel than the one of antiquity, who did not content himself with feeding the Christians to the wild beasts, but dreamed of seeing them *pricked to death by sewing machine needles?*"[91] Shortly after the release of Montesquiou's "review," Romaine's show traveled on to London. But the portrait of Winnaretta was not included: it disappeared from view, and has not surfaced to this day. That, however, did not put an end to the malicious gossip that Winnaretta seemed to inspire. It was a situation puzzling to one staunch friend, Meg de Saint-Marceaux. Not only was the Princesse de Polignac "part of the gang"—that is, one of society's leading ladies—but "among all the *grandes dames* she alone dominates with her intelligence. I can't believe what they say about her."[92]

Malice continued to find Winnaretta in unforeseeable ways. The previous year, Augustine Bulteau was considering having some of her *Figaro* articles published as a book of essays. She asked Winnaretta if she would be willing to translate the articles into English, in view of an eventual London publication. Winnaretta agreed enthusiastically, and for over a year she worked on the translation of a half-dozen articles.[93] Unfortunately, Bulteau happened to mention the project to their mutual acquaintance, British novelist Vernon Lee. A protégée of Henry James, and a gifted author of novels and short stories on the supernatural, Lee was one of the first fiction writers to apply psychological theory to literary and aesthetic criticism.[94] She had a strong possessive streak, however, especially with respect to Bulteau, with whom, at one time, she may have had an intimate relationship. When Lee learned of Winnaretta's and Bulteau's joint project, she asked that the translated articles be sent directly to her, so that she could offer her professional opinion. Apparently it was jealousy rather than altruism that motivated Lee's offer. Winnaretta's translations, Lee averred, had not captured the journalist's "robust and subtle style"; she did not write with enough abandon; the whole project, she implied, was unsalvageable.[95] Winnaretta wrote to Bulteau, "It's unfortunately not in my rotten character to let go, and I will only do it if you order me to do so in the most severe manner, but I don't like Vernon and I don't want to send her any more of my work."[96] Finally, after a year of labor, Winnaretta's translation project came to naught: none of the articles ever appeared in print.

Disgruntled, she left off pursuing artistic endeavors, devoting her energies to more mundane activities. Anna and Mathieu de Noailles had moved into a new apartment at 40 rue Scheffer, a quiet street abutting rue Cortambert. Their sunlit fifth-floor windows looked out onto Winnaretta's garden, and Winnaretta watched the Noailles's renovation going on just beyond the reach of her back yard. Joining in the spirit of taking things apart and putting them back together, she finished out the year 1910 by having her Cavaillé-Coll organ dismantled and rebuilt, all 3725 pieces of it.[97]

Winnaretta would not have to wait long to be back in the center of things. An important phase of her career as a music patron was about to begin.

The Astonishing Years

On a winter night in the Place de la Concorde, Jean Cocteau walked along with Diaghilev, seeking praise for his work, looking for a sign that the Russian was impressed with his flamboyant writings. Diaghilev issued his renowned directive, "Young man, astonish me!" With these words, the impresario summed up the essence of art, the irreducible elements that made it function: surprise, wonderment. "That phrase," Cocteau would later recall, "saved me from a flashy career. . . . I owe [the break with spiritual frivolity] to the desire to astound that Russian prince to whom life was tolerable only to the extent to which he could summon up marvels."[1] Ever since the days of The World of Art, Diaghilev's great gift had always been his ability to create works and realize spectacles that had never been seen, heard, or imagined before.

But such marvels could not reach their intended audiences without material support. If the colorful spectacles of Diaghilev's first Paris years left the Princesse de Polignac less than astonished, what the impresario summoned up in 1910 finally converted her from a somewhat detached admirer of Diaghilev's ideas and works into an active, public supporter of the Ballets Russes. The marvel was a musician, Igor Stravinsky.

Diaghilev's ability to astonish was not based solely on inspiration: he kept a weather eye on his audience—the aristocracy and the new moneyed class—and on the press, all of whom still gathered on a regular basis in the private salons. He took seriously the critical admonitions that music "of a more personal character" by young composers was needed if the Ballets Russes were indeed to represent the vanguard of modern synthetic art works.[2] The impresario immediately went on a search for young composers whose music had the power to rival the décors of Bakst and Benois, the choreography of Fokine, and the virtuoso dancing of Nijinsky and Karsavina. Diaghilev sought out the French composers with the greatest standing in the musical salons—Hahn, Debussy, Fauré, and Ravel—to produce new ballet scores.[3] Debussy and Fauré declined the commissions, but Ravel accepted, and began work on a Fokine/Bakst production, *Daphnis et Chloé*, while Hahn agreed to collaborate on an Orientalist work, *Le Dieu bleu*, with a librettist who represented his aesthetic antithesis: Jean Cocteau.

Fokine had created a new "Russian" choreography, which broke free from the French and Italian courtly forms upon which traditional Russian ballet was based. Up until now, his revolutionary dances had been set to colorful, brilliant "Orientalist" music, or potpourris of Russian music by the established masters—Borodin, Tchaikovsky, Rimsky-Korsakov, among others. As these works were proven crowd-pleasers, Diaghilev had not thought to deviate from this successful formula in planning his 1910 season. Even if the steamy and primitive *Schéhérazade* represented a new level of balletic eroticism even for Fokine, the music was already familiar to Paris audiences from the Ballets Russes's 1907 season, when Rimsky-Korsakov came to conduct his own work. But now, in seeking to bring to Paris "the *first* Russian ballet, since there is no such thing,"[4] Diaghilev was looking for a score by a young composer from his native land to accomplish this formidable task. In 1909, the impresario had become acquainted with the music of Rimsky-Korsakov's young student, Igor Stravinsky, whose *Fireworks* and *Scherzo fantastique* were being performed in St. Petersburg; at that time Diaghilev asked Stravinsky to arrange some Chopin piano works for a new Fokine ballet, *Les Sylphides*. The ambitious young composer accepted the task: he had heard about the fantastically successful Russian music programs mounted in Paris during the 1907 and 1908 seasons, and believed—correctly—that a connection with the Ballets Russes could help his career.

This first collaboration between Diaghilev and Stravinsky would have long-ranging and monumental consequences for the history of music. Making what was arguably one of the most astute decisions in his career as an impresario, Diaghilev commissioned Stravinsky to create the score for his new "Russian ballet," based on the libretto *The Firebird*. It was soon evident that Diaghilev had once again summoned up another marvel. Stravinsky fulfilled the commission in under six months, and *The Firebird* received its premiere at the Opéra 25 June 1910. The work was an instant success. Stravinsky's brilliantly orchestrated and executed music exploited every element of Russian musical "exoticism." It signaled the realization of The World of Art's original vision of a "total work of art": a successful integration of music, dance, and visual elements.[5] Diaghilev hastily added additional performances of *The Firebird* to his Paris season, and promised further commissions to his young "discovery."

In her memoirs, Winnaretta asserts that her appreciation of Stravinsky's talent was immediate: "From the first, it seemed to me impossible not to recognize the importance of this new genius."[6] Journalist Jean Desbordes would note her special interest in the young composer after the debut of *The Firebird*. "With his troupe, the extraordinary Nijinsky, with the works that he inspired and mounted, Diaghilev was preparing to change all the rules of art, preparing to change us, our era, the modern arts. . . . But among all the Russians, the Princesse Edmond went straight towards Stravinsky."[7] The slim, dandyish composer's aloofness appealed to her as much as his music. That fall she invited him to dine; he thanked her by sending tickets to concerts of his music.[8] The following spring the two spent time together in Rome, where Stravinsky was putting the finishing touches on his *Petrushka*.[9]

Her new friendship with Stravinsky brought Winnaretta into the midst of Diaghilev's coterie. Among this group she met the impresario's "muse," Mrs. Alfred Edwards, née Misia Godebska. A musical and artistic young woman of Polish descent, Misia had been married at age fifteen to Thadée Natanson, editor of the arts magazine *La Revue blanche*. Through Natanson, she became a friend of the young lions of the Paris avant-garde, whose members included Debussy, Mallarmé, and Valéry. A close friend of Ravel, she became the dedicatee of the composer's *Le Cygne* from *Histoires naturelles*, and *La Valse*. Her voluptuous figure and mysterious smile were immortalized in canvasses of Vuillard, Bonnard, Toulouse-Lautrec, Renoir, and Redon. She divorced Natanson to marry the fabulously wealthy Edwards, owner of the daily *Le Matin*. By time she met Diaghilev, Misia was separated from Edwards and living with Spanish painter José-Maria Sert, whom she would marry some years later. Misia gained a reputation as a formidable maneuverer on behalf of her friends in the artistic world. She became Diaghilev's closest confidant, and, frequently, his eleventh-hour financial savior: during many seasons, it would often fall to Misia to scare up the hefty sums owed to the impresario's creditors in order to bring up the curtain on certain Ballets Russes performances.[10]

Winnaretta didn't care much for the flamboyant Misia, but she liked her lover Sert, a Catalan native from a wealthy aristocratic family. The earthy, hedonistic artist had moved to Paris in 1899 and established a studio in the 7th *arrondissement*, where he gave notorious parties. He first came to the attention of the Paris art community with the acceptance and subsequent critical acclaim of his work in the 1908 Salon. Winnaretta surely met Sert around this time, possibly through their friend in common, Colette. By 1910 the artist was a member of the Diaghilev circle. More impressed by his canvasses than by his trademark cape and sombrero, Winnaretta invited him to show some of his paintings in her *atelier* in February 1911.[11] Sert had recently become interested in mural decorations, and was one of the first artists of his time to concentrate his creative efforts in that medium.[12] Winnaretta, who was now hosting many of her salon gatherings in the large avenue Henri-Martin music room, was seeking an audacious modernist artwork to adorn its walls. In 1911 she commissioned Sert to create a mural for the space. The artist customarily worked in bright primary colors, reflecting his Iberian heritage. But for Winnaretta's music room, with its high ceilings, somber dark green walls, Venetian chandeliers, and mirror-backed shutters, Sert created an elaborate set of murals over the capitals in black and gold, almost baroque in their opulence. In these scenes monkeys and eagles cavorted in the flora with satyrs, cupids, and frolicking female nudes. Sert's juxtaposition of a primitive and overtly sexual

subject matter with style elements of the high baroque was audacious, even
shocking. The murals certainly represented a change for Winnaretta, who
usually exhibited more discretion in sartorial and decorative matters. Clearly
the "exotic" influence of the Ballets Russes on fashion and interior design
was finally making its way into her house. When asked by a guest what
genre Sert represented, Winnaretta responded, "Genius genre."[13]

In Winnaretta's elegant music rooms a fascinating cross-section of the
avant-garde and the descendants of the *ancien régime* met, conversed, and
united through music. Here the Abbé Mugnier, convivial confessor to the
salon hostesses,[14] discussed the meaning of life with philosopher Henri
Bergson; here the writer Princesse Marthe Bibesco exchanged witticisms
with Jacques-Émile Blanche; here Jean Cocteau was introduced to Anna de
Noailles, whose corporeal fragility was belied by the astonishing volubility
of her speech. In recent years, Anna had turned her chronic ill health into
an art form. She would arrive bedecked in shawls and Turkish beads, collapse upon a divan, open wide her large black eyes, flutter her hands, and
launch into paroxysms of language—unstoppable, brilliantly incomprehensible monologues that would hypnotize those gathered around her.[15] Cocteau
was fascinated by the contrast between Anna's self-absorbed spectacle, and
the Princesse de Polignac's stoic demeanor, her profile resembling "a rock
worn away by the sea."[16] On one memorable June evening, Cocteau watched
Anna as "she talked, and talked, and talked; people started crowding the
room, youngsters at her feet and the older guests around her in a semi-
circle."[17] During this spectacle, Winnaretta, who was accustomed to Anna's
vocal outbursts, stood by, watching with a bemused smile, "wagging her
head like a malicious young elephant."[18]

Winnaretta was hiding more serious thoughts behind that smile. The
tenth anniversary of Edmond's death was approaching, and Winnaretta
had been reflecting for over a year on the best way to honor his memory.
The past thirty years had seen a proliferation of private philanthropic foundations in Paris, established to underwrite all manner of worthy projects.[19]
Winnaretta decided to create a charitable foundation that would link the
names of those she had most cherished: her father and her husband. In
1910, she established a "Fondation Singer-Polignac." Perhaps with the social barbs of the past year fresh in her memory, Winnaretta chose to preside
over the foundation the writer and political figure Comte Paul-Gabriel
d'Haussonville, one of the most esteemed members of the royalist faction
of the aristocracy.[20] In allying herself with the *ancien régime,* she thumbed
her nose at her detractors, and made herself into a patron to be reckoned
with.

In choosing an initial project for her new foundation, she remembered
that her father, in his last years, had expressed the desire to improve the
lives of working people in Paignton through an amelioration of housing
and schools in the village.[21] Winnaretta decided to realize Isaac's dream

through her own philanthropic work, by underwriting a public housing project in Paris. The need for affordable housing for the city's working class was particularly urgent. Day laborers with low-paying jobs lived in squalid, decaying buildings on crowded, narrow streets; hallways and alleyways in these terrible dwellings were strewn with refuse, and access to light and fresh air was almost non-existent. The district with the highest density of poorly housed workers was the Glacières section of the 13th *arrondissement,* on the Left Bank.[22] In this neighborhood, at 72 rue de la Colonie, near Paris's southern perimeter, Winnaretta bought a large plot of land on which to establish a low-cost housing site for working-class families. She engaged a young architect, Georges Vaudoyer, to design the buildings and oversee construction. Vaudoyer, from the fourth generation of a distinguished family of architects, had already gained a reputation as an innovator in public housing: Winnaretta's project was the third in a series of thirteen such housing projects that he would oversee between 1906 and 1930.[23] Vaudoyer's design consisted of two brick six-story buildings, which opened out onto a large courtyard and garden. The sixty-five apartments within, of varying sizes, were models of modern efficiency and comfort; all were equipped with modern kitchens and bathrooms, running water, and gas heaters, and were designed to give maximum access to fresh air and light. The rents were extremely modest, from 220 to 410 francs a year (roughly between three and six thousand dollars in today's currency). Families with children were more than welcome; indeed, large families were encouraged to apply for spaces. Two sets of bannisters, one at children's height, were installed in the stairwells. Forty individual garden plots had been laid out behind the courtyard; for a small supplemental fee, the inhabitants could rent a plot, where they could cultivate flowers and plants according to their own needs and tastes.[24] Vaudoyer's project, which was lauded by official architectural organizations in France, would serve as a prototype for future urban housing realizations. One contemporary critic remarked on the "pleasant aspect of the housing, where one lives happily. Everything here is cheerful. . . . [T]here is cleanliness and brightness, outside and inside."[25] Winnaretta's total contribution to the project was 600,000 francs, roughly nine million dollars in today's currency. At the official inauguration of the buildings in the spring of 1911, the Comte d'Haussonville urged the public sector to follow Winnaretta's lead. The Princesse de Polignac, he declared, had taken steps to resolve one of the most complex problems of current existence "through the inspiration of pure philanthropy."[26]

This was but the first of Winnaretta's tributes to her husband. Any suitable gesture honoring Edmond's memory, would, of course, have to involve music. To commemorate the tenth anniversary of his death, 8 August 1901, Winnaretta organized a musical matinee in June, at the height of the *grande saison,* featuring a diverse variety of "modern music" for solo piano, choir, and full orchestra.[27] The program featured an 1898 piece for mixed a cappella choir by Edmond de Polignac, *Le Vallon,* shockingly atonal for its time. The contemporary school of French music was represented by works of Florent Schmitt, Désiré Inghelbrecht, Claude Debussy, and, of course, Gabriel Fauré. Armande de Polignac's ballet score, *Les Mille et Une Nuits* received its first performance. Percy Grainger's *The Camp,* for mixed chorus, was the only non-French work on the program. The concert closed with a new classic, Ravel's *Pavane,* one of the first works by the young generation of composers to be dedicated to Winnaretta.

Winnaretta may have been rethinking her definition of modern music after seeing the astonishing first performance of *Petrushka* by the Ballets Russes at the Châtelet two nights later, on 13 June 1911. The premiere was a triumph, in part because of the "naïveté, sorrowful melancholy . . . [and] 'animal' grace"[28] that Nijinsky, in the title role, brought to Fokine's imaginative choreography. But just as impressive were what the papers would call the "little skillfully colored atoms"[29] of kaleidoscopically shifting rhythms and orchestral textures, brilliantly evoking the bustle and energy of the St. Petersburg fair. Stravinsky's angular music was much more than a colorful evocation of old Russia, however; it would challenge the listener's expectations of how melody and harmony interacted, and it would forever free rhythm from the tyranny of the barline. It would offer an exciting glimpse into the modernist music to come.

Winnaretta does not mention *Petrushka* specifically in her memoirs, but correspondence indicates that she went to visit the composer in Rome during the month of May, just as the finishing touches were being put on the new ballet music. No doubt the subject matter, one historically dear to her heart, appealed to her: pantomime, puppetry, the fair, the carnival—the entertainments of her childhood. However, another very specific element in Stravinsky's music may have resonated deeply with her. There is no way of knowing if she and the composer discussed the work's compositional elements—or, better yet, if Stravinsky played portions of this revolutionary piece for her. It will never be known if the composer might have mentioned (or demonstrated) that one of the principal organizing factors of the work was an eight-tone scale derived from Russian folk tradition. This scale had been appropriated and codified by his teacher Rimsky-Korsakov in 1867, and since that date put to copious use by most of the young composers in the Rimsky circle.[30] It is tantalizing to entertain the notion that at some point—during their conversations, or later, at the performance—Winnaretta recognized Stravinsky's scale as the same one that Edmond de Polignac believed himself to have "invented" in 1879, the octatonic scale. Perhaps Winnaretta saw Stravinsky as not just a gifted composer, but as the torch-bearer in the perpetuation of her husband's musical ideas.

The need to find a suitable means of perpetuating Edmond's memory continued to preoccupy her through the summer months. It was a topic of conversation with a young Englishman whose acquaintance Winnaretta made while in Venice. Sir Ronald Storrs, an intelligent and cultivated young man at the beginning of his diplomatic career, was making the first of what would become many visits to that city.[31] After serving in the Egyptian Civil Service, Storrs had recently been appointed Oriental Secretary at the British agency in Cairo. His keen intellect and fluency in several Arabic dialects allowed him to distinguish himself early on, and he would soon gain the good esteem of Lord Kitchener and Sir Henry McMahon. The two had much in common, including a passionate love of music, the classics, and contemporary literature. Storrs was also a homosexual man in a congenial marriage of convenience. He admired the princess for being a "liberal and evocative patroness." Winnaretta introduced her new friend to the poetry of Anna de Noailles and the music of Ethel Smyth. Evidently she trusted him to an unusual degree, and shared intimate memories of Edmond with him; she even allowed him to read the little notebook of Edmond's *bons mots* that she had collected. Storrs appreciated the prince's "chance pearls, preserved by her from oblivion," for example, his observation that "If I were cut in two, one half would speak badly of the other; but if I were reattached, I wouldn't hold a grudge."[32]

It was surely Storrs who suggested to Winnaretta that she establish a literary prize in Edmond's name. She liked the idea, and in late September she contacted the Academic Committee of the Royal Society of Literature in London, offering a substantial sum of money to establish a prize for literature as a memorial to the name of her husband. She proposed that, for a provisional period of five years, an "Edmond de Polignac Prize" of £100 would be awarded each November to a British author whose work had appeared the previous year.[33] During the month of October, while she entertained royalty from many nations at the palazzo,[34] she hammered out the details of the prize with the Academic Committee. It was to assist in the formation of literature and style, and to go to an individual who showed future promise.[35] One provision of the agreement upon which she insisted particularly was a clause stipulating that women would not be excluded from competing for the prize. Winnaretta knew well that even though no specific law barred women from being elected to one of the forty seats among the "immortals" of the Académie Française, "tradition [had] created an unwritten law."[36] In November she traveled to London for the awarding of the first Polignac prize, which went to Walter de la Mare for his supernatural novel, *The Return*. Winnaretta may not have been completely happy with the committee's choice, the story of the soul of a dead man that returns from its grave and fastens itself onto the flesh of the living. Winnaretta described the work to Bulteau as a "weird book."[37]

Winnaretta spent much of the first winter months with Anna de Noailles, seeing the New Year in with her. Anna's chronic ill health had recently taken a turn for the worse, in part due to strains in her marriage. Mathieu de Noailles, in all other respects a loving husband and father, had in recent years incurred crippling gambling debts. To help mend the marital as well as the financial damages of her friends, Winnaretta paid off a substantial portion of Noailles's debt, 150,000 francs.[38] Anna nonetheless decided to take the drastic step of legally separating from her husband, in order to avoid liability with his creditors for the remainder of the sum. On 14 February, the Tribunal of the Seine pronounced the separation of the couple. Winnaretta and Augustine Bulteau stayed close to Anna, to support her through this difficult period.[39]

Another member of this circle of friends sought Winnaretta's help at this time. In 1910, Ethel Smyth had fallen under the sway of the charismatic British suffragette Mrs. Emmeline Pankhurst, founder of the Women's Social and Political Union (WSPU), an organization fighting to secure the vote for women. So moved was Smyth by Mrs. Pankhurst and her indefatigable campaign for universal suffrage, that she put her compositional career on hold to devote all her energies to the movement. As suffragettes became more militant, their actions and their treatment by the police became more violent. After participating in a 1911 campaign to destroy property, Smyth was imprisoned at Holloway Jail with Mrs. Pankhurst, her daughters Christabel and Sylvia, and two dozen other women. When the protesters staged a hunger strike, they were force-fed by prison guards. Upon her release from Holloway, Smyth composed the Suffragette hymn, *The March of the Women*. The song served as a battle cry on the day that came to be known as "Black Friday," 2 March 1912, when hundreds of suffragettes marched through London carrying stones and hammers. The women smashed windows and threw stones at the prime minister's house, causing thousands of pounds of damage. Smyth was reincarcerated along with Mrs. Pankhurst and scores of other protesters, but Christabel Pankhurst fled to France to continue the work of the suffragettes while its other leaders were in prison.[40] Smyth got word to Winnaretta that Christabel would soon be arriving in Paris, and would require help getting settled. While the details are not documented, there is evidence that Winnaretta provided the suffragette with comfortable quarters and introductions to influential individuals sympathetic to her cause.[41] The struggle to gain the vote for women was not yet an issue whose time had come in France: left-wing politicians didn't promote the cause because they were afraid that women would vote for conservatives, and the Church opposed suffrage because it believed that the emancipation of women would break up the family.[42] Winnaretta's opinions about the suffrage movement are not known. Her feminism was subtle, directed rather towards women's creative accomplishments than political causes. She probably sympathized abstractly with the goals of suffrage, without feeling the desire to get actively involved. Whatever material aid was given to Christabel represented such a minute portion of Winnaretta's philanthropy that she surely gave it little thought, if any.[43]

Meanwhile, Christabel was directing the WSPU from Paris, communicating her plans of action through her appointed deputy, Annie Kenney.

Kenney, responsible for carrying out every aspect of the movement's work, would cross the Channel once a week to receive her instructions from the exiled suffrage leader. On one occasion Kenney arrived in Paris and was informed that Christabel had gone to the Princesse de Polignac's house. She went to avenue Henri-Martin to find her. It was a memorable experience for Kenney, a former mill worker from a poor Lancashire family. "I was shown into the largest room I had ever seen in a private house. I felt so tiny! There were beautiful books everywhere. I picked one up and found it to be a translation of Sappho's poetry. The colour of the leather binding was the shade of a ripe pink cherry."[44] Annie Kenney must have wondered at the dichotomy between the radical politics of Christabel Pankhurst and the kind of luxurious environment in which she was carrying forth the struggle. Christabel, in turn, apparently had nothing but laudatory things to say about Winnaretta and her benevolence, for shortly thereafter Ethel Smyth wrote to her old friend, much moved by her efforts on the suffragette's behalf. "C[hristabel] told us of all your kindness and generosity, which thrills us all. You *are* a brick, and I think Mrs. P.'s greatest comfort is to know she has friends like you."[45] In gratitude, Smyth composed a chorus for women's voices called *Laggard Dawn*, based on a melody by Edmond de Polignac.[46] It was published later that year, along with *March of the Women*, in a group of three choral works entitled *Songs of Sunrise*.

If Winnaretta's involvement in the political arena was a by-product of friendship, her interest in the sciences, especially the application of science to practical invention, was genuine. In recent years she had followed the work of the scientist Édouard Branly, whose experiments with radio-conductivity led to the first successful wireless telegraph transmissions, in 1899, by Gugliemo Marconi. Branly himself did not come to public prominence until 1911, when, after a politically charged campaign, he was elected to the Academy, defeating Marie Curie by one vote. Branly was hoping to devote more time to his scientific projects, but his faculty position at Paris's Institut Catholique required him to carry a full-time teaching load in exchange for access to the school's laboratory. The funding that would enable him to progress in his research was not easily forthcoming. His most pressing need was to build the apparatus which could test his theories. Winnaretta found out about the scientist's plight and in May 1912 she contacted Branly, offering to fund his laboratory with annual subventions of four thousand francs over a period of seven years.[47] The scientist's work was receiving much public attention at that time, not altogether in a positive light, for the importance and originality of his invention of the coherer was being negated by the Marconi "faction" of his profession. The "duel" was receiving much press coverage.[48] Winnaretta, still keeping a low profile in philanthropic circles, was nervous about having her name vaunted in association with this extremely generous act of *mécénat*. Shortly after the proposal of support was made to Branly, she wrote to Bulteau: "Everything is arranged now so that Branly can continue his work comfortably during the seven years that he owes to the Institut Catholique. I want to ask if you would be willing to use your great influence at the *Figaro* so that *my name won't come up* . . . it would be *very painful* for me. A word from you would arrange everything."[49]

Winnaretta seemed to be keeping a low profile in the musical realm as well: the musical offerings in her salon during the *petite saison* were relatively conservative in comparison to past years. On 15 February 1912, pianist Blanche Selva performed works by J. S. Bach and César Franck, selections from Albéniz's *Iberia,* and new works by her colleagues from the Schola Cantorum: Vincent d'Indy, Déodat de Séverac, Paul Le Flem, and Albert Roussel.[50] Only Roussel's Suite in F-sharp Minor was modernist in nature: although the titles of the movements (Prélude, Sicilienne, Bourrée, and Ronde) suggested the high baroque, the harmonic idiom was rich and daring, foreshadowing the composer's later style. Winnaretta's next gathering, on 22 February, featured Franck's long and penetrating D-Major String Quartet, played by the Geloso Quartet. The choice of repertoire was curious, given Winnaretta's professed antipathy towards Franck's music. The guests on this occasion included American expatriate writer Edith Wharton,[51] who had come with Winnaretta's niece Jane d'Oilliamson, Wharton's longtime friend and a translator of a number of her short stories.[52]

The program of 10 March was an even more elaborate affair, attended by a large crowd of ambassadors, aristocrats, and artists. It featured mezzo-soprano Claire Croiza, partnered at the piano by Reynaldo Hahn, who conducted his own works, performed by chamber orchestra, on the second half of the program.[53] The favor that Winnaretta showed to Hahn's compositions was not only a testimonial to twenty years of friendship, but was also was emblematic of her role as intermediary and negotiator between the private and public musical spheres. She still genuinely enjoyed Hahn's music, particularly some of his recent songs (especially his *Études latines*),[54] and devoted at least one program every season to her friend's music. Hahn's continued high standing in the salons (Stravinsky dubbed Hahn "the salon idol of Paris"[55]) bore fruit in the public arena: a "Reynaldo Hahn Festival" took place in Paris in May 1911.[56] The composer's popularity had not escaped the notice of Diaghilev, who relied on the wealthy salon hostesses to fill the seats and coffers of his ballet seasons. Looking to add another "exotic" production to his future Ballets Russes programs, and hoping to profit from Hahn's social connections, Diaghilev engaged him to write the score for a new Orientalist ballet, *Le Dieu bleu.* The librettists for the work were Frédéric "Coco" Madrazo (Hahn's cousin and a wealthy artistic dilettante), and Jean Cocteau, ecstatic to be invited, finally, into the bosom of Diaghilev's "family." A two-piano version of Hahn's lush ballet music—a "Polynesian idyll," loosely based on a Hindu legend—was performed in

1911 in St. Petersburg, where the composer met with cultural dignitaries and was feted as an important French musical celebrity. The first performance of *Le Dieu bleu* would be taking place in May 1912, the culmination of a season that would include the premiere of Hahn's ballet *La Fête chez Thérèse* at the Opéra, where the composer would also be conducting *Don Giovanni*. Winnaretta's own de facto "Hahn festival" in her salon reflected the high profile that her friend would be enjoying that spring.

Regrettably, success eluded Hahn and Cocteau and their Blue God in the public arena. Despite the spectacular décors by Bakst and the brilliant dancing by Nijinsky and Karsavina, the audiences apparently had had enough of formulaic exoticism. According to Benois, Hahn's score didn't rise above the level of "pleasant, drawing-room music," and was described by one chronicler as "India seen through the eyes of Massenet, sweet and insipid."[57] Even more devastating for Hahn was the subsequent *succès de scandale* accorded to his aesthetic nemesis, Debussy, after the notorious first performance, on 29 May, of his *Prélude à l'après-midi d'un faune*. The piece also marked Nijinsky's first assignment as choreographer for the Ballets Russes, and in this role the dancer introduced a revolutionary new style into his art. Nijinsky conceived a work in the style of Grecian bas-reliefs, and his choreography alternated angular movement and frieze-like poses of the dancers in profile.[58] The audience was confused and disappointed by the absence of Nijinsky's customary ecstatic leaps. The final gesture of Nijinsky's Faun was particularly shocking: a graphically masturbatory representation, evoked by manipulation of a scarf, of the Faun's passion for the Nymph. When the curtain fell, there was an uproar, and in defiance, Diaghilev ordered an immediate repetition of the ballet.

Winnaretta was in the audience with Augustine Bulteau that evening.[59] Her reactions to the revolutionary choreography are not noted, but the music surely carried her thoughts back to Edmond, with whom she had first heard Debussy's *Prélude* in 1894. Among her husband's papers was a letter that Debussy had written in 1895, in which the composer described his desire "to give a general impression of the poem," rather than to follow Mallarmé's text too closely,[60] thus in one stroke distancing himself from the Wagnerian drama of ideas and organizational use of leitmotifs. This was, in Debussy's words, "music without any respect for Key! and rather in a Mode that tries to contain all the nuances."[61] This very harmonic ambiguity and instability, which created the sensuality so alluring to the modernists, was the very trait that the conservative Hahn detested in Debussy's music. Hahn's opinion of Ravel's new *Daphnis et Chloé* was no better. He couldn't understand how Winnaretta could find pleasure in an aesthetic that he considered tasteless, and may have taken it as a personal affront when he discovered that she would be hosting a concert by the SMI in her *atelier* on 11 June 1912.[62] During this period of evolving musical modernism Winnaretta tried to convince her old friend that it was worth the trouble to struggle with certain works, while at the same time maintaining his own artistic integrity. Hahn addressed these issues some years later in a letter:

> I am happy that you always regard me as the opposite of *those people.* You know what care I have always taken not to give my allegiance to their odious associations. My music is *what it is* but it will never be *what they like,* and I'm very glad of it! . . . [Prince Edmond's] saying is very fitting, as was everything that he said and thought. Real taste doesn't indicate, certainly, that one has heart; but it signals a little corner of the heart, secret and privileged. Unfortunately, that little corner is very sensitive, very sad, and those who cultivate it rarely know "perfect happiness."[63]

The clash between old and new forms of art was a foreground topic when the 1912 Polignac Prize was awarded to John Masefield, for his 1911 realist narrative poem, *The Everlasting Mercy.* This work tells the story of Saul Kane, who begins as a liar, cheat, and drunken carouser, but experiences an epiphany that leads him to a love for nature and mankind, and ultimately to a state of grace and redemption. Public opinion of the work was strongly divided: while the poem, written in colloquial language, was denounced from church pulpits (and decried by Lord Alfred Douglas as being "nine-tenths sheer filth"), James M. Barrie, who presented Masefield with the award on 29 November 1912, described the work as "incomparably the finest literature."[64] Winnaretta, who greatly admired Masefield's "splendid" poems, received the news of the Academic Committee's decision to award him the Polignac Prize with "the greatest satisfaction."[65]

After the Paris season Winnaretta set off for her annual summer trip to England. Her sojourn included a weekend stop at Coombe Court, the country estate of her friends the Marquess and Marchioness of Ripon. The Ripons were London's leading patrons of the arts. Their particular passion was opera; in the words of their grandson Charles Duff, they "virtually ran Covent Garden."[66] Gladys Ripon was also a patron of progressive art: she sponsored Diaghilev's first London season, and often hosted the Ballets Russes artists and their coterie at Coombe Court. During Winnaretta's visit, the other guests included Diaghilev, Nijinsky, Mary Hunter (Ethel Smyth's sister), Bernard Berenson, Edith Wharton, and Percy Grainger.[67] As with Élisabeth Greffulhe, Winnaretta's relations with Gladys Ripon might best be described as friendly rivalry: although both women were imperious and controlling—especially when it came to "their" artists—they were able to surmount their similarities well enough to enjoy a cordial friendship.

From England, Winnaretta was off to Venice. The Palazzo Dario, former summer residence of the Comtesse de La Baume, Augustine Bulteau's companion, had been recently leased by a rather more colorful figure, symbolic of the "new," less quiet Venice: the Marchesa Luisa Casati. The Marchesa made herself legendary on the basis of her accoutrements: her lavish gowns, her expensive jewelry, and most especially the tiger that customarily lay stretched out at her feet. In 1910 Casati acquired the magnficent Palazzo Venier dei Leoni,[68] where, for the next fourteen years, she gave a series of fancy balls that added to her posthumous renown. At the height of the Ballets Russes mania, she appeared at the top of the steps leading to her garden in a splendiferous costume designed by Léon Bakst. The tiger was still at her feet, but it had been drugged for the occasion, so as not to frighten off the unitiated guests. At the end of the party some of the guests took the tiger to the Piazza San Marco, where the more sedate Venetians leaving the theatres were treated to a frightening sight as they alighted into the open air.[69] The animal, and its equally dangerous companions back at the Palazzo Venier, added to the Marchesa's carefully groomed mystique as a sex goddess, albeit a rather lurid one.

In early October, Winnaretta joined Lady Ripon for a brief stay in Ouchy, one of the charming resort towns around Lake Geneva. The two women stopped to look for Stravinsky in the neighboring town of Clarens, where the composer would be spending the winter months.[70] Stravinsky was nowhere to be found, however; he and his family were still en route from their Russian estate in Ustilig, and would not arrive until the end of the month.[71] Winnaretta was disappointed: she had been mulling over ideas for a project that would involve Stravinsky, and wanted to share her thoughts with the composer.[72] These thoughts had crystallized by the time Winnaretta set off for Stuttgart to attend the premiere of Richard Strauss's *Ariadne auf Naxos* on 25 October.[73] The new opera marked a radical point of departure for the composer from the controversial *Salome*: it signaled the beginning of Strauss's about-face towards a more conservative harmonic palette, and a classical-era conception of style, in which the music was set forth in clear forms, dominating the text, objective in its expression. Strauss's abandonment of his previous Wagnerian model also signaled the beginning of what would be labeled a decade later as "neoclassicism," a movement that would influence an entire generation of modern composers, especially French composers.

Listening to *Ariadne*, Winnaretta experienced something of an epiphany, setting her on a path that would define the rest of her life as a patron. She was struck by the opera's small dramatic proportions and play-within-a-play format, which included comic elements and characters drawn from the Italian *commedia dell'arte*. The music too was written for small ensemble, a chamber orchestra of thirty-six players. In short, *Ariadne* was a work that might fit comfortably into a sufficiently capacious home space like the Polignac salon. "I had the impression," Winnaretta wrote, "that, after Richard Wagner and [the earlier works of] Richard Strauss, the days of big orchestras were over and that it would be delightful to return to a small orchestra of well chosen players and instruments."[74] She started to imagine her salon as the ideal place to launch a new repertoire reflecting this new style, and she decided "to ask different composers to write short works for me for small orchestra of about twenty performers."[75] And the first composer who came to mind was the one that most represented to her the future of musical modernism: Stravinsky. By the time she returned to Paris Winnaretta's plan was fully formulated. She wrote to Stravinsky on 20 November.

> You know my very great admiration for your talent. You will not be surprised then that I thought of you in asking you to write for me a pantomime, or a symphonic work, which would belong to me and which I would have played in my music room which you are familiar with. It would obviously have to be a *short* work and for a small orchestra— maybe 30 to 36 musicians. Will you permit me to propose that you accept for this work a sum of 3000 francs—and to ask you if it could be finished around the 8th of April so that I can have it performed at my house around the end of April or the beginning of May.[76]

Stravinsky apparently responded to the plan with enthusiasm, offering Winnaretta the exclusive rights of performance until such time that the part would be published. She jumped into the details of the plan with fervor:

> Does the following orchestra suit you? 5 1st violins, 5 2nd violins, 3 violas, 2 cellos (or 3), 1 bass, 2 flutes, 2 oboes, 2 clarinets, 2 bassoons, 2 horns, 2 trumpets, 1 harp, 1 percussion. The performance date could be put off until the month of November next if your work prevents you from being ready earlier. I had thought of a piece which could last around 15 minutes.[77]

And two days later:

> To my list of yesterday there could be added perhaps a piano and a celesta—but do what will suit you best. Do you have something for 2 pianos or 4 hands that I could play?[78]

It is astonishing to read these words, in which Winnaretta essentially dictates the orchestration of the proposed work to the composer, but Stravinsky did not seem to take offense; on the contrary, he got into the spirit of things:

> Now having thought about my future work I have decided to compose a Concerto for Piano and Orchestra. So here are the instruments that I would need: 2 Flutes (the 1st changing to the piccolo), 2 Oboes, 2 Clarinets (the 2nd changing to the Bass Clarinet), 2 Bassoons (and the Con-

trabassoon if that would be possible), 2 Horns in F, 2 Trumpets in C, 2 Tympani, a Grand Piano (of course), a Harp, 2 Quartets (2 First Violins, 2 Second Violins, 2 Violas, 2 Cellos) and a Double Bass. . . . Unfortunately I have nothing to offer you in the way of 2- or 4-hand music except an old thing (4 *Études pour piano*—rather difficult besides) that you wouldn't like, I'm certain.[79]

Winnaretta responded on 12 December that "the combination . . . suits me perfectly."[80] It would be years, however, before Stravinsky actually began to compose the commissioned work, as he became swept up in the composition of *The Rite of Spring* and its aftermath.

Meanwhile, Winnaretta made a second substantial offer of support to her composer niece Armande. Marriage and motherhood had not slowed Armande down at all, and she continued to pursue her compositional activities with vigor. Even though she had received much of her training at the conservative Schola Cantorum, her studies had brought her into contact with modernist composers associated with the institution: Albert Roussel, Edgard Varèse, and Erik Satie (who, in 1905, at the age of thirty-nine, had entered the Schola to study counterpoint). Like many other young composers, Armande initially attempted to earn a reputation by writing operas. Her first work in this genre, *La Petite Sirène*, was based on the Hans Christian Andersen fairy tale, and had a libretto by Willy. When the opera received its first production by the Opéra de Nice in 1909, Armande herself conducted the work, apparently making her the first woman in France to conduct a symphony orchestra. Two more operas followed, *L'Hypocrite sanctifié* and *Les Roses de Calife*. While not particularly original, her scores were diverting and colorfully scored in the impressionist style, featuring the Orientalisms and *chinoiseries*—so-called "Chinese" harmonies in fourths and fifths—that were so much in vogue. With the arrival of the Ballets Russes, new dance scores replaced opera as the perceived surest road to fame. In 1912 Armande wrote a ballet, *La Source lointaine,* whose libretto by Goloubeff was inspired by a Persian legend.[81] The work received its premiere in January 1913 at the Théâtre des Arts, danced by actress Stacia Napierkowska.[82] The press generally wrote favorably, if cautiously, about her works. Reviewing *La Source lointaine,* Ravel wrote in 1913, "The form of this composition is a bit vague. On the other hand, one frequently encounters within it innovations, chiefly harmonic dissonances, whose daring does not exclude charm. It would be absurd to reproach Madame de Polignac this fortunate inquietude, the most noble gift that a sincere artist can possess."[83] Winnaretta, apparently impressed with Armande's talents, as well with as her plucky determination, offered to help produce her niece's next new work in a major Paris house.

At this time, either Winnaretta or Armande apparently met the sensational modern dancer Loïe Fuller.[84] The American-born Fuller had won

instant fame with Paris audiences in 1892, when she first performed her
exotic "skirt dances" at the Folies Bergère. These signature pieces consisted of the dancer-choreographer-producer, swathed in yards of billow-
ing silk, moving in swirling motions, sometimes graceful, sometimes fren-
zied, in synchronization with a continuously changing kaleidoscope of colored lights and magic-lantern projections. More interested in the "performance art" than in the technique of dance, Fuller's curiosity about the
employment of light for artistic effects led her to experiment with modern
technologies. She brought imaginative and sophisticated new uses of electricity and radium lamps to over one hundred dances, with titles like *But-
terfly, Clouds, Radium Dance*, and, with her troupe of young women, *Ballet of Light*. She was an early inspiration to Isadora Duncan, and a favorite
of avant-garde audiences. Robert de Montesquiou called her "a bonfire
inside a morning glory"; the press gave her the nickname "the Goddess of
Light."[85] Astruc engaged Fuller to perform a choreographed version of
Debussy's *Nocturnes* as a "prelude" to Fauré's new opera *Pénélope*, scheduled to receive its first performances in the spring of 1913. It may have
been the Astruc-Debussy connection that brought about a meeting between
the dancer and the Polignac women. One senses Winnaretta's presence (or
her money) behind a program for Fuller's 1914 season: Stravinsky's *Feux
d'artifice*, Debussy's *Children's Corner*—and Armande de Polignac's *Les
Mille et Une Nuits*, a score that had first been presented in Winnaretta's
atelier in 1911, and written, as Loïe Fuller's biographers assert, with the
dancer in mind.[86] It can be reasonably speculated that Winnaretta agreed
to underwrite at least a portion of this proposed concert.

In mid-January Winnaretta left for a month-long cruise to Egypt, ostensibly to visit Ronald Storrs, but also to soothe her brother Paris, who had
fled to the land of the Pharaohs after the most recent rupture in his stormy
relations with Isadora Duncan.[87] Arriving in Brindisi to board the ship,
Winnaretta learned that her lawyer, Raymond Poincaré, had been elected
President of the Republic, defeating Georges Clemenceau. Just before em-
barking for Cairo she wrote to Madame Poincaré offering her enthusiastic
congratulations: "The wishes of all those who love France are fulfilled!"[88]
Not all French patriots, particularly those of a pacifistic bent, would have
agreed. Poincaré, believing war with Germany to be inevitable, had worked
during his term as Foreign Minister to prepare France's armed forces for
the advent of hostilities. To what extent Winnaretta actually agreed with
the new president's policies is difficult to ascertain, for she was doggedly
apolitical. The previous year, when Toche Bulteau asked her a question
about Aristide Briand, Winnaretta responded that she knew nothing about
politics, and asked if Briand, the reform-minded socialist minister, was the
same person as Aristide Bruant, the combative balladeer from the cabaret
Le Chat Noir in Montmartre, famous for his black velvet cap and suit, and
immortalized in Toulouse-Lautrec's famous painting.[89]

During the winter of 1913, however, the tense political climate could not be avoided; it became a main subject of conversation in Winnaretta's social circles. This was the case at a dinner party given by Thérèse Murat, where Winnaretta was among a group of guests that included Anna de Noailles, Maurice Barrès, philosopher Henri Bergson, and the ever-present Abbé Mugnier. That evening Winnaretta spoke at length with Bergson, discussing France's current uneasy alliance with Russia.[90] Tsar Nicholas, a weak ruler who surrounded himself with reactionary and incompetent minsters, had recently reinstigated anti-Semitic pogroms and reprisals against the peasant population. Winnaretta wondered how a civilized leader could condone such intolerant policies. At the conclusion of her somber conversation with Bergson, her countenance was troubled and enigmatic; she seemed unreachable through the remainder of the soiree.[91] Some time later Thérèse Murat recounted Winnaretta's behavior on that evening to their mutual friend, Maurice Paléologue, French ambassador to Russia. Murat and Paléologue sought to understand the mysterious "Winnie," whose intelligence and culture couldn't hide the fact that she seemed so pathetic and alone. In thinking of her, Paléologue recalled the conclusion of Baudelaire's poem, *Femmes damnées*:

Faites votre destin, âmes désordonnées,
Et fuyez l'infini que vous portez en vous!
[Play out your destiny, disorderly souls,
And flee the infinite that you carry within!][92]

But if Winnaretta's inner state of mind was "disorderly," she gave no sign of it. Her sphinx-like inscrutability in social situations often seemed to add to her stature. Presiding from the center of the table at a dinner at Anna de Noailles's, Winnaretta seemed to painter Jacques-Émile Blanche to be "majestically silent."[93] The artist soon found that the imperious princess was a different, more approachable person away from groups of people.

Not long after Anna's dinner, Winnaretta commissioned him to paint her portrait. As gifted a conversationalist as an artist, Blanche began the preliminary sketches in 1913,[94] and these sittings gave the two old friends frequent opportunities to trade interesting tales about their shared acquaintances. Two portraits were completed in May 1914, depicting Winnaretta as a dignified woman of substance and complexity. The first portrait, traditional in style, depicts the Princesse de Polignac as a statuesque woman, with salt-and-pepper hair, her black velvet dress adorned with a white lace collar and a long single strand of pearls. Staring out of the picture, her gaze is direct and formdiable, but a smile plays around the corners of her mouth. The second portrait presents the same image in a more impressionist, highly colored rendering. Both canvasses were added to Winnaretta's quirky but impressive art collection, which now also included Blanche's enormous, colorful portrait of Nijinsky.[95] Around 1911 she acquired a small sketch by

Ingres, *Drawing of Félix Leblanc,* from her former teacher, Paul Mathey,[96] and subsequently purchased a pastel by Maurice Quentin La Tour, *Portrait of a Man.* In 1912 her collection became appreciably more important with the acquisition of two immense canvasses by Giovanni Paolo Pannini, painted in the mid-eighteenth century, the *Gallery of Views of Ancient Rome,* and the *Gallery of Views of Modern Rome.*[97]

During this period, Gabriel Astruc saw the fruits of a project to which he had given his heart and soul: the opening of a splendid new hall for the presentation of music and dance, the Théâtre des Champs-Élysées. The theater was situated on the fashionable avenue Montaigne in the 8th *arrondissement.* Designed by Auguste Perret in the Modern Style, it boasted a splendid Art Nouveau lobby, decorated with bas-reliefs and frescoes by Antoine Bourdelle and a series of paintings depicting the history of music by Maurice Denis.[98] Astruc had financed much of the hall's premiere season through subscriptions to his production company, the Société Gabriel Astruc.[99] Winnaretta, surely a major contributor, had purchased a box for the season; she attended the opening performances: a 2 April concert of French music, with Saint-Saëns, d'Indy, and Debussy conducting their works, and, the next evening, a gala performance of Berlioz's *Benvenuto Cellini.*[100] Upcoming highlights of the first season were to include Musorgsky's *Boris Godunov* and the Paris premiere of his *Khovantschina,* both starring Chaliapin, and a series of Ballets Russes programs that was to include three new ballets: Debussy's *Jeux,* Florent Schmitt's *La Tragédie de Salomé,* and Stravinsky's *Le Sacre du printemps* (The Rite of Spring).

Stravinsky's work on the *Rite* had preoccupied him through the end of 1912; the last additions to the score were finished only on 29 March 1913.[101] Winnaretta's commission, which, in principle, was supposed to be performed at her home in spring 1913, was far from his thoughts. In January and February the composer accompanied the Ballets Russes on its tour of continental Europe and London; he was present for the first performances of *Firebird* and *Petrushka* in a number of major cities. While in London during the month of February, the composer frequented the salons of Lady Ripon and her beautiful daughter Lady Juliet Duff.[102] Apparently, Stravinsky let slip that he was composing a new work that was *not* a Diaghilev commission. Whether he mentioned that the commission had come from Winnaretta and "would belong" to her is unclear. Plainly, however, Gladys Ripon foresaw a potential "scoop," and offered to give the London premiere of the composition in her home. It was not long before this piece of intelligence found its way to Paris. Winnaretta was not amused: she wrote to Stravinsky on 7 April 1913 upon his return to Clarens to assert her proprietary rights over the as yet unwritten work.

Sir, I would be very grateful if you could tell me around what date you could finish the piece that you have promised to write for me. It is important that I know when I will be able to have it played at my house. The Marquise de Ripon wants to include it on the program of a concert that she wants to give in London, but it goes without saying that it can't be performed at any concert before being played at my house, and that after having been played at my house it can't be played without my permission during a determined time. As far as the Marquise de Ripon's concert is concerned, I will be very happy for your work to be performed (after the 1st performance at my house) as long as it's mentioned [in the program] that it was written for me.[103]

The composer's response to this letter has not surfaced. And the resolution of the question of when the performance of Stravinsky's work would take place at the Princesse's house was long in coming—sixteen years long.

Later that month a tragedy befell Isadora Duncan and Paris Singer. Paris had just returned to the French capital after several months' absence. On 19 April, before leaving on a trip to Egypt, he enjoyed a pleasant lunch with Isadora, their six-year-old son Patrick, and Patrick's half-sister Deirdre. After the meal, the children got into the car with their governess to return to their country home in Versailles. En route, the engine stalled, and the driver got out to turn the crank in the front of the car. Suddenly the car lurched, and began to roll forwards. Before the driver could grab the door, the car gathered speed and plunged into the Seine, drowning the children and their governess. Paris Singer was the first to be told of the accident, and it was he who broke the horrible news to Isadora. "All Paris is in mourning," wrote the *New York Times*,[104] as family, friends, and total strangers came to the funeral to grieve for the unfortunate children. After the burial, Isadora Duncan left to travel in Turkey, and Paris Singer returned to London.

It seems strange that Winnaretta makes no reference to these events in her correspondence of this period. Although she was sympathetic to her brother's anguish over the children's deaths, his affair with the dancer had put her in an awkward position. It was not that Winnaretta had scruples about the affair per se: Paris had had many affairs, and given her own personal life, Winnaretta could hardly cast aspersions. The press had treated the issue of the children's parentage with discretion; newspaper reports of the funeral scrupulously avoided naming Paris Singer as Patrick's father, even after he threw himself onto the catafalque during the service.[105] The problem for Winnaretta was familial: she had a long, close relationship with Paris's wife Lillie and their five children (including a daughter named Winnaretta); even after the couple's separation, and despite the fact that the children were of adult age, Winnaretta surely felt her loyalties divided.

The story of the Duncan-Singer tragedy soon faded from the newspapers, as the Paris *grande saison* got underway. Winnaretta was soon wrapped up with all the pleasurable activities offered by Paris in May. She welcomed the visit of British composer Frederick Delius, who was living with his wife in Fontainebleau.[106] For years she had suggested performing one of Delius's works in her salon; it is not known whether this ever came to pass.[107] Most of Winnaretta's evenings during the month of May were spent at the Théâtre des Champs-Élysées. Astruc's beautiful new theater augured well to become an important center of new music and dance in the capital. On 9 May Winnaretta attended the first performance of the Debussy *Nocturnes*, danced by Loïe Fuller, and Fauré's new opera, *Pénélope*. Fauré had always been a slow composer—a fact of which Winnaretta was painfully aware. Because of his additional responsibilities as director of the Conservatoire, Fauré had taken five years to complete his new opera. *Pénélope* was a carefully crafted, subtly powerful lyric work, but its vocal lines bore more resemblance to Fauré's harmonically subtle songs than to the conventional showpieces of French opera.[108] Although the work was universally praised by the public and the press, it was unfortunately upstaged by the Ballets Russes premieres that began the following week.

Winnaretta invited a number of her Polignac relatives to join her in her box for the ballet performances; two of them left eyewitness accounts in their diaries. Comparing these entries to Winnaretta's memoirs, one can sense how forward-thinking Winnaretta was in her assessment of the new ballet scores. Comte Melchior de Polignac—one of the many Polignac nephews and nieces older than his aunt—attended the opening night performance on 15 May. The featured work was Debussy's *Jeux*, labeled a "cubist" ballet, presumably because of the inspiration drawn from the formal practices of Picasso and Braque. Its central plot device was a tennis game with ambiguous sexual overtones, played out by three dancers; the most dramatic moment occurred in the opening moments, when Nijinsky leapt onto the stage with a *grand jeté*, in pursuit of the tennis ball.[109] If the audience was puzzled by the work, they nonetheless responded with enthusiasm. Comte Melchior's scathing account of the premiere notes his distaste both for Debussy's work and for the "chic" audience's rubber stamp of approval of the Ballets Russes's productions.

> Noise, disorder, the notes chasing themselves around irrationally and awkwardly, like the three [dancers], including Nijinsky, who take their gambols on a plate of spinach. The world is being made fun of, but the "world" [*le monde*] doesn't see it, and applauds because Debussy represents the music of today, because he has succeeded—*Pelléas* and *L'Après-midi d'un faune*—and because the snobs want to give the impression that they understand. None of this has anything to do with art or intelligence; the hands, applauding loudly, make a chuckling noise.[110]

For the Marquise de Polignac, the highlight of the season was Musorgsky's *Khovantschina*, which received its first performance on 5 June: "very simple and interesting music," she noted in her diary, "splendid choirs (one in particular very religious and [sung] *à bouche fermée,* which simulates the organ)."[111]

But for Winnaretta, Stravinsky's new *Rite of Spring* was the unforgettable event of the season. The evening of the work's premiere, 29 May, has entered the annals of music history. The dissonance of Stravinsky's "pagan" score and raw primitiveness of Nijinsky's choreography shocked a good part of the audience, and the riots that ensued were attributed to the revolutionary nature of the work, which overturned every convention of classical ballet. "No one who was present at the first performance of *Le Sacre du printemps* can ever forget that evening," recalled Winnaretta in her memoirs,

for there was a real battle in the Théâtre des Champs-Élysées. The howls of some, the applause of others, went on for an hour—the orchestra reduced to silence. Here and there someone would rise and shout out his views at the top of his voice, each party abusing and insulting the other in the most violent way.

I was present each time a ballet was given, and until the end of the Season the same riotous scenes took place, sometimes lasting for more than an hour, the orchestra being reduced to silence. Still the army of admirers grew stronger and stronger, and Stravinsky was overwhelmed with applause when the curtain finally went down.[112]

After the uproar surrounding *The Rite of Spring,* Winnaretta's two musical gatherings in June seemed sedate by comparison, almost palliative. The programs rendered homage both to the Ballets Russes composers and to the classic masters. The first soiree, on 16 June, took place on a swelteringly hot night,[113] and the doors to the round reception hall, whose walls were now adorned with the enormous Pannini canvases, were left open. From the salon the audience of one hundred guests could look out into the adjoining garden, decorated with illuminated Venetian globes. Diverse works for solo soprano and flute were accompanied by orchestra; Ravel's *Pavane,* dedicated to Winnaretta, represented the "modern classic" among the evening's offerings.[114] Maurice Paléologue noted in his diary his admiration for both the program and the hostess, whom he called "the Oracle of Musicians."[115] One week later, the musical offering featured Vincent d'Indy and Blanche Selva, who performed Chabrier's *Trois Valses romantiques* for two pianos; on the second half of the program, Selva performed concertos by Schumann and Bach with a chamber orchestra under d'Indy's baton.[116]

By this time Winnaretta's Venetian salon had become as well known as the Parisian one. Many of the great artists, criss-crossing Europe on tour, would stop at the Palazzo Polignac to perform before Winnaretta's international audiences, especially during the fashionable summer months. The

English writer Cecil Roberts, a young boy in the pre-War years, recalled attending the Polignac salon with his parents during their Venetian vacations. Roberts remembered many pleasant hours spent in the "long salon with its Venetian Gothic windows overlooking the Canal. . . . [The Princesse] not only entertained lavishly, but was able to command the best artists. Paderewski, Jan Kubelik, Kreisler, Tetrazzini, Melba, Caruso, Pachmann, and many other stars played or sang for her. It was there I first heard the young Artur Rubinstein."[117]

That spring, Winnaretta participated in diverse occasions of high and low art. On 7 June she attended a "dance lesson" at the home of Princesse Amédée de Broglie (one of her niece Daisy's in-laws), where she may have learned the steps of the latest Parisian dance crazes, the Tango and the One-step.[118] Around the same period Winnaretta was introduced to a young composer who would figure prominently in her patronage career. Provence-born Darius Milhaud, only twenty years old, had just moved to Paris; an introduction to Jacques-Émile Blanche resulted in an invitation to perform his compositions before an audience of the artist's friends. These new-music recitals took place while Winnaretta was sitting for her portrait, and it was thus that she was called upon to turn pages when violinist Yvonne Giraud and pianist Georgette Guller performed Milhaud's new Violin Sonata, Op. 3, in the Blanche salon.[119] Winnaretta appreciated Milhaud as much for his refreshing irreverence as for his creative talent, and thereafter he became a regular in her salon gatherings.

That summer the Royal Society of Literature chose as the 1913 laureate of the Polignac Prize Dublin writer James Stephens, author of the mystical novel *The Crock of Gold*.[120] The prize came just in the nick of time for Stephens, who had discovered only the day before his notification by the Committee that his "total wealth in visible and moveable goods was one wife, two babies, two cats and fifteen shillings."[121] So impecunious was the novelist that, when summoned to London by William Butler Yeats to receive the prize money, he didn't even know if he could scrape up the round-trip train fare to and from Dublin in order to collect the check.[122] The Polignac Prize greatly enhanced Stephens's reputation, as well as his bank account.

Another author whose career would come to full bloom in the fall of 1913 was Marcel Proust. After receiving rejections from three publishers, his long manuscript was finally accepted by Bernard Grasset. Proust called the book *A la Recherche du temps perdu*; it was dedicated to *Le Figaro*'s Gaston Calmette, in gratitude for the editor's longstanding championship of his work. Winnaretta had lost touch with Proust, but read the first installment of his book, *Swann's Way*, soon after its release in November 1913, and loved it. She traveled to London shortly thereafter, where one evening she dined at the home of Lady Randolph Churchill. Seated beside her at dinner was British arts patron and author (and Sir Winston Churchill's former private secretary) Edward Marsh. Years later, Marsh would recall that Winnaretta spent the entire evening talking of nothing but this new work by Marcel Proust—an author not yet familiar to British readers. Some days later she gave Marsh her own copy of *Swann's Way*; it was a gift that he would cherish to the end of his days.[123]

The year did not end happily for many in Winnaretta's circle. Diaghilev was grief-stricken by the recent abdication of his choreographer, star dancer, and lover, Vaslav Nijinsky. While on tour in South America, Nijinsky had married a young Hungarian dancer, Romola de Pulzsky. Diaghilev was convinced that this artistic and personal betrayal signaled the end of the Ballets Russes. His worst fears seemed to be confirmed in November, when the fortunes of Gabriel Astruc foundered as well. Despite its adventurous programming and artistic brilliance (in the first four weeks alone the theater had presented five operas, two dance concerts, eight gala orchestral concerts, and a dozen recitals[124]), Astruc's season had been a financial failure. The increasingly xenophobic public accused the impresario of promoting foreign artists at the expense of French musicians and dancers.[125] His association with the Ballets Russes and the scandalous *Rite of Spring* was seen as proof positive of his unpatriotic stance. In early November, Astruc was forced to declare bankruptcy; he resigned as Director of the Théâtre des Champs-Élysées and disbanded his Société Musicale.[126]

A week later, Prince Camille de Polignac, Edmond's last surviving brother and Armande's father, died at the age of eighty-one while trying to solve a mathematical problem that had preoccupied him for the last ten years.[127] The family gathered to render homage to the fascinating old man. His mordant wit had sharpened in his last years: when asked by his nephew Charles why he had not written down the story of his fascinating life, Camille responded, "[My life] was made with a good sword, I won't spoil it with a bad pen."[128] Winnaretta mourned the loss of the noble soldier and intellectual who had been as close to her as a brother.

At Christmas, Winnaretta left Paris for the calm of Venice. She spent the holidays with the Marchioness de Ripon, the Stravinsky contretemps having apparently been resolved. The Marchioness had invited an international assortment of friends to her palazzo to celebrate the holiday. During the course of the evening, a Scottish lord arrived in a kilt, bearing two flaming plum puddings; his grand entrance was accompanied by the music of bagpipers, who entertained the assembled party with traditional melodies of the Highlands. Through the open windows the assembled party could hear the pealing of church bells and Christmas carols sung by children in passing gondolas.[129] But the shadow of impending war even fell over this peaceable gathering. As writer Paul Bourget stood by the window, a German prince came up to him and made an attempt to express a sense of international camaraderie. "My cousin the Emperor Wilhelm II likes France very much." Bourget smiled bitterly, and murmured, "Behold the announcement of war. This is how the world's enchantment will come to an end."[130]

Both the programs and the guests for Winnaretta's winter salon gatherings seemed to have been chosen in a spirit of multinational détente, as if the goodwill generated by music could stave off the pervasive political malaise in the air. The soiree of 17 February 1914 featured a mixture of instrumental repertoire by the great German masters—Handel, Mozart, and J. S. Bach—and modern music by French composers—Debussy and Ravel; the program also included a group of French songs by Duparc, Debussy, Alexandre Georges,[131] and Reynaldo Hahn, sung by celebrated soprano Ninon Vallin.[132] On 26 March, an audience of fifty guests from Russia, Germany, France, England, Italy and Greece listened to the diva Rose Féart and Spanish pianist Ricardo Viñes.[133] The soiree, given in honor of Grand-Duke Paul of Russia and his wife, may have been tied to fundraising efforts on behalf of the Ballets Russes: the double blow of Nijinsky's abdication and marriage, coupled with Astruc's bankruptcy, had once again forced Diaghilev to scramble around looking for last minute financial backing for his spring season.

Talk of the Ballets Russes's upcoming performances may have served as a convenient diversion from other recent and troubling events. Shock waves were still rippling through Paris after the dramatic assassination of *Le Figaro*'s Gaston Calmette. In January, Calmette, a staunch patriot and advocate of Poincaré's military policies, had used his editorial power to launch a series of vituperative attacks on Minister of Finance Joseph Caillaux, an equally ardent pacifist. Caillaux, convinced that war would ruin Europe, had pleaded the cause of peace between France and Germany. The usually reasonable Calmette had resorted to tactics of yellow journalism, publishing Caillaux's letters to his mistress, and consequently arousing the ire of the minister's wife. On 16 March, Henriette Caillaux entered *Le Figaro*'s offices and shot Calmette at point-blank range, killing him instantly.

Winnaretta's spring was filled with events—familial, musical, and spiritual—that brought solace. She became a godmother twice in six weeks, first on 2 April, when her niece Diane de Polignac gave birth to a little boy named Edmond (the first Polignac infant to be named for Winnaretta's husband), and again on 14 May, when Louis and Germaine Decazes also gave birth to a son, Élie. On 5 April she attended the first Paris concert performance of Stravinsky's *Rite of Spring* under the baton of Pierre Monteux. The work that had caused such uproar less than a year earlier was now enthusiastically applauded, and hailed by critics as a masterpiece.[134] Three days latter Winnaretta left for a cruise to Sicily, Greece, and Malta on the yacht *Narcissus*.[135] The ancient ruins of Greece thrilled her, arousing in her a spiritual connection to the world of antiquity. Anna, responding to a letter from Winnaretta, understood. "[The] mysterious quality of perfect beauty is destined to move you, to be revealed to you: it's the religious instinct, which demands reason and aspires to the divine, that Greece satisfies completely."[136]

Winnaretta was back in Paris in time to see Loïe Fuller and the young women of her dance school perform at the Théâtre du Châtelet on 5 May. Accompanied by the Concerts Colonne under the direction of Gabriel Pierné, the troupe danced to music by Mendelssohn, Stravinsky, and Debussy, and two scores by Armande de Polignac, *The Thousand and One Nights* and *The Orchestration of Colors.* Fuller's star had dimmed somewhat in recent years, as the inevitable comparisons were made with the Ballets Russes and the technical prowess of its star dancers.[137] Fuller's response was that her productions had more to do with "the harmony of sound, light, and music,"[138] and a faction of the press applauded her innovations in performance art. Critic Henri Quittard noted the strong link between the production and the music, and wrote favorably of the compatibility of Armande's music and Fuller's artistic vision. "In *The Thousand and One Nights* . . . Loïe Fuller has created her greatest deployment of sumptuous fabrics, of fantastic and dazzling lights: it's an orgy of colors."[139] "*The Thousand and One Nights* . . . whose ingenious music seemed so revolutionary some months ago, now rolled out its garlands of fifths and fourths with an air of classic innocence."[140] As astonishing as this first night spectacle had been, for the second performance the dancer and composer had reserved another surprise.

> In front of the bright gleam of lights that corresponded so well to the colored harmonies of the orchestration, the frail silhouette of a woman stood out above the musicians. The eyes of the entire hall were drawn to her: Madame Armande de Polignac was replacing M. Gabriel Pierné at the podium. With great modesty, wearing a black dress, her neck and fingers bare of any jewelry, the young woman conducted with an ease, a sureness, and an energy that enthused the audience.[141]

The Fuller troupe performed Armande's scores in eight Paris performances through the month of May, and subsequently presented the works at the Théâtre de la Monnaie in Brussels; in both venues, Armande conducted her own works to great acclaim.[142] She dedicated *The Thousand and One Nights* to her aunt. Through her patronage of her niece's work, Winnaretta helped to erode two barriers facing women musicians: their exclusion as composers in the public arena, and their even more firmly entrenched absence from the conductor's podium. Armande continued to mature and flourish as a composer for the dance, and her use of "Orientalist" materials became more sophisticated. In 1925, she would score a ballet, *Urashima,* for Japanese dancer Toshi Komori and his troupe, using authentic Japanese melodies. Of that ballet, critic Henry Prunières wrote that "[using] essentially European harmonic procedures, the composer has managed to give . . . the illusion of these musics from the Far East. . . . The cold sonorities of the piano accompaniment replaced fairly well the timbres of Oriental percussion instruments. . . . The art of Armande de Polignac has great finesse."[143]

Winnaretta's next acts of generosity were likewise of a familiar nature. Paris Singer, still hoping to reconcile with Isadora Duncan, had promised to undertake the complete funding of her dancing school—with no emotional demands attached. In 1912 he had purchased an enormous mansion in suburban Bellevue, the Hôtel Paillard (the former country house of Madame de Pompadour), to serve as the school's headquarters and dormitories.[144] Passion had made Singer reckless: the expense of underwriting the school and the property created an enormous drain on his cash flow, hobbling his ability to maintain the living expenses of his estranged wife and their five remaining children. He thought seriously of selling his London townhouse in Sloane Square, an act that would deprive his children of the home they had known since infancy—not to mention a key piece of their rightful inheritance. Winnaretta, having come so close to being deprived of her own legacy by her scheming stepfather, Victor Reubsaet, could not allow this to happen to her nieces and nephews: she intervened, determined to protect their interests when their father—her brother—wouldn't. On 25 May she addressed the following letter to her niece and namesake, Winnaretta Singer, Paris's twenty-three-year-old daughter:

> Dearest Winnie,
>   I have just heard of your Father's intention of selling his London house, and as I know how anxious you are to continue to live there, I feel sure you will want to buy it. I have no intention of buying it myself, but I should be very glad to know it is yours, so if it is convenient to you I will give you the money to help you to become owner of the house you have lived in so long.
>   With love, your affectionate Aunt
>   Winnaretta de Polignac[145]

Winnaretta's cultural *mécénat* that year embraced the new and old ends of the artistic spectrum. Perhaps as an adjunct to Loïe Fuller's Art Nouveau spectacles, Winnaretta turned her *atelier* into a gallery for an exhibition of drawings by Aubrey Beardsley, commemorating the twentieth anniversary of the artist's death.[146] Beardsley's art had never gone out of fashion: its embodiment of the curious, the grotesque, and the erotic, realized within the framework of delicate two-dimensional forms, was still as vibrant, troubling, and modern as it had been in the first bloom of the Belle Époque.

Winnaretta's home next became the setting for a concert sponsored by the International Music Society, Europe's first important musicological association, which was holding its 1914 conference in Paris.[147] Jules Écorcheville, president of the French branch of the Society,[148] had organized numerous musical events for the six hundred attendees of the conference, including concerts of medieval, Renaissance, and Huguenot music, early classical opera, and a Gluck "gala."[149] The penultimate concert, comprised exclusively of the works of Jean-Philippe Rameau, was held in Winnaretta's large music room. The program was organized by Camille Saint-Saëns, the *éminence grise* of French music and Rameau's most ardent twentieth-century advocate, who performed a recital of Rameau's works for keyboard and small ensembles, as well as conducting the overture to the opera *Zaïs*.[150] Tensions could not help but arise in a meeting of musical scholars speaking many languages and promoting different intellectual platforms,[151] but Winnaretta presided over her portion of this musical Tower of Babel with aplomb, perhaps believing that the power of music could still surmount national differences.

The Paris season was still in full swing on 28 June, the black day when a Serbian nationalist assassinated the heir to the Habsburg monarchy, Archduke Ferdinand, and his wife in Sarajevo. The explosive consequences of the murders had not yet penetrated the public consciousness. The papers devoted as much space to the upcoming garden parties and championship horse races as to the ensuing rioting in the Balkans and the national mourning in the Austro-Hungarian Empire. Winnaretta, who had just attended a grand formal dinner at the British Embassy,[152] left for England in the first days of July. There, she learned that the Royal Society of Literature had just chosen as the 1914 Polignac Prize laureate the poet Ralph Hodgson.[153] One of Hodgson's two prize-winning poems, "The Bull," described the impending doom of the aging leader of a proud herd of bulls. The poem's last verse could surely serve as a metaphor for the astonishing years of the Belle Époque, now coming to a precipitous end.

And the dreamer turns away
From his visionary herds
And his splendid yesterday,
Turns to meet the loathly birds
Flocking round him from the skies,
Waiting for the flesh that dies.[154]

Shelter from the Storm

Winnaretta's arrival in England in July 1914 coincided with the London Ballets Russes season. Diaghilev's influence was at its apogee in a British society seeking to leave the Victorian century behind; in London, as in Paris, the arbiters of culture had eagerly embraced the Russian troupe's colorful spectacles. The ballet enteprise had been brought under the aegis of conductor-impresario Thomas Beecham and his lover, California-born society hostess Lady Maud ("Emerald") Cunard, who used her influence to fill the theater stalls with royals and ministers, government officials and socialites.[1] Diaghilev's French coterie crossed the Channel to participate in the glittering British season. In honor of this international assemblage, Winnaretta arranged a recital of four-hand and two-piano music in her Chelsea townhouse, featuring herself and Percy Grainger as performers.[2]

After the recital, Grainger and the princess discussed the tense political atmosphere.[3] The assassination of Archduke Ferdinand had ignited the already fragile political tinder; the rejection of an ultimatum sent by Germany on 25 July demanding Serbian capitulation exploded it into flame. For the next several days, an uncertain European populace lived from one newspaper report to the next, fearing the worst. On 31 July Socialist leader Jean Jaurès, who had publicly opposed Poincaré's military expansion, was assassinated in Paris. Germany declared war on Russia on 1 August; two days later France joined the fight. The French currency was devalued, curfews and blackouts were imposed, and gathering places such as theaters and cafés were shut down. By month's end, Paris's citizenry was in a full state of panic: the Germans, having swept across Belgium, had broken the French lines on 23 August, forcing the retreat of the country's armies. Paris was in danger of being invaded at any time. Traffic all but ceased, as private cars were requisitioned by the army. Those still in possession of their vehicles were fleeing in increasing numbers, hoping to find enough gasoline en route to reach their destinations, but each day flight became more difficult, as roads in and out of the city were blocked to prevent the advance of the enemy.[4]

At the moment that war was declared, Winnaretta was visiting friends in Surrey. She wanted to return to Paris immediately, but Anna de Noailles urged her to stay where she was. "I think you [are] more secure in London, our provisions here not having been arranged at the present time, and the food supplies becoming difficult to find. *Of course if you come I will share everything I have with you.*"[5] Winnaretta reluctantly remained in England, frustrated to feel her usefulness limited "to [sending] as much money as I could drag from the Credit Lyonnais."[6] Anna contributed her friend's first check, for five thousand francs, to a French relief effort for indigent women and children.[7] She had intervened in the early days of the war to prevent Winnaretta's three cars from being appropriated by the army;[8] in late August, however, when one of the vehicles was requisitioned, Anna, in an "act of audacity and friendship,"[9] used it to depart for the south of France with her family, in a convoy with the Edmond Rostands.[10]

In mid-August Winnaretta went to Devonshire to join Paris and Lillie Singer (temporarily reunited), who had offered the Wigwam to the British Red Cross as a military hospital. The capacious house was converted into a facility of "two hundred beds, terrifying operating theaters, and X-ray rooms."[11] The first group of wounded soldiers arrived in September. Queen Mary herself traveled down to see the transformed Singer mansion, "stopping by the bed of each wounded man, to whom she spoke words of encouragement and comfort."[12] Winnaretta and Paris also organized a fifty-vehicle ambulance corps in Paris to be put at the disposition of Minister of War.[13] Upon her return to London, Winnaretta found ample work giving material aid to the French and Belgian refugees who had fled the Continent. "Notwithstanding the horrors," she continued to make music, finding it "the only solid thing left," turning, as always, "to John Sebastian [Bach] for comfort and strength."[14]

Finally, in October, Winnaretta returned to Paris. The city was still reeling from the assassination of Jean Jaurès and the departure of husbands, sons, neighbors, and friends. Currency had all but lost its value, and people were lined up in front of the banks to empty out their accounts. The subways were no longer running. Many newspapers had ceased publication; those that remained in circulation were devoted entirely to the war reports. The Abbé Mugnier spent his days sitting in the railroad stations, giving absolution and comfort to the brave and terrified men, young and old, departing for the front. Winnaretta was determined to stay in Paris, despite the potential dangers inherent in remaining. Given her delibitating fear of loud noises, the continual roar of warplanes and the distant thuds of bombardment posed a daily challenge to her equilibrium. Each day brought the news of the loss of a friend who had died on the battlefield. During some weeks, Winnaretta attended a funeral every day. Soon the losses became cruelly personal. On 25 September 1915 her nephew Henri, an army captain, was killed leading his squadron on the first day of a fierce offensive in the Champagne region—a prelude to the devastating battles that would be fought in Verdun the following year. Six months later, another nephew, Jacques Decazes, an aviator and the youngest of her sister Belle-Blanche's three children ("like a son to me," Winnaretta wrote to Stravinsky[15]), was struck down by enemy fire during an aerial combat mission.[16]

Winnaretta put her fortune to work for many wartime relief organizations. In March 1915 she met with Marie Curie, who was soliciting automobiles not yet requisitioned to convert them into mobile x-ray units: the scientist believed that X-rays would help to locate bullets and facilitate surgery near the battlefields, since the wounded often could not be moved. Curie herself trained a corps of one hundred fifty female attendants to operate the vehicles. Winnaretta donated one of her automobiles, and paid for the costs of the radiological equipment and its installation.[17] Through the spring and summer she continued to act as intermediary for Curie to secure car chassis from other aristocratic friends.[18] During the same period, Winnaretta joined the French branch of Ignace Paderewski's General Committee for Polish Relief, an organization that collected and distributed supplies to the needy population of war-torn Poland.[19] In October 1915 she became a driving force in the Franco-American Committee for the War Blind: she organized the purchase of an old hotel in the Paris suburb of Sceaux to be used as lodging for the blind, and helped raise large sums of money for the maintenance and staffing of the new facility. Appealing to columnist Joseph Reinach ("Polybe"[20]) for help, Winnaretta was able to secure the patronage of President Raymond Poincaré, whose name at the top of the list of contributors enabled the Committee to increase donations from America and other European countries.[21] At the end of the year Winnaretta became vice-president of another committee, founded by a group of Americans in association with the Belgium queen, to provide ambulances for Belgian soldiers and assistance to those mutilated in combat.[22]

Those who passed Winnaretta on the street would hardly have recognized her as a woman of means. She had always dressed simply, but during the war she became downright shabby, a gesture of contempt towards women who still continued to flaunt their wealth in the face of the general misery. One day, she walked to an outdoor benefit organized by the Paris police for their welfare fund. She waited in a long line to make her donation. Finally reaching the desk, she came face to face with an officious secretary, who, taking in Winnaretta's dowdy coat and worn shoes, thought that she was seeking a hand-out, and told her to come back the next day—whereupon Winnaretta handed the functionary a check for ten million francs, leaving him to gape in shock.[23]

Artistic *mécénat* had, of necessity, taken a secondary role, given the pressing material and medical needs. Nonetheless, Winnaretta continued to be solicited by artistic organizations that had depended on her help in the past. The Royal Society of Literature stayed in correspondence with Winnaretta, in the hopes of continuing to award the Edmond de Polignac Prize.[24] Although she asked the Society to forward to her copies of the prize-winning books, autographed by their authors,[25] Winnaretta did not send prize money to the Committee in 1915 or 1916; having apparently lost interest in the project, she used the war as a convenient excuse to cease funding the memorial to her husband.[26] Musical organizations solicited her aid as well. In the early months of the war, Jacques Rouché, who had been named General Director of the Paris Opéra in June 1914, had appealed to Winnaretta's generosity, in the hopes of keeping the house open during the war.[27] But Rouché's dream of maintaining a wartime opera season was not to be: the house closed soon after the letter was sent. The Opéra did not reopen until 9 December 1915, and then for matinees only, as the curfew was still in effect; evening performances, often interrupted by air raids, did not begin again until June 1916. Nonetheless, the recommencement of performances was felt to be, as the papers wrote, "the first shiver of Parisian life reborn, bringing us closer, it seems, to better times."[28]

During this period the private salons played an important role, providing a substitute for the still-dark theaters and concert halls, often serving as venues for charitable fundraising. Sometimes the salon served as a place of tribute to fallen artists: Natalie Barney's "Temple of Friendship" on the Left Bank was the scene of readings of works by poets killed during the war, accompanied by "sweet and sad music."[29] The salons also provided venues for performances of new music, as well as an opportunity for the musical hostesses to give some much-needed exposure and income to underemployed composers and musicians. And often the salons simply provided a way of finding solace in friendship and music. Throughout 1916 Winnaretta gave a series of small dinner parties followed by musical presentations. The first of these took place on 20 January, when organist Eugène Gigout performed a recital of works by Bach, Boëllmann, and Franck as a benefit for a charitable fund, "Affectionate Assistance for Musicians."[30] On 22 January Winnaretta's *atelier* was the scene of the premiere of a new work by Debussy, *En blanc et noir,* performed by duo-pianists Walter Rummel and his wife Thérèse Chaigneau.[31] These gatherings, apart from their musical importance, also served another purpose: they allowed friends to receive information about the war from members of the embassies and ministries privy to current news about the inner workings of international politics.

Paul Morand, a young attaché in the French foreign ministry and a budding author, chronicled many of these dinner musicales.[32] Morand's recollections of Winnaretta's lively dinners include incisive descriptions of "the celebrated Madame Bulteau . . . whose hard jutting chin contradicts the sweetness of her gaze,"[33] and of Athelstan Johnson, British *chargé d'affaires* in Budapest, "his face shriveled up under the ice cube of his monocle," who softened only when he heard the marvelous Borodin string quartet that followed the meal.[34] Morand's best-known anecdote concerns Winnaretta's querulous friend Madame Legrand.[35] The cantankerous "Cloton" visited

Winnaretta so frequently that she practically lived at avenue Henri-Martin. She was born into the socially prominent but cash-poor Fournès family, and Winnaretta's life of ease never ceased to arouse her ire. One evening, in a fit of jealousy, she spat out furiously, "Don't forget that the name Fournès is worth more than that of Singer." "Not at the bottom of a check," replied Winnaretta.[36]

As often as she could, Winnaretta fled Paris for short periods of time. She often booked a room at the Trianon Palace Hotel in Versailles. This tranquil haven, overlooking the palace gardens, became a home-away-from-home. In May, Versailles was the setting for a private performance of Reynaldo Hahn's new opera *Nausicaa*.[37] There, Winnaretta encountered Marcel Proust, who, happy to renew cordial relations with the Princesse, spent the next day accompanying her on her social rounds. Some months later Proust showed a cherished collection of old photographs to Paul Morand. Among snapshots of Princesse Mathilde, Robert de Montesquiou, Lucien Daudet, and Guy de Maupassant could be found photos of Edmond de Polignac in the company of Charles Haas (whom Proust had taken as a model for Swann in his novel) and Winnaretta in her thirties—already looking, Morand noted in his diary, "as she does today."[38]

During one of these suburban jaunts Winnaretta struck up a friendship with Princesse Eugène (Violette) Murat, who had a country house (built by Georges Vaudoyer[39]) in neighboring Jouy-en-Josas. Violette Murat had frequented Winnaretta's salon for more than a dozen years, but the two women had never been close.[40] Since the death of her husband in 1906, she lived openly as a lesbian, frequenting the Left Bank circles of Natalie Barney and Gertrude Stein, the cafés of Montparnasse, and the black nightclubs of Montmartre—the famous "revues nègres," epitomized by American performer Josephine Baker.[41] She attracted an impressive gathering of artists and musicians—particularly those of the avant-garde—to her salon; she was also one of the first in the aristocracy to become an inveterate opium smoker. In the past, Winnaretta, uncomfortable with Violette's open declarations of homosexuality and drug use, had kept a certain distance, but during the war years she came to appreciate her artistic tastes and devilish wit. They spent a good deal of time together, and often served on the same committees of charitable organizations. It was possibly Violette who coaxed her friend towards the Left Bank, metaphorically speaking, for during this period Winnaretta was introduced to both Pablo Picasso and Gertrude Stein.[42]

One of Murat's protégées was a twenty-five-year-old woman named Comtesse Isaure de Miramon. Exceptionally beautiful, artistically inclined, and a great music lover, Isaure was wed young to a military man, Baron de Laage, with whom she had two daughters. Unhappy in marriage and finding garrison life distasteful, she divorced her husband several years later. Upon her return to Paris, she took back her maiden name and began an artistic and literary salon, where Jean Cocteau was a constant presence. By this time Madame de Miramon had apparently acknowledged her attraction to women. It was probably through Violette that Winnaretta made her acquaintance in 1915 or 1916. Although the documentation is scant, it seems that Winnaretta was deeply in love with the beautiful young woman. She installed Isaure and her daughters in an apartment that she kept at 25 rue de Constantine, facing the Esplanade des Invalides.[43] After Isaure's operation for appendicitis, Winnaretta saw to her care and comfort, reading Anna de Noailles's new poems to the convalescent to cheer her up.[44] The Comtesse de Miramon subsequently took a Louis-XIV-style house in Versailles near Winnaretta's hotel; there, she held musicales in a high-ceilinged gold-and-white room with excellent acoustics, where the antique wainscotting was shaped like violins. The guests were an amalgam of Winnaretta's friends and a younger crowd of aristocrats with avant-garde pretensions.[45]

One friend who had been absent from Paris since the beginning of the war was Igor Stravinsky. The composer was living in the quiet countryside of Morges, cut off from the income from his property in Russia, and unable to reap any of the fruits of the success that had so recently greeted the 1914 orchestral performances of *The Rite of Spring*. With the exception of some performances of *The Firebird* in Geneva,[46] his works were not being played in Europe; communication with—and residual fees from—his German and Russian publishers had all but ceased.[47] Diaghilev had tours in Spain and America planned for 1916 that would include performances of *The Firebird* and *Petrushka,* but no performance royalties would be forthcoming in the foreseeable future. Living as an exile with a chronically sick wife and four children, Stravinsky was hard pressed to know how to support his family.

Nonetheless, the difficult year 1915 had yielded much musical fruit for the composer, and during his exile his style moved towards a new form of modernism, based on Russian folk sources. Stravinsky became preoccupied with the melodic and harmonic roots of the music of homeland, as well as with the syntactical possibilities of his native language. The racy texts of the folk poetry, the quirky rhythms of its speech cadences, and the tinkling sound of the syllables, words, and phrases, appealed to the composer, and he experimented with new ideas about rhythm and the relationship of text to music.[48] In contrast to the glittering ballet music for large orchestra from previous years, Stravinsky now sought to create music that was earthier, more angular, and much leaner. The notion of writing for smaller musical ensembles intrigued him. After completing a set of easy piano duets and some short vocal works based on Russian peasant songs, he began sketches for two new works, among them *Les Noces villageoises* (The Village Wedding). This important work would evolve into a kind of a modernist cantata, featuring the jangling speech phrases and short melodic

patterns that had preoccupied him of late. Diaghilev, much influenced at
the time by Futurist ideas, including Filippo Marinetti's tract "The Art of
Noises" and the noise machines of Luigi Russolo,[49] heard *Les Noces* as it
evolved through the year 1915, and loved it; he laid claim to the work as a
future production of the Ballets Russes, even though he had no idea when
his next Paris season would take place.

At the same time that *Les Noces* was taking shape, Stravinsky conceived
the idea of a chamber work for dancers and mimes with vocal accompaniment. The text was based on a well-known Russian "burlesque story," *The
Fox, the Cock, the Cat, and the Ram*, from Alexander Afanasyev's collection of children's tales,[50] and came to be known as *Renard*. Stravinsky had
already made some preliminary sketches of the work the previous spring
after combing through the different variants of the fable. The complete
libretto was culled from a hodge-podge of children's songs and nonsense
rhymes, which were traditionally accompanied by a Russian zither-like instrument, the gusli.[51] In the witty—but barely comprehensible—plot, Fox
tries to lure Cock out of his treetop aerie by flattery and seduction; Cock,
aided by two sidekicks, Cat and Ram, thwarts the wicked Fox. At the end
of the tale the four singers, two tenors and two baritones, crassly demand
to be paid by the audience for their efforts. The text's short, patter-like
phrases and verses, incorporating an endless variety of syllabic accents and
phrase lengths, are kaleidoscopically rendered by the four voices, and play-
fully accompanied by a "folk band" (evocative of the "authentic 'old-time'
Russian theater"[52]) that sometimes echoes, sometimes moves in contradic-
tion to, the prosodic stresses of the libretto. To evoke the distinctive folk
sounds of the gusli, Stravinsky included a Hungarian cimbalom in the small
orchestra.[53]

It was this work that the composer thought to offer to the Princesse de
Polignac as fulfillment of her commission, rather than the originally proposed piano concerto, but he hesitated to ask by letter. Winnaretta had
kept current with Stravinsky's work through contact with Diaghilev, who,
in December, returned to Paris to produce—against all odds—a performance of music and dance by the Ballets Russes at the recently reopened
Opéra. The concert, organized as a benefit for the British Red Cross of
Paris, included a performance of *The Firebird*. Stravinsky came to Paris to
conduct the work for the first time.[54] On 4 January 1916, he met with
Winnaretta at avenue Henri-Martin; after playing portions of *Les Noces,*
he proposed *Renard*—still in rough sketches—as the work to be written
"for her."[55]

He also used that meeting to renegotiate the commission's financial terms.
Stravinsky agreed to complete *Renard* by 1 July 1916. The Princesse would
pay a total of 10,000 Swiss francs for the work (instead of the original
3000 francs)—3500 to be paid immediately, 2500 on 4 April, and the remaining 4000 upon the work's completion.[56] At the time of final payment,

the Princesse would receive manuscripts of both the complete orchestra score and the reduction for piano and voice, and would have absolute control over performances of the work for a period of five years. The terms of this agreement became more or less the prototype for agreements that she made with composers in future years. In one important aspect, however, this commission was different from any other: it guaranteed Stravinsky a far larger fee for an original work than was ever offered by Winnaretta to any other artist, past or future. The fact that Winnaretta was willing to pay two and a half times the original price for the work is indicative of the high regard in which she held the composer. "I can't tell you enough how much I was happy to see you, to hear *Les Noces villageoises*, and to hear you speak of music. Everything that you said interests me intensely, and I'm happy to think that one of your first works in the form of 'chamber music' will be played at my house."[57]

On 7 February Winnaretta returned to Ouchy, Switzerland, where many of her friends had gone to wait out the war in the shelter of that country's neutrality.[58] She visited the Stravinskys in nearby Morges, and enjoyed a festive evening in their cozy little house.

> [Stravinsky's house was] all brilliantly lit up and decorated in the warm colors that the Russian Ballet had brought to Paris. Madame Stravinsky . . . looked like a princess in a Russian fairy tale. . . . I can never forget the delight of that evening at Morges: the table brilliantly lit with coloured candles, and covered with fruit, flowers and desserts of every hue. The supper was a wonderful example of Russian cuisine, carefully prepared by Madame Stravinsky and composed of every form of zakousky, then borscht, tender sterlets covered with delicious transparent jelly and served with a perfect sauce, various dishes of fowls and every sort of sweet, making it a feast always to be remembered.[59]

Winnaretta soon became involved in an effort to launch the Paris premiere of Stravinsky's early *Scherzo fantastique*. She had recently been in discussion with the Opéra's Jacques Rouché about the organization of a benefit concert for "Oriental refugees." The concert's patronage committee would include "an important group of political, artistic, and socially prominent figures,"[60] and Stravinsky's *Scherzo* was one of the works being considered for inclusion in the program. It is likely that Winnaretta had discussed the work with the composer when he came to see her in Paris in January; he may have played excerpts for her at that time. This 1908 composition was inspired by Maeterlinck's book *La Vie des abeilles* (The Life of the Bees);[61] it is ostensibly the work that brought Stravinsky to the attention of Diaghilev in 1909, and inspired the impresario to commission him to write music for the Ballets Russes.[62] The idea of turning the *Scherzo fantastique* into a work to be danced had been bandied about by the composer and Diaghilev since 1912.[63] Winnaretta's interest in the score can be easily surmised: four-square in its phrasing, but dissonant in its harmonic palette ("harsh, like a toothache," as Stravinsky described it to Rimsky-Korsakov[64]), the *Scherzo fantastique* is based exclusively on octatonic scales; it is, in fact, to quote Richard Taruskin, "one of the most single-mindedly octatonic pieces he or anyone ever composed."[65] Winnaretta would have been one of the few individuals in Paris, other than a handful of composers, to understand the importance and the modernist possibilities of these scales: these were Edmond's scales, the compositional building blocks with which he had been obsessed for the last twenty-odd years of his life. By presenting the premiere of Stravinsky's *Scherzo,* Winnaretta would also be vindicating her husband's belief in "his" scales.

Aside from the worthwhile charitable goals of the benefit concert, and the obvious coup of securing the participation of the author of *The Firebird* and *The Rite of Spring,* there would be that much more prestige surrounding the forthcoming performance of a newly commissioned Stravinsky work in the Polignac salon. Once again, unlike Élisabeth Greffulhe, who used her salon to negotiate entry into the public sphere, Winnaretta was using the public musical arena to promote the prestige and exclusivity of her salon.

For the next ten months (the concert date was ultimately set for January 1917) Winnaretta allowed herself to be used as intermediary for the practical and financial planning of the *Scherzo fantastique* premiere: the underwriting of the costs of a piano reduction of the score, the hiring of a rehearsal pianist, the expenses of Stravinsky's transportation to and lodging in Paris.[66] Even while mourning her nephew Jacques Decazes, Winnaretta saw to arrangements concerning the scenery and orchestral parts for the *Scherzo*—and as much as apologized to the composer for not being able to attend to these details sooner.[67] The letters of 1916 mark the beginning of a gradual shift in the power balance in Winnaretta's relations with Stravinsky. From that year onward, her correspondence with the composer reveals a deferential attitude not manifested towards any other creative or performing artist whom she supported. Stravinsky, while always respectful in tone, gives the clear impression—in the manner of Beethoven with *his* patrons— that he not only considered himself to be the equal of his patron, but that he had no compunctions about asking her to attend to certain tasks as if she were his personal errand-girl. Much of Stravinsky's language is couched behind the impersonal French *on,* "one." In response to letters from Rouché concerning the *Scherzo fantastique*'s practical and performance issues, the composer complained to Winnaretta, "Can one really do these things by letter? If one really has the intention of arranging [the production of] this show it must be done well. . . . I will only ask to be sent, several days in advance, some money for my trip (Paris round trip) and the stay in Paris (around ten days)."[68] In switching to a personal subject later in the same letter, he finally deigned to empower her: "I write to you, dear Princesse, because you're the one who wanted to take charge of the artistic side of this charitable project."[69] More surprising than Stravinsky's imperious tone was Winnaretta's willingness to be cast in the role of a titled Girl Friday. None of her efforts on Stravinsky's behalf could be considered selfless, however: in acceding to his numerous requests, moving his projects forward, and keeping him materially comfortable, Winnaretta was protecting her investment in "her" composer.

Her interest in Stravinsky's well-being did not, however, go so far as paying for goods not received. In June, just before the arrival of the contractual deadline for the completion of *Renard,* Stravinsky apparently wrote to the Princesse asking for the remaining four thousand francs of the commission, even though the completion of the work had been delayed by a trip to Spain with the Ballets Russes. Winnaretta's response left no room for argument: she reminded him that, "according to our agreement," the money would be sent "when the work is finished, and you must send me the manuscript or a copy, made by you, of the orchestral part and the reduction for piano and voice—when the work is finished."[70] On 11 July Stravinsky hastily sent his apologies for having made "a perfectly illegal request," offering as an excuse (echoing Carriès, echoing Fauré) the fact that he was not a businessman.[71] He assured her that "the work is finished"[72]—although the autograph of the piano-vocal score bears the date of 1 August.[73] The presentation copy of the orchestral score of *Le Renard, le coq, le chat et le bouc* was delivered into the hands of Isaure de Miramon, who had been in Switzerland that summer; she in turn delivered it to Winnaretta in Versailles. Dated "Lausanne, September 1916," the autograph, written in Stravinsky's precise, angular hand, was covered in a handsome red cloth with a Russian design, and bore the inscription (in French and Russian) "Very respectfully dedicated to Madame la Princesse Edmond de Polignac."[74] The composer visited his patron sometime in the early fall, and, to her delight, played her portions of "the magnificent Coq."[75] The work was the first commission to be completed that conformed to Winnaretta's modernist vision of music—it was even partially constructed on octatonic scales. And, significantly, in offering his patron not a piano concerto, but a work based on children's nonsense songs, a work that, in Afanasyev's words, evoked "a world of mockery, fun-and-games, tomfoolery, naughty satire . . . a profoundly indigenous *grotesque,*"[76] Stravinsky gave Winnaretta the thing she had been trying to recreate all along: the boisterous musicales and theatrical productions from her childhood at the Wigwam.

Winnaretta had apparently taken pity on Stravinsky and advanced him a thousand francs in July, for her final payment on the commission, credited to Stravinsky's Swiss bank, was for three thousand—not four thousand—francs.[77] More financial arrangements related to *Renard* were assumed before year's end. Winnaretta had agreed in February to the choice of Michel Larionov as *Renard*'s scenic designer, and to the payment of Larionov's fee of three thousand francs.[78] Additionally, it had been decided that the Russian text of Afanasyev's fable would need to be translated into French for presentation in the Polignac salon, and she offered to pay the translator's fee. For this work Stravinsky hired Swiss novelist Charles-Ferdinand Ramuz.[79] The composer had originally proposed three hundred francs for the translation, but the work proved longer and more difficult than anticipated,[80] and in October Stravinsky wrote Winnaretta a candid letter, asking her to augment the payment to five hundred francs, a fee more commensurate with Ramuz's efforts.[81] Winnaretta agreed to the new fee, and the check was dispatched on 25 October.[82]

Unbeknownst to Winnaretta, Stravinsky's financial machinations continued behind the scenes. In November he played portions of *Renard* to Violette Murat, who met the composer at one of her Paris soirees. So charmed was Murat that she offered to underwrite the cost of engraving some of his works.[83] In a letter on the subject, Stravinsky suggested that she consider, in addition to *Pribaoutki* and the *Berceuses du chat,* the publication of "my latest work . . . that I played for you when I had the pleasure of making your acquaintance: *Renard,* a burlesque piece (piano score only)."[84] The dedications, he continued, were unfortunately all spoken for, but he asked if she would "accept simply the homage of the manuscripts."[85] Technically, Stravinsky was entirely within his rights in offering the publication rights and the autograph of *Renard*'s piano reduction to Murat: his contract with his patron stipulated that the dedicatee of the work would receive "only" the piano-vocal score and the complete orchestra score; publication rights were never part of the package. But Winnaretta's reputation had surely preceded her: some twenty years earlier a parallel situation concerning the figurines of the "Porte de Parsifal" had brought threats of legal action hailing down upon poor Carriès. To what lengths might the indomitable Princesse de Polignac go to protect her proprietary interest in a work by Stravinsky? Murat evidently did not want to find out, for she wrote to Madame Stravinsky, "I can't tell you how much moved I was by M. Stravinsky's proposal to give me the manuscripts. . . . The only thing that could be a bit difficult is the question of 'Renard.' I thought that it belonged to the Princesse E. de Polignac, [who] could make trouble, or mount a lawsuit." (She added in a postscript, "since September I have not been speaking to the princesse de Polignac,"[86] although the reasons behind this statement are unknown.) Murat, acting anonymously,[87] did apparently keep her word to help Stravinsky publish his works: *Renard* and several other works came out under the imprint of Adolphe Henn, a Geneva publisher, in 1917.

If Murat's actions sprang from an unselfish desire "to please Stravinsky," Diaghilev's were motivated by jealousy. Through her independent projects with Stravinsky—*Renard* and the *Scherzo* production—Winnaretta had aroused the wrath of the pathologically jealous Diaghilev, who was still nursing his wounds from the defection of Nijinsky. The impresario, whose controlling nature rivaled that of the patron's, could not bear the thought that not one but two premieres of works by "his" composer would occur in situations not under his aegis, or that the Princesse might upstage him as a producer of Stravinsky works. The composer would later recall that "Diaghilev was furious with jealousy. . . . For two years he would not mention *Renard* to me, which didn't prevent him from talking about it to others: 'Our Igor, always money, money, money, and for what? This *Renard* is some old scraps he found in his dresser drawer.'"[88]

Whether Winnaretta was aware of all this behind-the-scenes drama is unclear. Even before Stravinsky's piece was completed, she began to formulate a project to commission additional new works for small ensemble (sixteen players[89]), to be written by a number of composers, which would be presented together on a salon program along with *Renard*. She turned her attention to Erik Satie as a possible candidate for such a commission. This curious figure, who had been composing since the 1890s, had been "re-discovered" by Debussy, Ravel, Cocteau, and Picasso in the pre-war years, and had subsequently become the darling of Paris's avant-garde circles. Satie's compositions—brief and deceptively simple, fashioned from the barest harmonic and contrapuntal materials—charmed the followers of his music with their qualities of gentle irony combined with pathos. In 1905 Satie had enrolled in Albert Roussel's counterpoint class at the Schola Cantorum, but found the theoretical rules incomprehensible; he did, however, form a warm friendship with fellow student Armande de Polignac.[90] Perhaps it was through her niece that Winnaretta first heard of Satie; she may have been in attendance at the "Festival Satie-Ravel" at the Salle Huyghens on 18 April 1916. She was fascinated with the odd titles of the compositions— *Music in the Shape of a Pear* and *Furniture Music*—as well as their equally odd tempo markings ("without sacrilegious exaltation" and "like an animal"). And she was surely informed that, following the concert, Cocteau had asked Satie to write the music for a new "cubist spectacle," a modernist evocation of the fairground, to be entitled *Parade*.[91]

She told soprano Jane Bathori, the featured singer at the Salle Huyghens concert, that she was "very anxious to know Satie," and asked her to arrange an introduction. Satie and Bathori came to dinner at avenue Henri-Martin late that summer. In her memoirs, Winnaretta recalled her vivid first impressions of the composer.

He was then a man of about 52 [he had actually just turned 50], neither tall nor short, very thin, with a short beard. He invariably wore pince-nez, through which one saw his kindly but rather mischievous pale blue eyes, always ready to twinkle as some humorous thought crossed his mind. I remember that the dinner included roast tongue, which he found particularly good, and when I asked him if he would have another slice, he at once answered, "Yes, yes, with pleasure, but . . . not the head, please, because head of veal makes me sick."[92]

After dinner Winnaretta spoke of an idea that had been turning in her mind for some time. She had kept the promise she had made to herself after her 1914 cruise to Greece: to learn classical Greek. By the time of Satie's visit, Winnaretta's capabilities had advanced to the point that she could read the *Dialogues* of Plato and the tragedies of Euripides in the original language.[93] Now she was thinking of finding a composer who would be willing to set music to *The Death of Socrates* from Plato's *Phaedo*. Something in Satie's music had seemed as "simple and poetical [as] Greek dances,"[94] and she was convinced that he was the man for the job. She apparently offered him terms similar to her original arrangement with Stravinsky: Satie would be paid two thousand francs immediately, and two thousand more upon the delivery of the piano-vocal score and the orchestral score.[95] The impoverished composer accepted right away: the idea of working with Plato's text held immediate appeal. Many discussions took place concerning production ideas. Originally Satie conceived of a scenario in which Winnaretta and two friends, all of whom were conversant in Greek, would take turns reciting the text, seated in armchairs, presumably while a chamber orchestra provided background music.[96] These discussions led to frequent invitations to dinner, and the impoverished Satie often made the trip from his shabby apartment in suburban Arcueil to partake of Winnaretta's hospitality. According to Morand, also present at a dinner on 6 October, Satie evoked the very likeness of Socrates: "His face is made of two half-moons; he scratches his goatee between each word. He doesn't speak of his genius, he has rather a cunning air." Morand was not impressed by Satie, who seemed to him to be a "half-bungler . . . crushed by Debussy . . . extremely jealous of Stravinsky."[97]

In fact, Satie, overwhelmed by the weightiness of the task that lay before him, was experiencing a crisis of confidence. He had never before attempted to compose such a large-scale musical work, nor had he ever grappled with such a serious text. To his friend, artist Valentine Gross, he confided, "I'm scared of 'failing' with this work that I wish to be as white and pure as Antiquity. I'm all over the place."[98] But two weeks later he wrote: "What am I doing? I'm working on the *Life of Socrates*. I've found a beautiful translation: that of Victor Cousin. Plato is a perfect collaborator, very gentle and never importunate. What a dream! I'm writing on this subject for the good Princesse. I'm swimming in happiness. Finally! I'm free, free as the air, free as water; like the wild sheep. Long live Plato! Long live Victor Cousin!"[99] The work on the Princesse's commission now became all-consuming; Satie even turned down a trip to Rome in February with Cocteau, Picasso, Massine, and Diaghilev for rehearsals of *Parade*—scheduled for presentation by the Ballets Russes that spring—so that he could work peace-fully on the work that he was now calling *Socrate*.

The year 1917 began with more sad news of war deaths and material privation (including sugar rationing, which began on 11 January).[100] Winnaretta devoted her own energy and financial resources to the charity concert at the Opéra, for which she had secured the patronage of Madame Raymond Poincaré.[101] Now entitled "For the Front," the event was billed as a "patriotic matinee," whose proceeds would benefit the Armies of the Land and Sea.[102] Winnaretta had personally pledged two thousand francs (roughly $50,000 in today's currency) to the campaign, and had also agreed to underwrite Stravinsky's travel and hotel expenses.[103] Despite a highly publicized war of letters between Maeterlinck and Diaghilev in the days before the event (the author claiming in the press that Diaghilev had stolen his libretto,[104] the impresario counterattacking that Stravinsky had only been "inspired" by *The Bees*),[105] the benefit concert was a brilliant, sold-out affair. In addition to the usual crowd of society patrons ("simply dressed . . .as an adaptation to the present conditions"), the audience was filled with a large number of wounded and convalescing military men. *The Bees*, a "white ballet" set to the music of the *Scherzo fantastique*, "geometri-cally" choreographed by Leo Staats and set in a beehive designed by Maxime Dethomas, was danced by the greatest stars of the Paris Opéra ballet troupe, including the prima ballerina Carlotta Zambelli. At the last minute, Stravinsky had fallen ill, and Camille Chevillard had conducted the perfor-mances.[106] Henri Quittard, the *Figaro*'s music critic, who had "never ap-proved" of *The Rite of Spring*, found the buzzing octatonicism of *The Bees* to be "delicately subtle . . . a delight to the ear."[107] The program was re-peated several more times; close to a million francs were raised for the patriotic charity.[108]

After the performances, Winnaretta mysteriously vanished. In March the reasons for her sudden disappearance became known, as the interna-tional papers picked up the tantalizing story: there was a warrant out for her arrest by the London police. She and her brother Washington were charged with conspiring to "evade the payment of income taxes," and thereby defrauding the British government of huge sums of money.[109] The Crown's case was based on Winnaretta's ownership of the house at 213 King's Road: as a London resident since 1908, she was therefore respon-sible for taxes owed since that date.[110] Winnaretta had known from the time of the purchase that property ownership in England brought with it tax liability; since the house was intended to serve only as a pied-à-terre for her short stays in London, she had, on the advice of her lawyer, put the property under her brother's name. Ironically, it was Winnaretta's unfore-seen extended stay in London at the outbreak of war that had tipped off the tax surveyors to her putative residency; their investigation revealed that it was she, not her brother, who was making all of the payments on the

property.[111] The Crown's lawyers turned her life upside-down in their quest
to prove her London residency. The press reported in meticulous detail
Winnaretta's yearly income from her Singer holdings. According to experts
brought in to bolster the Crown's allegations, Winnaretta's tax liability for
the years 1908 to 1916 came to £38,456.[112] On 18 April the trial against
the two Singer siblings and their British lawyer for fraud and conspiracy
began; Winnaretta, being tried in absentia, faced additional charges of per-
jury and concealment of evidence.[113] The case dragged on until late July, at
which time the only defendant assessed damages was the Singer lawyer,
Alfred Bird, who was obliged to pay £50. Washington Singer was completely exonerated of all charges.[114] Curiously, the outcome of the Crown's
case against Winnaretta was not reported in the papers. It can only be
speculated that a settlement was reached out of court, and most likely involved the payment of a hefty sum in back taxes to the Inland Revenue
Office.[115]

During the trial, friends on both sides of the Channel, hearing nothing
from Winnaretta, were worried. "I fear she is really ill," wrote Lady Helen
Radnor to Toche Bulteau. "I feel furious with those who advised and acted
for her!"[116] It was indeed illness that was the cause of Winnaretta's silence
in the spring—but not one brought on by anxieties over the trial. In April,
en route by train to a southern seaside resort, she had suddenly felt so
queasy that she had to ask the conductor to find a doctor among the passengers. "I looked at myself in the mirror," she wrote to Bulteau. "My
normal features were replaced by a purple pumpkin, with two strawberries
masquerading as eyes. 'It's not so bad,' [said the doctor], 'you have the
measles.'" Winnaretta was eventually able to make her way to Paris Singer's
estate in St.-Jean-Cap-Ferrat, where she recovered under the care of local
doctors and nurses. She asked Toche and her friends "not to talk about my
childish illness, no matter what happens."[117]

By the time she returned to Paris, no one was thinking of Winnaretta's
recent tribulations. All talk was of the March revolution in Russia.[118] Soon
thereafter the talk was of another revolution, this time an artistic one. On
18 May Winnaretta was in the audience for the premiere of the Cocteau-
Picasso-Massine-Satie spectacle, *Parade*. The "futurist ballet" was presented
at the Théâtre du Châtelet under the auspices of the Ballets Russes, which
was presenting its first Paris season in three years. Stravinsky's friend Ernest
Ansermet conducted. In keeping with Cocteau's and Diaghilev's new fascination with Russolo's noise machines, the score included parts for type-
writers, sirens, airplane propellers, Morse code tickers, revolver shots, and
lottery wheels. Picasso had designed ingenious cardboard costumes for a
cast whose characters included a Chinese conjuror, an American girl, and a
pair of blue acrobats. Massine created choreography in which the characters
mimed their occupations. Poet Guillaume Apollinaire described the ballet in
the program notes as "surrealist," using that term for the first time.[119]

The Paris public, starved for diversion during the long, cruel war, was apparently not prepared for such an iconoclastic entertainment, and reacted with a degree of violence reminiscent of the opening of *Le Sacre du printemps*. Poulenc recalled that "Satie's music, so simple, so raw, so naively intricate . . . shocked everyone with its breeziness. For the first time . . . the music hall invaded Art with a capital A."[120] Bedlam ensued, as *Parade*'s partisans applauded wildly, while its detractors, who perceived the novelty of the work as a deliberate insult to traditional patriotic values, booed and whistled. The authors were attacked at the conclusion of the performance by a wild cursing mob.[121] Poet Blaise Cendrars, a leader of the avant-garde movement during the war, declared that the aftermath of *Parade* signified "the first days of a new generation."[122] The press, for the most part, condemned the work. Satie took most umbrage at the vitriolic words of critic Jean Poueigh (a former student of d'Indy), who, hypocritically, had come up to congratulate him at the end of the performance. In *The Week's Notebook*, Poueigh attacked this "ballet that outrages French taste."[123] Satie responded on 30 May 1917 by sending Poueigh an open-faced postcard, writing in his inimitable calligraphy, "Sir and dear friend, you are an asshole—if I dare say so, an unmusical 'asshole.'"[124]

Two weeks later Satie found himself the defendant in a slander suit, in which he was attacked in court, as well as in the hostile press, as a *Boche* ["Kraut"] and a cultural anarchist.[125] On 12 July 1917 the composer was sentenced to a week in prison and a fine of a hundred francs, as well as the payments of a thousand francs in damages to Jean Poueigh. Although Satie's friends succeeded in getting the court to grant the composer an appeal, more powerful help would be needed.[126] Winnaretta subsequently arranged for Satie's case to be handled by jurist Henri Robert, whom Paul Morand dubbed "the lawyer of lost causes."[127] An attempt to secure a meeting between Satie and a low-ranking official in the Ministry of the Interior backfired, however: the official's secretary refused to schedule the appointment, saying, "It's a mistake for the Princesse de Polignac to get involved with these *Boches*."[128]

Despite his tribulations, Satie continued to work on *Socrate*. On the train to Versailles, he described the work to Morand as "a little simple thing, classic, lofty, for 4 sopranos, and amusing."[129] But the appeals process had exhausted his meager finances and his spirit. He dined with Winnaretta on 8 September, apparently hoping that she would take a more active role in getting his conviction overturned.[130] She may have encouraged him on that occasion to finish *Socrate* as soon as possible, the sooner to be paid. Satie wrote to his publisher, Alexis Rouart, "I have *two thousand francs* before me, waiting for me to put the word 'end' on a work already partially written."[131]

Meanwhile, Winnaretta started up her musical salon again, in Versailles that summer and in Paris at the start of the *petite saison*. Satie and brilliant young Russian pianist Juliette Meerovitch—dubbed "the piano-tamer" by Cocteau—played excerpts from Satie's *Parade,* arranged for piano four-hands.[132] On another occasion Winnaretta herself was the performing artist, in an evening of Bach organ works, executed, according to Paul Morand, "with intelligence and skill."[133] That season a talented new group of young musicians joined the Polignac circle. Spanish composer-pianist Manuel Infante played works by his countrymen, Albéniz and Granados.[134] Meerovitch played an equally virtuosic piano recital on 11 November.[135] That same evening a disciple of Fauré, Nadia Boulanger, a twenty-year-old organist and composer, performed on Winnaretta's Cavaillé-Coll.[136] Fifteen years later this marvelous musician would become a pivotal figure in the Polignac salon.

The Jazz Age came to rue Cortambert that autumn as well, and, with it, a future star in the firmament of American music. On 23 November, Paul Morand found himself amidst a group of Paris-based Americans, listening to "a young Yankee author on mission to Paris," who played a jaunty potpourri of popular piano music—rags, foxtrots, and United States Army marching band tunes.[137] One song, *San Francisco,* was especially captivating, with its "Negro [style] and pretty languidness."[138] Although unnamed in Morand's diary, the pianist can surely have been none other than twenty-six-year-old Cole Porter, newly arrived in Paris. Porter and the Princesse had several things in common besides their shared nationality and love of music: they were both wealthy, closeted homosexuals. It would not take long for the well-to-do and elegant Porter to establish a comfortable niche for himself in Paris. Fabricating a parallel life as a French Foreign Legionnaire for the American Press, he lived as a fast-rising socialite in Europe, giving elaborate and fabulous parties, welcoming the internationally rich, famous, and talented. The composer's wit, fabulous talent, and privileged economic status allowed him to circulate discreetly as a homosexual in sophisticated social strata without attracting scandal.[139]

Life was less amusing for Erik Satie. On 27 November 1917 he lost his court appeal. Winnaretta loaned Satie the eleven hundred francs needed to pay the fine and the damages,[140] and with Misia Edwards she continued to press the court for the composer's release. The support gave Satie a much-needed boost in morale. In mid-March, he wrote to Cocteau—on a piece of paper decorated with thick splotches of ink, representing falling bombs—that he had completed *Socrate,* a "symphonic drama with voices in 3 movements."[141] Some weeks later he wrote to editor Henry Prunières that Bathori had sung "a corner" of the piece to the Princesse.[142] There was more good news: on 15 March, the court agreed to suspend Satie's prison sentence "on the condition that he show proof of good conduct for five years."[143] The entire affair gave Satie a new cult status. Scholars have speculated that the composer may have seen in his own asceticm and legal victimization a reflection of the martyred Socrates.[144] Had not the great philosopher been condemned by an Athenian court because he failed to worship the officially recognized gods of the state, and because it was feared that he was corrupting the minds of the young?

The joy in the musical community over Satie's reprieve was interrupted by the death of Claude Debussy on 25 March 1918. Debussy had been diagnosed with cancer more than two years earlier; his great final compositions had been completed despite his continuous physical decline. He suffered through his final illness as the Germans began their long-range bombardment of Paris, and died on the day of the heaviest shelling; the last sounds he heard were those of exploding bombs. The annoucement of Debussy's passing was relegated to the back pages of the papers. Winnaretta was not in attendance at the hastily arranged funeral: she had left Paris just before the siege[145] for an extended sojourn in the resort town of St.-Jean-de-Luz, near the Spanish border.[146] By a sad coincidence, she had leased her "exquisite little house" on the recommendation of Debussy, who had vacationed there the previous year.[147] Her neighbor in St.-Jean was Ricardo Viñes, one of the most eloquent exponents of Debussy's piano music. Viñes spent hours playing "all the most wonderful pages" of the composer's music in Winnaretta's large music room, now serving as a sort of shrine to "Claude of France."[148] The young Francis Poulenc, awaiting his call to the Front, wrote to Viñes (his piano teacher) that "the presence of Madame de Polignac must give an immense musical effervescence to St.-Jean, and there must be nothing but celebrations and homages to the memory of Debussy."[149]

Winnaretta managed to receive news of Parisian friends and loved ones living through the awful days of the bombardment and the Allied counteroffensive. Satie, although "scared to death" by the cannon-fire, was preparing more performances of *Socrate* with Bathori; he hoped that Winnaretta could attend.[150] Anna de Noailles, plagued by chronic illness and insomnia, continued to write ardent verse. On 21 May, she sent Winnaretta a long poem "that I wrote for you" on the role of women in the war; the work was recited that month at the Sorbonne at a conference on women's rights.[151] In September, the welcome announcement of the successful counterattacks of General Foch's armies was mitigated by the sad news that Prince Jean de Broglie, Daisy Decazes's husband, had died in Algeria. (The beautiful Daisy would not mourn long, however: less than a year later she was remarried, to the Honorable Reginald Fellowes.)

One letter from Paris, from Marcel Proust, caused Winnaretta no little consternation.[152] After a ten-year absence from the Polignac salon, Proust had returned to rue Cortambert the previous winter to enjoy tea and organ recitals.[153] Winnaretta's benevolence towards the writer on those occasions made him wish to return a kindness with a kindness. The latest installment of his great novel, *A l'Ombre des jeunes filles en fleur,* was about to be printed. In the spring of 1918 he had the happy idea of dedicating the new volume to the dear and venerated memory of Prince Edmond de Polignac; homage from one to whom he showed so much kindness and who still admires, in the contemplation of memory, the remarkable nature of his delightful artistry and mind.[154]

The dedication would require Winnaretta's authorization. Proust, unaware of her departure for St.-Jean-de-Luz, made frequent, unsuccessful attempts to find her at avenue Henri-Martin. By time he was able to ascertain her whereabouts (which he learned from Reynaldo Hahn, home from the front), the matter had become urgent: the date of the novel's printing was imminent. Unfortunately, no doubt flustered by the approaching deadline, Proust sent Winnaretta a Proustian letter, filled with twisting, incomprehensible sentences and disturbing personal allusions (such as this one concerning Montesquiou: "you have a friend who is my enemy, and I have a friend—who will not remain my friend for long—with whom you have fallen out").[155] Despite Proust's assurances that not one character in his novel even remotely resembled her or the Prince, Winnaretta apparently responded to his request to dedicate the novel to Edmond with a resoundingly firm "no." Undaunted, the writer tried again in a second letter: "*I told you exactly the opposite of what you understood.*" Alluding to the unfortunate *Figaro* article of 1903, he hoped now that the homage to Edmond would dissipate twenty years of misunderstandings.[156] But Winnaretta, who feared such a dedication might suggest to the public a homosexual connection between Proust and the Prince, could not be swayed. The volume appeared without a dedication.[157]

Some weeks after the epistolary contretemps with Proust, Winnaretta received a poignant letter from Satie. Rather than pay the judgments, Satie had used the eleven hundred francs Winnaretta had lent him for his living expenses; by the summer he was in his customary impoverished state. The light, ironic tone of Satie's letter could not mask the desperation of his circumstances:

Dear and Good Princesse—I am writing to ask you a big favor. At the time of my sentencing, you very kindly sent me a sum of *eleven hundred* francs. Of this sum, I have paid out *211 f[rancs], 26 [centimes]*. There remains, then, *888f,74*.

It's about this that I address myself to you.

As a consequence of the misfortunes & peculiarities of the present war, I find myself deprived of sols, ducats & other objects of this genre. The lack of these trinkets results in my being not very comfortable. Yes—& *Necessity** forces me, Dear Madame, to turn to you, & prompts me to ask you to authorize me to make use of the above-mentioned *888f,74*.

You know, Princesse, that I have no intention of giving one cent to the noble critic who is the cause of my judiciary ills. One hundred francs should be sufficient to take to the [court] proceedings & ward off his evil blows, & stand up to him, if he attacks me.

May I dispose of this remainder? As an *advance?*

. . .

How are you doing? I heard about you from Madame Cocteau. Picasso told me that he had seen you. When will I have the pleasure?

I don't expect to send you *Socrate* before having submitted it.** I'm cleaning up the orchestral score. The work remains as we both discussed it, Dear & Good Princesse.

We will have a fine show with *Renard,* for Stravinsky's piece is good, *very good.* Come back soon, Madame; stay well; & believe me your respectful and devoted

Erik Satie[158]

*A very strange animal

**Read: before having submitted it *to you (at the performance).*

Satie's letter to Cocteau on 21 October suggests that "the Good Princesse" had assured his solvency, and that she was planning to give "her show"— the concert including *Socrate*—in the coming season.[159] For the moment, the composer felt secure; he was able to continue to indulge his penchant for buying a new umbrella every week.[160]

With Allied victory virtually a foregone conclusion, Winnaretta began to plan her return to Paris. She reasoned—accurately, as it turned out— that the war would probably be over by the next spring, and therefore foresaw July 1919 as a propitious time to present a program of works for small orchestra that she had commissioned. *Renard* and *Socrate* would not be sufficient to fill an entire evening, so she asked Armande de Polignac to write something for her; she also had it in mind to commission a work by Ravel.[161] Armande fulfilled the commission with a slight piece called *La Recherche de la vérité* (In Quest of the Truth);[162] regrettably, the Ravel commission seems never to have materialized.

Just before leaving for Paris, Winnaretta proffered one last commission to up-and-coming Spanish composer Manuel de Falla.[163] Born in 1876, Falla first established himself as a virtuoso pianist, performing his own first folk-inspired works in solo recitals. In 1907 he moved to Paris, where he became a protégé of impressionist composers Debussy, Ravel, and Paul Dukas, under whose guidance his style took on a new refinement. By the time that war obliged him to return to his homeland, Falla had completed a suite of seven Spanish folksong settings, and was in the process of composing *Nights in the Gardens of Spain.* Like Stravinsky, he was interested in integrating folkloric music with modernist harmonic constructions and theatrical forms. In 1917 he was "discovered" by Diaghilev, who, during a Ballets Russes tour of Spain, heard a colorful new pantomime by Falla, a predecessor of the composer's popular *Three-Cornered Hat.*

It was Ricardo Viñes who, during their evenings together in St.-Jean-de-Luz, introduced Winnaretta to Falla's music. Subsequently she found great challenge and pleasure in sight-reading through his piano works.[164] On 25 October Winnaretta wrote to Falla, proposing the same terms that she had offered to Stravinsky and Satie: to write a work for an ensemble of sixteen musicians, on a subject of the composer's choosing.[165] In a letter that has not surfaced, the composer apparently asked intriguing questions about how the work was to be staged, for Winnaretta wrote an equally intriguing response: "The work would not necessarily have to include marionettes."[166] The concept of utilizing marionettes does not seem to have originated with the patron; more than likely the idea came from Falla, who in the past had collaborated with his friend, the poet Federico Garcia Lorca, in mounting musical puppet shows based on a great variety of subjects. The notion of including puppetry in twentieth-century musical spectacles was initiated, of course, by *Petrushka,* and was moved forward by *Parade,* another work emblematic of the Futurist aesthetic of mechanical, disjunct movement.

Falla's ideas began to coalesce at the same moment that the armistice was being signed. By 9 December he had come up with a subject for his new composition: it would come from the twenty-sixth chapter of of Part Two of Cervantes's *Don Quixote,* entitled "El Retablo de Maese Pedro [Master Peter's Puppet Theater]."[167] In this story, Don Quixote attends a performance of a marionette show depicting a legend of knight errantry: Don Gayferos's freeing of his wife Melisendra, kidnapped by the Moors. Quixote, confusing the enacted story with his own mission as a knight-errant, finally ascends to the stage of the marionette theater, violently "slaying" the puppets and ranting about the glories of chivalry. Winnaretta responded with enthusiasm to Falla's proposal.[168] A contract was drawn up at the end of the year and signed in January.[169]

Upon returning to Paris, Winnaretta resumed her musical soirees and dinners. Starting in January 1919 the gatherings took place on a weekly basis, as if the hostess were making up for lost time.[170] A performance of *Socrate* (with piano) was scheduled for early February. Satie had abandoned his original idea of having *Socrate* performed by four sopranos, having been convinced by Cocteau to have it sung by a children's choir.[171] A number of people, including the Abbé Mugnier, gathered on the snowy winter evening of 7 February to hear the piece. Regrettably, the performance did not come off as planned. Later that night Mugnier wrote in his diary, "There was no music. The child who was supposed to play Alcibiade was in Argenteuil and couldn't come so far, held back by the snow or the ice, no doubt. Alcibiade at Argenteuil!"[172] Ultimately, it was Jane Bathori—alone—who sang the first performance of *Socrate* in the Polignac salon, accompanied by the composer. The rescheduled event probably took place on 16 February.[173] Regrettably, no documentation of this soiree has surfaced other than the date; despite the greatness of the music, the event passed by inauspiciously.

Happily, there were a number of reports of the next performance of *Socrate*, given on 21 March at La Maison des Amis des Livres, Adrienne Monnier's famous Left Bank bookshop on the rue de l'Odéon. Now that the obligation to give the first performance of the complete work in the Polignac *atelier* was fulfilled (though only with piano accompaniment), Satie was free—having secured Winnaretta's necessary approval[174]—to present *Socrate* to his friends from Paris's literary and artistic community: writers Paul Claudel, André Gide, Léon-Paul Fargue, Francis Jammes, James Joyce, and Paul Valéry; artists Georges Braque, Jacques Derain, and Pablo Picasso; composers Francis Poulenc, Darius Milhaud, and Igor Stravinsky.[175] Jean Cocteau introduced the work. The vocal part was sung by Suzanne Balguerie, with Satie again at the piano. Writer Maurice Sachs recorded his impressions of that memorable evening:

> We did not know at first just what was in store for us, and what amusement the serious-farcical Satie had prepared for us under the name of SOCRATES. . . . In truth, there were many tears in the eyes of those who listened to the death of Socrates, and [to] the last modulation, which resembled nothing else in our experience, and whose simplicity was more absolute than that of Greece itself. . . . [W]e were the witnesses to this phenomenon of which one speaks so often in the arts chronicles, and which is so rare: a revelation.[176]

The sober, pristine calm of Satie's music was at odds with the ebullient atmosphere that reigned in Paris at that moment, as leaders from all over the world converged in Versailles for the Peace Conference of 1919. Winnaretta's old refuge, the Trianon Palace Hotel, was converted into quarters for foreign dignitaries and political experts. Others came to launch campaigns of other kinds: Christabel Pankhurst, in Paris to promote the cause of women's rights, stopped by avenue Henri-Martin to introduce Winnaretta to her mother Emmeline.[177] With the signing of the armistice on 28 June, the city swelled with visitors. Sensing that good times were about to return, new revelers came to join the party. One of these was the audacious, warmhearted American Elsa Maxwell, soon to become one of Europe's leading hostesses, carving out a profession by showing rich people how to spend their money. Having secured an introduction to Britain's foreign secretary Lord Balfour, Maxwell had convinced Lady Colebrooke to throw a dinner party for him at the Ritz. Winnaretta was one of those invited, along with her old friends Comte Boni de Castellane and Sir Ronald Storrs. Another guest, Mrs. George Keppel, Edward VII's former mistress, would figure prominently in Winnaretta's life some years later, but it was Elsa Maxwell, who shared Winnaretta's sense of adventure along with her American, no-nonsense pragmatism, with whom she would form a warm, lasting friendship.[178]

Winnaretta was glad to reunite with family members dispersed through the war years. One favorite niece, Daisy Winnaretta Singer (Franklin Singer's daughter), had recently married François Dupré, a young financial advisor who would subsequently serve Winnaretta in this capacity. Several Polignac nephews who had served in the army now returned to civilian life, including Marquise Louise's sons Charles, an artist and violinist, and the handsome Jean, a great *mélomane* as well as an avid sportsman. The Polignac family met regularly for dinners and musicales; Winnaretta was frequently accompanied to these gatherings by Isaure de Miramon. That winter she hosted a series of musical matinees and soirees featuring standard repertoire. In December, Juliette Meerovitch performed works of Chopin and Lizst;[179] a month later, César Franck's Piano Quintet was performed by the Czech Quartet and an unnamed pianist.[180] Later that season, the young organist Marcel Dupré, recently acclaimed for his traversal of the complete organ works of J. S. Bach at the Trocadéro, played three recitals on Winnaretta's Cavaillé-Coll.[181]

Winnaretta had intended to present her soiree of premieres—*El Retablo, Socrate,* and *Renard*—at the end of the spring season, but there were problems with each work. The contractual deadline for the completion of *El Retablo* had come and gone. It had been a difficult year for Falla: both of his parents had died within a six-month period, even as his *Three-Cornered Hat,* performed in London by the Ballets Russes, was enjoying international success. Winnaretta's first impressions of the thin, diminutive Spaniard, whom she met for the first time when he came to stay with her at avenue Henri-Martin in mid-June 1919,[182] were recorded in her memoirs. She was struck by his "hard, emaciated features and dark complexion," which reminded her of "a figure carved out of walnut or a medieval saint in discolored stone."[183] Falla's opinions were as striking as his person. "He was very religious," she recalled. "He held strong political views, conservative and royalist; his hatred and indignation when any modern or democratic opinion was expressed amused me very much."[184] Whatever declarations the composer may have made during his visit concerning the speedy fulfillment of Winnaretta's commission, however, would prove to be optimistic: the *Retablo* would not be completed or performed until 1923.

As for *Socrate,* Winnaretta found her control over the work being wrested away by competing impresarios and *mécènes.* After its performance in the Polignac salon, Jean Cocteau took up the championship of *Socrate* in the public arena, arranging for two productions of the work for the 1920 season. Knowing how badly Satie needed the money and the good publicity, Winnaretta, swallowing her pride and envy, gave her authorization for the performances, despite the fact that it eroded the exclusive nature of her own "new music evening" projects.[185] She even loaned her own still unused set of orchestral parts for the event.[186] Satie understood the sacrifice of prestige that she was making for him: he asked the Comte and Comtesse

Étienne de Beaumont, sponsors of one of the 1920 performances, to give Winnaretta her due in the promotion of the event. "Would you please take care . . . with our good Princesse? She is precious, and I ask you, as a favor to me, to make an effort to get along with her."[187]

Winnaretta's greatest problems in organizing her soiree were caused by Diaghilev, who was resolutely obstructive in all matters related to *Renard*. For years he had been happy to tell all and sundry about *Les Noces*, in which he had a proprietary interest, but he would never mention *Renard*, a work which, according to Stravinsky, "left him completely indifferent (naturally, as does everything I write that is not for him)."[188] Diaghilev was anything but indifferent, however, when Winnaretta tried to schedule a first performance of *Renard* in her *atelier*, a performance that would necessitate the loan of the Ballets Russes's dancers and mimes. As far as the jealous impresario was concerned, the Princesse de Polignac had committed "treason" by commissioning a work from "his" composer. He wreaked his vengeance by finding myriad reasons to decline his help: the Polignac salon was not equipped to handle a theatrical production; the dancers were preparing for an upcoming tour, or were on tour, or were exhausted from their recent tour; the Ballets Russes would probably not last another year; and so forth.[189]

In the midst of her frustrated attempts to present important new works into her salon, Winnaretta received a piece of news in December that surely gave her pause. Proust's *A l'Ombre des jeunes filles en fleur* had been released—without a dedication to Prince Edmond—on 23 June 1919, five days before the signing of peace at Versailles. The book, like its predecessor, *Du Côté de chez Swann*, garnered a small number of passionate admirers, but it also had its detractors. All in all, the second installment of Proust's novel was considered to be a moderate success. On an impulse, the author decided in September to apply for the Goncourt Prize, France's most prestigious literary award. No one was more shocked than Proust to learn, on 10 December, that he had won it. This honor brought him the kind of fame that he had yearned for all his life. The newspapers were filled with articles about the heretofore-unknown author; by the end of the year he was a household name. "And that," Winnaretta would say self-deprecatingly many years later, recalling Proust's entreaties to associate Edmond's name with the novel, "is the story of how I turned down the dedication to a masterpiece."[190]

At least she could take satisfaction in the first public performances of *Socrate*. The work's premiere, sponsored by the Société Nationale, took place at the Ancien Conservatoire on 14 February 1920, with the soprano solos divided between Jane Bathori and Suzanne Balguerie. André Solomon was the pianist. The audience, expecting a work by Satie the humorist, was puzzled by the austere beauty and serious subject matter of *Socrate*, and regarded the whole performance as a joke. Some greeted *The Death of*

Socrates with laughter; many were simply bored. Satie may have anticipated the public's reaction, for in a pre-concert advertisement in the *Guide
du Concert* he had written: "Those who are unable to understand are requested by me to observe an attitude of complete submission and inferior-
ity."[191] But the work's vindication arrived four months later. On 7 June
1920, *Socrate*'s first performance with solo voice and chamber orchestra
was presented at the Salle Érard under the aegis of an "Erik Satie Festival,"
conceived by the composer and realized through the initiative of the Comte
and Comtesse de Beaumont. This time the performance was organized by a
professional concert agency, and promoted by a committee of powerful
society women, including Winnaretta.[192] Jean Cocteau introduced the concert. The vocal solo was sung by an eminent exponent of modern music,
Polish-born mezzo-soprano Marya Freund;[193] Satie's favorite conductor,
Félix Delgrange, was at the podium. With an audience full of wealthy and
influential partisans, the response was naturally more satisfying. Satie basked
in his "moral triumph," now that the press that had branded him a *Boche*
now declared him "more French than ever."[194] He had triumphed, thanks
to the friends who had believed in him.

And thanks, especially, to Winnaretta's love of classical literature. Through
her encouragement, Satie was able to remake the clarity and simplicity of
classicism within the framework of a modernist idiom.[195] The cool, objective
placidity with which he set the story of Socrates's death was in its own way as
radical as Stravinsky's angular, raucous *Renard*. It deeply impressed some of
the most distinguished critics and composers of the day.[196] A new generation
of young composers—Georges Auric,[197] Louis Durey, Arthur Honegger, Darius
Milhaud, Francis Poulenc, and Germaine Tailleferre (later known as "Les
Six")—became the composer's de facto disciples; before long their compositions would be featured in the Polignac salon alongside those of their "master." *Socrate* can be viewed retrospectively as the harbinger of one of the most
important aesthetic trends of the postwar years: neoclassicism.

For the Polignac family, however, the major event of 1920 was not musical but dynastic. That January, Winnaretta's nephew, Comte Pierre de
Polignac, became engaged to Charlotte Grimaldi, hereditary Princess of
Monaco. Handsome, refined, and witty (Proust had had a crush on him[198]),
a connoisseur of art and music, Pierre had had a brief career as a diplomat
in China. The impending alliance with Monaco brought new prestige to
the Polignac family. The pre-wedding festivities began in Paris six weeks
before the actual event. On 1 February, the two families attended a performance of Armande de Polignac's Orientalist orchestral work, *La Source
lointaine,* by the Concerts Lamoureux;[199] subsequent weeks brought a steady
stream of lunches and formal dinners honoring the couple.[200] On 16 March
the Polignac family arrived en masse in Monaco to attend three days of
garden parties, official lunches and dinners, parades and fireworks. On 20
March, the royal wedding took place under a brilliant blue sky.[201]

In the midst of the festivities, Winnaretta received some disquieting news. In recent years, Isaure de Miramon had mixed with a group of young aristocrats who used morphine as a recreational drug. Jean Cocteau and Violette Murat introduced her to opium; before long, she became addicted. Now, in Monaco, Winnaretta received a "heartrending" letter, apprising her that Isaure had suffered from a drug overdose, and was hospitalized by her family in a private clinic.[202] By the time Winnaretta returned to Paris, Isaure was being kept in seclusion, forbidden visitors.[203] That spring, although Winnaretta continued to appear in society (attending the orchestral premiere of *Socrate* in June, taking tea with Queen Marie of Romania in July),[204] she remained anxious about her lover's condition. At one point, it seemed that Isaure might surmount her addiction, but her health deteriorated precipitously over the summer. On 24 July 1920, the Comtesse de Miramon died of her "long and unfortunate illness," as the papers tactfully put it.[205] By eerie coincidence, 24 July was also the anniversary of Isaac Singer's death.

From that point on Winnaretta was inconsolable. To Bulteau, she wrote, "I can't tell you anything of myself except that I have lost *everything*."[206] In late August she traveled to Brittany to spend a month with Marquise Louise de Polignac and her family at Kerbastic. In her diary, Louise described days filled with the quotidian pleasures of reading, walking, and visits to the beach, and nights devoted to chess, card games, and sight-reading around the piano.[207] As Winnaretta was normally taciturn, no one questioned her periods of distraction and silence, although Louise noticed that her aunt was more willing than usual to go with her to take communion.[208] Finally, however, Winnaretta unburdened herself to her twenty-two-year-old nephew Jean, who in future years would become one of her closest confidants. Four years after the fact, on the occasion of another visit to the Palace of Monaco, Winnaretta recalled that sorrowful summer of 1920 in a letter to Jean, a letter revealing more emotional vulnerability than any other to be found in all of her extant correspondence.

> It was here, at the moment of Pierre's marriage, that a heart-rending letter informed me of Isaure's illness. Since that letter I have never known one hour, I won't say of happiness, but of real relaxation. We go on, because we have to, . . . but with a heart full of shadows and distress that time will not alter, at least for those with a sense of memory, who, *like you and I*, can't put up with vanity and "vain pleasures" and only have the taste for true happiness—which can only be *the giving of one's self* to someone *who is as we believe that person to be,* and to whom we will be able to say, at the moment of death, "I repent for everything, except for having loved you."[209]

Winnaretta returned to Paris in a state of nervous exhaustion. That fall she moved into a private rest home, where she stayed for the next several months.

In late November Manuel de Falla wrote to his patron, offering his excuses for not yet having completed the *Retablo*. He had been ill, but he promised to have the work finished by the end of the year; he asked Winnaretta to give him an idea of when she intended to have it presented in her salon.[210] Her response was terse and uncharacteristically lethargic:

9 December 1920

Dear Monsieur, I am completely saddened to know that you have been so ill. I myself have been sick all summer. Unfortunately I can't set any date for you for the performance. Take all the time you want to finish the work. I am still too unwell to make a plan for a long time. All my best wishes. Princesse Ed. de Polignac.[211]

Figure 16. Winnaretta in 1902. Bibliothèque nationale de France, Paris. Used by permission.

Figure 17. Winnaretta dressed for presentation at the British court, 1905. Private collection. Used by permission.

Figure 18. Portrait of the Princesse Edmond de Polignac by Jacques-Émile Blanche, 1914. Private collection. Used by permission.

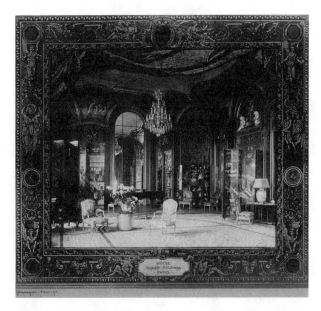

Figure 19. The Music Room at the Hôtel Singer-Polignac, Paris, ca. 1912. Ceiling capitals by José-Maria Sert. Private collection. Used by permission.

Figure 20. Winnaretta at the pre-wedding luncheon of Comte Pierre de Polignac and Princesse Charlotte de Monaco, at the Palace of Monaco, March 1920. Left to right: Comte Maxence de Polignac (father of the groom), Comte Maxence de Polignac (brother of the groom), Comtesse Maxence de Polignac, Winnaretta, Princesse Charlotte de Monaco, Comte Pierre de Polignac (the future Prince Pierre de Monaco), Marquis Melchior de Polignac, Comte Charles de Polignac. Collection of Prince Edmond de Polignac. Used by permission.

Figure 21. Printed program for the first performance of Manuel de Falla's *El Retablo de Maese Pedro* in the Polignac salon, 25 June 1923. Design by Hernando Viñes. Fundación Manuel de Falla. Used by permission.

Figure 22. Winnaretta and Igor Stravinsky on the balcony of the Palazzo Polignac, Venice, 1925. Private collection. Used by permission.

The Magic of Everyday Things

After the death of Isaure de Miramon, Winnaretta did not "receive" for almost two years; indeed, she shunned company. Her tendency towards asceticism became more pronounced. The empty house was kept at uncomfortably low temperatures. She ate little, but because she was less active, she gained weight. She read constantly, studied Greek, and spent long hours playing Bach's organ fugues. Her infrequent luncheon or dinner guests—mostly Anna or Hélène, or her nieces or nephews—were treated to meager repasts, during which Winnaretta gazed into space, beyond reach. Attempts by friends to engage her in activity were rejected. When Augustine Bulteau asked if she would be willing to host an evening of monologues by the British comedian Ruth Draper in her *atelier,* Winnaretta responded, "I would be very glad to meet her, but as I am no longer receiving, I have, I'm afraid, very little influence in the 'salons.'"[1]

These solitary years coincided with the successive deaths of various figures from her personal and artistic life, both friends and foes: Robert de Montesquiou, querulous to the end; the sensible and much beloved Louise de Polignac; her stepfather Paul Sohège; and saddest of all, her cherished friend and "spiritual advisor" Augustine Bulteau, who died in September 1922 while Winnaretta was away in Venice. The last significant death of that period was that of Marcel Proust, who succumbed on 18 November 1922 to the ill health that had pursued him for most of his life. Proust had chronicled one of Winnaretta's rare appearances in society during her self-imposed two-year exile when, in June 1921, the two had crossed paths at a party given in honor of the marriage of the Duke of Marlborough to another American "dollar princess," Gladys Deacon. On that occasion Winnaretta had seemed to Proust "icy as a cold draft, looking the image of Dante."[2] (What the writer perceived as coldness was more likely Winnaretta's shocked reaction to Proust's pallid, sickly complexion, as well as his to peculiar party attire: he had come dressed in a long seal-skin dressing gown that drooped around his ankles.[3]) Nonetheless, she had responded with undisguised delight when he informed her, "Paul Morand likes you very much." Proust had written to Morand later that night, "I must ask you not to contradict me . . . she'd be too disappointed otherwise." He added coyly, "Naturally, I didn't tell her you were in love with her!"[4] Although Winnaretta had never really liked Proust, she understood the larger significance of the loss: with the passing of the great chronicler of the Belle Époque, the door had closed definitively on a golden age. Recent political events had echoed the grim death knell of the Beautiful Era: on 27 October 1922, Benito Mussolini marched on Rome.

While Winnaretta was living in semi-withdrawal, the world and its artists were embracing with a feverish abandon the new decade, a period that would become known as *les années folles,* the crazy years. Paris in the 1920s was in the throes of a joyful recovery after the long dark years of the Great War. An exciting sense of endless possibilities impregnated the air. Suddenly, art and music spilled out of the museums and salons and into the cafés and the street fairs. Every day brought another new exhibition, or spectacle, or Dadaist manifestation, or costume ball, embodying a spirit of collaborative experimentation and innovation. These events took their inspiration from everyday objects and events, from the factory and the workplace. The concert halls now competed with the music halls, where aristocrats rubbed shoulders with the masses, sating themselves on the American rhythms of tango and ragtime, or the *chansons* of the curvaceous popular singer Mistinguett. It was the era of the cinema and the circus, and Jean Cocteau was the self-appointed ringmaster and town crier of the sophisticated vernacular, what one scholar has called "lifestyle modernism."[5]

Since the end of the War, Cocteau had taken to dining on Saturday evenings with the group of six composers, recent Conservatoire graduates, that Satie had named "Les Nouveaux Jeunes." Each night these six "young ones" would join Cocteau's large and boisterous group of companions: pianists Marcelle Meyer and Juliette Meerovitch, painters Marie Laurencin and Valentine Gross, and writers Lucien Daudet and Raymond Radiguet. After dinner the group would repair en masse to the Foire du Trône, or to the Médrano Circus to enjoy the mime shows of the Fratellini brothers. Afterwards they would all adjourn to Louis Moyse's Gaya Bar, where they listened to pianist Jean Wiéner play "Negro music": American blues and rags.

Jean Cocteau's 1918 manifesto *Le Coq et l'harlequin,* proposing the creation of a "typically French" music,[6] led to the publication of a series of articles on the same subject by critic Henri Collet in the French theater magazine *Comoedia.* It was Collet who, concurrently with the 1920 performance of *Socrate,* gave the Nouveaux Jeunes the collective appellation by which they would become known to posterity, "Les Six"—a direct reference to the Five Russians of the nineteenth-century nationalist music movement. Although their respective styles were quite different, the six composers had in common a shared admiration of Erik Satie, whom they regarded as a kind of spiritual mentor. They embraced the eccentricity and simplicity of Satie's writings and music as an artistic beacon, seeing no irony in the fact that while they spent their time reveling in society, their patron saint languished in poverty and incipient alcoholism. Despite the fact that Les Six participated together in only one project, an album of piano pieces, the articles by Collet resulted in overnight fame for these young composers. Winnaretta's assertion that "the days of big orchestras were over"—at least insofar as French music was concerned—found proof positive in the compositions of Les Six, which represented a turning away from the three most important pre-war influences on French composition: Wagnerian romanticism, Franckian religiosity, and Debussyian impressionism. Their music had in common a youthful freshness that was informed by—but distinct from— Stravinsky's; it had a gay and breezy insouciance that was instantly appealing to its audiences.

It also lent itself to the new spirit of collaboration permeating the arts. What Cocteau called "the music of everyday," a new hybrid of "art" music and popular entertainment—first signaled in *Le Coq* and realized in *Parade*—continued to bear fruit. Its first offspring of the decade was a "spectacle-concert" entitled *Le Boeuf sur le toit* (The Ox on the Roof, often known in English as The Nothing-Doing Bar). The work, financed by Comte Étienne de Beaumont, was the result of an impressive collaborative effort: a scenario by Cocteau, music by Darius Milhaud, and stage design by Raoul Dufy. Premiered on 21 February 1920 at the Comédie des Champs-Élysées, it was performed by the celebrated Fratellini Brothers clown troupe. The piece reflected the Parisian craze for all things American: it was set in an American saloon; under Cocteau's direction, the clown-actors, representing "typical" American archetypes (a barman, a bookie, a Negro boxer, a policeman, a woman in a low-cut dress), moved in slow motion to music based on tango and samba melodies. The enthusiastic audience was filled with the "lifestyle modernists," a growing segment of high society seeking sophisticated new forms of entertainment.[7]

After an evening's performance, everyone would go to the Gaya Bar, where Cocteau would read his latest poems, or Milhaud, Auric, and Polish pianist Arthur Rubinstein, a new arrival to the Paris scene, would play a six-handed version of *Le Boeuf* (Milhaud's work had fast become the bar's "party piece"). Two years later, Louis Moyse appropriated the title for his new bar and restaurant on rue Boissy d'Anglas. Henceforth Le Boeuf sur le Toit became the fashionable meeting place for artists and devotees of the avant-garde. On any given night the clientele was varied and lively; the ambiguous sexuality of those gathered contributed to the "chic" atmosphere. At one table, one might find André Gide debating Dadaism with Tristan Tzara. Alongside sat Diaghilev, his secretary Boris Kochno, Picasso, Chanel, and Misia Sert. Elsewhere, Satie exchanged witty aphorisms with René Clair and Jane Bathori. Cocteau and his new love, teen-aged poet Raymond Radiguet, discussed poetry with Anna de Noailles and Lucien Daudet. The "musicians in residence," Jean Wiéner and Clément Doucet, entertained the clientele with American jazz tunes.[8] Wiéner especially was a facile, multi-talented musician: he could switch back and forth with ease between Bach fugues and the *St. Louis Blues.*[9]

Salon life had not died out: it had simply mutated according to the so-cial needs of the period. A new breed of salons was on the rise, where artistic freedom, sexual liberation, opium smoking, and other manifesta-tions of avant-gardism were fostered. The Comte de Beaumont was one of the more intelligent and sophisticated hosts of this new type of salon. In the 16th *arrondissement,* the newly married Charles and Marie-Laure de Noailles redecorated their nineteenth-century mansion with the spare white furnish-ings of Jean-Michel Frank; their vacation home in Hyères was constructed in a cubist design. Under Cocteau's influence they became "godparents" to a young generation of surrealists—Luis Buñuel (whose films they under-wrote), Paul Éluard, André Breton, Max Ernst, Man Ray, and Jean Arp.[10] In subsequent years, the composers of Les Six would fall under their aegis as well. Ironically, for all that the Vicomte and Vicomtesse de Noailles became associated with the cutting-edge of the avant-garde, they were in a sense a throwback to the hosts of nineteenth-century salons: they entered the artistic arena not because of any innate artistic love or expertise, but because it was "chic."

This was not the case, however, in one Left Bank salon, where Natalie Barney, a beautiful and fearless millionairess from Ohio, held court in her hôtel on the rue Jacob. A summerhouse in her garden, flanked by Doric columns and called the Temple of Love, became the seat of one of the great literary salons, and perhaps the most open bastion of lesbianism, of the epoch. Natalie Barney welcomed both French and American writers to her circle, providing a meeting ground for the likes of Paul Valéry, Ernest Hemingway, Max Jacob, F. Scott Fitzgerald, André Gide, Gertrude Stein, Colette, and Ezra Pound. She hosted musical events as well, including the first performance of George Antheil's String Quartet No. 1, and keyboard recitals by Wanda Landowska and Virgil Thomson.[11] Unlike Winnaretta, she was courageously frank about her lesbianism. Over a thirty-year pe-riod, her long list of lovers included celebrated courtesan Liane de Pougy, Colette, Winnaretta's old flame Romaine Brooks, poet Renée Vivien, and Élisabeth de Clermont-Tonnerre, one of the few women of the old aristoc-racy to live openly as a lesbian. An excellent horsewoman, Natalie was known as "the Amazon of Letters" ("amazone," in French, means both an equestrienne and a lover of women); her memoirs, *Pensées d'une Amazone* (Thoughts of an Amazon), were considered to stand alongside the writings of Anna de Noailles and Colette.[12] She and Winnaretta were reputed to have met once, years earlier, at Montesquiou's Pink Palace in Versailles,[13] but Winnaretta, maintaining her distance from openly lesbian circles, ap-parently never came to call at rue Jacob.

If she eschewed participation in salon circles, Winnaretta nonetheless continued to champion the work of her friends. She was in Brussels with Anna de Noailles when the poet was inducted into the Belgian Academy of French Language and Literature.[14] She also kept current with the progres-

sive musical events taking place in Paris. She was on the founding committee of a new music magazine, *La Revue musicale,* whose editor, Henry
Prunières, was a scholar of wide-ranging interests.[15] Prunières launched a
series of concerts to acquaint the public with the composers and works
discussed in his magazine. It was thus that German modern music—notably Schoenberg's *Book of the Hanging Gardens* and the groundbreaking
Second String Quartet, music ignored by the Paris avant-garde—was first
introduced to Paris audiences.[16] During that same period, Jean Wiéner, seeking an outlet for his eclectic musical tastes and prodigious pianistic skills,
founded his own musical society. The Concerts Wiéner soon became one of
Paris's foremost venues for new music. Under Wiéner's auspices, Marya
Freund sang the first Paris performance of Schoenberg's *Pierrot Lunaire*—
on a program that also included Satie's *Socrate*—in December 1921, accompanied by an ensemble comprised of Wiéner at the piano and four
instrumentalists conducted by Darius Milhaud. Audiences may have been
puzzled by the juxtaposition of the two works: while Satie was by now
regarded as the *éminence grise* of avant-garde music,[17] Schoenberg's music
was barely known, much less understood or appreciated, in Paris new-
music circles. Indeed, Stravinsky had been perplexed by *Pierrot Lunaire*
after attending its Berlin premiere in November 1912: he "had never heard
anything like it in music," and could only describe it as resembling "the
designs of Beardsley."[18]

At that moment Stravinsky's thoughts were far from the perplexities of
German music. He was embroiled in the ongoing financial difficulties of
the Ballets Russes, which was preparing its 1922 spring season at the Opéra.
After the Russian Revolution the troupe had found itself facing competition with émigré dance companies and solo artists arriving in Paris from
the East. Music halls were now programming foreign ballet productions as
well as popular dance attractions. The "exotic" Ida Rubinstein and Rolf de
Maré's Ballets Suédois mounted competing productions of modernist ballet. While this explosion of dance activity created a new, wider interest in
the art form, it also undermined the unique and elite status that the Ballets
Russes had previously enjoyed with Paris audiences.[19] The decline in the
value of the franc coincided with a diminishment of Diaghilev's credibility
and financial power at the Opéra.[20]

Hoping to lure back his traditional audience, Diaghilev conceived of a
spring season of ballets based on "purely Russian" music. In addition to a
revival of *Petrushka* and first performances of Stravinsky's new opera buffa,
Mavra, and the "folk" ballet *Les Noces,* Diaghilev decided to mount a
great classic of the repertory, *Sleeping Beauty,* re-orchestrated by Stravinsky.
But the successful London performances of Tchaikovsky's ballet, which
preceded the Paris season, resulted in a financial calamity: Diaghilev was
unable to repay the 11,000 pounds advanced to him by his London pro-
ducers, and the Ballet Russes's sets and costumes were seized.[21] The

impresario was forced to withdraw the expensive and much anticipated full-length presentation of *Sleeping Beauty* from the forthcoming Paris season. Left with a large gap in the programming, he began to think about postponing *Les Noces* and presenting another work by Stravinsky, a work that he had been decrying for years out of sheer jealousy: *Renard*.

Renard, however, "belonged" to the Princesse de Polignac, and she would first have to be convinced to cede the debut performance of "her" piece to the Ballets Russes. Stravinsky was sent by Diaghilev to accomplish this delicate task. On 8 March 1922 the composer visited his patron, to whom he presented a dedicated copy of the published pocket score of *Renard*, which bore the printed inscription "very respectfully dedicated to Madame la Princesse Edmond de Polignac," as well as a handwritten inscription, "a souvenir from the very devoted author."[22] It seemed to be Winnaretta's destiny to relinquish works destined for her *atelier* to the public sphere. *Renard* received its premiere at the Opéra under the auspices of the Ballets Russes on 18 May 1922, paired with the final act of *Sleeping Beauty*.

It must have been strange for Winnaretta to see and hear the work intended for the intimacy of her *atelier* in the distinctly un-intimate Paris Opéra. The change of venue did not mar the work's reception: its artistic strength transcended its location. *Renard's* folk-like nature conformed perfectly to the ideals of 1920s modernism; it seemed, in the words of Dadaist Tristan Tzara, "as simple and naive as a child's drawings."[23] Tzara, writing about the piece for *Vanity Fair*, would call attention to the libretto's "clumsy and childish peasant talk," set to music that was "curious and fervently rich."[24] The work was—and still is—regarded as the perfect emblem of modernist creation: labeled by the composer as a "burlesque," it defies classification in a preexisting form or genre. Its angular music, clangorous and vibrant, ascribes no strong definition to the identity of its characters; the placement of the singers in the midst of the orchestra blurred the identification of a voice with its corresponding onstage character. Most importantly, the lines between sound and visual image are blurred.[25] And the inspiration for the work bears remembering: Winnaretta had commissioned a "pantomime" in 1912, not because of any conscious thought of the modernist possibilities of such a work, but because that kind of entertainment hearkened back to her happy childhood days at the Wigwam, when she and her siblings devised similar theaters piece in the Arena for her parents and the villagers of Paignton.

Winnaretta's beneficence towards the Ballets Russes that spring did not end with the ceding of *Renard*. As usual, Diaghilev experienced last-minute financial difficulties in the midst of the season; once again, Stravinsky was sent, the night before the last performance at the Opéra, and Winnaretta was asked, presumably by Stravinsky, to balance some of the Ballets Russes's accounts left outstanding at the Opéra. After the last performance, she wrote to the composer, "I hope that everything will work out without too much delay with Monsieur de Diaghilev, now that the accounts with the Opera seem to have been worked out in a satisfactory manner. . . . I hope that you will not hold it against me for adding to my letter this little souvenir [Winnaretta's code word for a check], and that you will permit me to wait a few days perhaps to clear up the accounts of which you spoke to me."[26]

Winnaretta sought to create other source of income for Stravinsky in addition to his work for the Ballets Russes. She introduced him to Jean Wiéner, in the hope that the pianist-producer would mount some performances of Stravinsky's pieces for small ensemble under the aegis of the Concerts Wiéner.[27] At the same time she contrived to secure additional revenue for him by suggesting that he teach composition—to Cole Porter. In 1919 Porter had married an American socialite, Linda Lee Thomas, who shared his taste for high living; the couple would enjoy a long and happy *mariage blanc*. In the early years of his marriage Porter had not yet achieved the popular success that he later attained, and was experiencing some creative self-doubts. In 1920, he had enrolled at the Schola Cantorum to study harmony, counterpoint, and orchestration; he ultimately left, finding that the teaching interfered with his creative instincts.[28] Linda Porter, who was not above social climbing on behalf of her husband, encouraged him to develop his talents for "serious" music by studying harmony and composition with Stravinsky.[29] Porter asked composer Paul Thévanez to arrange an introduction; Thévanez described Porter to Stravinsky in the following manner: "He will pay absolutely whatever you want. He's a very nice young man, intelligent and gifted, and a multi-millionaire."[30]

It fell to Winnaretta to arrange a meeting between the two men. How serious the raffish Porter actually was about becoming Stravinsky's student is questionable, however, and the naturally misanthropic older composer may have caught the scent that Porter was seeking only to make an advantageous professional contact with a celebrated "colleague." Stravinsky asked Porter to sign a contract, requiring that the latter commit to taking a certain number of lessons, at a presumably hefty fee. The older composer was insulted when Porter came back with a counterproposal, offering a fee that was but half of what Stravinsky had quoted. When Stravinsky would not alter his initial conditions, Porter backed out of the arrangement altogether in a rather typical American fashion—by having his lawyer send Stravinsky a letter of refusal. On 18 July 1922, Stravinsky wrote to Winnaretta, "I will not hide from you that his way of acting rather irritated me, and I also regret very much that he bothered you for nothing."[31]

Winnaretta was not concerned. Ready to resume her role as musical hostess after two years of absence, she hoped to commission some members of the new generation of composers to write works for performance in her *atelier*. In 1920s Paris, the most interesting compositions were coming from the pens of the young—not only Les Six, but also the members of an offshoot group known as the "Arcueil school," whose best-known member was Henri Sauguet. Albert Roussel, a former Schola student, now a member of its faculty, would attract great attention with an exotic opera-ballet, *Padmâvati,* based on Hindu melodies and scales.[32] In Venice Winnaretta made the acquaintance of the twenty-seven-year-old Italian composer and pianist Mario de Castelnuovo-Tedesco, one of his country's rising young creative talents;[33] she encountered him again in Florence in early September, where he came to play for her several times, presenting her with dedicated scores.[34] Germaine Tailleferre, the first of Les Six to develop a real friendship with Winnaretta, came for a visit to Venice in mid-September.[35] Tailleferre was a fine exponent of the burgeoning neoclassical trend. Winnaretta was particularly taken with the young woman's compositional style: crisp and contrapuntal, sparkling and rhythmically charged, infused with the style and spirit of J. S. Bach.

Before Winnaretta could embark on new commissioning projects, however, she needed to divest herself of other patronage responsibilities, both familial (often requested "in the name of Uncle Edmond"[36]) and artistic.[37] One ongoing charge was particularly troublesome: the Ballets Russes. Winnaretta must have had a sense that she was pouring money into a bottomless pit of financial need—but what to do? If she were to refuse, she would be leaving not just Diaghilev in the lurch, but many of her composer friends, especially Stravinsky. Relief arrived in the person of Prince Pierre de Monaco, who came to visit his aunt during that summer. Pierre was seeking to add more panache to the principality's cultural offerings. According to family legend, that summer in Venice included numerous conversations about Diaghilev and his troupe. Winnaretta: "Oh, how I wish I could rid myself of that bothersome Diaghilev!" Pierre: "I can solve your problem: send him to me, I'll bring the Ballets Russes to Monte Carlo. What a coup for my cultural prestige!"[38] It was thus that in September 1922, the Ballets Russes were installed in Monaco under the aegis of the Société des Bains de Mer, the managing organization of the Théâtre de Monte Carlo, steps away from the principality's famous Casino. For the next seven years the company was able to mount a full annual season with a subsidized budget; Diaghilev's troupe subsequently became known as the "Ballets Russes de Monte Carlo."[39]

While Winnaretta was rethinking the course of her charitable giving, the value of her portfolio was increasingly exponentially, a direct result of the American economic boom taking place during Warren G. Harding's presidency. Elected in 1920 in a landslide victory, Harding had taken the steps necessary to eliminate World War I controls, cut taxes, and promote growth. By 1923, the American economy was at its peak, and investors like Winnaretta experienced a vast rise in dividends from her substantial Singer Sewing Machine stock. François Dupré, Daisy Singer's husband, had become Winnaretta's financial advisor at the beginning of the decade. Initially he took a conservative approach to the management of her Singer fortune; now he counseled her to take aggressive steps to capitalize on her windfall. In 1923 Winnaretta bought two hotels in the 8th *arrondissement*: the Plaza Athénée, which would become one of Paris's most luxurious hotels, and the Hôtel La Trémouille, a smaller but no less elegant establishment. Several years later she would become a major investor in an even more luxurious hotel, the George V. Since her young adulthood Winnaretta had viewed real estate as a solid, dependable investment; the acquisition of the three hotels conformed to that spirit—and added consistently and significantly to her already impressive fortune.

Not only did the year 1923 begin well in financial terms, it started on a high note, musically speaking. On 10 January Manuel de Falla wrote to his patron that he had completed the piano-vocal score of *El Retablo,* and asked her to accept the dedication.[40] The complex production details of the work were still being discussed: Falla wrote that he was thinking of having the dramatic action done entirely by marionettes, and having the three singers join the chamber orchestra off-stage (perhaps Falla was influenced by the use of similar procedures in *Renard* and *Les Noces*). This idea of adding a more fantastic aspect to the performance through "dislocation" of the voice was one that would work well in the setting of a salon, a space large enough for the concept to be effective, but not so large that the audience's recognition of "play" on the spatial relationships would become moot. Winnaretta was delighted with the idea, and on Falla's recommendation, she commissioned two distinguished Spanish artists, Hermengildo Lanz and Manuel Angeles Ortiz, to create the marionettes and the stage design.[41] Although she diplomatically professed to having been "surprised" by the composer's long delay in completing the piece (a condition which, contractually, was to have been met by July 1919[42]), she could not have helped being moved by the conclusion of Falla's letter of 20 February 1923:

> As far as the long delay suffered by the composition of this work (independent of the care necessitated by my health and all the reasons you know), the cause was the unexpected development *for me*—I'm speaking from the point of view of my own growth as a composer—of a work that I began with the intention of creating a simple light piece. As things stand now, it represents, among my compositions, that to which I have given my deepest creative commitment [*celui où j'ai mis plus d'illusion*].[43]

Could any words make a patron more proud?

That year Winnaretta initiated a vigorous campaign to commission new works from young composers. François Dupré helped her to establish an "artistic budget" that, in addition to promoting musical modernism, probably alleviated some significant portion of her tax burden as well.[44] Over the next several years she would commission, on average, two to three works per year. Frequently she would ask for a work in a particular genre. During her two-year "sabbatical" from salon culture, Winnaretta had received from Manuel Infante the dedication of a colorful work for two pianos—*Ritmo,* the first of the composer's three *Danses andalouses.*[45] Perhaps inspired by the dedication, she decided to begin her commissions project with works in that genre. Although each individual commissioned was encouraged to explore his or her particular creative path, Winnaretta's penchant for classicism, the literature of antiquity, and her unequivocal adoration for the music of J. S. Bach was well known, and a fair number of the commissioned works reflected her taste.

The first commission of 1923 was given to Germaine Tailleferre. Tailleferre, like Cole Porter, was also slated to create a score for the 1923 season of the Ballets Suédois. Written within the space of one month, February 1923, Tailleferre's ballet *Le Marchand d'oiseaux* (The Bird-Seller) would come to be considered as one of her most successful works. Combining the humorous pomposity of light eighteenth-century ballet music with the pungent harmonies recalling the language of Fauré and Ravel, the score is infused with the rhythmic verve of the neo-baroque style that seemed to bring out the best of the composer's talents.[46] *Le Marchand* was dedicated to a gifted young amateur singer associated with Les Six, Marguerite Jacquemaire, whom Winnaretta had just recently gotten to know—and who would very shortly come to play a major role in her personal and musical life. Impressed with Tailleferre's new ballet, Winnaretta commissioned a piano concerto from her, with the stipulation that it should be written in the same neo-baroque style, a challenge that the composer accepted with delight.[47] Winnaretta probably asked for a work that could be performed either with orchestra or for two pianos.

Winnaretta next offered a commission to Mario Castelnuovo-Tedesco, whom she saw in the course of a mid-winter visit to Florence, and again in April in Brioni, one of the ports of call visited during a Mediterranean cruise on the yacht *Zara.* The young composer was invited to dine on her yacht, and Winnaretta asked him to write a piece for her for two pianos. (According to Castelnuovo-Tedesco, that year Winnaretta was commissioning pieces for that specific ensemble.)

We were seated on the upper deck having our coffee, when the sound of a little Viennese tune reached our ears. I then proposed the idea that came to mind of a kind of "triptych" that would describe the "dance history" of Vienna: from the old waltz (*Alt Wien*) seen as a caricature; then a nocturne (*Nachtmusik*), an evocation of the Romantic period, but still with nostalgic echoes of the waltz; finally, a "tragic Fox-Trot" (*Memento Mori*), in which the old aristocratic society "crumbles" at the sound of this lugubrious dance rhythm. She was pleased by this idea, and thus was born *Alt Wien, Rapsodia Viennese*.[48]

The work was completed in August 1923 in its version for two pianos, and Winnaretta added the autographs to her manuscript collection.[49] *Alt Wien* enjoyed a considerable success during that era: it was performed most frequently in a version for solo piano that appeared often in the recital programs of Walter Gieseking; a transcription by Mario Corti for violin and piano figured frequently in the recital programs of Jascha Heifetz.[50]

Winnaretta had always made a point of keeping current with the latest trends in literature as well as in music. One of her favorite poets of that period was the young Léon-Paul Fargue,[51] a true "people's poet." A shining example of Montparnasse's more colorful denizens, he felt as comfortable with Winnaretta in her avenue Henri-Martin mansion as he did with the fruit-seller or the bus driver. For her part, Winnaretta thought of the iconoclastic poet as "a modern François Villon . . . eloquent, truculent, and original." He had become a regular member of her salon gatherings; he would show up late, unkempt, poorly dressed, distracted, but he was always forgiven by the hostess because of his literary genius. Winnaretta had invited Fargue to join her on the *Zara* during its sunny voyage from the south of France to Italy. There was only one condition: he must be strictly punctual about returning from his on-shore excursions, for the sailing schedule had been minutely planned. "Invariably," recalled Winnaretta, "as the launch glided away with the rest of the party soon after breakfast, we would see Fargue, disheveled, rushing up on deck waving his arms frantically, having just awakened after a night spent on deck looking at the stars in the summer sky and drinking endless whiskies and sodas. I am sure Fargue saw nothing between Marseilles and Venice except in his imagination, which was apparently quite sufficient."[52]

It may have been her friendship with Fargue that inspired Winnaretta to include poetry readings and literary lectures in her salon activities; she decided to allocate a portion of her 1923 "artistic budget" to this goal. If she had had any thought of asking Fargue to inaugurate these activities, she soon changed her mind. The poet had recently quarreled with the "Comte de X," who had invited him to recite his work in the midst of a boisterous party. Fargue apparently took umbrage at his host's behavior that evening, however, for a fight ensued, and the decision was made that a duel must be fought. The unnamed Count was a convivial host, but notorious for his poor spelling. Consequently when he challenged Fargue to "choose his weapons" for the duel, the rapier-tongued poet replied, "For my weapon I choose spelling—you are dead!"[53]

To inaugurate her literary activities, Winnaretta chose a writer who was as cool-headed as Fargue was tempestuous—the poet and essayist Paul

Valéry. A former protégé of Mallarmé's, Valéry had worked for the last twenty-two years as the private secretary of an executive for the Havas news agency, while privately developing his ideas on the intellect and the creative process. The publication of several major poems in 1922 brought him sudden fame, and he soon gained the position as France's most significant contemporary poet.[54] However, the death of his employer during the same period put Valéry in the strange position of being both highly renowned and impecunious. In January 1923, possibly at the performance of *Socrate* at the Théâtre des Champs-Élysées, Winnaretta chanced to see Valéry[55] and subsequently invited him to avenue Henri-Martin to hear a piano recital by Ricardo Viñes.[56] By then she had been apprised of the poet's difficulties. To his utter astonishment, Valéry received a letter from Winnaretta a few weeks later, in which she offered him a stipend of twelve thousand francs to organize a series of monthly lectures in her home over the course of the next year. He would be allowed to choose whatever topics interested him, as long as they fell under the general rubric of "Poetry and Music."[57]

The proposal was quickly accepted. While Valéry's association with the Polignac salon was viewed as a sign of prestige by some of his associates, others were dubious. A woman who had also worked at Havas pulled the poet aside one day to query him about Winnaretta. "She is very nice. Is it true? They say that she is a little *pédéraste* . . ."[58] Valéry's projected lecture series aroused out-and-out rancor in the soul of his lover, Catherine Pozzi, a former acolyte of Toche Bulteau's—and, coincidentally, the daughter of Dr. Samuel Pozzi, Edmond de Polignac's London traveling companion in 1885. Catherine Pozzi felt that by agreeing to speak in a *mondain* setting, Valéry was being "bought," sacrificing his integrity by "peddling" his art.[59] Privately, she felt intimidated, "frozen," by the Princesse with "eyes of blue steel."[60] In her diary, she referred to Winnaretta with denigrating nicknames such as "Croesus," and "Pilate-mouth," and wrote that she "killed her mistresses."[61] Despite her fulminations, Pozzi came to hear Valéry deliver his lectures, which were held in the rotunda that abutted the music room at avenue Henri-Martin; there, the poet would deliver his oration to a rapt audience from behind a large antique desk, with the enormous Pannini "Gallery" paintings in the background.[62]

During the spring 1923 "season," Winnaretta welcomed some new faces into her circle: Nadia Boulanger, whose devotion to Stravinsky garnered her the occasional invitation to the rue Cortambert musicales, and Polish pianist Arthur Rubinstein, recently arrived from the United States and introduced to Winnaretta by Elsa Maxwell. During that period, there was much enthusiastic anticipation of Stravinsky's *Les Noces,* to be presented as an avant-première at Winnaretta's on 10 June, three days before its first public performance by the Ballets Russes at the Théâtre de la Gaîté-Lyrique. This work, first conceived as a successor to the Russian composer's post-

Rite of Spring folk-inspired style, underwent choreographic and design changes after the Revolution, altering the sense of what being "Russian" meant, artistically speaking. To correspond with Stravinsky's angular, almost savage score, full of changing meters and accents and fragmented folk melodies, Bronislava Nijinska created a choreography emphasizing geometric shapes and collective group motion—a perfect emblem for the new Soviet state.[63] The dance and musical rehearsals took place in Winnaretta's *atelier.*

Les Noces was scored for an orchestra of four pianists and six percussionists. A young, impressionable Nadia Boulanger recalled "the famous evening when [Winnaretta's] butler entered, appalled: 'Madame la Princesse, four pianos have arrived. . . .'"[64] "Let them come in," responded Winnaretta, as if the instruments were invited guests.

The young dancer Serge Lifar had just joined the Diaghilev troupe that spring. He remembered the ebullient atmosphere that pervaded the first rehearsals of *Les Noces.*

> Stravinsky was conducting. Round Diaghilev were Nijinska, all our leading artists, and the whole musical world of Paris. I sat on the floor, absorbing the music and rhythms, and floating away, as it were, into the inner world of this ballet. The powerful sounds enthralled me, swept me on, thrilled me with their mystery, their timelessness and illimitable space, their wild Russian upsurge. . . . Diaghilev looks at us kindly and smiles the smile of a great, loving, omniscient father. Princesse de Polignac embraces Stravinsky.[65]

It was much easier for Winnaretta to adopt a beneficent attitude towards the Ballets Russes, now that she had divested herself of much of the responsibility for the troupe's care and financing. The *avant-première* was a grand affair, redolent of Russian imperial splendor. And the proportions of the work—compact, spare, contained—seemed ideally suited to a salon presentation. The four pianists—Georges Auric, Édouard Flament, Hélène Léon, and Satie's friend Marcelle Meyer—were placed right at the front of the set, almost as an organic part of the scenery, as it were.[66] Reception to the work, both in Winnaretta's music room and in the public theater, was enthusiastic; the public seemed to welcome the return of Stravinsky the folklorist after the many years that he had spent honing the purity of his neoclassicism.[67]

On Sunday, 17 June, four days after the public premiere of the work at the Gaîté-Lyrique, the American expatriates Gerald Murphy (model for the protagonist of F. Scott Fitzgerald's *Tender is the Night*) and his wife Sara hosted a party to honor the Ballets Russes and its new production. The celebration was held on a barge tied up in the Seine in front of the Chambre des Députés. The first person to arrive was Stravinsky, who seemed pleased to discover that, according to the place cards, he was to be seated at the right hand of the Princesse de Polignac.[68] The other forty-odd guests included Diaghilev, with his secretary Boris Kochno in tow, Pablo Picasso, Darius Milhaud, Jean Cocteau, *Les Noces* conductor Ernest Ansermet, the production's husband-and-wife designers Natalia Goncharova and Michel Larionov, Germaine Tailleferre, Marcelle Meyer, Dadaist exponents Tristan Tzara and Blaise Cendrars, and a half-dozen dancers from the Ballets Russes. The Murphys' party went on to achieve a sort of legendary status in the annals of 1920s cultural lore; Calvin Tomkins, the couple's biographer, referred to the gathering as "a kind of summit meeting of the modernist movement in Paris."[69]

Winnaretta's prestige as a modernist musical hostess continued to rise. On 25 June the avenue Henri-Martin salon was the setting for the first staged performance of Falla's *El Retablo de Maese Pedro* (a concert version having been performed in Seville two months earlier). Once again the select audience had the privilege of bearing witness to the birth of a masterpiece. Vladimir Golschmann conducted the chamber orchestra. Falla had written an elaborate harpsichord part into the work—the first time that this instrument was incorporated into a modern work—and on this occasion it was played by no less august an executor than Wanda Landowska. Madame Henri Casadesus played the harp and lute. Ricardo Viñes, assisted by his piano student Francis Poulenc, manipulated the movements of the large Don Quixote marionette. The singers were placed in the midst of the orchestral instruments. The role of Quixote was sung by Hector Dufranne, leading bass-baritone of the Opéra Comique. The audience in the Polignac salon doubled as the de facto spectators of the puppet show.[70]

For this work Falla turned away from the exotic, sensual Andalusian style of Spanish music found, for example, in his *El Amor Brujo,* a style generally thought of as "typically" Spanish; rather, in seeking to evoke the time and place of the masterpiece of Castilian literature, Cervantes's *Don Quixote,* Falla adopted the style of the more austere and refined Castilian music, and infused it with his own pungent harmonic language. The result was something wholly original in all of Spanish music.[71] Each of the three characters in the story has a different type of music to sing—popular songs for Master Peter, lyrical, neo-Renaissance melodies for Don Quixote, street cries and old Romances for the Trujamán, the crier-boy—but every line is informed with a splendor and power, and an intensity and maturity that represents an important breakthrough in Falla's writing. The elaborate play-within-a-play tells the story of Don Quixote, represented by a life-size marionette, who watches the hand puppets from Master Peter's theater reenact the story of Don Quixote's rescue of the beautiful Melisendra from the evil moor. The knight-errant becomes so wrapped up in the tale being told by the puppets that he loses his sense of reality, and frequently interrupts the puppet play to complain about the crier-boy's narration, to the distress of Master Peter (also portrayed by a life-size marionette). Convinced that the puppets are real, and outraged by what he perceives as monstrous distortions of the heroic tale, Don Quixote leaps up and attacks the puppet theater with his sword, wrecking Master Peter's puppets and livelihood, obliviously shouting a paean to knighthood and knight-errantry.

After the triumphant performance, no one could find the painfully shy Falla. He was discovered sitting alone in the darkened music room behind the puppet theater, cradling one of the hand puppets.[72] The performers, meanwhile, were angry because Winnaretta had not invited them to the private dinner held before the performance; they felt they were being treated like servants rather than distinguished artists. The hostess's actions were no doubt less the result of parsimony than absent-mindedness: she had simply forgotten that the musicians would have no chance to eat between the final rehearsal and the performance. Unfortunately, the incident reinforced Winnaretta's reputation of using an outward show of *mécénat* for purely self-serving purposes.[73] But given the important and long-ranging consequences of the salon performance for many of the key participants, this viewpoint can hardly be sustained. Through her contact with Falla and Poulenc during the *Retablo* rehearsals, Wanda Landowska was able to add two new important works to the modern repertoire that she was seeking to develop for the harpsichord: Falla's Concerto for Harpsichord and Six Instruments, and Poulenc's *Concert champêtre*.[74] Falla, for his part, saw the *Retablo* quickly snatched up for productions in many venues, including the Bristol Operatic Festival, the Opéra-Comique in Paris,[75] and the Zurich Festival of the International Society for Contemporary Music. The Orchestral Society of Granada took the work on a seven-city tour in 1925.[76]

Winnaretta was indeed well on her way towards fulfilling "the work to which she aspired," as she had told the Comtesse Greffulhe twenty years earlier: to make her home a thriving center for new music. But strangely, her successes seemed to reinforce her loneliness. She missed Edmond. The absence of her cherished partner stung even more sharply at the end of this most successful season. Shortly after the *Retablo* performance, Winnaretta traveled to Kerbastic, the summer home of her nephew Comte Jean de Polignac, who had inherited the Brittany estate after the death of his mother, Marquise Louise de Polignac. Among her family members, Jean was Winnaretta's closest confidant. Although his principle interests were horses and boating, he was also a passionate music-lover and, naturally contemplative, an attentive and sensitive listener as well. He and his aunt spent a companionable week together in July, during which Winnaretta gave no indication that she harbored any troubling thoughts. It wasn't until Jean took her to the train station for her return trip to Paris that Winnaretta's true loneliness broke through: tears shone underneath her veiled hat. She could not bear her life without Edmond, she confessed. And the anniversary of her father's death, always a difficult day, would occur in two days. All of her activities, all of her so-called success meant nothing.

Jean responded with compassion.

I can understand better than anyone how cruel separation can be. I knew
that's what you were feeling, and that all your momentum and intellectual activity, pursued alone, could not be experienced without some bitterness. I wouldn't say that the fact that people and things have begun to
interest you again means that you are happy, because one cannot consider oneself happy when one has lost all happiness. But to have re-
gained those interests, while your heart still retains a deeply felt memory,
is already to be living with intensity.[77]

Jean de Polignac's understanding of his aunt's loneliness was not merely
theoretical. Four years earlier he had met the woman of his dreams. Marguerite Jacquemaire, the daughter of Emilio di Pietro and the *couturière*
Jeanne Lanvin, was young, beautiful, charming. Men adored her, and her
sweetness disarmed even the most hard-hearted female detractors. Beneath
her natural sense of elegance, she possessed a mischievous sense of humor
that made her all the more irresistible. A gifted pianist and soprano, Marguerite was sought after—despite her "amateur" status—by Satie, Caplet,
Auric, Tailleferre, and Poulenc, to perform their music.[78] As for Jean de
Polignac, she loved him, but could not marry him: she was already married, to her childhood sweetheart, scientist René Jacquemaire, grandson of
France's "Tiger," Georges Clemenceau. Marguerite was discontent in her
marriage, but her natural passivity, coupled with the high public profile of her
husband's family, rendered any thoughts of separation impossible.

It was in fact Arthur Rubinstein who brought the stalled love affair to a
happy conclusion. Rubinstein, a notorious womanizer, had pursued Marguerite relentlessly since meeting her at Poulenc's house. Dr. Jacquemaire
had remained unruffled by the pianist's advances towards his wife, but
Jean de Polignac, whose sense of chivalry was offended by the Polish
Lothario, took it upon himself to defend the virtue of his ladylove. Moved
by Jean's ardor on her behalf, Marguerite Jacquemaire left her husband in
early 1923 and subsequently divorced him; in April 1924 she became the
Comtesse de Polignac. As a symbol of her desire to "whitewash" her past,
she changed her name from Marguerite to Marie-Blanche. Arthur Rubinstein
was henceforth dubbed the "godfather" of the Polignacs' marriage.[79]

Winnaretta was one of the few family members to whom Jean had confided his hopes for personal happiness during the difficult years of emotional stalemate. In the fall of 1923, when Jean's impending alliance became a matter of common knowledge in the Polignac family, she wrote to
her nephew, confiding one of her deepest wishes to him.

I know how loyal you are to the memories of the past, and that you
understand the great place that the memory of Edmond occupies in my

life. In my solitude, there remains the pride of having shared the life of the noblest being I have ever known, of having had the privilege of knowing a mind without parallel. I would like to think that, after I'm gone, some pious hands will gather together the manuscripts that he left, and that one of his own family will take care of his admirable musical works. Almost all of these works were engraved and published long ago. . . .

I would like to ask you to accept this responsibility, especially now that I know, since our last conversation, that you will be helped in your task by someone who will certainly be moved by the beauty and the purity of this work.[80]

(The outcome of this request must be set aside for now.)

Winnaretta's pensive state of mind that summer in no way inhibited her social life after her arrival in Italy. Venice always drew an interesting group of summer residents from all over Europe. In 1923 Cole and Linda Porter rented the Ca'Rezzonico, the Venetian palace where English poet Robert Browning had died. They soon latched onto Diaghilev and the circus-like coterie that swarmed around the impresario. Winnaretta was frequently invited to the Porters' dinner parties, where the other guests included Diaghilev, Serge Lifar, Vittorio Rieti, and Boris Kochno;[81] the Porters, in turn, were soon in regular attendance at the Polignac salon. That summer Elsa Maxwell acted as social director at the two palazzos, organizing stunts, games, and musicales.

At the Palazzo Polignac, Porter met Darius Milhaud, who took an instant liking to the suave American songwriter, and arranged for him to meet Rolf Maré, director of the Ballet Suédois. The result was Maré's commission of Porter's only ballet, *Within the Quota*. Porter's librettist was Gerald Murphy; together the two compatriots created a scathing satire on the values of the American "roaring 1920s." The work, whose stage decoration featured a large Empire State Building, is notable for being the first ballet with an American theme set to music by an American composer. It was performed at the Théâtre des Champs-Élysées on 25 October 1923, on a double bill with Milhaud's *La Création du monde*.[82]

That summer, Winnaretta was introduced by Daisy Fellowes to a witty, eccentric composer from the British aristocracy, Gerald Tyrwhitt, better known as Lord Berners.[83] Berners had struck up a friendship with Stravinsky many years earlier, and eventually gravitated towards the Ballets Russes circle. Winnaretta and Berners regarded each other as somewhat odd, but this mutual bemusement at the other's quirks made for a lifelong friendship.[84] That summer Winnaretta also welcomed Arthur Rubinstein to the palazzo for the first time. The pianist found his hostess to be a willing and capable two-piano partner; at one of her soirees they teamed up for a rousing performance of Chabrier's *Valse romantique*.[85]

As a longtime summer resident of Venice, Winnaretta had established a circle of friends among that city's old Italian aristocracy; among her companions she counted members of the Mocenigo, Robilant, and Morosini families. In particular, Contessa Anina Morosini was often Winnaretta's companion in quotidian pleasures that included trips to the Lido in the morning, coffee in the piazza San Marco in the late afternoon, and music-making or bridge games in the evening. A voluptuous redhead, Morosini was reputed to have been the mistress of the Kaiser. She was well known for her imperious beauty, her empty-headed vanity, and her sense of drama; she often treated the world as if it were her personal theater. One day, she and Winnaretta were together among a group of friends. Turning towards Winnaretta with an expression of world-weariness, Morosini sighed, "How lucky you are, Winnie, to not be beautiful." "Perhaps," replied Winnaretta, "but I have a small compensation—I am intelligent."[86]

Since Winnaretta was one of Venice's more visible celebrities, this kind of anecdote became grist for the local gossip mill. Sometimes, however, the gossip had a sharper edge. It was reported that Winnaretta had invited to dinner a beautiful Englishwoman, for whom she had a soft spot, without the woman's husband. The uninvited spouse, upon learning of his wife's whereabouts, arrived at the Palazzo Polignac in a heightened state of jealousy and inebriation. He pushed his way past the servants, entered the dining room, and delivered a furious challenge to his putative rival: "If you are the man you pretend to be, come and fight a duel tomorrow at the Lido!" He was eventually ushered from the room, but not before he had flung the place settings and candlesticks into the Grand Canal. These items were reportedly recovered the next day, but by then, the previous evening's events had already circulated among the purveyors of gossip, providing entertaining material for mischievous tongues.[87]

Winnaretta's social life continued to be a topic of conversation even after she left Venice. Upon returning to Paris that fall, she was introduced to a intriguing and vivacious young woman with whom she would soon embark on a tumultuous ten-year affair, the British-born Violet Trefusis. Violet's mother, Alice Keppel, was the most famous of Edward VII's many mistresses, and Violet, in her later years, loved to make the apocryphal boast that His Majesty was her true father. The royal affair, while commonly acknowledged in British society, had been carried on discreetly, bringing a wealth of social advantages to Mrs. Keppel. However, in 1918, Violet created a scandal when she began a love affair with writer Vita Sackville-West, whose husband, Harold Nicolson, was a prominent historian and diplomat, and also a homosexual.[88] Unlike her mother, Violet could not comply with the hypocritical conventions of Edwardian England: she defiantly flaunted her obsessive passion for Vita in society, and was subsequently shunned by that society for her behavior. Mrs. Keppel, in order to quash the social damage, arranged for her daughter to marry Denys Trefusis, an army officer. But, even after her marriage, Violet continued her affair with Sackville-West until, after much anguish for all concerned, the women parted company in 1921. That year Denys Trefusis was offered a post in Paris, and Violet went with him.

It was probably through musical circles (Denys was a great music-lover) that Winnaretta met the Trefusises in the fall of 1923. The attraction between the two women was immediate. Violet was twenty-nine, with dramatic dark good looks, a quick wit, and an alluring spontaneity—a mode of behavior that Winnaretta would later come to view as erratic and volatile. For her part, Violet was drawn to the older woman's "rocky profile . . . her face more like a landscape than a face." She soon discovered that Winnaretta's "imperturbable, inscrutable" demeanor masked a penetrating intelligence and a dry, trenchant humor. Violet was invited to an afternoon tea in the *atelier,* during which a young society debutante asked Winnaretta in an ingratiating manner, "Will you be in Paris for some time, Princesse?" "For the next thirty years, I should think," was Winnaretta's annihilating reply.[89] Violet, who liked to portray herself as a hapless victim of circumstance or fate, admired the Princesse de Polignac's strength; she came to lean on it, to see herself as a willow to Winnaretta's oak. Tellingly, Winnaretta's nickname for Violet was "Mouse"[90]—but this was a Mouse that roared.

Denys sought independence and travel, and his wife distraction; Winnaretta was able to satisfy both their needs. She introduced Violet into the highest echelons of Paris society. Alice Keppel condoned their affair, glad that her daughter had fallen under the aegis of someone so powerful, and relieved that Winnaretta's discretion in affairs of the heart matched her own. In December Winnaretta planned a cruise to Egypt and Algeria, and asked Violet to accompany her. In order to avoid the appearance of scandal, the women adopted a modus operandi that would become a prototype in the future for similar situations: Winnaretta invited the Trefusises as a couple to be her guests on the cruise, and the Keppels as well. And so, in late December, the boat began its slow ascent up the Nile. Winnaretta's other guests included Jean de Polignac and his fiancée Marie-Blanche, Germaine Tailleferre, and the young pianist Jacques Février. Février's role, it seemed, in addition to playing piano on board, was to amuse Violet, while Winnaretta played bridge on an upper deck with the Keppels.[91]

In January 1924 the group disembarked in Algeria at the Bordj Polignac, the former mountain retreat of Edmond's brother Ludovic, subsequently inherited by Winnaretta's nephew Charles de Polignac. The property's panorama, encompassing both snow-capped mountains and endless stretches of desert, was inspirational. Here Germaine Tailleferre completed the piano concerto commissioned by Winnaretta earlier in the year,[92] and Winnaretta, who, twenty years earlier, had translated Thoreau's *Walden* in these same surroundings, now began a new translation project. Some months earlier she had read the text of a speech given by the new American president,

Calvin Coolidge, called "The Classics for America."[93] Coolidge, who had suddenly ascended to the presidency in August 1923 after the death of Warren G. Harding, was known for his entrenched taciturnity, but in fact "Silent Cal" was a highly educated man who had been brought up with a solid foundation in the Greek and Latin classics. In his speech, Coolidge had advocated a return to the study of classical languages and literature as a means of forming character and reawakening the world to "the value and the righteousness of democracy. . . . [America's] power depends on [its] ideals. . . . The great and unfailing source of that power and these ideals has been the influence of the classics of Greece and Rome. Those who believe in America, in her language, her arts, her literature and in her science, will seek to perpetuate them by perpetuating the education which has produced them."[94] Winnaretta, a lifelong lover of classical language and culture, was deeply moved by Coolidge's thoughts, and while in Algeria set about translating the entire speech. The completed translation was submitted and accepted six months later for publication by the literary journal, *La Revue de Paris*.

On her way back to Paris, Winnaretta stopped in Monaco to attend the new season of the Ballets Russes de Monte Carlo. While staying at the palace, a wellspring of powerful memories flooded up—of Edmond, of her sister, of Isaure de Miramon.[95] She thought about the musical friends of her youth, many of who were now elderly or deceased. Fauré, her first important mentor, was now approaching his eightieth year. When she had attended a "National Homage to Fauré" at the Sorbonne two years earlier, she was sad to see her old friend "bowed with age and nearly stone deaf. . . . At the end of the concert all those present turned spontaneously towards him with overflowing hearts and many with tears in their eyes; he could neither hear the music nor the loud applause, but he stood there in the balcony looking down with an unutterably melancholic smile on his handsome face."[96] His last letter to her was filled with the gallantry and enthusiasm of the composer's young years.

> *Chère Princesse amie,* your delightful note enchanted me. I've already told you, but it's always an exquisite pleasure to read [your letters]: I see you too rarely and I think very often of the marvelous hours spent in Paris that I owe all to *you, you,* the unique Winnie in the world! I embrace you with all my heart.
>
> Gabriel Fauré[97]

These reflections on the past must have been salutary for Winnaretta, for she returned to Paris well rested, in love, and in a beneficent frame of mind. That winter she established a travel fund at the Université de Paris, enabling classics students to spend four months in Greece. Her *mécénat* in 1924 was personal as well as institutional. Colette had decided in January to divorce her second husband, Henry de Jouvenel. In their separation agreement, Jouvenel had promised to buy Colette a new car. When the vehicle did not materialize after several months, Winnaretta bought Colette the car—a bright red Renault. This gift was followed, several months later, by another—an antique writing table that permitted Colette to write in bed.[98]

Such was Winnaretta's generosity with a friend; what would she not do for a lover? That year Mr. and Mrs. Keppel purchased a beautiful property in Tuscany, which they named L'Ombrellino, and which quickly became a gathering place for the international elite. Winnaretta visited the villa several times with Violet and others of her own entourage; photographs show her on the terrace with Hélène de Chimay, with François Dupré, with Mrs. Keppel.[99] But Violet wanted to escape from her mother's milieu, to find independence. And so Winnaretta helped her buy and renovate a tower that had once been part of an eleventh-century abbey in the hilltop town of St.-Loup-de-Naud (from whence Proust took the name of the character in *A la Recherche du temps perdu*). This "romantic and mysterious" tower became the place where the women were to pursue their relationship in tranquility, away from the watchful eyes of society.

But Winnaretta could not abandon that society for long. That spring she hosted a brilliant series of musical gatherings. The first was devoted to the music of Stravinsky. Earlier in the year the composer had begun work on a piano concerto, commissioned by conductor Serge Koussevitzky. Koussevitzky encouraged his compatriot to perform as soloist in his own work, but Stravinsky, who suffered from stage fright, was extremely nervous about the prospect of appearing in public as a pianist.[100] The conductor asked Winnaretta if she would host an *avant-première* performance of the new concerto in her salon, in order to provide a "safe" venue for Stravinsky to test his wings as a soloist. Winnaretta was delighted to help Stravinsky; she even suggested that he fill out the evening's program with performances of *L'Histoire du soldat* and the Octet for Wind Instruments.[101] Jean Wiéner was engaged to conduct *L'Histoire* and to play the thorny orchestral reduction of the concerto on a second piano.[102] On 14 May 1924, Winnaretta's guests assembled, waiting with anticipation for the music to begin. The musicians made their entrance, and the room fell into a hush. Stravinsky, collecting his nerves, sat silently for a long moment at the piano. Just then, Anna de Noailles, who apparently perceived the silence as an invitation to fill it, spontaneously launched into one of her rapid and rhapsodic discourses. Winnaretta was scandalized. With an icy authority she turned to her friend, "Anna, please, the guests are here for the music, despite the suavity of your own." At which point, Anna fell, remarkably, silent.[103] Stravinsky and Wiéner acquitted themselves splendidly, and were roundly cheered by the audience.[104] While the press was ambivalent about the concerto after its first public performance,[105] the work proved to be an important one for Stravinsky: he played it constantly over the next five years, and it became one of his best-known works of this period.

Winnaretta's next soiree featured Debussy's *Trois Chansons de Charles d'Orléans,* some of Edmond de Polignac's a cappella works, and Germaine Tailleferre's new Piano Concerto, with the composer as soloist and Jean Wiéner at the second piano.[106] Tailleferre's presentation manuscript was bound in an ornate book decorated with baroque designs, and the flowing contrapuntal lines of the music were written in calligraphy reminiscent of J. S. Bach's handwriting.[107] Plainly influenced by the Brandenburg Concertos of Bach, the sparkling three-movement work was also conceived in the spirit of Stravinsky-like brevity and wit. The Tailleferre concerto would be performed in Winnaretta's salon many times over the next dozen years, both in two-piano form, and with chamber orchestra.

Winnaretta had planned to engage Arthur Rubinstein to play a recital in her salon that season, but plans went awry when she asked him what his fee would be. The pianist directed her to contact his manager, Marcel de Valmalète. Shortly thereafter, Rubinstein heard that Winnaretta refused to pay Rubinstein's fee, claiming that it was too high for a private concert. The pianist, outraged by the Princesse's stinginess, refused to play at avenue Henri-Martin for less money. The recital was called off, and relations between Winnaretta and Rubinstein cooled considerably. However, the story did not end there. Winnaretta learned that King George of Greece was coming to Paris in early July, and that one of her friends from the Greek diplomatic corps, Stéphane Vlasto, was organizing a dinner and reception in the monarch's honor.[108] One day Vlasto paid a visit to Rubinstein. "The Princesse de Polignac suggested that I ask you to play a recital for the King of Greece at my house." The pianist directed the gentleman to Valmalète. This time the manager charged two thousand francs more than his client's usual fee—and Vlasto accepted without hesitation. Winnaretta was at the reception for King George, on which occasion Rubinstein played brilliantly. At the buffet Winnaretta approached the pianist, a wicked grin on her face. "You see, dear Arthur, I *did* provide you with the fee that you asked for— and you even took good advantage of it!"[109]

On 24 April Winnaretta attended the first performance of Lord Berners's new "opera-ballet," *Le Carrosse du Saint-Sacrement,* on a program that also included Stravinsky's *L'Histoire* and Henri Sauguet's *La Chatte.* The offerings of the Ballets Russes de Monte Carlo were equally interesting; Winnaretta, seated in a box with Pierre and Charlotte de Monaco,[110] listened attentively to the latest works of recent habitués of her salon: Auric's *Les Fâcheux,* Poulenc's *Les Biches,* and Milhaud's *Le Train bleu.* Erik Satie's music was represented in the form of some "completions" composed for Gounod's comic opera, *Le Médecin malgré lui.* By now, Satie was an internationally renowned composer; his music was being performed throughout Europe and the United States as well as in France. In a futurist tract, Marinetti named Satie as one of the "creators of modernity, futurists without knowing it." That fall *Socrate* would be performed in Salzburg at the festival of the International Society for Contemporary Music, conducted by the Italian composer Alfredo Casella and sung by Marya Freund.[111] In September, Winnaretta arranged for a "run-through" performance of *Socrate* at the Palazzo Polignac, with Freund as soloist.[112] Satie was not present for any of these performances of his music: he was already feeling the ill effects of the cirrhosis of the liver that would end his life five years later.

That summer, Winnaretta's translation of Calvin Coolidge's "classics" speech was published in *La Revue de Paris*.[113] She sent a copy of the journal to the American president, who had formally authorized her work.[114] She traveled to England, where she decided that, "were I not [so old], I wouldn't hesitate to come back again to Cambridge to pick up a degree— what a delicious life, between the Pepys Library, the river, and the King's Chapel organ." That summer in Venice, Winnaretta received a letter from Stravinsky containing an unexpected and joyful surprise: the composer was on the verge of completing a new piano sonata, and he wanted to dedicate it to Winnaretta, in gratitude for the *avant-première* of the concerto in her salon some months earlier.[115] The sonata, completed on 11 October, paid multiple homages to its dedicatee's tastes. The outer movements were modernist remakings of J. S. Bach's fast-tempo preludes from the *Well-Tempered Clavier*. The first movement was written in a terse sonata form, in a manner similar to some of Beethoven's late works. And superimposed on the baroque and classic references was an amiable, undulating first theme, harmonized by chains of thirds, like a Neapolitan barcarolle sung on a Venetian canal.

Perhaps the anticipation of seeing Stravinsky's new score jogged Winnaretta's memory that Falla too owed her a score: his promise to deliver the autograph of the *Retablo* in May was still unfulfilled. Winnaretta wrote Falla a polite but firm letter, reminding him of his commitment.[116] But the Spaniard was overwhelmed with work, too busy that summer with concerts and festivals to be able to attend to a five-year-old obligation.

Winnaretta spent the month of October living a life of "straordinaria" austerity, as she wrote to Marie-Blanche de Polignac:

> Up at dawn, I do a series of boring and completely useless things, interspersed by lunches, always alone (menu: green beans, yogurt, a pear), then I seize my oar, and, with the fidgety [gondolier] Antonio, I row for an hour and a half, in the vain hope of tiring myself out. Finally an hour of "L'Uomo Finito"[117] (which is never finished), an hour of Bach or Biches, an hour and a quarter of Mah Jongg at the Robilants,[118] and I go to bed at 9:30, to sleep "like a log."[119]

Shortly after Winnaretta's return to Paris, she received sad news: Gabriel Fauré was dead, having passed away peacefully in his sleep on 4 November.

Winnaretta joined the throngs who filled the Church of the Madeleine to mourn the passing of the fondly loved man and musician. Fauré had been the first composer to dedicate his scores to her, the first from whom she commissioned new music. Now, thirty-five years later, she was Paris's foremost patron of new music. In 1924 alone she had commissioned three new pieces, from Karol Szymanowski, Jean Wiéner, and Darius Milhaud; salon programs featuring these new works were anticipated for the forthcoming year.

Winnaretta had met Polish composer Karol Szymanowski through Arthur Rubinstein, an ardent champion of his compatriot's music. After years of exploring Germanic and French composition, Szymanowski had recently begun to integrate the harmonies and melodies from his homeland into his works. To young Polish composers he was a hero, but in Western Europe his music remained largely misunderstood. Szymanowski was exactly the kind of composer that Winnaretta liked to support: an iconoclast experimentalist, whose art was still waiting to be discovered. He was subsequently invited to meet with Winnaretta to discuss the possibility of writing a piece for the Polignac salon. She was quite specific about her requirements: she wanted a piece for soloists, choir, and orchestra with a Polish text. Szymanowski accepted the commission; he thought of writing a "peasant requiem . . . naively devotional, a sort of prayer for souls."[120] However, he took umbrage with what he perceived to be a new set of conditions imposed by the patron: a limit of twenty performers and a completion date of May 1925. On 29 December 1924 he wrote to Winnaretta, "Since I haven't heard from you in three weeks, would you be so kind as to let me know if you have changed your mind about the project, because I am loaded down with work, and my health is not very good."[121] If and in what manner Winnaretta responded to the letter is not known, but the commission was never fulfilled. The whole incident embittered Szymanowski, who later wrote to a friend, "A certain rich lady in Paris asked me to produce [strange] things, but she was most sordidly avaricious and we quarrelled over the price (we must keep silent as to her name). I cannot imagine what, for instance, the Princesse de Polignac would think of this, but I do hope that she would be too sensitive to limit the freedom my imagination requires."[122] Szymanowski did in fact write a religious choral work in 1925, a *Stabat Mater,* inspired by the death of his young niece. The work came to be considered one of the composer's masterpieces, but it was not dedicated to the Princesse de Polignac.

A happier conclusion, if not as great a piece of music, resulted when Winnaretta commissioned a piano concerto from Jean Wiéner. The young impresario-pianist-conductor was, according to Rubinstein, "the most capable propagator of jazz in Europe."[123] For Winnaretta Wiéner wrote an exuberant pastiche, entitled *Concerto franco-américain,* which received its first performance in the Polignac salon in 1924. Wiéner always found it curious that, even after having invited a hundred-odd guests to attend her musical gatherings, Winnaretta took steps to make it seem as if she were alone in the room. "In order to listen without being disturbed, she sat right in front of the stage, on an embroidered armchair with a very high back; to further [assure] her isolation, she then placed the chair a good meter in front of the first row of guests."[124] The concerto subsequently received its public première, with the pianist as soloist, under the auspices of the Concerts Pasdeloup on 24 October 1924. Critic Boris de Schloezer wrote:

> There's a little bit of everything in this 'franco-american' piece: . . . some Bach, some Stravinsky . . . and some jazz in the first movement; some Milhaud . . . and some Blues in the second; some polkas and again some Bach in the Finale, all of which is ground up and amalgamated in a very skillful fashion, and played with lots of gusto. . . . There's nothing wrong with writing a piece whose only goal is to distract and amuse its auditors . . . and, in this, [Wiéner] has succeeded.[125]

The last commission of 1924 was given to a member of Les Six, Darius Milhaud. In the decade that Winnaretta had known Milhaud, he had become one of the most highly regarded of the young French composers.[126] The composer and his new wife Madeleine frequently attended Winnaretta's salon, although the couple had no interest in joining in the accompanying *mondanités* that some of the more urbane young musicians—Tailleferre and Poulenc, in particular—accepted with ease. It did not escape the notice of Madeleine Milhaud that many of Winnaretta's guests seemed more interested in the post-concert repast than the music itself. Often, after the last note had sounded, and the inevitable stampede towards the buffet began, the Milhauds would duck out quickly to go for a sandwich and a beer. Yet Madame Milhaud could not help but admire Winnaretta: "She was one of those delightful American ladies," she would recall. "She was not at all fashionable; she was not a smiling, charming type: she barked. Her ideas were her own. She did just what she wanted, which, in a way, is very American."[127]

It was Darius Milhaud's interest in writing a dramatic work based on the Orpheus legend that prompted Winnaretta to offer the composer her next commission. The resulting work, *Les Malheurs d'Orphée* (The Misfortunes of Orpheus), was the first of Milhaud's many chamber operas. Its libretto, written by Armand Lunel, the composer's childhood friend, updates the story of Orpheus and Eurydice to the twentieth century, in a Provençal setting. Orpheus is recast as a simple peasant who tends to sick animals, Eurydice as a nomadic gypsy. The dénouement is as tragic as the original: far from her homeland, Eurydice dies of a mysterious disease, and is lamented by Orpheus's animal friends; the unfortunate peasant returns to the village only to be brutally stabbed by Eurydice's sisters. Milhaud returned to his native Provence to write the work, completing it in less than two months. In view of a salon performance, the composer made every aspect of the starkly beautiful work compact: the libretto was written in the form of short, concentrated scenes; the individual musical numbers were each only a few minutes long, bringing the total length of the work to thirty-five minutes; the orchestra was reduced to thirteen players. Milhaud sent the Princesse a presentation score in February 1925—the fastest delivery of a commissioned work that Winnaretta would ever experience.[128]

Everything augured well for an imminent first performance in the Polignac salon, with all the anticipated compensations—a sophisticated audience, attention from the press, the possibility of future performances. There was but one difficulty: Winnaretta, after hearing a private reading of the opera, decided she didn't like it. Privately, she confided to Marie-Blanche that she found it so boring she would never consent to have it presented in her salon.[129] And yet she did not want to cast aspersions on Milhaud or on his music—or on her own publicly known support of them. What to do? No documentation survives to fill in the details, but Winnaretta's solution may be imagined: she found pretexts to delay the salon performance; at the same time, she used her many contacts to secure the chamber opera's debut in an important public venue. Thus Milhaud's *Les Malheurs d'Orphée* received its premiere at the Théâtre de la Monnaie in Brussels on 7 May 1926, a theater with a tradition of presenting unusual new operas. The imaginative Provençal-style costumes and stage sets were designed by Jean Hugo.[130] Of course, Winnaretta made the trip to Brussels to hear the opera that she had commissioned. Perhaps she regretted her decision not to present Milhaud's work in her salon, for the press was unstinting in its praise. "Rarely have we heard music so rich in melodies, so fine in dramatic import, so soberly moving," wrote Belgian critic Paul Collaer. "The audience listened to *Les Malheurs d'Orphée* in a religious silence. . . . One was gripped by the grandeur of the emotions that burst forth from this work. . . . *Orphée* is Milhaud at his best."[131]

Winnaretta continued to mediate between the private and public spheres. It was well known in musical circles that a performance in the Polignac salon was but a stepping-stone to a wider audience, particularly if Winnaretta herself made a personal intercession on behalf of the composer. After its first performance at avenue Henri-Martin, Germaine Tailleferre's Piano Concerto was quickly snapped up by Koussevitzky for inclusion in his 1925 season.[132] Boris de Schloezer was impressed by the work, which he found to be "very Bach and very Scarlatti, although one finds the personality of Germaine Tailleferre in the melodic abundance of this music . . . in its light voluptuousness." The intimacy of the writing, ideal for a salon performance, did not translate well into a larger venue: Schloezer complained that much of the charm of the work was lost in the enormous space of the Opéra, and that the soloist was completely overpowered by "the orchestral tempest raised by Koussevitzky."[133]

Besides the music, part of the appeal for Winnaretta in organizing her home soirees was the opportunity to bring together interesting friends from different milieux who might never meet otherwise. Since the earliest days of her salon, when the irrepressible Chabrier had shocked her aristocratic friends, she had enjoyed "mixing things up," putting avant-garde artists and musicians next to the denizens of the firmly closed Faubourg, using music as the common coin. In 1925, only the names had changed. Léon-Paul Fargue, invariably late, unkempt, and mud-spattered, was only the most extreme example of the nobility's view of artists. Colette, for all her fame, still had the ability to shock, with her thick Burgundian accent, heavy eye-makeup, and open sandals from which bright red toenails were on full display. A similar sense of discomfort was experienced by the artists themselves, although for different reasons: they found the aristocrats to be so utterly lacking in life as to appear embalmed, dragged out of their mausoleums for the occasion. Poet and composer Max Jacob gave a trenchant account of the mutual mistrust with which Winnaretta's guests eyed their neighbors at supper.

Sometimes before the concerts, thanks to Bathori, I was invited to a grand dinner. As always, one saw there a mixture of intellectuals and society people. In the eyes of some of the latter, this mixture was acceptable for a soiree, but was not to their taste for a "private" dinner. I know that very "chic" people declined this invitation because they might have to rub shoulders with artists! I myself was honored by the confidence of an unknown noble who, evidently not knowing who I was, said to me, "One meets the strangest people here . . . ARTISTS!"—as if he had been speaking of the mania of his hosts for monkeys and parakeets![134]

Of course, some encounters among individuals of disparate worlds were more successful; sometimes, lasting friendships were formed. Francis Poulenc became a cherished friend both of Marie-Blanche (to whom he would eventually dedicate fourteen songs and two piano works) and Jeanne "Pata" de Montagnac, the future wife of Comte Charles de Polignac. In her childhood, Pata's neighbors had included Meg de Saint-Marceaux and Jacques Février; the Saint-Marceaux salon had been an integral part of her young adulthood. Pata had a beautiful singing voice, and would become a frequent participant in the Polignac musicales *en famille*.

Winnaretta took a similar pleasure in introducing her artistic and musical friends to each other. The meeting of Colette and Anna de Noailles in the Polignac *atelier* resulted in a lasting camaraderie between the two writers. Colette's introduction to Maurice Ravel yielded even more productive fruit: she asked the composer to write the music for a libretto that would accompany a ballet, *L'Enfant et les sortilèges* (The Child and the Magic Spells). The pairing of Ravel and Colette did not seem to all to be a natural match: he was cerebral, fascinated with clocks and mechanical devices; she was a sensualist, a creature of instinct. But the writer and the composer shared a common trait: they were both keenly attuned to the magic of everyday things. *L'Enfant et les sortilèges* reflected the personalities of both: it was a fantastical tale of a child's adventures among the objects in his nursery—a teapot, a clock, a Chinese cup—which, through the casting of a spell, suddenly become animated. The first performance, which took place at the Opéra de Monte Carlo, was choreographed by Diaghilev's latest discovery, a talented newcomer from Soviet Georgia: George Balanchine. Winnaretta was in Monte Carlo for the first performance, on 21 March 1925. "It's exquisite," she wrote to Falla, "and the success was very great."[135] Shortly thereafter, Winnaretta visited Falla in Granada, where he dwelt in "monastic" simplicity with his elderly unmarried sister. Despite the composer's ascetic way of living, Winnaretta's most striking memory of her visit was the sensually charged evening when Falla and guitarist Andres Segovia took her to the Alhambra. Under a beautiful moonlit sky, the three sat in an empty garden, where Segovia filled the quiet night with "strange old Spanish music."[136]

Winnaretta's spring salon season began with brio. Poulenc's music was featured in the matinee of 7 April, when soprano Claire Croiza sang the composer's *Poèmes de Ronsard*.[137] At a soiree organized by Elsa Maxwell on 13 May, Falla's *Seven Popular Spanish Songs* were sung by Vera Janacopoulos, in the presence of the composer.[138] The evening was not entirely successful: the weather was unusually cold that night, and Winnaretta, unprepared for nature's vagaries, had not thought to heat the *atelier*. "We froze," wrote Marie-Blanche, "despite our fur coats."[139] Two weeks later it was the boisterous behavior of the guests that brought warmth to the salon. On 28 May Winnaretta presented a recital by pianist Alexander Borovsky and a Belgian trio. At the reception following the matinee, the antics of "three clowns" named Colette, Anna de Noailles, and Léon-Paul Fargue, resulted in the overturning of a full punch bowl, an event as entertaining to the guests as the preceding music.[140]

The next program, held on a beautiful June night, was the one that made Winnaretta most proud: its centerpiece was the first performance of Stravinsky's new Piano Sonata, dedicated to her.[141] The soiree also included a repeat performance of the Piano Concerto, which had received its premiere in the Polignac salon the previous year. Marie-Blanche's ambivalent reaction to Stravinsky's lean, austere neoclassical style, recorded in her diary, is noteworthy:

Soiree at Tante Winnie's. Stravinsky played the first performance of a sonata for piano that he had dedicated to her, and whose interest escaped me. But how can one judge a first performance of [a work by] Stravinsky? I had the answer right away, since the Concerto for Two

Pianos that he played with Wiéner seemed to me to be ten times more magnificent than [when I heard it] last year. With a genius like that one, one can trust him [*on peut lui faire confiance*].[142]

Another important Russian composer made his début in the Polignac salon two weeks later, on 21 June. Serge Prokofiev had met Winnaretta as early as May 1920, when he came to the *atelier* to play his piano music for her following a breakfast *à deux*; the composer was surprised to learn that she was already familiar with his compositions.[143] It was not until the spring of 1925, however, that Prokofiev was invited to present a concert of his works at avenue Henri-Martin. To accommodate the "chamber" proportions of the salon, he rewrote his Third Piano Concerto for a small orchestra of thirty-two players, the major reduction being in the string sections.[144] Winnaretta proudly told her guests that Prokofiev had rewritten the work "especially for her." The composer, who was the concerto soloist under Roger Désormière's baton, followed his performance with a traversal of some of his solo piano music. Prokofiev, despite being put off by the "stiff" atmosphere, was pleased by the attentiveness of the audience, which included both aristocrats and musicians; he deemed the concert a "great success"[145] (although Arthur Rubinstein recalled the concerto receiving only "polite applause.")[146] Nonetheless, for the next few years Serge Prokofiev was a regular attendee of the Polignac salon—the only Russian modernist composer besides Stravinsky to achieve a certain "celebrity" status in that milieu.

The season closed on a sorrowful note: Erik Satie died on 1 July of cirrhosis of the liver. This loss, coming close on the heels of Fauré's death the previous November, saddened Winnaretta. For the last six months she had helped the Comte de Beaumont pay the expenses of Satie's medical care at the Hôpital Saint-Joseph,[147] where, like the Socrates he had so eloquently portrayed in music, he waited calmly for death. Winnaretta came often to visit the quirky composer whom she regarded as "the gentlest and kindest of men."[148] It was said that after Satie's death, his friends went to clear out his shabby little apartment in Arcueil, and discovered hundreds of brand-new umbrellas.[149]

Winnaretta continued to see Violet Trefusis, whose affair with the Princesse de Polignac gave her access to a ready-made circle of interesting friends. On one fine Saturday evening in June, Violet gave a dinner party in the garden behind her tiny rue de Ranelagh apartment. The garden was adorned with Japanese lanterns; during coffee a black *chanteuse* sang Gershwin tunes. The next afternoon the Trefusises and Jean and Marie-Blanche drove down to the suburb of Jouy-en-Josas, where Winnaretta had rented decorator Henri Gonse's villa, built the previous year by Georges Vaudoyer. The group was treated to a private recital by Arthur Rubinstein, who played "like a god" in a program ranging from Albéniz's *Iberia* to a transcription of Wagner's *Ride of the Valkyries*.[150] Violet and Rubinstein were both Winnaretta's guests at the palazzo in September, where there was "mad and constant music-making" every night with Stravinsky, Casella, Malipiero, Lord Berners, and the Cole Porters.[151] At close range, Rubinstein found Violet to be "complicated": he liked her sensuousness and spontaneity, and admired the attentive sensitivity with which she listened to him practicing Chopin on Winnaretta's new Bechstein piano. But Rubinstein also noticed that much of the young woman's "irrepressible" behavior seemed to be a form of rebellion against Winnaretta, whose personal passions were always carefully hidden from public view.[152]

Winnaretta's time in Venice was chiefly taken up with the Festival of the International Society for Contemporary Music, which was, like the previous year, featuring music associated with her *mécénat*: Stravinsky's Piano Sonata. When it was presented on the Festival's final program, the Sonata was greeted with the same puzzlement as in Winnaretta's salon. Henry Prunières wrote, "Igor Stravinsky appeared and played . . . his admirable Sonata, realized in the style of J. S. Bach. The international audience, sweltering in La Fenice's concert hall, didn't understand why the author of *Le Sacre* and *Les Noces* felt the need to write a sequel to *The Well-Tempered Clavier*."[153] In seeking to explain this ostensibly sudden movement "back to Bach," Prunières, recalling the first wave of ebullient musical activity in the early 1920s, asked, "Are we now going to see a new classicism succeed the anarchy of these last few years?"[154] The "new" classicism, could, in part, be traced back to Winnaretta's commission of *Socrate,* a work that had presaged the movement towards the Apollonian in music years before Stravinsky led the march down this new path. In any event, the incomprehensibility of Stravinsky's music didn't stop the public from flocking around Stravinsky the celebrity. Italian composer Gian-Francesco Malipiero recalled "the flower of international *snobisme* that gathered in Venice that September. In the salon of the Princesse de Polignac . . . men and women paid court to the Russian composer. He was surrounded by a perpetual buzz of 'mon cherr. . . .'"[155]

In these last happy years, Winnaretta had come close to creating the world of security, love, and music that she always dreamed of. Now she would bravely approach a new frontier: she was going rediscover America, the land of her birth.

Cottages of the Elite, Palaces of the People

In the second half of the 1920s Winnaretta devoted her energies to publicly oriented works of *mécénat*. This change of direction in her patronage activities—away from musical projects, and towards houses, buildings, and institutions—began, oddly enough, with her brother Paris's newest financial scheme: the opening of a luxury country club in South Florida.

The publicity and royal accolades that Paris Singer had garnered from the conversion of the Wigwam into a war hospital failed to attract the wealthy investors to his European business ventures as he had hoped. His affair with Isadora Duncan had ended unhappily, despite his offer to purchase Madison Square Garden for her use as the New York branch of her dancing school.[2] At the same time his wife Lillie, fed up with his amorous dalliances, obtained a French divorce. Plagued with financial woes and chronic heart problems, the indefatigable entrepreneur relocated to Florida and, in 1919, acquired a large property in the middle of a swamp, with a single dirt road running through it. He devised a plan to convert "Joe's Alligator Farm" into a convalescent and rehabilitation facility for wounded French and English officers returning from the war. To build the facility, Paris called upon the talents of another eccentrically brilliant amateur architect, Addison Mizner, who, with the Singer fortune at his disposal, built a manor house in "Bastard-Spanish-Moorish-Romanesque-Gothic-Renaissance-Bull-Market-Damn the Expense Style."[3] Paris solicited investors from the same group of wealthy Europeans who had endowed beds at the Wigwam. Unfortunately, the facility failed to attract convalescing soldiers. Facing the grim prospect of another financial failure, Paris had the idea of converting the building into a private social club. He had Mizner build a ring of private residential "cottages" to surround the manor house; he financed the transformation of the property's dusty dirt road into Worth Avenue—Palm Beach's future equivalent of Hollywood's Rodeo Drive. The Duchesse de Richelieu—the recently widowed Princesse Alice of Monaco—was enlisted to take charge of the décor. The success of the newly-born "Everglades Club" was instantaneous: from the first launch of advance publicity in 1925, the elite of two continents made plans to travel to Florida in order to discover this new palace of elitism.

In December 1925, Winnaretta crossed the Atlantic to attend the club's official opening in the company of Violet and Denys Trefusis.[1] It was her first visit to America in almost sixty years. After being met in New York by Violet's relatives, the Marshall Fields (of department store fame),[4] the threesome took the train down to Florida. The large Singer clan was already gathered there; Jean and Marie-Blanche de Polignac arrived some weeks later. Winnaretta's first impressions of her homeland were far from positive: "What a country!" she exclaimed upon her niece and nephew's arrival. "Have you noticed how nothing works? Do you still have all your bags? I'm amazed."[5] A daily ritual was begun to see who could find the most ridiculous articles in the papers ("we had too great a choice," wryly commented Marie-Blanche[6]). Another recent arrival, Britain's Sir Oswald Mosley (one of Winnaretta's frequent salon guests before his fall from political grace in the 1930s),[7] was astonished one morning to hear the Princesse excoriating the management on the subject of her broken lavatory in decidedly un-noble language: "What is the use of being as nasty as Americans if you are as inefficient as Sicilians?"[8]

She was, however, impressed with the club's just-completed Music Room. Classical music recitals, Winnaretta told her brother, were needed to provide the new facility with an air of "pure 16th [*arrondissement*]"—that is, upper-class chic.[9] Paris Singer followed her advice, and hired a string quartet to play an hour of chamber music every day following afternoon tea.[10] The first recital took place on 28 January, with a performance of a Beethoven quartet. Marie-Blanche recalled "a delicious atmosphere: wood fire, flowers, a forgotten book, etc."[11] Winnaretta had succeeded, as usual, in imposing her strong will on her surroundings in order to achieve her perpetual dual goal: creating a niche in which she could feel useful, and bringing music (and, thus, an inner sense of security) into whatever house she happened to be inhabiting at the moment. She took to reading chamber music in the mornings with members of the string quartet, whom she gamely joined one afternoon for an after-tea performance of the Schumann Piano Quartet.[12] She encouraged Marie-Blanche to follow suit. Since her marriage to Jean de Polignac, the very musical countess had, with regret, relinquished her public concert performances; all of her musicmaking now took place strictly within the family circle. It was therefore with "insane joy" that she accepted the challenge of performing, on three days notice, Schumann's Piano Quintet.[13] This recital would signify only a first step in the renewal of Marie-Blanche's musical life, which would blossom in Tante Winnie's salon, eventually leading to performances on international concert stages.

Winnaretta planned to travel north in mid-February, stopping first in Washington, D.C. (It is not clear whether these plans included the Trefusises.[14]) Just before leaving from Palm Beach, Winnaretta spontaneously decided to try to arrange a meeting with President Calvin Coolidge. She wired French Ambassador Henri Béranger on 8 February, seeking an appointment at the White House; she asked Béranger to remind the president of her translation and publication, two years earlier, of Coolidge's speech on the classics.[15] When Winnaretta arrived in Washington a few days later, she was handed a letter informing her that the president would receive her on 18 February 1926 at 11:45 a.m.[16] There is unfortunately no record of the substance of the conversation between these two taciturn individuals, but one can imagine that, each in his or her own laconic way, the president and the Princesse managed to communicate to each other the depth of their respective passions for the world of antiquity.

Winnaretta has left no written account of her American travels. In passing through its eastern cities by train, however, she must surely have noted the sad shantytowns of the poor lining the railroad tracks, a dramatic contrast with the opulence of the Everglades Club. Perhaps it was this experience that caused her to renew her interest in the plight of the indigent in Paris. One cold night after her return from Europe, she saw on the street a group in heavy military-looking coats with braided decorations. Some of them were feeding soup from a large iron cauldron to a group of indigents; others were standing in a huddle, singing hymns. Moved by the sight, she went out to meet the people coming to the aid of the hungry. It was thus that Winnaretta was introduced to the work of the Salvation Army, the champion of the poorest and most disenfranchised citizens of Paris.[17]

The commander of the Army's French branch was Commissioner Albin Peyron, son-in-law of the movement's British Protestant founder, William Brooks. Peyron was a charismatic, eloquent man, and he knew how to use these traits to attract wealthy and influential individuals of many faiths and political affiliations to his cause. Thanks to his winning personality, he was able to raise large contributions for the social welfare and building programs launched by the Army in the 1920s. Several successive French prime ministers as well as local politicians, hard-pressed to satisfy the urgent need for public housing, agreed to become members of Peyron's patronage committee: their support of the Salvation Army's public works projects enabled them to reap the benefits of Peyron's excellent press relations, and spared them the burden of actually having to fund these badly needed municipal services.[18] By 1925, Peyron had already created two new shelters: one for young women in the suburb of Asnières and another for men in Paris's 13th *arrondissement,* named "Le Palais du Peuple."

In 1926, the Salvation Army launched a new fundraising campaign to purchase and renovate a large dormitory-style building in the 11th *arrondissement,* destined to house and give job skills to women abused by their husbands or abandoned by their families. Despite her privileged circumstances, Winnaretta understood well what it meant to be abused by a husband and abandoned by a family. That spring she sought out Peyron; presumably she told him of the low-cost housing project that she had underwritten in 1911. Together they went to visit the projected site of the women's dormitory; this was followed by a visit to the Palais du Peuple, where Winnaretta was moved by the work being done to "ease [such] great misery."[19] She was impressed by the Army's compassionate campaign, through its well-organized programs and hierarchical structure, to ease the plight of single mothers, who, forced to work, needed a safe place to leave their children.[20] She joined the founding committee for the reconstruction of the women's hostel. The building, renamed Le Palais de la Femme, was dedicated on 23 June 1926; in its renovated form it was able to provide housing for 800 women.[21] Shortly thereafter Winnaretta, Peyron, and an official from the Ministry of Labor and Hygiene met for lunch. Peyron spoke of a new building project that he had in mind, the addition of an annex to the existing Palais du Peuple, which would provide shelter for another 120/130 homeless persons.[22] An architect had drawn up a plan for the building; 500,000 francs had already been raised for the building campaign.[23] Would the Princesse be willing to contribute to such a worthy cause? Now, Winnaretta was a businesswoman: she never simply donated money to anyone or anything, no matter how gifted (or needy) the artist, no matter how worthwhile the cause. Her *mécénat* usually came with strings attached. In the case of her proposed donation to the Salvation Army's building fund, an extraordinary piece of blackmail entered into the equation.

From the renovations of her properties to the 1911 public housing project undertaken with Vaudoyer to the purchase of the Paris hotels, Winnaretta had always been interested in houses and housing. Architecture interested her on the intellectual plane as well: she had done a great deal of reading on the subject, from the histories of the cities of antiquity right up to the most recent trends in modern design. One young architect whose ideas held particular appeal for her was Charles-Édouard Jeanneret, better known by the name he adopted in 1920, Le Corbusier. In 1926 Le Corbusier was considered to be radical even among the most forward-thinking members of the avant-garde. He had aroused great controversy and often derision at the previous year's Exhibition of Decorative Arts by presenting models of spare, boxlike buildings devoid of ornamentation. Winnaretta, however, had been interested in his work for years: she was one of the first subscribers to *L'Esprit nouveau,* a periodical launched by Le Corbusier in 1920 to disseminate his original, often radical ideas on architecture and urban design.[24] She subsequently read his other writings on the decorative arts and modern cities,[25] and was surely intrigued by the parallels that he drew between architecture and music. Le Corbusier's most basic tenet was that harmony in the elements of construction—the precise relationship of finite quantities—was the key to the realization of a building, just as in a musical composition.[26] The modern city, he wrote in 1924, must incorporate both diversity and unity: "chaos and turmoil in the general plan (meaning a composition full of contrasting elements—as in a fugue or symphony), uniformity in the details (meaning decency, restraint, and conformity in the details)."[27] Le Corbusier came by these musical metaphors naturally: his brother Albert was a composer, a friend of Fauré, and, at one time, a professor at the Schola Cantorum. Both of the brothers Jeanneret were avid concertgoers, and it may have been at some musical event, perhaps even at a recital in a private salon, that Winnaretta was first introduced to Le Corbusier.[28]

In May 1926 Winnaretta informed Peyron that she was considering the underwriting of the bulk of the construction costs for the annex to the Palais du Peuple, but only under certain conditions. She was not entirely satisfied with the design submitted by the Salvation Army's architect, a Monsieur Préau. Given the extent of her proposed largesse, it seemed to her that she "had the right" to designate the architect of her choice for the project.[29] In fact, she informed the astonished Peyron, she had an architect in mind, one whose "methods and procedures worked better than any other,"[30] and who, she was certain, could complete the project less expensively than Préau.[31] Shortly after this conversation Winnaretta wrote to Le Corbusier, with whom she had never had any prior professional contact.[32] She bluntly exposed the manner in which she had imposed her choice of architect on the commissioner, effectively letting Le Corbusier know that he must underbid Préau in order to win the project.[33] Shortly thereafter Winnaretta left Paris for the summer. During her absence, Le Corbusier went to see the Palais du Peuple, where he was "moved by the beauty of the [charitable] work" being done there.[34] By late September, the Salvation Army and the architect had reached an agreement, both in terms of the design plan and the financial terms. "Our stripped-down dormitory will be modest compared to San Marco or the marble [circle] of Il Rendentore," Le Corbusier wrote to Winnaretta, "[but] we can bring to the Palais du Peuple's humble frame the unsuspected riches born of its proportions."[35]

Coincidentally, during the summer, Winnaretta received a letter from another great artist pursuing the dream of "being in one's own home."[36] Igor Stravinsky was hoping to buy a beautiful but dilapidated house in Nice, situated on a large piece of garden property. He had enough money to pay half the purchase price, but could afford neither the reconstruction costs nor the taxes. He asked Winnaretta if she knew of a bank that would offer a loan at a favorable interest; perhaps he was secretly hoping that she would simply front the money, or co-sign the loan.[37] Winnaretta contacted a real estate office in which she "had an interest," intimating that this agency would offer the composer a loan at a rate appreciably lower than the one he had been offered in Nice.[38] "How well I understand your desire to have a home to your liking, in the Midi, where you can find the calm that you need, and I will be more than happy if I can help you to find the means to realize your plans."[39]

During that same period, however, the American composer Virgil Thomson was unsuccessful in securing Winnaretta's aid. Newly arrived in

Paris, Thomson had been introduced to Elsa Maxwell who, after taking her compatriot under her ample wing, outlined for the composer "a custom-made career"—the first step of which was to be a work commissioned by Winnaretta, "to be performed the next season" at one of gatherings in the Polignac salon.[40] But Maxwell had overestimated her influence with the Princesse: after initially agreeing to meet Thomson at lunch one spring Saturday at avenue Henri-Martin, Winnaretta ultimately cancelled the appointment; the composer never knew "whether Miss Maxwell's plans encountered resistance, or whether she had been bluffing all along."[41] Cocteau, apprised of this confusing situation, offered to write to Winnaretta explaining that Thomson "was not to be judged from [his] acquaintances in café society."[42] It is possible that the composer's close friendships with Natalie Barney and Gertrude Stein, two of the more prominent members of the Left Bank's lesbian artistic community—a community that Winnaretta carefully eschewed—may have contributed to her refusal to meet with the American. No introduction was ever made, even though Winnaretta was to be seen at performances of Thomson's music in later years.

During 1926, Winnaretta was preoccupied with projects of a more far-reaching nature. She decided to seek the advice of Maurice Paléologue, who came to Venice for a visit at the beginning of September. The evening of his arrival she took him out for a gondola ride, and in the small boat she poured forth her heart to him. Years later, Paléologue would remember her every word.

> I wanted to see you in Venice, in my dear Venice, to speak to you of a thing which I have pondered for a long time in my heart. . . . You understand that I am indebted to my father for my considerable fortune. But I am sixty-one years old; I am now seriously preoccupied with the arrangements that I have to make concerning the future of this fortune. I have made a cult of the memory of my father, and it is in him above all that I want to find the inspiration for the future use of my inheritance. I need a foundation with which I can associate myself during my lifetime. Instruct me; advise me.[43]

Paléologue advised Winnaretta to form a new version of the "Fondation Singer-Polignac" that she had instituted in 1910, one that could sponsor and underwrite a broad range of projects to support or advance creative and scientific activity. He further advised that she put the foundation under the auspices of the Collège de France. While cruising in the Mediterranean in October, Winnaretta sat on the deck sketching out the philosophical tenets that she would wish to govern such an organization. By time the cruise was over, she had created a plan, a combination of Paléologue's suggestions and her own ideas;[44] she submitted the proposal to Raymond Poincaré, who, over the next two years, took the legal steps to put the plan into action.

Winnaretta returned to Paris in late November. On 3 December she gave a dinner party for a small number of family members and friends. Unfortunately, the repast bore the hallmark of stinginess that formed the opposite pole of Winnaretta's largesse. Knowing full well that their aunt had never been famous for the bounteousness of her table, Jean and Marie-Blanche nonetheless made the long trip from Brittany especially to attend the dinner. Afterwards Marie-Blanche complained in her diary, "Pitiful to think of that! What a fall from grace. We ended up with empty stomachs—the same imbecility over costs [as if she were trying to feed] one hundred fifty people!"[45] Marie-Blanche, however, quickly forgave her aunt, who, if not a source of good food, was always a source of good gossip: when the two women lunched together with Cole Porter a few days later, Winnaretta broke the news to her niece about the surprise marriage of Germaine Tailleferre to the much-married American millionaire Ralph Barton.[46]

In the first months of 1927 Winnaretta hosted a series of Monday afternoon musical matinées.[47] Catherine Pozzi wrote in her diary of hearing a Bach cantata performed "*chez Croïsos*" before an audience of "one hundred empty-headed women." If Pozzi disliked the the ambiance, she found the music to be "perfection . . . so fine, so happy, so full, so pure, that all that we are—our dresses, our lapdogs, our furs, our pearls—becomes terribly diminished."[48] The next week Pozzi attended a five o'clock Polignac gathering—this one including a larger number of men, mostly political figures—where the musical fare of the day was a recital of keyboard works by Rameau, Albéniz, and Chopin performed so beautifully by pianist Marcelle Meyer that Pozzi had the impression that she was "leaving her body."[49]

Winnaretta spent much time during this period in the company of Colette and Anna de Noailles. The two writers, introduced by Winnaretta, had developed a close friendship of their own.[50] In an unpublished sketch, Anna evoked a late-night dinner at Colette's "bizarre and seductive" apartment on rue Beaujolais, attended by herself, her sister Hélène, Winnaretta, and the ever-present Cloton Legrand. Seated on an Oriental carpet, the five women feasted on rack of lamb, a "voluminous" cake, and hot Burgundy wine, trading popular stories, while Colette's many cats circled the group, echoing the feline glances of their owner.[51] Winnaretta also continued to see Violet Trefusis, although Violet's indiscretions—particularly her habit of flirting aggressively with other women during her visits to the Polignac *hôtel*—came back to haunt Winnaretta in the form of malicious gossip.[52]

Her unfettered social life came to a sudden halt that winter when she became, unexpectedly, for the second time, a foster parent. For nearly a year, her niece Diane de Polignac had been at wit's end, not knowing how to cope with the temper tantrums of her youngest son, Winnaretta's godson Edmond. Twelve-year-old Eddy had always been the most rebellious and impetuous of Diane's six children; his violent flare-ups had become so frequent that she could no longer stand to have him in the house. Neither boarding school nor the influence of other relatives generated any improvement of his behavior. Finally, in desperation, Diane sent Eddy to live with Winnaretta, the only family member who could stand up to him.

The boy had grown up in affluence, in a carefree familial atmosphere, surrounded by numerous siblings and cousins; there were at least twenty people at the table for any given meal. Consequently, he was taken aback by the cold asceticism of Winarretta's rue Cortambert *hôtel*. The house was dark, minimally furnished, minimally heated, and devoid of any of the accoutrements that would give pleasure to a child; it reflected instead the living style of a world-wary hermit. On the first day, Eddy was ushered into his aunt's *atelier*. Winnaretta seemed to him as glacial as her house, seated at her organ, silent and enigmatic. "Sit down and watch," she instructed him; he found it curious that the instruction was to watch, and not to listen. Later, he realized that this was her way of examining the intellect and the spiritual makeup of each person presented to her.[53] It took a long time for the boy to surmount his intimidation, and he relied heavily on Winnaretta's Russian secretary, Sonia Galperine, to offer some modicum of maternal warmth. As the months passed, however, Eddy came to admire his inscrutable and authoritarian aunt, who spent most of her waking hours "working, working, working at her music."[54] He silently registered his impressions of the fascinating people who came to visit: François Dupré, precise and courteous, the fluttering and indiscreet Violet Trefusis, the exotic, garrulous Anna de Noailles, and the urbane, charming Jean Cocteau.[55]

Cocteau was hoping to put his charm to good use with the Princesse, for he needed her financial support for a new project: a collaboration between himself and Stravinsky. Shortly after his Venice performance of the Piano Sonata in 1925, Stravinsky had conceived the notion of creating music for a staged work in Latin based on the Oedipus myth. He asked Cocteau, whose version of *Antigone* he had recently read and enjoyed, to be the librettist for "a tragedy of the ancient world that everyone would know."[56] Stravinsky extracted a promise from Cocteau, not the most discreet of friends, to keep their collaboration secret: he had it in mind to prepare this new *Oedipus Rex* as part of a surprise performance to be given in the Ballets Russes's 1927 summer season, commemorating Diaghilev's twentieth anniversary as director of the company.[57] The secret was successfully maintained right up until January 1927, when Cocteau sent Stravinsky the first part of the completed libretto, in Jean Daniélou's Latin translation. It was now time to expose their project to certain dependable *mécènes*, because funding had to be secured in order to hire the soloists, the chorus, and the orchestra. Stravinsky, still in Nice, entrusted the financial details to Cocteau.

Winnaretta, informed of the project in the last days of 1926, was delighted to hear of the collaboration, especially one involving a work of Sophocles. Nonetheless, she was cautious when Cocteau asked her to make a financial committment to the project. As always, her business sense over-rode artistic considerations: she agreed only to look over the lists of figures with lawyer André Aron;[58] if satisfied, she would then contribute 20,000 francs, the sum necessary to pay for the performers—but would release the funds only on the condition that Cocteau could find additional backers to fund the balance of the staging and production costs, estimated at 100,000 francs.[59] Winnaretta had reason to act with caution: she did not completely trust Cocteau, and had serious doubts about his ability to find other back-ers for *Oedipus*. She was also familiar with the crises that invariably pre-ceded each Ballets Russes production, as well as the intrigues and jealou-sies that swirled within Diaghilev's circle. It was wise to maintain the secret about the new piece, she told Cocteau: "She foresaw a drama with Serge, who was counting on a work [by Stravinsky] that he could parade around to draw attention to his productions."[60] Although grateful for her offer of financial backing, Cocteau felt nervous about the Princesse's apparent need to control the production, even as she decried the same tendency in Diaghilev. "She understood the reverse of my ideas," wrote Cocteau, " . . . and she got everything mixed up, as society people tend to do, even the nicest ones."[61] The meeting ended on a more or less optimistic note, with Winnaretta declaring that *Oedipus* was "a capital event, the music of our times, so we will succeed and we will present it," although she concluded darkly, "but not without backstabbing," a thinly-veiled allusion, thought Cocteau, to "Serge, Misia and company."[62]

Cocteau, however, could suppress his gossipy inclinations for only so long. To Stravinsky's great displeasure, he began to confide details of the performance to Diaghilev's "muse," Misia Sert, a devoted *mécène* but also an incorrigible meddler. Misia confidently assured Cocteau that fashion designer Coco Chanel, Stravinsky's former lover, would certainly be will-ing to underwrite the staging costs of the performance.[63] Chanel, however, was in London at the time that her friends were so cavalierly taking her support for granted. With blind optimism, Cocteau took no additional steps to find other backers, and was therefore unable to secure a firm commit-ment from the Princesse de Polignac. Consequently, as late as the month of March, there was still no budget for a first staged performance projected for 30 May, and no practical preparations could be undertaken. Stravinsky, who, up until that time, had disassociated himself from the practical and financial arrangements for the work's production, now wired his collabo-rator about the urgent need to hire soloists and choir, and to engage an orchestra.[64] Cocteau pleaded with him to write personally to Winnaretta, convinced that an initiative by the composer would yield more fruitful re-sults.[65]

Stravinsky, who had written to the poet to "stop paying attention to gossip,"[66] undertook the financial wooing of his patron in several steps. Immediately after completing *Oedipus Rex*—a work he was now calling an "opera-oratorio"—the composer arranged for a rehearsal of the work in Winnaretta's *atelier* on 17 March.[67] On that occasion, Stravinsky asked his patron if she would be willing to host an *avant-première* of the work before the public presentation; apparently he also made a passing reference to the finances necessary to launch the public performance. Winnaretta was no fool: she could foresee the request for funding that was inevitably coming. In a letter, she told Stravinsky that she would be "proud and happy" to present this "admirable work" of "powerful and noble austerity" in her salon. But in the same letter she claimed (or feigned) ignorance of the results of Cocteau's non-existent search for other financial backers. She coolly reasserted her previous promise to underwrite Stravinsky's conductor's fee of fifteen hundred dollars, and to contribute twenty thousand francs to the general production expenses—but *only* after "Cocteau [had] found among his friends the necessary support."[68] Stravinsky, undaunted, addressed the issues of his own practical concerns, stressing the need to engage the soloists and choir immediately, and asking her to underwrite those costs.[69] Chanel would not be coming back for another week, he explained, and "as Cocteau wants to present the situation to her in person, things are dragging on a bit."[70]

Why did Winnaretta play so hard-to-get in a situation where she could have easily helped out her beloved Stravinsky, especially given that the amount of money involved was—for her—not a particularly large sum? It seems that she did not wish to have her name connected in an act of *mécénat* with the names of women whom she felt to be beneath her, or whom she simply didn't like. If the Princesse disapproved of Misia Sert, she felt outright disdain for Chanel. Once when asked by Vera Sudeikina (Stravinsky's mistress and, later, the second Mrs. Stravinsky) why she didn't invite Chanel to her soirees, the daughter of the sewing machine manufacturer replied, "I don't entertain my tradespeople."[71] This statement is curious, for ordinarily Winnaretta admired hard-working, self-made women. Some particular sort of jealousy, perhaps related to Stravinsky, perhaps related to the competition between Chanel and Marie-Blanche's mother Jeanne Lanvin, may have come into play. In any event, the very self-confident Chanel was unperturbed by the Princesse de Polignac's attitude. Once she had even bested Winnaretta in an act of *mécénat*. On that occasion, one of Diaghilev's quotidian cash crises, the impresario had run around Paris trying to find a thousand pounds for his creditors, else the curtain would not rise for a Ballets Russes performance that night. He ran to Lady Maud Cunard, he ran to the Princesse de Polignac. His last stop was the home of Coco Chanel. He arrived at her doorstep, hands clasped, sweating profusely. "I've been to the Princesse—she gave me seventy-five thousand francs!" exclaimed Diaghilev. "Oh, but she's a grand American lady," Chanel said. "I'm only a French *couturière*. Here's two hundred thousand."[72]

But on this occasion, Chanel, who arrived back in Paris on 1 April to find that her friends were considering her financial support to be a fait accompli, declined to be generous. It was Misia's fault, wrote Cocteau to Stravinsky. "Misia said to her: 'Everybody's waiting for you, dear—you're holding the purse strings.' [Chanel:] 'Who said that?' [Misia:] 'The Princesse de Polignac.' You can imagine that Madame de P. never said things of that kind."[73] With the failure of *Oedipus* imminent, Cocteau finally wrote in desperation to Winnaretta for help, but she stood firm, her conditions for participation unchanged.[74] In mid-April, Chanel finally agreed to fund a stage production, but by then it was too late: Stravinsky had already revealed the "surprise" to Diaghilev, who put the performance under the aegis of the Ballets Russes.[75] The impresario pragmatically observed that there was not enough time to give *Oedipus* a stage setting, and that it would have to be presented in concert form, sandwiched between two ballets.[76] He envisioned a dramatically stark setting, with "no décor, and the cast in evening dress, sitting on the stage in front of black velvet curtains. Musically it will even gain."[77] At that point, Winnaretta suddenly "found" a solution to the financial quagmire that made the public performance of *Oedipus Rex* dependent on the salon presentation: in a "sweet letter,"[78] she offered Stravinsky a very handsome sum—paid in advance—to conduct the *avant-première* in her *atelier*. Stravinsky promptly turned over the fee to Diaghilev to finance the public performance.[79] In the final analysis, Winnaretta was *Oedipus*'s sole patron: her total contribution to the project was 70,000 francs (over $10,000 dollars in today's currency).[80]

With the *Oedipus* conflict resolved, Winnaretta set sail on 22 April on the yacht *Sayonara* for a three-week cruise along the coast of Spain, in the company of Violet and Denys Trefusis, Jean and Marie-Blanche, Charles and Pata, and her nephew Edmond, who had just celebrated his thirteenth birthday.[81] It was a particularly memorable trip for the young Edmond, who had become quite fond of his iconoclastic aunt.

> [The] cruise [seemed] like her attempt to leave her own self behind. . . .
> On board, when she was relaxed, she organized games of devilish leap-frog or hide-and-seek, running out of breath and bursting into strident laughter as she lifted me off the floor and hoisted me onto her shoulders. Then, brusquely, she became serious again: game time was over. And the fascinating conversations—about the arts, about life—resumed; I participated alongside the adults, since she always invited me to give my opinion, strange [to me] as that seemed.[82]

The on-land excursions were a study in extreme contrasts for the impressionable boy. He accompanied Winnaretta when she paid a visit to Manuel de Falla, still living in ascetic simplicity with his unmarried sister in their little home in Granada.[83] The next visit could not have been more strikingly different: invited by the King of Spain, Alphonse XIII, to the

Feria of Seville, Winnaretta took her nephew "in a pompous coach hitched up to two coffee-colored mules, garnished with red pompons." When they arrived at the royal palace, the major-domo asked Winnaretta what names he should announce. Her response was "The Prince and Princesse Edmond de Polignac." Many smiles accompanied their descent down the grand staircase.[84]

The pleasure of the cruise did not prevent the return of Winnaretta's oldest fears—of the sea, of storms. As in her youngest years, the confrontation with the untamable forces of nature became a personal test of courage. On one turbulent night, however, she could not manage to surmount her terror. Edmond recalled, "As the wind rose, the waves grew full, pitching and tossing the boat, Tante Winnie, very seasick, called to me. 'We're going back to port, warn the pilot!' And me, with my childish logic: 'But, my aunt, you're the only one who can speak to the pilot.' 'Come here,' she said. And cutting three gold ribbons, she stuck them on the sleeve of my peacoat, 'Go, you're the captain now.'"[85] The group was back on land in time to celebrate, along with all of Paris, the successful trans-Atlantic crossing of Charles Lindbergh.[86]

Meanwhile, while the *Sayonara*'s passengers were struggling against the storm, Stravinsky had been struggling to complete the orchestration of *Oedipus Rex* in time for its first performance. He finished the work in the early morning hours of 10 May,[87] and the first rehearsal with the choir took place only two days before Winnaretta returned to Paris, on 19 May.[88] In all, the work only received four full-length rehearsals; the singers had barely had time to learn the notes.[89] The *avant-première* took place at avenue Henri-Martin on 29 May, the night before the public performance, before a "colossal gathering" of guests; the composer accompanied the singers and choir at the piano, with Serge Prokofiev "helping" (probably doubling the singers' vocal parts at a second piano).[90] Marie-Blanche de Polignac found Stravinsky's composition to be "a beautiful work, very austere, very stark . . . an oratorio as poignant and detached as a Passion of Bach."[91] The response of the Paris ballet audience the next night at the Théâtre Sarah Bernhardt was more muted. The ascetic, sparely orchestrated work—presented on a bare stage, sandwiched in between two ebullient one-act ballets by Berners and Sauguet and a reprise of *The Firebird*—held little appeal for a ballet audience.[92] Diaghilev, who had never cared for *Oedipus Rex*'s archaic Latin text and austere music, acerbically observed that Cocteau and Stravinsky had given him "a very macabre present."[93] Winnaretta, however, was surely moved by the new work, which paid homage both to the powerful myth of antiquity and the contrapuntal rigors of the baroque. She may have enjoyed reading the words of journalist Janet Flanner in the *New Yorker*: "Stravinsky, who, having once struck his century's new creative high C, in his latest work returned to the old and lower B major—Bach."[94]

Winnaretta presented only one other musical soiree that season, a recital by Vladimir Horowitz. Horowitz, like so many other great artists, was first introduced to Paris audiences through the world of the private salon. His 1925 recital at the home of Madame Jeanne Dubost, performed at the behest of the Soviet ambassador to France, was a consequence of the French business community's attempt to make inroads into newly opened Eastern markets. From the moment that the pale, awkward young Russian launched into a fiery performance of a work by Liszt, the small audience gathered in Madame Dubost's living room recognized that they were in the presence of greatness.[95] Horowitz took a liking to Paris and its elegant culture; he would make the city the base of his European career. Even after his 1926 debut catapulted him to instant stardom,[96] he continued to frequent the city's musical salons.[97] That he should gravitate to the Polignac salon was only a matter of time. On 15 June 1927 the pianist performed a program at avenue Henri-Martin that included a toccata by J. S. Bach and the Liszt Sonata. It was "a revelation," recalled Marie-Blanche; Horowitz played "with such emotional intensity that an entire roomful of people held their breath, people who usually only came there to chatter. Tante Winnie, overcome with emotion, doubled his fee on the spot."[98] Horowitz's charming letter of thanks expressed the hope that he would see his hostess again soon "in Italy or in America."[99] The two would in fact establish a close relationship in the decade to come, after the pianist's 1933 marriage to Wanda Toscanini.

The *avant-première* of *Oedipus Rex* and the Horowitz recital seem to have been the only two musical gatherings that Winnaretta hosted in that spring season. She had turned down a request to host a private performance of Falla's new Harpsichord Concerto by Wanda Landowska: the date that Falla proposed conflicted with Horowitz's concert, and she offered him no other.[100] Instead, Winnaretta ended her season by attending the inauguration of Le Corbusier's recently completed dormitory annex to the Palais du Peuple.[101] The four-story homeless shelter had been renovated to provide shelter for a hundred indigent people; its construction had totalled 350,600 francs, of which Winnaretta contributed 296,313.[102] The annex, tucked discreetly behind an unassuming facade on a quiet street in the 13th *arrondissement,* faced onto a beautiful garden. Winnaretta had instructed that the new wing be named the "Fondation Edmond de Polignac." A commemorative plaque had been affixed to the wall at the entrance of the annex wing; upon it was inscribed a phrase in Latin from the Twenty-third Psalm, one that Winnaretta felt would best remind its readers of the goal of the foundation: "Non timebo mala quia tu mecumes" (I shall fear no evil, for Thou art with me).[103]

Winnaretta began her summer travels with a trip to the medieval tower that she had purchased for Violet Trefusis, La Tour de Saint-Loup.[104] Her annual Venetian sojourn was especially memorable that year, for it brought Winnaretta in contact with one of the city's most extraordinary native sons, a musical prodigy, Bruno Maderna.[105] Maderna had begun his musical studies on violin at the age of four; now, recently turned seven, he played with the virtuosity and maturity of a seasoned artist. He was invited to the Palazzo Polignac that summer, and Winnaretta was astonished by the boy's remarkable gifts. She immediately arranged performances for him to launch his fledgling career, and agreed to underwrite his formal musical education, including his first studies in composition. Winnaretta's patronage, which continued for the next dozen years,[106] bore fruit: Bruno Maderna would become one of Italy's best-known conductors and composers and play an essential role in the development of its avant-garde movement.

Upon her return to Paris, Winnaretta resumed a custom that she had abandoned because of her frequent absences: she started up again her "Piano Fridays." Some of these were formal piano recitals, such as the one given by Serge Prokofiev on 16 December.[107] But often the "Fridays" consisted of long sight-reading sessions of original four-hand and two-piano works, as well as all sorts of transcriptions for two and three pianos. Winnaretta and often Marie-Blanche were joined in these keyboard adventures by whatever pianists happened to be available that day. Some were already great keyboard luminaries, such as Horowitz and Rubinstein; other young artists who came to these sometimes raucous gatherings were destined to become well-known names: Francis Poulenc, Jacques Février, Henri Sauguet, Jean Françaix, Jeanne-Marie Darré, and Magda Tagliaferro.[108]

Among the newcomers at these sessions in 1927 was one of the greatest artists ever to join the Polignac musical circle, the young Romanian pianist Clara Haskil. Born in 1895, Haskil was, from her youngest years, hailed as a prodigy, and seemed destined for a great career as a performing artist. But her early professional life was marred by misfortune. In 1913, her first European concert tour was interrupted by complications of scoliosis, the first in a lifelong series of illness. Nonetheless, Haskil managed to resume her concert career in 1918. Winnaretta may have heard this extraordinary pianist for the first time in duo-recital with Romanian composer and violinist Georges Enesco, who had played often in the Polignac salon.[109] Winnaretta surely recognized instantly the artistic genius of the subtle, sober musician. But by 1921, when the two women were introduced,[110] Haskil had been overshadowed in the concert world by more extroverted virtuosos such as Cortot and Horowitz. Not only was her performing style devoid of flamboyance, she was also plain, skeletally thin, and extremely timid. Many of her contemporaries felt that the Haskil was a finer pianist even than Horowitz, but without the suave good looks and debonair social skills of the Russian virtuoso, she was incapable of reestablishing her professional reputation.[111]

The Princesse de Polignac adopted the shy pianist as her next "project." From 1927 through 1939, she provided Haskil with a small monthly allowance, which permitted her to live in modest comfort. The "arrangement" also included lodgings: in the first years the pianist more or less lived at avenue Henri-Martin. The servants became very fond of her, and it was not uncommon to see the butler or the cleaning woman pause in their tasks to listen to the beautiful piano music floating through the house.[112] In exchange, Haskil was required to be "on call" for Winnaretta's "Piano Fridays," participating in these gatherings of young musicians; additionally she was frequently featured as solo recitalist in Winnaretta's more formal soirees. Thanks to her patron's contacts, Haskil was able to secure more playing engagements, and formed important musical friendships with Stravinsky, Poulenc, Rubinstein, and Sauguet. But while Winnaretta's promotion of Clara Haskil helped to re-establish the pianist's career, it also brought to the fore the more unpleasant aspects of the patron's personality. Haskil found herself obliged to "snap to" whenever Winnaretta required her to perform. Her position as "house musician"—in the most servile definition of the term—required her attendance at Winnaretta's countless dinners and receptions, both in Paris and Venice. These *mondanités* were a form of torture for the painfully shy pianist, who, to the hostess's great irritation, often tried to escape them by hiding behind a door, or scurrying into the kitchen to eat with the servants.[113]

In 1928, Winnaretta received good news: the Minister of the Interior had accepted the proposal for her reconstituted Fondation Singer-Polignac; the decree was published on 25 March.[114] Raymond Poincaré had agreed to become the Foundation's first president.[115] Winnaretta's initial gift to the Foundation of three million francs was to be used, as she wrote Poincaré, "to underwrite without delay the needs of the French arts and sciences, in cases where the resources of the State are insufficient or even powerless."

> American by birth, French by my alliances, I have always had the desire to participate in my modest measure in the expansion of French culture. . . . [T]he awarding of the fund's revenues should be undertaken with the greatest liberty, [but] those who attend to this task should consider uniquely the essential goal of the foundation, which is, I repeat, the favoring of French culture.
>
> In particular, the [fund] could institute a large scientific experiment, in physics, chemistry, astronomy, etc., be it the organizing or underwriting of a geographic or archeological exploration, facilitating the publication of a great literary, historical or epigraphic work, aiding the State in the enrichment or the conservation of its museums and monuments, or finally the awarding of a grand prize to a great artist, thinker, or writer, whose work should be brought to public attention. . . .
>
> The enumeration that I've given is in no way limiting. It indicates, however, the spirit and the role of the foundation to which I hope to attach the memory of those who were dear to me, and my own name.[116]

Her foundation successfully launched, Winnaretta plunged into the Paris *grande saison* with a light heart. The month of June was the period of grand balls, many of which required costumes based on a particular theme. Some balls provided opportunities for cross-dressing. Madame Cardinal's ball required that her guests come disguised as literary figures; Winnaretta appeared as the dramatist Tristan Bernard, with the Marchesa Casati on her arm dressed as Bernard's wife. That same month Daisy Fellowes gave a ball where the theme was Paris personalities; both her aunt and Elsa Maxwell came dressed as Aristide Briand, each woman sporting the same distinctive mustache.[117]

In younger, fashion-oriented circles, Winnaretta was known not because of her musical *mécénat,* but because she was Daisy Fellowes's aunt. By the late 1920s Daisy had positioned herself as a major figure in society. Although not conventionally beautiful, she had an innate sense of style, and was a pacesetter in fashion, wearing tuxedos long before Marlene Dietrich turned the same outfit into a sartorial trend. Despite her lack of background in journalism, Daisy was frequently hired to write feature articles for the Paris edition of *Vogue*; in 1933 she would become an editor at the Paris bureau of *Harper's Bazaar.*[118] As a result, Winnaretta's name or picture began to appear in fashion magazines.

In the spring of 1928, the Princesse de Polignac was asked to write an article on music for French *Vogue.* Winnaretta's dense prose mystified much of the readership, but she poured her heart into this one-page piece, extolling not only the musical works of the Masters, but the song inherent in Nature: "We don't ask that music be the multiple science that it has become through the course of time; it can be every cry, every call, or every outline of a melodic idea which, harmoniously, breaks the silence. The simplest song can be as evocative as sophisticated polyphony."[119] Abbé Mugnier had another point of view on the nature of music: "Music is also a sedative. The Church understood that quite well."[120] Winnaretta and the urbane priest met from time to time to exchange ideas on philosophical matters. In November, after introducing the Princesse to a "thought" from Pascal's *Pensées* previously unknown to her ("anguish, in all things, is only a form or an effect of ignorance"), Mugnier was treated to a private organ recital in the *atelier.*[121]

Two weeks later, Winnaretta attended the first performance Stravinsky's *The Fairy's Kiss,* conducted by the composer and danced by Ida Rubinstein, who had just formed a new company under her own name. Winnaretta found herself surrounded by the Ballets Russes regulars—those whom Lifar referred to as "all our people": Comte Étienne de Beaumont, Stravinsky, the Serts, Picasso, Kochno, as well as Diaghilev himself, who, resentful of Rubinstein's "defection," had come to deprecate the spectacle, claiming that it "breathed a provincial boredom."[122]

That fall, Winnaretta joined the founding committee of a major new Paris orchestra, the Orchestre Symphonique de Paris (OSP), an ensemble whose goal was to bring a full season of excellently played symphonic music—including new music—before the public. The OSP's founding committee, which, in addition to Winnaretta, included Coco Chanel, Alfred Cortot, David Weill, Christian Lazard, and the Pleyel brothers, determined that it was "necessary that an orchestra in service of Music find financial support to guarantee both material stability and financial independence."[123] If musicians were given better working conditions, the reasoning went, they would play better. To ensure a consistently high quality over the course of an eighty-concert season, the organization's music directors and principal conductors—Alfred Cortot, Ernest Ansermet, and Louis Fourestier[124]—staffed the orchestra with mostly young, recent conservatory graduates. The players were given substantial salaries in exchange for a daily three-hour rehearsal period; substitutes were forbidden.[125] Ansermet was the driving force in the programming of new music in the OSP's repertoire, mounting a "Honegger festival" and a series of all-Stravinsky concerts in the orchestra's inaugural season.[126] The critics lauded the OSP for its "ardor, freshness, and youth," noting that "[its] musicians . . . already possess a collective spirit, and that's the highest praise that one can give."[127] The ensemble continued to perform until the end of World War II, and held an important place in the contemporary music scene of the epoch. Winnaretta's role in relation to the group was the customary mixture of enlightened philanthropy and unembarrassed self-interest: her generous subventions of the OSP gave her license to employ the group as her personal "house orchestra" through the 1930s.

On 4 January 1929, Winnaretta left with the Trefusises, the Keppels, and a half-dozen of her Singer and Polignac relatives for six weeks of cruising on the Nile aboard her brother Paris's yacht (named *The Duncan*).[128] *Vogue*'s photographer snapped pictures of the group in Egypt riding on camels, the women wearing white gloves.[129] Winnaretta's idyll came to an abrupt end, however, when she returned to Paris. During that glacially cold winter, Hélène de Caraman-Chimay fell ill with double pneumonia and died on 4 March. For almost twenty-five years, since the death of Belle-Blanche Decazes, Hélène had been Winnaretta's closest friend and confidant. The loss of this kind, gentle companion shook her to her core. She wrote to Jean de Polignac: "You know how much I needed her, her incomparable affection, her judgment, her mind, and don't have to be told how alone I feel. . . . I've become irresolute, incapable of action or decision, idle, unable to become interested in anything."[130]

However, her deeds belied her words. To shake off her grief, Winnaretta threw herself into a myriad of projects. She made appearances publicizing the Fondation Singer-Polignac's first major donation of scientific equipment: an electromagnet and a cathode oscillograph, to be used for biological research sponsored by the Collège de France.[131] She joined a committee of guarantors underwriting a Paris production of Wagner's *Ring* cycle by the Bayreuth company; final arrangements were being made for a June performance—although, as she confided to Jean, "if it's Siegfried Wagner who's conducting, it won't be so marvelous."[132]

And she pressed for the realization of a wish long unfulfilled. The Ballets Russes was presenting a revival of Stravinsky's *Renard* that spring, with a new staging and choreography by Diaghilev's "star" dancer and intimate companion, Serge Lifar; the first performance was scheduled for 21 May.[133] For a decade Diaghilev had successfully obstructed the presentation of *Renard* in the Polignac *atelier*; now, once again, Winnaretta found herself pleading with the impresario to allow the dancers and mimes of his troupe to perform the work, at long last, in her home, as an *avant-première* of the new production. Diaghilev would not deign to be involved with such a project; he suggested that she contact Stravinsky directly to work something out.[134] And contact Stravinsky she did, with vigor: "What time period would be convenient? How could we arrange the stage? Under what [financial] conditions could Diaghilev's troupe and his artists come?"[135] The composer did try to negotiate the situation with Diaghilev, but was obliged to return with the disappointing news that it would "unfortunately not be possible (given the lack of space) [!] to perform *Renard* at your house with the dancers and mimes."[136] Nonetheless, Stravinsky continued magnanimously, if the Princesse were willing to present the music alone (she would "only" have to pay for the four singers and fourteen musicians), he would be too happy—"at least this time"—to pay homage to her by conducting the work free of charge.[137] And it was thus that, at last, one of her dearest wishes was finally granted: on Monday, 20 May 1929, reported *Le Figaro*, "a small group of music-loving listeners had the pleasure of hearing . . . the performance of *Renard* by Stravinsky, interpreted by Messieurs Raissow, Tkhoryevsky, Maltzoff et J. Nedre, the orchestra directed by the maestro himself."[138] In some ways, however, it must have been a disappointing affair. When Winnaretta first commissioned the work, she had anticipated an exciting artistic adventure: a raucous, modern multimedia show, conceived in the spirit of the Wigwam's free-spirited burlesques and musicales. Musically, Stravinsky's brilliant cacophony was there in full, but as for the rest, it was—in all senses of the word—a reduction.

However, she did have the satisfaction of seeing *Renard* associated with her salon. That same spring, another lasting legacy of her *mécénat* was realized, this one associated with her ongoing commitment to housing for the poor. In the two years since she had underwritten the annex of the Salvation Army's Palais du Peuple, Commissioner Albin Peyron had vigorously pursued his goal to provide shelter and social services for Paris's underprivileged citizens. One of the Army's major goals was the creation of programs to reintegrate the poor into the existing economic system through education and job training.[139] In 1929 the Salvation Army embarked on an ambitious fund-raising campaign to create a "Cité de Refuge." Once again, Le Corbusier was engaged to design and construct the building, whose construction costs were estimated at six million francs.[140] Winnaretta was of course contacted as a potential contributor to the campaign fund. Peyron came several times to avenue Henri-Martin to discuss the building project, often dressed in his resplendent Salvation Army uniform. Eddy de Polignac was so impressed with this magnificent garb that he nicknamed Peyron "Monsieur Royal."[141]

One day shortly after the *Renard* performance, the commissioner came to call. Eddy answered the door. He ran up the grand staircase to his aunt's office to announce her visitor's arrival: "It's Monsieur Royal, Tante Winnie." "Ah," she replied, "come in, I need you to do an errand for me." She put something that she had just written into a little envelope, sealed the envelope, and handed it to her nephew. "Give this to Monsieur Peyron. I want you to tell me what happens; give me the *exact* details of his reaction." Eddy dutifully obeyed his aunt's wishes; he bounded down the stairs and handed Peyron the envelope. The commissioner opened the flap, unfolded the check contained within, turned pale, and, to Eddy's astonishment, collapsed onto the floor in a dead faint. Winnaretta had written the Salvation Army a check for 1.8 million francs.[142] In fact, by the time the Cité de Refuge project was fully realized, the Princesse de Polignac had contributed over three million francs to the Army's building fund.

The school year had come to an end, and Eddy had just received his *brevet* (middle-school certificate). He was feeling buoyant: he was on vacation, he had just attended the "dancing soiree" that Winnaretta had given for Daisy Fellowes's eldest daughter Emeline,[143] and he had just been given his allowance of ten francs, a princely sum in 1929. Eddy asked, "Can't we go out to celebrate my *brevet*, Aunt? Can't we go to the movies?" Winnaretta accepted, and the two took a cab to the movie theater, on the Champs-Élysées. Winnaretta got out first, and said to her nephew, "Pay the taxi driver." Eddy was stunned, but he relinquished the ten-franc note, crestfallen to see his fortune depleted nearly by half. He went to the ticket window, where his aunt awaited. "Pay for the tickets," she instructed her nephew, adding lightly, "It's customary for the gentleman to pay when taking out a lady." He could not disobey; after the purchase of the tickets he was left with empty pockets. Upon returning to avenue Henri-Martin after the show, Eddy quickly retired to his room, flat broke and desolate. Winnaretta came in and sat on the bed. "So what did you think of our evening together?" "I would have rather kept my ten francs for myself, Tante Winnie." "Ah," she said, "you have learned an important lesson this week. To hand someone a check for a million francs—that's nothing, it's just a piece of paper. But to take ten francs out of your own pocket—now *that's* painful!"[144]

Another one of those "pieces of paper" yielded fruit that season: in June, Wagner's *Ring* was performed by the Bayreuth company at the Théâtre des Champs-Élysées. For four consecutive evenings, Winnaretta, Jean, and Marie-Blanche were "submerged, crushed" by this powerful music.[145] That spring, for his annual costume ball, Comte Étienne de Beaumont required his guests to come dressed as characters from operas, and Winnaretta, Jean, Marie-Blanche, Charles, and Pata arrived as the entire personnel of *The Ride of the Valkyries*.[146] Another costume ball was given at the home of Charles and Marie-Laure de Noailles, who, following Winnaretta's example of musical *mécénat*, had commissioned a piece by Francis Poulenc, *Aubade*, especially for the occasion.

Winnaretta's spring ended sadly, however. Denys Trefusis was suffering from the chronic chest infection that would end his life in early September. Winnaretta, who enjoyed a warm friendship with her lover's husband, spent long hours at his bedside at the American Hospital in Neuilly. "I can only suppose they talked about music," wrote Violet, "as I was not encouraged to be present.[147] On 24 June, Winnaretta's older brother, Sir Adam Mortimer Singer, died in England of an overdose of sedatives. Suffering from intestinal troubles and chronic insomnia, the sixty-five-year-old Sir Mortimer had taken nearly two hundred times the prescribed dosage of Veronal, claiming in a letter, "I am still wide awake, notwithstanding all the drugs I have taken. I cannot stand it any longer."[148] The obituaries remembered him as a champion horse breeder and a gentlemanly philanthropist.[149] Like his sister, Sir Mortimer had taken an active interest in public works projects; he left instructions in his will that a substantial part of his fortune be given to charities and research concerned with "the technical education of the professional classes and the helping of workers of all classes."[150]

Upon returning from her brother's funeral, Winnaretta terminated her two-year stint as a "foster mother": she packed up her nephew Eddy and sent him home to his family. She spent the month of July at a peaceful mountain resort in Germany, where she enjoyed "delicious air . . . big sleeping porches, simple but excellent food, and a total absence of children (I think they're killed at the border just to be sure)."[151] From there, Winnaretta traveled to Mannheim to visit her brother Paris, who was still seeking the elusive cure for his chronic heart problems; she went on to Baden-Baden, where Violet Trefusis was also taking a "cure" in a sanatorium, while her husband languished close to death in Paris.[152]

The Baden-Baden music festival, a bastion of avant-gardism of the period, took place during that month. Winnaretta was interested in hearing the latest work of a young Berlin composer, Paul Hindemith, who was rapidly gaining a reputation as a major force in new music. His new piece, *Lehrstück,* was awaited with special interest, particularly because of its "utilitarian" text by the controversial Bertolt Brecht. Upon her arrival, Winnaretta crossed paths with Diaghilev, also in Baden-Baden to hear

Hindemith's piece: he had just engaged the German composer to write a new ballet.[153] The impresario was in the company of his newest "composer-discovery" and last love, seventeen-year-old Igor Markevitch. Winnaretta had met Markevitch in July, when the fragile, angular prodigy had played a private performance of his remarkable new piano concerto for her and Misia Sert in the *atelier*.[154] In Baden-Baden, however, Winnaretta barely noticed Markevitch: she was distracted by Diaghilev's unhealthy demeanor. She remarked to Nicolas Nabokov, also in attendance at the festival, that he "seemed like a changed man." Nabokov concurred, recognizing in his compatriot's puffy, sallow face the ravages of diabetes.[155] It was the last time either of them would see the man who had had such a powerful influence on their lives. Diaghilev died in Venice on 19 August, surrounded by Lifar, Misia, and Kochno, and was buried on the nearby island of San Michele.[156] With his death, the Ballets Russes lost its brilliant beacon light, the imperious, far-seeing, and irreplaceable genius that had led the troupe into glory, and all of Western Europe into the new world of modernism.

Winnaretta was visiting the Jean de Polignacs at Kerbastic at the time of Diaghilev's death.[157] Upon her arrival in Venice in September, she was immediately preoccupied with a houseful of guests: Jean and Marie-Blanche, Solange d'Ayen,[158] and Arthur Rubinstein. Rubinstein's frequent recital partner, violinist Paul Kochanski,[159] was also visiting Venice that summer. On one memorable evening, as the magical light of late summer filtered through the Lombard-style windows of the palazzo, Rubinstein and Kochanski enchanted a group of Winnaretta's guests with a spellbinding recital.[160]

But when the summer faded and all her guests departed, Winnaretta paid a visit to Diaghilev's gravesite in the Greek cemetery at San Michele, facing out onto the silent lagoon. In the last years she had seen so many homes, great and small, from the American White House to Falla's simple white house in Granada. She had stayed in the opulent "cottages" of the Everglades Club; she had helped to build a "palace" for the poor. Now, eight months after paying homage to the pharaohs in their pyramids, she stood in front of Diaghilev's final safe haven: his little tomb, upon which was engraved a phrase translated from the Russian, "Venice, the eternally calming inspiration."[161] In the years to come, on each 1 November, the Day of the Dead, Winnaretta would return to that lonely spot to leave flowers on the visionary impresario's grave.[162]

13

A Pride of Protégés

The economic and political stability of the 1920s came to a sudden halt in late October 1929, with the crash of the American stock market. For Americans thriving in Paris on favorable exchange rates and growing stock dividends, it meant the end of a decade-long party. Many talented, wealthy expatriates who had come to feast on the lively artistic scene—including the writers of the "Lost Generation" such as Ernest Hemingway, F. Scott Fitzgerald, and John Dos Passos—packed their bags and returned home.

It took a while for French people, other than those with significant American investments, to feel the economic blow of the Great Depression. In Winnaretta's case, her wealth appears to have remained untouched: her Singer dividends, emanating from a Canadian trust, and capably and conservatively managed by her Paris business manager, François Dupré, continued to fill her bank accounts. Most of her investments were in real estate, and her considerable charitable activities offset her equally considerable tax liabilities. Consequently, unlike most of the people she knew, she did not suffer financial reverses in the early 1930s; on the contrary, there is every indication that she thrived during these economically uncertain years. Only months after the crash, she bought the Jouy-en-Josas country house built by Vaudoyer that she had rented for several summers from decorator Henri Gonse; after assuming ownership, she had the villa redecorated by Paris's most sought-after designer, Jean-Michel Frank.[1] Later that year she treated a dozen of her family members and friends—including Violet Trefusis and her mother—to a two-week cruise to the Greek Islands and Dalmatia, on a ship called, appropriately enough, the *Sans Peur—Fearless.*[2]

The healthy state of her portfolio allowed her to help others in less fortunate economic circumstances. Winnaretta's help generally came, however, with the same proviso that she had imposed in the case of *Oedipus Rex*: she would provide financial aid only if additional *mécènes* were found to supplement her contribution. This was her modus operandi in her latest involvement with the Salvation Army, which, in 1929, began a fundraising campaign for a new Paris shelter, one that could house as many as five hundred men and women. Winnaretta made the organization an irresistible offer: after an initial gift of 1.8 million francs, she promised to augment the amount to a total of three million francs—if Le Corbusier were once again engaged as architect, and if supplementary assistance could be found within the Paris business and philanthropic communities. Winnaretta's gift inspired Commander Peyron to seek the additional help required; he eventually found twenty thousand new donors. On 24 June 1930, Winnaretta laid the foundation stone at the building site.[3]

Winnaretta employed a similar technique when she came to the aid of Colette the following year. The writer, now world-renowned for her *Claudine* books, found herself in serious financial straits at the beginning of the new decade. Her new husband, Maurice Goudeket, a diamond dealer, had been hurt by the Depression, as had other purveyors of luxury goods. Colette hit upon the idea of opening her own line of cosmetics. Winnaretta agreed to give her friend 20 percent of the one million francs necessary to mount the business. Colette was able to use Winnaretta's support as leverage to find four other primary investors to supply the remaining 80 percent, and La Société Colette was founded in early 1932.[4] By June customers could come to the storefront on the rue de Miromesnil to buy beauty products, or even have their makeup done by the celebrated writer herself.[5]

Another beneficiary of Winnaretta's largesse, albeit in a more modest way, was American-born violinist, Olga Rudge. Rudge had begun a promising concert career in Europe during the Great War. She was as eloquent as an interpreter of new music—especially the compositions of her compatriot George Antheil—as she was of the Sonatas and Partitas of Bach. In 1923 she began a lifelong love affair with American expatriate poet, Ezra Pound, with whom she had a child in 1925. Rudge continued to play concerts in England, France, and Italy, visiting the married Pound when his wife was absent. Her artistry was praised by Benito Mussolini, for whom she performed a private recital in 1927. In 1929, just at the moment that she had bought a small house in Venice, the American stock market crashed, and she found herself without resources. About this time Rudge met Winnaretta through their mutual friend, Venetian pianist Giorgio Levi. Levi had discreetly hinted to the Princesse of Rudge's financial difficulties since the crash. Winnaretta, who was particularly impressed by the violinist's interpretation of an Ernest Bloch Violin Sonata,[6] came to her aid with the offer of a "princely" sum to rent her Venetian house for several months.[7] Rudge subsequently became a regular guest at the Palazzo Polignac, playing recitals with Giorgio Levi and sight-reading Bach sonatas with Winnaretta herself;[8] when Pound was in Venice, he too was invited to join in the musical festivities.[9]

Most of Winnaretta's generosity, however, was oriented towards her great love, music. When pianist-conductor Alfred Cortot, who had become director of the École Normale de Musique, sought contributions for the construction of a new concert hall for the school, Winnaretta urged him to hire Auguste Perret, architect of the Théâtre des Champs-Élysées, and paid Perret's fee.[10] The new Salle Cortot—acoustically, among the finest concert venues in Paris—was dedicated on 25 June 1929. Winnaretta also continued her financial support of the Orchestre Symphonique de Paris, whose 1930 season included the works of, among others, Falla[11] and the Alexandria-born Italian Vittorio Rieti.[12] She would often be called upon to rescue the OSP from acute financial deficits. In June 1931 the orchestra couldn't find the money to pay Vladimir Horowitz the 25,000 francs they owed him for concerto performances—there were only five thousand francs remaining in the account, and the Princesse de Polignac was solicited to make up the shortfall. She agreed to give part of the balance, on the condition that three other people were found to do the same. They were found.[13] By the end of the same year more requests would come for projects related to Stravinsky (which will be discussed in more detail later on). If Winnaretta was not completely open-handed with the OSP, she made up for it by hiring the musicians to perform works that she commissioned, both in her salon and in the concert hall. By hiring the OSP for her own projects, she was assured of having a reliable group of orchestral musicians at her disposal who had the skills to play complex new scores. She kept the OSP busy with her numerous projects throughout the 1930s.

In the meantime, the salon gatherings continued. The musical programs often comprised recent works by young composers, but, almost as often, Bach was the featured—and favored—composer; Winnaretta referred to the German master's music as "l'alimentation complète," a complete diet.[14] By this time the Polignac musicales, so frequent as to be difficult to count precisely, could be broken down into two categories: the somewhat casual afternoon gatherings and the more formal soirees. The "Piano Fridays," organized around tea at five o'clock, were now held on a regular basis. On other afternoons there were chamber music recitals. Generally it was Clara Haskil who dutifully played with whatever other musicians had been hired for the occasion. Despite a slight increase in the number of her public concerts, Haskil was still essentially without resources. For all intents and purposes she now lived at avenue Henri-Martin, in a small room on one of the upper floors of the lonely mansion. After Winnaretta bought the house in Jouy-en-Josas it was simply assumed that Haskil would come with her, to be "on call" for weekend music-making. The pianist was as bored by the country as she was by her benefactress's urban *mondanités*. In a certain sense, the country was worse, because there was nothing to do and nowhere to go. One day, when she learned that Winnaretta would be returning to Paris for the day to attend to some errands, Haskil dressed and waited by the front door of the house, hoping (without daring to speak up) that the Princesse would notice and offer to take her with her. But Winnaretta pretended to notice nothing, and swept out, with an imperious, "See you this evening!"[15]

Clara Haskil found the "Piano Fridays" pleasant, because of the excellence of the other musicians who came to join her in music-making. In 1930 the Italian virtuoso Renata Borgatti, a former lover of Romaine Brooks, was frequently engaged to partner Haskil in traversals of the four-hand or two-piano repertoire. Despite marked differences in their temperaments and performance styles—Borgatti was a tempestuous virtuoso, Haskil a model of nuance and refinement—the pairing was successful; with Winnaretta's help, the two women were able to secure concert engagements playing the Mozart two-piano concerto in venues beyond the confines of the Polignac salon.[16] Another new initiate into the "Fridays" circle was eighteen-year-old composer-pianist Igor Markevitch, whose star had continued to ascend even after the death of Diaghilev. Winnaretta presented Markevitch to Clara Haskil just around the time that the two newly acquired Steinway grands were delivered to the *atelier*; she asked the two pianists to break in the instruments with a sight-reading session—very likely before an audience—of the Brahms Piano Quintet, Op. 34, in its two-piano version. Sight-reading had never been Markevitch's strength, but seeing that the Princesse would not take no for an answer, he decided to rely on sheer bravado, and sat down at one of the instruments. At the other piano, Clara Haskil began with assurance; Markevitch (as he himself later recalled) muddled through his part, conscious that his partner was irritably marking time with her foot so that the ensemble wouldn't fall apart. As the piece came to a close, the young man finally got back on track just in time to finish with a grand flourish, as if the whole enterprise had been a delightful frolic.[17]

The atmosphere at the soirees, however, was less boisterous. Although the dinner parties that usually preceded the music were often intimate and relaxed in character, the recitals and concerts themselves were large, formal affairs. It is interesting to read the contrasting impressions of these events chronicled by various friends and guests. When Colette proffered an invitation on Winnaretta's behalf to her neighbor, the painter Dunoyer de Segonzac, for a dinner followed by music in the *atelier*, she emphasized the convivial aspect of the gathering. "The Princesse de Polignac asked me to write you to deliver an invitation to dinner on Sunday. . . . The dinner and the soiree will be nice and intimate, in the *atelier* at the back—do you know it?—with the Luc-Morhanges,[18] Germaine Taillefer [*sic*], the Carcos,[19] Février. . . . A suit or *smoking* [dinner jacket], as you wish, there will be both. A bit of good music without rows of chairs, a big fire in the fireplace."[20] A more jaded viewpoint of this kind of evening, however, was offered by another author, Élisabeth de Gramont. Separated from her husband, the Duc de Clermont-Tonnerre, Gramont was among the first in the aristocratic community to live openly as a lesbian, frequenting the Left Bank avant-garde circles of Natalie Barney and Gertrude Stein. Her description of Winnaretta's salon, written with equal parts affection and disdain, reflects a growing opinion that salon culture was a holdover from a faded era.

At avenue Henri-Martin, the home of the Princesse Edmond de Polignac, a large room is reserved for music. The platform is at the far end, and the Princesse rustles her train of silver-grey satin, going up and down the middle of the nave, while the faithful gather to the right and left waiting for the beginning of the service. Automatically the groups go to their places: the first three rows for the American billionaires, white hair and diamonds, and the British duchesses; three other rows for the important French women with tinted hair; the divine youth gather at the back, murmuring to each other amid the jostled chairs.

Gathered around the doors are the old esthetes, standing up, the Princesse's companions from her youth. Abbé Mugnier, Jacques-Émile Blanche, Paul Valéry, Abel Bonnard, the faithful quartet, listen quietly to the suave music; sometimes Colette; Madame Legrand sitting on a couch, and the Comtesse de Noailles reining in her voluble emotions. The composers come at their turn. . . .

The Princesse Edmond de Polignac is the only hostess in Paris whose eyes are not turned towards the door when the concert begins; they are filled with the ecstasy produced by a duo, a trio, a quartet, an orchestra, a sonata of Lekeu, a concerto of Bach.[21]

If Gramont viewed Winnaretta's musical gatherings as relics of a faded age, the composers and musicians who had enjoyed the first glory days of the Polignac salon continued to show their pleasure. Reynaldo Hahn, despite his disapproval of Winnaretta's modernism, did not turn down an opportunity for an *avant-première* of his new Piano Concerto, played by Magda Tagliaferro.[22] And when the aging Vincent d'Indy wrote to Winnaretta in November 1930, finalizing plans for an upcoming performance of Bach concertos by the faculty and students of the Schola Cantorum in the *atelier,* he nostalgically evoked the salon of earlier days: "Be assured that it will not be without emotion that I will find myself in this hospitable house, where so many comrades, for the most part deceased, gathered with such joy: Chabrier, Fauré, Messager, Maus . . .!"[23]

But the younger audience members had no such historical or sentimental perspective. Writer Julien Green's account of a salon program of Bach concertos, performed at Winnaretta's on Christmas Day 1930, was dry-eyed, to say the least.

A soiree at Madame de Polignac's. Many elegant society people there. Three Bach concertos were played. After the second concerto there was a more or less general stampede toward the buffet, and the third was played to barely half the audience. The murmur of the other half carried right up the music room, and sometimes, in the softest passages, it invaded, battling victoriously with the orchestra. "I detest this contemplative atmosphere," whispered one lady to her neighbor. Finally, no longer able to hang on, they, too, went to the buffet.[24]

Green's sardonic reportage of the *mondain* salon was a reflection of the attitudes of his era. The younger generation of artistically inclined aristocrats didn't host traditional salons: influenced by the lifestyle modernism of Jean Cocteau, music halls, black jazz, and the cinema, they hosted not just musical gatherings, but "happenings" with music. Étienne de Beaumont's masked balls and "Soirées de Paris"; Charles and Marie-Laure de Noailles's showings of surrealist films by Man Ray, Luis Buñuel, and Jean Cocteau at their mansion in the place des États-Unis; the outdoor "spectacle-concerts" organized around Poulenc's *Le Bal masqué* and *Aubade* at the Noailles' cubist villa in Hyères[25]—these were the alternatives to the conventional offerings of the rue Cortambert *atelier* being offered to young Parisian high society. The press had all but ceased to devote space to the musical salons. Much more attention was given in the society columns to embassy receptions, the festivities that followed the horse races at Longchamps, and the arrival of movie stars and other celebrities to the capital. In 1930 *Le Figaro* gave a total of one line to Winnaretta's prodigious salon activities, but devoted two separate articles to her Greek islands cruise, noting the name of every guest aboard the *Sans Peur.*

Winnaretta's salon might have faded entirely from public view were it not for another mutually beneficial marriage of a titled male Polignac and a female daughter of commerce. In April 1931, Winnaretta's nephew Prince Guy de Polignac exchanged wedding vows with Gladys Dupuy, daughter of an American mother and French newspaper magnate, Paul Dupuy. The Dupuy family, which had begun its ascent in the journalism industry thirty years earlier with the purchase of the popular daily *Le Petit Parisien,* now ran a publication empire that comprised more than a dozen illustrated dailies and magazines intended for the "popular classes."[26] The clan was a major sponsor of highly visible events: it was one of the main sponsors, for example, of Lindbergh's trans-Atlantic flight in 1927. In recent years, Dupuy had added an important jewel to its crown: a copiously illustrated daily newspaper devoted to society life, entitled *Excelsior.* After the repeal of Prohibition in America, the Polignac-Dupuy-Pommery combine assiduously courted American champagne and cinema industry interests; subsequently Dupuy-owned theaters and movie distributors had first access to popular American films, and were the first to show Mickey Mouse cartoons in French cinemas.[27] Winnaretta was a frequent guest at the celebrated dinner parties of Madame Dupuy, Prince Guy's mother-in-law, considered to be among the most powerful of Paris's wealthy upper bourgeois hostesses. Thus, after the 1931 Polignac-Dupuy marriage, musical events in the various Polignac households once again became newsworthy items in *Excelsior.* The paper even included, on one occasion, a picture of Winnaretta playing the Cavaillé-Coll organ.[28] Not to be outdone, *Le Figaro* and *Le Gaulois* returned to carrying items about the salon of the Princesse de Polignac in their society pages.

Winnaretta's renewed interest in commissioning music was piqued by the rising career of the young Igor Markevitch. Self-taught until the age of fourteen, the composer had come to Paris from Kiev to study theory with Nadia Boulanger, whose reputation as a composition teacher was steadily growing. Thanks to Diaghilev's influence, Markevitch's music had been brought to the attention of the directors of the Orchestre Symphonique de Paris. In June 1930 his Cantata was given its first performance by the OSP, under the baton of Désormière. The critics praised his orchestration, calling it "bright, dense, and dissonant, but not aggressive."[29] On 8 December Winnaretta had occasion to hear another work by Markevitch, his Concerto Grosso, included in a program that also included works by Haydn and Sauguet, and Stravinsky's *Renard*. When she first heard the young composer play through some of his music in 1929, in the presence of Diaghilev and Misia Sert, the impresario had told Winnaretta, "This young man is less well-behaved than he seems, and maybe just as impertinent as his music."[30] Winnaretta may have had an inkling of this impertinence when Markevitch read through the Brahms Quintet with Clara Haskil, but it didn't lessen her regard for his brash compositional style. It was this characteristic that the press underlined in its review of the Concerto Grosso, "a work that refers to the classics by its form, and to the more [modern] composers by its absence of lyricism [and] its disjunct, bumpy writing, from which emanates a heightened sense of rhythm."[31]

Winnaretta wrote to Markevitch the following week, congratulating him on this "vigorous and beautiful work . . . a new expression of your strong personality."[32] Shortly thereafter the composer came to rue Cortambert with the manuscript of the score in hand, though whether Winnaretta had asked to buy the autograph or whether Markevitch was offering it as a gift is not known. The young composer proposed the idea of writing another piano concerto, in *concertante* style, for performance in the Polignac salon.[33] Winnaretta accepted, and in February 1931 formalized the commission with a letter of agreement that offered terms similar to those proposed to Stravinsky, Satie, and Falla.[34] Markevitch was offered eight thousand francs to write the work, which was to be completed by early May 1931; four thousand would be paid in two installements in March and April, and the remainder would be paid upon delivery of the manuscript.[35] The young composer accepted the terms, although he made an inadvertent gaffe in implying that Winnaretta should pay for the orchestral parts.[36] The mediation of his teacher, Nadia Boulanger, was required to straighten out the misunderstanding.[37]

Winnaretta was enjoying a certain renown at that moment, having just been named a *Chevalier* of the Legion of Honor as a result of her "generous and discreet philanthropy, as well as the enlightened and informed support that she has brought to the arts, and, in particular, to music."[38] Paul Valéry, who sponsored her induction, presented her with the rosette.[39]

Winnaretta was able to share the prestigious evening with Anna de Noailles, who was inducted as Commandant of the Legion of Honor, the first woman to receive that distinction.[40] That spring Winnaretta was honored at a dinner hosted by the Collège de France for the important work being accomplished by the Fondation Singer-Polignac.[41] In June, her Manet painting, *La Lecture,* was loaned out for a Paris exhibition. She took pleasure in telling her guests that when she bought it forty-five years earlier for three thousand francs, her family had thought her completely crazy: to squander money on a picture showing a woman clad in white, sitting on a white sofa—what madness! In 1914, when it appeared in a London exhibition, it had been evaluated at thirty thousand francs.[42] Now, in 1931, she had been offered 1.5 million francs for the work fifteen minutes after the Paris show opened.

But good luck was not always on her side. Her spring salon season got off to a bumpy start. The musical offering of 31 March 1931 was to be the first Paris performance of Paul Hindemith's new *Konzertmusik* for piano, harp, and brass instruments. Hindemith's music was relatively unknown in France, and it was perhaps Milhaud and Poulenc, two of the composer's champions, who had recommended it to Winnaretta, always on the lookout for an interesting musical "scoop."[43] At the moment the recital was to begin, the "natural harps," indispensable for the execution of the Hindemith concerto, had not yet arrived from Pleyel,[44] and the harpists insisted that it was impossible to play the work on conventional chromatic instruments. To placate the audience, Winnaretta asked a singer who was among the audience members to perform some songs; the woman—according to the novelist Julien Green, "a large German"—obliged the hostess, and sang some *Lieder* by Brahms and Richard Strauss.[45] Finally the instruments arrived, and the concerto "burst forth like a storm" in the small *atelier,* which could barely support the loud sonority of the brass. "Boring," concluded Green;[46] "a great success," declared *Le Figaro.*[47]

There were further upsets to the plans for Winnaretta's spring season: Markevitch had not yet completed his piece, a work for piano and chamber orchestra, to be entitled *Partita.* Winnaretta had already made plans to hire the OSP for a May performance;[48] now the premiere was put off indefinitely. Undaunted, Winnaretta turned her attention to two other composers in her circle, Henri Sauguet and Francis Poulenc. Sauguet was commissioned to write a two-piano suite; it was completed in 1932, and called *Les Jeux de l'amour et du hasard* (The Games of Love and Chance). Sauguet was a member of the École d'Arcueil, another group of composers who had gathered in 1923 under the leadership of Satie, naming themselves for the suburb where their teacher lived.[49] He wrote music in many genres, including film music; his ballets were produced by Diaghilev and Ida Rubinstein.

As a friend of Marie-Blanche and Pata, Poulenc held a special place in

the Polignac circle. In 1931 he found himself without sufficient commissions to guarantee a reasonable income for the year. It is possible he hinted
to Winnaretta that he would like to write a work for her salon; if so, the
hint was not taken. That summer the composer turned to Pata for help,
hoping that she would be able to influence her aunt. "You *can't imagine*
[how] the commission of which I spoke would change things. To be able to
work again without nightmares, think of it! Of course the dedication, manuscript, first performance, all would belong to your aunt."[50] Pata's intervention worked, for on 24 August Winnaretta wrote to the composer, asking if
he could "foresee the possibility of writing a work for my 'collection.' . . .
I would be so happy to add your name to those of Stravinsky, Fauré, Falla,
Satie, who were willing to write . . . the beautiful pages that you are familiar with." Winnaretta suggested that he write a piano concerto, with a
reduction "for three pianos: a solo part, and two [accompanying]"—thinking, no doubt, of making the work accessible for the "Piano Fridays." The
proposed fee was indicative both of her high regard for the composer and,
perhaps, of Pata's influence, for she offered Poulenc a payment of twenty
thousand francs—more than twice what she had offered Markevitch less
than a year earlier—plus five thousand for the performance of the solo part
by the composer.[51] In the fall, Poulenc proposed a different configuration
of the work, one that his patron happily accepted: a concerto for two pianos and orchestra (or third piano).[52]

Winnaretta was kept apprised of Poulenc's progress that summer at the
Palazzo Polignac; even before the work's completion, she was investigating
performance venues in which to present it—"in Paris, and also in Venice,
where there will be some big musical festivities next year."[53] Venice was, at
that moment, looking for ways to rid itself of the image of being a "museum" city, devoted only to the glories of the past. Winnaretta was on a
committee of *mécènes* and musicians—including Giorgio Levi and Guido
Bianchini, director of La Fenice—who were interested in bringing new artistic life to Venice and its musical institutions. The committee sought to
mount concerts and festivals featuring the composers of the "young school"
of European composers. Poulenc's name naturally came up during the ple-
nary meetings hosted by Winnaretta at the palazzo.

Olga Rudge also came often to the palazzo, to dine, to "listen in" to
radio broadcasts of the Berlin Philharmonic, or to read through Bach violin sonatas with her hostess.[54] The violinist also partnered pianists Clara
Haskil and Renata Borgatti, both of whom were taking "working vacations" in Venice.[55] Rudge gently but persistently tried to interest the Princesse
in Ezra Pound's musical compositions (the poet was also an amateur composer),[56] but Winnaretta had other ideas in mind for the violinist, who was
planning to spend the winter in Paris. Marie-Blanche had expressed an
interest in organizing, in conjunction with her aunt, regular sight-reading
sessions of the piano-trio literature, and Winnaretta thought that Rudge

might find it "amusing" to participate in these sessions. "No guests, just my nieces and nephews, who also play [instruments]," Winnaretta wrote to Rudge. "We would do the 1st Schumann, the 1st Mozart and the 1st Mendelssohn, and the 3rd or 4th and 7th Beethoven. We have a cellist, and we would do the piano parts *à tour de rôle* [taking turns]. If this doesn't terrify you and you can accept the very modest [fee] of 100 francs, we could begin early in December."[57] Winnaretta surely thought that she was doing a kind thing in contributing to the violinist's income—despite the fact that she was still a year late in paying Rudge the two thousand francs that she owed her for the summer rental of her house.[58] In December, the first "sight-reading session" with Olga Rudge as violinist took place in Winnaretta's *atelier*.[59] Three piano trios were read through by Rudge, an unnamed cellist, and, as pianists, Winnaretta, Clara Haskil, and Marie-Blanche de Polignac, respectively. As Marie-Blanche began her traversal of Schubert's B-flat trio, Stravinsky arrived just in time to turn pages, beating time with his cigarette, while Poulenc and Février followed the score, humming the beautiful themes along with the pianist.[60]

Rudge loved listening to Winnaretta tell stories about her past. In one amusing tale, Winnaretta recalled going out one evening to hear a performance of a Bach cantata. Forgetting that the performance was taking place in a Protestant chapel, and not in a concert hall, she had turned up in an evening gown and ermine cloak. The usher said, "You are not wearing a hat, Madame," and refused to let her in. Having decided that she *would* hear the Bach, and having already sent away her chauffeur, Winnaretta turned to a man sitting in the back of the church, snatched the hat off the astonished gentleman's head, and walked to her place, prominently sporting the "nice little bowler" that accompanied her evening clothes. "She's really nice," Rudge later wrote to Ezra Pound, "and I hope she will soon remember the two thousand francs that she owes me!"[61]

That winter, Winnaretta maintained a schedule that would be daunting even to a younger woman, much less one of sixty-five years. Her first soiree of the *petite saison* featured a performance by Haskil and Borgatti of Mozart's Two-Piano Concerto, K. 365. "It was very good, only people talked all the time," wrote Rudge to Pound.[62] On 25 November, at 11 o'clock at night, Winnaretta gave an impromptu organ recital in the *atelier* for her nieces and nephews.[63] The next weekend she traveled down to the Loire Valley for a luncheon at Poulenc's house, where the other guests included Colette and Georges and Nora Auric.[64] Two nights later, back in Paris, she gave a dinner party, followed by "an hour of music" by soprano Madeleine Grey, who, "with remarkable artistry," performed songs by Chabrier and Ravel, including the latter's *Four Folk Songs* (each song in a different language—Spanish, French, Yiddish, and Italian).[65] The following week another soiree featured works for wind instruments and piano by Poulenc, Stravinsky, and Weber.[66] Julien Green was again in attendance; he noted the presence of "many very elegant people, who would have been completely happy if the musicians had consented to shut up, allowing them to chatter on. The writer 'M.' [possibly Paul Morand] said, 'I admire those who can distinguish Poulenc from Stravinsky.'" Green himself was content to savor the romanticism of a Carl Maria von Weber Clarinet Sonata, also presented that evening, "something truthful and serious, [exuding] a deep nocturnal emotion."[67]

Meanwhile, Poulenc was hard at work on "Winnaretta's" concerto, which was "not going too badly," as he wrote to Marie-Laure de Noailles. "The first movement is very Balinese."[68] On 19 December the composer played portions of the work for its dedicatee; Winnaretta declared herself "*enthusiastic* about what you played for me today, and very proud to hear my Concerto."[69] Poulenc's elevated status as a commissioned composer did not deter Winnaretta from engaging him to "arrange . . . some musical surprises" for her New Year's Eve supper and soiree—"a singer ([for] 'Boléro'[70]), or instruments, or something else."[71] In addition to being put in charge of finding a piano "thumper" (*tapeur*) and a dance band for the post-supper festivities, the composer was hired to play a two-piano recital with Février before the meal.[72] Among the "musical surprises" of that evening was "a rather beautiful reading" given by Poulenc and Février (at two pianos) of Ravel's new G-Major Piano Concerto;[73] this may very well have been the first performance of this "marvelous work," which would not receive its public premiere with orchestra for another two weeks.[74]

The most anticipated event of the season, however, was the repeat performance of Stravinsky's much-acclaimed *Symphony of Psalms,* which had received its premiere by the OSP under the direction of Ernest Ansermet at the Théâtre des Champs-Élysées in February 1931. The OSP had wasted no time in taking advantage of Winnaretta's integral connection to the composer: Ansermet had written to the patron in February, asking her to contribute between thirty and fifty thousand francs towards the advance costs necessary to produce the début performance.[75] It is safe to assume that Winnaretta contributed at least a portion of this sum to defray the costs. But a new round of requests for aid came ten months later, when the OSP programmed a new all-Stravinsky program, consisting of *Oedipus Rex, The Rite of Spring,* and the *Symphony of Psalms.* The OSP faced a new deficit in December, and asked Stravinsky to find a less expensive work to replace the *Symphony of Psalms,* one that did not involve chorus. The composer wanted "at no price to abandon the *Symphony.*" On 24 December he wrote to his "very dear friend" Winnaretta, asking her to provide emergency funds to hire choristers for the work.[76] True to form, she agreed to "accept the responsibility of paying for half the cost," a total of thirty-five hundred to four thousand francs.[77] But the OSP's administrator, Georges Marie, pressed harder, asking the composer if he couldn't "kindly obtain a little more ([a total of] 5,000 francs, for example)."[78] In January Stravinsky went to Winnaretta's to plead the case to her directly.[79] It was impossible to resist Stravinsky's entreaties, especially when it concerned what the patron referred to as "this most beautiful work of all, the *Symphony of Psalms.*"[80] She agreed to underwrite the cost of the choir, and the OSP was able to hire a first-rate ensemble, the Vlassoff Chorus. Later, Winnaretta's generosity would be repaid by the composer in a shockingly ungenerous manner.

The 1931–32 season was a particularly lively period for modernist music in Paris, as a spate of fledgling contemporary music enterprises sprang up. Elizabeth Sprague Coolidge, the wealthy American *mécène*, was in Paris in October 1931, presenting works by Prokofiev and Malipiero under private auspices.[81] Katherine Heyman, an American expatriate pianist, presented a series of lecture-concerts on such topics as "Music as Pattern in Space" and "Neither Major nor Minor" that featured, among others, the music of American composer Charles Ives.[82] In 1932, a chamber music ensemble called Le Triton gave a series of concerts that presented recent works of an international array of composers, including Schmitt, Hindemith, Bartók, and Stravinsky.[83] But by far the most visible of all the new music enterprises was La Sérénade, founded and directed by the violinist Marquise Illan de Casa Fuerte,[84] née Yvonne Giraud. Madame Casa Fuerte had studied violin at the Conservatoire, where she formed a close musical friendship with Darius Milhaud, and played the composer's new violin sonata in Jacques-Émile Blanche's salon. Under the Marquise's capable leadership, the Sérénade would soon become well known for its imaginative programs featuring the music of Les Six and the École d'Arcueil.[85] The first program, held on 1 December 1931 at the Salle Pleyel, included first performances of works by Markevitch, Rieti, and Sauguet. Even though Winnaretta was on the founding committee of the Sérénade,[86] she clearly felt some ambivalence about the organization, perhaps feeling that it stole some of her thunder as Paris's premiere private presenter of new music. She did not attend the inaugural concert, instead hosting her own soiree with Madeleine Grey that evening. Neither did she attend the second concert on 22 February 1932—making her perhaps one of the only absentees from the *tout-Paris* audience who came to hear works by Stravinsky, Sauguet, Milhaud, Poulenc, and Satie.[87]

The reasons for Winnaretta's chilly attitude towards the Sérénade may have had to do with behind-the-scenes machinations pertaining to Markevitch's new *Partita,* recently published by the German firm of Schott.[88] Yvonne de Casa Fuerte apparently had proposed a first public performance of the work under the auspices of the Sérénade. Correspondence suggests that Markevitch had hinted to Casa Fuerte that the Polignac salon could be used as a venue for a "dress rehearsal." This was hardly what Winnaretta had in mind in commissioning the work: she was not about to see the prestige of a first performance of a work that existed due to her generosity relegated to the lowly status of "dress rehearsal," certainly not for the likes of a competing operation run by an *arriviste* like the Marquise de Casa Fuerte. She had her secretary inquire of Markevitch about his "plans on the subject of the concert of which you spoke to [the Princesse]," adding, for emphasis, "it is completely impossible for her to organize a concert at her house whose costs would be too high."[89] She became obstructive when Markevitch proposed a first performance during the month of April, to be followed by a public performance with the Sérénade in May. She could not schedule the performance before the end of April, she wrote, and she wished to remind him of their contractual agreement that "the first performance must take place at her house."[90] The wrangling over the *Partita* continued for several months.

Winnaretta's imperious attitude towards the maladroit Markevitch (now being tagged with the nickname "Igor II"[91]) could not have been more different from the solicitude she showed to Poulenc in the same period. Despite new strictures on culture imposed by the Fascist regime, the directors of the 1932 Venice Biennale had decided to organize an International Festival of Music as an adjunct to its prestigious art exhibition. Winnaretta was asked to organize the French section; she declined the invitation, becoming instead honorary president. In this capacity she was able to influence the choice of works selected by the artistic committee. She recommended, among "her" works, Falla's *Retablo* and Poulenc's as yet unfinished two-piano concerto. The committee informed her that she should reserve for Venice the first performance of Poulenc's concerto[92]—and this time, for Poulenc and the honor of having "her" concerto heard in the context of a prestigious international venue, Winnaretta acquiesced.[93]

Poulenc was being rewarded as much for his devotion to Winnaretta as for his wonderful music. He was charming and funny; his gracious flattery came from the heart—and he was better at it than the immature Markevitch. The composer was a constant presence at his patron's home during the early part of the year. He loved the lively atmosphere: "Lots of dinners at avenue Henri-Martin in the *atelier* with Stravinsky, Colette, Aunt Anna [de Noailles],[94] more prodigious than ever with her golden bowler hats, black sequins, pink plumes, chantilly lace, Carco, Max Jacob (Aunt Anna's buddy), Segonzac, Misia, Marthe Hyde, Solange [d'Ayen]. . . ."[95] "Poupoule"—as he was called by his closest friends—was also in attendance for the "first music [gatherings] at the Jean de Polignacs in a room with marvelous acoustics. Little trios '*en famille*,' very nice, like everything that happens at their house."[96]

It is doubtful, however, that one of those most involved in those "little trios" would have agreed with Poulenc's assessment that everything was "nice." Olga Rudge had quickly begun to realize that in agreeing to serve as a "house musician" for Winnaretta—and now for Marie-Blanche as well[97]—she was obliged to suffer the less beneficent side of the Princesse's character. For six weeks Rudge received requests, tantamount to commands, to be on call for readings of difficult piano-trio repertoire that would some-times occur on less than a day's notice, all for the inadequate compensation of one hundred francs (approximately twenty dollars), not including travel fare. A typical such "invitation" was sent one Saturday in February: "Dear Miss Rudge, . . . If you are free on Sunday—tomorrow—will you come to Jouy en Josas till Monday? You will find a good train at 3:20 and another at 3:40. Will you telephone here which you will take. I am here till 10 o'clock Sunday. Anyhow I look forward to these trios on Tuesday 4:30 at 16 rue Barbet de Jouy. Yours sincerely, SP."[98] Another note, sent two days later, informed the violinist that "my niece wants to play the 2nd Schubert trio. We will also do the 1st Mendelssohn and the Beethoven we already read over one day—3rd or 4th I think."[99] Rudge fought back her indignation over this denigrating attitude as best she could; finally, she decided "down in the pride of my heart to *show* her. I like the old girl . . . but I doubt that I made her understand."[100] There were, of course, perks to being in fre-quent close proximity to the Princesse. When Daisy Fellowes rented the Théâtre du Vieux-Colombier for a private showing of Cocteau's new film, *The Blood of the Poet*, Rudge was invited to attend.[101] And it was possible to hear musical works in Winnaretta's salon that were unlikely to be played anywhere else in the city, such as the first Paris performance of Alban Berg's *Lyric Suite*,[102] played by the celebrated German ensemble, the Kolisch Quar-tet.

A series of complications around her commissioned works—the ceding of the two-piano concerto to the Venice Biennale, the inability of the Sérénade to finalize a concert date—forced Winnaretta to cancel the pro-jected May soiree that would have featured the first performances of the Markevitch and Poulenc commissions; ultimately she relinquished the pre-miere of the *Partita* to the Sérénade.[103] The month of May, as it turned out, was an inauspicious time for gaiety. The stormy weather that refused to relent for the first half of the month augured ominous portents: the recent "theatrical blows" in Germany, where elections had just brought Adolf Hitler to power; the assassination on 7 May of French President Paul Doumer by a Russian terrorist; the kidnapping story of the Lindbergh baby, which, days later, came to its tragic conclusion. The atmosphere in Paris was anxious. Winnaretta soothed her nerves by attending concerts—Horowitz with the OSP on 4 May, Yehudi Menuhin in recital at the Salle Pleyel on 11 May.[104] She began a new charitable project, raising money for the Hôpital Foch.[105] She made frequent visits to Anna de Noailles, whose chronic illnesses had kept her bedridden since the month of March.[106] They were as close as sisters, and Anna had paid tribute to their long friendship in dedicating to Winnaretta her collection of poetic prose pieces, *Exacti-tudes*: "I was fifteen years old when I had the good fortune to know, with dear Edmond and my beloved sister Hélène, what the nobility of a friend-ship like yours really means. Compassion in times of sadness, strength in times of adversity, your friends find these in you, and thanks to you, *the world is less bitter.* Thank you for the diamond loyalty of which your affection is made, intermingled with my whole life."[107]

Winnaretta herself was ill the night of the Sérénade's third concert on 19 May, and missed the premiere of the work she had commissioned from Markevitch, performed by pianist Marcelle Meyer with the OSP under the baton of Roger Désormière. "From all directions I'm being told of the enormous success of the *Partita,*" she wrote the next day. "What great regret for me not to have been there for this triumph."[108] Later that week she finalized plans to have the work performed in her salon on 2 June.[9] Olga Rudge was underwhelmed by "Igor II" and his music: "He's doing what George [Antheil] was doing ten years ago—he has talent, but he's very young, of course, eighteen."[110] Apparently, however, the work was well received. The three-movement concerto was a successful blend of classical forms and dissonant harmonic idioms; its title, with its baroque associations, surely appealed to its dedicatee. Marie-Blanche noted in her diary, "Markevitch's *Partita,* played at Tante Winnie's, was even more gripping than [it was] at the Sérénade. Implacable music, serene in its nastiness, perfectly constructed. Despite its harshness, one had the satisfaction that is given by perfect things, by closed circles. One mysteriously perceived that within, a mathematical problem was resolved."[111] The performance of the soloist, Marcelle Meyer, was excellent—and provided some extramusical drama as well. Meyer, married to celebrated actor Pierre Bertin, was now nine months pregnant, and some audience members seemed nervous that she might go into labor during the concert. Meyer was nonplussed by her condition, however; according to Markevitch's memoirs, she played with energy and flair. At the conclusion, Winnaretta, visibly satisfied with "her" work, asked for a second performance, after which Markevitch was amused to hear one gentleman whisper that "he would slip out before the third," whereas the person to whom he spoke responded that he was mistaken, that they had played two different works, and that she "preferred the second."[112]

Winnaretta organized two final musical gatherings that month. The first, at Jouy-en-Josas on Sunday, 12 June, was held on a terrace ringed by chestnut trees, with the valleys of Versailles at their feet. The guests stretched out on chaises longues while Clara Haskil's violinist sister Jeanne and "the customary cellist" sight-read Haydn and Schubert trios with Marie-Blanche and Haskil.[113] The soiree of 15 June was held in the Paris *atelier.* Suzanne Peignot gave a fine rendition of Poulenc's recent *Five Poems of Max Jacob,* and Jacques Février played a "serious and well-developed" piano sonata by Georges Auric. Finally, Sauguet's four-movement two-piano suite, *Les Jeux de l'amour et du hasard,* was given its first performance, performed by the composer himself and Poulenc, whom Sauguet described as a "dazzling pianist."[114] Winnaretta's reaction to the work that she had commissioned is nowhere noted. Its first public performance took place in a Sérénade concert at the Salle Gaveau on 4 February 1933; Henry Prunières, writing for *La Revue musicale,* reacted with deadpan bemusement: "Sauguet's flat improvisations are delightful. . . . [They] run along, trickling on until the faucet is turned off."[115] In Marie-Blanche's estimation, the piece was "frankly bad."[116]

On 23 June 1932, Paris Singer died suddenly and alone in a London hotel.[117] Winnaretta traveled to England for the funeral, held five days later, and quickly returned to France. After so many years of worry and care, her brother's passing seemed to leave her relieved, and she set off for Venice and the Biennale in August in a mournful but liberated state of mind.

That summer the palazzo was perpetually full, with guests that included Poulenc, Falla, and Février. Arthur Rubinstein and his new bride Nela (née Aniela Mlynarska) arrived soon thereafter. They had just been married in London on 27 July, and their stay at the palazzo would constitute a second honeymoon.[118] Every day Winnaretta's beautiful black gondola waited at the train station to pick up the next arrival of guests. During the day, when not in rehearsals, the group would explore the pleasures of Venice, enjoying its gastronomic delights in small, out-of-the-way restaurants, sunbathing at the Lido, or playing golf. Some attended to individual pleasures: Poulenc went on sorties in quest of encounters with handsome men—encounters that inevitably proved to be, in Marie-Blanche's words, "rapid, fatal, like the first act of *Tristan.*"[119] The religious Falla, on the other hand, went daily to morning Mass at Winnaretta's neighborhood church. Poulenc, whose earthier interests had caused him to abandon the rituals of the church, accompanied his composer friend on one occasion, and had the astonishing experience of watching Falla "[sink] down in prayer, [like] certain saints who in ecstasy suddenly vanish from the sight of the profane." While Falla prayed, the parish's organist played a Frescobaldi work on the magnificent organ that had been restored by Winnaretta; the music seemed to Poulenc to be purity itself, "for us alone."[120] There were musical pleasures to be had within the palazzo itself, in the drawing rooms filled with pianos. Once, upon returning after Mass, Falla had the pleasure of hearing his own *Nights in the Garden of Spain,* played in its two-piano version by Rubinstein and Poulenc.[121]

Excursions to nearby scenic sites provided variety. One day, Winnaretta and her guests visited Jean Hugo and his new wife, the former Duchesse de Gramont, née Maria Ruspoli, at their newly restored Vigoleno castle, a medieval fortress at Salsomaggiore, near Milan.[122] At night the group attended concerts at the Fenice or the Goldoni Theater. The Music Committee had done its best to be all-inclusive in its choices of repertoire, and there was an embarrassment of riches: among others, works by Ottorino Respighi and Alfredo Casella ("interminable," reported Marie-Blanche), George Gershwin's Concerto in F, and Palestinian-Jewish composer Joseph Achron's

The Golem. But the assessment of critics and audience alike was that Falla's *Retablo* and Poulenc's Two-Piano Concerto (finished only three days before leaving for Venice[123]) outstripped all other offerings in terms of musical interest. Falla's work could be presented only in concert version (a fully staged version being too complicated and expensive), but the composer had agreed to conduct the performance. He allowed his hostess to attend most of the rehearsals. At the dress rehearsal Winnaretta was startled to see that the composer's face was covered with cotton tufts. He had suffered an attack by mosquitoes the night before, and the ammonia-soaked cotton wads applied to soothe the sting had stuck to his skin, giving a comic aspect to his dark, sober visage.[124] But there was nothing comical about the performance, which was masterful. Winnaretta told Falla that "in the opinion of all, your admirable *Retablo* was the high point of the Festival, and I am so proud of your precious dedication."[125] It was Poulenc's Two-Piano Concerto, however, that critic Henry Prunières deemed to be "the great event of the Festival."[126] The work was given a brilliant performance by the author and Jacques Février, accompanied by the Orchestra of La Scala of Milan under the direction of Désiré Defauw. The Balinese gamelan[127] effects in the first movement made a great impression, as did the Mozartian second movement, and the lightning-fast finale. Poulenc thought the orchestral accompaniment "a miracle at every moment."[128]

After the concerts, the musicians and their friends gathered for supper on the Piazza, celebrating in the intoxicating atmosphere of the warm night air, returning afterwards to the Palazzo Polignac to make more music. One night, after a concert, Arthur Rubinstein sat at the piano; Nela, tossing her shoes across the salon, began dancing with astonishing grace, "giving us the [kind of] joy that Isadora must have given people thirty years ago," wrote Marie-Blanche. It was only one of many unforgettable moments shared by the occupants of the palazzo that month. "This visit was so full of rare pleasures," wrote Marie-Blanche, "and Tante Winnie was the magician."[129]

The "magician" had unfinished business with one of her guests, however. During the course of his visit, Winnaretta gently reminded Falla that he had yet to deliver the two manuscripts of the *Retablo,* as promised in their 1919 contract. Falla had been promising for years that the scores would be finished "soon,"[130] but the promise had never been fulfilled. Winnaretta keenly wished to see the material proofs of her *mécénat* added to her manuscript collection. In 1928, she had paid the composer an additional seven thousand francs to spur his efforts,[131] but even the force of the franc had failed to achieve the desired conclusion. Apparently fearing that Falla would never complete the task, Winnaretta proposed a compromise: she would accept a much shorter manuscript of her favorite portions of the piece. Falla, surely grateful to be relieved of the larger burden, readily agreed.[132] During one of the many festive evenings at the palazzo, the composer sat quietly in a corner, writing out two excerpts from the *Retablo*: the seventh part, "Melisendra," and Don Quixote's final solo, a paean to knight errantry and the lady Dulcinea. Falla bound the pages in a gilt-edged cover, on which he inscribed in gold letters, "I am at the Princesse de Polignac's house."[133] Of all the happy hours they enjoyed during the Festival, the most wonderful for Winnaretta was surely the moment when the composer placed his long-awaited manuscript in her hands.

Even after the Festival ended and the guests went home, Winnaretta did not slow her pace. She went to Chioggia to watch the competition of the small fishing boats. Olga Rudge returned in Venice in October and was promptly invited to the Palazzo Polignac to play chamber music.[134] There were still performances ongoing at the Fenice, and Winnaretta attended with her British friends Gerald Berners and Emerald Cunard. Later that month she drove to Vienna "for a few days of operas and concerts," including a recital where "Horowitz played so beautifully."[135] Her plans for the next season's soirees were already in motion, including readings of the Mozart Two-Piano Concerto and the introduction of several newly commissioned works.[136] Germaine Tailleferre was commissioned to write a short orchestral piece; she produced an *Overture,* which, subsequent to its salon performance, emerged as the highlight of the OSP program given on Christmas Day 1932.[137] Nicolas Nabokov, a former member of the Diaghilev "clan," was invited to write a work for solo voice, chorus, and small orchestra. The composer, whose creative style featured stylized, tuneful renditions of Russian idioms (an approach that already seemed archaic in light of Stravinsky's revolutionary music), chose as a text the story of Job.

Winnaretta's next commission was given to Igor Markevitch. Whatever reservations she may have had about the young man's maturity and savoir-faire, there was no denying the power of his music or the impact his works had made on the Paris public in the last three years. Winnaretta wrote to Markevitch right after the conclusion of the Venice Festival, reminding him that he had yet to send her the piano reduction of the *Partita,* at the same time inviting him to write a new work "for a small number of instruments (or voice), which you would do under the same conditions as *Partita*— dedication, first performance, manuscript, etc."[138] She offered, however, a higher fee for this work: ten thousand francs, as opposed to the eight thousand paid for the *Partita.*[139] Markevitch accepted the commission with pleasure; by February 1933, what he called the Princesse's "little darling" [*le chou de Madame de Polignac*], a multi-movement orchestral piece entitled *Hymnes,* was "well under way," with one movement already completed.[140]

Winnaretta's final commission was the most surprising of all, for it was offered to a composer whom she barely knew: Kurt Weill. The German-Jewish composer already had quite a following among the artistic denizens of Montparnasse and Montmartre, as well as the "chic" Parisians who followed the avant-garde trends. His reputation had been built on his status as the founder of a new school of popular opera, what critic Henry Prunières, one of his staunchest French champions, hailed as a genre destined "to renew the decrepit lyric drama."[141] The *Threepenny Opera* had brought him international renown; Stravinsky told Weill that it was the most talked-about contemporary German work of art.[142] The work's librettist, poet and playwright Bertolt Brecht, contributed texts that were scathing, astute lampoons of contemporary political and social culture; these were set to seductive melodies and grinding harmonies, whose rhythms evoked the dance hall and the cabaret. On the surface, Weill's music seemed to embody the amalgam of music-hall esthetics and classical forms that Jean Cocteau had espoused for years. If the realism of *Threepenny Opera* was harsher and grittier than what Cocteau and Les Six had in mind in their championship of the "music of everyday," Weill was still viewed as a composer for the everyman, an artist-hero for the working class—and for the "chic" aristocrats who paid lip-service to these values.

Winnaretta was surely familiar with Weill's music—it had been receiving performances in Paris since the mid-1920s—but it was undoubtedly the younger, "trendy" members of the aristocracy who were responsible for her serious interest in the composer. After the enormous success of the 1932 Paris production of *Threepenny Opera*, Charles and Marie-Laure de Noailles contacted Weill, offering to present *Mahagonny*[143] and *Der Jasager* in November in their home;[144] at the same time, Yvonne de Casa Fuerte arranged to present a second, public, semi-staged performance of these works at the Salle Gaveau under the auspices of the Sérénade.[145] In October, encouraged by this unexpected and long-hoped-for opportunity to capitalize on his previous Paris triumph, Weill began discussion with his publisher about the possibility of "an important French production" of his works, perhaps a "first-class" revival of *Threepenny Opera*. He mentioned that "the Princesse de Polignac was particularly interested in the project,"[146] but Winnaretta had an even more interesting—and self-serving—project in mind. On 7 November Weill wrote to his publisher, "I have . . . received from the Princess Polignac a commission to write an orchestra work to be premiered in her house and to be dedicated to her."[147] Further correspondence indicates that Weill was offered twenty thousand francs for this work—his Second Symphony.[148]

Weill arrived at the Gare du Nord on 7 December, the day of the private concert of the Noailles. He was given a celebrity's welcome: Yvonne de Casa Fuerte had arranged for press photographers to record his arrival. The society press, which trotted out the inevitable litany of society names associated with the Weill performances (including Winnaretta's), was slyly cutting in its reports of the reception accorded the composer (who was dubbed "The Man of the Day"): "They're talking only of him, as if Bach, Beethoven, Chopin, Liszt, Wagner, and Debussy had been reborn in a single man."[149] Prunières lauded the Salle Gaveau performances, writing, "One had the surprise of seeing this musician of aristocratic tendencies converted to the entirely new cause of popular art."[150] But the *Figaro*'s critic, Stan Golestan, was forthrightly hostile, both to Weill and to his music. Although the overt signs of French anti-Semitism—dormant since the conclusion of the Dreyfus Affair—had only just begun to resurface,[151] Golestan's attack on Weill—while making no mention of Jewishness—was so scathing that one might have thought him to be in collusion with the officials of the Third Reich, whose list of "decadent composers" was topped with Weill's name.

The Sérénade just gave its first concert of the year, and a motley crew . . . filled the Salle Gaveau. . . . A group of people in strange get-ups rubbed elbows with a rather sizeable audience of snobs, whose mentality has never allowed them to penetrate the mysteries of a true work of art. The most favorable welcome was given to the music of the poorest quality, by those who carry within them the seed of the complete decay of all loftier sentiments.

A great publicity campaign has been made around Mr. Kurt Weill, who is considered among certain German musicians to have completely emancipated opera from tradition. . . . His surrealist opera, *Mahagonny,* is nothing but an incoherent babble, devoid of action or life. . . . The music, occasionally pleasant in itself, was best aided by its jazz rhythms [and] Negro refrains. But we've heard more enjoyable music at [the black jazz clubs] where the working-class strains are less pretentious and more honestly rendered.

Needless to say, the crowd went wild, and Mr. Kurt Weill rushed to the stage to bask in the applause of the snobs, unleashed in an excessive frenzy.[152]

Regrettably, Winnaretta left no personal impressions of Weill's music. Was she frightened by the political overtones? (Hitler's appointment as Chancellor on 30 January 1933 would signal the end of the Weimar Republic, forcing Weill to flee from his native soil.) One also wonders how the Princesse must have felt about being grouped with those "snobs" who attended fashionable musical events only in quest of reflected glamor. Did she perhaps have second thoughts about being influenced by Marie-Laure de Noailles—the embodiment *par excellence* of a "chic" patron—in awarding a commission to Weill? Was she indeed supporting "decadent" music?

Winnaretta had always sought a kind of personal purity through her engagement with music. She would soon discover the very embodiment of that purity in a woman, a musician, whose piety and seriousness of purpose would inspire her to the end of her days.

Mademoiselle

The 1932 Paris winter season was in full swing, and brilliant. One eagerly awaited musical event was an upcoming recital to be given by Stravinsky and Russian violinist Samuel Dushkin.[1] The two musicians had decided to embark on a duo partnership, and Stravinsky had written some new pieces for their collaborative programs: a *Suite italienne* based on his Pergolesi-inspired ballet *Pulcinella,* and a Duo Concertant.[2] These works were scheduled to receive their Paris debut on 8 December 1932 at the Salle Pleyel. Winnaretta's seats for the recital were already reserved. She had invited Igor Markevitch, now a "regular" in the Polignac salon, to join her in her loge, with a promise to introduce him to Stravinsky afterwards.[3] At the moment, Markevitch was in a bit of an awkward position vis-à-vis his patron: she had recently asked him to write a new work for small ensemble, a request that surely delighted the composer; on the other hand, she had not yet sent the final payment of four thousand francs for his *Partita,* due at the time of the manuscript's delivery. After the financial misunderstandings that had taken place the previous year, Markevitch did not feel capable of broaching the subject of money with Winnaretta. He wrote to his teacher, Nadia Boulanger, to ask for help.[4] Boulanger was accustomed to acting as emissary on behalf of her talented but unworldly young students. On 15 November 1932 she called at rue Cortambert, expecting, no doubt, to carry out a relatively simple errand on Markevitch's behalf.[5] Little did she imagine that her visit would set in motion a chain of events that would change her own life, and Winnaretta's, forever.

Nadia Boulanger's strength of character had been forged from many personal and professional disappointments. Born in 1887, she was the daughter of composer and Prix de Rome winner Ernest Boulanger and his wife Raissa (his former voice student), who claimed descent from a family of Russian princes. The young Nadia had shown early promise as a musician. At the Conservatoire she studied harmony, piano accompaniment, and organ; in 1901 (the year of Edmond de Polignac's death) she entered the composition class of Gabriel Fauré. While still a student, she met the pianist and composer, Spanish-born Raoul Pugno, who became her mentor and, subsequently, her lover. Pugno encouraged the young woman to compose, even to submit her works to the Prix de Rome committee. Boulanger entered the prestigious contest three times, but the odds of a woman composer winning the prize were virtually non-existent—she received the back-handed compliment of a second grand prize after her third try.[6] Nonetheless, through her own efforts, and with Pugno's help, she gained a reputation in the Paris musical community as an estimable young composer and pianist.[7] A number of her works were published, and a 1912 opera, *La Ville morte* (The Dead City), on a libretto by Gabriele d'Annunzio, seemed assured of a prestigious first performance.

The first of the many halts to Nadia's professional progress and personal happiness came in 1913 when her younger sister Lili, to the astonishment of all, won the Prix de Rome. Lili Boulanger was suddenly hailed as a "genius," whereas Nadia was regarded merely as a "talent." A stunning blow was dealt in 1914, with the sudden death of Raoul Pugno; crueler yet was the premature passing, in 1918, of the chronically ill Lili, whom Nadia devotedly loved. More disappointments followed: because of her gender, Nadia was passed over for important posts at the Conservatoire, and not until the mid-1920s was she able to secure positions at the École Normale and at the American Conservatory at Fontainebleau, where her students included young American composers such as Aaron Copland, Roy Harris, Virgil Thomson, and Walter Piston. She subsequently became a private teacher of composition, organ, piano, and theory. Her reputation for an extraordinary ability to illuminate both the stuff and the soul of a musical score quickly spread, and her salon at 36 rue Ballu became a seat of the most important pedagogical activity in Paris. Boulanger's ability to demystify the complexities of modern works was soon put to the service of contemporary composers. She had made a serious study of the works of the so-called Second Viennese School composers—Schoenberg and his disciples Webern and Berg—but soon rejected their aesthetics and techniques for those of Stravinsky, her devotion to whom was unconditional. She gave frequent lectures on his most recent scores, often timed to coincide with his Paris premieres.

In 1932, Nadia Boulanger was still living in the apartment where she was born, caring for her aging mother and mourning her dead. She devoted the rest of her time to studying scores, teaching an ever-larger number of students, going to concerts and listening to radio broadcasts to keep abreast of international world premieres and music-making, and maintaining epistolary contact with composers, students, friends, and professional acquaintances. If indeed she had ever entertained any hopes of personal happiness through the conventional routes of love, marriage, or children, these dreams had probably, by this point, been laid to rest. Her life was a testament to the power of music, discipline, and self-abnegation.

Boulanger had visited Winnaretta's *atelier* before, had even performed there many years earlier, but it was the first time that the two women had ever engaged in a quiet *tête-à-tête*. Winnaretta was intrigued by Boulanger, twenty-two years her junior, who presented herself so simply and modestly, yet whose quiet fervor for the music that she loved communicated itself so powerfully. During the rehearsals and *avant-premières* of Stravinsky's works at rue Cortambert, Boulanger had had the opportunity to observe the Princesse de Polignac at close range and to judge her character. Despite her pious demeanor, Boulanger possessed a strong careerist streak—as much, if not more, for her students as for herself. She knew well what the support of the Princesse de Polignac could mean to a young musician's future.

The conversation between the two women surely moved quickly beyond the latter's errand on behalf of Markevitch. They could have spoken about their mutual admiration for Stravinsky, about Markevitch and his talent as a composer, and about another young composition student of great promise, twenty-year-old Jean Françaix. (Winnaretta offered to accompany Boulanger to a concert of Françaix's works the following week.) They could have discussed organ repertoire and their mutual love for Renaissance and baroque music, especially their veneration of the music of J. S. Bach. In 1931 Boulanger had begun giving a weekly course on the cantatas of Bach, in her apartment on rue Ballu in the 9th *arrondissement*. Every Wednesday about thirty singers, instrumentalists, and composition students would gather; two or three cantatas would be read through, after which Boulanger would explain the structure and the emotional meaning of these remarkable works. She invited Winnaretta to attend.

A few days after Boulanger's visit, Stravinsky contacted Winnaretta to ask if she would be willing to host an *avant-première* of his recital with Dushkin at her house.[8] Winnaretta accepted and immediately sent a check for ten thousand francs as advance payment—as much money as she would be paying Markevitch for his new work.[9] Invitations were hastily sent out to the soiree; Nadia Boulanger's name was included on the guest list. The society columnist from *Le Figaro* who attended the event praised the audience for "listening with the attentiveness deserved by the eminent composer and his works," while describing the works themselves, rather vaguely, as having been "composed [with] profound skill and originality, comprising harmonies of an indisputable quality that belong to [Stravinsky] alone."[10] Accounts of the Salle Gaveau recital the following evening were muted—the music community and press were caught up by the premiere of Kurt Weill's *Mahagonny*.[11]

But the concert of the Société Musicale Indépendante that Winnaretta attended on 12 December would prove to have a much greater impact on her musical future than the Stravinsky or Weill concerts. From her seat she spotted Nadia Boulanger in another loge, and went to greet her; the next day, Winnaretta went to rue Ballu to hear Boulanger's Bach cantata class (Boulanger marked both visits in her datebook),[12] and was "delighted by the youthful and enlivening atmosphere."[13] From that point on she became a regular attendee of the classes, and persuaded Marie-Blanche to join her. Marie-Blanche immediately fell under the sway of "the marvelous Nadia

Boulanger." "The atmosphere of this house is captivating," she wrote. "The students come from every corner of the world. . . . [Boulanger] subjugates them, uplifts them, and makes them live in this deep love that she has for her art. She is the apostle and they are really her disciples."[14]

Boulanger offered to give Winnaretta some lessons on a favorite Handel organ concerto at no charge, which would explain Winnaretta's response: "I will wait for you with joy, but I'm embarrassed at your going out of your way for me."[15] The Princesse was soon able to repay the kindness: knowing that Boulanger was a great admirer of Francis Poulenc's music, she arranged a private reading in the *atelier* of the composer's Two-Piano Concerto, the manuscript of which had been delivered on New Year's Eve.[16] Before long, the Princesse and her quietly powerful new mentor had filled their 1933 datebooks with events to be enjoyed together: an organ lesson on the Handel concerto, a concert of the Société Musicale Indépendante on 22 January,[17] the private reading of the Poulenc concerto on the 23rd, sight-reading sessions, and so forth.[18]

Around that time, Winnaretta crossed paths with Alfred Cortot, whom she had not seen since the dedication of the new concert hall at the École Normale. She was pleased to learn that Cortot and the directors of the Orchestre Symphonique de Paris had decided to honor her with a concert at the Salle Pleyel, consisting exclusively of works that she had commissioned and that were dedicated to her. The orchestra's members had agreed to waive their fees in honor of the "protector of the arts"; profits from ticket sales would go into a fund for unemployed musicians. Georges Marie, the OSP's administrator, had contacted the composers who had received commissions, to solicit their participation; Cortot had already received a firm commitment from Ravel, who had agreed to come to conduct his *Pavane*.[19] Not surprisingly, Winnaretta's first thought was to contact Stravinsky. "You understand how proud I am of *Renard*, among all the works that are dedicated to me," she wrote, "and how much I would like to have it played in this concert."[20] No answer was forthcoming. On 5 February she wrote again. "I would be inconsolable if, at the Salle Pleyel concert . . . I won't hear the magnificent *Renard*, conducted by one of whom I'm so proud. I've asked Monsieur Marie to schedule [the concert] for a date that would permit you to be in Paris." The letter concluded with a little bribery: she was hoping to organize a private performance of his new *Apollon musagète* "in private surroundings"—would the composer permit her to underwrite his five hundred dollar conducting fee?[21] There was no answer. Georges Marie wrote again to Stravinsky on 8 February; still there was no response.

Finally, in mid-February, the composer wrote a brief note to inform his patron that he was free neither in March nor April, and could not participate in the concert.[22] In fact, Stravinsky was embroiled in one of his busiest seasons ever: in February he was performing in Munich with Dushkin, continuing on to Milan, Turin, and Rome, and then to Lausanne to begin another series of concerts with Dushkin. Winnaretta did not know this, and was stunned by the cursory tone of the letter, which arrived on 15 February. She had been planning to attend Boulanger's Bach cantata class that day, but was too upset to leave her house. She sent a note to Boulanger excusing herself for her absence, claiming fatigue and a cold—only briefly mentioning Stravinsky's refusal, almost as an afterthought.[23] Boulanger, however, could read between the lines, and, without Winnaretta's knowledge, wrote to Stravinsky.

Dear Friend,
    Forgive me for bothering you about something that, in principle, doesn't concern me. . . . Would you accept, *without anybody's knowing* (*no* exceptions, word of honor), a compensation of five, perhaps six thousand francs to come and conduct *Renard*. I can get [the money] without fearing *the least indiscretion*. It is urgent that you wire me [your response], because the OSP is supposed to make a decision [about the concert programming] Tuesday at the latest. It seems impossible that you wouldn't be there, and it would be so beautiful to hear *Renard* with you. Forgive me, and know how faithfully I am your
                                    NB[24]

Stravinsky's terse answer, by telegram, was dismissive, even exasperated. "Have 19 March concert OSP, *Psalms Rite Nightingale,* and 21 March concert with Dushkin Lausanne. Have however clearly explained to our friend. Best, Stravinsky."[25] What made the composer's response all the more shocking was his offhand reference to *Psalms*: had he forgotten that it was only because of Winnaretta's generosity that the performance of the *Symphony of Psalms* was taking place at all? Georges Marie's embarrassment over the situation was evident in a letter sent to the composer (with a duplicate copy sent to Winnaretta), informing him that, "despite the enormous disappointment that your absence from the concert dedicated to her has caused her," Winnaretta had given the OSP her assurance that she would honor her commitment to pay the fee of the Vlassoff Choirs for the *Symphony of Psalms* performance, only two days before her own concert.[26] Stravinsky was impervious to guilt. Finally, Marie was obliged to write to Winnaretta: "we should no longer count on the participation of Monsieur Stravinsky."[27]

Winnaretta's disappointment was kept carefully hidden behind her "sphinx" persona. She tried to cheer herself up by spending an evening with Pata in Colette's cozy apartment, where the writer had prepared two favorite treats from her native Burgundy: *galette* washed down with ambrosia.[28] The Wednesday cantata classes continued to be an inspiration, as did Boulanger's frequent and salutary visits to rue Cortambert and Jouy-en-Josas. On another occasion, Boulanger came bearing new musical delights: scores of the organ works of Frescobaldi and Buxtehude, composers unfamiliar to Winnaretta.[29] But the name of a composer well known to both of them kept creeping into their conversations, and into Winnaretta's notes to Boulanger: Stravinsky would be conducting the *Symphony of Psalms* with the OSP; Stravinsky would be returning to Paris in May; Radio Turin would be giving several broadcasts of Stravinsky's concerts.[30] Finally, in the midst of a sight-reading session (during which Boulanger introduced the patron to the works of her sister Lili),[31] Winnaretta worked up the courage to ask the question that was really on her mind: did Mademoiselle Boulanger know the *real* reason why Stravinsky would not be participating in her concert?[32] Alas, there was no explanation to be given. Marie-Blanche's comment: "He just didn't want to be bothered, which really wasn't very classy [*ce qui n'était vraiment pas très chic*]."[33]

The Salle Pleyel concert honoring Winnaretta took place on 21 March 1933. The hall was packed with the patron's family and friends. The only person missing (besides Stravinsky) was Nadia Boulanger, who was unable to attend: every year she observed a month-long mourning period, beginning on March 15, to commemorate the death of her sister Lili. The atmosphere was festive, and the music superb, as Henry Prunières noted in a long article about the event and Winnaretta's importance as a patron.

The only problem was what to choose for the program of this concert. . . . It would take, I think, several evenings, if one wanted to hear all the music that [the Princesse de Polignac] generated or inspired. There are many Parisian salons where good music is made, but the only one that has gained widespread renown is the one on avenue Henri-Martin.

The players of the OSP surpassed themselves under the direction of Cortot and Désormière. The Suite from *Pelléas et Mélisande* by Gabriel Fauré was played to perfection, as was the *Overture* of Germaine Tailleferre. . . . Maurice Ravel, Darius Milhaud, and Igor Markevitch [conducted] their own works. . . . [T]he Concerto for Two Pianos and Orchestra of Francis Poulenc had the effect of a ray of sunshine [and] was applauded frenetically.

The *Partita* of Markevitch already represents the past of this adolescent, but what force, what sense of architecture is manifest there. . . . [I]t affirms an original and dominating temperament.[34]. . . The *Overture* of Germaine Tailleferre . . . was for me a revelation. . . . It's a beautiful piece, full of robust life, exuding good health.[35]

During the intermission, Cortot made an elegant little speech in the foyer, praising Winnaretta and offering her a medal on behalf of all the musicians in the orchestra. At supper afterwards Ravel was engaged in a very deep *tête-à-tête* with another American-born princess, Audrey Illinska,[36] "who,"

Winnaretta surmised, "had never heard of him before, as she was not very interested in music." Winnaretta inquired about the subject of their conversation. "Oh! We are talking about death," replied Ravel.[37] Winnaretta was surprised, since the odd couple seemed to be in high spirits when the exchange was concluded. She would have sorrowful reason to recall that lively discussion some months later, when it was revealed that Maurice Ravel had been diagnosed with an incurable brain disease, which would claim his life in late 1937 at the age of sixty-two.[38]

The day after the Salle Pleyel tribute, Winnaretta left for a vacation in Morocco and Italy in the company of great-nephew Olivier de La Moussaye (husband of Daisy Fellowes's daughter Isabelle), Violet Trefusis, and Mrs. Keppel. From the moment of their departure, the normally calm, blue Mediterranean turned rough and dark; the stormy voyage would serve as a metaphor for the three weeks that Winnaretta and Violet spent together in Morocco and Italy. As much as Winnaretta loved Violet, she was exasperated by her childish self-indulgence and public indiscretions, calculated to draw maximum attention.[39] "Violet's moaning and groaning defies description," Winnaretta wrote to Pata. "Her mother scolds her, uselessly."[40] For Winnaretta, the need to keep her private life private and maintain her good name was paramount; yet, the younger woman persisted in publicly testing of the limits of respectability—and of Winnaretta's patience.[41] Finally, when Violet's rebelliousness extended to a dangerously indiscreet flirtation with Olivier de La Moussaye—a married man—Winnaretta decided she'd had enough.[42] When the two women parted ways at the end of the vacation, it effectively represented the end of their ten-year relationship. Upon her return to Paris, Violet gave a ball on the first level landing of the Eiffel Tower—as if to announce that, henceforth, she would have no need to rely on the support of the Princesse de Polignac.[43]

Winnaretta fled to the refuge of Jean and Marie-Blanche's house outside of Antibes; apart from two evenings attending Ballets Russes performances in Monte Carlo, she stayed in, playing four-hand piano music with Marie-Blanche and talking quietly with her niece. Nadia Boulanger constantly occupied her thoughts—at the Ballets Russes premieres of new scores by Boulanger's students Markevitch and Françaix,[44] when she and Marie-Blanche spoke "of cantatas sung in my absence," and when she practiced at a local church the Vivaldi D-Minor Organ Concerto that Boulanger had encouraged her to learn.[45]

Winnaretta planned to see Boulanger immediately upon her return to Paris on 26 April, but was instead confronted with another upset in her personal life: Anna de Noailles was on her deathbed. In her last years the capricious, self-absorbed poet had cut a pathetic figure, suffering from "hideous troubles." But even in a frail and feverish state, she was still spellbinding. Marie-Blanche was invariably willing to be her audience when Anna would stretch out melodramatically on the divan of Winnaretta's salon, "playing out her theatricalities at the expense of innocent victims."[46] Despite her ailments, she had released an autobiography in 1932, *The Book of My Life*.[47] It was to be her swan song. During her last months her most frequent visitors were doctors of all specialties, who could do nothing to cure the buzzing in her ears or her worsening insomnia. By the time of Winnaretta's return, her friend was already yearning for death. It came on 30 April 1933. In her grief, Winnaretta cancelled all of her appointments but one: she attended Boulanger's cantata class on 3 May,[48] two days before Anna's funeral at the Church of the Madeleine.

The rupture with Violet Trefusis and the death of Anna de Noailles caused Winnaretta to draw nearer to Nadia Boulanger in the spring of 1933, for musical as well as personal succor. The almost daily meetings between the two women would evolve into a rich, productive, but also complicated, friendship; it would become the pre-eminent relationship of the last decade of Winnaretta's life. Boulanger's asceticism and propensity for grueling work resonated with the Princesse, who had her own Spartan tendencies, and who lived in constant quest of keeping her time fully occupied in order to stave off loneliness. That their interactions were filtered through musical discourse and activity no doubt provided a necessary zone of comfort for both women, both of whom were negotiating power levels in their relations. Boulanger took on the complex role of both mentor/teacher and supplicant, seeking favors of patronage for her students, and, eventually, for herself as well. Winnaretta, for her part, was unusually willing to submit to Boulanger—a testament to her admiration for Nadia's musical wisdom.[49]

Boulanger discovered early, however, that Winnaretta did not cede power easily. "She was not blind—she would discriminate," the musician would recall years later. "She wasn't easily influenced. She used to say, 'I shall see.' And she would see. And if it didn't please her, she wouldn't see."[50] Boulanger's first experience of Winnaretta's "discrimination" occurred during the spring of 1933, when she attempted to secure a commission for one of her talented young students, François Olivier. Olivier was subsequently invited to rue Cortambert to discuss the project, and Winnaretta did in fact offer the young man a commission, for a short instrumental work, to be completed by October.[51] The money she offered, however, was not enough to make the project worthwhile for Olivier. The young man apparently pressed the point with the patron: he could not give up other work to take on a new project for such a modest sum; could she not increase the amount of money for the commission? Winnaretta responded by letter on the day of her departure for Morocco: she understood Olivier's situation *perfectly*; nonetheless, her other commitments made it difficult to take on a new project, she had offered what she was able to offer *at that time*—and besides, she hardly knew Olivier's work; all conversations pertaining to the commission, therefore, were to be put on hold until next year.[52] Exasperated, Boulanger wrote in her datebook, "Olivier caused the plan for a commission from the Princesse de P. to fail because of his tactlessness, and she has left for Morocco."[53]

If Boulanger was not yet skilled in negotiating commissions from the patron, she was successful in opening the door to her own professional advancement. Just before Winnaretta's departure for Morocco, she offered to organize and conduct two musical matinees, one in Jouy and one in Paris, featuring arias from the Bach cantatas that had been sung during the year by her student choir.[54] She offered a challenge to Winnaretta and Marie-Blanche as well: to perform as concerto soloists for the occasion. Winnaretta had often played piano and organ in her own salon, but this would be her "debut" as soloist. Boulanger had decided that the Vivaldi D-Minor Organ Concerto would suit her new student perfectly, and Winnaretta set to the task of learning the piece with determination. Marie-Blanche, on the other hand, was reluctant to participate. As fine an artist as she was, and as much practice as she had had in recent months at the "Piano Fridays," she was overcome with fear at the idea of appearing in a "formal" concert setting, even in a private salon. But Boulanger was brilliant in her ability to encourage her students and colleagues to surpass their perceived "personal best" in music-making. Finally, "out of pride and heroism," Marie-Blanche consented to play the virtuosic piano solo in J. S. Bach's Fifth Brandenburg Concerto for keyboard, violin, and flute at the matinee, despite her trepidation over the work's long and difficult cadenza.[55] The musical and practical planning for the two concerts provided the excuse for Winnaretta and Boulanger to meet frequently, for organ lessons and reading sessions, cantata classes, lunches, and dinners, in Paris and in Jouy.[56] Like two children before a large box of candy, they picked and chose: which of the delicious arias and choruses from the Bach cantatas should be sung and played?

Winnaretta, in mourning for Anna de Noailles, had cancelled all musical activity in her salon in the first part of the spring.[57] Her first reception took place on 23 May, when she arranged a performance with chamber orchestra of Satie's *The Death of Socrates*, played as memorial tribute to Anna.[58] After the concert Winnaretta, Marie-Blanche, and Boulanger sat in the little salon adjacent to the *atelier*, its walls lined with Manet and Monet paintings, and read Anna's poems.[59] They discussed the full schedule of musical programs planned for the month of June, including the first performance of Igor Markevitch's *Hymnes*, recently completed and dedicated to Winnaretta. As was his wont in the previous year, the twenty-year-old Markevitch committed numerous blunders of tact and protocol with his patron; fortunately for him, her respect for his talent—and perhaps Boulanger's intervention—enabled her to remain unruffled in the face of his gaffes. First, Markevitch tried to convince Winnaretta to allow *Hymnes* to be performed in a Sérénade concert before being performed at her house; she refused, just as she had the year before, citing the terms of their agreement.[60] Then, on 12 May, while visiting rue Cortambert to play excerpts of the new work for Winnaretta, the composer asked to receive the final payment for the commission in advance of delivery of the manuscript. Again citing their contractual arrangement, the patron responded, imperturbably but firmly: "The letter [concerning our agreement] that I addressed to you in the first days of November was perfectly clear. . . . You have not yet delivered the manuscript, but in waiting for you to do so, I will be happy to deliver the last quarter [of the payment] when I have the pleasure of seeing you."[61]

The menacing political situation in Germany had an impact on Paris musical life that spring. With Hitler's ascendancy to the Chancellorship in January 1933, antagonism escalated toward Jewish artists and writers and others deemed "decadent" by the Nazi regime. Kurt Weill was a prime target of the Nazi authorities' repressive policies. Realizing that he was no longer safe in Germany, Weill left for France on 21 March; when he arrived in Paris two days later, he had with him one small suitcase, filled with the sketches for the symphony commissioned by Winnaretta. In mid-April he moved to the Charles de Noailles's country house in suburban Louveciennes, where he could work in tranquility.[62] Weill was not the only Jewish composer to seek safe haven in Paris. That spring Arnold Schoenberg, though he had converted to Lutheranism in 1898, was forced to flee Germany, arriving in Paris in mid-May.[63] It is likely that he was introduced to Winnaretta shortly after his arrival, and was subsequently invited to her salon for the first performance, on 9 June, of Markevitch's *Hymnes*,[64] played by the OSP under the baton of Désormière to an enthusiastic audience of friends and colleagues.[65] Poulenc was among the admirers. "I was *very much taken* by your *Hymnes*," he wrote to his younger colleague. "I always believed in you, always admired what you did, I'm happy today to be able to *love* it."[66] The program also included a performance of the Brahms Piano Quintet, Op. 34, and a group of Romantic piano works played by twenty-five-year-old American pianist Beveridge Webster, a longtime student of Boulanger.[67]

In between the rehearsals and arrangements for the upcoming Bach concerts, Winnaretta and Boulanger found time almost every night to partake of the musical offerings of the lively 1933 spring season.[68] Boulanger joined Winnaretta in her box at the Opéra for the Wagner season (*Tristan* and *Die Walküre*, conducted by Fürtwangler). The two woman attended performances by the new incarnation of the Ballets Russes, *Les Ballets 1933*, choreographed by Georges Balanchine and designed by Boris Kochno, and funded by English millionaire and self-styled poet Edward James. Among the seven new ballets presented by the troupe at the Théâtre des Champs-Élysées was a work commissioned by Winnaretta for her *atelier*, Nicolas Nabokov's new *Job*. The Old Testament text, adapted by Jacques Maritain (later a prominent professor of religion), was scored for two solo voices, male chorus, two pianos, and orchestra.[69] The work ultimately proved to be too large in scope to be presented in the *atelier,* and, once again, Winnaretta ceded its first performance to the public arena. The pianists for the choreographed performance were Jacques Février and Jean Doyen; Maurice Abravanel was the conductor. The stage décor consisted of slides of William Blake's illustrations for the *Book of Job,* projected behind the orchestra. Winnaretta may have been reminded of a similar kind of *mise-en-scène* pioneered by her husband forty years earlier.

On 17 June, Boulanger, Polish soprano Maria Modrakowska,[70] a group of students from the Bach cantata class, and a chamber orchestra all took the suburban train out to Jouy to perform on the Princesse de Polignac's veranda.[71] The program, in addition to excerpts from the Bach cantatas, included works from the French Renaissance and baroque eras, as well as pieces by Fauré and Stravinsky, performed by Paris's finest wind and string players.[72] The audience, small but enthusiastic, included Prince Pierre de Monaco, who would soon become one of Boulanger's closest friends and confidants. Meanwhile, as the Paris concert approached, Winnaretta immersed herself in the Vivaldi concerto. If she felt nervous, she kept her fears well concealed. Boulanger had written out a version of the organ part suited to the Cavaillé-Coll and to her student's abilities, and reorchestrated the instrumental accompaniment to fit the acoustics of the space.[73] And Marie-Blanche, customarily so hypercritical of the musical performances of others, found herself living through "two weeks of joy and horror, working six hours a day, making the ends of my fingers explode—so unaccustomed were they to so much effort—living more or less alone, [acting] unbearably to everybody, in a terribly neurotic state."[74] But it was too late to back out. The newspapers carried advance notice of the upcoming Bach concert.

On the great day, 30 June 1933, a thirty-voice chorus and twenty-three-piece orchestra filled the *atelier,* nearly outnumbering the guests. The concert began with three arias from Bach cantatas, sung by Modrakowska and the chorus. This was followed by the Vivaldi concerto. Winnaretta was garbed in a splendid evening gown, but wore tennis sneakers to facilitate playing the pedals. Boulanger had solicited the help of two of her students for the performance, one to turn Winnaretta's pages, the other to change the organ stops as necessary. It fell to a young American student, twenty-four-year-old Elliott Carter (also a member of the bass section in Boulanger's choir), to attend to the latter task. While Winnaretta played, Carter stood by the organ, as Boulanger whispered directions to him for changing the stops with a dizzying frequency.[75] Then, after another group of Bach arias, came the Brandenburg Concerto, performed by internationally acclaimed violinist Paul Kochanski, OSP flutist Roger Cortet, and Marie-Blanche, who handled the long, difficult piano cadenza with aplomb.[76] Reports of the soiree ran in all the major Paris newspapers. *Excelsior* put its article on the front page, with a large picture of Winnaretta seated at the Cavaillé-Coll organ.[77] The newspapers gave warm praise to the performances of Marie-Blanche, Modrakowska, and Winnaretta, but were positively effusive in their enthusiasm for Nadia Boulanger, "who led the choruses, sung by her students and accompanied by orchestra, with her habitual mastery"[78]—a curious statement, given that it was Boulanger's first time conducting an entire performance. However, the most beautifully written compliment came from Colette:

> To find friendship, to give it, means first crying out: "shelter, shelter!"
> My dear Winnie, I only cried out to you before in a whisper, but your ear is so fine.
>   Your Colette
> The music of Bach is a sublime sewing machine.[79]

Three days after the concert, Winnaretta brought Boulanger with her to London for a week, where she introduced the musician to "the National Gallery, the British Museum and a few corners of [the city] that I love very much."[80] During the next seven days, when not seeing the sights, the women packed in a dizzying number of dinners with Winnaretta's friends and Boulanger's students.[81] Boulanger was both exhausted and exhilarated by her hostess's daily agenda. "Everywhere she went, Greek was translated, Latin was translated, music was made. She'd arrive in London and an hour later, you'd be playing music or reading poems."[82] David Ponsonby, a former Boulanger student, commented bemusedly on the pace of the "vacation," and encouraged his teacher to find a way of keeping up: "I'm sure that the Princesse will know how to find a solution so that you can finish your trip in a restful and charming manner. Besides, I think that simply the fact of being together with her and enjoying the richness of her mind, put at the disposition of her friends with such benevolence and humor, will suffice to render every circumstance charming."[83]

The time spent together deepened the already close bond between the two women. Winnaretta began to sign her letters "W" and addressed Boulanger now as "Nadia" rather than "Mademoiselle"—although Boulanger never ceased to call her student-patron "Princesse." After Boulanger returned to France, Winnaretta joined her brother Franklin on his yacht in Devonshire. As always, she experienced "the great joy of seeing this marvelous drowsy country again, where I spent such wonderful years of childhood."[84] Her lightness of heart opened her pocketbook as well. Releasing Clara Haskil from her iron grip, materially as well as symbolically, she arranged for the fragile pianist to take a small but comfortable apartment on the avenue Malakoff, and provided her with a monthly stipend of five hundred francs.[85] Out of the blue, Igor Markevitch, who was suffering from serious pulmonary ailments,[86] received a generous check from the Princesse, to provide him with the wherewithal "to rest quietly in Switzerland, after the tiring experiences of your brilliant season in Paris, where *Icare* and *Hymnes* had such a magnificent success."[87]

Markevitch knew that Boulanger was the force and the inspiration behind this spontaneous gesture, and wrote to thank her. "The Princesse wrote
to me in a manner at once noble and charming, which touched me greatly,
and she gave me the aid necessary for the reestablishment of my health."[88]
Without financial burdens, he was able to complete a new piece that summer, entitled *Psaume*. Boulanger kept Winnaretta apprised of her student's
progress.[89] The two women saw each other almost daily during the last
two weeks of July, in Fontainbleau, where Boulanger prepared for the opening of her summer school, the American Conservatory, and in Jouy, where
the musician spent weekends filled with music-making amidst Winnaretta's
friends and family.[90] Boulanger met a dizzying array of people during those
two weeks: Elsa Maxwell, Eugène and Kitty de Rothschild, Cloton Legrand,
the Alex de Castéjas (Daisy Fellowes's daughter Emeline and Emeline's husband), and Lady Sibyl Colefax. One typical weekend at Jouy included performances by Jean Françaix and the Pasquier Trio of Françaix's new String Trio
and Fauré's C-Minor Piano Quartet.[91] After so many years of relentless hard
work, Boulanger's world was rapidly expanding, and she was grateful. Her
letters to Winnaretta from this period have not survived, but Winnaretta's
responses indicate clearly that the sense of gratitude was mutual: "Your letter
touched me very much, and was a great help to me in a period of anxiety and
emotional depression. I would like to think that you will come soon."[92]

Boulanger knew the cause of this depression: Winnaretta's brother Washington was in London, wasting away with a lingering illness; despite his
worsening condition, he was expected to live for a long time, in terrible
pain.[93] On 11 August Boulanger accompanied Winnaretta to Jouy for the
weekend. Sometime during those three days the Princesse suddenly collapsed into grief-stricken tears. Winnaretta was no less shocked than her
guest at her own outburst: she never allowed herself to cry, even in front of
her closest family members. She wrote to Boulanger, "I must excuse myself
for having let my feelings show too much the other day, when I was in a
state of despondency that I couldn't control. The news of my brother is
always awful, and . . . I couldn't hide my feelings of very great sadness.
Your presence was a real comfort for me. I want to tell you that again, [as
well as] my deep affection."[94]

In September, Winnaretta arrived in Venice for her two-month sojourn.
Despite the prematurely autumnal weather, she "was able to fish out some
pianists" with whom to play four-hand music: conductor Sir Thomas
Beecham and virtuoso Marguerite Long.[95] Madame Long was introduced
to Winnaretta's protégé Bruno Maderna, and was impressed by his magnificent violin playing; she offered her assistance in helping the young prodigy
advance in his promising career.[96] Nadia Boulanger and Pierre de Monaco
arrived later in the month; in their honor, Olga Rudge came to stay at the
palazzo, to provide command performances of Bach sonatas and Schubert
and Beethoven trios.[97] By this point Ezra Pound had already begun to write

his pro-Fascist manifestos; Rudge showed them to Winnaretta, who found them "very well done *indeed*."[98] The most generous interpretation here is that Winnaretta, adamantly apolitical, only wanted to compliment Rudge's lover. Of more interest to her, however, were Pound's recent musical projects. That year he had inaugurated a series of concerts in his hometown of Rapallo. The first of these was so successful that the mayor offered the Municipal Hall for the next concert, which would take place in November and feature Olga Rudge.[99] Winnaretta promised that she would try to attend. Meanwhile, musical events beckoned elsewhere. On 23 and 24 September Poulenc and Février were in Venice for performances of Poulenc's Two-Piano Concerto; at the conclusion of the first night's concert, at which the pianists "played like angels," Winnaretta, Boulanger, and Pierre de Monaco "applauded furiously," thrilled to watch "the entire house rise to its feet!"[100] Prior to her visit, Boulanger had suggested that Winnaretta consider making some changes in the registration of her Cavaillé-Coll organ,[101] and Winnaretta authorized her friend to initiate the work with Gonzales, Paris's premier organ-builder and technician.[102] She also sought to have the works of Boulanger's students played in the 1934 Biennale, then in its planning stages, proposing "an orchestral work by Markevitch" to the Festival Committee, headed by composer Alfredo Casella.[103] And, thanks to her influence, Markevitch's work was subsequently accepted by the Committee.[104]

Restless without Boulanger, Winnaretta left for Vienna, where Arturo Toscanini was to conduct a series of concerts with that city's Philharmonic. Boulanger, who idolized Toscanini for "the liberty that [paradoxically] existed [in his] regular, severe, immutable pulse,"[105] had extolled the combination of her favorite conductor and the Vienna orchestra. Winnaretta made the trip with Toscanini's daughter Wally and Wally's husband, Conte Emanuele Castelbarco. "You would have been proud of your old Zia [aunt]," Winnaretta wrote to Pata, "for on leaving Venice I drove two hundred kilometers by car to see several cities along the way, then, taking the night train to the frontier, I arrived in Vienna at 8 o'clock in the morning, and at 10 a.m. I was at the rehearsal, which lasted until 1 p.m."[106] An added attraction to Winnaretta was the concerto soloist, Vladimir Horowitz, who, two weeks earlier, had announced his engagement to Toscanini's younger daughter, Wanda.[107] After the first beautiful concert, Winnaretta attended the Toscanini rehearsals every morning. "It was just as you said," she wrote to Boulanger, describing her awe of "the respect and *mesmerized* attention of the Philharmonic."[108] Viennese cultural life appealed to her, as she wrote to Pata. "[These] rehearsals are incomparable lessons and I wouldn't have missed hearing them for anything in the world. Besides the music, the museums here are splendors, and the life is amusing—theaters and even dancing and bars, for one finds everywhere two Steinways and musicians of the first order, and (something that thrills me), everything starts and ends at a reasonable hour."[109]

Winnaretta continued her Italian peregrinations. In Rome, she stayed at the Farnese Palace and visited her English composer friend, Gerald Berners; she met with Alfredo Casella to further discuss the planning of the 1934 Venice Festival, and was introduced by the composer to an obscure but delightful opera by Paisiello, *Nina, pazza per amore*.[110] A few days later, in Siena, she made the acquaintance of Count Chigi, the "*mécène* of Siena" and Olga Rudge's patron.[111] On 14 November Winnaretta continued on to Rapallo, to hear the concert organized by Ezra Pound.[112] She asked Pound to reserve a seat for her in a part of the hall that was "not too conspicuous, as I shan't have time to dress."[113] Pound gallantly responded that "You needn't bother about tickets and I function as doorkeeper or whatever honorary title is required and I trust you will regard yourself as a guest of honor (anonymous and incognito if you like)."[114] And, indeed, when Winnaretta arrived at Rapallo's Sala del Municipio, newly built and ornately decorated with murals and *trompe l'oeil* designs, there was Pound, distributing programs and holding out his big wide-brimmed hat to collect donations. Winnaretta and her Venetian friends the Robilants sat together amidst an audience of Italian aristocrats sympathetic to the Fascist regime. Olga Rudge and her pianist Gerhard Münch shone in performances of works by Bach, Debussy, and Corelli.[115] The next day Winnaretta spent the afternoon at Pound's house, where the two discussed their favorite Renaissance and early baroque works. Winnaretta delighted in Pound's ability to discover the progressive tendencies in music that was over three hundred years old. She introduced to him one sixteenth-century French composer with whom he was not familiar: Clément Janequin, best known for witty *chansons* filled with sound effects, such as bird calls, battle cries, hunting calls, and street noises. Winnaretta had featured Janequin's *Chant des Oiseaux* and *La Bataille de Marignan* in her salon performances since the early 1890s, long before the current early music revival. When she returned to Paris she sent a number of her favorite Janequin scores to Pound, who noted insightfully that certain "verbal values . . . had been overthrown in *Le Chant des Oiseaux* for the sake of the counterpoint"; referring to the Futurist leader Filippo Marinetti's love of noise machines, Pound noted that "*Marignan* seems finally to dispose of Marinetti's illusion that he had invented something."[116]

Winnaretta's time was already much spoken for by the time she returned to Paris. The major event of the month of December was the inauguration of the Salvation Army's newly built Cité de Refuge, the five-hundred bed shelter designed and constructed by Le Corbusier and his brother Pierre Jeanneret. The enormous, costly, and controversial edifice, situated in a working-class neighborhood near the Seine in the 13th *arrondissement*, had taken three full years to complete. The construction costs had constantly gone over budget, and even in the final months of work, Winnaretta was obliged to infuse an additional 1.25 million francs into the Salvation Army's treasury to ensure the building's completion.[117]

The Cité was Le Corbusier's most important building to date, and represented more than any other of his creations the architect's utopian philosophies of communal living within an urban setting. Taking his idea of a building as a "machine for living" to its most radical extreme, Le Corbusier had designed a hermetically sealed structure. Its most distinctive feature was its southern exposure, a thousand-square-meter facade of unbroken window wall.[118] The architect had equipped the building with the most technologically innovative features available, including a dust-free air circulation and climate control system.[119] The lower floors of the building had been equipped with canteens, laundries, and other trade workshops, designed to give the residents of the shelter a means of learning a trade. Le Corbusier acknowledged Winnaretta's role in allowing him to achieve the tangible results of his research on urban habitations. "You were willing to have faith in me and to impose me, more or less, on Commissioner Peyron. The result was . . . a rather eloquent demonstration of everything that could be done if one set to the construction of the habitation with a good spirit, and applied progressive methods to a corps of trades stagnated by routine."[120] The Cité de Refuge was inaugurated by President of the Republic Albert Lebrun on 7 December under the name "Singer-Polignac Refuge"; Winnaretta was given the honor of installing the cornerstone in its place, and, as honorary President, was given an office in the building.[121]

Winnaretta was starting to receive more solicitations on behalf of Jewish refugee musicians, who were fleeing Germany and Austria in ever-increasing numbers. Sauguet wrote to the Princesse in December, asking for her help on behalf of a German early-music vocal group. "I know well that in these times, your clairvoyant and benevolent generosity must often be solicited," wrote the composer, "but . . . perhaps you might be interested in [presenting] 'The Madrigal' at your house. You would fulfill the wish of these excellent choristers; at the same time you would permit them to enjoy a less cruel existence for a few days."[122] Winnaretta's response has not surfaced; perhaps she felt that she was doing her part by having one German-Jewish musician under her charge. Kurt Weill was hard at work on his symphony, and his patron sent him the first installments of the commission payment. "La Polignac has already paid one-third [of 20,000 francs]," Weill wrote to Lenya on 8 December, "and that's given colossal wings to my imagination."[123] The next week Weill wrote to Winnaretta to tell her that he had finished the first draft of the symphony.[124] The work was completed two months later, and the manuscript, dated "Louveciennes, February 1934," was delivered to its dedicatee.[125]

Winnaretta spent the last two weeks of December in bed with the flu. She was obliged to cancel a musical matinee that would have featured Olga Rudge, who would have been glad for the income.[126] It is not certain whether she was able to hear a performance by her niece Marie-Blanche, who had been persuaded, reluctantly, by her composer friends to expand her musical activity as a soprano beyond the walls of her aunt's salon. On 16 December Marie-Blanche participated in the ninth concert of La Sérénade at the Salle Gaveau, her first public performance since her marriage to Jean de Polignac.[127] She gave the premiere of Georges Auric's song cycle, *Alphabet,* accompanied by the composer.[128] Later in the program she sang a musical adaptation of La Fontaine's celebrated *Fables* by André Caplet, accompanied by Poulenc. Although shivering with what she later described as fever brought on by intense stage fright, Marie-Blanche astonished the sold-out house with her artistry.[129] One critic in attendance wrote, "The Comtesse de Polignac takes her rank, right off the bat, among the most subtle, the most infallible interpreters of modern music."[130] In subsequent years, both Winnaretta and Nadia Boulanger would make good use of Marie-Blanche's talent.

Even though Winnaretta was forced to languish at home during the gayest part of the winter season, roses sent by Nadia Boulanger filled the *atelier* with color. Winnaretta sent her grateful thanks in a letter, alluding to the many projects that the two women had planned for 1934. Up until this point Boulanger had performed her function of concert organizer and conductor in Winnaretta's *atelier* for no compensation. This couldn't continue, averred Winnaretta.

> I want to talk to you of our plans for January. Do you remember the "solemn vow" you made to me last summer? Some little performances of music in the intimacy of my *atelier* would be a joy for me, but I don't want to bother you "for nothing," and I ask you to permit me to send this check, which will build a little fund, and which you can use as you wish for the benefit of those who will take part in these intimate concerts.[131]

No sooner were the Christmas holidays finished than Nadia Boulanger's "cantata Wednesdays" recommenced, and, with them, Winnaretta's musical matinees and soirees. Marie-Blanche became a linchpin in both groups of gatherings.

> Thanks to Nadia Boulanger there were [so many] beautiful musical performances at Tante Winnie's. Lots of Bach, sublime cantatas. . . . Each week, I would come home, elated, from [Boulanger's] Wednesday classes. No one loves and no one can make me love music the way she does. Her explanations are marvelous, and her way of playing is moving. She takes such pleasure in hearing an unusual modulation that her eyes close at that moment, her breathing stops, and everyone responds with an attentive silence within which the long-awaited chord expands and lingers. . . . And yet, her implacable rhythm didn't falter for a second.[132]

Boulanger subsequently undertook most of the practical aspects involved with arranging Winnaretta's salon programs that had been assumed in the past by Bordes and Astruc: the choice of music, the hiring of musicians, the arrangement of rehearsals, and the payment of the musical personnel. Winnaretta's first salon gathering of the new year took place "before an intimate audience" on 8 January 1934; the program, organized and conducted "magisterially" by Boulanger, consisted of J. S. Bach's Fourth Brandenburg Concerto, soprano duos from Cantatas 184, 163, and 78, and Mozart's Clarinet Concerto.[133] The next program, performed on 21 January, was larger in scope. Bach's Cantata 4, *Christ lag in Todesbanden,* was performed in its entirety; the rest of the program consisted of songs and arias by Fauré, Hindemith, Mozart, and Lully, Stravinsky's *Pastorale,* and Bach's C-Major Concerto for Two Pianos and Orchestra. Winnaretta and Boulanger were the piano soloists for the Bach Concerto.[134] Public performance apparently held no terror for the hostess.

Washington Singer died unexpectedly in his sleep in London three weeks later.[135] "I knew he wasn't going to get better," Winnaretta wrote to Boulanger, "and [although] this gentle end was what he wanted . . . it is hard to bear these wrenching events, even when we know that they're inevitable and when we're supposed to be prepared."[136] She did not linger in London after the funeral, but came back quickly to France, the sooner to conceal her sorrow in musical activity. She saw Kurt Weill frequently upon her return. He was, with a will, staying within his patron's sightline: he had delivered to her the promised manuscript of his new Symphony—but she had not deliver the promised check. On 20 February he wrote to Lenya, "Sunday I'm invited to [Polignac's house], and I'm ready to string her up on one of the pipes of her organ if she doesn't give me my money."[137] "It was very nice at Polignac's house," he reported to Lenya later in the week, "but that beast hasn't given me my money."[138] Presumably Weill was paid shortly thereafter, as the topic did not arise again in his correspondence.[139]

When her month of mourning was finished, Winnaretta left for Rome to attend a new music festival, the Concerti di Primavera, named for the spring months during which the concerts were to take place. Organized by Comtesse Laetitia (Mimi) Pecci-Blunt and leading Italian composers, the Primavera was launched with the goal of promoting contemporary music, particularly French contemporary music, in Rome. Mimi Pecci-Blunt was as interesting a *mécène* as Winnaretta: the daughter of Italian and Spanish nobility, niece of Pope Leo XIII (Conte Pecci), she married banker and art collector Cecil Blunt in 1919.[140] The Pecci-Blunt salons in Paris and Rome became havens for musicians and artists such as Dali, Valéry, Claudel, and Poulenc. The Primavera concerts were presented in the couple's Roman palazzo on the Piazza Aracoeli, in conditions similar to those at avenue Henri-Martin.

The festival was already in progress when Winnaretta arrived in Rome on 7 March. Françaix's String Trio and Markevitch's new *Psaume* had already been performed, to great success.[141] Winnaretta was greeted by the

Pecci-Blunts (in whose palazzo she was staying), Jean and Marie-Blanche, and Poulenc and Février, who would be performing the Two-Piano Concerto at the festival. Igor Markevitch was there with his new lover, Marie-Laure de Noailles, who had created a minor scandal by leaving her husband to live with the young composer in Switzerland. "She's playing Madame d'Agoult and Cosima," was Marie-Blanche's wry comment.[142] The group of friends toured the city together, lunching en masse, joining Mimi Pecci-Blunt every evening for cocktails, dinners, and after-concert suppers. Only Markevitch seemed not to be enjoying himself: the anxieties surrounding the rehearsals for his Cantata (on a text by Cocteau), which he would be conducting, were wreaking havoc on his nerves. His worse fears were realized: at the dress rehearsal, the musicians didn't know the parts, and refused to accept criticism from the composer-conductor. Marie-Blanche watched as Markevitch did everything in his power to impose his musical desires on the recalcitrant orchestra members, with little success; the performance, held the same day, was an uphill battle as well.

> Trembling with fever, he conducted with a sureness and an admirable sense of will. He knew so well what he wanted to hear, that he could tell each instrumentalist the [correct] fingering, the places to breath, the desired sonority. In front of this astonishing genius, this twenty-year-old boy who looked like he was dying, who gave all his energy and intensity to his work, the musicians brought [to the task], as always, the souls of mediocre functionaries. . . .
>
> The concert took place before a barely competent audience, but one that sensed that the work being heard was noble and deserving of respect. It was all that one could ask of these beautiful Italians, in a hurry to return to their bridge and backgammon tables, where they spent 365 days a year.[143]

Markevitch himself told a similar story in a letter to Boulanger, noting that "in all the agitation of the preparations for the concert and the receptions, it was a great joy for me to see the Princesse [de Polignac], whom . . . I like more every day." He was happy to report that, all things considered, "the concert in Rome went very well—the best success in the most atrocious conditions."[144] The critical notices were favorable. This was more than could be said for the Poulenc Two-Piano Concerto. "Our friend Poulenc didn't have much success in Rome," Winnaretta wrote to Boulanger, "the critics were often not very friendly. I see that he felt it, and that he was wounded."[145] It surely cannot have pleased Winnaretta either that "her" concerto had not received a better critical reception. Nonetheless, she conducted her habitual behind-the-scenes machinations on behalf of her stable of composers and artists; by the Festival's end, she had secured a promise from Alfredo Casella to mount a spring concert for Olga Rudge.[146]

In Paris musical circles, the most anticipated event of the spring was the upcoming premiere on 30 April of Stravinsky's ascetic ballet-oratorio *Perséphone,* with a libretto by André Gide, presented by the Ida Rubinstein Ballets, with Rubinstein in the title role and the composer serving as conductor.[147] Winnaretta was not in Paris for the first performance, however: the premiere of *Perséphone* was originally supposed to have taken place in January, and Winnaretta had long ago made plans to spend late April and early May with Charles and Pata at the Bordj Polignac. She was obliged to content herself with the glowing reports that she received from Boulanger,[148] who had given an *avant-première* performance for her students at rue Ballu some days before the official opening.[149] Determined to return to Paris in time to see the last performance on 16 May, Winnaretta cut short her trip. She arrived on 13 May, only to discover that the final performance of *Persephone* had been cancelled, possibly due to critical notices that had been, at best, ambivalent and, at worst, scathing.[150] "It's a very terrible disappointment for me," she wrote to Stravinsky. "Not to hear this admirable score, of such lofty and pure beauty, performed with orchestra fills me with immense regret. I can hardly express it."[151]

The Stravinsky cancellation was not the only musical disappointment that Winnaretta experienced that spring. Hermann Scherchen, the distinguished German conductor, had agreed to lend his talents to a 1934 Paris festival of contemporary music, organized by Henry Prunières. Winnaretta joined a number of other *mécènes* in funding the event, which would feature performances of great modern works (including Stravinsky's *Les Noces* and *L'Histoire du soldat* and the Alban Berg Violin Concerto) in private homes. A highlight of the festival was to be Arnold Schoenberg's *Pierrot Lunaire,* to be sung by Marya Freund, who had given the Paris premiere of the work in 1921. This performance may have been scheduled for Winnaretta's *atelier.*[152] All went smoothly until Scherchen first met with the French orchestral musicians, who apparently balked at the grueling rehearsal schedule. To the astonishment of all, Scherchen, who had been paid in advance, left Paris surreptitiously just before the first performance—leaving only a short note of explanation: "I regret the trouble that I've caused, but in Paris, there are no means for making music." Freund's son Doda Conrad recalled in his memoirs that, when apprised of the calamity, "the Princesse de Polignac fulminated, it seems!"[153] That is surely an understatement.

But the salon performances that did take place that spring in the Paris *atelier* and at Jouy more than made up for the Scherchen debacle. Jean Françaix wrote a Serenade for Twelve Instruments, dedicated to Winnaretta, for one gathering. Modern music took center stage in other programs as well. One matinee featured the music of Fauré's student Roger-Ducasse, Spanish composer Joaquin Nin,[154] and Arthur Honegger, represented by his vaudeville operetta, *La Belle de Mondon.*[155] The most remarkable of the spring's offerings, however, was a grand soiree with soloists, chorus, and full orchestra, held on 17 May. The program opened with Bach's Cantata 104, followed by Fauré's song cycle *La Bonne Chanson,* performed by Modrakowska and Boulanger. Two of Edmond de Polignac's a cappella choruses, *Ave Maris Stella* and *Aubade,* were paired with a chorus from Haydn's *Creation.* The program closed with excerpts from Stravinsky's *Persephone.*[156] Stravinsky's work was as puzzling to many of Winnaretta's guests as it had been to the audiences who had heard the public performances. Although novelist Julien Green was impressed by "the cyclopean power of the rhythms," he found that "the intervening sections often drift, and the parts seem weakly connected to one another."[157] Marie-Blanche had entertained similar thoughts some weeks earlier: "Nadia brought the manuscript to the house, and played through the score for us; it sounded beautiful to me, but dry and austere . . . and I didn't understand it until much later."[158] Winnaretta, however, must have been particularly pleased—musical reasons apart—to have Stravinsky's new work performed in her salon: the mountain had come to Mohammed, as it were.

These spring programs in all ways exemplified the perfectly meshed musical interests of Winnaretta and Nadia Boulanger. Considering that it was now Boulanger who was planning the programs, the similarity of this May 1934 program to the staple repertoire of the Polignac salon in its first years—Renaissance rarities, baroque masterworks (especially those by Bach), the compositions of Fauré, and "modern music"—is remarkable. The curious fact, forty years later, was not that Winnaretta's tastes had not changed, but that it had taken so long for the public to catch up with them. Now, with the beneficent presence of Boulanger in her musical and personal life, the dreams of Winnaretta's "ideal" salon were realized concretely. Maurice Paléologue expressed the power of "Mademoiselle" in a letter written after the 17 May concert.

> Princesse and dear friend,
>   I didn't thank you enough the other night for the elevating and mystical emotion inspired in me by the Bach *Cantata.* Certainly, I owe much of it to the great artist who seemed to embody and personify within herself all the dynamism of the magisterial work that she conducted. She was as interesting to watch as she was to hear. In the smallest of her gestures, what intelligence and what fire! It brought to mind this beautiful verse of Livy: "Never did Apollo possess more fully the limbs of one of his priestesses."
>   Your loyally devoted Paléologue[159]

Nadia Boulanger, of course, benefitted as well. Winnaretta's connections with Alfred Cortot led him to invite Boulanger to conduct the orchestra of the École Normale, where she was on the music theory faculty. This concert, which took place on 13 February 1934, featured several works that had been performed in the Polignac salon;[160] the event garnered much critical praise.[161] In the spring, Winnaretta arranged for another highly visible, albeit "private," performance venue for Nadia Boulanger and her students at the Cercle Interallié. An elite men's club, whose founding committee included Prince Pierre de Monaco, the Cercle also served as the location for the fundraising events of the Foch Foundation, a women's organization that raised money for the Foch Hospital. Probably Prince Pierre and Winnaretta both used their influence to involve Boulanger in the well-publicized monthly musicales associated with the organization.[162] The successful Cercle Interallié performance, on 22 May 1934, was followed by two concerts in the public arena. The first of these was held under the auspices of the Sérénade. Boulanger conducted the first half of a program that, once again, included repertoire previously performed in Winnaretta's salon. The second half of the concert was conducted by Markevitch, who presented the Paris debut of his *Psaume*. The association of the three names— Boulanger, Markevitch, and Polignac—helped solidify the prestige of each.[163]

After the first concert at the École Normale, Boulanger undertook to present a second, more ambitious one. She decided to build her program around repertoire for two sopranos, and engaged Modrakowska and Marie-Blanche to sing the solos. Marie-Blanche had grown as an artist under Boulanger's tutelage in the Bach cantata classes. Boulanger had come to appreciate the pure, silvery voice of the charming Comtesse de Polignac, who also brought a touch of worldly panache to the enterprise. Yet, as well as she responded to Boulanger's high standards of artistic excellence, the hypersensitive Marie-Blanche was still insecure about performing in public. Although she had agreed earlier in the year to participate in Boulanger's spring concerts, by the month of May she had changed her mind; she declined to sing, even giving up her participation in the "Cantata Wednesdays." But Boulanger refused to accept the refusal, and was not above using guilt to secure Marie-Blanche's participation: Modrakowska was counting on this concert to pay her debts, so Marie-Blanche's cancellation would put her colleague in the poorhouse.[164] Besides, Winnaretta had commissioned a work specifically for the occasion from one of Boulanger's students, composer-pianist Marcelle de Manziarly: *Three Duos for Two Sopranos,* set to fourteenth-century French poetry by anonymous authors.[165]

Happily, the music itself, and the "pure joy of the rehearsals, often five hours at a stretch," helped relieve Marie-Blanche's anxieties.[166] The concert took place on 14 June 1934; it may have been underwritten, at least in part, through the "little fund" that Winnaretta had established for Nadia Boulanger's performances. The program chiefly featured duets for women's voices.[167] Although Winnaretta had commissioned only one work for this concert, two other Boulanger students took the initiative to write music especially for the Modrakowska-Polignac soprano duo. Jean Françaix wrote

Three Duos for Two Sopranos on texts of Aristophanes; Bernard Schulé wrote *Mariae-Sehnsucht,* on poems by Eichendorff.[168] Unlike the society people who made up most of the audiences in Winnaretta's salon, those in attendance at the École Normale were mostly musicians and music students. The École Normale concert confirmed Marie-Blanche's status as a first-class vocal artist. She was elated to receive the enthusiastic compliments of composers Roland-Manuel and Stravinsky. What made her most proud, however, was the approbation of Nadia Boulanger, "thanks to [whom] we realized something very refined and musical."[169] After the concert, Boulanger told Marie-Blanche that the pleasure of listening to her "was equal to that given to her by Isaye [*sic*] and Pugno!"[170]

For Winnaretta as patron, this event was important for numerous reasons. First, she helped bring into being a new subrepertoire of works that, even if not commissioned, were still associated with her *mécénat.* Since more or less the same program was repeated in different venues the following season, the newly written works by Françaix, Manziarly, and Schulé had the benefit of multiple performances in 1934 and 1935.[171] Second, the concert served to place her *maîtresse-de-chapelle* Nadia Boulanger squarely into the public eye. In the fall Boulanger was invited to assume the directorship of the Cercle Interallié's monthly concerts; these concerts were broadcast on the radio, further increasing her audience for the repertoire associated with the Polignac salon.[172] Finally, Winnarctta's behind-the-scenes support of performances in external venues for "her" salon artists and composers effectively moved her into the role once filled by Élisabeth Greffulhe: that of a salon hostess whose "inside" activities were but a stepping-stone towards the larger, more prestigious public arena.

Nadia Boulanger finished out her 1934 musical season with an outdoor concert on Winnaretta's veranda in Jouy. The program consisted of short pieces spanning four centuries: excerpts from Bach cantatas and Lully's *Amadis,* instrumental works by Boismortier, Gervaise, Gluck, Fauré, and Stravinsky, and three choruses "from the time of Ronsard" by Janequin, Lasso, and Le Jeune.[173] Unfortunately, despite the glorious program, the day did not bring out the best in the hostess, as Marie-Blanche recalled in her diary.

> The heat on that Sunday afternoon was torrid. All the chorus and orchestra members arrived in big vans—rented at their own expense. These poor sixty-odd people, dripping sweat, were parked on the veranda steps in the blazing sun. When I asked Tante Winnie if she couldn't give them a glass of water or orangeade, she said, jutting out her jaw with ill humor, "This is a surprise, I don't want to deal with it."[174]

Winnaretta's refusal to alleviate, or even acknowledge, the discomfort of her performers was not out of keeping with her habitual modus operandi, for the frugality of her hospitality was already a matter of notoriety. But the incident reveals an even more striking aspect of her character: she wanted *nothing* to interrupt her immersion in the pleasures of music. During this period, it seemed that many of her reactions to the physical or emotional distress of those around her were couched in musical terms. When Pata complained of a head cold, Winnaretta exhorted her to "get well soon so that you can sing Schumann and Mozart."[175] When Marie-Blanche opened her heart to her aunt about a perceived slight from a family member, Winnaretta responded, "In the same circumstances, those [like me] who have only *The Well-Tempered Clavier* to sustain them are more sorely tried."[176]

Her determined obliviousness to physical and practical matters took its toll on her health. After years of alternating Spartan repasts at home with rich feasts at receptions and restaurants, she had gained a dangerous amount of weight. She began to experience shortness of breath. Her doctor put her on a strict diet and gave her injections to promote weight loss.[177] This did not prevent her, some months later, from attending a "charming supper" after one of Ethel Smyth's concerts in Manchester, England, where she joined Smyth, Ronald Storrs, Maurice Baring, and Sir Thomas Beecham in imbibing "a drunkard's quantity of Pommery champagne."[178]

With her doctor's admonitions to live prudently having already gone out the other ear, Winnaretta began her summer travels. In August, she made her second and last trip to North America, starting in Québec and finishing in Bar Harbor, Maine. While in Venice in September she spent a good deal of time with her fourteen-year-old protégé, Bruno Maderna, advising him about his future studies.[179] Olga Rudge and Ezra Pound performed a recital at the palazzo whose program consisted of the fruits of their recent project: transcriptions for modern instruments of pieces for lute, collected by Italian musicologist Oscar Chilesotti.[180] Pound's research had attracted the attention of Mussolini, who was greatly interested in Italy's musical patrimony. The recital at Winnaretta's was, in fact, a runthrough for the grand concert that Rudge and Münch would give at the Fascist Institute of Culture in Genoa in November 1934.[181]

Winnaretta seemed completely oblivious to the implications of being involved with crypto-Fascist musical activities. It was surely due more to a form of willful blindness than to any political stance on her part. In mid-September, she hosted an official tea for the International Music Congress, which was being held in Venice that year.[182] The musical dignitaries who came to the palazzo included Stravinsky, Alban Berg, Leone Sinigaglia,[183] Henri Büsser,[184] Vladimir Horowitz, and Richard Strauss. Strauss's presence certainly raised some hackles: during the previous year, he had been appointed by Goebbels as president of the notorious Reichs-Musikkammer (State Music Bureau), the office that had hounded Kurt Weill out of Germany. Winnaretta, however, willfully ignored politics: she didn't hesitate to use her influence with Strauss to promote the cause of French music, eliciting from the composer a promise to have the Fauré *Requiem* performed in Berlin that winter. In the course of her tea party she also learned (presumably not from Strauss) that, in October, "her" Kurt Weill symphony would receive its first public performance with the Concertgebouw of Amsterdam, conducted by Bruno Walter.[185] Ironically, Walter, as a Jew, would soon be replaced by Strauss at German podiums.

Winnaretta defied more than politics that summer. As if determined to ignore her doctor's orders, during the month of September she took to inviting her Venetian friends on outings in search of interesting new cuisine as an accompaniment to some artistic pleasure. Guido Bianchini, administrator of La Fenice, fondly remembered these jaunts.

> This fairy godmother of artists, especially musicians, loved culinary "folk-lore." She frequently organized for some elite group, refined and sensitive people, some succulent little suppers in the islands of the estuary or in some little neighboring regions, noted for their original and characteristic dishes. In general the supper was the excuse and the crowning glory of an artistic event. Certain "birds in the bush," the pride of a renowned little inn of Castelfranco, would never have been appreciated if there hadn't been, in the town's Cathedral, the admirable Madonna of Giorgione. We would never have gone to Cortina d'Ampezzo either, to taste the famous "elk of Antelao," if there hadn't been the delicious prelude of Giorgio Levi at the piano: the *Préludes* of Debussy.[186]

En route to Cortina,[187] where the Debussy and the elk awaited, Winnaretta experienced a sharp pain in her finger. She ignored it, but by the end of the concert, the finger had swollen horribly. Bianchini recognized the affliction as being a "phlegmon," an infected, possibly gangrenous, lesion; he called a surgeon friend who lived two hours away by car. Winnaretta arrived at the clinic and was immediately sent into surgery without anesthetic, submitting to the procedure, according to Bianchini, "with sang-froid and admirable courage." Afterwards, the doctor informed her that, had she waited any longer, she would have lost both her finger and her arm.[188] Winnaretta wrote to Marie-Blanche that the whole incident was "uninteresting," although she was annoyed that she would have to wait until the end of October to play the piano.[189] A few days later she took another group of musicians on a two-day automobile trip to Brescia, Vicenza, Bergamo, and Gardone, where the culinary specialty was trout stuffed with salmon.[190]

The central artistic event of Winnaretta's summer was the music festival of the 1934 Biennale, which she described to Boulanger as being "very amusing," apart from certain performances that were "indescribably boring: a night of the Nordics, of young Italians, of ghastly 'chamber operas'" (Strauss's *Die Frau ohne Schatten* was grouped in this last category).[191] But there were superb performances as well, which she often attended in the company of Bruno Maderna: Stravinsky's *Capriccio* and Mozart's *Così fan tutte*, and, best of all, a splendid Verdi *Requiem* on the Piazza San Marco, "well sung and tastefully conducted by Serafin." After this last performance, Winnaretta chanced upon Toscanini, who "transfixed" her with a piercing stare as she communicated her impressions to him.[192] The maestro presented an altogether more affable demeanor later in the week, when he came to Winnaretta's palazzo after a performance at La Fenice, in the company of the Horowitzes and the Castelbarcos, to prepare pasta in her kitchen.[193]

Winnaretta continued to feast even though she knew that her portfolio had suffered a blow that year. The slow but inevitable decline in the European economy brought about by the Great Depression finally trickled down sufficiently to have an effect on the wealthy of France—that is, those who had not already lost everything in the Crash.[194] The collapse of the dollar in late 1933 finally brought the situation home to Winnaretta.[195] The point of her trip in August to Canada had probably been to meet with Singer Trust administrators.

Still, Winnaretta was feasting on her dreams, as she wrote Nadia Boulanger, "of cantatas, of Heinrich Schütz, of concerts in my *atelier* that I would like to be very numerous."[196] Schütz was one of her favorite baroque composers, and in the upcoming season she hoped to present his masterwork, the *Auferstehungs-Historie* (History of the Resurrection), first performed in her salon in 1896. Winnaretta had also been considering commissioning a new work for organ and small instrumental ensemble to be performed at the Cavaillé-Coll, with herself as soloist. The idea for an organ piece may have first been suggested by Francis Poulenc in late July, just before Winnaretta's departure for Canada.[197] Winnaretta reintroduced the subject in a letter to Poulenc written in mid-September from Venice.

> You have written to me so frankly that it allows me to tell you very simply that, thanks to Mr. Roosevelt, my musical budget has been very considerably reduced. I will only be able to offer you half of what you accepted for the [Two-Piano] Concerto, that is to say 12,500 francs. Under these conditions, are you interested in writing for an instrument that is not widely used? I hope that you will do it all the same, perhaps in view of my Cavaillé-Coll, whose stops you would have to study a bit. Nadia would give you some precious instructions.[198]

Boulanger was notified right away of these developments, and wrote Poulenc shortly thereafter. "The Princesse de Polignac tells me of your intention of writing something for her, for organ. Do I need to tell you how much this project interests me, and gladdens my heart—and my ears! I always have confidence in you, but I wonder, however, if you really know know the rue Cortambert organ—its resources, its drawbacks."[199] Clearly

Winnaretta was setting up a situation in which the realization of the commission would be accomplished by a triumvirate: Poulenc the composer, Boulanger the conductor and advisor, and herself the instigator and performing artist. She decided to expand her idea into a full evening of first performances of works for organ. On 23 September she wrote to Boulanger, "Do you think that Jean Françaix would like to write something for me, maybe for small orchestra with organ (an easy organ part)? Would he accept 12,000 francs? If you see him, would you present the subject to him, before writing to me?"[200] Boulanger put the second project into motion. That Winnaretta expected to be the organ soloist for the commissioned works is made clear by her letter to Boulanger of 6 October: "Will the works of Poulenc and of Jean Françaix be for small orchestra? As I hope, with an organ part that isn't too difficult?"[201] She was looking forward to discussing so much with Boulanger—books, music, travel—"and I can only do it *with you*, because it's only with you that I ('la silencieuse') become a veritable CHATTERBOX."[202]

In choosing to travel to Vienna to hear Toscanini conduct Beethoven's Ninth Symphony,[203] Winnaretta abandoned her plans to attend the premiere of the Kurt Weill symphony in Amsterdam on 11 October. Weill's completed work, a "song symphony," made frequent use of styles and dance-band rhythms that would not have been out of place in a music theater piece. The first performance, by Bruno Walter and the Concertgebouw Orchestra,[204] elicited two diametrically opposed reactions, one from the critics, who dismissed the work as "banal," "disjointed," and "Beethoven in the beer garden,"[205] and one from audiences, who greeted the work and its composer with enthusiasm.[206] Belgian critic Henri Monnet summed up the situation concisely: "The Dutch critics and the specialists . . . condemned this Symphony in Songs, which the public, astonished by a pleasure that is refused it so often, gave the work a warm and appreciable welcome."[207] None of Winnaretta's own reactions to Weill's work have surfaced. Perhaps the "popular" quality of the symphony and her possible unease about the piece's reception account for her absence from the Concertgebouw premiere. But there may have been another factor at play. The fact that Winnaretta did not impose a first performance of the Weill in her salon, nor rush to Amsterdam to hear the public debut, signaled a recent and important change in attitude towards her commissions: like a mother acknowledging that her children are capable of going off into the world without her, she was allowing the music to "leave the nest" at the time that suited the composer's needs, not her own.

Winnaretta's relinquishment of her former possessiveness can surely be attributed to the presence in her life of Nadia Boulanger. Daily contact with the woman whose intelligence and integrity, and passion for her art, caused music to come to life, brought Winnaretta a happiness that she had not known in forty years, since the happy days of her marriage to Edmond.

She knew it, and she was able to express it to Boulanger: "I [had lost] my emotional equilibrium just at the precise moment where fate sent me one of the most precious gifts: your friendship, without which I don't know how I would have ever gotten through these last two years."[208] As with Edmond, Winnaretta's relationship with Boulanger was chaste: in place of sex, they had a salon. As with Edmond, their communion was shared on the high plane where great art illuminates the spirit.

Figure 23. Winnaretta and friends in Italy, 1932. Left to right: Mme Jean Hugo, née Maria Ruspoli, violinist Olga Rudge, pianist Arthur Rubinstein, Winnaretta, society hostess Elsa Maxwell. Collection of Prince Edmond de Polignac. Used by permission.

Figure 24. Winnaretta at the Cavaillé-Coll organ in the rue Cortambert *atelier,* Paris, 1933. Private collection. Used by permission.

Figure 25. Winnaretta laying the foundation stone at the French Salvation Army's Cité de Refuge, designed by Le Corbusier, 24 June 1930. The Salvation Army, Paris. Used by permission.

Figure 26. Winnaretta and her painting, *Santa Maria della Salute* (Venice, 1902), 1936. Private collection. Used by permission.

Figure 27. The Nadia Boulanger Ensemble on the *S. S. Champlain* en route to the United States, 1938. Seated: Gisèle Peyron, Nadia Boulanger at the piano. Standing: Irène and Nathalie Kédroff, Doda Conrad, Comtesse Jean (Marie-Blanche) de Polignac, Hugues Cuénod. Collection of the author.

Figure 28. Winnaretta and Colette in the garden of the Hôtel Singer-Polignac, Paris, ca. 1938. Collection of the author.

Figure 29. Winnaretta and Dame Ethel Smyth, Surrey, 1942. Collection of the author.

All Music is Modern

By the mid-1930s the musical salon was an anachronism. The younger generation of "chic" Parisians had little interest in the musicales hosted by this duchess or that countess. The space formerly reserved in newspapers for the private gatherings of the *gratin* was now filled with photographs of socialites in Chanel gowns and Schiaparelli hats, of princes perched in their Renault sports cars or twin-engine airplanes, and of movie stars (mostly American) in full-page photomontages. Thanks to her Dupuy connections, Winnaretta's salon gatherings still received occasional coverage in *Le Figaro, Excelsior,* and *The New York Herald.* But the reportage took place in a climate of shifting political winds, one that would culminate the following year in the election of Léon Blum and a government dominated by the Popular Front, a coalition Leftist party. At this moment when the working class was on the ascent, the idle aristocracy and its leisure pursuits—of which the salon was an icon—were objects of derision. Winnaretta's musical activities were lampooned for their elitism by the unfriendly factions of the press. One such article appeared in *Vendémiaire,* signed by a reporter called "Snob."

> Attendance at public concerts is not entirely recommended for those who wish above all else to be considered music lovers. Rather, the smart society woman should try to become part of that musical Olympus, at the summit of which reigns the Princesse Edmond de Polignac. . . .
>
> When [she] has managed, thanks to Mademoiselle Boulanger's courses, to know her Bach and her Mozart right down to the tips of her fingers, and is able to sight-read Stravinsky's *Perséphone* better than the score of [Irving Berlin's] *Top Hat,* she may begin to go to the concerts, without fear of confusing the music of Poulenc with that of Auric, or of sleeping during the performance of the masterworks of Honegger.[1]

Winnaretta was not necessarily better served by her advocates in the press. In late 1934 a full-page article by Jean Desbordes[2] appeared in *Paris-Midi* under the expansive headline, "Great Ladies of Paris: The Princesse E. de Polignac, or the Genius of the Arts." Extolling her artistic prescience, "intuitive, illuminated, . . . infallible," Desbordes hailed Winnaretta as "the chosen one . . . of an extra-terrestrial tribunal"; if "her heart stirred at the approach of such and such an artist, obscure or well-known, she knew that her heart never erred, and that it only beat thus when in the presence of greatness."[3] The best phrase in the article was a quote from Winnaretta, describing her lifetime adoration of Bach: "Everything in there is taut, incisive, useful. Every stroke, every note is expressive, musical, alive, like the line of a drawing by Ingres or Manet."[4]

Despite the march of time, the change in tastes, the aspersions of naysayers and the hyperbole of high-culture pundits, the musical salon of the Princesse Edmond de Polignac had lost none of its luster. On 8 January 1935 Winnaretta turned seventy. To celebrate the event, she gave herself a grand birthday party: a musical soiree in the *atelier,* organized by Nadia Boulanger, who conducted an ensemble of fifty-nine musicians—vocal soloists, chorus, and orchestra—in a performance of Heinrich Schütz's *Auferstehungs-Historie,* a work that had first been performed in the *atelier* thirty years earlier by Charles Bordes and the Chanteurs de Saint-Gervais.[5] Hearing "this work of such great beauty" interpreted by Boulanger, Winnaretta found it "more marvelous than ever."[6]

She sent a copy of the Schütz program to Ezra Pound, with whom she maintained a lively correspondence about very old and very new repertoire.[7] Pound had taken to making suggestions of modernist repertoire unknown to Winnaretta for possible inclusion in her salon; in 1935 he was particularly enthusiastic about Béla Bartók's ballet *The Miraculous Mandarin,* and a new work, *Music for Strings, Percussion, and Celesta.*[8] Winnaretta does not seem to have taken Pound's advice, at least insofar as Eastern European composers were concerned. She reported the upcoming February programs to Pata: Germaine Tailleferre's Piano Concerto (in its two-piano version), a recital by a young Boulanger protégé, pianist Clifford Curzon,[9] and a Bach cantata evening.[10] In the same letter, Winnaretta enclosed a copy of a cherished photograph from 1899: the group of friends at the Brancovan estate in Amphion. She was able to identify just about everyone from that long-ago time—Edmond, Proust, Abel Hermant, Léon Delafosse, Anna and Hélène, and Constantine de Brancovan—but claimed not to remember the name of the woman sitting right next to her, turned in profile towards her[11]—the Marquise de Monteynard, Winnaretta's first friend in the aristocracy, later her cousin by marriage, and perhaps her lover. Clearly she was whitewashing her past for future generations.

Even at the age of seventy, Winnaretta's energy was astonishing. She hosted an elegant dinner to commemorate the thirtieth anniversary of Arthur Rubinstein's Paris recital debut.[12] Through the Fondation Singer-Polignac, she gave 100,000 francs to underwrite an archeological dig of a necropolis dating from the seventh and sixth centuries B.C.E. in Vari, Greece, organized by the Greek Archeological Society.[13] As honorary president of the Cercle Interallié, she organized fundraising drives for the Pasteur Institute and the Foch Foundation, which subsidized a health-care facility for low-income families. A founding member of the "Friends of Anna de Noailles," Winnaretta contributed to the establishment of a commemorative "Amphion Garden." On the musical front, she arranged for Nadia Boulanger to make her Rome debut under the auspices of La Primavera.[14] But this plan was soon abandoned: Boulanger's mother, Raissa, was on her deathbed. Winnaretta, traveling in Portugal, received an anguished letter from her friend. "So many bereavements, sorrows, efforts, and renunciations have accumulated, that my heart is at the end of its strength. And yet I must, however, work, smile, and hang on. I think I can do it, but how to achieve that 'on the inside'? You will help me, dear Princesse, I'm sure of it, in the hours when courage fails me."[15] Madame Boulanger died on 19 March, and her daughter plunged into mourning. Winnaretta sought to comfort her distraught friend. "You draw courage from your faith, from your disciplined nature . . . but I also know that even the strongest beings can't go through such trials without some bitter hours, lassitude, and limitless sorrow. . . . All I ask is that you count me among those who would do anything at all for you."[16]

However, the two women did not see each other for some time. After her mother's death, a part of Boulanger seemed to close down permanently, as if, in Hugues Cuénod's words, "she lived in a cult of unhappiness."[17] Winnaretta had been correct about the importance of work in helping the musician to recover. In May, Boulanger resumed her Wednesday cantata classes. Even though she had cancelled all performances through the spring and fall, she was already formulating an important long-range project: the creation of a small ensemble of professional singers, technically and musically equipped to handle the vast amount of repertoire that she hoped to present in future seasons. By the fall Boulanger had chosen her singers: sopranos Marie-Blanche de Polignac and Gisèle Peyron (the young new wife of Commissioner Albin Peyron of the Salvation Army), the Russian cousins Irène and Nathalie Kédroff, mezzo and contralto respectively, tenors Hugues Cuénod and Paul Derenne, and bass Doda Conrad.[18]

Meanwhile, Winnaretta continued her dizzying array of projects. On 31 May an exhibition of twenty-four of her paintings, representing fifty years of her artistic output, opened at the Galerie Jean Charpentier. Minister of Fine Arts Georges Huisman presided over the inauguration.[19] *Le Figaro* featured a picture of Winnaretta, surrounded by her canvasses, lauding her as a "distinguished artist-painter."[20] On 24 June a performance of Kurt Weill's commissioned Symphony was given in the large music room of avenue Henri-Martin, along with works by Beethoven and Chabrier.[21] She helped plan the spring gala of the Foch Foundation, whose goal that year was the construction of a new public health facility.[22] She made her round of family visits in the early summer, and set off for Venice in the fall. Her gondola had become so inadequate for the comings and goings of herself and her guests that she bought a little motorboat and named it *The Rose of*

Devon. People would stare in wonderment to see this elderly woman with the granite-like face motoring down the canal to the Lido, to the train station, to her pink palazzo. Winnaretta's letters in August and September were filled with news of a houseful of guests, a Titian exhibition, and an automobile trip to Salzburg to hear *Fidelio* and *Don Giovanni* under Bruno Walter. But from time to time she would admit to various loved ones that she was experiencing inexplicable depressions, passing through a period "of physical and emotional malaise."[23] Winnaretta's depression may have had to do with loss of control—of death, of the passage of time, of musical projects, and of Nadia Boulanger, who assuaged her grief through grueling work rather than personal confidences. In October, having returned to Paris, Winnaretta wrote to Boulanger of her wistful hope that her friend would soon have a free day to see her "for a long time."[24]

The fall season held numerous pleasures: a luncheon with Marie-Blanche and the actress Claudette Colbert, a performance in her salon by the Kolisch Quartet later the following week, a Toscanini series, and the recommencement of the Wednesday cantata classes.[25] Igor Stravinsky returned to Paris to give the first performances of his new Concerto for Two Solo Pianos with his son Soulima.[26] Winnaretta was not able to attend the first performances, but she had the pleasure of a personal introduction to "this admirable and magisterial concerto" in her own *atelier* through the good graces of Nadia Boulanger, who finally found time for a long visit with her patron in mid-November.[27] Two weeks later she entertained British art critic Clive Bell, who, like his celebrated sister-in-law Virginia Woolf, was a member of the Bloomsbury Group.[28] Winnaretta was an ardent admirer of Virginia Woolf's novels, and she pressed Bell to introduce her to his sister-in-law. Woolf, who knew of the Princesse de Polignac only by reputation—as her friend Ethel Smyth's "old flame"[29]—did indeed meet Winnaretta for lunch in London on 12 December, but, regrettably, she left no impressions of this encounter. The two women would meet again over the next several years, and it would require the fullness of time for Virginia Woolf to warm to the enigmatic princess.

The remainder of the month was filled with friends and music-making in the *atelier.*[30] Boulanger was enticed to attend an informal 9 o'clock dinner at rue Cortambert for which Colette prepared truffles "[arrived] from Cahors at 7 p.m." While Colette saw to the requisite slow cooking of the culinary treat, Boulanger and her hostess worked out fingerings for a Bach organ fugue.[31] Winnaretta paid Boulanger the high compliment of allowing her to borrow one of her prized manuscripts, the autograph score of Igor Markevitch's *Hymnes.* The favor was granted not without trepidation: "It's a unique [copy of the] manuscript, it seems; I separate myself from it trembling."[32] Winnaretta's fears, as it turns out, were justified: Boulanger never returned the manuscript; it was found among her papers after her death.[33]

In early 1936, all of Winnaretta's soirees were planned and conducted by Nadia Boulanger. "All music is modern," asserted the musician, and the programs bore out this point of view. That of 7 February included new pieces for string quartet by Paul Hindemith, and a chamber music work, *As It Fell upon a Day,* by one of Boulanger's former American students, Aaron Copland.[34] Three Monteverdi madrigals—*Hor che'l ciel e la terra, Lamento della ninfa,* and *Chiome d'oro*—rounded out the program; they would soon number among the Boulanger Ensemble's signature pieces.[35] The second performance, on 13 February, was even grander: Winnaretta hired the Orchestre Symphonique de Paris to perform in her large music room, under Boulanger's baton. The program included a Haydn symphony and Mozart's Concerto for Two Pianos, performed by Marie-Blanche and Jacques Février. Hindemith's Five Pieces for Violin were played by a young violinist, Paul Makanowitzky, who was partnered by Boulanger for the premiere of Jean Françaix's Sonatine for Violin and Piano.[36] The third program, given on 22 February, featured Italy's most distinguished violin virtuoso, Gioconda de Vito,[37] accompanied by an orchestra led by Boulanger.[38]

If the performances in Winnaretta's *atelier* were "of supreme elegance," as the newspapers would say, the remuneration of the artists involved in these events was less than satisfactory. Winnaretta had from time to time given Boulanger a check for ten thousand francs to add to a general "fund" for salon musicales, with the understanding that Boulanger should use her discretion in paying the musicians. But given the large number of personnel involved in many of these performances, the division of Winnaretta's "fund" often resulted in insultingly low fees for the artists. Boulanger, as contractor, was put in an awkward position vis-à-vis her colleagues. Eventually she addressed this situation with Winnaretta, who sent an additional two thousand francs "for the artists who were paid too little."[39] Generally, the musicians who performed in the Polignac salon understood that the prestige of playing in this venue outweighed monetary compensation. This viewpoint was expressed by violinist Paul Makanowitzky.

> I would be happy to make music with you in November at the Princesse's house. . . . Don't you think, dear Mademoiselle, that it would be prudent [for you] to keep mum about the fee that the Princesse would like to offer me on this occasion? Because I think that everyone in London will find it very very insufficient, and that this would make a bad impression. Don't you agree with me? Nonetheless this soiree will be very interesting for me because of the fashionable audience that will be there.[40]

Boulanger understood better than anyone the far-ranging benefits of the Princesse's patronage: Winnaretta had just arranged for her to conduct the OSP in a public performance of the Schütz *Auferstehung.*[41]

Unconsciously, Makanowitzky had come close to articulating the paradox of the Princesse de Polignac: the disparity between the appearance of opulence and elegance at avenue Henri-Martin and the meager payment of the musicians was mirrored in the disparity between Winnaretta's rich inner world and her plain, even austere way of life. To Maurice Goudeket, who in 1935 had become Colette's third (and most beloved) husband, Winnaretta always seemed like a guest in her own house. Goudeket believed that Colette had "adopted" her because she looked like, in his words, "a millionaire orphan." He liked her wry, self-deprecating humor. "My dear," she said to Colette after the renovation of the house in Jouy, "I have no luck. I buy a little cottage in the country [and] tell my architect to add a tiny little wing to it while I am in Venice. I return, and what do I find? The Louvre"—a word that, emanating from Winnaretta's clenched jaw, came out sounding like "the Lrrrvvre." Winnaretta seemed to find more rusticity in Colette's top-floor apartment in the Marignan Building on the Champs-Élysées than in her own country retreat. She would determinedly climb the many flights of stairs, where, once arrived, a feast awaited her: a cheese orgy, served with Colette's famous mulled wine.[42] Marie-Blanche, who sometimes joined the party at the Goudekets, found her aunt to be a different person in their company: there was no high-flown intellectual talk in the homey apartment; the conversations turned around topics such as plants and herbs, wine and cheese, dogs and cats.[43]

Since the death of Anna de Noailles, Colette had become the woman friend—other than her nieces—to whom Winnaretta turned most frequently for quotidian companionship (as opposed to the loftier, musically oriented friendship that she shared with Nadia Boulanger). It was not unusual for Winnaretta to show her affection in grandiose ways. On 21 January 1936, she gave an elegant dinner in honor of Colette's promotion to the rank of Commander of the Legion of Honor.[44] On another occasion, she sent Colette a pot of flowers; the writer discovered a diamond necklace nestled in the stems.[45] The greatest testimony of friendship was rendered in the month of April. Colette had been nominated to Belgium's Royal Academy of French Language and Literature, to fill the seat previously held by Anna de Noailles.[46] Custom dictated that a new academician deliver an encomium praising the predecessor. In this case, custom and affection coincided: the vivid portrait of the fragile poet written by Colette for the Academy was a tribute to a true friend. Winnaretta accompanied the Goudekets to the ceremony, just as she had accompanied Anna fourteen years earlier. But when the train to Brussels stopped at the French-Belgian border, it was discovered that Colette's passport had never been renewed, and an officious Belgian security controller was ready to remove the writer from the train. At that point Winnaretta fixed the functionary with her cold blue gaze and said, "Your Academy is expecting Madame for a speech, and they can't begin without her." This statement had no meaning for the controller, who still intended

to eject Colette from her compartment. "I tell you the passport is not in order," said he. "And I tell you that without Madame there will be no speech,"
repeated the Princesse, gnashing the words through her clenched jaw. The
functionary retreated, presumably to check with his superior; shortly thereafter Colette and her companions were allowed to continue their journey.[47]
After delivering her moving speech to the Academy, Colette gave Winnaretta
her handwritten copy, as a souvenir of their Belgian adventure.[48]

That spring, the Cercle Ronsard, a charity organization that raised money
for indigent artists, sponsored three fundraising concerts. The first of these
took place at Winnaretta's house on 15 May; the performance featured the
Nadia Boulanger Ensemble singing choral music spanning three centuries,
including J. S. Bach's cantata *Jesu meine Freude*. Marie-Blanche was the
featured soloist in Monteverdi's *Lamento della ninfa*; bass Doda Conrad
offered a moving account of Poulenc's *Épitaphe*.[49] Conrad was an enterprising young musician. The young bass had recently been invited by the
fledgling British Broadcasting Company (BBC) to sing a series of song recitals organized by the musicologist and critic Michel Calvocoressi, entitled "Foundations of Music."[50] While in London in June 1936 for an all-
Ravel broadcast, Conrad proposed to the BBC's artistic director that the
Nadia Boulanger Ensemble be engaged to perform five broadcasts in the
same series. Calvocoressi, who had known Boulanger at the Paris
Conservatoire, was enthusiastic about the idea. Conrad then carried out a
second, more fantastic idea: he found, with the help of British musical phi-
lanthropists, a venue for Boulanger to conduct Fauré's *Requiem,* which,
unbelievably, had never been performed in London.[51]

Winnaretta happened to be in London at the time of Conrad's broadcasts.[52] On 11 June, she attended a lavish dinner, hosted by Lady Sibyl
Colefax, who lived on King's Road, right next to the townhouse that had
caused Winnaretta so much grief. The guests included King Edward VIII
and his mistress, Baltimore-born Wallis Simpson, the Winston Churchills,
National Gallery director Kenneth Clark and his wife, Noel Coward, the
Arthur Rubinsteins, and diplomat Harold Nicolson. Rubinstein had consented to play a recital after the meal. People drifted in and out of the
music room, but Winnaretta planted herself next to the piano so as not to
be distracted. "I have seldom seen a woman sit so firmly: there was determination in every line of her bum," recalled Nicolson. Rubinstein played
Chopin until after midnight. As Winnaretta tapped her foot with impatience, waiting for the next piece, the King approached, thanking Rubinstein
in a peremptory manner that indicated the concert was over. As goodbyes
were being said, more guests arrived, including Gerald Berners. The new
group gathered around the piano, as Noel Coward sat down and began to
play and hum one of his jaunty songs. The King promptly returned to his
seat to listen. "I much fear," wrote Nicolson, "that Rubinstein and Madame de Polignac must have thought us a race of barbarians."[53]

On 7 July, back in Paris, Winnaretta gave a dinner party followed by "a little music."[54] Doda Conrad was one of the performers that evening; he sang some Schubert *Lieder* and the bass recitative and aria from Bach's Cantata 70 that had so moved his hostess at a previous soiree.

A few days later Conrad received a phone call from Winnaretta, inviting him to spend the weekend with her at Jouy. "Bring a volume of Schubert," she instructed him. The following Friday afternoon, with stormy skies menacing, Conrad met Winnaretta's chauffeur-driven Packard limousine at the appointed hour. He attempted to make conversation with his hostess, who offered not one word of response; she remained huddled in her corner of the back seat, silent and distracted. Conrad, perplexed and offended, was about to ask the chauffeur to stop the car and let him out on the sidewalk, when suddenly the skies turned black and opened up with torrential rain. "Stop the car," shrieked Winnaretta to the chauffeur, "get me to shelter!" The chauffeur stopped at a cafe, and the three dashed inside. At each thunderclap, she trembled more violently, prey to her irrational fear of storms and loud noises. As the rains ceased, Winnaretta's demeanor relaxed; she commenced pleasant conversation with her guest as if nothing had happened. That night the two sight-read through most of the book of Schubert *Lieder* into the wee hours of the morning. Conrad had the impression that his imperious hostess became like "a timid little girl" when making music. By the end of the evening a new friendship had been formed. However, Conrad's warm feelings towards his hostess cooled again the next morning, when he discovered that Winnaretta had gone out for her morning constitutional, without making any provisions for his meals.[55]

Later that day, the two went for a walk in the park at Versailles, where they discussed the London project. Winnaretta and Boulanger had already met to decide on programs; both agreed that Schütz's *Auferstehung* and the Fauré *Requiem* would be good companion pieces for a Queen's Hall concert.[56] But problems related to the concert's financing were already foreseen. The rental of Queen's Hall—London's preeminent performance venue—cost 150 pounds. Robert Mayer was prepared to guarantee one-third of the sum, but two other "guarantors" would have to be found.[57] Winnaretta immediately agreed to contribute fifty pounds towards the rental, and asked Conrad to keep her apprised of any further difficulties.[58] Indeed, other obstacles had presented themselves by mid-July. Marchioness Sibyl Cholmondeley, one of London's prominent arts patrons, wrote to Marie-Blanche on 12 July, "Frankly I'm afraid that these concerts would not cover their costs, because the musical [audience] that could appreciate the beautiful and rare music in the Schütz *Resurrection* is rather small. . . . I'm afraid that concentrating all these concerts into eight days will render the enterprise rather difficult, because you're addressing the *same* audience for this genre of very good music."[59] Winnaretta, however, was intent on hearing the Schütz performed. As a way of generating publicity and strong ticket sales, she proposed hosting two private salon concerts in London featuring the Boulanger Ensemble, to be held in borrowed music rooms. She asked Boulanger to plan two programs that would be simple to perform, and whose costs would not exceed four thousand francs per concert. "Naturally you will stay with me in London," Winnaretta informed Boulanger, "and I will be seriously wounded if you do not permit me to take care of all your travel expenses—as many tickets as you would like, Paris London Paris London Paris London!"[60]

Winnaretta's summer was hardly a restful one. The London concert represented merely one of her occupations. Business related to the archeological dig in Vari, Greece, needed attending to. The dig had yielded some extraordinary treasures: the discovery of many intact tombs, which contained giant ornamented snake figures, black ornamental cups engraved with figures, and a sphinx (minus its head).[61] Her nephew, Louis Decazes, chronically ill for many years, had to be moved from Lausanne into a clinic,[62] although Winnaretta also found time while in Switzerland to study German literature with a visiting professor of that subject, and to play two-piano music with a local pianist.[63]

On her last day in Switzerland before her departure for Venice, Winnaretta chanced to meet tenor Hugues Cuénod, who, as it happened, was also departing for Venice the next day. Winnaretta proposed that they travel together. Cuénod, with some embarrassment, confessed that he would be traveling second-class. "Don't worry," said Winnaretta, "meet me in front of my train car tomorrow, and I'll arrange for your ticket. But please buy a *ticket de quai*." In those days, persons accompanying travelers to the train to see them off were required to purchase a twenty-five-centime "*ticket de quai*," which allowed access to the train platform; the ticket was then given to a comptroller upon leaving the platform. Cuénod was puzzled by Winnaretta's request, but he purchased his *ticket de quai,* and found Winnaretta in front of the first-class train cars. "Ah, good, you're here!" she exclaimed, "Please give me your *ticket de quai*." She then handed her chauffeur (who had shown the controller Cuénod's first-class ticket in order to enter the platform) the *ticket de quai,* so that he could leave the platform. With this act she gave living proof of the economic philosophy that she had imparted to her nephew Eddy: a check for a first-class train ticket was but an abstraction, a piece of paper, but pulling twenty-five centimes out of her pocket to buy a *ticket de quai*—now *that* was painful![64]

In Venice, however, Winnaretta seemed to Cuénod the soul of graciousness and enlightenment. It was an emotional moment for the tenor, who sang Fauré's *Cinq Mélodies de Venise* at a musical soiree shortly after his arrival, when he realized that he was being accompanied by the dedicatee of the songs, in the very room where Fauré had probably played his new songs for the first time.[65] Cuénod was only one of a steady stream of guests that summer, for whom Winnaretta arranged excursions to the famous Harry's Bar and teatime recitals featuring Clara Haskil.[66] But for most of the summer Winnaretta was preoccupied with the plans for London. She corresponded regularly with Doda Conrad about the financial viability of the project; she awaited confirmation from the French Ambassador and Maud "Emerald" Cunard about using their music rooms for her private recitals; she arranged for Ronald Storrs to write some publicity articles about the music of Heinrich Schütz.[67] As unforeseen expenses mounted, Winnaretta agreed to underwrite the additional costs, so keen was her desire to see the project realized. When Boulanger praised her commitment to the project and to great music, Winnaretta responded, "Your affectionate words [are] much too laudatory, for there's nothing praiseworthy about loving what one loves and what is essential and indispensable to our existence."[68]

In the midst of these plans, Winnaretta received a discouraged letter from Henry Prunières, editor of Paris's most important music journal, *La Revue musicale*. Despite its healthy readership, the *Revue* was foundering on the verge of bankruptcy; Prunières asked Winnaretta, already a benefactor, to contribute more than the eight thousand francs she had already pledged.[69] Winnaretta never altered her peculiar way of being generous. She agreed to augment her contribution, but only on the condition that Prunières find other subscribers to shore up the deficit.[70] The editor didn't have time to find more subscribers, especially during the summer holidays. Bankruptcy was imminent. Prunières devised a brilliant solution, one to which Winnaretta gladly agreed: he would put Boulanger on the Board of Directors of the *Revue*; through this device, the Princesse de Polignac could make a contribution "in the name of Nadia Boulanger," so that the musician could become a stockholder.[71]

In the last weeks of October the sunny Italian skies turned gray, and Winnaretta's guests departed. Once again she suffered the customary illness and depression that accompanied her solitude. There was another depressed soul in Venice at that moment—Vladimir Horowitz. The renowned pianist had married Wanda Toscanini in 1933; almost immediately, the effects of living with the Toscanini family had taken a toll on his nerves. Wanda was overly protective of her husband, who had formerly enjoyed a very active social life; there were very few connections with people outside the Toscanini circle. At the relatively young age of thirty-three, Horowitz's grueling life as a concert artist, coupled with the new pressures that came with the recent birth of his daughter, provoked a series of physical ailments, including high blood pressure and paralyzing stage fright. In February 1936, exhausted and overworked, Horowitz suffered a nervous breakdown, and for the next year and a half ceased all performing activities. He had come to Venice that summer to recuperate,[72] and it was there that he found Winnaretta. The two were well suited as companions in consolation:

compared to life with his in-laws, Horowitz probably found Winnaretta's enigmatic silences refreshing. The princess and the pianist took walks along the beach; sometimes Horowitz accompanied Winnaretta on little jaunts down the canal in her motorboat, *The Rose of Devon*.[73]

These walks were the last moments of calm that Winnaretta would enjoy for the next month. In early November she left for England. After a whirlwind of last-minute preparations, the members of the Nadia Boulanger Ensemble crossed the Channel on 10 November. Winnaretta had arranged lodgings for the group at the Hotel Claridge. She was staying in an apartment on the top floor; its salon was equipped with a piano, which would double as a rehearsal space.[74] The week was scheduled to begin with an elegant luncheon at the Ritz hosted by Mr. and Mrs. Robert Mayer, the principal London benefactors of the concerts. Dorothy Mayer had also volunteered to host an "at home" concert on 19 November in her music room at St John's Wood, in order to introduce Boulanger to London society.[75] Even before meeting the Mayers, Winnaretta was predisposed to dislike them: there had been friction in their communications during the summer, over both money and artistic control, and Doda Conrad had often been put in the uncomfortable role of mediator.[76]

On the night of the Ensemble's arrival, when Winnaretta reminded Conrad that she would be seeing him the next day at the Mayers's luncheon, he told her, with much embarrassment, that he had not been invited. Winnaretta became enraged. "These are *your* friends; how could they treat you so rudely? In any event, be at the Ritz tomorrow at 12:45—I will take care of things." The next day, Winnaretta found Conrad at the appointed hour, and brought him into the dining room, where they took a table for two. Moments later, the Mayers arrived with Nadia Boulanger and the Jean de Polignacs, and approached the table of their guest of honor, the Princesse de Polignac. "Who is this fellow disturbing our lunch?" Winnaretta coldly asked Conrad, who rose, discomfited, to make the awkward introductions. Robert Mayer reddened as he suddenly realized his social gaffe, but it was too late. Winnaretta, impervious to the general embarrassment of all, did not budge: "I expected to lunch with Doda, and I *shall* lunch with Doda!" The Mayers departed, minus their guest of honor. From then on, Winnaretta excused herself from all social functions involving the Mayers, including their "at home"—although, at Conrad's behest, she grudgingly invited them to Lady Cunard's private concert.[77]

For the remainder of the week, Winnaretta's main concern was the care and comfort of Nadia Boulanger. Knowing that Boulanger still considered herself to be in mourning, Winnaretta organized small dinners for her in her top-floor hotel suite, so that the musician could see former students and friends, such as Prince Pierre de Monaco, in tranquil surroundings. The rest of the time was packed with frenetic activity. The musical repertoire chosen for the BBC broadcasts was a fascinating mix of old and new:

madrigals by Orlando di Lasso, French chansons, and choruses by Debussy, Fauré, and Stravinsky. The music of Poulenc was inserted in between works from the sixteenth century.[78] One entire broadcast was devoted to the Monteverdi madrigals. Thanks to the help of Ronald Storrs and Daisy Fellowes, the newspapers were full of articles about the broadcasts and the forthcoming Queen's Hall concerts, placing particular stress on Winnaretta's patronage of the Boulanger Ensemble.[79] On 22 November, Emerald Cunard's salon was "borrowed" for two musicales hosted by Winnaretta—a matinee of vocal and two-piano works, performed by Marie-Blanche, Boulanger, and Clifford Curzon, and a grand soiree presented that same evening featuring the full Ensemble, which sang works ranging from Monteverdi to Debussy, as well as new works by British composer Lennox Berkeley, a former student of Boulanger.[80] The Monteverdi madrigals, unknown to the audience, proved to be the sensation of the soiree; they were fast becoming the pieces with which the Boulanger Ensemble was mostly closely identified.[81]

Due to scheduling difficulties, the soiree of 20 November that was to have taken place at the French Embassy was cancelled at the last minute. The program was to have included first performances of two works commissioned by Winnaretta, Françaix's Serenade and Lennox Berkeley's *Two Poems of Pindar (Dithyrambe and Hymn)*.[82] Boulanger convinced Winnaretta to allow Berkeley's new piece to be included in the Queen's Hall concert. This unforeseen performance in such a prestigious venue had consequences for both Berkeley and Winnaretta: it gave an important boost to the young composer's career, and established Winnaretta as a patron of young *British* composers.[83] But in more important ways, the entire Queen's Hall concert was a revelation. It was the first time that a woman had ever conducted the London Symphony, and Nadia Boulanger was the heroine of the British press and public. The Schütz *Auferstehung* enjoyed, as Sibyl Cholmondeley had predicted, only a *succès d'estime*, but the performance of the Fauré *Requiem* was warmly praised. One critic called Boulanger's conducting "an essay in restraint, in delicate tones. . . . Mademoiselle Boulanger [is] a great interpreter of music."[84]

Winnaretta, Boulanger, and Marie-Blanche stayed in London to enjoy the city after the other musicians returned to France. On 25 November, Winnaretta joined Clive Bell, Virginia Woolf, writer Rosamond Lehmann, Lord Sackville, and Lord Berners for lunch. Woolf noted that Winnaretta, "a waxy solid handsome lady with kind eyes," seemed "out of things"[85]—not very surprising, given the whirlwind of events of the previous week. But the writer began to take Winnaretta's full measure at a luncheon at Claridge's the following day. "I was much impressed by Madame de Polignac," she wrote to Ethel Smyth, "[I] thought her reserved, distinguished, not an oyster to be opened with one flick of the knife."[86] To another friend Woolf confided, "I saw La Princesse de Polignac. . . . [W]hatever she was born she's grown into the image of a stately mellow old Tory; to look at [her] you'd never think she ravished half the virgins in Paris."[87]

Winnaretta's ostensible "mellowness" was shattered during her last few days in London by upsetting news of a general strike in Paris initiated by the Popular Front. Originally founded to stave off fascism in France, The Front had recently implemented a legislative program that included a forty-hour workweek, an increase in wages, and collective bargaining rights. But despite these victories, the Front continued to mount strikes to press for further reforms, instilling unease in a population that quaked at the word "communism" as vehemently as they quaked at the idea of "fascism." After reading the British press accounts about the violent after-effects of the strike, Winnaretta, according to Marie-Blanche, "trembled like a leaf, and was unable to collect herself." She declared that she would not return to France, that she wanted to stay in London. Only the reassurances of Nadia Boulanger that she would stay by her side calmed her down.[88]

The strike had been quelled by the time the group returned to Paris, and Winnaretta was immediately involved with an important new project, one that, in a certain sense, paid tribute to Edmond, for it involved an amalgamation of old music and modern technology. Doda Conrad was a recording artist for His Master's Voice (HMV, London). While in London, Jean de Polignac had approached Conrad with the idea of underwriting a recording of Marie-Blanche singing Monteverdi's *Lamento della ninfa,* and giving the copies to their friends for Christmas. When Conrad broached the subject with Georges Truc, the director of HMV, Truc conceived of an even more adventurous plan: to make an album of Monteverdi madgrials, sung by the Boulanger Ensemble, for commercial release on HMV's Red Label series. After hearing the Ensemble at the Cercle Interallié in December, Truc was sufficiently impressed to give Conrad an advance contract for the recording, on the condition that fifty thousand francs could be found to cover the risks of a financial deficit. Jean de Polignac had originally consented to contribute ten thousand francs for the original, smaller project. Conrad approached Winnaretta for a subvention towards the remainder. Her response was a reprise of the familiar refrain: she would contribute ten thousand francs, but only if other subscribers could be found.

Conrad succeeded in finding other *mécènes* to cover the rest of the expenses. The last, most difficult, step would be to convince Nadia Boulanger, who was vigorously opposed to the fixed nature of musical recording. "Music is, and should remain, fleeting."[89] Winnaretta advised Conrad to present the project to Boulanger as one of historical necessity. With Winnaretta's coaching, Conrad presented such a cogent argument that Boulanger finally consented to the recording project.[90] In February 1937, the first recordings of Monteverdi Madrigals were made in Paris's Columbia Studios, in a remote corner of the 14th *arrondissement.*[91] Winnaretta was right: when released later that year, the Monterverdi album proved an

instant success, and in the long run proved indeed to be of immense importance in arousing public interest in early music. It is worth noting that these
historic recordings have never left the catalogues: they are still in record
stores today.[92]

Winnaretta was not an auditor at the recording sessions: a new bout of
health problems laid her low during the first months of 1937. While vacationing in the south of France in early January, a *phlegmon* of the thumb,
similar to the affliction she had suffered three summers earlier, necessitated
an emergency operation in Monte Carlo. For the next two weeks she remained immobilized, unable to speak or write.[93] "Take the greatest precau-
tions, as long as necessary, I beg you," wrote Colette. "I'm wary of your
terrible impatience, and of the rash things that you are capable of doing in
the name of the piano and the organ. I hope that these deadly instruments
have not penetrated the Principality."[94] Illness continued to plague
Winnaretta upon her return to Paris; in the midst of her musical season,
she was confined to her room.[95] Winnaretta continued to plan soirees from
her sickbed. "I want to know about the program for Friday night [19 Feb-
ruary]," she wrote to Boulanger. "Maybe the Brahms Waltzes, the Fauré
Madrigal, among others? Have you received my check for 10,000 francs?"[96]

On her first day out of bed, Winnaretta rushed to Marie-Blanche's house
to listen to the rehearsals of the Brahms *Liebeslieder Waltzes*: she was interested in the extraordinary Romanian pianist Dinu Lipatti, Boulanger's
composition student and protégé since 1934 and her two-piano partner for
the Brahms.[97] The 19 February program was one of Boulanger's most imaginative assemblages of repertoire: three sonatas of Scarlatti, two sixteenth-
century *chansons*, and the popular *Madrigal* of Fauré. Françaix's Serenade
for Twelve Instruments, a work commissioned by Winnaretta in 1934, received its first performance that evening; this was followed by Poulenc's
Suite française and his song *A sa guitare*. The ebullient *Liebeslieder Waltzes*
by Brahms, with the vocal quartet accompanied by Boulanger and Lipatti,
closed the program.[98] Despite the imaginative programming, the evening
was not a success. Boulanger and the singers were exhausted, their nerves
on edge after a long and stressful week of recording sessions; the rehearsal
for the soiree took place only hours before the event. The avenue Henri-
Martin music room, its dark green walls adorned by Sert's lurid frescoes, was poorly lit, creating a gloomy atmosphere. Winnaretta insisted
on keeping the room at an uncomfortably low temperature; the musicians,
forewarned, were wearing "woolies" underneath their evening attire.
Boulanger, probably as a result of fatigue, conducted "ten times too slowly."
When Marie-Blanche looked out into the audience, she saw "faces that
were literally sleeping, despite the exasperated clicking of Madame de Ludre's
rosary."[99]

The next soiree, held in the *atelier* on 23 February, was a far more light-
hearted event. That evening began with a dinner given in honor of

Winnaretta's new friend and guest, the celebrated British novelist Rosamond Lehmann.[100] Lehmann, who lived rather simply in the English countryside, was dazzled by daily life at avenue Henri-Martin. "I have had the most fantastic time that ever was," she wrote to her brother. "Yesterday I lunched with Valéry. Today with Cocteau. I suppose I've met 500 people at the least. . . . Really, I don't know where I am, what with Mauriac, Morand, Maurois, Giraudoux, Jaloux, Gabriel Marcel etc. etc."[101] In addition to the literary stimulation, Lehmann loved the fact that music was such an integral part of her hostess's world. "In the intervals the Princess plays me Bach preludes and fugues on the organ. She is a grand old girl with a rocky masculine aquiline profile. . . . She gives ravishing concerts in her salon every week. There was one the night I arrived, another tonight. She is very witty, trenchant and autocratic and likes me very much!"[102] It was the beginning of a warm friendship between the two women.

Marie-Blanche, Hugues Cuénod, and Nadia Boulanger were slated to perform a recital after the dinner party. The Monteverdi recording sessions had left no time for preparation, and so the musicians opted to skip Winnaretta's dinner and rehearse at the last minute.[103] "It was divine to sight-read with Cuénod and Nadia," wrote Marie-Blanche in her diary, "but a bit worrisome [knowing] that [the music had] to be performed ten minutes later." However, fears abated when the trio arrived at rue Cortambert, where they found the festive gathering of writers enumerated by Lehmann gathered around the banquet table, joined by yet more writers: Colette, Albert Flament, and poet Louise de Vilmorin. Winnaretta hushed her guests, and the music began. "Very quickly, the atmosphere became pleasant, and I felt how charming it was, and how much less disconcerting, to sing before intelligent people, whom you might not get along with, but who would always have something [of substance] to say."[104]

Just before the after-dinner music, Marie-Laure de Noailles arrived to join the party. The striking Vicomtesse had in recent years earned two unfortunate nicknames: "la Vicomtesse rouge," because of her associations with the avant-garde and the political left, and "Marie-Laure d'Agoult," because of her liaison with the much younger Igor Markevitch.[105] Through her reckless behavior she had become the scourge of the aristocracy, having breached one of that class's cardinal rules: to avoid scandal at all cost. Noailles had flouted this convention in full measure, much to her own social detriment; public opinion was squarely behind her discreet, self-effacing, uncomplaining husband, Charles de Noailles. Marie-Blanche de Polignac's disapproval of the "Vicomtesse rouge," noted in her diary, drips with sarcasm. "[She made] a sensational entry in Communist attire: ten rows of pearls, diamond broaches, forty clips of gemstones in her hair around the feather of a circus horse,[106] lace gloves pinned with orchids." Noailles, whose novel, *Dix Ans sur terre,* had recently been released to small effect, was obliged to join a prestigious group of her literary colleagues. With a laugh that betrayed her nervousness in such company, she sat down next to Lehmann. Marie-Blanche was struck by the contrast between the two women: Noailles with her feathers and jewels, Lehmann very simply dressed, "like an overgrown girl."[107] There can be no question that, in inviting Noailles to this estimable gathering, Winnaretta was sending the signal that she intended to seat this writer among her colleagues. In using the full weight of her social standing, she showed her support for the unhappy woman, who, like her, had been determined to pursue a fulfilling personal life, whatever the risks and costs.

Winnaretta's compassion for Marie-Laure de Noailles put a permanent chill into her relations with Igor Markevitch. The composer, who, over the last several years, had relied on the admittedly mercurial Noailles for every kind of support—material, medical, emotional, and professional—had begun a revisionist campaign against his former lover; he portrayed himself as the prey of a wealthy, emotionally needy older woman who had used him "to fill her idle hours and sharpen her egocentricity by creating imaginary dramas of which she was the victim."[108] In 1936 Markevitch married Kyra Nijinsky, daughter of the celebrated dancer; by the following year he had become a father. Winnaretta expected her protégés to play by society's rules as well as be artistically brilliant; Markevitch had broken a cardinal rule of her circle by airing his dirty linen in public. This was surely on her mind when she read a letter from the composer, received the same day as the 23 February soiree.

> It has seemed to me over the past year that you have lost some of your good opinion of me, and I must tell you that I have really suffered for it. . . . You know how I have always gone out of my way to give you loyal proof of my gratitude and my affection, and how, with all my heart, I have tried to justify your trust by writing the *Hymnes* and *Partita.*
>
> You know no doubt that I have decided to orient my life in a new way and to make a career as a conductor. . . .[109] My engagements begin in the month of September. . . . I have to get through another six months, six months without work, six months in which I have to live, six months during which I would like to complete a work that I have in my head, a chamber music work that will be certainly far and away the best that I could imagine. . . . In order to work in complete tranquility, I would need five thousand francs per month until September, a sum that I promise, on my honor, to return to you in the course of next year. Something tells me that you . . . will never abandon someone who has attempted to never betray the trust that you placed in me.[110]

Markevitch offered to dedicate his next work to her as a testimony of gratitude. But Winnaretta would have none of it. Supporting an entire family for eight months exceeded even her most expansive definition of *mécénat.*

Moreover, the impudence of Markevitch's attempt to impose a commission project on her was more than she could tolerate. She responded immediately.

> My dear Igor,
>
> . . . I hasten to respond to [your letter] with great candor. You have never consulted me about your plans, so I therefore feel not the least responsibility as far as the consequences of your decisions. My admiration for your musical genius is still very great, as you know, but I have not always approved of your attitude towards [our] mutual friends, and you are not mistaken in thinking that my feelings of friendship are less keen than before. . . .
>
> You have made me a proposal that I cannot accept. This year I have asked several musicians to write some works for me, and I just gave a series of concerts that has, for the moment, exhausted my musical budget. I wouldn't dream of your dedicating your next masterwork to me— given the current conditions I couldn't accept the honor of a dedication. Permit me to send to your newborn son a small baptismal gift that you will choose for me, in accepting the enclosed check for 5000 francs. Believe in all my admiration and my sincere best wishes.[111]

It is not clear to whom Winnaretta was referring when she wrote that "several musicians" were writing music for her, but her musical budget was certainly not quite exhausted. On 12 March 1937 she hosted a grand concert with full orchestra and concerto soloists.[112] The program included two works that she had commissioned, Germaine Tailleferre's 1932 *Overture,* and Fauré's Suite from *Pelléas and Mélisande,* Op. 80, as well as Henri Sauguet's Piano Concerto, performed by Clara Haskil, and Tailleferre's Violin Concerto, played by the work's dedicatee, violinist Yvonne Astruc.[113] As moving as this concert was, Nadia Boulanger's absence was sorely felt: the conductor was in the United States, the first of many trips there, where she was engaged in a full schedule of teaching and lectures; she also had arranged for some radio broadcasts, which would feature repertoire from the Polignac salon.[114] On her side of the Atlantic, Winnaretta was planning a second London performance for Boulanger in November. This time the patron would not rely on the Mayers: she was making all the arrangements herself.

With her "music director" in America, Winnaretta's musical salon activities that spring seem to have slowed, if not stopped altogether. Boulanger's return to Paris on 11 May did not make her any more available to her patron. The musician plunged immediately into her own very full, very public spring season, which included a live broadcast for French Radio from the Schola Cantorum,[115] a performance at the Cercle Interallié, and a four-concert series at the Théâtre des Champs-Élysées.[116] During this same period the Monteverdi album was released, and recording sessions for a second project, an album pairing Brahms's *Liebeslieder Waltzes* with J. S. Bach's Cantata 4, were already underway.[117]

Winnaretta found herself obliged to relinquish her propietary hold, real or imagined, on Nadia Boulanger. However she may have felt about her protégée's new public standing and success—a success in which she played an integral role—she seems to have kept her distance from Boulanger's activities. She traveled all summer; upon her arrival in Venice in August, she kept the palazzo filled with guests. Stravinsky came in August for concerts of his music during the city's annual music festival.[118] September brought visits from Pata and Pierre de Monaco. Pierre introduced Winnaretta to a young British couple that he saw often in London: Anthony Chaplin, an amateur composer and student of Boulanger, and his beautiful wife Alvilde.[119] Winnaretta also welcomed *Le Figaro*'s Gérard Baüer,[120] who chronicled a particularly amusing example of his hostess's dry sense of humor. At a dinner party, one of the Italian guests in attendance spent the evening lamenting the high taxes imposed upon the Italian citizenry. These complaints were poured out in a voluble stream of adjectives and superlatives, punctuated by expressive hand movements; they increased as the guest warmed to his subject: the tax burden was unbearable, excessive, *pesantissimo, esageratissimo.* "The government has put taxes on everything," he said, "I wonder what there is left to tax?" "And calmly" (in Baüer's words), "with her voice of a Roman emperor," the Princesse answered, "Adjectives."[121]

There was constant music-making during those months. Olga Rudge's daughter Mary could always tell when her mother was going to play at the Palazzo Polignac because of "her intensive practicing beforehand and the elegance of her clothes."[122] And, indeed, Rudge, now the de facto "house violinist," came regularly to play Mozart and Beethoven sonatas with Winnaretta. Sometimes the two women were joined by Yvonne de Casa Fuerte (who still played violin as an amateur) for readings of the two-violin concertos of J. S. Bach and Antonio Vivaldi—"also very beautiful," Winnaretta wrote to Boulanger of this latter, "if something *could* be beautiful compared to Bach."[123] In fact, that summer, Winnaretta's soirees featured a good deal of Vivaldi's music. Earlier that year, Olga Rudge had discovered a large number of manuscripts of violin concertos by Antonio Vivaldi in a library in Dresden, Germany. Rudge and Pound became interested in making these scores available to scholars and students. By the time Winnaretta arrived in Venice, the couple was deeply involved in the process of assembling a catalogue of the works.[124] The Polignac salon was the setting for the first performances in perhaps two hundred years of many of the Vivaldi scores discovered by Rudge. Stravinsky was the volunteer pageturner for the violinist, who performed from the scores that she had laboriously and lovingly transcribed by hand.[125]

On 1 October, on his thirty-fourth birthday, Vladimir Horowitz ended a two-and-a-half year withdrawal from concert life to play a private concert at the Venetian home of his sister-in-law, Wally Castelbarco. Among the works on the program was one of his signature pieces, the Schumann *Fantasy*. Afterwards, Winnaretta wrote to Wally, "I've heard some great musicians in the course of my long life, but never, I think, a performance as *sublime* as Horowitz's. He is more marvelous than ever; these long sad months have given to his genius an almost superhuman intensity and depth. I will remember this revelation forever."[126]

Preparations for the London trip occupied most of the month of October. Three broadcasts on the BBC were arranged;[127] a performance in Cambridge was planned for the Ensemble on 7 November. Winnaretta also hoped to host a private salon performance in a "borrowed" music room on 8 November; her new friend Alvilde Chaplin undertook many of the logistical arrangements for this soiree. The Queen's Hall concert would, unquestionably, be the major event of the week; its program was to include a repeat of the Fauré *Requiem*, as well as Monteverdi's *Lamento della Ninfa*, and excerpts from Rameau's *Dardanus*, a work that Winnaretta and Edmond had reintroduced into French cultural life in 1895. This time Boulanger would not conduct a mere freelance ensemble: her patron had hired the Royal Philharmonic Orchestra for the occasion. Indeed, Winnaretta had formulated all of the London events with the odd mixture of frugality and generosity that governed so many of her actions. She asked Boulanger to organize the salon concert on a narrow budget of three thousand francs, but added in the same letter that she hoped the musician would "agree to be my 'guest' like last year, whether at Claridge's or in a hotel at Piccadilly (without music)." The letter concluded with the wistful hope that she would see Boulanger a little more often in Paris.[128] It was a wish left unfulfilled: the musician was preoccupied with rehearsals, the copying of scores, and other pre-departure chores. Winnaretta was only able to see her busy friend when she "presided" (as honorary president) over the Ensemble's performance at the Cercle Interallié,[129] two days before the departure for England. In London, Boulanger was immediately surrounded by the press when she arrived at the train station on 1 November. This concert would break new ground—the first time that a woman had ever conducted a major orchestra in England. Many newspapers carried long interviews and photographs of the Frenchwoman.[130]

With Boulanger much occupied, Winnaretta spent time with old friends: Ronald Storrs, Ethel Smyth, Gerald Berners, and the Kenneth Clarks. She also began to see a good deal of Prince Pierre's friends, the Chaplins. Marie-Blanche described the young couple as "very nice, unfortunately no longer happy together, exuding sadness." Indeed, Anthony Chaplin[131] was courteous, but seemed largely indifferent to other people. He actually preferred animals: in addition to being an amateur composer and harpsichordist, he was also a zoologist.[132] Winnaretta had to mask her terror every time she entered his library: it was there that Anthony kept a boa constrictor, which lay curled behind the books, just at the height of Winnaretta's ears.[133] Alvilde Chaplin was grateful for the older woman's company. Like Winnaretta, her childhood had been shaped by a powerful and charismatic father, Colonel Tom Bridges, who, in addition to his military training, possessed a broad literary culture. When Bridges was named governor of South Australia, his wife remained behind in England; Alvilde, in her teenaged years, was required to serve as hostess for her father's official functions. Pretty, intelligent, and vivacious, she arrived at marriageable age with a formidable set of social skills. However, her marriage to Chaplin, arranged by her father, was an unfortunate one. Now twenty-eight, Alvilde had few outlets for her intelligence and drive. She surely looked up to Winnaretta as a woman who had been able to accomplish what she could not. Even though both women were naturally autocratic, this did not impede the blossoming of their friendship: Alvilde's intense admiration for Winnaretta was unmistakable.[134]

The week's activities began and continued at a dizzying pace. The BBC broadcasts were organized as a survey of French opera, featuring arias and choruses ranging from Grétry and Rameau to Berlioz, Gounod, and Chabrier. Marie-Blanche described being accompanied by the BBC Orchestra as the "greatest musical excitement" of her life.[135] The Boulanger Ensemble also performed at a private soiree, organized by Winnaretta and held at the home of Lady Ravensdale. In between rehearsals and broadcasts, Winnaretta took care to see that the group was entertained in grand style. On 3 November the entire entourage—musicians, family, friends—attended a performance of Beethoven's Ninth Symphony at Queen's Hall, conducted by Toscanini; afterwards they were all invited to dine with the maestro at the home of the Marchioness Sybil Cholmondeley. Doda Conrad was so awestruck to be at the same table as Toscanini that he could barely eat. Toscanini never noticed: all his attention was directed towards Richard Wagner's granddaughter, seated beside him.[136] The crowning event of the week was no less thrilling. The Queen's Hall concert the following evening was a sold-out affair, and an enormous success with both the audience and the critics.[137]

Thanks to the London concerts, underwritten by Winnaretta, Nadia Boulanger achieved legitimacy as an international orchestral conductor. Within months she was engaged to perform with major orchestras in the United States, and set sail, accompanied by the Ensemble, in late January 1938. Winnaretta, on the other hand, despite the glory her patronage had brought to the public musical sphere, and to her personally, wanted nothing more than to return to her private music room and the intimate soirees held for her family and friends. And Boulanger, even with the prospects of an international career looming before her, remained actively involved in the life of the Polignac salon. In the months prior to her departure for the United States she reassumed her role as advocate for one of her composition students, Jean Françaix. Three years earlier, Winnaretta had asked Françaix to write a work for organ, either a concerto with chamber orchestra or a solo suite; she had offered him twelve thousand francs for the work.[138] The young composer had accepted the commission, but the project had stalled. Françaix's style was elegant, dry, clear, polished; perhaps his ebullient nature resisted the idea of writing for so "serious" an instrument. In 1937 he began work on a chamber opera based on Alain-René Lesage's story, *Le Diable boîteux* (The Limping Devil), a tale of magic and immortality. The piece, for tenor, bass, and small orchestra, was written with the voices of tenor Hugues Cuénod and bass Doda Conrad in mind. Newly married and underemployed, Françaix wrote to Boulanger in October 1937, asking if she thought that Winnaretta would be willing to substitute the new opera for the abandoned organ work. He thought it would be "marvelous to premiere the *Diable* at rue Cortambert, with those good Parisian musicians."[139] Boulanger proposed the idea to Winnaretta, who agreed to the plan. Two weeks later, Françaix wrote to his teacher, "I've finished *Le Diable boîteux,* which I dedicate to a woman, although she is neither a devil, nor limping!"[140]

Winnaretta planned a January 1938 soiree in the *atelier* to precede Boulanger's departure; the program would consist of first performances of Françaix's chamber opera and Poulenc's long-awaited Organ Concerto. But Winnaretta fell ill after her return from London, and considered postponing the soiree until the following June, after Boulanger's return from the United States.[141] Françaix was going on the American tour with the Ensemble. Anticipating the January presentation of *Le Diable boîteux* (which would fulfill his contractual obligation of a first performance in Winnaretta's *atelier*), he hoped that his opera could then be introduced in the United States. Now it seemed that his hopes were to be dashed. "The delay of *Le Diable* is . . . annoying," he wrote to Boulanger, "because in America, [the performance] would have been so good for my propaganda! Is there really nothing, nothing that can be done?"[142] Boulanger kept a close watch on the state of Winnaretta's health, but time was growing short. Finally, it became clear that the soiree could not take place in January, and it was rescheduled for June 1938.

Boulanger and her Ensemble set sail in January. In Boulanger's absence, Winnaretta found alternate ways to keep occupied with *mécénat*. When Henri Sauguet could not find a publisher for the score of his new opera, *La Chartreuse de Parme,* he enlisted private "subscribers" to underwrite the costs of a private printing. Winnaretta was among the first to help to underwrite the publication.[143] She maintained a lively correspondence with Ezra Pound, who, with Olga Rudge, was consumed with the cataloguing and microfilming of the Vivaldi violin concertos. There is some indication that Winnaretta offered a small subvention towards the realization of the project.[144] She kept involved with the activities of the Fondation Singer-Polignac, which was supporting an impressive number of scientific projects ranging from oceanographic research (organized by scientists using as their base a ship called the *Winnaretta Singer*) to conferences on hormones, from the creation of scholarships for students interested in doing scientific research under the auspices of the Institut Pasteur to the restoration of the Hagia Sophia in Istanbul.[145]

Winnaretta also began to set her house in order, as it were. She wrote her will, and started to give away some treasured objects. One morning, her great-nephew, Élie Decazes, who had married the previous November, received a phone call from his godmother: she had a belated wedding present for him and his bride; could he stop by rue Cortambert to pick it up? When Decazes arrived, he found Winnaretta waiting at the door with the life-size portrait of her painted by John Singer Sargent in 1889. She put the canvas into his arms, leaving him thoroughly perplexed as to how to get the enormous piece home.[146]

That winter Winnaretta began an affair with Alvilde Chaplin. Like her father Isaac Singer, Winnaretta's powerful charisma did not diminish with age; even young beautiful women like Alvilde still fell in love with her. As with Olga Meyer, the relationship involved numerous crossings between Paris and London. As with Violet Trefusis, the husband in question, Anthony Chaplin, was tolerant, even encouraging, of the affair: he had been neglectful of Alvilde since the early days of their marriage, and by 1938 had taken up with a French mistress. To avoid the appearance of scandal, Winnaretta used the modus operandi that had worked successfully with the Trefusises: when she traveled with Alvilde, Anthony was often invited to come with them. When Anthony was not available, Winnaretta's family acted as a social shield. In April the two women spent five days together in Amsterdam, in the company of a pack of Polignacs, plus Ronald Storrs. En masse, they roamed the city and visited its museums.[147]

On Sunday afternoon, 10 April, the entire group attended the Concertgebouw Orchestra's annual performance of J. S. Bach's *St. Matthew Passion*, conducted by Willem Mengelberg.[148] After the concert, Mengelberg, hearing that Winnaretta and her entourage were staying in the same hotel as he, spent the evening with them. Still "lively and ardent," even after the intensity of the Bach concert, he recounted the thrill of having been able to study the scores of the Beethoven symphonies annotated in Beethoven's own hand. The conversation drifted into a discussion of Mengelberg's theories of phrasing, which seemed to echo the ideas of line and structure so often expressed by Nadia Boulanger.[149] Winnaretta's thoughts turned towards her absent friend. Boulanger had been keeping her apprised of the Ensemble's musical activities far away in her native America. "What travels, what fatigues, what enthusiasms!" Winnaretta wrote. "But don't fall too deeply in love with this country that tears you away from those who love you and have such great need of you here. . . . Don't forget Poulenc's new work, and that of Jean Françaix, and the *atelier,* and me, who misses you so much."[150] Despite Boulanger's absence, Winnaretta began organizing spring musicales. On 17 May, Dinu Lipatti and a Romanian cellist performed at the Cercle Interallié in a program of Chopin, Poulenc, Beethoven, and Fauré. That same night Winnaretta hosted a soiree in the *atelier* in honor of the Kenneth Clarks, featuring the Budapest String Quartet playing Mozart's Quartet in B flat, K. 458 ("The Hunt").[151]

Anticipating the grand event of her season, the first performances of the Françaix and Poulenc commissions, Winnaretta contacted Francis Poulenc to inquire about the organ concerto. For the last two years, "Poupoule" had been telling his friends and colleagues that the work was "almost finished," but, in fact, its completion was achieved slowly and painfully. To Marie-Blanche, he had written on 30 April 1936, "The concerto is nearing conclusion. It has given me many problems, but I think, such as it is, it is good and will please you. This is not the amusing Poulenc of the Concerto for Two Pianos, but rather a Poulenc on his way to the cloister, very 15th-century, if you will."[152] Several months later, he wrote her that the work had taken him in a "very new direction"[153]—an astonishing echo of the words expressed by Carriès, Satie, Falla, and other artists whose work, commissioned by Winnaretta, had taken an unexpected and exciting creative turn. But at this point, Winnaretta was not interested in knowing how her commission had inspired Poulenc—she just wanted the piece to be completed. She wrote to Poulenc on 24 May 1938, "I would like to think that the beautiful work that you are writing for me is *finally* finished, and I just want to ask you about the composition of the orchestra, to see if it would be possible to have it performed on 20 June, at the same time as Jean Francaix's work."[154] Winnaretta received a prompt response from the composer, but not the one she had hoped for.

Dear Princesse,
Yes you are *finally* going to have your concerto, this word *finally* summing up for me the joy of having obeyed my conscience, and even more, of having obeyed my artistic conscience, for the work now is really almost done—never, since I've been writing music have I had so much trouble finding my means of expression. . . . Now, after so many other indulgences, I'm going to make one more appeal to your goodness—I fervently ask you not to give the [premiere of] the concerto on 20 June, for the numerous reasons that I'm going to spell out.
First, there will barely be time to copy out the orchestral parts. Then, and this is *capital,* there will certainly be some details of changes in the organ part to be worked out with Nadia, in addition to the *delicate* and *long* work on the registrations, which will perhaps lead me to make

changes in the orchestration. All that cannot practically be done between the 13th and the 20th. . . . I also have to find an organist and have him rehearse—in addition, this Concerto [wouldn't suit] a brilliant June soiree; I see, in saying that, Daisy's dress, Misia's pout etc.

It would be for me a great joy if, at the end of June, you would be willing to assemble the *few* string instruments that I would need one afternoon in your *atelier,* and then we would read through the work for you alone with Nadia, stopping and starting, etc. . . . then we could play it publicly in the fall. . . . I'm *counting* essentially on this private reading session, which will be for me the proof of my success or my error. . . .

Dear Princesse, you see that, once again, my fate is in your hands. . . .

Francis[155]

Winnaretta (who had renounced the role of organ soloist) acceded to Poulenc's request, writing, "We will wait for Nadia's return for the reading that you suggest."[156] She wrote to Jean Françaix to inform him that, once again, the premiere of *Le Diable boîteux* would have to be postponed until a "later date." Françaix's bad news did not end there. A Cercle Interallié concert conducted by Boulanger was to take place on 21 June, and Françaix had hoped that, with his obligation for a first performance in the salon fulfilled, his work could be also included in the Cercle's program. But Winnaretta clung to her conventions: "I prefer that *Le Diable boîteux* not be played at the Cercle Intérallié before being heard at my house," she informed her hapless young protégé. Françaix had convinced his German representative from Schott Editions to make a special trip to Paris for the performance; now that, too, would have to be cancelled. "Nothing is going as it should!" wrote Françaix to Boulanger. "This news is rather disagreeable, especially since I've been listening to Poulenc talk about the composition of his work for two years. . . . There's nothing left to do but play Chopin's *Funeral March* while awaiting better times!"[157]

Françaix's sentiments, unbeknownst to him, echoed Winnaretta's very own: nothing was going as it should! All her life, she had wanted nothing but to use her fortune to bring music and art into the world. All that she had asked in exchange was that "her" artists fulfill their written contracts and deliver their works on time. Now here she was, at the age of seventy-three, still having to deal with delays, complications, abrogated commitments, personality clashes, and jealousies. And the person who was supposed to attend to all of that, to smooth over the problems, a woman whom she loved and supported and relied on, was off in America! All of the players in this drama, it seemed (Poulenc, Françaix, and Winnaretta), were paralyzed by Nadia's absence. Winnaretta's mood turned foul. Marie-Blanche noticed that her aunt was out of sorts when she and Jean went to Jouy for lunch on a Sunday afternoon in June. "A hen party: Alvilde Chaplin, Pata, and Clara Haskil. Strange atmosphere when we arrived: Tante Winnie was clearly in a bad mood. When Pata smothered poor Clara with her careful solicitudes, 'some more of these marvelous potatoes? a little of this terrific cider?' Tante Winnie, between two clenched jaws, shot out, 'Please, Pata, leave Clara alone. It's a custom of the household: she'll eat when she's hungry.'" The moment the tense luncheon concluded, Marie-Blanche and Haskil lunged for the piano, evading the hostess's stony gaze by sinking into the ecstasies of the Schubert F-Minor *Fantasy*.[158]

But by the next day Winnaretta's good humor had returned. She brought Marie-Blanche with her to the dress rehearsal of a Sérénade concert, featuring the Paris premiere of Stravinsky's new *Dumbarton Oaks Concerto* for fifteen instruments. The work had been written for Winnaretta's American counterparts in artistic *mécénat*, Robert and Mildred Woods Bliss.[159] Boulanger, who had helped negotiate the commission for Stravinsky, had conducted the world premiere in the Blisses' music room outside Washington, D.C. one month earlier. Stravinsky would be conducting his own work for the Sérénade performance.[160] The Polignac women were delighted when the composer came up to them and gave them a score to follow; they were "dazzled, moved, transported" by this new work, which Marie-Blanche described as "at once classic and free . . . the blossoming of everything that he's tried for the last ten years."[161]

The following weekend Stravinsky visited Winnaretta's country home in Jouy. Among the other guests who had gathered for a Sunday afternoon of music-making by Lipatti and Haskil were poet Louise de Vilmorin and her new husband, Hungarian count Paul (Pali) Palffy, and Alvilde and Anthony Chaplin. Anthony Chaplin, still pursuing his avocation of zoology, had brought along a guest as well: a rare bird from the Andes, worth millions of dollars.[162] Two evenings later, 14 June, Winnaretta hosted a soiree in the Paris *atelier,* an all-Schubert program, organized by a newly formed "Schubert Society," founded by Doda Conrad, and on whose Board of Directors Winnaretta served.[163] The concert included the two piano trios, Opp. 99 and 100, a work for solo woman's voice accompanied by chorus, with Marya Freund as soloist, and a group of *Lieder* sung by Doda Conrad.[164] It is only thanks to Marie-Blanche that the names of the mother-and-son vocal soloists, Freund and Conrad, have been passed down to posterity in connection with this program: the by-laws of the Society stipulated that none of the names of the performers ever appear on the printed programs of any of the concerts, "leaving the place of honor to Schubert alone."[165]

Nadia Boulanger had returned to Paris after her trans-Atlantic voyage the day before the soiree. It must have been *very* shortly after her feet had alighted on French soil that she let Winnaretta know, in a way that brooked no opposition, that there could be no second postponement of *Le Diable boîteux*. Thus, on 30 June 1938 (only ten days after the originally rescheduled date), Françaix's sparkling chamber opera was heard twice—at the beginning and the end of the program—in Winnaretta's music room, with Cuénod and Conrad as soloists, the ensemble of fourteen instruments conducted by Nadia Boulanger.[166] The performance was a great success. Françaix had multiple reasons to be jubilant: with the salon premiere behind him, he was now able to secure (with Winnaretta's permission) performances in other venues, including one conducted by Boulanger at her Fontainebleau festival, a highly publicized BBC broadcast in November,[167] and a December performance directed by Charles Munch under the auspices of La Sérénade.[168] More good news followed: Françaix's representative from Schott, in attendance at the salon performance, was so impressed with the work that he agreed on the spot to have it published.[169]

Poulenc, on the other hand, continued to fret about his own work. After consulting with Boulanger on the technical aspects and the registrations of the Organ Concerto, he found it necessary to rewrite significant portions of the piece. Fortunately, he been invited by Jean and Marie-Blanche to spend ten days with them at Kerbastic. In the quiet and calm of Brittany, Poulenc finally completed the concerto at the end of July 1938—almost four years to the day after first discussing the commission with Winnaretta.[170] He came to Winnaretta's *atelier* to play the work for her on 4 August. She seemed happy with the piece, but her physical state concerned the composer, who wrote to Marie-Blanche, "*Just between the two of us*, I didn't find her in very good health that evening. She had a mild dizzy spell leaving the Chaplins' house, where we had dined. After dinner (at avenue Henri-Martin, where I was alone with her), I had been singing Nadia's praises, and she is—you were right—a little jealous, especially because she hadn't seen her in several days, [while] Solange [d'Ayen] had had her to lunch."[171]

Winnaretta's physical and emotional malaises were playing out against the terrible atmosphere of insecurity that permeated Europe. Everyone expected war, or at least hoped that, in a best-case scenario, hostilities could be staved off until the month of October—until after vacation. In that spirit, Winnaretta, the Chaplins, and nine of Winnaretta's relatives (the youngest of whom was fifteen-year-old Prince Rainier of Monaco) left Venice on 17 August for a two-week cruise to Greece. Winnaretta's enthusiasm for the land of antiquity was boundless: each time the group arrived in a new place, she would recount with passion the history and mythology associated with its temples and ruins. After sailing around the islands, the group stopped in Athens, where Winnaretta visited George Oekonomos, the archeologist in charge of the dig in Vari that she had underwritten.[172] The dig had been more successful than anticipated, revealing an intact seventh-century B.C.E. necropolis, containing a chariot with bizarre-looking death figures carved into its roof.[173] The trip brought disappointments, too, however. Age had begun to slow Winnaretta's pace. Although initially she bravely climbed up and down, in and out of ruins and museums, by the end of the two weeks she was obliged to lean on someone's arm for support when she walked. She acknowleged with chagrin that she was too tired to climb up to the Acropolis with the rest of the group.[174] But, as she wrote Boulanger, "I did my best and *es is genug* [that's enough]."[175] She had one compensation upon returning to Venice: she discovered with delight that Poulenc was there—with the completed manuscript of the Organ Concerto in hand, ready to be delivered to its dedicatee.[176]

Back in Paris, Winnaretta reaped the fruits of some musical matchmaking undertaken earlier that year. During the spring recording of Brahms's *Liebeslieder Waltzes,* she had had the happy idea of bringing Dinu Lipatti together with his Romanian compatriot Clara Haskil. The two pianists were ideally suited in both musical and personal temperament. In October 1938, at Winnaretta's first soiree of the season, they performed Mozart's Concerto for Two Pianos, K. 365, accompanied by an orchestra conducted by Boulanger.[177] Lipatti wrote his own cadenzas for the concerto, which he dedicated to Haskil. This performance was only the first of many collaborations by these two gifted pianists. Another of Winnaretta's "matchmaking" maneuvers proved equally fruitful. For the 30 June concert two months earlier, Winnaretta had insisted that, between the two performances of *Le Diable boîteux,* Doda Conrad sing the bass aria from the Bach cantata *Ich habe genug.* Unbeknownst to Conrad, he was being "auditioned" for an important engagement: a duo partnership with the celebrated Hungarian pianist Lili Kraus. That spring, Winnaretta had passed by Kraus's door as she was practicing at the Beaurivage hotel in Switzerland. Fascinated by the beautiful music emitting from the room, she knocked on the door and introduced herself. Winnaretta invited the pianist and her husband to dinner, during which the subject turned to the great *Lieder* cycles. Winnaretta, having heard Conrad's recent traversals of this repertoire in concerts and broadcasts, thought of pairing the bass and the pianist. Kraus and her husband-manager came to the 30 June soiree and heard Conrad sing the Bach. By the end of the evening, a concert tour of Holland was planned for the two musicians.[178]

For unknown reasons, Winnaretta did not accompany the Nadia Boulanger Ensemble to England for their third round of concerts and broadcasts in early November 1938. Perhaps she felt that she simply was not needed, perhaps after the Greek cruise she had lost her taste for looking after a large group of people in complicated circumstances.[179] Many of Winnaretta's friends volunteered to see to the needs of Boulanger and her group: Boulanger stayed with Lord Berners; Sybil Cholmondeley hosted a dinner for the group, attended by Arthur Rubinstein; *Art and Travel* magazine sponsored a soiree in Lady Londonderry's music room; another soiree was hosted by the Kenneth Clarks. The BBC broadcasts went flawlessly; the Queen's Hall concert was sold out; the press was ecstatic about the "woman conductor."

Winnaretta followed Gerald Berners's glowing reports of Boulanger's successes with pride; she was eager to see her friend upon her arrival in France. But Boulanger did not call; she sent only a terse note, apparently informing Winnaretta that she did not want to see her, because her "attitude had changed." Winnaretta was stupefied. "To my knowledge my attitude is exactly what it has always been, [one] inspired always by the best feelings of admiration and friendship. . . . If I never see you, is that my fault? It is you who are (fortunately) always busy, and not I. I am ineloquent, devoid of trickery, absolutely innocent of all changes of attitude. . . . I remain more and more amazed by you, and my tender friendship is immeasurable."[180] The strained relationship between the two women permeated the arrangements for the premiere of the Poulenc Organ Concerto, scheduled for 16 December. Boulanger did not bother to alert Winnaretta to the preparations made for rehearsals in the *atelier,* and the latter, still mystified and wounded by the unexplained rift in their relations, was reduced to begging Poulenc for details.[181] (Conrad later claimed that a contretemps between Boulanger and Winnaretta was caused by the latter's instigation of the Kraus-Conrad meeting.)[182]

The long-awaited premiere of Poulenc's Concerto for Organ and String Orchestra was the grand finale of a program that included a suite of Purcell songs (arranged by Boulanger for string ensemble), a trio sonata by J. S. Bach, and two sets of Poulenc's songs (including the *Trois Poèmes de Louise Vilmorin*), sung by their dedicatee, Marie-Blanche de Polignac.[183] The concerto was given a brilliant performance by organist Maurice Duruflé and an orchestra conducted by Boulanger. Poulenc himself considered this premiere in the Polignac salon to surpass the first public performance, given six months later by Marcel Dupré under the baton of Roger Désormière;[184] he would write to Boulanger, who was in America and unavailable to conduct, "How I mourned [your absence] (in every sense of the word) for the premiere of the Concerto. Désormière was perfectly competent, but you also had the heart and the lyricism, and God knows that my music needs it."[185] Winnaretta has left no detailed account of her own impressions of this strange and magnificent work, but its echoes of baroque masters, especially Buxtehude, as well as its complex and changing moods—austere, episodic, dark, exploratory—surely touched her.

Paris became oppressive for Winnaretta. She attended a performance of *Cyrano de Bergerac* at the Comédie Française with Alvilde Chaplin, only to find herself flanked on one side by Violet Trefusis and on the other by her niece Daisy Fellowes, with whom she had fallen out.[186] Nadia Boulanger was soon leaving for six months in the United States, and their misunderstanding had not been resolved. The political atmosphere was intensely pessimistic, as the rants of Mussolini joined those of Hitler. Winnaretta spent the latter half of January 1939 in England with Alvilde. She became acquainted with the music of the Benjamin Britten, including the young composer's *Variations on a Theme of Frank Bridge*.[187] She also contacted Virginia Woolf. The two women had seen each other on occasion since their first meeting; after one encounter, Woolf had described Winnaretta in her diary as "a perfectly stuffed cold fowl."[188] Yet something about the Princesse clearly fascinated the writer, who invited her to her home.

On 29 January 1939, on a gray Friday afternoon when Barcelona fell to Franco and Hitler addressed the German masses, Winnaretta climbed the many flights of stairs to take tea in Virginia Woolf's apartment. The long ascent exhausted her; she couldn't catch her breath, and, once arrived, had to take two aspirin. But then the two women sat by the fire and talked about literature and music. "[She] was very gracious," Woolf wrote to Ethel Smyth, "something like an old manor house with the sun in its window."[189] The writer was curious to learn of Winnaretta's and Edmond's friendship with Proust, and she was rewarded with stories about how Proust had taken notes about their lives, which Winnaretta, at his request, used to correct.[190] Winnaretta also reminisced about the birthday party for which she had requested a performance of Beethoven's C-sharp Minor String Quartet. By this point Woolf was fascinated by everything Winnaretta had to say, and asked if she wouldn't be willing to write down her recollections. A short time later, Winnaretta sent Woolf a present, a recording of two Beethoven String Quartets, Opp. 130 and 131. Woolf's responding letter of thanks received this reply:

Dear Mrs Woolf,
(When will you allow me to call you Virginia, and when will you call me Winnaretta?)
It wasn't the wonderful Cavatina, but the beginning of the XIVth quartet, Opus 131, that I longed to hear on my 13th birthday.[191] I must have also sent you that record, with the Opus 130. Anyhow here are the opening bars—they have always been one of the greatest comforts of my life, together with the Prelude of the 23rd fugue in Bach's *48*. Alas! I can't write myself, but I will try to dictate all I can remember about my 13th birthday, as you are good enough to care what happened on that particular birthday—which touches me deeply.
Here is a letter from Proust found in an odd corner, and it will show you how badly we got on, though I owe him great gratitude for all the beautiful pages of the Pléiade and Baudelaire's *Poemes as prose* that he made me read. I admired him, but could not like him. If it isn't too much trouble, will you ask your secretary to send me back Proust's letter some day? I shall never forget that hour with you by the fire—it is locked away in my heart forever.
Yrs gratefully and affectionately
Winnaretta (de Polignac)[192]

In March, Anthony and Alvilde Chaplin followed Winnaretta back to Paris. As a trio they attended dinners and musical events (the dress rehearsal of Henri Sauguet's new opera, *La Chartreuse de Parme*,[193] a Liszt recital by Clifford Curzon[194]). Clara Haskil continued to provide afternoon music for Winnaretta's teatime visitors.[195] In April, Nadia Boulanger, still in America, finally sent a sign of détente: pictures of her deceased mother and sister.[196] Winnaretta fell ill in May; Marie-Blanche arrived at rue Cortambert one evening late in the month to hear a performance by Poulenc and his longtime musical partner, baritone Pierre Bernac, only to discover that her aunt was not even present at her own gathering.[197] When Marie-Blanche came to visit some days later, she found Winnaretta convalescing in the little green salon next to her bedroom, decorated with her three beautiful Monet paintings; she was wrapped in blankets, ensconced in an armchair next to the little lemonwood side table that Edmond had had made for her birthday thirty years earlier.[198]

The Bernac-Poulenc soirée was repeated two nights later, as a paying charity event. The *atelier* was incapable of holding the throngs of people who sought admission to the heretofore inacessible Polignac salon. An article the next day in the newspaper *L'Ordre* mocked both Winnaretta and her guests.

> The High Priestess [of the] Music-Lovers is called Princesse Edmond, and it's at her house that the faithful assemble regularly to worship a new polyphonic discovery and to bow down before a work of Sauguet or Markevitch. These little [musical] ceremonies are usually . . . surrounded by the most complete, the most absolute of mysteries. . . . That is why it's easy to imagine the joy of all the music- lovers when they learned that for the modest sum of 50 francs they had the right to penetrate this paradise, forbidden to common mortals, to hear Messieurs Pierre Bernac and Francis Poulenc. . . . [N]ever have the lovers of counterpoint and fugue felt such a marvelous and paradisiacal pleasure.[199]

In June Alvilde left her husband and came to live at avenue Henri-Martin with Winnaretta. Marie-Blanche had some reservations about her aunt's new attachment. "Looking at her radiant happiness, one is frightened despite oneself. I'm afraid that she would not be able to bear any more break-ups."[200] A musical soiree was planned for 22 June, and Winnaretta was of course present for the rehearsals. But her mind was not on the music. Marie-Blanche noted, "Tante Winnie's presence saddens me a little now. She is so obsessed by her love affair (a happy love, thank God), that no one can communicate with her anymore: she is absent."[201]

The Paris season had begun, much muted, and, with it, Winnaretta's soirees. The first gathering featured chamber music and vocal repertoire for solo voice and chorus. Pierre Bernac sang *mélodies* by Poulenc, accompanied by the composer; Marie-Blanche followed with a group of songs by Schubert, Caplet, and Roussel. Yvonne Gouverné's chorus performed choral works by Schumann, Poulenc, and Edmond de Polignac. Winnaretta accompanied her husband's *Choeur d'Esther* on the piano; the audience, mostly family members, was moved by the sight of their Tante Winnie, still so devoted to Edmond's memory.[202] The second soiree, a grand affair, took place on 3 July, timed to coincide with Nadia Boulanger's return to France after an absence of six months. "It would be *marvelous* if you could come! even late," Winnaretta wrote in anticipation of her friend's arrival, "I hope that you will make an effort to fill us with joy." [203] Whether Boulanger came is not known.

As with so many soirees in the Polignac salon, the focus of the evening was the new music of a promising young composer, the pianist Dinu Lipatti. The *New York Herald-Tribune* wrote a long and detailed account of the event, enumerating the works—the Third Brandenburg Concerto, played by a full orchestra conducted by Charles Munch, the Mozart and Busoni Two-Piano Concertos, played by Lipatti and Haskil, and Lipatti's compositions, a Concertino for Strings, arranged for two pianos, and a *Suite Classique*, conducted by Munch. It was a glorious event, and friends and family representing Winnaretta's past and present filled the large music room on avenue Henri-Martin, gathering at the buffet that followed, to offer heartfelt congratulations to the artists and the hostess.[204]

Winnaretta would never hear music in that room again.

16

The Beautiful Kingdom of Sounds

In July 1939, Winnaretta received notification that she was to be promoted to the rank of Officer of the Legion of Honor for "fifty-four years of service rendered to the sciences, letters, and the arts."[1] The nominating committee cited her numerous acts of generosity for the public good, including her beneficence towards to the Salvation Army and the Hôpital Saint-Louis, and her countless activities on behalf of the arts: her organization of concerts in France and abroad, her articles in the *Renaissance latine* and the *Revue de Paris,* and the exhibitions of her art at the official Salon and the Galerie Charpentier. Her creation of the Fondation Singer-Polignac was cited as the culminating gesture of her long career as a *grande mécène.*[2]

The subject of honor—of a more personal sort—was discussed when Winnaretta's nephew Edmond de Polignac came to visit at avenue Henri-Martin. As the expectation of war loomed, the imminent conscription of young men was on the minds of French families everywhere. Anticipating his "call to the flag," Eddy had come to bid farewell to his aunt. In parting, Winnaretta said to her godson, "Never forget that, no matter what happens, you are the son of your father—a man of honor *par excellence*—and that you are the nephew of the uncle for whom you were named, the only man besides my own father that I respected and that I loved. Remember that you are bound, by your blood and by your name, to honor your family."[3] Within a month Edmond de Polignac would be conscripted and sent to defend his country on foreign soil. At almost the same time, on 10 August 1939, Winnaretta's brother Franklin Singer, the youngest of Isaac's twenty-four children, died in Paris. Winnaretta accompanied the body back to England for its burial in the Singer family crypt. As the boat bearing the coffin approached Torquay, Winnaretta thought of the lines by Tennyson:

And the stately ships go on
To their haven under the hill;
But O for the touch of a vanished hand,
And the sound of a voice that is still![4]

After the funeral ceremonies Winnaretta decided to stay in England until the end of the month to attend to some family business. She took a hotel room in Rottingdean, Sussex, where the Chaplins had a house. On 3 September, just as Winnaretta was preparing to return to mainland Europe, Britain and France declared war on Germany. Despite her anxious wish to be back in Paris, Winnaretta was urged by her family to remain in England until her safe passage could be secured.[5] She returned to Devonshire, where, as she wrote to Marie-Blanche, "my father came from Paris in 1870, fleeing the Germans and the Commune, where I feel less dispossessed than elsewhere in England, where I spent my childhood and long periods later with Edmond and my brothers. Edmond loved this countryside. . . . [H]e lies in the Torquay Cemetery with my father and my brothers, and it consoles me to be so close to them."[6] She moved into a seaside hotel, assisted with what relief efforts she could: organization of ambulance corps, health efforts on behalf of impoverished children evacuated from London. François Dupré promised to come to London in October to accompany her back to France. However, the difficulty of travel, even across the Channel, caused him to postpone his plans several times.[7] To stave off depression in the face of "long and empty days [that] colorlessly slide by," she challenged herself to learn by memory a few lines of a Bach fugue every day—"which is very difficult for me!" She confided her best hopes, as always, to Nadia Boulanger.

Before what seems like the end of everything for an old lady like me, I console myself as I always have with music, painting, and books . . . and I keep my sanity. As someone said: I believe the way of beauty is the *wiser* as well as the wider way. It is God's own most perfect way to himself.[8]

From Paris, where the days were punctuated by the sounds of gunfire and nights by alert sirens, Colette wrote, "I flatter myself with the idea that you have ordered an underground music-room for your friends. . . . I entrust you to your friends, to music, to the benevolence of fate."[9] And almost reflexively, Winnaretta started organizing musical gatherings in Devonshire. With Audrey Parr-Colville and Boulanger's student David Ponsonby she sponsored a series of charity recitals at local hotels to raise money for the Red Cross; through these activities she was able to meet many fine musicians living in the area. Friends came to visit: Lord Berners, Ethel Smyth, Ronald Storrs, and Alvilde Chaplin, whose husband had joined the Royal Air Force.[10] She traveled often to London, where daily concerts at the National Gallery, performed by pianist Myra Hess and other great artists, allowed the audience to forget their sorrows for an hour.[11] "I would like to ask Benjamin Britten to write something for me," she wrote to Boulanger, declaring that she would always be "like the fine lady in the Nursery Rhyme: she shall have music wherever she goes!"[12] Britten was in America at the time, however; instead Winnaretta asked Peter Pope, a British student of Boulanger's, to write a piano trio "which would be played at my home in Paris—as soon as possible!"[13]

She vacillated about returning to France. In February 1940, having decided finally to make the trip, Winnaretta was told to expect the imminent arrival of François Dupré, who would accompany her across the Channel. But Dupré never came. Elisabeth and George Chavchavadze, old friends who rented the top floor of the Palazzo Polignac, made plans to leave for America; Winnaretta was urged to go with them, but she could not face the long plane trip.[14] That spring an old friend, Prince Jean-Louis de Faucigny-Lucinge, a member of the French Economic War Mission in London, told Winnaretta that he had access to special travel permits. Each time that he offered to bring her back to Paris with him, she would pack her bags—and then cancel at the last minute. Faucigny-Lucinge saw Winnaretta for the last time in May 1940 in Cornwall: they had both come for the funeral of their friend in common, pianist Audrey Parr-Colville, who had been killed on the road driving an ambulance for the Red Cross. That afternoon, the news of the Nazi invasion of Holland and Belgium was announced to the assembled mourners. Winnaretta trembled and insisted on returning to London by the next train—the one that necessitated the most transfers. Faucigny-Lucinge met up with Winnaretta on the last leg to London, where he found her close to panic. Suddenly a siren signaling a blackout broke the silence of the night, and the train stopped at a small, poorly lit station in the middle of nowhere. After an agonizing wait in the darkness, Winnaretta stood up. "I'm leaving," she announced to Lucinge. And before he could stop her, she had grabbed her bag, descended to the platform, and disappeared into the night.[15]

After making her way back to London, Winnaretta continued to waver about leaving England. Her niece Daisy Dugardin (Franklin Singer's daughter, now married to third husband Hervé Dugardin) received a frantic cable: "French Mission difficult to telephone, try to have me out of here."[16] That month and the next, Winnaretta and Alvilde listened to the radio broadcasts announcing the occupation of the Netherlands and Belgium. Shortly thereafter, France was overrun by German armies; Maréchal Pétain, a long-time family friend of the Polignacs, signed an armistice with Hitler on 22 June. In the fall Nadia Boulanger sailed from Lisbon for America and a teaching post at Harvard University. Winnaretta cabled: "From the depths of my distress I bid you adieu." In a second telegram, she wrote, "Implore news family, Jeans [de Polignac], Dupré."[17]

Indeed, François Dupré seemed to have disappeared, and, along with him, Winnaretta's access to her bank funds. The story told by the Singer family is that during the war Dupré embraced, chameleon-like, whatever end of the political spectrum seemed most expedient at any particular moment; in doing so, he managed to keep his own—and Winnaretta's—financial and property holdings intact throughout the German occupation. He managed to pull off a clever maneuver on Winnaretta's behalf: he had a postcard sent to the Duc Decazes, ostensibly from Winnaretta, through a friend in Chile. Henceforth, the Gestapo, believing the Princesse de Polignac to be in a neutral country, made no attempts to appropriate or damage her house on avenue Henri-Martin.[18] These kinds of machinations required that Dupré maintain a very low profile; for long periods of time his family would have no idea of where he had alighted. Winnaretta did not know any of this, however, and was panic-stricken to find herself—in extremely relative terms—without money. Yet, as much as she suffered from constant uncertainty, from "the despoliation of our country, the [separation] from all that defines my life, . . . the death of loved ones," Winnaretta understood quite well that her own personal tragedies were paltry in comparison to the devastating fates of others. "I'm amazed by the courage—the *gay* courage of each person [who utters] not one word of complaint. Those who live in the midst of this hell have but one thought: to resist until the end."[19]

Winnaretta did not count herself among those who could resist until the end. In February she wrote to the Blisses and to Colonel Jacques and Consuelo Balsan,[20] asking if they would be willing to sponsor her emigration to the United States. A financial guarantee of Winnaretta's upkeep in America would be required (a *temporary* guarantee, Winnaretta hastened to assure her addressees), since she had no bank accounts or other assets in the United States.[21] Mildred Woods Bliss was taken aback by the request. After consulting with Consuelo Balsan, she wrote to Boulanger. Sadly and ironically, Winnaretta was going to get a taste of her own medicine when it came to giving money with an open hand. Mrs. Bliss responded:

> [Mme. Balsan] will contribute $500—if a group of friends gets together to create a fund whose total will permit Winnie to live in this country. But she cannot accept the financial responsibility for W. de P., as she already has countless human ruins [*épaves*] to attend to. It's the same with us. . . . It seems unbelievable to all of us that the huge fortune that she and her family have at their disposal would be inaccessible. Also, we pity her very little if she has removed all of her fortune from here and put it in France or England. . . . She should be writing to her family [to secure funds] for the trip and her upkeep here. . . .
>
> Old age is atrocious, loneliness sometimes terrible and this cataclysmic war an anguish every hour. . . . That she wants to come I understand, but the unfortunate from the invaded countries . . . present more urgent cases than that of poor Winnie, who, God knows, also has much to lament. Who doesn't, these days?[22]

And so another escape exit closed. Ironically, as Mrs. Bliss was wondering why Winnaretta's American family had not come to her aid, an article on the Singer family, "Women, Wealth: Isaac Singer, an Habitual Lover," appeared in New York's *Sunday News*. The article rehashed all the sordid old stories about Isaac "Uncle Ike" Singer—his fortune, his mistresses, his scandals. It was revealed that many of the Singer heirs in the United States were indigent: "Most of Singer's legitimate descendants are grubbing to make a living, while many of his illegitimate descendants are still foraging on the greenbacks Singer captured so unjustly. Eight of his descendants have died bankrupt." The article continued, "Before war put an end to the monthly checks from France, a child of his second marriage was coming to the aid of offspring of his first marriage—a bond between Singer's only two lines of legitimate descendants." This was surely a reference to the monthly checks that Winnaretta had been sending since 1905 to her half-brother William Singer and—after William's death—to his children. "If this is confusing," continued the report, "it is no more mixed up than was Singer's domestic life. Simultaneously, he had one wife, three mistresses and 18 children in New York. Then to top things off, he took another lawful wife in his old age [Isabella Boyer] and had six more children. . . . What a man!"[23] It is unlikely that Winnaretta saw this article. She spent the remainder of 1941 in Paignton. With her estranged husband in the Royal Air Force, Alvilde Chaplin moved with her daughter down to Devon to live with Winnaretta. "I don't really believe [Winnie] would be happier [in America] than here," wrote Alvilde to Boulanger. "I have been with her nearly all the time, and so far have managed to guide her footsteps into peaceful ways!"[24]

Finally resigned to remaining in England for the duration of the war, Winnaretta sought out activities to relieve her boredom and anxiety. In the fall an apartment in Torquay at the edge of a cliff became available, and Winnaretta moved in; it was "like living on a yacht." She assisted in relief efforts for the refugees in the region; painting and voracious reading occupied her solitary hours. "Remember [that] you are of the 'Jack-in-the-box tribe,'" she wrote to Daisy Dugardin, "and nothing can keep you down for very long."[25] Earlier in the year, Ronald Storrs had elicited from Winnaretta a promise that she would write her memoirs. Originally, Storrs had brought over a recording machine, so that she could speak extemporaneously, but the speaking voice captured on wax cylinder, uttered through clenched jaws, was so difficult to understand that the idea was abandoned. Instead, Winnaretta spent long hours in her yacht-like apartment typing out a lifetime's worth of memories—"a day of Fauré, of Ravel, of Jean Françaix, or of Francis Poulenc." The task, which preoccupied her for over a year, allowed her to relive many happy hours of her life in Paris and Venice.[26] While many of these written recollections were informative and witty, many of the stories were garbled, conflated with other incidents, or simply inaccurate. Eventually journalist Raymond Mortimer was soliticited for the daunting task of editing the typewritten text so that it could be presented coherently.[27]

Gradually, Winnaretta was able to glean information about those she had left behind in Europe. Her nephew Duc Louis Decazes had died in

April 1941. Jean and Marie-Blanche had remained at Kerbastic. Before the outbreak of war, Jean had been elected mayor of Guidel, the seaside village in whose jurisdiction the property fell. The occupation of the town by the Germans now required his vigilant attention on behalf of the besieged citizenry. And from Elisabeth Chavchavadze came upsetting news: the Fascist-ruled Venetian municipal government had appropriated the Palazzo Polignac—on official occasions, a banner displaying the swastika could be seen hanging from the palace's upper balconies.[28] Soon thereafter, Winnaretta received a sad letter from the "poor Mouse," Violet Trefusis, informing her that Alice Keppel was ill, and that Violet was soon leaving for L'Ombrellino. "The tone of the [Italian] press is so disgusting that I can't imagine going there now," responded Winnaretta. "Is St. Loup a comfort? I hope so. I don't like to think you are sad and *dépaysée* [disenfranchised]."[29]

Eventually, Winnaretta gravitated back to London. In the fall of 1942 she moved into a small four-room apartment at 55 Park Lane in the Mayfair district of London, where her niece Élisabeth Noailles Macready also had a flat. This would be Winnaretta's last home. She had an upright piano moved into the small salon, and shortly thereafter wrote to Boulanger, "I have derived great benefit by memorizing many preludes and fugues of our great Johann Sebastian Bach. . . . It is an excellent exercise."[30]

Her musical life became lively again. She took to prowling around Wigmore Hall, cajoling the pianists who were practicing there into joining her for some four-hand reading sessions.[31] Despite the Blitz, the number of literary and musical activities had continued to proliferate in London. Winnaretta took an interest in the young composers still in London, especially Gerald Berners, whom she visited frequently at his estate in Faringdon, and Boulanger's former student Lennox Berkeley.[32] Winnaretta continued to see Ethel Smyth, whom she described to Boulanger as "84 years old, [with] *complete* self-assurance," despite her poor health.[33] The composer was still a force of nature: "You must always be ready to *begin again,* a fresh start," she declared to Winnaretta. "I am now writing a new book."[34] New friendships were formed with pianists Myra Hess and Clifford Curzon, whose performances Winnaretta attended avidly. Another new musical friend was William McKie, organist at Westminster Abbey, who met Winnaretta during his two years stationed at the Royal Air Force base at Torquay. McKie, invited to dinner at the Wigwam, was thrilled to be able to discuss Poulenc's Organ Concerto with the woman who had brought it into being.[35]

Winnaretta's musical *mécénat* made an impact even during the war. The Piano Trio that she had commissioned from Boulanger student Peter Pope was now being performed at various festivals, with much success.[36] Despite her current limited finances, Winnaretta thought about commissioning music. Hervé Dugardin, Daisy Singer's husband, was the French director of the Italian music-publishing house Ricordi; Winnaretta wrote to Daisy that she was formulating a plan "[to] have a good many works by [Ricordi's] composers written for me."[37] In 1942 Benjamin Britten returned to London from his four-year sojourn in the United States. Later that year Winnaretta was finally brought face to face with the composer whose works she so admired, when Alvilde Chaplin invited Britten, in the company of his partner, tenor Peter Pears, to a luncheon at the Café Royal. There is some evidence that a commission project may have been discussed, but the details are not known.[38]

To Nadia Boulanger, Winnaretta summed up the gratitude that she felt at having spent a life in music: "Dear Nadia, I don't see any possibility of resuming *together* our former life, but even while separated, you in Cambridge, me here, we are reunited by this or that chord, by a Bach chorale, which, *in an instant,* reconstitutes the past, and proves to us that we had a reason for living *on this rock*: to live in the beautiful kingdom of sounds."[39] And in a second letter: "I think with such great emotion of all that music has done for me, of the immense consolation, the marvelous refuge that it was for me at all times—Bach, Monteverdi, so many others."[40]

Curiously, in London's wartime cultural circles, Winnaretta became as well known for her literary associations of yesteryear as for her musical involvement. It dawned on the younger generation of British writers that here in their midst was a direct link to Marcel Proust and his world. Stephen Spender was invited to Winnaretta's for dinner on 25 February 1943.[41] Winnaretta probably wanted to discuss the young man's poetry and his new novel *The Backward Son,* but her guest diverted the conversation towards the subject of Proust. Winnaretta shocked the bisexual Spender with a disconcerting story about his neurasthenic literary hero. Proust liked to indulge an odd fancy: he would hire a taxi, ride it for a hundred yards, and then tip the driver one hundred francs just to see his reaction. Very often this extravagant gesture was interpreted by the cabby as a sexual proposition. The story apparently ended the conversation, but the next day Spender reported that Winnaretta's stories about Proust had been "fascinating." He was pumped for information: was Winnaretta *really* the model for Madame Verdurin?[42]

The next young writer to be thrown in the path of the Princesse de Polignac was James Lees-Milne, secretary of the six-year-old National Trust. As ambassador and aesthetic assessor of Great Britain's architectural treasures, Lees-Milne was accustomed to showing charming solicitude towards potential donors to the Trust, mostly patrician and eccentric octogenarians, holdovers from the Victorian age. Compared to these last, Winnaretta, whom he met at a party, seemed to Lees-Milne simple and delightful. The young writer wanted to ask a myriad of questions about Proust and his world, but thought better of it; he was rewarded for his reserve when Winnaretta began to tell him about her relationship with the young Marcel Proust. Some months later Lees-Milne happened upon Winnaretta at a party at Sibyl Colefax's house on King's Road. Winnaretta spent the entire evening ensconced on a sofa, "immobile, with a hat on, like a large Buddha." There was something "very godlike" about her, and Lees-Milne repressed his desire to query her some more about Proust. She seemed indifferent to her surroundings, but when Lees-Milne told her that he had absolutely no idea who the other guests were, she "chortled," as though she and the young man had shared a private joke. The illusion was shattered only a moment later, when Winnaretta asked Lees-Milne what his name was.[43] Two months later, however, Winnaretta invited him to dinner, on which occasion Lees-Milne was finally able to ask his hostess about her relationship with Proust. Winnaretta told him that "it was impossible to endure [Proust's] company for a long time. . . . He was touchy and took umbrage at every supposed slight," and, she thought, enjoyed quarreling with his friends. That evening she also dispelled the rumor that she was the model for Madame Verdurin. After the publication of *Swann's Way,* she told Lees-Milne, she used to entertain her Proust-loving friends in the King's Road by playing a game in which everyone present assumed the name of one of the novel's characters: one was Cottard, another Brichot, and she was Madame Verdurin.[44]

In October Winnaretta was informed of the death of Jean de Polignac, at Kerbastic. Despite this loss, Winnaretta seemed, as her nephew Fred Singer wrote to Boulanger, "in excellent health and full of activity. She is astonishing."[45] On 7 October Winnaretta attended a grand reception given by Sir Henry Channon for Field Marshal Wavell and his wife. A hundred people milled around, not all of whom Winnaretta was glad to see: Violet Trefusis was "grandly got-up in an 1860 affair"; Daisy Fellowes circulated among the guests, elegant and dangerous. When the blackout fell at seven o'clock, during the meal, the guests all rushed simultaneously to find taxis. Winnaretta was too anxious and exhausted to join the fracas; she sat waiting in the porter's chair for an hour until a car became available to take her home. All the while people milled around her, as if she were invisible, conversing and making dates.[46]

As the air raids increased that fall, the terrifying nocturnal noise plunged Winnaretta into a more or less permanent state of anxiety. On 3 November, invited to her apartment for dinner, James Lees-Milne was shocked, upon his arrival, to discover his hostess seated on a milking stool in the alley, waiting for the air raid to end, while Alvilde attended to the meal. Winnaretta scarcely spoke a word all evening; occasionally she would make a terse contribution to the conversation, uttered "in a deep voice and trenchant manner," ending each thought with an unintelligible French epithet. Among the guests that evening was a visiting Frenchman, Prince Marc de Beauvau-Craon, who had just escaped from Paris to take refuge in London. The news of the French capital was grim. Traffic around Paris had all but ceased: there were no cars, taxis, or buses, and the Métro was running only three hours a day. High society figures were now indistinguishable from the general population, forced to walk or ride bicycles like everybody else. The Opéra gave a presentation every night, but only German officers and their wives attended. A meal at a fine restaurant cost one thousand francs. French radio had been usurped by the Nazis, and the French people had taken to listening to the BBC. Beauvau-Craon reported that his compatriots were united as never before, and that the Resistance was successfully carrying out its activities underneath the noses of the captors. The young aristocrat laughed when he described how the Germans had hacked apart all of the furniture in the family chateau, simply to amuse themselves; his voice caught, however, when he told of the Nazis destroying his cousin's Rubens and Van Dyck canvases because the relative had refused to collaborate.[47]

By the end of the month, Winnaretta was suffering as many as twenty angina attacks daily. The worst attacks occurred at night, with the onset of the bombings; drugs no longer seemed to help. Nonetheless, when James Lees-Milne came to dine with her and Alvilde on 24 November, he was struck by Winnaretta's dignity as she walked, slowly and sedately, into the small parlor wearing a green dress, her thick gray hair unadorned. Even though "her remarkable face, like some mountainous crag" was bright pink from shortness of breath, she seemed to sustain herself by evoking the redemptive powers of art, literature, and, music. That night she spoke again of Proust, and of her latest literary passion, the works of E. M. Forster.[48] The next day she lunched with Sir Edward Marsh and Raymond Mortimer, during which Mortimer waxed enthusiastic about Benjamin Britten's genius. Marsh, however, was concentrating on Winnaretta, whom he considered to be "a most remarkable woman, a very great lady, intelligent and cultivated to the last degree."[49] An orchestral score of Britten's was playing on the radio that night, and Winnaretta listened to the broadcast at Sibyl Colefax's house, in the company of Alvilde, Ronald Storrs, and James Pope-Hennessy; she probably still dreamed of commissioning a new work from the brilliant young British composer. At the broadcast's conclusion Storrs brought Winnaretta and Alvilde back to Park Lane in a taxi; during the short trip home Winnaretta began to feel ill and short of breath. Storrs brought her into her building and waited with Sons in the hall until her palpitations had stopped. But once inside her apartment she had another attack. Alvilde called a doctor, but there was really nothing to do. On 25 November 1943, at 2 o'clock in the morning, Winnaretta suffered massive heart failure and died.[50]

Nelly de Vogüé, Pata's daughter, was in London at the moment of Winnaretta's passing: a pilot in the Resistance, she was flying reconnaissance missions back and forth between London and the European mainland. In the morning Alvilde asked Nelly to keep vigil while she made funeral arrangements.[51] A young artist from the Royal Academy, Thomas Monnington, was engaged to make a sketch of Winnaretta on her deathbed; the portrait that he painted showed an angular but dignified profile, finally at rest.

A Requiem Mass for Winnaretta was celebrated on 1 December 1943 at the Church of the Immaculate Conception on Farm Street. William McKie had been engaged to play the organ. Most of the music was, appropriately, by J. S. Bach: four Chorale Preludes for organ, and the *Benedictus* from Bach's B-Minor Mass; the choir also sang Mozart's *Ave Verum Corpus*, and *In Paradisum* from Fauré's *Requiem*, with the tenor Peter Pears at soloist.[52] The service concluded with the playing of the *St. Anne's Fugue* by Bach. "There are so many who are mourning the death of Winnie de Polignac," wrote Rosamond Lehmann in *The London Times*,[53] and it was true: the large number of people in attendance at the funeral—aristocrats, diplomats, artists, writers, musicians—testified to the profound impact that Winnaretta had made on the lives of so many; there was a communal feeling of loss and warmth among those gathered at the church on that somber Wednesday.[54] Alvilde Chaplin arranged for the transfer of Winnaretta's body to the family crypt in Torquay. "France has lost a generous and noble friend," she wrote in a letter to the *Times*, "whom we in England are proud to have had with us these last years, in spite of the sad reason that brought her here."[55]

Winnaretta was buried alongside her husband and her father in the Singer crypt, high on a cliff overlooking the town of Torquay and the sea beyond. The plaque bearing her name was placed below Edmond's, which honored him as a "Composer of Music"; Winnaretta had instructed that her own plaque identify her simply as "Wife of the Above." In spirit, they shared the same epitaph: "Selig in Glaube, Selig in Liebe" (Happy in faith, Happy in love). Even in death, Winnaretta and Edmond lay at rest in "the beautiful kingdom of sounds," as the humming breezes blew over the crypt, wending their way eastward towards the Channel, in the direction of France.

Postlude

Some months after Winnaretta's death, Lennox Berkeley wrote to Nadia Boulanger,

> I often wonder whether the old patrons had so much taste as people think, apart from a few Razumovskys and Esterhazys. . . . You will have heard the very sad news of the death of the Princesse de Polignac. It was a real shock to me, as I had come to like and admire her greatly. I know what a blow this news will have been to you. I was just speaking of patrons: was she not the perfect patron?[1]

In December 1944, *Le Figaro* published a commemorative article, expressing regret that, when she had died a year earlier, "the events and the subjugation that weighed on all free expression in France did not permit us to speak as we would have wished." The article, praising her lifelong contribution to the arts, concluded that "it will be impossible to write the chronicle of the twentieth century without including the salon on Avenue Henri-Martin and the palazzo on the Grand Canal. . . . Music has forever inscribed her name at the top of some of the classic works of our time." [2]

A large memorial gathering in Winnaretta's honor was held in Paris sometime in 1944. Many family members, friends, and distinguished members of the European cultural community celebrated the life of this "eight-thousand-volt being," as Armande de Polignac aptly described her aunt.[3] Shortly thereafter Winnaretta's will was read. In addition to the bequests of money and objects that she had made to various family members and friends, the document testified to her commitment to art, artists, and charitable institutions. Generous legacies were left to Colette, Nadia Boulanger, Clara Haskil, Giorgio Levi, Renata Borgatti, Jacques Février, and Léon-Paul Fargue (Fargue's bequest was the last codicil to be added to the will, in 1939). Institutions such as the Hospice for the Women of Calvary, the Society for the Preservation and Rehabilitation of Young Girls, and the Pasteur Institute (to which she endowed two scholarships) were also beneficiaries of her posthumous largesse. She donated the wainscotting from her library to the Musée des Arts Décoratifs; to the Louvre she left her beloved Manet canvas, *La Lecture,* as well as the Ingres drawing, the two large Paninis, and the three Monets—including the *Champs de tulipes en Hollande* that had brought her into competition with Edmond for its purchase.

In addition to the sizeable capital endowment that she had given to the Fondation Singer-Polignac at its founding, she gave a bequest of an additional 1.5 million francs to the institution bearing her name. She instructed that part of the money be used to pay a salary to Nadia Boulanger for the direction of musical activities at the Fondation. A commemorative book-let, *Les Heures de musique à la Fondation Singer-Polignac,* testifies to the brilliant, imaginative programming ideas that Boulanger continued to bring to the task. Jean Françaix assumed the role of concert director at the Fondation after Boulanger's death in 1979, functioning in this capacity until his own death in 1996.

At the approach of the centenary year of Winnaretta's birth (1965), Nadia Boulanger planned a special concert honoring her memory. Not surpris-ingly, one of her first thoughts was to contact Igor Stravinsky, who had benefitted more than any other composer or artist from the Princesse de Polignac's largesse. In November 1964, Boulanger wrote to Stravinsky, then living in Hollywood, California, and asked him to write a work in honor of his patron. It would be a commission from the Fondation Singer-Polignac, she informed him, and he would be paid ten thousand dollars.[4] Three days later she received a telegram from the composer.

SINCERE REGRETS, BUT RECEIVE TODAY TEN THOUSAND DOLLARS TO CONDUCT A CONCERT, AND NOT LESS THAN TWENTY FIVE THOUSAND FOR THE COMMISSION OF A SHORT WORK. THANK YOU VERY MUCH NONETHELESS.[5]

Quite a cavalier, not to say callous, dismissal of two such loyal friends who had so steadfastly encouraged and supported the composer over a thirty-year period. The concert took place without him, on 7 December 1965. Fauré's *Mélodies de Venise* were performed by baritone Gérard Souzay and pianist Dalton Baldwin. A chorus led by Boulanger sang works by Schubert and excerpts from four Bach cantatas. Pierre Fresnay recited ex-cerpts of Paul Valéry's most famous poem, *Le Cimetière marin.* And two of Stravinsky's works were included as well, the *Elegy in Memoriam John F. Kennedy* and the *Introitus* from his new *Mass*—for, finally, how could a memorial concert to the Princesse de Polignac take place without including music by Stravinsky?[6]

The Fondation Singer-Polignac continues to give monthly concerts in the avenue Henri-Martin music room. It grants funds for scholarly research and holds numerous conferences on historical, literary, and scientific subjects.

The Cavaillé-Coll organ and music library—including the manuscripts of commissioned works and dedicated scores—were left to Marie-Blanche de Polignac, who continued to perform with the Boulanger Ensemble and hold weekly musical gatherings in her townhouse on rue Barbet-de-Jouy. After Marie-Blanche's death in 1958, the organ and music library were inherited by her nephew, Prince Louis de Polignac. The organ was sold to a seminary in Merville, in the north of France. The music library is currently housed in a private collection.

To her nephew and godson Edmond, whom she ultimately saw as the spiritual heir to her Polignac legacy, Winnaretta left her husband's musical manuscripts. In recent years, Prince Edmond, now in his eighties, has sponsored concerts featuring the music of the uncle he never knew, the composer for whom he was named. Winnaretta, in 1923, had expressed the hope that, "after I'm gone, some pious hands will gather together the manuscripts that he left, and that one of his own family will concern himself with his admirable musical works." Eighty years later, Winnaretta's wish has been granted.

Appendix A

Musical Performances in the Salon of the Princesse Edmond de Polignac

The following listing represents but a scant fraction of the musical programs presented in the salons of the Princesse Edmond de Polignac. Regrettably, there are very few printed programs extant in the Polignac archives. The information listed here has been culled from every available source: books, printed programs in public and private archives, letters, diaries, and newspaper reports of the events. Often the data on the event is incomplete; every effort has been made to identify the date, location, composers, works, artists presented, guests, and sources for the information.

Asterisks (*) indicate works dedicated to the Princesse Edmond de Polignac

Date: Tuesday, 22 May 1888
Location: Avenue Henri-Martin, Paris
Composers/Works: Emmanuel Chabrier, *Gwendoline,* opera; Gabriel Fauré, *Clair de lune,* voice and piano (orchestrated version); works of Vincent d'Indy and Ernest Chausson
Artists: Thuringer, mezzo-soprano; Edmond Vergnet, tenor; Baldo, voice; Gabriel Fauré, harmonium and conductor; Emmanuel Chabrier, piano and conductor; Georges Marie, conductor; Vincent d'Indy and André Messager, percussion; the choruses and orchestras of Concerts Lamoureux and the Conservatoire
Sources: *Figaro,* 16 and 24 May 1888; Poulenc, *Chabrier,* 80–81

Date: mid-July 1889
Location: Avenue Henri-Martin, Paris
Composers/Works: Vincent d'Indy, Piano Trio (first performance)
Source: Vincent d'Indy to WSP, 19 July 1889, Fondation Singer-Polignac, Paris

Date: June 1891
Location: Venice
Composers/Works: Gabriel Fauré, *Mandoline,** *En Sourdine,** voice and piano (premieres)

Artists: Amélie Duez, soprano; Gabriel Fauré, piano
Source: WSP, "Memoirs of the Late Princesse Edmond de Polignac," *Horizon*

Date: September 1892
Location: Avenue Henri-Martin, Paris
Composers/Works: poems of Robert de Montesquiou
Artists: Sarah Bernhardt
Sources: Robert de Montesquiou to WSP, 20 August and September [undated] 1892, Fondation Singer-Polignac, Paris; WSP to Robert de Montesquiou, 28 August 1892, Bibliothèque nationale de France, Nafr 15115

Date: Early 1894
Location: Rue Cortambert *atelier*, Paris
Composers/Works: works for organ
Artists: various Parisian organists, including Alexandre Guilmant, Eugène Gigout, and Louis Vierne
Source: *Figaro*, 5 June 1894

Date: Monday, 21 May 1894
Location: Rue Cortambert *atelier*, Paris
Composers/Works: Gabriel Fauré, songs
Artists: Marguerite de Saint-Marceaux, soprano; Maurice Bagès, tenor
Source: Marguerite de Saint-Marceaux, daily diary, edition forthcoming (Paris: Fayard)

Date: Sunday, 20 January 1895
Location: Rue Cortambert *atelier*, Paris
Composers/Works: chamber music
Artists: Delsart String Quartet (André Tracol, violin; Mathieu Crickboom, violin; Louis van Waefelghem, viola; Jules Delsart, cello)
Source: *Figaro*, 21 January 1895

Date: Wednesday, 6 February 1895
Location: Rue Cortambert *atelier*, Paris
Composers/Works: Gabriel Fauré, *Nell, Les Roses d'Ispahan, En Prière, Mandoline,** voice and piano; *Elégie* for cello and piano; *Berceuse* for violin and piano; Edmond de Polignac, *Au Pays où se fait la guerre*, voice and piano; *Chant de Blancheflor*, voice, 2 violas and cello; unknown composer, *La Romanesca* and *Menuet* for guitars; Robert Schumann, Piano Quartet, Op. 47
Artists: Jeanne Remacle, soprano; Gabriel Fauré, piano; Jaime Bosch, Comte Guy de Polignac, guitars; WSP, guitar and piano; Delsart String Quartet

Source: Marcel Proust to Edmond de Polignac, archives of Prince Edmond de Polignac; *Figaro*, 8 February 1895

Date: Friday, 3 March 1895
Location: Rue Cortambert *atelier*, Paris
Composers/Works: works for string quartet
Artists: Delsart String Quartet
Source: *Le Gaulois*, 5 March 1895

Date: Monday, 23 April 1895
Location: Rue Cortambert *atelier*, Paris
Composers/Works: Heinrich Schütz, *Je veux louer le Seigneur constamment, Dialogo per la Pasqua*; Jean-Philippe Rameau, *Dardanus*, opera (Act II complete, extracts of Acts I, III, IV, V)
Artists: Éléonore Blanc, soprano; Marcella Pregi, soprano; Clément, Soulacroix, Challet, men's voices; Chanteurs de Saint-Gervais, Charles Bordes, conductor
Sources: *Figaro*, 4 and 22 April 1895

Date: Sunday, 16 June 1895
Location: Rue Cortambert *atelier*, Paris
Composers/Works: Gabriel Fauré, *Mandoline,** voice and piano; Edmond de Polignac, *Lauda Sion*, choir a cappella, *Au Pays où se fait la guerre, Noël*, voice and piano, *Martha et Maria*, men's chorus a cappella, *Le Vallon*, 3 solo voices and chorus (*bouche fermée*), *Chant de Blancheflor*, soprano, 2 violas and cello, final chorus from *Pilate livre le Christ*, chorus and organ
Artists: Jeanne Remacle, soprano; Delsart String Quartet; Gabriel Fauré, piano; WSP, piano and organ; Chanteurs de Saint-Gervais, Charles Bordes, conductor
Sources: printed program, private collection; Marcel Proust to Edmond de Polignac, archives of Prince Edmond de Polignac; *Figaro*, 15 and 23 June 1895; *Le Gaulois*, 18 June 1895, 19 September 1895

Date: Sunday, 5 January 1896
Location: Rue Cortambert *atelier*, Paris
Composers/Works: Gabriel Fauré, songs, [Piano] Quartet [no opus no.]
Artists: Comtesse de Guerne, soprano; Delsart String Quartet; Gabriel Fauré, piano
Source: *Figaro*, 9 January 1896

Date: Sunday, 7 January 1896
Location: Rue Cortambert *atelier*, Paris
Composers/Works: C. W. Gluck, arias from *Iphigénie in Aulide*

Artists: Marguerite de Saint-Marceaux, soprano, unnamed pianist
Source: Marguerite de Saint-Marceaux, daily diary, edition forthcoming
  (Paris: Fayard)

Date: Tuesday, 25 February 1896
Location: Rue Cortambert *atelier*, Paris
Composers/Works: Gabriel Fauré, songs; Richard Wagner, Overture from
  Die Meistersinger (arr. piano solo); piano works of Frédéric Chopin
  and Franz Liszt; C. W. Gluck, excerpts from *Orphée*; Edmond de
  Polignac, *Salve Regina*, chorus a cappella
Artists: Aguiar, soprano; Gabriel Fauré, piano; Édouard Risler, piano; Ro-
  maine Bussine, conductor; unnamed choir
Sources: *Figaro*, 27 February 1896; Jean Gallois, *Ernest Chausson*; Mar-
  guerite de Saint-Marceaux, daily diary, edition forthcoming (Paris:
  Fayard)

Date: Friday, 1 May 1896
Location: Rue Cortambert *atelier*, Paris
Composers/Works: songs and a trio for harp, cello, and organ by unnamed
  composers
Artists: Anita Kinen, soprano; Princesse Amédée de Broglie, harp; Prince
  Pierre de Caraman-Chimay, cello; WSP, organ
Source: *Figaro*, 3 May 1896

Date: Tuesday, 12 May 1896
Location: Rue Cortambert *atelier*, Paris
Composers/Works: Edmond de Polignac, *Lamento*, voice and piano, *Robin
  m'aime*, chamber orchestra, Andante for violin and orchestra, "Queen
  Claribel's Aria" from *La Coupe du Roi de Thulé*, opera, *Tarantelle*,
  orchestra; C. W. Gluck, extracts from *Armide*; Heinrich Schütz, *Dialogo
  per la Pasqua*; Gabriel Fauré, extracts from the incidental music to
  Shylock
Artists: Lovano, soprano; Jeanne Raunay, soprano; Tosti, mezzo; Cheyret,
  tenor; Maratet, tenor; Auguez, baritone; Fernandez, violin; Gabriel
  Fauré, piano; WSP, piano and organ; unnamed orchestra, Charles
  Bordes, conductor
Sources: *Figaro*, 8 and 13 May 1896; Marguerite de Saint-Marceaux, daily
  diary, edition forthcoming (Paris: Fayard)

Date: Sunday, 12 June 1898
Location: Rue Cortambert *atelier*, Paris
Composers/Works: W. A. Mozart, arias from *The Magic Flute*, *The Mar-
  riage of Figaro*, and *Così fan tutte*; J. S. Bach aria; Gabriel Fauré, *Les
  Berceaux, Automne*, voice and piano; Edmond de Polignac, *N'écris*

pas, voice and piano, *Chant de Blancheflor,* voice, two violas and cello, and *Cantilène,* flute and cello

Artists: Comtesse de Guerne, soprano; Mary Ador, mezzo-soprano; Morel, tenor; Jullien, unspecified voice; Edmond de Polignac, piano

Source: Figaro, 14 June 1898

Date: Monday, 20 June 1898
Location: Rue Cortambert *atelier,* Paris
Composers/Works: Polignac, *Le Vallon, Ave maris stella,* chorus a cappella
Artists: Chanteurs de Saint-Gervais, Charles Bordes, conductor
Source: Figaro, 22 June 1898

Date: Friday, 8 July 1898
Location: Rue Cortambert *atelier,* Paris
Program co-sponsored by the Schola Cantorum
Composers/Works: J. S. Bach, Toccata and Fugue in D Minor, organ; Chorales No. 37 and 45, organ; Prelude in B Minor, piano; Fantasy and Fugue in G Minor, organ; Paul Jumel, Three Motets for four voices and *Prière,* organ; Léon Saint-Réquier, *Alleluia, Salve Virgo,* and *Alleluia, Senex portabat,* chorus a cappella; Henri Estienne, Suite; motets for four voices by Charles Bordes, Abbé C. Boyer, Léon Saint-Réquier; songs for voice alone by Auguste Serieyx, Pierre Coindreau, Marcel Levallois, Déodat de Séverac; Albert Dupuis, Prelude; François de La Tombelle, Two Motets; Guy Ropartz, *Pièce de concert sur un thème breton;* Orlando di Lasso, *Nos qui sumus in hoc mundo;* Tomas-Luis da Victoria, *Gaudent in coelis;* Alexandre Guilmant, *Offertoire sur un thème grégorien,* organ; Edmond de Polignac, *Deux Madrigaux spirituels*
Artists: Mlle de Jerlin, voice; Béchard, voice; Albert Dupuis, organ; J. Beyer, piano; Albert Decaux, organ; Louis Aubert, piano; Chanteurs de Saint-Gervais; Alexandre Guilmant, organ
Source: Figaro, 9 July 1898

Date: Saturday, 28 January 1899
Location: Rue Cortambert *atelier,* Paris
Composers/Works: J. S. Bach, cantata
Artists: Alexandre Guilmant, organ; Chanteurs de Saint-Gervais, Charles Bordes, conductor
Source: Marguerite de Saint-Marceaux, daily diary, Saint-Marceaux family archives

Date: Thursday, 9 February 1899
Location: Rue Cortambert *atelier,* Paris
Composers/Works: Gabriel Fauré, *La Bonne Chanson*

Artists: Maurice Bagès, tenor; unnamed string quartet or piano
Source: Marguerite de Saint-Marceaux, daily diary, edition forthcoming (Paris: Fayard)

Date: Wednesday, 22 March 1899
Location: Rue Cortambert *atelier,* Paris
Composers/Works: Edmond de Polignac, String Quartet in F Major (1860); Armande de Polignac (Comtesse de Chabannes-La Palice), String Quartet in E Major; J. S. Bach, unspecified keyboard concerto
Artists: string quartet comprised of musicians from the Orchestre des Concerts Lamoureux (Dezso Lederer, 1st violin; Alfred Forest, 2nd violin; Pierre Monteux, viola; René Carcanade, cello); WSP, piano
Sources: unpublished letter from Marcel Proust to Prince Edmond de Polignac, 22 March 1899, Polignac family archives; *Le Figaro,* 23 March 1899

Date: Thursday, 25 May 1899
Location: Rue Cortambert *atelier,* Paris
Composers/Works: C. W. Gluck, Pâris's aria from the opera *Pâris et Hélène*
Artists: Pauline Roger, soprano
Source: Marquise Guy de Polignac, daily diary, archives of Prince Edmond de Polignac

Date: Tuesday, 6 March 1900
Location: Rue Cortambert *atelier,* Paris
Composers/Works: Gabriel Fauré, *La Bonne Chanson, En Sourdine,* Les Roses d'Ispahan, La Fée aux chansons,* and *Arpège,* voice and piano
Artists: Jeanne Remacle, soprano; Gabriel Fauré, piano
Source: *Figaro,* 10 March 1900

Date: 24 March 1900
Location: Rue Cortambert *atelier,* Paris
Composers/Works: C. W. Gluck, "Pâris's aria" from the opera *Pâris et Hélène*; Wagner, *Das Rheingold* (1st and 4th scenes), "Isolde's Death" from *Tristan und Isolde,* Franz Liszt, Hungarian Rhapsody for piano; Franz Schubert, songs
Artists: Pauline Roger, soprano; Alfred Cortot, pianist; Maurice Bagès, tenor
Source: *Figaro,* 26 March 1900

Date: Saturday, 31 March 1900
Location: Rue Cortambert *atelier,* Paris
Composers/Works: Jules Bouval, organ work; Félix Godefroid, *Danse des Sylphes*; Gioacchino Rossini, Duo from the Mass; Alphonse Hasselmans, Menuet for Harp; Charles-Marie Widor, *Ave Maria*; Edmond

de Polignac, *Choeur d'Esther,* women's chorus and piano; Charles Gounod, six excerpts from *Mors et Vita*
Artists: Jules Bouval, organ; Comtesse de Guerne, soprano; Anita Kinen, mezzo-soprano; Mlle Leroux, soprano; Millot, tenor; Pierron, soprano; Chanteurs de Saint-Gervais, Charles Bordes, conductor; Ada Sassoli, harp
Source: *Figaro,* 1 April 1900

Date: Thursday, 18 April 1901
Location: Rue Cortambert *atelier,* Paris
Composers/Works: G. F. Handel, chorus from *Alexander's Feast*; Hubertus Waelrant, *Adieu mon frère* (16th century), chorus a cappella; Gabriel Fauré, *Nell, Le Voyageur, Notre Amour,* voice and piano, *Pavane* and *Madrigal,* chorus and piano; Edmond de Polignac, *Choeur de buveurs, Madrigal, Ave maris stella, Aubade,* chorus a cappella; Johannes Brahms, *Liebeslieder Waltzes*
Artists: Pauline Vaillant-Couturier, soprano; Gaétane Vicq, soprano; Mlle Marteau, soprano; Euterpe Chorus, Duteil d'Ozanne, conductor
Source: printed program, archives of Prince Edmond de Polignac; *Figaro,* 19 April 1901

Date: Wednesday, 22 May 1901
Location: Rue Cortambert *atelier,* Paris
Composers/Works: "Dance Idylls"
Artists: Isadora Duncan, dancer; Ada Sassoli, harp
Sources: invitation card, Isadora Duncan papers, NYPL; *Figaro,* 19 and 24 May 1901

Date: Monday, 27 May 1901
Location: Rue Cortambert *atelier,* Paris
Composers/Works: Camille Chevillard, String Quartet; Tomaso Vitali, *Chaconne* for violin; Alexis de Castillon, Sonata for Violin and Piano
Artists: The Geloso String Quartet (Geloso, violin; Tracol, violin, Pierre Monteux, viola; Schneeklud, cello); Mme Schmidt, violin (Paris début), Octave Maus, piano
Source: *Figaro,* 29 May 1901

Date: Monday, 11 May 1903
Location: Rue Cortambert *atelier,* Paris
Composers/Works: Gabriel Fauré, songs, Sonata in A Major for Violin and Piano, Op. 13
Artists: Lydia Eustis, soprano; Georges Enesco, violin; Gabriel Fauré, piano
Source: *Figaro,* 12 May 1903

Date: Monday, 25 May 1903
Location: Rue Cortambert *atelier*, Paris
Composers/Works: J. S. Bach, Sonata for Violin and Piano [unspecified],
    Roffredo Caetani, Sonata for Violin and Piano, Richard Wagner,
    Siegfried Idyll, transcribed for violin and piano
Artists: Eugène Ysaÿe, violin; Raoul Pugno, piano
Sources: *Figaro*, 26 May 1903; Marguerite de Saint-Marceaux, daily diary,
    edition forthcoming (Paris: Fayard)

Date: Wednesday, 3 June 1903
Location: Rue Cortambert *atelier*, Paris
Composers/Works: [Unspecified] organ works; Gioacchino Rossini,
    Canzonetta from *La Cenerentola*; Edvard Grieg, *Im Kahne*, voice and
    piano; Ambroise Thomas, Mignon's aria from *Mignon*; Jules Massenet,
    extracts from *Les Erinnyes*
Artists: M. Loth, organist; Lucile Marcel, soprano; Jules Massenet, piano
Source: *Figaro*, 3 June 1903

Date: Tuesday, 31 January 1905
Location: Grand salon, Avenue Henri-Martin, Paris
Composers/Works: two French folksongs, harmonized by Julien Tiersot, *Noël
    aux champs* and *Vive la rose!*; Edmond de Polignac, *Ave maris stella*,
    Aubade, and *Hirondelles*; Gabriel Fauré, *Pavane*, Op. 50, and *Madrigal*,
    Op. 35; Johannes Brahms, *Liebeslieder Waltzes*, Op. 52 No. 1
Artists: Euterpe Chorus, Duteil d'Ozanne, conductor; César Estyle, piano
Source: *Figaro*, 2 February 1905

Date: Wednesday, 15 February 1905
Location: Rue Cortambert *atelier*, Paris
Composers/Works: Leoncavello, aria from *Pagliacci*; Léon Moreau, songs;
    Claude Debussy, *Masques* and *L'Ile joyeuse*, piano (premieres)
Artists: Charles Rousselière, tenor; Ricardo Viñes, piano
Source: *Figaro*, 16 February 1905

Date: Friday, 3 March 1905
Location: Rue Cortambert *atelier*, Paris
Composers/Works: Johannes Brahms, songs; Robert Schumann, songs;
    operatic arias for baritone
Artists: Mme Blach, soprano; M. Baldelli, baritone
Source: *Figaro*, 5 March 1905

Date: Tuesday, 28 March 1905
Location: 51 Rue de Varennes, Paris
Composers/Works: Works of Edmond de Polignac

Source: Marguerite de Saint-Marceaux, daily diary, edition forthcoming (Paris: Fayard)

Date: Sunday, 10 December 1905
Location: Rue Cortambert *atelier,* Paris
Composers/Works: J. S. Bach, Concerto in D Minor for Three Pianos, other unspecified works
Artists: Blanche Selva, piano; Marcel Labey, piano; WSP, piano
Sources: *Figaro,* 12 December 1905; Marguerite de Saint-Marceaux, daily diary, edition forthcoming (Paris: Fayard)

Date: 17 December 1905
Location: Rue Cortambert *atelier,* Paris
Composers/Works: Claude Debussy, songs and new works for piano; Maurice Ravel, Sonatine, piano (premiere), *Schéhérazade,* voice and piano; Modest Musorgsky, songs; Mili Balakirev, songs
Artists: Ricardo Viñes, piano; Mme Fourrier, soprano
Sources: *Figaro,* 12 and 19 December 1905

Date: 14 January 1906
Location: Rue Cortambert *atelier,* Paris
Composers/Works: J. S. Bach, choral prelude for organ; Eugène Gigout, Toccata for organ; J. S. Bach, alto aria from the cantata *Bleib bei uns,* with English horn obbligato; Heinrich Schütz, *Dialogo per la Pascua*; Hector Berlioz, *Le Repos de la Sainte Famille*; J. S. Bach, duo from the cantata *Pour tous les temps*; Heinrich Schütz, *Alleluia*; J. S. Bach, duo from the cantata *Wachet auf*; Giacomo Carissimi, *O Vulnera doloris*; Gabriel Fauré, *Pavane* and *Madrigal,* chorus and piano
Artists: Mme Tracol, soprano; Mary Pironnay, soprano; Rodophe Plamondon, baritone; M. Gebelin, voice; M. Mondain, voice; Eugène Gigout, organ; Gabriel Fauré, piano.
Sources: invitation card and printed program, Fonds Gabriel Astruc, Archives Nationales; *Figaro,* 23 January 1906

Date: Monday, 22 January 1906
Location: Rue Cortambert *atelier,* Paris
Composers/Works: Claude Debussy, String Quartet; Borodin, String Quartet; Mili Balakirev, songs; Maurice Ravel, *Chansons populaires grecques,* voice and piano
Artists: Geloso String Quartet (Alfred Geloso, violin; André Bloch, violin; Pierre Monteux, viola; Jules Tergis, cello); Mlle Thomasset, soprano; Marcel Chadeigne, piano
Source: handwritten program, Fonds Gabriel Astruc, Archives Nationales; *Figaro,* 23 January 1906

Date: Sunday, 28 Janaury 1906
Location: Rue Cortambert *atelier,* Paris
Composers/Works: René de Castéra, Piano Trio in D Major; Pierre Coindreau, Piano Trio, Op. 8; Alfred Roussel, Piano Trio, Op. 2.
Source: Marguerite de Saint-Marceaux, daily diary, edition forthcoming (Paris: Fayard)

Date: Sunday, 11 February 1906
Location: Rue Cortambert *atelier,* Paris
Composers/Works: J. S. Bach, [unspecified] organ works; Giacomo Carissimi, organ works; Claude Debussy, piano works; two popular songs, *Sainte Geneviève* and *Vive la rose!,* harmonized for chorus by Julien Tiersot; two sixteenth-century pavanes; Edmond de Polignac, two works for chorus a cappella, *Ave maris stella* and *Hirondelles*; piano works by Frédéric Chopin and Isaac Albéniz; Ravel, *Alborado del Gracioso*; Claude Debussy, *Prélude à l'après-midi d'un faune,* arranged for two pianos
Artists: The Euterpe Choir, Duteil d'Ozanne, conductor; WSP, organ; Ricardo Viñes, piano
Sources: invitation card and printed program, Fonds Gabriel Astruc, Archives Nationales; *Figaro,* 14 February 1906

Date: Sunday, 25 February 1906
Location: Rue Cortambert *atelier,* Paris.
Composers/Works: works performed on harpsichord: J. S. Bach, Suite; William Byrd, *La Volta*; Jacques Champion de Chambonnières, *La Volta*; Thomas Morley, *La Volta*; works performed on fortepiano: J. S. Bach, Polonaise in E-flat Major; Franz Schubert, *Valse Nobles and Valses Sentimentales*; works performed on piano: J. S. Bach, *Sarabande* and *Passepied*; Berlioz arr. Liszt, *Valse des Sylphes*; Frédéric Chopin, [unspecified] Waltz
Artist: Wanda Landowska, harpsichord, fortepiano, and piano
Sources: invitation card and typed program, Fonds Gabriel Astruc, Archives Nationales

Date: Sunday, 4 March 1906
Location: Rue Cortambert *atelier,* Paris
Artists: Société des Instruments à Vent (Philippe Gaubert, flute; Prosper Mimart, clarinet; Louis Bleuzet, oboe; Charles Bourdeau, bassoon, Louis Vuillermoz, horn)
Source: correspondence, Fonds Gabriel Astruc, Archives Nationales

Date: Sunday, 18 March 1906
Location: Rue Cortambert *atelier,* Paris
Composer/Works: J. S. Bach, sonatas for flute and keyboard in E Minor, E Major, and B Minor.

Artists: Philippe Gaubert, flute, and unspecified pianist
Source: correspondence, Fonds Gabriel Astruc, Archives Nationales

Date: Sunday, 25 March 1906
Location: Rue Cortambert *atelier,* Paris
Composers/Works: Déodat de Sévérac, *En Languedoc,* piano
Artists: Blanche Selva, piano; Mary Tracy, soprano
Source: *Figaro,* 3 April 1906.

Date: Sunday, 1 April 1906 and Monday, 2 April 1906
Location: Rue Cortambert *atelier,* Paris
Composers/Works: two songs for voice and piano: Charles Gounod,
   "Cantilène" from *Sapho*; Gabriel Fauré, *Le Ruisseau,* chorus and pi-
   ano; choral works for women's voices and piano: C. W. Gluck, two
   "Choruses of the Priestesses" from *Iphegenia in Taurus*; Edmond de
   Polignac, *Choeur d'Esther*; A. Duteil d'Ozanne, *La Légende du torrent*
   (*Choeur des Ondines*); César Franck, *La Vierge à la Crèche*
Artists: The Euterpe Chorus, Duteil d'Ozanne, conductor; Comtesse de
   Guerne, soprano; unnamed pianist
Sources: printed program, Fonds Gabriel Astruc, Archives Nationales;
   Figaro, 29 March and 3 April 1906

Date: Sunday, 27 May 1906
Location:
Composers/Works: Déodat de Sévérac, *Le Coeur de Moulin*
Source: Marguerite de Saint-Marceaux, daily diary, edition forthcoming
   (Paris: Fayard)

Date: Thursday, 11 April 1907
Location: Grand salon, Avenue Henri-Martin, Paris
Composers/Works: Vincent d'Indy, *Chansons et danses,* flute, oboe, 2 clarinets, horn, 2 bassoons; W. A. Mozart, Andante from [unspecified] Serenade for Winds; Camille Saint-Saëns, aria from *Le Timbre d'argent,*
   voice and string quartet; Gabriel Fauré, *Les Roses d'Ispahan, Clair de
   lune,* voice and piano; Reynaldo Hahn, *O Fons Blandusiae* (text on an
   ode by Horace), soprano solo and female chorus, and *Le Bal de Béatrice
   d'Este,* soprano, violin, wind ensemble, and piano
Artists: Mlle Leclerc, soprano; M. Quesnor, violin; Gaston Blanquart, flute;
   Lucien Leclercq, oboe; Jean Guyot, Louis Cahuzac, clarinets; Petit, trumpet; Capdevielle, François Mellin, horns; Hermans, A. Vizentini, bassoons; Reynaldo Hahn, piano and conductor
Sources: *Figaro,* 13 April 1907; Marguerite de Saint-Marceaux, daily diary, edition forthcoming (Paris: Fayard); Proust, *Correspondence,*Volume 7: 139; Marquise Guy de Polignac, daily diary, archives
   of Prince Edmond de Polignac

Date: Thursday, 25 April 1907
Location: Rue Cortambert *atelier,* Paris
Composers/Works: Frédéric Chopin, mazurkas for piano, and Benjamin Godard, *En Courant,* piano
Artists: unnamed eighteen-year-old Polish woman pianist
Source: Marquise Guy de Polignac, daily diary, archives of Prince Edmond de Polignac

Date: early September 1907
Location: Palazzo Polignac, Venice
Artists: Reynaldo Hahn, piano
Source: *Echo de Paris,* 5 September 1907

Date: Sunday, 24 November 1907
Location: Rue Cortambert *atelier,* Paris
Composers/Works: Blanche Selva, *Les Ancêtres du Lys* for piano
Artists: Blanche Selva, piano
Source: dedicated score of Selva's *Les Ancêtres du Lys,* Polignac family music library

Date: Thursday, 2 January 1908
Location: Rue Cortambert *atelier,* Paris
Composers/Works: Isaac Albéniz, extracts from *Iberia* for piano
Artists: Blanche Selva, piano
Source: Deledique, *Isaac Albéniz*

Date: Sunday, 5 April 1908
Location: Grand salon, Avenue Henri-Martin, Paris
Composers/Works: Gabriel Fauré, songs, voice and piano, *Madrigal* and *Pavane* for vocal quartet and piano
Source: *Figaro,* 6 April 1908

Date: Saturday, 11 April 1908
Location: Rue Cortambert *atelier,* Paris
Composers/Works: Isaac Albéniz, extracts from *Iberia,* Books 1–3
Artists: Jane Bathori, soprano; Blanche Selva, piano; Louis Aubert, piano
Sources: *Figaro,* 12 and 13 April 1908

Date: Tuesday, 2 June 1908
Location: Grand salon, Avenue Henri-Martin, Paris
Composers/Works: "Tableaux vivants" of the works of Aubrey Beardsley
Artists: Orchestra conducted by Désiré Inghelbrecht
Source: *Figaro,* 4 June 1908

Date: Friday, 8 January 1909
Location: Rue Cortambert *atelier*, Paris
Composers/Works: works for voice and piano: Claude Debussy, *Fêtes galantes, Les Ingenues* and *Le Colloque sentimental*; Gabriel Fauré, *Le Secret*; Henri Duparc, *L'Invitation au voyage*; works for piano: Robert Schumann, *Aufschwung* and *Wirren* from *Fantasiestücke*; Claude Debussy, *Estampes* (*Pagodes, Soirée dans Granade*, and *Jardins sous la pluie*); Franz Liszt, *Jeux d'eau de la ville d'Este*; Armande de Polignac, *Miroitement*; Maurice Ravel, *Ondine* from *Miroirs* (premiere)
Artists: Maggie Teyte, mezzo-soprano; Ricardo Viñes, piano
Source: *Figaro*, 9 January 1909

Date: Tuesday, 4 May 1909
Location: Rue Cortambert *atelier*, Paris
Composers/Works: J. S. Bach, Sonata for Cello and Piano and *Capriccio on the Departure of a Beloved Brother*, piano; Reynaldo Hahn, *Variations chantantes sur un thème ancien*, piano; Claude Debussy, *Menuet*; songs by Robert Schumann, Gabriel Fauré, and Reynaldo Hahn; works for piano by Jean-Philippe Rameau, Domenico Scarlatti, and Isaac Albéniz
Artists: Louise Durand Texte; Georges Picth
Source: *Figaro*, 6 May 1909

Date: Saturday, 18 December 1909
Location: Rue Cortambert *atelier*, Paris
Composers/Works: works for piano by Robert Schumann, Jean-Philippe Rameau, Camille Saint-Saëns, Theodore Leschtizky, Maurice Ravel, Gabriel Fauré, Claude Debussy; works for voice and piano by Camfra, Robert Schumann, Henri Duparc, Gabriel Fauré, Ernest Chausson, Claude Debussy
Artists: Ethel Leginska, piano; Mary Pironnay, soprano
Source: *Figaro*, 19 December 1909

Date: Wednesday, 19 January 1910
Location: Rue Cortambert *atelier*, Paris
Composers/Works: Claude Debussy, *Poissons d'or*, piano, *Chansons de Bilitis*, voice and piano
Artists: Germaine Sanderson, soprano; Ricardo Viñes, piano
Sources: *Figaro*, 13 and 21 January 1910

Date: Wednesday, 23 February 1910
Location: Rue Cortambert atelier, Paris
Composers/Works: works for piano by François Couperin, W. A. Mozart, and Isaac Albéniz; works for voice and piano by Henri Duparc and Claude Debussy; Edmond de Polignac, *Aubade, Ave maris stella*, and

Hirondelles, for a cappella chorus; Claude Debussy, *Trois Chansons de Charles d'Orléans* for a cappella chorus
Artists: Blanche Selva, piano; Maggie Teyte, soprano; Chorus of the Concerts Colonne; Désiré-Émile Inghelbrecht, conductor
Source: Figaro, 24 February 1910

Date: Thursday, 9 June 1911
Location: Rue Cortambert *atelier,* Paris
Composers/Works: Florent Schmitt, *Puppazzi,* orchestral suite; Percy Grainger, *The Camp,* chorus; Edmond de Polignac, *Robin m'aime,* orchestra, *Le Vallon,* chorus a cappella, *Lamento,* voice, chorus, and orchestra; Gabriel Fauré, *Pavane, Madrigal,* and two choruses from *Caligula;* Armande de Polignac, *Les Mille et Une Nuits,* ballet music; Claude Debussy, *Prélude à l'après-midi d'un faune;* Désiré Inghelbrecht, *Deux Esquisses antiques,* orchestra; Maurice Ravel, *Pavane pour une infante défunte**
Artists: Mary Pironnay, soprano; unnamed chorus and orchestra
Sources: Figaro, 11 June 1911; Marguerite de Saint-Marceaux, daily diary, edition forthcoming (Paris: Fayard); Marquise Guy de Polignac, daily diary, archives of Prince Edmond de Polignac

Date: Thursday, 15 February 1912
Location: Rue Cortambert *atelier,* Paris
Composers/Works: works for piano of J. S. Bach, César Franck, Albert Roussel (Suite)
Artists: Blanche Selva, piano
Source: Figaro, 18 February 1912

Date: Thursday, 22 February 1912
Location: Rue Cortambert *atelier,* Paris
Composers/Works: works of César Franck
Artists: Geloso String Quartet
Source: Figaro, 25 February 1912

Date: Sunday, 10 March 1912
Location: Grand salon, Avenue Henri-Martin, Paris
Composers/Works: works for voice and piano: Gabriel Fauré, *Les Berceaux, Nell;* C. W. Gluck, aria from *Pâris et Hélène;* Henri Duparc, *Chanson triste;* Pierre de Bréville, *Les Lauriers sont coupés* and *Le Furet;* Ernest Chausson, *Les Papillons;* W. A. Mozart, *Menuet* from Serenade for Winds; Vincent d'Indy, *Chansons et Danses;* Reynaldo Hahn, *Le Bal de Béatrice d'Este,* orchestra, Variations for Flute and Piano
Artists: Claire Croiza, soprano; Gaston Blanquart, flute; Société des Instruments à Vent (Philippe Gaubert, flute; Prosper Mimart, clarinet; Louis Bleuzet, oboe; Charles Bourdeau, bassoon; Louis Vuillermoz, horn); Reynaldo Hahn, pianist and conductor

Sources: Figaro, 12 March 1912; Marguerite de Saint-Marceaux, daily diary, edition forthcoming (Paris: Fayard)

Date: Sunday, 22 December 1912
Location: Rue Cortambert *atelier,* Paris
Composers/Works: works for piano by Frédéric Chopin and Johannes Brahms
Artists: M. Amelungen, Austrian pianist
Source: Figaro, 24 December 1912

Date: Monday, 16 June 1913
Location: garden of Avenue Henri-Martin, Paris
Composers/Works: J. S. Bach, Suite in B Minor for Flute and Orchestra; Brahms, *Mädchenlied* and *Thérèse,* voice and piano; Maurice Ravel, *Pavane pour une infante défunte,** orchestra; Roger Quilter, *Passing Dreams,* voice and piano; unknown composer, *Open My Window To The Stars,* voice and piano; Richard Wagner, *Siegfried Idyll,* orchestra; Hugo Wolf, two songs; Debussy, *Petite Suite,* orchestra; Florent Schmitt, *Reflets d'Allemagne,* orchestra
Artists: Ernest Millon, flute; Betty Calish, soprano; unidentified orchestra and conductor
Sources: Figaro, 17 June 1913; Maurice Paléologue, *Journal,* 156

Date: Monday, 23 June 1913
Location: Grand salon, Avenue Henri-Martin, Paris
Composers/Works: Emmanuel Chabrier, *Trois Valses romantiques* for two pianos, and work for two pianos and chamber orchestra; J. S. Bach, Concerto for two pianos; Robert Schumann, work for two pianos
Artists: Vincent d'Indy, piano; Blanche Selva, piano; unnamed chamber orchestra
Source: Marquise Guy de Polignac, daily diary, archives of Prince Edmond de Polignac

Date: 17 February 1914
Location: Grand Salon, Avenue Henri-Maritn, Paris
Composers/Works: G. F. Handel, *Concerto Grosso* in D Minor; W. A. Mozart, Quintet for Clarinet and Strings in A Major, K. 581; songs for voice and piano by Henri Duparc, Claude Debussy, Alexandre Georges, and Reynaldo Hahn; Claude Debussy and Maurice Ravel, unspecified works arranged for harp; J. S. Bach, unspecified sonata for flute and piano
Artists: Ninon Vallin, soprano; Boisné, flute; Bineau, clarinet; Gaston Lefeuve, violin; H. Delange, violin; unnamed violist; Delobel, cello; Mlle Auckier, harp; Henri Morin, conductor
Sources: Figaro, 19 February 1914

Date: Thursday, 26 March 1914
Location: Rue Cortambert *atelier,* Paris
Composers/Works: unspecified works for piano; songs and arias of Carl
  Maria von Weber, Gabriel Fauré, and Claude Debussy
Artists: Ricardo Viñes, piano; Rose Féart, soprano
Source: Figaro, 28 March 1914

Date: Wednesday, 10 June 1914
Location: Grand salon, Avenue Henri-Martin, Paris
Composers/Works: Jean-Philippe Rameau, works for keyboard and small
  ensembles, Overture to the opera *Zaïs*
Artists: Camille Saint-Saëns, pianist and conductor
Sources: printed program, Bibliothèque nationale de France; *Figaro,* 5 May
  1914

Date: mid-July 1914
Location: 213 King's Road, Chelsea, London
Composers/Works: two- and four-hand works for piano
Artists: WSP, piano; Percy Grainger, piano
Source: John Bird, *Percy Grainger*

Date: Thursday, 20 January 1916
Benefit Concert for "Aide affectueuse aux Musiciens"
Location: Rue Cortambert *atelier,* Paris
Composers/Works: works for organ by J. S. Bach, Boëllmann, and César
  Franck
Artists: Eugène Gigout, organ
Sources: Norbert Dufourcq, "Eugène Gigout," *L'Orgue Cahiers et
  Mémoires,* 1, no. 27 (1982): 13

Date: Saturday, 22 January 1916
Location: Rue Cortambert *atelier,* Paris
Composers/Works: Claude Debussy, *En blanc et noir* for two pianos (pre-
  miere)
Artists: Walter Rummel and Thérèse Chaigneau Rummel, pianists
Source: François Lesure, *Catalogue Claude Debussy*

Date: Sunday, 3 December 1916
Location: Rue Cortambert *atelier,* Paris
Composers/Works: Borodin, String Quartet
Source: Paul Morand, *Journal,* 98

Date: Monday, 14 May 1917
Location: Rue Cortambert *atelier,* Paris

Composers/Works: Ludwig van Beethoven, Sonata for piano in F Minor, Op. 57 ("Appassionata"); Robert Schumann, *Carnaval* for piano, Op. 9
Artists: unnamed pianist
Source: Paul Morand, *Journal,* 237

Date: Sunday, 11 November 1917
Location: Rue Cortambert *atelier,* Paris
Artists: Juliet Méerovitch, piano; Nadia Boulanger, organ
Sources: Paul Morand, *Journal,* 417–18; WSP to Nadia Boulanger, 6 November 1917, Bibliothèque nationale de France, NLa 94, 193

Date: Saturday, 17 November 1917
Location: Rue Cortambert *atelier,* Paris
Composers/Works: organ works by J. S. Bach
Artists: WSP, organ
Source: Paul Morand, *Journal,* 424

Date: Friday, 23 November 1917
Location: Rue Cortambert *atelier,* Paris
Composers/Works: American rags (including *San Francisco*), foxtrots, U.S. Army marching tunes performed on piano
Artists: unnamed "Yankee" pianist, probably Cole Porter; Harry Lear, piano; Consuelo Yzsnaga, singer
Source: Paul Morand, *Journal,* 430–31

Date: Saturday, 1 December 1917
Location: Rue Cortambert *atelier,* Paris
Source: Paul Morand, *Journal,* 436

Date: Sunday, 9 December 1917
Location: Rue Cortambert *atelier,* Paris
Source: Marcel Proust, *Correspondance,* Volume 16: 344–45

Date: Sunday, 16 December 1917
Location: Rue Cortambert *atelier,* Paris
Composers/Works: works for organ
Artists: WSP, organ
Source: Marcel Proust, *Correspondance,* Volume 16: 363–64

Date: Sunday, 19 January 1919
Location: Rue Cortambert *atelier,* Paris
Source: Marquise Guy de Polignac, daily diary, archives of Prince Edmond de Polignac

Date: Friday, 7 February 1919
Location: Rue Cortambert *atelier,* Paris
Composers/Works: Erik Satie, *Socrate*
Artists: Unspecified boy soprano, children's choir
Source: Abbé Mugnier, 8 February 1919, *Journal,* 350
Comments: The performance did not take place, because, according to
    Mugnier, "the child who was supposed to play Alcibiade was in
    Argenteuil and couldn't come so far, held back by the snow or the ice,
    probably."

Date: Sunday, 16 February 1919
Location: Rue Cortambert *atelier,* Paris
Composers/Works: the cancelled performance of Satie's *Socrate* may have
    been rescheduled for this date.
Source: Marquise Guy de Polignac, daily diary, archives of Prince Edmond
    de Polignac

Date: Sunday, 25 May 1919
Location: Rue Cortambert *atelier,* Paris
Artists: chorus conducted by Reynaldo Hahn
Source: *Figaro,* 16 May 1919

Date: Sunday, 1 June 1919
Location: Rue Cortambert *atelier,* Paris
Source: Marquise Guy de Polignac, daily diary, archives of Prince Edmond
    de Polignac

Date: Sunday, 14 December 1919
Location: Rue Cortambert *atelier,* Paris
Composers/Works: Franz Liszt, Sonata in B Minor, piano; Frédéric Chopin,
    works for piano
Artists: Juliette Méerovitch, piano
Source: Marquise Guy de Polignac, daily diary, archives of Prince Edmond
    de Polignac

Date: Friday, 30 January 1920
Location: Rue Cortambert *atelier,* Paris
Composers/Works: Czech piano quintet (probably by Antonin Dvořák, Op.
    81); César Franck, Piano Quintet
Artists: Czech Quartet (Karel Hoffman, violin; Josef Suk, violin; Jiri Hérold,
    viola; Ladislav Zelenka, cello); Blanche Selva, piano
Sources: *Figaro,* 28 January and 1 February 1920

Date: Sunday, 29 February 1920
Location: Rue Cortambert *atelier,* Paris

Composers/Works: works for chorus by Orlando di Lasso, *Domine convertere* and *Du fond de ma pensée* (Clément Marot); folk songs for chorus, *Chanson Poitevine, Chanson du Vivarais, Entre le Boeuf et l'ane gris* (Christmas folk song), J. S. Bach, final chorus from the *St. Matthew Passion*; works for piano by Isaac Albéniz, Frédéric Chopin, and Robert Schumann
Artists: The chorus of the Manécanterie [choir school] des Petits Chanteurs à la Croix de Bois; Manuel Infante, piano
Source: *Figaro*, 1 March 1920

Date: Sunday, 14 March 1920
Location: Rue Cortambert *atelier*, Paris
Artist: Maria Olenina-d'Alheim, mezzo-soprano
Source: Claude Terrasse to WSP, 9 March 1920, archives of Prince Edmond de Polignac

Date: Saturday, 19 June 1920, Saturday, 26 June 1920, and Thursday, 16 July 1920
Location: Rue Cortambert *atelier*, Paris
Composers/Works: J. S. Bach, works for organ
Artists: Marcel Dupré, organ
Source: Marcel Dupré, "Concerts," Bibliothèque nationale de France, Rés. VmF ms58, 6

Date: Sunday, 21 January 1923
Location: Rue Cortambert *atelier*, Paris
Artist: Ricardo Viñes, piano
Source: WSP to Paul Valéry, Bibliothèque nationale de France, MF 2800, 248

Date: Sunday, 10 June 1923
Location: Grand salon, Avenue Henri-Martin, Paris
Composers/Works: Igor Stravinsky, *Les Noces* (premiere)
Artists: Georges Auric, Édouard Flament, Hélène Léon, Marcelle Meyer, pianos
Source: Stephen Walsh, *Stravinsky*, 366

Date: Monday, 25 June 1923
Location: Grand salon, Avenue Henri-Martin, Paris
Composers/Works: Manuel de Falla, *El Retablo de Maese Pedro*, chamber opera (first staged performance, Paris premiere)
Artists: Hector Dufranne, baritone (Don Quixote); Thomas Salignac, tenor (Master Peter); Manuel Garcia, boy soprano (Announcer); Mme Henri Casadesus, harp; Wanda Landowska, harpsichord; twenty musicians from the Golschmann Concerts Orchestra, Vladimir Golschmann, conductor; Ricardo Viñes, Francis Poulenc, puppeteers
Sources: printed program, Archivo Manuel de Falla; Paul Sacher Stiftung; Stravinsky and Craft, *Memories and Commentaries*, 80

Date: summer 1923
Location: Palazzo Polignac, Venice
Composers/Works: songs by Robert Schumann, Franz Schubert
Artists: Olga Lynn, soprano; WSP, piano
Source: Olga Lynn, *Oggie,* 80

Date: Saturday, 1 December 1923
Location: Rue Cortambert *atelier,* Paris
Source: *Figaro,* 4 December 1923

Date: Saturday, 8 December 1923
Location: Rue Cortambert *atelier,* Paris
Source: *Figaro,* 5 December 1923

Date: Wednesday, 14 May 1924
Location: Grand salon, Avenue Henri-Martin, Paris
Composers/Works: Igor Stravinsky, Piano Concerto (premiere);
    L'Histoire du soldat, narrator and chamber ensemble; Octet for
    Wind Instruments
Artists: Igor Stravinsky, piano soloist; Jean Wiéner, second piano and con-
    ductor; Société Moderne des Instruments à Vent
Source: printed program, reprinted in Wiéner, *Allegro appassionato*; *Figaro,*
    26 May 1924

Date: between 15 and 25 May 1924
Location: Grand salon, Avenue Henri-Martin, Paris
Composers/Works: Claude Debussy, *Trois Chansons de Charles d'Orléans,*
    chorus a cappella; J. S. Bach, [unspecified] concerto for piano (reduction
    for two pianos); Germaine Tailleferre, Concerto for Piano (premiere, re-
    duction for two pianos); Edmond de Polignac, works for chorus a cappella.
Artists: Germaine Tailleferre, solo pianist; Jean Wiéner, second piano; un-
    specified chorus
Source: *Figaro,* 26 May 1924

Date: early September 1924
Location: Palazzo Polignac, Venice
Composers/Works: Satie, *Socrate*
Artists: Marya Freund, mezzo-soprano
Source: WSP to Marya Freund, undated letter, archives of the author

Date: October 1924
Location: Rue Cortambert *atelier,* Paris
Composers/Works: Jean Wiéner, Concerto franco-américain
Artists: Jéan Wiener, solo pianist; unnamed second pianist
Source: Boris Schloezer, *La Revue musicale,* 1 December 1924

Date: Wednesday, 7 January 1925
Location: Rue Cortambert *atelier,* Paris
Composers/Works: J. S. Bach, unspecified concerto
Sources: Figaro, 10 January 1925; WSP to Paul Valéry, Bibliothèque
  nationale de France, MF 2800, 240

Date: Tuesday, 7 April 1925
Location: Rue Cortambert *atelier,* Paris
Composers/Works: Francis Poulenc, *Poèmes de Ronsard*
Artists: Claire Croiza, mezzo-soprano; Francis Poulenc, piano
Sources: Figaro, 4 and 9 April 1925

Date: Wednesday, 13 May 1925
Location: Rue Cortambert *atelier,* Paris
Composers/Works: Manuel de Falla, *Seven Popular Spanish Songs*
Artists: Vera Janacopoulos, soprano, unnamed pianist
Source: Comtesse Jean de Polignac, private diary, archives of Prince Edmond
  de Polignac

Date: Thursday, 28 May 1925
Location: Rue Cortambert *atelier,* Paris
Artists: Alexander Borovsky, piano; Trio de La Cour de Belgique (Alfred
  Dubois, violin; Maurice Dambois, cello; Emile Bosquet, piano)
Sources: Comtesse Jean de Polignac, private diary, archives of Prince Edmond
  de Polignac; WSP to Serge Prokofiev, 16 May 1925, Serge Prokofiev
  Archive, Goldsmiths College, London

Date: Sunday, 7 June 1925
Location: Jouy-en-Josas
Composers/Works: Isaac Albéniz, selections from *Iberia*; Richard Wagner,
  The Ride of the Valkyries, transcribed for solo piano
Artist: Arthur Rubinstein, piano
Source: Comtesse Jean de Polignac, private diary, archives of Prince Edmond
  de Polignac

Date: Tuesday, 9 June 1925
Location: Grand salon, Avenue Henri-Martin, Paris
Composers/Works: Igor Stravinsky, Piano Sonata (premiere), Concerto for
  Piano and Wind Instruments, arr. two pianos
Artists: Igor Stravinsky, solo pianist; Jean Wiéner, second piano
Sources: Figaro, 8 June 1925; Comtesse Jean de Polignac, private diary,
  archives of Prince Edmond de Polignac

Date: Thursday 21 June 1925
Location: Grand salon, Avenue Henri-Martin, Paris

Composers/Works: Serge Prokofiev, Concerto No. 3 in C Major, Op. 26,
for piano and orchestra, and solo piano works: *March and Scherzo*
from the opera *Love for Three Oranges,* Op. 33, transcribed; four
Visions fugitives, Op. 22; two Gavottes, Opp. 25 and 32; Toccata
Artists: Serge Prokofiev, piano; chamber orchestra; Roger Désormière, conductor
Sources: Serge Prokofiev, diary entry of 20 June 1925, in his *Dnevnik,
1907–1933,* 330; *Figaro,* 24 June 1925; unpublished correspondence
of WSP and Serge Prokofiev between 10 April and 13 June 1925, Serge
Prokofiev Archive, Goldsmiths College, London

Date: Monday, 29 June 1925
Artists: Arthur Rubinstein, piano
Location: Grand salon, Avenue Henri-Martin, Paris
Source: Figaro, 2 July 1925

Date: Friday, 28 May 1926
Location: Grand salon, Avenue Henri-Martin, Paris
Composers/Works: Ernest Chausson, *Poème de l'Amour et de la Mer,* Op.
19, voice and piano; Maxime Jacob, *Six Poèmes de Jean Cocteau,* voice
and piano
Artists: Jane Bathori, soprano; Maxime Jacob, piano
Sources: Clouzot, *Souvenirs à deux voix de Maxime Jacob à Dom Clément
Jacob,* 114–16; Serge Prokofiev, diary entry of 28 May 1926, in his
Dnevnik, 1907–1933, 408

Date: Monday, 22 November 1926
Location: Rue Cortambert *atelier,* Paris
Composers/Works: J. S. Bach, unspecified work
Artists: Marguerite de Saint-Marceaux, soprano; unnamed instrumentalists
Source: Marguerite de Saint-Marceaux, daily diary, edition forthcoming
(Paris: Fayard)

Date: Monday, 24 January 1927
Location: Grand salon, Avenue Henri-Martin, Paris
Artists: Henri Sorin, conductor
Sources: Figaro, 25 January 1927; Henri Sorin to Serge Prokofiev, 27 April
1927, Serge Prokofiev Archive, Goldsmiths College, London

Date: Monday, 31 January 1927
Location: Grand salon, Avenue Henri-Martin, Paris
Composers/Works: J. S. Bach, unspecified cantata
Source: Catherine Pozzi, *Journal,* 358

Date: Monday, 7 February 1927
Location: Rue Cortambert *atelier,* Paris

Composers/Works: works for piano by Jean-Philippe Rameau, Isaac Albéniz, Frédéric Chopin
Source: Catherine Pozzi, *Journal,* 360–61

Date: Sunday, 29 May 1927
Location: Grand salon, Avenue Henri-Martin, Paris
Composers/Works: Igor Stravinsky, *Oedipus Rex,* opera-oratorio (premiere)
Artists: Belina-Skupervski, tenor (Oedipus); Hélène Sandoven, mezzo-soprano (Jocasta); G. Lanskoy, bass-baritone (Creon); K. Japorojetz, bass (Tiresias); D'Arial, tenor (The Shepherd); Lanskoy, baritone (The Messenger); Claude Brasseur (The Narrator); Igor Stravinsky, piano; Serge Prokofiev, piano
Sources: Walsh, *Stravinsky,* 446; Maurice Paléologue to WSP , 1 June 1927, Fondation Singer-Polignac; Comtesse Jean de Polignac, private diary, archives of Prince Edmond de Polignac; invitation card from WSP to Serge Prokofiev, Serge Prokofiev Archive, Goldsmiths College, London; Serge Prokofiev, diary entry of 29 May 1927, in his *Dnevnik, 1907–1933,* 563

Date: Wednesday, 15 June 1927
Location: Grand salon, Avenue Henri-Martin, Paris
Composers/Works: J. S. Bach, Toccata in C Major; Franz Liszt, Sonata in B Minor
Artists: Vladimir Horowitz, piano
Sources: Comtesse Jean de Polignac, private diary, archives of Prince Edmond de Polignac; invitation card from WSP to Serge Prokofiev, Serge Prokofiev Archive, Goldsmiths College, London

Date: "Piano Fridays," November and December 1927; January 1928
Location: Rue Cortambert *atelier,* Paris
Artists: Clara Haskil, Arthur Rubinstein, Francis Poulenc, Jacques Février, Henri Sauguet, Jean Françaix, Jeanne-Marie Darré, Magda Tagliaferro, pianists
Source: Jérôme Spycket, *Clara Haskil,* 95

Date: Friday, 16 December 1927
Location: Rue Cortamber *atelier,* Paris
Composer/Works: Serge Prokofiev, solo piano works
Artist: Serge Prokofiev, piano
Sources: correspondence of WSP and Serge Prokofiev, October-December 1927, Serge Prokofiev Archive, Goldsmiths College, London

Date: Monday, 16 January 1928
Location: Rue Cortambert *atelier,* Paris
Sources: Figaro, 19 January 1928

Date: Friday, 1 June 1928
Location: Grand salon, Avenue Henri-Martin, Paris
Source: *Figaro,* 20 May and 3 June 1928

Date: Monday, 20 May 1929
Location: Grand salon, Avenue Henri-Martin, Paris
Composers/Works: Igor Stravinsky, *Renard,* burlesque
Artists: Messieurs Raissow, Tkhoryevsky, Maltzoff, J. Nedre, singers; unspecified orchestra, Igor Stravinsky, conductor
Sources: Figaro, 22 May 1929; Serge Prokofiev, diary entry of 20 May 1929, in his *Dnevnik, 1907–1933*

Date: Monday, 17 February 1930
Location: Rue Cortambert *atelier,* Paris
Source: WSP to Paul Valéry, Bibliothèque nationale de France, MF 2800, 244–45

Date: Saturday, 13 December 1930
Location: Grand salon, Avenue Henri-Martin, Paris
Composers/Works: J. S. Bach, concertos
Artists: Vincent d'Indy
Source: Vincent d'Indy to WSP, 27 November 1930, Fondation Singer-Polignac, Paris

Date: Thursday, 25 December 1930
Location: Grand salon, Avenue Henri-Martin, Paris
Composers/Works: J. S. Bach, concertos
Source: Julien Green, *Journal,* 28

Date: Tuesday, 31 March 1931
Location: Grand salon, Avenue Henri-Martin, Paris
Composers/Works: Johannes Brahms, songs; Richard Strauss, songs; Paul Hindemith, *Konzertmusik* for Piano, Harp, and Orchestra
Sources: Figaro, 2 April 1931; Julien Green, *Journal,* 37

Date: Friday, 20 November 1931
Location: Rue Cortambert *atelier,* Paris
Composers/Works: W. A. Mozart, Concerto for Two Pianos, K. 365
Artists: Clara Haskil, Renatta Borgatti, pianos; unnamed orchestra
Sources: Previously unpublished letter, Olga Rudge to Ezra Pound, 17 November 1931, Olga Rudge Papers, Beinecke Library, Yale University, YCAL 54/279; Anna de Noailles, datebook entry, Archives Princesse Eugénie de Brancovan (communicated by Mignot-Ogliastri)

Date: Tuesday, 1 December 1931
Location: Rue Cortambert *atelier,* Paris
Composers/Works: Maurice Ravel, *Chansons populaires grecques,* voice and piano; Emmanuel Chabrier, songs
Artists: Madeleine Grey, soprano; Maurice Ravel, piano
Source: Figaro, 4 December 1931

Date: Thursday, 10 December 1931 and Friday, 11 December 1931
Location: Grand salon, Avenue Henri-Martin, Paris
Composers/Works: Carl Maria von Weber, Sonata for Clarinet and Piano; additional works for wind ensemble
Artists: Société des Instruments à vent
Sources: Figaro, 4 December 1931; Julien Green, *Journal,* 60; Anna de Noailles, datebook entry, Archives Princesse Eugénie de Brancovan (communicated by Mignot-Ogliastri)

Date: Thursday, 31 December 1931
Location: Rue Cortambert *atelier,* Paris
Composers/Works: Maurice Ravel, Concerto in G for piano, with 2nd piano reduction (possibly premiere)
Artists: Jacques Février, Francis Poulenc, pianos
Source: Francis Poulenc to Nora Auric, 12 January 1932, in Poulenc, *Correspondance,* 360–61

Date: Friday, 15 January 1932
Location: Rue Cortambert *atelier,* Paris
Source: Anna de Noailles, datebook entry, Archives Princesse Eugénie de Brancovan (communicated by Mignot-Ogliastri)

Date: Friday, 5 February 1932
Location: Rue Cortambert *atelier,* Paris
Composers/Works: Alban Berg, *Lyric Suite*
Artists: Kolisch String Quartet
Sources: Anna de Noailles, datebook entry, Archives Princesse Eugénie de Brancovan (communicated by Mignot-Ogliastri); WSP to Olga Rudge, undated [6 February 1932], Olga Rudge Papers, Beinecke Library, Yale University, YCAL 54/1675

Date: Friday, 12 February 1932
Location: Rue Cortambert *atelier,* Paris
Source: Anna de Noailles, datebook entry, Archives Princesse Eugénie de Brancovan (communicated by Mignot-Ogliastri)

Date: Wednesday, 15 June 1932
Location: Rue Cortambert *atelier,* Paris
Composers/Works: Francis Poulenc, *Cinq Poèmes de Max Jacob,* voice and piano; Georges Auric, Piano Sonata; Henri Sauguet, *Les Jeux de l'Amour et du Hasard,* two pianos
Artists: Suzanne Peignot, soprano; Georges Auric, piano; Francis Poulenc, piano; Henri Sauguet, piano
Sources: Comtesse Jean de Polignac, daily diary, archives of Prince Edmond de Polignac; Sauguet, *La Musique, ma vie,* 302

Date: Wednesday, 7 December 1932
Location: Grand salon, Avenue Henri-Martin, Paris
Composers/Works: Igor Stravinsky, works for violin and piano. *Suite italienne* on themes of Pergolesi; *Duo concertante* (premiere); Violin Concerto, transcribed for violin and piano; four arrangements for violin and piano (Aria from *Le Rossignol,* Scherzo and Berceuse from *L'Oiseau de feu,* "Danse Russe" from *Petrushka*)
Artists: Samuel Dushkin, violin; Igor Stravinsky, piano
Sources: printed program, Paul Sacher Stiftung; *Figaro,* 9 December 1932

Date: Tuesday, 23 May 1933
Concert in memory of Anna de Noailles
Location: Rue Cortambert *atelier,* Paris
Composers/Works: Gavriil Popov, Septet (later renamed Chamber Symphony) (Paris premiere); Erik Satie, "La Mort de Socrate" from *Socrate* *
Sources: Nadia Boulanger, Datebook, 23 May 1933, Bibliothèque nationale de France; Comtesse Jean de Polignac, Datebook , 23 May 1933, archives of Prince Edmond de Polignac

Date: Friday, 9 June 1933
Location: Rue Cortambert *atelier,* Paris
Composers/Works: Igor Markevitch, *Hymnes* * (premiere); Johannes Brahms, [unspecified] Quintet for Strings; unnamed solo piano works
Artists: Orchestre Symphonique de Paris, Roger Désormières, conductor; members of the OSP (in the Brahms); Beveridge Webster, piano
Sources: WSP to Igor Markevitch, 9 May 1933, Fonds Markevitch, Bibliothèque nationale de France; Nadia Boulanger, datebook entry of 9 June 1933, Bibliothèque nationale de France, VmF ms 99/2; Marie-Blanche de Polignac, datebook entry of 9 June 1933, archives of Prince Edmond de Polignac; Francis Poulenc to Igor Markevitch, undated letter [late May 1933], in Poulenc, *Correspondance,* 387; undated card from WSP to Arnold Schoenberg, archives of the Arnold Schönberg Center

Date: Monday, 17 June 1933
Location: Jouy-en-Josas
Composers/Works: J. S. Bach, excerpts from Cantatas 206 and 104; Boismortier, Adagio; J. S. Bach, March; Jean Baptiste Lully, trio from *Amadis*; Orlando di Lasso, *Bon jour mon coeur*; Claude Janequin, *Ce moys de May*; Le Jeune, *Revecy venir*; C. W. Gluck, Minuet from *Orphée*; Claude Gervaise, *Pavane* and *Galliarde*; Gabriel Fauré, "Nocturne" from *Shylock*; Igor Stravinsky, *Pastorale*
Artists: Roger Cortet, flute; Gérard Masson, flute; Jullien, violin; Figueroa, violin; Blanpain, viola; Bartsch, cello
Sources: Brooks, "Nadia Boulanger," *Journal of the American Musicological Society* 46, no. 3 (Fall 1993): 415–68

Date: Friday, 30 June 1933
Location: Rue Cortambert *atelier,* Paris
Composers/Works: J. S. Bach, excerpts from Cantatas 41, 71, 137, 151, 78, 3, 8, 208, and 60; Brandenburg Concerto No. 5; Antonio Vivaldi, Concerto in D Minor, organ and strings, transcribed by Nadia Boulanger
Artists: Maria Modrakowska, soprano; WSP, organ; Paul Kochanski, violin; Roger Cortet, flute; Marie-Blanche (Comtesse Jean) de Polignac, soprano and piano; chorus (including Elliott Carter, bass) and string orchestra, Nadia Boulanger, conductor
Sources: printed program, Fondation Internationale Nadia et Lili Boulanger; printed program, archives of Prince Edmond de Polignac; *Figaro,* 29 June and 1 July 1933

Date: Saturday, 22 July 1933
Location: Jouy-en-Josas
Composers/Works: Jean Françaix, String Trio; Gabriel Fauré, Piano Quartet in C Minor, Op. 15; Franz Schubert, unnamed work
Artists: Pasquier Trio (violin, viola, cello), Jean Françaix, piano; "Horodjski," perhaps pianist Mieczyslaw Horszowski
Sources: Jean Françaix to Nadia Boulanger, 10 July 1933, Bibliothèque nationale de France, NLa 71, 64; Nadia Boulanger, datebook entry of 22 July 1933, Bibliothèque nationale de France, VmF ms 99/3

Date: Monday, 8 January 1934
Location: Rue Cortambert *atelier,* Paris
Composers/Works: J. S. Bach, excerpts from Cantatas 78, 163, and 184; Brandenburg Concerto No. 4; W. A. Mozart, Clarinet Concerto
Artists: Henri Bronschwak, violin; Roger Cortet, flute; Gérard Masson, flute; Louis Cahuzac, clarinet; chorus and orchestra, Nadia Boulanger, conductor
Sources: printed program, Fondation Internationale Nadia et Lili Boulanger; printed program, archives of Prince Edmond de Polignac; *Excelsior,* 11 January 1934

Date: Sunday, 21 January 1934
Location: Rue Cortambert *atelier,* Paris
Composers/Works: J. S. Bach, Cantata No. 4 (*Christ Lag in Todesbanden*); Gabriel Fauré, "Nocturne" from *Shylock;* Paul Hindemith, *Gebürt Maria,* voice and piano; W. A. Mozart, duo, "Che soave zefiretto," from *The Marriage of Figaro;* Stravinsky, *Pastorale;* Jean-Baptiste Lully, trio from *Amadis;* J. S. Bach, Concerto in C for Two Pianos
Artists: Maria Modrakowska, soprano; Marie-Blanche de Polignac, soprano; Frédéric Anspach, tenor; François Narçon, bass; WSP, piano; chorus and orchestra, Nadia Boulanger, piano and conductor
Sources: printed program, Fondation Internationale Nadia et Lili Boulanger; printed program, archives of Prince Edmond de Polignac; *Excelsior,* 22 January 1934

Date: Wednesday, 16 May 1934
Location: Grand salon, Avenue Henri-Martin, Paris
Composers/Works: Arthur Honegger, *La Belle de Mondon*, operetta; vocal
    works of Roger Ducasse and Joaquin Nin
Artists: Gabrielle Gills, soprano; Jacques Neilz, tenor; J. Peyronnet, so-
    prano; Andrée Vaurabourg-Honegger, piano; Arthur Honegger, piano
Source: *Figaro,* 17 May 1934

Date: Thursday, 17 May 1934
Location: Grand salon, Avenue Henri-Martin, Paris
Composers/Works: J. S. Bach, Cantata 104; Gabriel Fauré, *La Bonne Chan-
    son,* voice and piano; Edmond de Polignac, *Ave maris stella, Aubade,*
    chorus a cappella; Franz Joseph Haydn, "Nun schwanden" from *The
    Creation*; Igor Stravinsky, excerpts from *Perséphone*
Artists: Maria Modrakowska, soprano; Nadia Boulanger, piano and conductor
Sources: printed program, Fondation Internationale Nadia et Lili Boulanger;
    printed program, archives of Prince Edmond de Polignac; Julien Green,
    Journal, 165

Date: Sunday 10 June 1934
Location: Rue Cortambert *atelier,* Paris
Composers/Works: Franz Joseph Haydn, Divertimento for Flute, Violin,
    Cello; George Frederick Handel, Sonata in C Minor for Flute, Violin,
    Cello, and Bass
Artists: Quintette Instrumental de Paris (René Le Roy, flute; Pierre Jamet,
    harp; René Bas, violin; Pierre Grout, viola; Roger Boulmé, cello)
Source: *Figaro,* 12 June 1934

Date: Thursday, 17 January 1935
Location: Rue Cortambert *atelier,* Paris
Composers/Works: Claudio Monteverdi, *Lasciatemi morire* and *T'amo mia
    vita*; Paul Hindemith, *O Herr, gib jedem* and *Wer sich die Musik erkiest*;
    Jean Françaix, *Trois Duos*; Heinrich Schütz, *Historia der Auferstehung*
Artists: Maria Modrakowska, soprano; Natalie Kédroff, soprano; Marie-
    Blanche de Polignac, soprano; Mmes Gresle, J. Lemoine, Manziarly,
    Rauh, voices; Frédéric Anspach, tenor; Benedetti, violin; Figueroa, vio-
    lin; Quattrochi, viola; Bartsch, cello; A. Cellier, organ; E. Passani, harp-
    sichord; chorus and orchestra conducted by Nadia Boulanger
Sources: printed program, Fondation Internationale Nadia et Lili Boulanger;
    printed program, archives of Prince Edmond de Polignac; *Figaro,* 21
    January 1935

Date: Thursday, 28 February 1935
Location: Rue Cortambert *atelier,* Paris

Composers/Works: Henry Purcell, extracts from *King Arthur*; Igor Markevitch, chorale from *Cantate*; W. A. Mozart, *S'Altro che lagrime*; André Grétry, *Sérénade de l'amant jaloux*; Jean Françaix, *Pour un anniversaire*; Marcelle de Manziarly, *Hélas que je suis désolée* and *J'aimeray mon amy*; Igor Stravinsky, *Ave Maria*; J. S. Bach, Cantata 150 *Nach dir verlanget mich*
Artists: Marie-Blanche de Polignac, soprano; Maria Modrakowska, soprano; J. Lemoine, mezzo-soprano; Hugues Cuénod, tenor; D. Harris, baritone; Gromer, oboe; Proffit, violin; Migliorini, violin; Quattrocchi, viola; Bartsch, cello; Annette Dieudonné, organ; chorus and orchestra conducted by Nadia Boulanger
Sources: printed program, Fondation Internationale Nadia et Lili Boulanger; printed program, archives of Prince Edmond de Polignac

Date: Saturday, 25 January 1936
Location: Rue Cortambert *atelier*
Composers/Works: piano works
Artists: Clara Haskil, piano
Source: Doda Conrad, *Dodascalies*, 134

Date: Friday, 7 February 1936
Location: Rue Cortambert *atelier*, Paris
Composers/Works: W. A. Mozart, *Petit Ouverture*; John Dowland, *Lachrimae antiquae novae, King of Denmark's Galliard*, and *Semper Dowland, Semper Dolens*; Anonymous, *Bransle simple*; J. S. Bach, "Seligster Erquickungstag" for bass voice from Cantata 70, *Wachet, betet, seid bereit allezeit*; Paul Hindemith, Two Pieces for String Quartet, Op. 44 and *Tummel dich*, Op. 33, No. 6; Albert Roussel, *Rossignol, mon amour*; Aaron Copland, *As It Fell upon a Day*; William Boyce, Symphony No. 1; Claudio Monteverdi, *Hor che'l ciel, Lamento della ninfa*, and *Chiomo d'oro*
Artists: Marie-Blanche de Polignac, soprano; Hugues Cuénod, tenor; Paul Derenne, baritone; Doda Conrad, bass; Roger Cortet, flute; chorus and orchestra conducted by Nadia Boulanger
Sources: printed program, Fondation Internationale Nadia et Lili Boulanger; printed program, archives of Prince Edmond de Polignac

Date: Thursday, 13 February 1936
Location: Rue Cortambert *atelier*, Paris
Composers/Works: Franz Joseph Haydn, Symphony in C Major; Paul Hindemith, Five Pieces (*Zusammenspiel*), Op. 44; Carl Maria von Weber, *Die fromme Magd* and *Mein Schätzerl*; Jean Françaix, Sonatine, violin and piano (premiere); W. A. Mozart, Concerto for Two Pianos, K. 365
Artists: Marie-Blanche de Polignac, soprano; Irène Kédroff, soprano; Gisèle Peyron, soprano; J. Lemoine, mezzo-soprano; Natalie Kédroff, mezzo-

soprano; Warner, mezzo-soprano; Monteil, mezzo-soprano; Rauh, alto;
L. Vergniaud, alto; Paul Makanowitzky, violin; Jacques Février, piano;
Orchestra de la Société Symphonique, conducted by Nadia Boulanger
Sources: printed program, Fondation Internationale Nadia et Lili Boulanger;
printed program, archives of Prince Edmond de Polignac

Date: Saturday, 22 February 1936
Location: Grand salon, Avenue Henri-Martin, Paris
Composers/Works: Franz Schubert, Octet, Op. 166; Tomas Vitali, *Ciaccona*
for solo violin; W. A. Mozart, tenor aria from *La Clemenza di Tito*;
Igor Stravinsky, *Chant dissident*; J. S. Bach, *Bist du bei mir* and Violin
Concerto in E Major, BWV 1042
Artists: Hugues Cuénod, tenor; Gioconda de Vito, violin; André Vacellier,
clarinet; Reumond, horn; Grandmaison, bassoon; Bronschwak, violin;
Migliorini, violin; Blanpain, viola; Lancy, cello; Georges Marie, bass;
chorus and orchestra conducted by Nadia Boulanger
Sources: printed program, Fondation Internationale Nadia et Lili Boulanger;
printed program, archives of Prince Edmond de Polignac

Date: Friday, 15 May 1936
Location: Grand salon, Avenue Henri-Martin, Paris (benefit concert for
the Cercle Ronsard)
Composers/Works: Franz Schubert, *Gott ist meine Zuversicht* and
Mondenschein; Robert Schumann, *Ländliches Lied*; Felix Mendelssohn,
Gruss; Francis Poulenc, *Épitaphe*; Claudio Monterverdi, *Lamento della
ninfa*; Gabriel Fauré, *Madrigal*; John Dowland, *Flow My Tears* and *If
My Complaints*; Thomas Campion, *Through Your Strangeness* and
Jack and Joan; J. S. Bach, *Jesu meine Freude*
Artists: Marie-Blanche de Polignac, soprano; Gisèle Peyron, soprano; Irène
Kédroff, soprano; Warner, mezzo-soprano; Monteil, mezzo-soprano;
Vergniaud, alto; Natalie Kédroff, alto
Sources: printed program, Fondation Internationale Nadia et Lili Boulanger;
printed program, archives of Prince Edmond de Polignac; *Figaro,* 2
May 1936

Date: Tuesday, 7 July 1936
Location: Rue Cortambert *atelier,* Paris
Composers/Works: Franz Schubert, *Lieder*; J. S. Bach, "Seligster
Erquickungstag" for bass voice from Cantata 70
Artists: Hugues Cuénod, tenor; Doda Conrad, bass; Nadia Boulanger, piano
Source: Nadia Boulanger, datebook entries of 3 and 7 July 1936,
Bibliothèque nationale de France, VmF ms 100/3

Date: Sunday, 22 November 1936 (two concerts, morning and evening)
Location: "borrowed" salon of Lady Maud Cunard, London

Composers/Works: Morning program: works for soprano and two pianos. Evening program: Claudio Monteverdi, *Hor che'l ciel, Lamento della ninfa, Chiomo d'oro*; Hector Berlioz, "Tout n'est que paix" from the opera *Les Troyens*; Gabriel Fauré, *Madrigal*; Claude Debussy, *Dieu, qu'il la fait*; W. A. Mozart, Sonata for Two Pianos; Carl Maria von Weber, *Die fromme Magd, Liebeslied,* and *Mein Schätzerl*; Franz Schubert, *Mondenschein* and *Andantino varié*, Op. 84, No. 1; Johannes Brahms, *Die Schwestern* and *Liebeslieder Waltzes*, Op. 52, No. 1; J. S. Bach, "Seligster Erquickungstag" from Cantata 70; Rosseter, *When Laura Smiles*; Lennox Berkeley, *Polka*

Artists: Morning program: Marie-Blanche de Polignac, soprano; Clifford Curzon, piano; Nadia Boulanger, piano; Evening program: Nadia Boulanger Ensemble (Polignac, Kédroff, Peyron, Kédroff, Cuénod, Derenne, Conrad), Clifford Curzon, piano; Nadia Boulanger, piano and conductor

Sources: printed program, Fondation Internationale Nadia et Lili Boulanger; printed program, archives of Prince Edmond de Polignac

Date: Monday, 18 January 1937

Location: Rue Cortambert, *atelier,* Paris

Composers/Works: works for piano: Padre Soler, Sonata in F-sharp; Amteo Albeniz, Sonata; Gluck, arr. Saint-Saëns, Airs de ballet d'*Alceste*; Claude Debussy, *Les Collines d'Anacapri, Poissons d'or*; Maurice Ravel, *Oiseaux tristes, Fox-trot*; Erik Satie, *Croquis et agaceries d'un gros bonhomme en bois: Tyrolienne turque, Danse maigre, Espanana*; Francis Poulenc: Suite; Isaac Albeniz, *Évocation* and *El Puerto* from *Ibéria*; Frédéric Mompou, *Chanson et danse*; Ernest Halffter, *Danse de la Gitane*

Artist: Ricardo Viñes, piano

Source: printed program, archives of Prince Edmond de Polignac

Date: Friday, 5 February 1937

Location: Rue Cortambert *atelier,* Paris

Composers/Works: Marc-Antoine Charpentier, *Pestis Mediolanensis*; Claudio Monteverdi, *Lasciatemi morire, O Mirtillo, T'amo mia vita, Zefiro torna, Chiome d'oro*; Gabriel Fauré, "Nocturne" from *Shylock*; Francis Poulenc, *Litanies pour la vierge noire*; Igor Markevitch, *Deployez-vous d'un vol adorable*; J. S. Bach, chorale from *Wachet, betet*

Artists: Nadia Boulanger Ensemble, Nadia Boulanger, piano and conductor

Source: *Figaro*, 3 February 1937

Date: Friday, 19 February 1937

Location: Grand salon, Avenue Henri-Martin, Paris

Composers/Works: Domenico Scarlatti, three sonatas (orchestrated by Jean Françaix); Francis Poulenc, *A ma guitare*, voice and piano, and *Suite*

française, orchestra; Crequillon, *Cessez mes yeux;* Sermisy, *Tant que vivray;* Gabriel Fauré, *Madrigal;* Jean Françaix, Sérénade for Twelve Instruments, Op. 58; Johannes Brahms, *Liebeslieder Waltzes,* Op. 52, No. 1

Artists: Marie-Blanche de Polignac, soprano; Irène Kédroff, soprano; Hugues Cuénod, tenor; Doda Conrad, bass; Roger Cortet, flute; Henri Gromer, oboe; André Vacellier, clarinet; G. Grandmaison, bassoon; Vuillermoz, Adriano, Alviset, unspecified instruments; Bas, violin; Migliorini, violin; Schmitt, viola; Roger Boulmé, cello; Georges Marie, bass; Dinu Lipatti, piano; Nadia Boulanger, pianist and conductor

Sources: printed program, Fondation Internationale Nadia et Lili Boulanger; printed program, archives of Prince Edmond de Polignac; *Figaro,* 10 February 1937

Date: Tuesday, 23 February 1937
Location: Grand salon, Avenue Henri-Martin, Paris
Composer/Works: Vocal duets of Mendelssohn, Schubert (duet from *Mignon*), Schumann
Artists: Marie-Blanche de Polignac, soprano; Hugues Cuénod, tenor; Nadia Boulanger, piano
Sources: Comtesse Jean de Polignac, private diary, archives of Prince Edmond de Polignac; Rosamond Lehmann to John Lehmann, Princeton University Library

Date: Friday, 12 March 1937
Location: Grand salon, Avenue Henri-Martin, Paris
Composers/Works: Germaine Tailleferre, *Ouverture,** orchestra; Henri Sauguet, Concerto No. 1 for Piano and Orchestra (premiere); Gabriel Fauré, Suite from *Pelléas et Mélisande,* Op. 80,* orchestra; Germaine Tailleferre, Concerto for Violin and Orchestra
Artists: Yvonne Astruc, violin; Clara Haskil, piano; members of the Concerts Lamoureux Orchestra, Eugène Bigot, conductor
Sources: printed program, Fondation Internationale Nadia et Lili Boulanger; printed program, archives of Prince Edmond de Polignac

Date: Friday, 12 November 1937
Location: "borrowed" salon of Lady Ravensdale, London
Composers/Works: Charles Gounod, excerpts from *Philémon et Baucis;* Thomas Tallis, *O Nata Lux;* John Dowland, *Flow My Tears,* Henry Purcell, *How Blest are the Shepherds,* J. S. Bach, "Seligster Erquickungstag" from Cantata 70; Emmanuel Chabrier, *Ah! d'amour plus un mot;* Francis Poulenc, *Avant le cinéma,* voice and piano; Hector Berlioz, "Tout n'est que paix" from *Les Troyens;* Gabriel Fauré, *Madrigal;* Johannes Brahms, *Liebeslieder Waltzes,* Op. 52, No. 1
Artists: Nadia Boulanger Ensemble (Polignac, Kédroff, Peyron, Kédroff,

Rauh, Cuénod, Derenne, Bastard, Conrad); Clifford Curzon, piano; Nadia Boulanger, piano

Sources: printed program, Fondation Internationale Nadia et Lili Boulanger; printed program, archives of Prince Edmond de Polignac

Date: Thursday, 2 June 1938
Location: Rue Cortambert *atelier*, Paris
Artists: unnamed Hungarian pianist, student of Arthur Schnabel
Source: Comtesse Jean de Polignac, private diary, archives of Prince Edmond de Polignac

Date: Sunday, 12 June 1938
Location: Jouy-en-Josas
Artists: Clara Haskil, piano; Dinu Lipatti, piano
Source: Comtesse Jean de Polignac, private diary, archives of Prince Edmond de Polignac

Date: Tuesday, 14 June 1938
Location: Rue Cortambert *atelier*, Paris
Composers/Works: works by Franz Schubert. Piano Trio in B flat Major, Op. 99; Piano Trio in E flat Major, Op. 100; a group of songs; work (unnamed) for solo woman's voice accompanied by chorus
Artists: Marya Freund, mezzo-soprano; Doda Conrad, bass
Source: Comtesse Jean de Polignac, private diary, archives of Prince Edmond de Polignac

Date: Thursday, 30 June 1938
Location: Rue Cortambert *atelier*, Paris
Composers/Works: Jean Françaix, *Le Diable boîteux,** tenor, bass, chamber orchestra (premiere, played twice, once at the beginning and once at the end of the concert); J. S. Bach, excerpts from cantatas *Beglückte Herde, Jesu Schafe, Der Tod bleibt doch, Selig sind die Toten, Es ist genug,* men's voices and orchestra; Gabriel Fauré, *La Bonne Chanson,* voice and string quartet
Artists: Marie-Blanche de Polignac, soprano; Hugues Cuénod, tenor; Doda Conrad, bass; Roland Charmy, violin; Chedical, violin; Benoit, viola; Paul Tortelier, cello; Georges Marie, bass; Roger Cortet, flute; Henri Gromer, oboe; André Vacellier, clarinet; G. Grandmaison, bassoon; Blot, bassoon; Adriano, trumpet; André Lafosse, trombone; Félix Passerone, percussion; Lily Laskine, harp
Source: printed program, Fondation Internationale Nadia et Lili Boulanger

Date: Saturday, 16 December 1938
Location: Rue Cortambert *atelier*, Paris
Composers/Works: Henry Purcell, Suite for ensemble; J. S. Bach, sonata

(unspecified); Francis Poulenc, songs dedicated to Marie-Blanche de Polignac, including *Trois Poèmes de Louise de Vilmorin,* and Concerto for Organ* (premiere)

Artists: Marie-Blanche de Polignac, soprano; Francis Poulenc, piano; Maurice Duruflé, organ

Sources: printed program, Fondation Internationale Nadia et Lili Boulanger; Comtesse Jean de Polignac, private diary, archives of Prince Edmond de Polignac

Date: Wednesday, 24 May 1939 and Friday, 26 May 1939 (the second is a paying concert)

Location: Rue Cortambert *atelier,* Paris

Composers/ Works: songs of Francis Poulenc

Artists: Pierre Bernac, baritone; Francis Poulenc, piano

Sources: Comtesse Jean de Polignac, private diary, archives of Prince Edmond de Polignac; Les "Indiscrétions de Saint-Loup: Les Mystères de l'atelier," *L'Ordre,* 27 May 1939

Date: Thursday, 22 June 1939

Location: Rue Cortambert *atelier,* Paris

Composers/Works: J. S. Bach, Sonata in E flat Major, flute and piano; Francis Poulenc, songs for baritone and piano; Franz Schubert, *Ständchen,* voice and piano; André Caplet *Viens, ma flûte, invisible surprise,* voice and piano; Albert Roussel, *Rossignol, mon mignon,* voice and piano; Francis Poulenc, *Quatre Motets pour un temps de pénitence,* chorus and piano; Robert Schumann, choral work for solo voice, flute, horn, chorus, and orchestra; Edmond de Polignac, *Choeur d'Esther,* women's voices and piano

Artists: Marie-Blanche de Polignac, soprano and piano; Pierre Bernac, baritone; Francis Poulenc, piano; Yvonne Gouverné Chorus, Yvonne Gouverné, conductor; unnamed flutist

Source: Comtesse Jean de Polignac, private diary, archives of Prince Edmond de Polignac

Date: Monday, 3 July 1939

Location: Grand salon, Avenue Henri-Martin, Paris

Composers/Works: J. S. Bach, Brandenburg Concerto No. 3; W. A. Mozart, Concerto for Two Pianos, K. 365; Frederich Busoni, Concertino for Two Pianos; Dinu Lipatti, *Suite Classique* for Piano and Chamber Orchestra, and Concertino for Strings, arranged for two pianos

Artists: Dinu Lipatti, piano; Clara Haskil, piano; orchestra conducted by Charles Munch

Sources: WSP to Nadia Boulanger, Bibliothèque nationale de France, NLa 94; *New York Herald Tribune,* 5 July 1939

Appendix B

Guests in the Salon of the Princesse Edmond de Polignac

ABDY, Lady (1 Jun 28); **ADHÉMAR**, Comtesse Marie d' (19 Jan 19, 16 Feb 19); **ALBUFERA**, Duchesse d' (9 Jun 11); **ANCILOTTO**, Comte (31 Mar 00); **ANDLAU**, Comtesse d' (11 Apr 07, 16 May 34); **ANET**, Claude (8 Jan 09, 9 Jun 11); **ANDRÉ**, Mme Édouard (31 Mar 00, 23 Feb 10); **ARAMON**, Comte/Comtesse Paul d' (18 Dec 09); **ARENBERG**, Princesse Pierre d' (10 Mar 12); **ARGENSON**, Marquis/ Marquise (3 Mar 05, 11 Apr 07, 11 Apr 08, 8 Jan 09, 4 May 09, 23 Feb 10, 9 Jun 11, 10 Mar 12); **ARGYROPOULOS**, Mlle (23 Feb 10); **ARNIM**, Mme/Mlle (31 Mar 00); **ASTIER DE LAVIGERIE**, Baron d' (16 Jun 13); **ASTRUC**, Gabriel (14 Jan 06, 2 Jun 08); **AURIC**, Georges (21 June 25); **AVARAY**, Marquise d' (18 Apr 01); **AYEN**, Duchesse Jean (Solange) d' (21 Jun 25, 7 Feb 27, 10 Jun 34, 17 Jan 35); **AZEVEDO**, Comte/Comtesse d' (20 Jun 98)
BACON (United States Ambassador)/Mrs./Miss (10 March 12); **BAILBY**, Léon (10 Mar 12); **BAILLEUL**, Marquise de (25 Feb 96, 26 Apr 98, 20 Jun 98, 11 May 03, 11 Apr 07, 4 May 09, 16 May 34); **BAKST**,Léon (22 Feb 12, 14 May 17); **BALLI**, Mme/Mlle (9 Jun 11, 10 Mar 12); **BARTHOLONI**, M./Mme de (20 Jun 98); **BASSANO**, Duchesse de (31 Mar 00, 18 Apr 01); **BASSIANO**, Prince/Princesse de (31 Jan 05, 10 Jun 34); **BAUGNIES**, M./Mme Jacques (11 Apr 07, 23 Feb 10, 10 Mar 12); **BEAUCHAMP**, Comtesse de (10 Mar 12, 16 Jun 13, 3 Jul 39); **BEAU-MONT**, Comte/Comtesse Étienne de (2 Jun 08, 22 Feb 12, 10 Mar 12, 16 Jun 13, 16 Dec 17, 21 Jun 25, 7 Feb. 35); **BÉARN**, Comte/Comtesse René de (22 Apr 95, 31 Mar 00, 11 Feb 06, 11 Apr 07); **BEAUVAU**, Prince de (11 Apr 07, 5 Apr 08, 11 Apr 08, 2 Jun 08, 8 Jan 09, 23 Feb 10, 9 Jun 11, 1 Jun 28); **BEAUVAU-CRAON**, Prince/Princesse de (3 Jul 39); **BEECHAM**, Sir Thomas (July 1914); **BÉHAGUE**, Comtesse de (17 Jan 35); **BÉNARDAKY**, M./Mme de (20 Jun 98, 31 Mar 00); Benkendorff, M. (2 Jun 08); **BERCKHEIM**, Baron/Baronne "Toto" de (31 Mar 00, 14 May 17, 11 Nov 17); **BERNILLE**, Marquise de (10 Mar 12); **BERRY**, Walter (17 Nov 17, 21 Jun 25); **BERTEUX**, Comtesse Jean/Mlle de (31 Mar 00, 10 Mar 12); **BERTIER DE SAUVIGNY**, Comte L. de (31 Mar

00); **BERTOUX,** Comtesse Jean de (18 Dec 09); **BIBESCO,** Prince Georges/Princesse Marthe (5 Apr 08, 22 Feb 12, 26 Mar 14); **BISACCIA,** Duc/Duchesse de (25 May 03, 31 Jan 05, 5 Apr 08, 9 Jun 11, 16 Jun 13, 17 Jan 35); **BLANCHE,** Jacques-Émile (20 Jun 98, 18 Apr 01, 11 Apr 08, 2 Jun 08, 8 Jan 09, 4 May 09, 10 Mar 12, 21 Jun 25); **BLUMENTHAL,** Mme (16 May 34); **BOISROUVRAY,** Comte/Comtesse Amaury de (18 Dec 09, 1 Jun 19, 16 May 34); **BOLDINI,** Giovanni (20 Jun 98); **BONNAMY,** Mrs. (16 May 34); **BONNARD,** Abel (23 Feb 10, 10 Mar 12); **BONNAT,** Léon (16 Jun 95); **BONNIÈRES,** M./Mme Robert de (3 Mar 95, 16 Jun 95, 5 Jan 96, 20 Jun 98, 22 May 01, 27 May 01); **BONVOULOIR,** Comte Guy de (10 Mar 12, 16 Jun 13); **BORGHESE,** Prince/Princesse Giovanni de (24 Mar 00, 16 Jun 13); **BOROVSKY,** Alexander (21 Jun 25); **BOURG DE BOZAS,** Comtesse du (9 Jun 11); **BOULANGER,** Nadia (10 Jun 23, 21 June 25, 23 May 33, 9 Jun 33); **BOURBON-PARME,** Prince/Princesse Sixte de (1 Jun 28); **BOURGET,** Paul (26 Mar 14); **BOUTRAY,** Baronne de (20 Jun 98); **BOZANO,** Dchsse/Mlle (31 Mar 00); **BRABANT,** Comtesse de (16 May 34); **BRANCOVAN,** Prince de (16 Jun 95, 2 Jun 08); **BRANCOVAN,** Prince/Princesse Constantine de (2 Jun 08, 23 Feb 10); **BRANCOVAN,** Princesse Rachel de (3 Mar 95, 12 Jun 98, 22 May 01, 27 May 01, 31 Jan 05, 11 Feb 06, 11 Apr 07, 23 Feb 10, 9 Jun 11, 22 Feb 12, 22 Dec 12); **BRANTES,** Mme de (22 Apr 95, 16 Jun 95, 1 May 96, 12 Jun 98, 22 May 01); **BRANTES,** Marquis/Marquise de (2 Jun 08, 10 Mar 12); **BRÉGUET,** Mme (16 May 34); **BRETEUIL,** Marquis/Marquise de Breteuil (11 Apr 08, 10 Mar 12); **BRIAILLES,** Comte/Comtesse R. Chandon de (5 Apr 08); **BRIEY,** Comtesse Th. de (5 Apr 08, 2 Jun 08, 23 Feb 10); **BRIGODE,** Comte/Comtesse de (22 Apr 95, 16 Jun 95, 31 Mar 00, 11 May 03, 25 May 03, 2 Jun 08); **BRIMONT,** Mme de (17 Nov 17); **BROGLIE,** Prince/Princesse Amédée de (25 Feb 96, 1 May 96, 12 Jun 98, 20 Jun 98); **BROGLIE,** Prince/Princesse François de (12 Jun 98, 15 Feb 05, 3 Mar 05); **BROGLIE,** Princesse Jacques de (14 May 17); **BROGLIE,** Prince/Princesse Robert de (1 Jun 28); **BROISSIA,** Mme de (16 Jun 95); **BROU,** Marquise de (22 Apr 95, 31 Mar 00); **BRUNEEL,** Comte/Comtesse (23 Feb 10)

CADAVAL, Comtesse Olga de (1 Jun 28); **CAETANI,** Don Roffredo (31 Jan 05);, **CAMPOSELICE,** Duchesse Victor de (22 May 88); **CAPPIELLO,** M. L. (2 Jun 08, 1 Jun 28); **CAPUS,** A. (26 Mar 14); **CARAMAN,** Comte E. de (11 Apr 08); **CARAMAN-CHIMAY,** Prince/Princesse Alexandre de (18 Apr 01, 22 May 01, 11 Feb 06, 11 Apr 07, 11 Apr 08, 23 Feb 10, 9 Jun 11, 22 Feb 12, 21 Jun 25, 17 Jan 35); **CARAMAN-CHIMAY,** Prince Philippe de (11 Apr 08, 4 May 09); **CARAMAN-CHIMAY,** Prince/Princesse Pierre de (15 Feb 05, 2 Jun 08); **CAROLUS-DURAN** (16 Jun 95); **CARRABY,** Mme (31 Mar 00); **CASA-FUERTE,** Marquis/Marquise Illan de (2 Jun 08); **CASERTA,** H. R. H. Comtesse (wife of the head of the royal family of Bourbon-Sicily) (31 Mar 00); **CASTÉJA**, Comte/Comtesse de (31 Mar 00, 31 Jan 05, 11 Apr 07, 5 Apr 08, 2 Jun 08, 8 Jan 09, 23 Feb 10, 9 Jun 11, 21 Jun 25); **CASTÉJA**, Comtesse Alex de (16 May 34); **CASTÉJA**, Comte/Comtesse Stanislas de (11 Apr 07, 16 Jun 13, 1 Jun 28); **CASTÉJA**, Marquise de (18 Apr 01); **CASTELAJAC**, Comte/Comtesse de (9 Jun 11); **CASTELLANE**, Comte/Comtesse Boni de (16 Jun 95, 25 Feb 96, 11 May 03, 15 Feb 05, 11 Apr 07, 5 Apr 08, 11 Apr 08, 2 Jun 08, 4 May 09, 9 Jun 11, 22 Dec 12, 26 Mar 14); **CASTELLANE**, Comte/Comtesse Jean de (31 Mar 00, 31 Jan 05, 11 Apr 07, 2 Jun 08, 10 Mar 12, 22 Dec 12, 16 Jun 13); **CASTELLANE**, Marquis de (22 Apr 95; 16 Jun 95); **CASTELLANE**, Marquise de (12 May 96, 18 Apr 01); **CHABANNES-LA-PALICE**, Comte/Comtesse Alfred (née Armande de Polignac) (16 Jun 95, 12 Jun 98, 2 Jun 08); **CHABRILLAN**, Comte/Comtesse Aynard de (25 May 03, 4 May 09, 23 Feb 10, 16 Jun 13, 21 Jun 25); **CHADOURNE**, M./Mme Paul (10 Jun 34); **CHAMBRUN**, Comte de (10 Mar 12); **CHANDON DE BRIAILLES**, Comtesse G. (9 Jun 11); **CHANDON DE BRIAILLES**, Comtesse G. (16 Jun 13); **CHANDON DE BRIAILLES**, Vicomtesse de (22 May 88); **CHAPLIN**, Anthony/Alvilde (12 Jun 38); **CHAPONAY**, Marquis/Marquise Pierre de (16 Jun 95, 15 Feb 05, 3 Mar 05, 16 Jun 13); **CHARMES**, Francis (23 Feb 10); **CHAULNES**, Duchesse de (1 Jun 28); **CHAUSSON**, Ernest (25 Feb 96); **CHÉRAMY**, M. (11 Apr 08, 8 Jan 09); **CHEVIGNÉ**, Comte/Comtesse Adhéaume de (11 Apr 07, 5 Apr 08, 2 Jun 08, 4 May 09, 16 June 13); **CHEVILLARD**, M./Mme Camille (27 May 01); **CHEVREAU**, Comtesse Urbain (23 Feb 10); **CHILDE**, M./Mme Edward Lee (16 Jun 95, 11 Apr 08, 2 Jun 08); **CLAIRIN**, Georges (11 Apr 08); **CLAPIERS**, Comte de (26 Apr 98, 2 Jun 08); **CLAPIERS**, Marquis/Marquise de (11 Apr 07); **CLERK**, Lady (wife of the British ambassador to France) (17 Jan 35); **CLERMONT-TONNERRE**, Comtesse de (12 Jun 98, 20 Jun 98); **CLERMONT-TONNERRE**, Duchesse de (11 Nov 17); **CLERMONT-TONNERRE**, Marquise de (22 May 88); **COCHIN**, Denys (27 May 01); **COCTEAU**, Jean (22 Feb 12, 29 May 27); **COLEBROOKE**, Lady (11 Feb 06, 4 May 09, 22 Feb 12); **COLETTE** (22 May 01, 21 Jun 25, 30 Jun 33, 23 Feb 37); **COLONNE**, Édouard (25 May 03); **CONRAD**, Doda (25 Jan 36); **CONROBERT**, Maréchal de (22 May 88); **CONTADES**, Vicomte/Vicomtesse Antoine de (1 May 96, 12 Jun 98); **CONTADES**, Comtesse A. de (26 Apr 98); **COSSÉ-BRISSAC**, Comte/Comtesse de (10 Jun 34); **COSTA DE BEAUREGARD**, Comte/Comtesse de (22 May 88, 31 Mar 00); **COUTRIÈRE**, Princesse de (23 Feb 10); **COURCY**, Marquise de (22 May 88); **CROISSET**, Francis de (8 Jan 09); **CUNARD**, Lady Maud (July 1914); **CUNARD**, Lady Violet (1 Jun 28) **DANILOFF**, Mme (16 May 34); **DAUDET**, Lucien (11 Apr 08, 2 Jun 08, 4 May 09); **DECAZES**, Comte Louis (2 Jun 08); **DECAZES**, Duc Élie (26 Apr 98, 12 June 98, 31 Jan 05, 3 Mar 05, 2 Jun 08, 8 Jan 09, 4

May 09, 18 Dec 09, 23 Feb 10); **DECAZES**, Duchesse Élie (25 Feb 96, 12 May 96); **DECAZES**, (dowager) Duchesse Louis (16 Jun 95); **DECAZES**, Duchesse Louis (1 Jun 28, 16 May 34, 17 Jan 35); **DECAZES**, Mlle Daisy (4 May 09, 18 Dec 09, 23 Feb 10); **DECAZES**, Marquis and Marquise (3 Jul 39); **DESLANDES**, Baronne [de] (3 Mar 95); **DIAGHILEV**, Serge (2 Jun 08, 21 Jun 25); **DOUDEAUVILLE**, Duc/ Duchesse de (1 May 96, 12 May 96, 16 June 13); **DRAKE**, Mrs. John (16 May 34); **DREUX-BRÉZÉ**, Comtesse de (22 May 88); **DREXEL**, Mme Y. A. (16 May 34); **DUEZ**, M./Mme Ernest (Jun 91); **DUKELSKY**, Vladimir (21 Jun 25); **DÜLBERG**, M. (29 May 27); **DUPERRÉ**, Vice-Admiral (31 Jan 05); **DUPRÉ**, M./Mme François (3 Jul 39); **DUPUY**, Mme Paul (3 Jul 39); **DURFORT**, Comte/Comtesse Bertrand de (20 Jun 98, 2 Jun 08, 18 Dec 09, 9 Jun 11, 10 Mar 12, 16 Jun 13); **DUSSAUD**, Mme (16 May 34); **DU BOS**, M./Mme/Mlle (23 Feb 10)

ÉCORCHEVILLE, Jules (10 June 14); **EHRENSVAD**, Comte (Minister from Sweden)/Comtesse (1 Jun 28); **EIGNY**, M. (8 Jan 09); **ENGLAND, PRINCE EDWARD** of (8 Dec 23); **EPHRUSSI**, Charles (25 May 03); **ESPINAY**, M. d' (12 May 96); **ESTAMPES**, Marquise d' (22 May 88); **ESTAUNIÉ**, Mme Édouard (7 Feb 27); **EUSTIS**, Miss Lydia (31 Mar 00); **EYRAGUES**, Marquis/Marquise Étienne-Charles d' (16 Jun 95, 11 May 03, 25 May 03, 2 Jun 08)

FAUCIGNY-LUCINGE, Prince/Princesse Ferdinand de (23 Feb 10); **FAUCIGNY-LUCINGE**, Prince/Princesse Guy de (18 Dec 09, 22 Dec 12, 16 Jun 13, 17 Jan 35, 3 Jul 39); **FAUCIGNY-LUCINGE**, Princesse Jean-Louis de (1 Jun 28, 3 Jul 39); **FAUCIGNY-LUCINGE**, Prince/ Princesse Rogatien de (23 Feb 10, 1 Jun 28); **FAURÉ**, Gabriel (3 Mar 95, 11 Feb 06); **FELLOWES**, Hon. Mrs. Reginald (17 Jan 35); **FELS**, Comtesse de (21 Jun 25); **FÉO**, M. de (18 Dec 09); **FILOSE**, Contessa (31 Mar 00); **FITZ-JAMES**, Comtesse Robert de (11 May 03, 31 Jan 05, 15 Feb 05, 11 Apr 07, 2 Jun 08, 8 Jan 09, 10 Mar 12); **FLAMENT**, Albert (2 Jun 08, 16 Jun 13, 23 Feb 37); **FORAIN**, Jean-Louis (16 Jun 95, 5 Jan 96, 25 Feb 96, 22 Feb 12, 14 May 17); **FORTUNY** (25 May 03, 8 Jan 09); **FOUQUIÈRES**, Comte André de (4 May 09, 18 Dec 09, 23 Feb 10, 10 Mar 12, 16 Jun 13, 1 Jun 28); **FOURNIER-SARLOVÈZE**, M. (8 Jan 09, 23 Feb 10, 9 Jun 11, 10 Mar 12); **FOY**, Comtesse/Mlle (31 Mar 00); **FRANCESCHINI**, M./Mme (16 May 34); **FRANQUE-VILLE**, Comte/Comtesse François de (2 Jun 08, 23 Feb 10); **FURSTENBERG**, Prince de (9 Jun 11)

GABRIAC, Comte Alexandre de (25 Feb 96, 1 May 96, 26 Apr 98, 12 Jun 98); **GABRIAC**, Comte/Comtesse Arthur de (24 Mar 00, 31 Mar 00, 25 May 03, 31 Jan 05, 2 Jun 08, 8 Jan 09, 18 Dec 09, 14 May 17); **GABRIAC**, Comte Ernest de (18 Dec 09, 23 Feb 10, 22 Feb 12, 10 Mar 12, 16 Jun 13); **GABRIAC**, Marquis/Marquise de (12 Jun 96, 20 Jun 98); **GAIGNERON**, Comte de (22 Feb 12); Gaigneron, Vicomte/

Vicomtesse de (15 Feb 05, 2 Jun 08, 23 Feb 10, 26 Mar 14); **GALLIFET,** Marquise Gaston de (16 Jun 95,); **GANAY,** Comte/Comtesse André (5 Apr 08, 2 Jun 08, 23 Feb 10); **GANAY,** Comte/Comtesse Gérard de (11 Apr 07, 16 Jun 13); **GANAY,** Comtesse J. de (22 Apr 95, 12 May 96, 26 Apr 98, 31 Mar 00); **GANAY,** Marquis/Marquise de (3 Mar 95, 12 May 96, 22 Apr 95, 25 Feb 96, 11 Feb 06, 11 Apr 07, 2 Jun 08, 23 Feb 10, 26 Mar 14, 21 Jun 25, 16 May 34, 17 Jan 35); **GARETS,** Vicomtesse de (22 May 88); GAULT-SAUSSINE, Comte/Comtesse/Mlle du Pont de (3 Mar 95, 9 Jun 11); **GAY,** Walter /Mme (4 May 09); **GERMINY,** M. de (11 Apr 08); **GERVEX,** M./Mme/Mlle (9 Jun 11, 10 Mar 12); **GHIKA,** Prince/Princesse Jean (16 Jun 13); **GIRAUDOUX,** Jean (11 Nov 17, 17 Nov 17, 23 Feb 37); **GONTAUT,** Comte Joseph de (2 Jun 08, 4 May 09, 14 May 17); **GONTAUT-BIRON,** Comte/Comtesse Bernard de (12 June 98; 20 Jun 98, 5 Apr 08, 2 Jun 08, 9 Jun 11, 22 Dec 12); **GONTAUT-BIRON,** Comte/Comtesse Joseph de (16 Jun 95); **GONTAUT-BIRON,** Comtesse Louis (9 Jun 11); **DE GOUY,** Marquis de (26 Apr 98); **GOYENA,** Mme de (8 Jan 09); Graham, M. (4 May 09, 10 Mar 12); **GRAMONT,** Comtesse de (22 May 88, 25 May 03); **GRAMONT,** Comte/Comtesse Armand de (3 Mar 05, 2 Jun 08); **GRAMONT,** Comte/Comtesse Arnaud de (22 May 01, 8 Jan 09, 4 May 09, 9 Jun 11, 22 Dec 12); **GRAMONT,** Comtesse Élisabeth de (17 Jan 35); **GRAMONT,** Comte Louis-René de (10 Mar 12); **GRAMONT,** Duc/Duchesse de (1 May 96, 26 Apr 98, 12 Jun 98, 20 Jun 98, 24 Mar 00, 31 Mar 00, 18 Apr 01, 15 Feb 05, 9 Jun 11, 10 Mar 12, 16 Jun 13, 1 Jun 28, 10 Jun 34); **GREEN,** Julien (25 Dec 30, 31 Mar 31, 11 Dec 31, 17 May 34); **GREFFULHE,** Comtesse Henri (Élisabeth) (22 Apr 95, 26 Apr 98, 12 Jun 98, 20 Jun 98, 24 Mar 00, 31 Mar 00, 22 May 01, 25 May 03); **GREFFULHE,** Mlle. Elaine (31 Mar 00); **GROSCLAUDE,** M./Mme Étienne (10 Mar 12, 26 Mar 14, 17 Nov 17, 7 Feb 27); **GRUENBERGER,** M. (former Minister from Austria)/Mme (17 Jan 35); **GUDIN,** Comtesse de (22 May 88); **GUERNE,** Comte/Comtesse de (26 Apr 98, 12 Jun 98); **GUICHE,** Duc de (11 Apr 08, 22 Feb 12, 10 Mar 12, 16 Jun 13); **GYLDENSTOPE,** Comte (Swedish Minister)/Comtesse (4 May 09)

HAAS, Charles (3 Mar 95, 22 Apr 95, 5 Jan 96, 25 Feb 96, 12 May 96); **HARCOURT,** Comte Eugène d' (22 Apr 95, 20 Jun 98, 25 May 03); **HARCOURT,** Duchesse d' (31 Jan 05, 5 Apr 08, 21 Jun 25); **HARCOURT,** Vicomte d' (3 Mar 95); **HAUSSONVILLE,** Comte/Comtesse d' (16 Jun 95, 25 Feb 96, 11 May 03, 25 May 03, 31 Jan 05, 26 Mar 14); **HAUSSONVILLE,** Marquise d' (12 May 96); **HELLEU,** Paul (5 Jan 96, 2 Jun 08, 4 May 09); **HENNESSY,** Mme Jean (9 Jun 11); **HERMANN,** M. Édouard (23 Feb 10); **HERMANT,** Abel (18 Apr 01); **HERVIEU,** Paul (23 Feb 10, 10 Mar 12, 16 Jun 13); **HESSE,** Edmond (16 Jun 13); **HESSE,** Landgrave of (27 May 01); **HEUGEL,**

Mme Jacques (16 May 34); **HINNISDAL**, Comtesse d' (31 Mar 00); **HOHENLOHE**, Prince Nicolas von (10 Mar 12); **HUMIÈRES**, Robert d' (3 Mar 95); **HYDE**, Mrs. Martha (17 Jan 35)

IGNIATIEFF, Comte/Comtesse (16 Jun 13); **ILON**, M. l' (5 Apr 08); **INES**, Mme (16 May 34); **INDY**, Vincent d' (3 Mar 95, 22 Apr 95; 16 Jun 95, 25 Feb 96, 20 Jun 98, 24 Mar 00); **ITURBIDE**, M. (11 Nov 17, 17 Nov 17); **IZVOLSKY**, Alexander (Ambassador of Russia)/Mme Izwolsky (10 Mar 12)

JAMES, Mme Max (11 Apr 07); **JALOUX**, M./Mme Edmond (2 Jun 08, 23 Feb 37); **JAMESON**, Mme (31 Mar 00); **JANZÉ**, Vicomte/Vicomtesse Léon de (11 May 03, 31 Jan 05, 23 Feb 10); **JAUCOURT**, Marquise de (10 Jun 34); **JAUNEZ**, Mme Max (2 Jun 08, 4 May 09, 23 Feb 10); **JAVAL**, Mlle (16 May 34); **JOHNSON**, Athelstan (3 Dec 16, 11 Nov 17); **JOURDAIN**, M./Mme Roger (Jun 91); **JUMILHAC**, Comtesse de (16 May 34)

KERGARIOU, Comte/Comtesse de (22 Apr 95, 2 Jun 08); **KERGIOU**, Vicomte/Vicomtesse de (9 Jun 11); **KERGOLAY**, Comtesse Jean de (31 Mar 00); **KERJÉGU**, M. de (20 Jun 98, 3 Mar 05, 5 Apr 08); **KERSAINT**, Comte/Comtesse de (22 Apr 95, 16 Jun 95, 25 Feb 96, 12 May 96, 24 Mar 00, 3 Mar 05, 4 May 09); Comte **KHEVENMÜLLER-METSCH** (Austro-Hungarian ambassador) (31 Jan 05, 15 Feb 05, 3 Mar 05, 11 Feb 06); **KINEN**, M./Mme/Mlle (1 May 96, 18 Apr 01, 11 May 03, 11 Apr 07, 11 Apr 08, 10 Mar 12); **KINGSLAND**, Mrs. Walter (3 Jul 39); **KNOBLOCK**, Lt. (11 Nov 17); **KLEMPERER**, Otto (29 May 27); **KOCHANSKI**, Paul (21 Jun 25)

LABORDE, Comte Alexandre de (20 Jun 98, 11 Apr 07, 5 Apr 08, 4 May 09); **LA FERRONNAYS**, Comte/Comtesse Fernard de (25 Feb 96, 31 Mar 00, 3 Mar 05); **LAFOND**, Comte/Comtesse/Mlle (3 Mar 05, 23 Feb 10); **LANGERON**, Mme (16 May 34); **LA GANDARA**, Antonio de (3 Mar 95, 20 Jun 98, 18 Apr 01, 25 May 03); **LA GLORIETA**, Princesse (31 Mar 00); **LA HOUSSAYE**, Marquise de (9 Jun 11); **LAHOVARY**, J. (11 Nov 11); **L'AIGLE**, Comtesse (16 May 34); **LAMBERTYE**, Comtesse Marie de (31 Mar 00, 17 Jan 35); **LA MORLIÈRE**, Comtesse/Mlle (31 Mar 00); **LA MOTHE-HOUDAN-COURT**, Duchesse de (24 Mar 00, 18 Apr 01, 9 Jun 11); **LA MOUSSAYE**, Comte/Comtesse de (11 Apr 07, 2 Jun 08, 4 May 09, 10 Mar 12); **LANVIN**, Mme Jeanne (3 Jul 39); **LARIBOISIÈRE**, Comte/Comtesse de (31 Mar 00, 4 May 09, 9 Jun 11); **LA ROCHE-FOUCAULD**, Comte/Comtesse de (3 Mar 95, 12 Jun 98, 24 Mar 00); **LA ROCHEFOUCAULD**, Comte/Comtesse Aimery de (22 Apr 95, 25 Feb 96, 18 Apr 01, 11 May 03, 25 May 03, 23 Feb 10); **LA ROCHEFOUCAULD**, Comte/Comtesse Édouard de (1 May 96, 5 Apr 08); **LA ROCHEFOUCAULD**, Comtesse Édouard de (31 Jan 05); **LA ROCHEFOUCAULD**, Comte/Comtesse Gabriel de (26 Apr 98, 18 Apr

01, 4 May 09, 16 Jun 13, 10 Jun 34); **LA ROCHEFOUCAULD**, Comte Guy de (25 May 03); **LA ROCHEFOUCAULD**, Duchesse de (1 Jun 28, 17 Jan 35); **LA ROCHE-GUYON**, Duchesse de (22 Apr 95); **LASTEYRIE**, Comte de (11 Apr 08); **LA TOUR D'AUVERGNE**, Duchesse de (1 Jun 28); **LA TOUR D'AUVERGNE**, Prince de (12 Jun 98); **LA TOUR D'AUVERGNE-LAURAGUAIS**, Prince/Princesse de (18 Dec 09); **LA TOUR DU PIN**, Vicomte/Vicomtesse de (10 Mar 12); **LAU**, Marquis de (16 Jun 13); **LAUBESPIN**, Marquise de (22 May 88); **LAWRENCE**, Mme (10 Mar 12, 14 May 17, 23 Nov 17); **LEAR**, Harry (23 Nov 17); **LEBEY**, André (14 May 17); **LEFEBVRE**, Baronne E. (16 May 34); **LEGHAIT**, M. (Belgian minister)/Mme (11 Apr 07, 4 May 09); **LE GONIDEC**, Comte Guy (11 Apr 07, 2 Jun 08, 18 Dec 09, 23 Feb 10, 22 Feb 12, 10 Mar 12, 26 Mar 14); **LEGRAND**, M./Mme Gaston ("Cloton") (22 May 01, 11 May 03, 31 Jan 05, 11 Apr 07, 5 Apr 08, 11 Apr 08, 8 Jan 09, 4 May 09, 18 Dec 09, 23 Feb 10, 22 Feb 12, 10 Mar 12, 16 Jun 13, 26 Mar 14, 23 Nov 17, 21 Jun 25, 1 Jun 28, 16 May 34, 17 Jan 35); **LEHMANN**, Rosamond (19 Feb 37, 23 Feb 37); **LEMAIRE**, Madeleine/Mlle (8 Jan 09, 9 Jun 11); **LE MAROIS**, Comte/Comtesse (11 Apr 07); **LESPARRE**, Duchesse de (22 May 88); **LÉVIS-MIREPOIX**, Comtesse A. de (4 May 09); **LÉVIS-MIREPOIX**, Marquis/Marquise de (16 Jun 13); **LIANCOURT**, Duc/Duchesse de (21 Jun 25); **LIFAR**, Serge (31 Mar 31, 17 Jan 35); **LIGNE**, Princesse de (24 Mar 00); **LISTER**, Hon. Reginald (11 Apr 07, 5 Apr 08); **LOUÿS**, Pierre (12 May 96); **LOYS-CHANDIEU**, Marquise de (1 Jun 28); **LUBERSAC**, Comte/Comtesse (11 Apr 08, 9 Jun 11); **LUBERSAC**, Marquise de (24 Mar 00); **LUDRE**, Marquis/Marquise de (18 Apr 01, 11 Apr 07, 2 Jun 08, 4 May 09, 16 Jun 13, 19 Feb 37); **LUR-SALUCES**, Comtesse de (12 Jun 98, 20 Jun 98); **LUYNES**, Duc/Duchesse Honoré/Mlle de (16 Jun 95, 12 May 96, 12 Jun 98, 3 Mar 05, 5 Apr 08, 4 May 09, 23 Feb 10, 10 Mar 12, 16 Jun 13, 26 Mar 14); **LUYNES**, Duchesse Yolande de (22 Apr 95, 12 May 96, 18 Apr 01, 11 May 03, 25 May 03)

MADRAZO, Frédéric de (23 Feb 10); **MAILLÉ**, Comtesse de (22 Apr 95); **MAILLÉ**, Comte/Comtesse de Foulques de (20 Jun 98); **MAILLÉ**, Duchesse de (12 May 96, 16 May 34); **MALEISSYE**, Comtesse (18 Apr 01); **MANCHESTER**, Duchess of (12 May 96); **MARCEL**, Gabriel (23 Feb 37); **MARÉ**, Rolf de (Summer 1923); Marlborough, Duchess of (18 Apr 01); **MARLBOROUGH**, Duchess of [Gladys Deacon] (21 Jun 25); **MARKEVITCH**, Igor (7 Dec 32); **MARSHALL**, Mrs. (16 May 34); **MASSA**, Duc de (22 Apr 95); **MASSA**, Marquis de (22 Apr 95); **MAURIAC**, François (23 Feb 37); **MAUROIS**, Claude (23 Feb 37); **MAX**, Mme Charles (11 Apr 08, 8 Jan 09, 23 Feb 10); **MAXWELL**, Elsa (20 Apr 23, 13 May 25, 3 Jul 39); **MERODE**, Princesse de (3 Jul 39); **MESAGNE**, Prince (31 Mar 00); **MILHAUD**, Darius (Summer

1923, 23 May 33, 17 Jan 35); **MILLERAND**, Mme Jacques (16 May 34); Miquel, M. de (3 Mar 05); **MIRAMON**, Comtesse Isaure de (17 Nov 17); **MODÈNE**, Marquis/Marquise de (15 Feb 05, 18 Dec 09, 23 Feb 10, 9 Jun 11, 22 Dec 12); **MONACO, PRINCE PIERRE** de (17 Jan 35, 22 Jun 39); **MONTAGLIARI**, Marchesa (11 Apr 07, 23 Feb 10); **MONTAGNINI DI MIRABELLO**, Monsignor (31 Mar 00); **MONBRISON**, M. de (18 Dec 09, 23 Feb 10); **MONTALEMBERT**, Comtesse de (16 Jun 95); **MONTALEMBERT**, Marquise de (22 May 88); **MONTEBELLO**, Comtesse Fernand de (11 Apr 07); **MONTESQUIOU-FEZENSAC**, Comte F. de (3 Mar 95, 16 Jun 95); **MONTESQUIOU-FEZENSAC**, Comte/Comtesse Odon de (16 Jun 95, 11 Apr 07, 2 Jun 08); **MONTESQUIOU**, Mlle de (31 Mar 00); **MONTEYNARD**, Marquis de (20 Jun 98, 27 May 01, 11 Apr 07, 8 Jan 09, 10 Mar 12); **MONTEYNARD**, Marquise de (22 May 88, 3 Mar 95, 5 Jan 96, 20 Jun 98, 31 Mar 00, 22 May 01, 11 Feb 06, 11 Apr 07, 11 Apr 08, 2 Jun 08, 8 Jan 09, 4 May 09, 23 Feb 10, 22 Feb 12, 10 Mar 12, 16 Jun 13, 26 Mar 14, 21 May 94); **MONTHOLON**, Marquis/Marquise de (2 Jun 08); **MONTJOU**, Comtesse Alice de (3 Jul 39); **MOORE**, Mme (25 Feb 96, 2 Jun 08, 9 Jun 11, 26 Mar 14); **MOOS**, M. (9 Jun 11); **MORAND**, Paul (3 Dec 16, 14 May 17, 11 Nov 17, 17 Nov 17, 23 Nov 17, 1 Dec 17, 9 Dec 17, 23 Feb 37); **MOROSINI**, Conte/Contessa (18 Dec 09); **MORTEMART**, M. de (18 Dec 09); **MSURUS BEY**, M. (9 Jun 11); **MUGNIER**, Abbé (7 Feb 19); **MÜHLFELD**, Mme Lucien (11 Apr 08, 2 Jun 08, 4 May 09, 23 Feb 10); **MUN**, Comte/Comtesse Albert de (3 Mar 95, 11 Apr 07, 9 Jun 11); **MUN**, Marquise de (10 Mar 12); **MUN**, Comte/Comtesse Bertrand de (5 Apr 08, 2 Jun 08, 4 May 09); **MUN**, Comtesse Henri de (1 Jun 28); **MUN**, Marquise de (11 Apr 07, 4 May 09); **MURAT**, Comte/Comtesse Joachim (11 Apr 07, 5 Apr 08, 18 Dec 09, 23 Feb 10, Jun 34, 17 Jun 35; 13 Jul 39); **MURAT**, Prince Eugène (31 Mar 00); **MURAT**, Princesse Eugène (22 Feb 12, 10 Mar 12); **MURAT**, Princesse Lucien (11 Apr 07, 11 Apr 08, 2 Jun 08, 10 Mar 12) s

NEU, Marquise de (23 Feb 10); **NOAILLES**, Comte Mathieu/Comtesse Anna (12 Jun 98, 15 Feb 05, 11 Feb 06, 18 Dec 09, 22 Feb 12, 22 Dec 12, 25 May 19, 21 Jun 25, 7 Feb 27, 5 Feb 32); **NOAILLES**, Comtesse Anne-Jules de (17 Jan 35); **NOAILLES**, Comtesse Charles (Marie-Laure) de (23 Feb 37); **NOAILLES**, Duc/Duchesse de (25 Feb 96, 12 Jun 98, 27 May 01, 23 Feb 10, 16 Jun 13, 21 Jun 25, 1 Jun 28, 10 Jun 34); **NOAILLES**, Marquis de (4 May 09); **NOVION**, Comtesse de (16 May 34)

ODELIN, Abbé (31 Mar 00); **OILLIAMSON**, Comtesse Guillaume (Jane) d' (5 Apr 08, 11 Apr 08, 4 May 09, 22 Dec 12); **OILLIAMSON**, Marquise d' (3 Jul 39); **ORIGNY**, Vicomte/Vicomtesse d' (23 Feb 10, 10 Mar 12)

PALÉOLOGUE, M./Mme Maurice (16 Jun 13, 7 Feb 27, 29 May 27, 16 Dec 27, 17 May 34); **PALFFY**, Comte Paul (12 Jun 38); **PALLADINI**, Princess (21 Jun 25) **PASTRÉ**, Comte/Comtesse André (26 Apr 98, 11 Apr 07, 16 Jun 13); **PASTRÉ**, Comte Jean (16 Jun 13); **PELOUX**, Vicomtesse de (16 May 34); **PÉRIGORD**, Comte/Comtesse L. de (16 Jun 95, 25 Feb 96, 31 Mar 00, 2 Jun 08); **PFEIFFER**, G. (16 Jun 95); **PIERREBOURG**, Baronne A. de (23 Feb 10, 10 Mar 12, 16 Jun 13); **PIERREDON**, Comte de (2 Jun 08); **PILLET-WILL**, Comtesse (31 Mar 00, 22 May 01); **POINCARÉ**, M./Mme Raymond (23 Feb 10, 9 Jun 11); **POIX**, Princesse de (2 Jun 08, 21 Jun 25); **POLIGNAC**, Comte Charles de (11 Apr 07, 22 Feb 12) ; **POLIGNAC**, Comte/Comtesse Charles de (2 Feb 27, 1 Jun 28, 17 Jan 35); **POLIGNAC**, Comte Jean de (11 Apr 07, 17 Jan 35); **POLIGNAC**, Comte/Comtesse Jean (7 Apr 25, 13 May 25, 28 May 25, 7 Jun 25, 9 Jun 25, 21 Jun 25, 7 Feb 27, 29 May 27, 15 Jun 27, 16 Dec 27, 9 Jun 33, 12 Jun 38, 3 Jul 39); **POLIGNAC**, Comte Maxence de (15 Feb 05); **POLIGNAC**, Comte/Comtesse Melchior de (11 Apr 07, 2 Jun 08, 4 May 09, 10 Mar 12); **POLIGNAC**, Comtesse Melchior de (7 Feb 27, 1 Jun 28, 3 Jul 39); Polignac, Duc de (21 Jun 25); **POLIGNAC**, Marquise Guy de (26 Apr 98, 25 May 99, 11 Apr 07, 25 Apr 07, 5 Apr 08, 2 Jun 08, 9 Jun 11, 10 Mar 12, 23 Jun 13, 1 Jun 19, 14 Dec 19); **POLIGNAC**, Marquis Melchior de (11 Apr 07, 10 Mar 12); **POLIGNAC**, Prince/ Princesse Henri de (15 Feb 05, 11 Apr 07, 18 Dec 09, 10 Mar 12, 16 Jun 13); **POLIGNAC**, Princesse Henri (19 Jan 19, 16 Feb 19, 1 Jun 28); **POLIGNAC**, Prince Ludovic de (16 Jun 95, 20 Jun 98, 11 May 03, 25 May 03); **POLIGNAC**, Vicomte/Vicomtesse de (25 May 03, 11 Apr 07, 9 Jun 11); **PONTÈVES**, Comte de (31 Mar 00); **PORGÈS**, Mme/Mlle Jules (20 Jun 98, 31 Mar 00, 2 Jun 08, 18 Dec 09, 9 Jun 11, 10 Mar 12); **PORTER**, Cole and Linda (Summer 1923); **POTOCKA**, Comtesse N. (22 Apr 95, 16 Jun 95, 5 Jan 96, 18 Apr 01, 11 Apr 07); **POULENC**, Francis (21 June 25, 29 May 27, 9 Jun 33, 17 Jan 35); **POUQUET**, Mme. (7 Feb 27); **POURTALÈS**, Comtesse Edmond de (25 May 03, 31 Jan 05, 11 Apr 07, 5 Apr 08, 2 Jun 08, 23 Feb 10); **POURTALÈS**, Comte/Comtesse Jacques de (15 Feb 05, 8 Jan 09, 18 Dec 09, 22 Feb 12); **POURTALÈS**, Comtesse Paul de (31 Mar 00); **POUY**, Vicomte de (16 Jun 95, 25 Feb 96); **POZZI**, Catherine (31 Jan 27, 7 Feb 27); **PRACOMTAL**, Marquis/ Marquise de (31 Jan 05, 15 Feb 05, 2 Jun 08, 4 May 09, 23 Feb 10, 9 Jun 11, 10 Mar 12, 3 Jul 39); **PRÉVOST**, M./Mme Marcel (10 Mar 12); **PRIMOLI**, Comte Joseph (11 Apr 07, 2 Jun 08, 16 Jun 13); **PROKOFIEV**, M./Mme Serge (9 Jun 25, 29 Jun 25, 28 May 26, 29 May 27, 15 Jun 27); **PROUST**, Marcel (6 Feb 95, 3 Mar 95, 23 Apr 95, 16 Jun 95, 22 Mar 99, 11 Apr 07, 2 Jun 08, 16 Dec 17, 25 May 19); **PUYSÉGUR**, Comtesse de (2 Jun 08, 9 Jun 11)
QUÉLEN, Comtesse B. de (12 May 96); **QUÉNÉTAIN**, Comte/Comtesse de (20 Jun 98)

RADNOR, Lady (8 Jan 09); RADOLIN, Prince (Ambassador to Germany)/ Princesse (4 May 09); RADWAN, M. Auguste de (31 Jan 05, 3 Mar 05, 11 Apr 08, 23 Feb 10, 17 Jan 35); RADZIWILL, Prince/Princesse D. de (11 Apr 08, 4 May 09); RADOLIN, Princesse (25 May 03); RAFFIGI, Contessa (31 Mar 00); RAIBERTI, M. (2 Jun 08); Ranuzzi dei Bianchi, Monsignor (31 Mar 00); RAOUL-DUVAL, Mme (18 Apr 01); RAPANI, Contessa (31 Mar 00); RAVIGNAN, Baron de (26 Apr 98); RECOULY, M. (17 Nov 17); RÉGNIER, M./Mme Henri de (3 Mar 95, 16 Jun 95, 18 Apr 01, 2 Jun 08, 23 Feb 10); REINACH, Joseph ("Polybe") (14 May 17); RENAULT, Léon (4 May 09); RIDGELEY-CARTER, M./Mme (1 Jun 28); RIPON, Marchioness Gladys of (26 Mar 14); ROBILANT, Conte/Contessa (18 Dec 09); ROCCA, Principe della (31 Mar 00); ROCHE, Jules (25 May 03, 4 May 09, 9 Jun 11, 10 Mar 12, 26 Mar 14); ROCHECHOUART, Marquise de (25 May 03, 11 Apr 07, 22 Feb 12, 26 Mar 14); ROCHEMONTEUX, Marquise de (16 May 34); RODIER, Georges (8 Jan 09, 18 Dec 09, 22 Dec 12, 23 Nov 17); ROHAN, Vicomte/ Vicomtesse Jéhan de (5 Apr 08, 18 Dec 09, 21 Jun 25); ROHAN, Duc/ Duchesse de (20 Jun 98, 10 Mar 12, 16 Jun 13); ROSTANG, Comtesse de (16 May 34); ROTHSCHILD, Baron Eugène de (17 Jan 35); ROTHSCHILD, Baronne Henri de (9 Jun 11); ROTHSCHILD, Baron/ Baronne Maurice de (9 Jun 11, 3 Jul 39); ROTHSCHILD, Baron/ Baronne Robert de (9 Jun 11, 9 Jun 25, 28 May 26, 16 Dec 27, 3 Jul 39); ROUGEMONT, Comte/Comtesse René du Temple de (1 Jun 28, 3 Jul 39); ROUJON, Henry (10 Jun 14); RUBINSTEIN, Arthur (20 Apr 23, 21 Jun 25); RUDGE, Olga (20 Nov 31); RUDINI, Marquise di (16 Jun 13); RUSSIA, GRAND-DUKE ANDRÉ of (2 Jun 08); RUSSIA, GRAND-DUKE CYRILLE of (2 Jun 08); RUSSIA, GRAND-DUKE PAUL of/Hohenfelsen, Comtesse (consort of Grand-Duke Paul of Russia) (11 Apr 07, 5 Apr 08, 2 Jun 08, 23 Feb 10, 9 Jun 11, 10 Mar 12, 16 Jun 13, 26 Mar 14); RUSSIA, GRAND-DUCHESS VLADIMIR of (2 Jun 08)

SAINT-ANDRÉ, M. de (4 May 09, 9 Jun 11); SAINT-ANDRÉ, Mme de (11 Apr 07); SAINT-BRISSON, Marquise de Ranst de (16 May 34); SAINT-CHAMANS, Mme de (16 May 34); SAINT-DENYS, Marquise d'Hervey de (12 Jun 95); SAINT-GILLES, Comte/Comtesse de (16 Jun 95, 20 Jun 98); SAINT-MARCEAUX, Marguerite de (28 Jan 99, 9 Feb 99, 22 May 01, 25 May 03, 28 Mar 05, 10 Dec 05, 28 Jan 06, 27 May 06, 11 Apr 07, 23 Feb 10, 10 Mar 12); SAINT-MARCEAUX, René de (25 May 03); SAINT-MAURICE, Mme de (16 May 34); SAINT-PAUL, Comtesse Diane (16 Jun 95, 16 May 34); SAINT-PHALLE, Comte de (16 Jun 95) ; SAINT-SAUVEUR, Comte/Comtesse Armand de (4 May 09, 18 Dec 09, 16 Jun 13); SALA, Cte Antoine (16 Jun 13); SALLES, Georges (10 Jun 34); SAMAZEUILH, Gustave (23 May 33); SAN FAUSTINO, Princesse de

(26 Mar 14); **SAN MARTINO,** Comte de (29 Jun 25); **SAUGUET,** Henri (28 May 26, 23 May 33); **SAUSSINE,** Comte/Comtesse de (3 Mar 95, 16 Jun 95); **SAVILLE,** Lady (11 Feb 06); **SCHOENBERG,** Arnold (9 Jun 33); **SCHLUMBERGER,** Gaston (2 Jun 08, 4 May 09, 16 Jun 13); **SÉGUR,** Comte Henri de (16 Jun 95, 5 Jan 96, 12 Jun 98, 31 Mar 00); **SEILLIÈRES,** Baron/Baronne Raymond (16 Jun 95); **SERT,** Mme José (Misia) (21 Jun 25); **SESMAISONS,** Comtesse de (31 Mar 00); **SEYNES,** Mme de (16 May 34); **SINGER,** Mme Paris/Mlle Winnaretta (26 Mar 14, 3 Jul 39); **SINGER,** Paris (16 Dec 17); **SINGER,** M./Mme Franklin/ Mlle Daisy (20 Jun 98, 8 Jan 09; 18 Dec 09, 23 Feb 10, 11 Nov 17, 3 Jul 39); **SIZERANNE,** M. (20 Jun 98); **SOHÈGE,** M./Mme Paul (5 Jan 96); **SOUDAYS,** M./Mme (11 Nov 17); **SOUTZO,** Princesse Hélène (11 Nov 17, 17 Nov 17, 16 Dec 17); **SPARTA,** Duc de (9 Jun 11); **STANDISH,** Mme Henry (31 Mar 00); **STAPFORD,** Albert (2 Jun 08); **STIRBEY,** Princesse de (22 May 88, 9 Jun 11); **STRAVINSKY,** Igor (21 Jun 25, 12 Jun 38); **STURCK,** Comtesse (16 May 34); **SWETCHINE,** M. (20 Jun 98); **SZECSEN,** Comte (Austrian-Hungarian Ambassador)/Comtesse (10 Mar 12, 16 Jun 13); **SZYMANOWSKI,** Karol (21 Jun 25)
TAIGNY, Olivier (22 Feb 12, 10 Mar 12, 16 Jun 13, 1 Jun 28); **TALLEYRAND,** Comte/Comtesse de (16 Jun 95); **TALLEYRAND,** Comtesse Vera de (10 Mar 12, 16 Jun 13); **TALLEYRAND-PÉRIGORD,** Comtesse de (31 Jan 05, 3 Mar 05, 2 Jun 08); **TALLEYRAND-PÉRIGORD,** Marquise de (2 Jun 08); **TECK,** Prince Francis von (11 Apr 07); **TERNAUX-COMPANS,** Mme/Mlle (11 Apr 08, 8 Jan 09); **TERRASSE,** Claude (14 Mar 20); **TEYSSIER DE SAVY,** M. (9 Jun 11); **TREFUSIS,** Denys/Violette (7 Jun 25, 7 Feb 27, 16 Dec 27); Trouard-Riolle, M. (26 Mar 14); Troubetzkoï, Prince de (22 Apr 95); **TRUELLE,** M. (11 Nov 17); **TYSZKIEWICZ,** Comtesse Jean (11 Apr 07, 2 Jun 08, 4 May 09, 18 Dec 09, 9 Jun 11)
UZÈS, Duc/Duchesse d' (25 May 03, 18 Dec 09, 16 Jun 13)
VACARESCO, Mlle Hélène (16 May 34); **VALÉRY,** Paul (21 Jan 23, 7 Jan 25, 1 Jun 28, 17 Jan 35); **VALLOMBROSA,** Comtesse de (8 Jan 09); **VALLOMBROSA,** Duc de (22 Apr 95, 18 Apr 01); **VALLOMBROSA,** M. Amédée de (31 Mar 00); **VEDEL-JARLSBERG,** Baron (Minister from Norway)/Baronne de (1 Jun 28); **VERDÉ-DELISLE,** Comtesse/ Mlle de (31 Mar 00); **VERDÉ-DE L'ISLE,** M./Mme Didier (2 Jun 08, 16 May 34); **VERNEAUX,** Comte de (2 Jun 08); **VESNITCH,** Mme (16 May 34); **VIBRAYE,** Comte/Comtesse de (31 Mar 00); **VIEL-CASTEL,** Comte de (9 Jun 11); **VIGGIANO,** Princesse/Mlle de (9 Jun 11, 10 Mar 12); **VIGIER,** Vicomte/Vicomtesse René (16 Jun 13); **VILMORIN,** Louise de (23 Feb 37, 12 Jun 38); **VIRIEU,** Marquis/ Marquise de (27 May 01, 4 May 09); **VITALI,** Comtesse G. (20 Jun 98, 24 Mar 00, 31 Jan 05, 11 Feb 06, 10 Mar 12, 22 Dec 12); **VOGÜÉ,** Comte de (11 Apr 07); **VOGÜÉ,** Comtesse Arthur de (10 Mar 12);

VOGÜÉ, Comte/Comtesse Félix de (16 Jun 13); **VOGÜÉ,** Comtesse Jean de (10 Jun 34, 23 Feb 37); **VRIÈRE,** Baronne de (31 Mar 00)

WAGNER, Siegfried (24 Mar 00); **WAGRAM,** Princesse de (12 May 96, 20 Jun 98); **WALDNER,** Baron/Baronne de (11 Apr 07, 10 Mar 12, 16 Jun 13); **WARRENDER,** Lady Maud (26 Mar 14); **WARU,** Comte/Comtesse Jacques de (26 Apr 98, 15 Feb 05, 2 Jun 08, 4 May 09); **WEBER,** M. (23 Nov 17); Weill, David (23 May 33); **WENDEL,** Mme Guy de (22 Feb 12); **WHARTON,** Edith (22 Feb 12, 22 Dec 12); **WHITE,** Henry (United States Ambassador to France) (2 Jun 08); **WIBORG,** Miss Mary Hoyt (3 Jul 39); **WOLKENSTEIN-TROSTBURG,** Ambassador/Comtesse (Austria-Hungary) (20 Jun 98, 24 Mar 00, 18 Apr 01)

YTURBE, Mme d' (9 Jun 11); **YZNAGA,** Miss Consuelo (23 Nov 17)

ZURLO, Principessa (31 Mar 00)

Appendix C

Works Commissioned by and Dedicated to The Princesse Edmond de Polignac

Works Commissioned by and Dedicated to the Princesse de Polignac

Lennox Berkeley
  Deux poèmes de Pindare: Dithyrambe et Hymne (1936)
Mario Castelnuovo-Tedesco
  Alt Wien, Rhapsody for Two Pianos (1923)
Manuel de Falla
  El Retablo de Maese Pedro (1923)
Jean Françaix
  Le Diable boîteux, opera-cantata (1937)
  Sérénade pour douze instruments (1934)
Marcelle de Manziarly
  Trois Duos pour deux soprani (1934): 1. *J'aimeray mon amy*; 2. *Hélas, que je suis désolée!*; 3. *M'y levay par ung matin*
Igor Markevitch
  Partita for Piano and Orchestra (1930)
  Hymnes (1934)
Darius Milhaud
  Les Malheurs d'Orphée, opera (1924)
Nicolas Nabokov
  Job, oratorio (1933)
Armande de Polignac
  La Recherche de la vérité, ballet (1918)
Peter Pope
  String Trio (1940)
Francis Poulenc
  Concerto for Two Pianos and Orchestra (1932)
  Concerto for Organ, Tympani, and Strings (1938)
Erik Satie
  Socrate, drame symphonique (1918)
Henri Sauguet
  Les Jeux de l'amour et du hasard for Two Pianos (1932)

Igor Stravinsky
  Renard (1916)
Germaine Tailleferre
  Concerto for Piano (1923)
  Ouverture for Orchestra (1932)
Kurt Weill
  Symphony No. 2 (1932)
Jean Wiéner
  Concerto franco-américain for Piano and Orchestra (1924)

Works Dedicated to the Princesse de Polignac

Joseph Bonnet
  Prélude au Slave Regina, Op. 7, No. 7, for organ (1910)
Anthony Chaplin
  Sarabande sur le nom de Gabriel Fauré (1945—in memory of the
    Princesse Edmond de Polignac)
Emmanuel Colarocco
  . *Il Giganto del lago* (1933)
Gabriel Fauré
  Larmes, Op. 51, No. 1 (1888)
  Cinq Mélodies de Venise, Op. 58 (1891): 1. *Mandoline*; 2. *En Sourdine*;
    3. *Green*; 4. *A Clymène*; 5. *C'est l'extase*
  Incidental Music to *Pelléas et Mélisande,* Op. 80 (1898)
Winifred Gordon
  Meditation for Cello and Piano (date unknown)
Manuel Infante
  Ritmo from *Trois Danses andalouses* for two pianos (1921)
Daniel Lazarus
  Toccata for piano (date unknown)
Adela Maddison
  Soleil couchant for two women's voices or women's chorus (1895)
Armande de Polignac
  Les Mille et Une Nuits, ballet (1914)
Maurice Ravel
  Pavane pour une infante défunte (1899)
Ethel Smyth
  The Wreckers, opera: Prelude to Act II, "On the Cliffs of Cornwall"
    (1909)
Igor Stravinsky
  Piano Sonata (1924)

Abbreviations

The following abbreviations are used in the notes: INT = interview with the author; MF = microfilm; MS = manuscript.

With respect to certain unpublished primary material, the following abbreviations are used: Db = datebook (brief jottings of daily events); DD = daily diary (a dated book large enough to include one or two paragraphs recounting the day's events, not of an intimate nature); PD = private diary (notebooks dated by hand by the author, with longer accounts of events, usually of a more personal nature).

AB	Augustine Bulteau
ADLN	Archives départementales de la Nièvre
AMF	Archivo Manuel de Falla, Granada
AN	Archives Nationales, Paris
ANo	Comtesse Mathieu de Noailles, née Anna de Brancovan
APEP	Archives of Prince Edmond de Polignac, France
ASM	Archives of the Saint-Marceaux family, France
BMFP	Music library, Polignac family, France
BNF-Mss	Bibliothèque nationale de France, Manuscripts Department
BNF-Mus	Bibliothèque nationale de France, Department of Music
CUL	Cambridge University Library, UK
EP	Prince Edmond de Polignac
ES	Erik Satie
FGA	Fonds Gabriel Astruc
FLC	Fondation Le Corbusier, Paris
FP	Francis Poulenc
FSP	Fondation Singer-Polignac, Paris
GA	Gabriel Astruc
GAP	Gabriel Astruc Papers
GF	Gabriel Fauré
HCC	Princesse Alexandre de Caraman-Chimay, née Hélène de Brancovan
IBS	Isabella Boyer Singer
IM	Igor Markevitch
IS	Igor Stravinsky
JC	Jean Cocteau
JP	Comte Jean de Polignac
KWF	Kurt Weill Foundation
LC	Le Corbusier
LMLV-F	"Le Monde et la ville" (society column), *Le Figaro*, Paris
MBP	Comtesse Jean (Marie-Blanche) de Polignac, née Marguerite di Pietro

MBSM	Marguerite Baugnies, after 1892 Marguerite de Saint-Marceaux
MF	Manuel de Falla
MP	Marcel Proust
NAfr	Nouvelles Acquisitions françaises, Bibliothèque nationale de France, Paris
NB	Nadia Boulanger
NLa	Nouvelles Lettres autographes, Bibliothèque nationale de France, Paris
NYPL	New York Public Library
ORP	Olga Rudge Papers, Yale University Library, New Haven, Conn.
PP	Comtesse Charles (Pata) de Polignac, née Jeanne de Montagnac
PSS	Paul Sacher Stiftung, Basel
RM	Comte Robert de Montesquiou
RSL	Royal Society of Literature Archives, London
SHSW	Singer Manufacturing Company Manuscript Collection, State Historical Society of Wisconsin
SMI	Société Musicale Indépendente
SNM	Société Nationale de Musique
WS, WSP	Winnaretta Singer, later Winnaretta Singer-Polignac
YCAL	Yale Collection of American Literature, New Haven, Conn.

Notes

Introduction

1. Winnaretta Singer-Polignac, "Memoirs of the Late Princesse Edmond de Polignac," *Horizon* 12, no. 68 (August 1945): 134.

2. Boris de Schloezer, "'El Retablo' de Manuel de Falla (Concert Wiéner)," *La Revue musicale* 5, no. 2 (1 December 1923): 192–93.

3. Philip Brett, "Music, Essentialism, and the Closet," in *Queering the Pitch: The New Gay and Lesbian Musicology*, ed. Brett et al. (New York: Routledge, 1994), 11.

4. Ibid., 17.

5. Elizabeth Wood, "Sapphonics," in *Queering the Pitch*, ed. Brett et al., 47. Similarly in need of correction, sometimes, are capsule portrayals in musicological writing, generally, of WSP's allegiances and activities. See the too-simple reference to her political orientation (as a member of the "liberal Right") and to the composers and musical organizations that she did or did not support in Jane F. Fulcher, *French Cultural Politics and Music: From the Dreyfus Affair to the First World War* (New York and Oxford: Oxford University Press, 1999), 167, 217. Further on Fulcher's pathbreaking but uneven study, see Carlo Caballero's review of her book in the *Journal of the American Musicological Society* 55, no. 3 (Fall 2002): 563–78.

6. It is difficult to ascertain the point that Wood is making in her listing of visitors to WSP's salon: she includes both known homosexuals (such as Landowska and Diaghilev) and heterosexuals (such as Pablo Picasso, Anna de Noailles, Paul Valéry, and John Singer Sargent).

Chapter 1

1. WSP to AB, 26 March 1906, NAfr 17554:101–2.

2. Most of the biographical information on Isaac Merritt Singer in this chapter comes from Ruth Brandon's *Singer and the Sewing Machine: A Capitalist Romance* (London: Barrie & Jenkins, 1977).

3. "The Singer Will," *The New York Herald*, 18 November 1875. This and other articles related to the Singer family are in a scrapbook of press clippings in the Singer Manufacturing Company Manuscript Collection, State Historical Society of Wisconsin (SHSW), Box 1/1, RLIN Number WIHV87–A1164.

4. "Singer's Varied Wedlock," *The New York Sun*, 8 July 1878, SHSW, Box 1/1.

5. This nomenclature is used in the marriage and death certificates of Isabella's sister, Jeanne-Marie Boyer.

6. Ruth Brandon, *Dollar Princesses: Sagas of Upward Mobility 1870–1914* (New York: Knopf, 1980), 180.

7. WS to Raymond Poincaré, 24 December 1905, NAfr 16013:119.

8. Brandon, *Singer and the Sewing Machine.* Brandon gives the location of Madame Boyer's *pension* as rue Jacob, on the Left Bank. However, Isabella's letters to her mother written during the years 1863–66 give her mother's address as 12 rue des Écuries d'Artois (today, rue d'Artois), in the 8th *arrondissement* close to the Champs-Élysées.

9. Isabella Boyer Singer (IBS) to Pamela Boyer, 23 June 1863, private collection.

10. Duc Élie Decazes, INT, 26 November 1993, New York City.

11. Brandon, *Singer and the Sewing Machine,* 174–75.

12. "Stories of Life Abroad," *The New York Times,* 27 May 1883; Brandon, *Singer and the Sewing Machine,* 175–76.

13. The extant letters from IBS to her mother Pamela Lockwood Boyer, housed in a private collection, date from the time of her marriage to Isaac Singer in New York in June 1863. In these letters Isabella speaks fondly of her daughter, left behind in Paris. She also asks her mother if she has received the money sent from Glasgow.

14. IBS writes to her mother on 10 April 1864 (private collection) that "it is thirteen months since I kissed you goodnight at the door of your house, little thinking that I would not see you again for so long." Isaac Singer's will makes clear that Isabella was going under the name of "Isabella Eugenie Summerville" at the time of their marriage.

15. IBS to Pamela Boyer, 23 June 1863, private collection.

16. Ibid.

17. Ibid.

18. The archives of St. John's Episcopal Church, New York, contain a record of the marriage of Isaac Singer and Isabella "Summerville" by Reverend Edwin Cook. I am grateful to C. Robert Spooler, Warden Emeritus of St. John's, for communicating the details of the entry to me.

19. IBS to Pamela Boyer, 23 June 1863, private collection.

20. Birth records for 1863 (microfilm), Hall of Records, City of New York.

21. IBS to Pamela Boyer, 23 June 1863, private collection.

22. Ibid., 10 April 1864.

23. Ibid., July 1864.

24. Ibid.

25. "Singer's Varied Wedlock," *The Sun* (New York), 1 July 1878, SHSW, Box 1/1.

26. IBS to Pamela Boyer, July 1864, private collection.

27. Ibid.

28. It was an accepted part of Singer family lore that the name "Winnaretta" was of "Red Indian" origin. Apparently, after WSP's death, when a funeral mass was being said for her, the presiding priest experienced a moment of panic in trying to find an equivalent saint's name in the Catholic calendar. One of WSP's nieces, Daisy Singer Dugardin, suggested the name "Marguerite," which the priest accepted, with no other choice available.

29. IBS to Pamela Boyer, 9 March 1865, private collection.

30. Ibid.

31. Ibid., 9 June 1865.

32. Ibid., 23 February, 22 August, and 29 December 1866.

33. The portrait of Isaac Singer by Edward May (1824–1887) now hangs in the National Portrait Gallery of the Smithsonian Institute, Washington, D.C.

34. The story of WSP's rescue by Turgenev is recounted in Peter Quennell's review of Michael de Cossart's *The Food of Love* in *The Financial Times of London*, 30 March 1978. Sir Peter Quennell (1905–1994), author and journalist, was the editor of *History Today*. As the story is not mentioned in WSP's memoirs, it may be assumed that WSP herself told Quennell the story during her stay in England between 1939 and 1943.

35. WSP, "Memoirs of the Late Princesse Edmond de Polignac," *Horizon* 12, no. 68 (August 1945): 111.

36. Ibid.

37. Brandon, *Singer and the Sewing Machine*, 187.

38. *The Torquay Directory*, 14 May 1873.

39. Ibid., 11 August 1875.

40. Brandon, *Singer and the Sewing Machine*, 189.

41. Ibid., 191.

42. WS to Raymond Poincaré, 24 December 1905, NAfr 16013:119.

43. IBS to Pamela Boyer, 12 August 1875, private collection.

44. Brandon, *Singer and the Sewing Machine*, 194.

45. SHSW, various articles.

46. Isaac Singer's will is on record with the Westchester County (New York) Surrogate Court, File Number 302–1875.

47. WSP to her niece Daisy Singer, daughter of Franklin Singer, undated [1930–39], private collection. Reference is made to Emily Bronte's poem "Remembrances"; WSP misquotes the final line of the poem, which is actually "how could I seek the empty world again?"

48. WSP to Pamela Boyer, 18 May 1878, private collection.

49. Ibid.

50. Ibid.

51. Alain Ollivier, Interview, 21 June 1992.

Chapter 2

1. Christian Blanchet and Bertrand Daud, *Statue of Liberty: The First Hundred Years,* trans. Bernard A. Weisberger (New York: American Heritage, 1985), 48.

2. "The Mrs. Singer Who Became Duchess of Camposelice," clipping from unidentified newspaper, undated, SHSW 1/1.

3. "Stories of Life Abroad," *The New York Times*, 27 May 1883.

4. Ibid.

5. Ibid.

6. Isabelle-Blanche Singer to Pamela Boyer, 20 February 1878, private collection.

7. WS to Pamela Boyer, 18 May 1878, private collection.

8. Isabella Boyer Singer's mansion at 27 avenue Kléber no longer exists. In its place stands a building constructed in 1907.

9. WSP, "Memoirs of the Late Princesse Edmond de Polignac," *Horizon* 12, no. 68 (August 1945): 111.

10. Cécile Tardif, "Les Salons de musique à Paris sous la Troisième République" (M.A. thesis, Université de Montréal, 1994), 4.

11. "Court Journal," article from an unspecified newspaper, 16 July 1881, SHSW, SA-1/1.

12. In her "Memoirs," 111, WSP writes that it was her *mother* who, "after much research," assembled the collection of Stradivarius instruments.

13. I am grateful to Philip J. Kass for communicating to me a list of the stringed instruments bought by the Duc de Camposelice, fifteen in total. Sources that mention Camposelice's instruments include W. Henry Hill et al., *Antonio Stradivari: His Life and Work* (New York: Dover, 1963), Ernest N. Doring, *How Many Strads? Our Heritage from the Master* (Chicago: William Lewis and Sons, 1945), Herbert K. Goodkind, *Violin Iconography of Antonio Stradivari* (New York: Goodkind, 1972), W. Henry Hill et al., *The Violin Makers of the Guarneri Family (1626–1762): Their Life and Work* (London: Holland Press, 1965), and Charles-Eugène Gand, *Cahiers* (Paris, 1998).

14. "Stories of Life Abroad," *The New York Times,* 27 May 1883.

15. WSP, "Memoirs," 111.

16. "Court Journal," article from an unspecified newspaper, 16 July 1881, SHSW, SA-1/1.

17. WSP, "Memoirs," 111–12.

18. Félix Barrias (1822–1907). Barrias won the Prix de Rome in 1844.

19. WSP, "Memoirs," 112.

20. Ibid., 114–115.

21. Ibid., 112.

22. Ibid.

23. Ibid., 113.

24. Ibid.

25. Ibid., 111. In a 1939 letter to Virginia Woolf (see chapter 15), WSP asserts that the performance of the Beethoven quartet took place on the occasion of her thirteenth, not fourteenth, birthday, that is, in January 1878. It seems more logical, however, that the performance took place in Paris, and not in Paignton.

26. Philip Brett, "Music, Essentialism, and the Closet," in *Queering the Pitch: The New Gay and Lesbian Musicology,* ed. Philip Brett et al. (New York: Routledge, 1994), 11.

27. Alexandre Guilmant (1837–1911) was one of Paris's foremost nineteenth-century organists. He was organist at the Trinité, and became closely associated with the great organ-builder Aristide Cavaillé-Coll. See Carolyn Shuster-Fournier, "Les Orgues Cavaillé-Coll au salon, au théâtre et au concert" (Ph.D. diss., Université François-Rabelais de Tours, 1991), 274–77. The Palais du Trocadéro was built specially for the 1878 Paris World's Fair.

28. Émile Bourgeois (1849–1922) made opera reductions during the 1880s for such composers as Paladilhe, Victor Massé, and Ferdinand Poise.

29. The catalogue of the Music division of the BNF lists close to one hundred of

Bourgeois's works, composed between 1872 and 1914. What appears to have been one of his most popular works, a song, *La véritable Manola,* on a poem by Théophile Gautier, was reprinted no fewer than nine times over the years, in versions for voice and piano, piano four hands, mandoline and piano, and violin and piano. Coincidentally, in 1887 Bourgeois's name appears on a program of the works of Edmond de Polignac, Winnaretta's future husband.

30. The presence of the "American" Singer family at the Château de Blosseville inspired novelist Ludovic Halévy—best known as the co-librettist of Bizet's Carmen—to write a novel, *L'Abbé Constantin* (1881), which vibrantly depicted the elegant and lively atmosphere that reigned at the estate and the fascination with which the denizens of Pennedepie regarded the château's inhabitants. Halévy's novel enjoyed considerable success, and was later adapted for the stage. I am grateful to Bernard Gorgeu, Mayor of Pennedepie, for calling my attention to this work.

31. WSP, "Memoirs," 118.

32. Ibid., 121.

33. Gabriel Fauré, *His Life through His Letters,* ed. Jean-Michel Nectoux, trans. J. A. Underwood (New York: Marion Boyars, 1984), 156.

34. Jean-Louis Forain (1852–1931).

35. Gérard Bauer, "Une Initiatrice de la musique contemporaine," *Le Figaro,* 2 December 1944, 2.

36. WSP, "Memoirs," 116–17.

37. As quoted in Ruth Brandon, *The Dollar Princesses: Sagas of Upward Mobility 1870–1914* (New York: Knopf, 1980), 182.

38. Ruth Brandon, *Singer and the Sewing Machine: A Capitalist Romance* (New York: Kodansha Globe, 1996), 172.

39. Ibid.

40. *The New York Times,* 1 November 1877.

41. Ibid.

42. "Court Journal," article from an unspecified newspaper, dated Saturday, 12 May 1883, SHSW, SA-1/1.

43. WSP, "Memoirs," 113.

44. Ibid.

45. Frederick Boyer appears to have been influenced in his career choice by WSP's younger brother Washington, who had "resolved as a young man to make a career for himself as a rancher in the Far West" (*The Times* of London, 12 February 1934). Washington was persuaded by Mortimer Singer to remain in England, but Frederick, with Mortimer's financial backing, went on to California alone.

46. Andrew Thomson, *Vincent d'Indy and His World* (Oxford: Clarendon Press, 1996), 69.

47. Félix Barrias, *Winnaretta Buonaparte,* dated Hyères, 31 August 1885, private collection.

48. Paul Mathey (1844–1929). Mathey's 1887 portrait of his student, *Winnaretta Singer,* is in a private collection.

49. *Catalogue du Salon de 1885,* Item 2264 (Paris: E. Bernard, 1885).

50. *Catalogue du Salon de 1886,* Item 2206 (Paris: Dupont, 1886). The portrait of Isabelle-Blanche Singer hangs today above the Great Staircase of the Fondation Singer-Polignac in Paris.

51. 'D. Hawley' ledger re Singer estate, 1878–1884, SHSW, Box 200. In 1877, Winnaretta received outright $115,000, her share of her father's estate; an additional distribution of $50,507 was also made after the final disputes over the Singer will were settled. By 1886, WS's net worth was ten times greater than it had been less than a decade earlier.

52. A more exact idea of Winnaretta's net worth can be derived from a description of the financial status of the other Singer daughter, Isabelle-Blanche. Winnaretta and Belle-Blanche had received equal portions of money and stock, according to the Singer will. In 1888, at the time of the Belle-Blanche's marriage to Duc Élie Decazes, an Iowa newspaper (December 20, 1888, located in SHSW, SA-1/1) printed the following report on the finances of the future Duchesse Decazes. It serves to describe Winnaretta's approximate holdings as well. "The [Singer children] draw upon Mr. Hawley as they need money. They have their own horses and carriages, and tutors and servants. They are worth $1,500,000 each. When Surrogate Coffin of Westchester County made his decree of distritbution, Oct. 31, 1877, [Isabelle-Blanche] was awarded $174,437.02 in money, 3,487 shares of the singer manufacturing Company, the par value of each of which is $100, and the market value of which was put at $699,525, making her share, in all, $783,962.02. Today she is worth, Mr. Hawley says, $1,385,075, invested, about half of it in Singer Manufacturing stock, one-quarter in United States 4 and 4 ½ percent bonds, and one-quarter in cash in bank. In addition she has an interest worth about $200,00 in certain real and personal property in England which she will be entitled to receive in 1891 when her brother Franklin becomes of age."

53. Proceedings of the Isaac M. Singer estate trial, Westchester County Archives (N.Y.), Series 16, A-0255 (122) 2, call number 1875–302.

54. Ibid.

55. WSP, "Memoirs," 113; Richard Ormond and Elaine Kilmurray, *John Singer Sargent: The Early Portraits*, vol. 1 of *Complete Paintings* (New Haven: Yale University Press, 1998), 190–91.

56. Previously unpublished letter from Olga Rudge to Ezra Pound, Monday [22 June 1931], ORP1–YCAL 54/263, ©2003 by Mary de Rachewiltz; Julien Green, 22 June 1931, *Journal 1928–1958* (Paris: Plon, 1961), 35.

57. Daniel Wildenstein, *Monet ou le triomphe de l'Impressionisme*, 4 vols. (Cologne: Taschen, 1996), 3:403, #1067. Wildenstein puts the purchase date as July 1886.

58. Hill, *Antonio Stradivari*, ch. 11.

59. "The Mrs. Singer Who Became Duchess of Camposelice," article from an unidentified newspaper, 1 December 1886, SHSW, SA-1/1.

60. Ibid.

61. "Americans in Europe," *The New York World*, 30 July 1887, SHSW, SA-1/1.

62. Prince Jean-Louis de Faucigny-Lucinge, *Un Gentilhomme cosmopolite* (Paris: Perrin, 1990), 98.

63. Comte Louis de Beauchamp, *L'Hôtel de la Princesse Edmond de Polignac* (Paris: Fondation Singer-Polignac, 1983), 6.

64. Ironically, one of his uncles was a student at the Conservatoire de Paris during the same years as Winnaretta's second husband, Prince Edmond de Polignac.

65. Brandon, *Dollar Princesses*, 1–6.

66. George Woodruff to WS, 24 June 1887, private collection.

67. Ibid.

68. "Americans in Europe," *New York World,* 30 July 1887.

69. Déodat de Sévérac (1872–1921) received his training at the Schola Cantorum with Vincent d'Indy. He wrote works in the musical idiom of his native southwestern France.

70. Wedding menu, signed by the guests, FSP.

71. Brandon, *Dollar Princesses,* 183. Ms. Brandon, INT, 22 August 1998, affirmed that she had heard the story from Singer family members when researching her book in the mid-1970s.

72. *Le Figaro,* Friday, 2 September 1887, p. 1.

73. "A Duke's Funeral," *The Herald-Tribune,* 7 September 1887.

74. Ibid.

75. "Singer and His Families," *The World* (NY), 2 September 1887.

Chapter 3

1. Paris Singer to WSP, 15 January 1888, private collection.

2. WSP, "Memoirs of the Late Princesse Edmond de Polignac," *Horizon* 12, no. 68 (August 1945): 124–25.

3. Ibid.

4. The scrapbook of articles in SHSW, SA-1/1, contains this and similar articles about the Singer-Decazes marriage.

5. SHSW, SA-1/1.

6. *L'Art et la mode,* 4 May 1888; *The New York Herald,* 29 April 1888.

7. Cécile Tardif, "Les Salons de musique à Paris sous la Troisième République" (M.A. thesis, Université de Montréal, 1994), 46.

8. Ibid., 55.

9. George D. Painter, *Marcel Proust: A Biography,* 2 vols. (New York: Vintage Books, 1978), 1:107–8.

10. Édouard André and his wife, née Nelly Jacquemart, devoted their lives to the collection of artworks from the Italian Renaissance. Their music salon took place in one of the gallery-reception rooms in their sumptous *hôtel* on Boulevard Haussmann. The building is now the site of the Musée Jacquemart-André.

11. Alphonse Daudet (1840–1897) was a well-known novelist and short-story writer. He wrote the libretto for Bizet's opera, *L'Arlésienne.*

12. Tardif, "Les Salons de musique," 27–37; Myriam Chimènes, "La Musique dans les salons de la Belle Époque aux années Cinquante," in *Musique et musiciens au Faubourg St-Germain,* ed. Jean Gallois, 89–101 (Paris: Délégation à l'Action Artistique de la Ville de Paris, 1996).

13. WSP, "Memoirs," 139–40.

14. Ibid.

15. MBSM as quoted in Colette, *Journal à rebours* (Paris: Fayard, 1941), 53.

16. Ibid.

17. WSP, "Memoirs," 123.

18. Colette, *Journal à rebours,* 53.

19. WSP, "Memoirs," 127.

20. Ibid., 122–23.

21. Ibid.

22. Ibid.

23. Anne de Cossé-Brissac, *La Comtesse Greffulhe* (Paris: Perrin, 1991), 84.

24. Ibid.

25. Emmanuel Chabrier to Ernest Van Dyke, 7 April 1888, in Francis Poulenc, *Emmanuel Chabrier* (Paris: La Palatine, 1961), 80–1.

26. A score of *Gwendoline*, given as a gift to WS, bears the following dedication: "A Madame la Princesse de Scey-Montbéliard, Hommage reconnaissant & dévoué, Emmanuel Chabrier, 1888," BMFP.

27. WSP, "Memoirs," 122.

28. "A travers Paris: Dans le monde," *Le Figaro*, 16 May 1888, 1.

29. "A travers Paris: Dans le monde," *Le Figaro*, 24 May 1888, 1.

30. WSP, "Memoirs," 122.

31. The word derives from the family name Caius Maecenas, a wealthy Roman statesman under Caesar Augustus and patron of literary figures such as Virgil and Horace.

32. Among the many organizations in existence since 1870 committed to the advancement of contemporary French music, the Société Nationale de Musique was unique in that it was composer-run, private, and self-financed.

33. A set of sketches drawn by WSP during a visit to Madame de Monteynard's Château de Tencin, dated 14 July 1888, is in the possession of Mme. Pierre Rigaud, the Marquise de Monteynard's granddaughter. The sketches include caricatures of the Singer family and Mme. de Monteynard, as well as a floral design drawn around the text of Verlaine's poem *Clair de lune*.

34. Albert Lavignac, *Voyage artistique à Bayreuth* (Paris: Delagrave, 1897), 555.

35. GF to MBSM, undated [27 July 1888], in Gabriel Fauré, *Correspondance,* ed. Jean-Michel Nectoux (Paris: Flammarion, 1980), 142–43. This correspondence is also published in English as *Gabriel Fauré: His Life through His Letters,* trans. J. A. Underwood (New York: Marion Boyars, 1984.

36. I date this manuscript by its inclusion in a volume of diverse pieces by Fauré including the most recent, the song *Larmes,* dedicated to "Mme la Princesse Wynaretta de Scey-Montbéliard."

37. "The Singer Festivities," *The Totnes Times* (England), 17 November 1888. Paris Singer had married a young Australian, Lillie Graham, at approximately the same moment as his sister Winnaretta's marriage.

38. Ibid., 25.

39. "Many Wives and Millions," article from an unidentified New York paper, 20 December 1888, SHSW, SA-1/1.

40. IBS to David Hawley [1889], as quoted in Ruth Brandon, *Singer and the Sewing Machine: A Capitalist Romance* (New York: Kodansha Globe, 1996), 214. Regrettably, all of IBS's letters to Hawley have been lost.

41. WS's correspondence with sculptor Jean Carriès places her at rue de Lübeck between November 1889 and October 1891. The original *hôtel* is still extant, its beautiful ornate facade and grand entry-hall still intact. It is owned by and serves as the headquarters for France's National Center for Cinematography.

42. A number of scores of Gigout's original organ works with inscribed dedications in the BMFP show his long and productive relationship with WSP. The first, Gigout's *Cent Pièces brèves pour orgue ou harmonium* (1888), is dedicated to

"Madame Winnaretta Singer, Respectueux hommage, Eugène Gigout," BMFP. His *Dix Pièces pour grand orgue*, dated January 1906, bears the dedication "A Madame la Princesse Edmond de Polignac, en souvenir de studieuses et très agréables heures organistiques, Eugène Gigout."

43. Printed program of SNM concert, 6 April 1889, folder of "programmes imprimés," BNF-Mus. The 6 April 1889 concert featured Chausson's *La Caravane*, two movements from the Suite in D Major by d'Indy, and the first concert performance of the incidental music from Fauré's *Caligula*; the program also included first performances of works by Ernest Bernard, Alfred Bruneau, and Camille Benoit. An undated letter, in the archives of the Fondation Singer-Polignac, Paris (FSP), was subsequently sent to WSP by the Committee of the Société Nationale de Musique; its author is Vincent d'Indy and it is signed by César Franck, Emmanuel Chabrier, d'Indy, Gabriel Fauré, Camille Benoit, and Pierre de Bréville. The letter thanks the Princesse for her past support, and expresses the hope of continued future support.

44. GF to WS, 9 April 1889, FSP. Some thirty letters sent to WSP, dated 1889–1924, including related letters addressed to Fauré by Paul Verlaine and Maurice Bouchor and included in his own correspondence, are still extant. The texts to some of these letters can also be found in Fauré, *Correspondance*, chapter 5.

45. Vincent d'Indy to WS, 19 July 1889, FSP.

46. Lavignac, *Voyage artistique à Bayreuth*, 557.

47. Poulenc, *Emmanuel Chabrier*, 152–53.

48. Probably the Marquise de Monteynard, WSP's friend since 1888.

49. The two paintings are listed in the 1889 catalogue *Salon, Exposition des ouvrages de peinture* (Paris: Paul Dupont, 1889), 189. The "Portrait de M. Félix Barrias," listed in the 1890 catalogue, now hangs in the *salle de concert* of the Fondation Singer-Polignac, Paris.

50. Daniel Wildenstein, *Monet ou le triomphe de l'Impressionisme*, 4 vols. (Cologne: Taschen, 1996), 3:435–36, #1151. Wildenstein lists WSP as being the first owner of the canvas. In a letter from Claude Monet to WS, dated Giverny 22 July 1889, the painter thanks her for "the five thousand francs that [John Singer] Sargent sent on your behalf. . . . I am so happy and flattered that you like my painting" (FSP).

51. Monet to WS, Giverny, 31 July 1889, FSP. He thanks her for her "generous participation in the Manet subscription."

52. WSP, "Memoirs," 115; Stanley Olson, *John Singer Sargent: His Portrait* (London: Barrie & Jenkins, 1989), 71–73.

53. Richard Ormond and Elaine Kilmurray, *John Singer Sargent: The Early Portraits*, vol. 1 of *Complete Paintings* (New Haven, Conn: Yale University Press, 1998), 190–91, 258–59. Art historians speculate that WSP's portrait may have been exhibited by Sargent under the title "Portrait de Madame . . ." in the 1890 exhibition of the Société Nationale de Beaux-Arts.

54. *World's Columbian Exposition 1893 Official Catalogue*, 26.

55. WSP to GF, undated [July 1894], FSP.

56. Painter, *Marcel Proust*, 1:229.

57. WS to Jean Carriès, 23 November 1889. Complete correspondence between WS and Jean Carriès (1889–92) is located in the Archives départementales de la Nièvre (ADLN), France, Box 73, folders J4 and J5.

58. John Deathridge et al., eds., *Wagner Werk-Verzeichnis (WWV): Verzeichnis*

der musikalischen Werke Richard Wagners und ihrer Quellen: erarbeitet in Rahmen der Richard Wagner-Gesamtausgabe (Mainz; New York: Schott, 1986), 538–49.

59. The absence of documentation concerning WS and the *Parsifal* manuscript has been confirmed in correspondence with the author by Dr. Sven Friedrich, Director of the Richard Wagner Museum and National Archives, and The Research Center of the Richard Wagner Foundation, Bayreuth.

60. The most recent study of the *Porte de Parsifal* is Patrice Bellanger, *Jean-Joseph Carriès, 1855–1894* (Paris: Galerie Patrice Bellanger, 1997), 21–29, 82–90.

61. Arsène Alexandre, *Jean Carriès, imagier et potier: Étude d'une oeuvre et d'une vie* (Paris: Librairies-Imprimeries Réunies, 1895), 134–35.

62. WS to Jean Carriès, 20 March 1890, ADLN, 73 J4.

63. Ibid.

64. Productions notes of the modeler, Ginet, in ADLN, 73 J4.

65. Carriès's studio still exists, in the village of St-Amand-en-Puisaye, La Nièvre. It is now the site of a museum and a pottery school based on the artist's principles.

66. WS to Jean Carriès, 14 December 1890, ADLN, 73 J4.

67. Jean-Michel Nectoux, editor's notes in Fauré, *His Life through His Letters*, 156, 158–59.

68. Cécile Tardif, "Fauré and the Salons," in *Regarding Fauré*, ed. and trans. Tom Gordon (Newark, N.J.: Gordon and Breach, 1999), 1–14.

69. GF to WS, undated [17–19 January 1891], FSP, reprinted in Fauré, *Correspondance*, 161–62. The "Fridays" that Fauré mentions are the weekly salon gatherings of Madame de Saint-Marceaux.

70. Neither this letter nor its response survives. WS refers to this correspondence in a later (undated) letter, written from Paignton, probably in June 1894. Both this 1894 letter and Fauré's response, also undated, presumably from August 1894, can be found in FSP.

71. Jann Pasler has pointed out that the fee proposed to Fauré by WSP was more than twice the annual salary paid to composer Ambroise Thomas in his capacity as Director of the Paris Conservatoire.

72. WSP to GF, undated (June 1894), FSP.

73. The story of the Fauré-Verlaine incident was first published in an article by Georges Jean-Aubry, "Gabriel Fauré, Paul Verlaine et Albert Samain, ou les tribulations de 'Bouddha,'" in *Le Centenaire de Gabriel Fauré*, a special edition of *La Revue musicale*, 1945.

74. WSP, "Memoirs," 120.

75. Paul Verlaine to GF, 21 January 1891, FSP, reprinted in Fauré, *Correspondance*, 162–63.

76. GF to WS, undated [30 January 1891], FSP, reprinted in Fauré, *Correspondance*, 163–66..

77. GF to WS, 18 January 1891, FSP, reprinted in Fauré, *Correspondance*, 161–62.

78. GF to WS, 30 January 1891, FSP, reprinted in Fauré, *Correspondance*, 163–66.

79. Ibid.

80. Ibid.

81. Sketch of Paul Verlaine by Gabriel Fauré, FSP, reprinted in Fauré, *Correspondance*, 165.

82. Paul Verlaine to GF, 6 April 1891, FSP, reprinted in Fauré, *Correspondance*, 166.

83. GF to WS, undated [late April 1891], FSP, reprinted in Fauré, *Correspondance*, 169–71.

84. WSP, "Memoirs," 119–20, 129. The Casa Wolkoff is now owned by actor-director Woody Allen.

85. Ibid., 120.

86. Dedication manuscripts to four of the five songs can be found in the BMFP. *Mandoline*, dedicated to "la Princesse W. de Scey," is dated 7 June 1891. *En Sourdine*, dedicated "à Madame la Princesse de Scey," is dated Venice-Paris–June 1891. *Green*, dedicated "à Mme la Princesse de Scey-Montbéliard," is dated Paris, July 1891. *A Clymène*, bearing the same dedication, is dated "Paris, August 1891." All four manuscripts bear Fauré's signature on the title page. The whereabouts of the fifth, *C'est l'extase*, are unknown.

87. WSP, "Memoirs," 120.

88. Nectoux, editor's note, in Fauré, *His Life through His Letters*, 158–59.

89. All of these works are housed in the BMFP.

90. GF to MBSM, undated [12 June 1891], in Fauré, *Correspondance*, 174–76.

91. Ralph P. Locke, "Cutthroats and Casbah Dancers, Muezzins and Timeless Sands: Musical Images of the Middle East," *19th-Century Music* 22, no. 11 (Summer 1998): 20–53.

92. Maurice Bouchor wrote the poem *Poème de l'amour et de la mer*, which was set to music by Ernest Chausson.

93. GF to Paul Poujard, undated [6 June 1891], in Fauré, *Correspondance*, 171–72, and to WS, two undated letters [28 June 1891 and 22 August 1891], FSP, reprinted in Fauré, *Correspondance*, 181–83 and 184–85.

94. GF to MBSM, undated [12 June 1891], in Fauré, *Correspondance*, 181.

95. Paul Verlaine to GF, 2 June 1891, FSP, reprinted in Fauré, *Correspondance*, 181.

96. WSP, "Memoirs," 120–21.

97. Nectoux discusses at length Fauré's diffidence towards certain texts in his introduction to chapter 5, Fauré, *Correspondance*, 158–60, and *His Life through His Letters*, 157–58.

98. GF to WS, undated [late August 1891], FSP, reprinted in Fauré, *Correspondance*, 184–85.

99. Nectoux, editor's note, in Fauré, *Correspondance*, 158–60; see also *His Life through His Letters*, 157–58.

100. GF to WS, undated [late August 1891], FSP, reprinted in Fauré, *Correspondance*, 163–66; and in English in *His Life*, 167–68.

101. Fauré is referring to his First Piano Quintet, a work that had an exceedingly long period of gestation; still only in draft form in 1894, it was not taken up again by Fauré until 1903, and completed in 1905.

102. GF to WS, Paris, Monday 22 June [1891], FSP, reprinted in Fauré, *Correspondance*, 178–79.

103. GF to WS, undated [late July 1891], FSP, reprinted in Fauré, *Correspondance*, 183–84. The line "Ne le déchirez pas avec vos deux mains blanches" is from Verlaine's poem *Green*. "Le" is the poet's heart.

104. WS to Jean Carriès, 2 August 1891, ADLN, 73 J4.

105. WS to Jean Carriès, 25 January 1892, ADLN, 73 J4.

106. Bellanger, *Jean-Joseph Carriès*, 27.

107. Jean Carriès to Maurice Lobre, undated [1891–92], as quoted in Alexandre, *Jean Carriès,* 160.

108. Jean Carriès to WS (rough draft), 10 February 1892, ADLN, 73 J3.

109. WS to Jean Carriès, 12 February 1892, ADLN, 73 J4.

110. Even though Fauré referred to her as the "Princesse de Scey," Winnaretta signed her letters "WS," Winnaretta Singer.

111. According to William Kass, IBS began to sell the stringed instruments from the collection amassed by the Duc de Camposelice back to the British Hill brothers in 1891. Provenance papers for the 1734 "Duc de Camposelice" Guarneri del Gesù violin now owned by concert artist Cho-Liang Lin give a date of sale (to Frankfurt dealer Franz-Charles Edler) of 1895.

112. All of the information about the Comtesse Greffulhe in this chapter comes from Cossé-Brissac, *La Comtesse Greffulhe,* except where otherwise noted.

113. "Les Compositeurs français en France," *Le Figaro,* 10 April 1890, 1; Cossé-Brissac, 87.

114. GF to WS, undated [late April 1891], FSP, reprinted in Fauré, *Correspondance,* 169–71.

115. Document in a folder bearing the inscription "Pour servir aux mémoires de la comtesse Greffulhe," Archives Comtesse Greffulhe, carton 149. These archives are no longer accessible for perusal. I am grateful to Anne de Cossé Brissac for communicating the text to me.

116. In an undated letter [Spring 1891] to WSP, Helleu writes, "With great pleasure, I will come to work in your magnificent atelier, and I look forward to having you and your friends pose for me." FSP.

117. Excerpt from *La Vie parisienne* (no date provided), as cited in Jean Adhémar, preface to Bibliothèque nationale (France), *Helleu [Exposition, 16 mai–15 juin 1957]* (Paris, 1957), 12.

118. WS to MBSM, sent from "Blosseville, Villerville," undated, probably written 24 July 1891, ASM.

119. Prince Edmond de Polignac, INT, 23 January 1999, Paris. Prince Edmond, Winnaretta Singer-Polignac's great-great-nephew and godson, recalled being told this story often during his childhood.

120. The royal wedding took place on 6 July 1891.

121. WS to MBSM, 8 July [1891], ASM.

122. Ibid.

123. WS to MBSM, undated [24 July 1891], ASM.

124. WS to MBSM, 14 August 1891 (letter no. 1), ASM.

125. Ibid.

126. WS to MBSM, undated [September 1891], ASM.

127. One can compare, for example, the letters of GF to the Comtesse Greffulhe. See Fauré, *Correspondance,* chapter 4.

128. GF to WS, undated [28 June 1891], FSP, reprinted in Fauré, *Correspondance,* 181–82.

129. WS to MBSM, 14 August 1891 (letter no. 1), ASM.

130. WS to MBSM, 14 August 1891 (letter no. 2), ASM.

131. WS to MBSM, 24 August 1891, ASM.

132. WS to MBSM, undated [September 1891], ASM.

133. GF to WS, undated [September 1891], FSP, reprinted in Fauré,

Correspondance, 187–88. According to Fauré's letter, Winnaretta had asked him in July to submit the song to *Le Figaro* with the dedication "To Mme Winnaretta Singer." When *Mandoline* appeared in that publication on 2 November 1891, it bore the dedication "A Madame la princesse de Scey-Montbéliard," a reflection, no doubt, of the paper's policy of pandering to the *noblesse*.

134. WS to MBSM, undated [September 1891], ASM.

135. GF to WS, undated letter [22 August 1891], FSP, reprinted in Fauré, *Correspondance*, 184–85.

136. Albert Samain to his sister, 9 January 1892, as quoted in Fauré, *Correspondance*, 155–56.

137. Ibid., 31 December 1891, 155.

138. Georges Servières, "Musique," *La Revue indépendante* 23, no. 66 (April 1892): 130–31.

139. GF to WSP, 7 January 1892, FSP.

Chapter 4

1. Comte Melchior de Polignac, unpublished *Souvenirs de famille* (1906), APEP.

2. Ibid.

3. Duc Jean-Héracle de Polignac, *La Maison de Polignac: Étude d'une évolution sociale de la noblesse* (Le Puy: Éditions Jeanne d'Arc, 1975), 27.

4. Jules de Polignac was given his first title of *principe romano* in 1822 by a breviary of Pope Pius VII. Ibid., 129.

5. Pierre Robin-Harmel, *Prince Jules de Polignac, Ministre de Charles X (1780–1847)* (Paris: Aubanel Père, 1950), 165.

6. Ibid., 169.

7. Comte Melchior de Polignac, unpublished *Souvenirs de famille* (1906), APEP.

8. Ibid.

9. Robin-Harmel, *Prince Jules de Polignac*, 169.

10. Alphonse Thys (1807–1879) was best known as an author of *romances* (light popular songs) and other easy pieces for piano; although he was less successful as a composer of comic operas and operettas, many of his works were performed at Théâtre du Gymnase and the Opéra-Comique. He was a frequent contributor to *Le Ménéstrel*, which printed several of his *romances*. See, for example, Thys's "Enfant légère," *Le Ménéstrel*, No. 257, 4 November 1838, 48–49.

11. French music students, even to the present day, receive "prizes" instead of grades. In the four years that Edmond studied at the Conservatoire, 1855–59, his highest award was a Second Prize (1856), his lowest a Third Runner-Up (1858). AN, AJ^{37}, 353.

12. Princesse Charlotte de Polignac to Prince Ludovic de Polignac, 15 February 1859, APEP. The letter, with the exception of the above-cited phrase in French, is written in English.

13. Elisabeth Ann Levinge to Prince Ludovic de Polignac, 19 May 1864, APEP; Comte Guy de Polignac to Prince Ludovic de Polignac, Aix-les-Bains, 12 October 1886, APEP.

14. Richard Wagner, *My Life*, ed. Mary Whittall, trans. Andrew Gray (New York: Da Capo Press, 1992), 639.

15. Charles Bordes to EP, undated [18 April 1896], APEP.

16. MP [Horatio], "Le Salon de la Princesse Edmond de Polignac," *Le Figaro,* 6 September 1903. Of EP's music, MP wrote, "The outdoors suited his music better than the concert hall."

17. Philippe Gumplowicz, *Les Travaux d'Orphée, 150 ans de vie musicale amateur en France, Harmonies, chorales, fanfares* (Paris: Aubier, 1987), 55, 57.

18. Gounod, who served on the faculty of the Conservatoire, had marked "Très bon" in one of Edmond's composition notebooks, BMFP.

19. Edmond de Polignac, String Quartet in F Major (Paris: Richault, 1864).

20. The libretto, *La Coupe du Roi de Thulé,* had been chosen in a separate, earlier contest. The writers of the winning book were Édouard Blau and Louis Gallet. Both men went on to enjoy successful careers as librettists; Gallet, in particular, wrote numerous texts for major composers, including Massenet, Bizet, Saint-Saëns, and Gounod.

21. "Concours de Grand Opéra," *Le Ménéstrel,* 28 November 1869, 413.

22. Eugène d'Harcourt, "Un Prince musicien," *Le Figaro,* 9 August 1901, 1.

23. EP to Prince Ludovic de Polignac, 30 July 1880, APEP.

24. Henry James to RM, 1 July 1885, NAfr 15335:45–46.

25. EP to RM, undated [July 1888] NAfr 15343:68.

26. Debussy apparently liked EP's music. See his letter of 23 February 1895 to Pierre Louÿs, in Claude Debussy, *Letters,* ed. François Lesure and Roger Nichols, trans. Roger Nichols (Cambridge, Mass.: Harvard University Press, 1987), 77.

27. The first performance of one of EP's works under the aegis of the SNM took place on 7 March 1891. This was the *Chant de Blancheflor, complainte gothique* for voice, strings, and piano. Subsequent performances of EP's works under the SNM's auspices took place in 1895 and 1896. He was a member of the organization until his death in 1901.

28. Vincent d'Indy et al., *Le Schola Cantorum: Son histoire depuis sa fondation jusqu'en 1925* (Paris: Librairie Bloud and Gay, 1927), 5.

29. Andrew Thomson, *Vincent d'Indy and His World* (Oxford: Clarendon Press, 1996), 81.

30. Rimsky-Korsakov's works—notably *Sadko,* the first composition to be identified by the composer as being based on what is now referred to as the octatonic scale—were first performed in Paris during a series of concerts of Russian music performed at the 1878 World's Fair. The conductor Pasdeloup subsequently championed *Sadko,* which was included in an 1882 Russian Music Festival, organized in Paris by Pasdeloup and Anton Rubinstein.

31. "Mondanités," reported by "Étincelle" in *Le Figaro,* 17 May 1888, 1. Pierre Loti (1850–1923), French novelist and naval officer, is considered to be the initiator of modern French exotic fiction. He was at the height of his popularity in 1888, the period of the performances of Polignac's octatonic music.

32. Comte Melchior de Polignac, unpublished *Souvenirs de famille* (1906), APEP.

33. MP, *Le Figaro,* 6 September 1903.

34. Archives Comtesse Greffulhe, communicated by Cossé-Brissac.

35. EP to RM, undated [1892], NAfr 15032:130–31.

36. Gautier's haunting *Lamento* (incipit: "Connaissez-vous la blanche tombe") was also set to music by Duparc and Berlioz; the latter included it in his cycle *Les Nuits d'été* under the title *Au Cimetière.*

37. EP does not specify the venue of the performance in his letter; it is probably the Cercle de l'Union artistique.

38. Soprano Rose Caron (1857–1930) was one of the great divas of the Paris Opéra, lauded as much for her acting as her singing.

39. The French method of singing *à bouche fermée,* literally "with closed mouth," is a modified form of humming; the singer closes the teeth and leaves the lips partly open while producing sound.

40. EP is describing rhythmic augmentation and diminution of the main theme.

41. EP refers to the natural minor scale.

42. EP to WS, 4 April 1892, FSP.

43. The printed program of the SNM concert (30 April [1892], BNF-Mus) indicates that the concert was being given "under the patronage of Madame W. S." The concert also included works by Chausson, Bréville, Benoit, Bordes, and d'Indy.

44. The print of WS's painting (title unidentified) was enclosed in the deluxe edition of *La Revue indépendante,* 23 (April–June 1892).

45. Edgar Munhall, *Whistler and Montesquiou* (New York: The Frick Collection, 1995), 36.

46. WS to RM, 8 May 1892, NAfr 15122:95.

47. RM to WS, 12 May 1892, FSP.

48. WS to RM, undated [13–16 May 1892], NAfr 15168:177. WS subsequently bought one of Helleu's paintings, *Sailing Boats at Cowes.*

49. RM to WS, 5 June 1892, FSP.

50. George D. Painter, *Marcel Proust: A Biography,* 2 vols. (New York: Vintage Books, 1978), 1:29.

51. RM to WS, 20 August 1892, FSP.

52. WS to RM, 28 August 1892, NAfr 15115:57–58; RM to WS, undated letter [September 1892], FSP.

53. WS to RM, 28 August 1892, NAfr 15115:57–58.

54. Wilde's *Salome* was written expressly to be performed by Bernhardt. *Salome* was already in rehearsal in London, when the production was stopped by Lord Chamberlain, who informed the playwright that it was blasphemous to stage a play with biblical characters.

55. WS to RM, undated [November or December 1892], NAfr 15115:59.

56. Pictures of WSP and EP, Cowes, England, July 1893, private collection.

57. EP to RM, 19 November 1892, NAfr 15113:91–92.

58. EP to WS, 27 September 1893, FSP.

59. Ibid.

60. WS to the Comtesse Greffulhe, 9 November 1893, NAfr 15115:60.

61. "Belle" [Isabelle-Blanche] Singer to WS, undated [November or December 1893], private collection.

62. "A travers Paris," *Le Figaro,* 16 December 1893.

63. "Belle" Singer Decazes to WSP, undated [November or December 1893], private collection.

64. Ruth Brandon, *The Dollar Princesses: Sagas of Upward Mobility 1870–1914* (New York: Knopf, 1980), 27.

65. Comtesse Jane d'Oilliamson to Prince Ludovic de Polignac, 28 December 1893, APEP.

66. Jacques-Émile Blanche, *La Pêche aux souvenirs* (Paris: Flammarion, 1949), 249.

67. EP to RM, 18 January 1894, NAfr 15115:49–50.

68. MP, *Le Figaro*, 6 September 1903.

69. Blanche, *La Pêche aux souvenirs*, 249.

Chapter 5

1. Unpublished poem by EP to WSP, undated. Ironically, these verses ended up in the Montesquiou papers, NAfr 15115:10.

2. EP to WSP, [Summer 1895], FSP.

3. Ibid.

4. WSP to EP, undated, private collection.

5. Comtesse Amélie Rozan to Prince Ludovic de Polignac, undated, APEP.

6. Edmond de Goncourt, diary entry of 18 April 1894, in Edmond and Jules de Goncourt, *Journal: Mémoires de la vie littéraire*, ed. Robert Ricatte, 3 vols. (Paris: Robert Laffont, 1989), 3:946.

7. André Germain, "Robert de Montesquiou," typed text numbered "33" with accompanying autograph by André Germain, 15–16, private collection, as quoted in Antoine Bertrand, *Les Curiosités esthétiques de Robert de Montesquiou* (Geneva: Droz, 1997), 517.

8. Ibid.

9. Comtesse Edmond de Pourtalès to RP, NAfr 15112:126.

10. RM clearly knew WSP's artistic tastes well: blue and green were her favorite colors.

11. At French aristocratic dinners parties the host and hostess were seated in the middle. Guests were seated around them according to their rank, while those placed at the *bouts de table*, that is, the far ends of the table, were generally literary or artistic figures whose purpose was to entertain those seated near them. Edith Wharton, in *A Backward Glance* (London, 1972), provides a commentary on this custom: "The *bouts de table* are at once the shame and the glory of the French dinner-table; the shame of those who think they deserve a better place . . . the glory of hostesses ambitious to receive the quickest wits in Paris."

12. RM, *Vinaigrette, portrait satirique*, excerpt from *Quarante bergères*, 3rd series, No. 20 (private printing). The autograph can be found in the NAfr 15115:54.

13. Armande de Polignac (Comtesse de Chabannes), speech, "Homage" (1944), APEP.

14. Jeanice Brooks, "Nadia Boulanger and the Salon of the Princesse de Polignac," in *Journal of the American Musicological Society* 46, no. 3 (Fall 1993): 415–19.

15. Alexandre Guilmant's reputation as a Bach interpreter was confirmed after his 22 January 1892 presentation of J. S. Bach's *Christmas Oratorio*, the work's first performance in France, presented under the auspices of Greffulhe's Société des Grandes Auditions. A copy of the program of J. S. Bach's *Oratorio de Noël* is preserved in the BMFP, although it is not clear whether it was WSP or EP who was present for the performance.

16. "Courrier des théâtres," *Le Figaro*, 9 January 1894.

17. "Boîte à lettres," *Le Figaro*, 24 February 1894.

18. "Boîte à lettres," *Le Figaro*, 28 February 1894.

19. "A travers Paris," *Le Figaro*, 5 May 1894.

20. "A travers Paris," *Le Figaro*, 18 May 1894.

21. *Le Figaro*, 22 March 1890, 1.

22. "Graceful as a Bride," *New York Herald*, 16 December 1893. An idea of the room's décor can be gleaned in John Singer Sargent's *Portrait of Princesse de Scey-Montbéliard*, private collection.

23. MP [Horatio], "Le Salon de la Princesse Edmond de Polignac: Musique d'aujourd'hui; Échos d'autrefois," *Le Figaro*, 6 September 1903, 2.

24. EP to Ludovic de Polignac, undated [early June 1894], APEP.

25. "A travers Paris," *Le Figaro*, 5 June 1894.

26. MBSM, excerpt from an unpublished diary entry of 21 May 1894, forthcoming in an edition by Myriam Chimènes (Paris: Éditions Fayard).

27. Ibid.

28. Ibid.

29. GF to WS, undated [late July or early August 1892], FSP.

30. WSP to GF, draft, June 1894, FSP, reprinted in Jean-Michel Nectoux, "Gabriel Fauré," *Le Monde de la musique*, no. 142 (March 1991): 64–70.

31. Ibid.

32. GF to WSP, undated [July 1894], FSP, reprinted in ibid.

33. Ibid.

34. WSP, "Memoirs of the Late Princesse Edmond de Polignac," *Horizon* 12, no. 68 (August 1945): 121.

35. Arsène Alexandre, *Jean Carriès, imagier et potier: Étude d'une oeuvre et d'une vie* (Paris: Librairies-Imprimeries Réunies, 1895), 166.

36. Edmond Pottier, "Les Salons de 1892," *Gazette des beaux-arts* (July 1892): 38–39.

37. Ibid.

38. Joseph Uzanne to Jean Carriès, undated [1893–84], ADLN, 73 J4; Paul Ménard-Dorian to Jean Carriès, 13 March 1894, ibid.

39. Marquise Guy de Polignac, DD, 5–18 August 1894, APEP.

40. LMLV-F, 10 September 1894, 2.

41. MP [Horatio], *Le Figaro*, 6 September 1903, 2.

42. According to Edmond de Goncourt's diary entry dated 30 December 1894 (Edmond and Jules de Goncourt, *Journal: Mémoires de la vie littéraire*, ed. Robert Ricatte, 3 vols. [Paris: Robert Laffont, 1989], 3:1066), Antonio de La Gandara had just completed his lithograph of WSP, *Femme en robe noire*. The work was subsequently exhibited in Siegfried Bing's "Salon de l'Art Nouveau" in the spring of 1895. One of twelve copies made of the lithograph is in the collection of the Zimmerli Art Gallery, Rutgers University, N.J.

43. Paul Helleu's drypoint, *Chez la Princesse de Polignac; Tissot et trois jeunes femmes* is difficult to date. It may have been executed as early as 1891, during the period when WSP commissioned the album of her women friends, although the title suggests that it was done after her marriage. The work is reproduced in Paul Helleu, *Catalogue des pointes-sèches d'Helleu* (Paris: Imprimerie Lemercier, 1897), plate no. 56, and in Christopher Wood, *Tissot* (London: Weidenfeld and Nicolson, 1986), 132.

44. Charles Yriarte, in "Beaux Arts: Troisième Exposition des Femmes Artistes," *Le Figaro*, 16 January 1895, 2, wrote, "The exhibition of Madame Winnaretta Singer (princesse Edmond de Polignac) is one of the most personal, she even has the temperament of a *coloriste* (as evidenced in *The Pool* and *The Portrait of Sir R. S.*)."

45. LMLV-F, 21 January 1895, 2.

46. LMLV-F, 4 February 1895, 2.

47. LMLV-F, 8 February 1895, 2.

48. The members of the Delsart Quartet were also specialists in early music. The group's violist, Van Waefelghem, was often called upon to play viola d'amore in performances of Renaissance and baroque repertoire in the Polignac salon.

49. LMLV-F, 8 February 1895, 2.

50. Identical press releases announcing the Bach-Schütz concerts "sous la patronage de Mme la princesse de Polignac" appeared on 7 February 1895 in, among other papers, *La Libre parole, America Register, La Libéral, Gil Blas, La République française,* and *France Nouvelle.* These news clippings are gathered in scrapbooks tracing the musical career of Comte Eugène d'Harcourt, housed in the archives of Madame Carmen Zayas-d'Harcourt.

51. Anselm Gerhard, *The Urbanization of Opera: Music Theater in Paris in the Nineteenth Century,* trans. Mary Whitall (Chicago: University of Chicago Press, 1998), 36–40.

52. The Vicomtesse de Grandval, née Marie Reiset (1830–1906), composed a dozen operas which were performed in major Paris houses between 1859 and 1892. Her *oeuvre* also includes symphonic works and large religious works.

53. Augusta Holmès (1847–1903).

54. For a fuller discussion of Holmès's importance as a composer, see Jann Pasler, "The Ironies of Gender, or Virility and Politics in the Music of Augusta Holmès," *Women and Music* 2 (1998): 1–25.

55. Vincent d'Indy to Henry Gauthier-Villars, 23 January 1895, FSP.

56. Armande de Polignac (Comtesse de Chabannes), speech, "Homage" (1944), APEP.

57. A *halling* is generally a heavily accented Norwegian dance in duple meter. It is not clear why WSP chose this title, as her work is in 6/4, and is delicate and lilting.

58. Armande de Polignac (Comtesse de Chabannes), speech, "Homage" (1944), APEP.

59. James Lees-Milne, *Diaries: 1942–1945 (Ancestral Voices; Prophesying Peace)* (London: John Murray, 1995), 190. WSP's description of MP was made in the course of an evening spent with Lees-Milne on 22 July 1943. It is not clear in this diary entry whether Lees-Milne is quoting WSP directly, or paraphrasing her words.

60. Jean-Yves Tadie, *Marcel Proust: A Life,* trans. Euen Cameron (New York: Viking, 2000), 156–57.

61. Marcel Proust, *Correspondance de Marcel Proust,* ed. Philip Kolb, 20 vols. (Paris: Plon, 1970–93), 2:439, n. 3.

62. MP to Mme. Jean Hennessy, in Proust, *Correspondance,* 16:322. The Théâtre Libre was founded by André Antoine in 1887. As a center for the promotion of naturalist drama, it produced the first Paris performances of works by Hugo, Strindberg, and Ibsen.

63. Ibid., 189–90, 192.

64. See Jean-Jacques Nattiez, *Proust Musicien,* part 2 (Paris: Christian Bourgeois, 1999), 79–151; George D. Painter, *Marcel Proust: A Biography,* 2 vols. (New York: Vintage Books, 1978), 2:242–44.

65. MP [Horatio], *Le Figaro,* 6 September 1903, 2. The writer probably refers to Fauré's A Major Violin Sonata and to Brahms's Hungarian Dances.

66. MP to EP, undated [7 February 1895], APEP.

67. LMLV-F, 23 April 1895, 2.

68. Prior to being played in the Polignac salon, the most recent Paris performance of Rameau's *Dardanus* had taken place as part of a program given by the Concerts du Conservatoire in March 1887; on that occasion, too, only excerpts were performed. See the review in *Le Ménéstrel*, 6 March 1887.

69. LMLV-F, 23 April 1895, 2.

70. Program notes by Edmond de Polignac in the printed program of the concert, private collection. A portion of these notes were included in LMLV-F, 15 June 1895, 2.

71. Charles Bordes to EP, undated [May–June 1895], APEP.

72. Ibid.

73. MBSM, excerpt from an unpublished diary entry of 25 February 1896, forthcoming in an edition by Myriam Chimènes (Paris: Éditions Fayard).

74. In addition to reports about musical events in the Polignac home itself, LMLV-F, cites the Polignacs' presence at numerous social activities hosted by members of the noblesse more than fifty times during the years 1894–99.

75. LMLV-F, 16 June 1895, p. 2.

76. MP [Horatio], *Le Figaro*, 6 September 1903, 2.

77. Ibid.

78. EP to WSP, St-Gervais, undated [summer 1895], FSP.

79. EP to RM, undated, NAfr 15343:66. EP had visited Morris's studio with Montesquiou in London 1885, and had also gone to see an exhibition of Morris's fabrics in Paris.

80. MBP-PD, 27 May 1939, APEP. Two of EP's side tables were exhibited in the 1897 and 1898 Salons de Beaux-Arts (EP to WSP, undated [1897–98], FSP).

81. Gabriel Fauré, *Lettres intimes,* ed. Philippe Fauré-Fremiet (Paris: Grasset, 1951), 24.

82. Mrs. Patrick Campbell, née Beatrice Tanner (1865–1940), was a tall, graceful English actress whose talent was matched by her beauty and wit. For over twenty years, she was one of London's most popular, if often controversial, stage personalities. She created the role of Mélisande in Maurice Maeterlinck's *Pelléas et Mélisande* in its London opening in 1898. Her close friendship with George Bernard Shaw led her to create the role for which she was best-known: that of Eliza Doolittle in Shaw's *Pygmalion* (1912).

83. LMLV-F, 29 November 1895, 2. WSP mistakenly writes in her "Memoirs," 119, that the event took place in 1896.

84. Adela Maddison son (1866–1929).

85. The score of Maddison's *Twelve Songs*, Op. 9 & 10 (London: Metzler, 1895), given as a gift to WSP, bears the inscription "à Madame de Polignac from Adela Maddison." BMFP.

86. GF to Madame Ménard-Dorian, undated [1896] APEP.

87. LMLV-F, 9 January 1896, 2.

88. Jean Gallois and Isabelle Brétandeau, *Ernest Chausson, choix et présentation des écrits inédits* (Monaco: Éditions du Rocher, 1999), 435.

89. D'Indy to WSP, 14 April 1896, FSP; Charles Bordes to EP, 18 April 1896, APEP.

90. EP's *Martha et Maria* had just been performed by the Chanteurs de Saint-

Gervais, conducted by Charles Bordes, on 15 February 1896 at a concert of the SNM (printed program, BNF-Mus).

91. D'Indy to WSP, 14 April 1896, FSP.

92. See, for example, *Le Ménéstrel*, 22 March 1896, 21 January 1900, and *Le Journal*, 7 February 1900, concerning Paris performances of Handel's *Messiah*.

93. In the "partie documentaire" of Vincent d'Indy et al., *Le Schola Cantorum: Son histoire depuis sa fondation jusqu'en 1925* (Paris: Librairie Bloud and Gay, 1927), d'Indy devotes a chapter to "Concerts donnés par La Schola," 228–37. This detailed chronicle makes no mention of a performance of Bach's *St. John Passion*.

94. MBSM, excerpt of an unpublished diary entry of 12 May 1896, forthcoming in an edition by Myriam Chimènes (Paris: Éditions Fayard).

95. Ibid., 21 May 1894.

96. Claude Francis and Fernande Gontier, *Creating Colette*, 2 vols. (South Royalton, Vt.: Steerforth, 1998–99), 1:187.

97. Prince Jean-Louis de Faucigny-Lucinge, *Un Gentilhomme cosmopolite* (Paris: Perrin, 1990), 99.

98. LMLV-F, 15 January 1895, 1.

99. Stories about Isabelle Singer Decazes's "melancholy" are part of family lore; there is no documentation of this apparent chronic depression, however, and certainly no clinical proof.

100. LMLV-F, 15 January 1895, 2.

101. LMLV-F, 30 May 1896, 2.

102. EP to WSP, 17 July 1896, FSP.

103. LMLV-F, 7 August 1896, 2.

104. EP to WSP, 17 July 1896, FSP.

105. Ibid.

106. Ibid.

107. GF to his wife Marie, Bayreuth, 4 August 1896, in *Lettres intimes*, 15.

108. In a letter to WSP (FSP, undated, presumably from summer 1896), Mottl indicates that he will be happy to meet Fauré and looks forward to knowing his music.

109. GF to his wife, Marie, Bayreuth, 7 August 1896, in *Lettres intimes*, 17.

110. A letter from Paul Boyer, "Photographie inaltérable," dated October 1896 (APEP), invites EP to have his picture taken in order to be included in the Automobile Club of France's first portrait album of its members.

111. *Le Figaro*, 18 November 1896, 1.

112. LMLV-F, 16 November 1896, 2; EP to Ludovic de Polignac, 22 February 1897, APEP.

Chapter 6

1. EP's present to WSP, an 1851 edition of the complete works of J. S. Bach (21 volumes), was published by the Leipzig Bach-Gesellschaft, edited by Hauptmann, Jahn, Becker, and Moscheles. It is housed today in the BMFP.

2. France began the national registration of automobiles in 1892.

3. Marquise Guy de Polignac noted in her daily diary on 30 April 1897 (APEP), "the telephone is installed!"

4. Marquise Guy de Polignac noted in her daily diary on 8 February 1899 (APEP), "the *théâtrophone* is installed (*Meistersinger*)." Each broadcast cost ten francs. During April and May 1899 the Marquise also heard performances of the Orchestre Colonne, *Tannhäuser, Die Walküre* and *Manon.* The device remained in use for a long time: Proust listened to the Opéra's production of *Parsifal* on the *théâtrephone* in early 1914 (Jean-Yves Tadié, *Marcel Proust: A Life,* trans. Euen Cameron [New York: Viking, 2000], 613).

5. WSP, "Memoirs of the Late Princesse Edmond de Polignac," *Horizon,* 12, no. 68 (August 1945):117.

6. Barbara W. Tuchman, *The Proud Tower: A Portrait of the World before the War, 1890–1914* (New York: Macmillan, 1966), 202.

7. Jacques Chastenet, *Histoire de la Troisième République,* Vol. 3: *La République triomphante, 1893–1906* (Paris: Hachette, 1955), 118.

8. Maurice Barrès, *Scènes et doctrines du nationalisme* (Paris: Éditions des Trident, Diffusion Librairie Francaise, 1987), 152.

9. Marquise Guy de Polignac, DD, 9 May 1897, APEP.

10. Vincent d'Indy et al., *Le Schola Cantorum: Son histoire depuis sa fondation jusqu'en 1925* (Paris: Librairie Bloud and Gay, 1927), 228.

11. Armande de Polignac (Comtesse de Chabannes) to EP, undated, "Saturday" [end of July 1897], APEP. A bill from the Rechnung von Carl Boller, Bayreuth, made out to "Ihre Hoh. Prinz & Prinzess de Polignac, Paris," (APEP) indicates that their stay in Bayreuth lasted from 1 to 10 August 1897.

12. Armande de Polignac (Comtesse de Chabannes), speech, "Homage" (1944), APEP.

13. Camille de Polignac to EP, 18 August 1897, APEP.

14. LMLV-F, 18 August 1897, 1.

15. *The Torquay Times,* 12 October 1897.

16. WSP, "Memoirs," 117.

17. Ibid.

18. Ibid.

19. LMLV-F, 28 April 1898, 2.

20. LMLV-F, 29 May 1898, 2.

21. LMLV-F, 22 June 1898, 2.

22. MP to EP, 25 June 1898, APEP. Two years after EP's death, MP would write in *Le Figaro* (6 September 1903, 2) of the astonishing impression left by the composer's audiovisual experiments: "All of today's innovations, the union of music and visual effects, accompaniment by music of spoken recitations, [EP] was one of their original promoters. And, whatever progress or imitations have occurred since then, the sometimes inharmonious decorations of the rue Cortambert hôtel have remained entirely 'new.'"

23. Jean-Michel Nectoux, *Gabriel Fauré: Les voix du clair-obscur* (Paris: Flammarion, 1990), 282.

24. The autograph manuscript of Fauré's Prelude to *Pelléas et Mélisande,* arranged for piano four-hands, is dedicated in Fauré's hand "à la Princesse Edmond de Polignac," and is housed in the BMFP. The Incidental Music is Fauré's Op. 80.

25. LMLV-F, 9 July 1898. See Appendix A for a full listing of works, as well as d'Indy et al., *La Schola Cantorum,* 228.

26. Madeleine Lemaire to EP, "Hotel Vatel, Versailles," undated [July 1898], APEP.

27. EP to WSP, 16 July (mistakenly written 6 July) 1898, FSP.

28. Pierre Monteux (1875–1964) began his career as a violist, but came to fame as conductor of Diaghilev's Ballets Russes, leading the first performances of Stravinksy's *Petrushka* and *The Rite of Spring,* and Ravel's *Daphnis et Chloé.* He went on to conduct the Boston and San Francisco Symphonies, the Concertgebouw Orchestra, and the Orchestre Symphonique de Paris.

29. LMLV-F, 23 March 1899, 2.

30. MP [Horatio], *Le Figaro,* 6 September 1903.

31. MP to EP, "Wednesday night" [22 March 1899], APEP.

32. WSP to Virginia Woolf, 24 February 1939, The Monk's House Papers, University of Sussex, U.K.

33. Ibid.

34. MP to RM, 21 April 1899, in MP, *Correspondance,* 2:284.

35. George D. Painter, *Marcel Proust: A Biography,* 2 vols. (New York: Vintage Books, 1978), 1:237. MP's guests included poets RM, Anatole France, and ANo, MP's parents Dr. and Mme. Proust, the great salon hostess Mme. Arman de Cavaillet, Madeleine Lemaire, Mathieu de Noailles, and Léon Bailby, the editor of *La Presse.*

36. A copy of Perosi's *La Risurrezione di Cristo* (1899) in the BMFP bears the dedication "A Madame la princesse Edmond de Polignac, L. Perosi, Roma, Mayo 99." After serving as choirmaster at San Marco, Perosi went on to assume that post at the Sistine Chapel.

37. LMLV-F, 19 May 1899, 2.

38. A sizeable number of Maddison's works, including several song collections and a Piano Quintet, were released by the Parisian music publishers Choudens, Quinzard, and Fauré's publisher, Hamelle.

39. Frederick Delius to his wife Jelka Rosen (March 1899), in *Delius: A Life in Letters 1862–1934,* ed. Lionel Carley (London: Scolar Press in association with the Delius Trust, 1983), 1:149.

40. Ibid.

41. Colette, *Journal à rebours* (Paris: Fayard, 1941), 53.

42. Ibid. Colette would always regret losing "the flattering little sketch" that EP made of her on one such occasion.

43. Ibid.

44. WSP, "Memoirs," 127.

45. Maurice Ravel, *Pavane pour une infante défunte* (Demets, 1901), BMFP.

46. *La Presse,* 4 September 1899.

47. MP to Jeanne Proust, 19 September 1899, in *Correspondance de Marcel Proust,* ed. Philip Kolb, 20 vols. (Paris: Plon, 1970–93), 2:305. It was widely assumed among many in the aristocracy that WSP was of Jewish origins, even though both of her parents were brought up, more or less, in the Protestant faith.

48. Ibid.

49. MP to Jeanne Proust, 11 September 1899, ibid., 268.

50. Abel Hermant, *Souvenirs de la vie mondaine* (Paris: Hachette, 1935), 220, 223.

51. MP to Jeanne Proust, 11 September 1899, in Proust, *Correspondance,* 2:308.

52. MP to Jeanne Proust, 12 September 1899, ibid., 310.

53. *Le Figaro,* 20 September 1899, 1.

54. "Retire de la vie: Chez Joris-Karl Huysmans," *Le Figaro,* 3 February 1900, 1.

55. "Censure et *La Belle Hélène," Le Figaro,* 22 January 1900, 1.

56. Colette, *Journal à Rebours,* 53.

57. Ibid.

58. WSP, "Memoirs," 128.

59. EP to WSP, undated [Spring 1899], FSP.

60. *Pilate livre le Christ* was published in full orchestral score, a set of separate orchestral parts, and piano-vocal reduction.

61. *Autographs, Exposition Universelle de 1900,* in twenty volumes, collected by Charles Malherbe, Bibliothèque de l'Opéra, Paris.

62. Of Chevillard's performance of the third act of Wagner's *Götterdämmerung* at the Cirque d'hiver, *Le Figaro* wrote on 15 April 1900: "It is impossible to imagine a more faithful, sensitive, attentive, or warm interpretation than this one."

63. LMLV-F, 27 April 1900, 2.

64. Louis Mors (1855–1917) and his brother Émile were among the first French manufacturers of high-quality automobiles and racing cars. A generous music lover and patron, Louis Mors established a Chair in Musicology at the Collège de France.

65. LMLV-F, 27 April 1900, 2.

66. LMLV-F, 26 March 1900, 2.

67. LMLV-F, 10 March 1900, 2.

68. LMLV-F, 1 April 1900, 2.

69. *Le Figaro,* 13 April 1900, 6.

70. MP to HCC, 23 August 1917, in Proust, *Correspondance,* 16:210.

71. Marie Dujardin, "Marcel Proust à Venise," *Le Figaro,* 10 October 1931, 7. Dujardin erroneously identifies MP's visit to Venice as taking place in the spring of 1901.

72. WSP, "Memoirs," 129.

73. *Le Figaro,* 4 May 1900, 6; Henry Février to EP, 12 May 1900, APEP.

74. EP to WSP, undated [8 July 1900], FSP.

75. GF to his wife, Marie, 26 August 1900, in Fauré, *Lettres intimes,* ed. Philippe Fauré-Fremiet (Paris: Grasset, 1951), 48.

76. The first performance of Fauré's *Prométhée* at the Théâtre des Arènes had been scheduled for 26 August 1900. The actual première took place on 27 August. "Everything worked out marvelously, I got a standing ovation," GF wrote to his wife on 28 August 1900 (*Lettres intimes,* 50).

77. Comtesse Gontraud de La Baume-Pluvinel wrote novels under the *nom de plume* Laurent Evrard.

78. Jean-Louis Vaudoyer, "P.-J. Toulet et Madame Bulteau," *La Revue de Paris,* 34/3 (1 August 1924), 801.

79. HCC, various letters, NAfr 17473–75; see also Claude Mignot-Ogliastri, *Anna de Noailles, une amie de la Princesse Edmond de Polignac* (Paris: Fondation Singer-Polignac and Méridiens-Klincksieck, 1986), 109.

80. AB to WSP, undated [probably 1900], private collection.

81. WSP, "Memoirs," 131.

82. Ibid. WSP remembered Léon Daudet as "one of the most brilliant and cultured men I have ever known."

83. WSP to AB, 2 October 1900, NAfr 17554:6.

84. WSP to AB, 15 December 1900, NAfr 17554:8–9. WSP thanks her new friend "for having brought the Tiepolos to my attention." The purchase of the Tiepolo frescoes was concluded with the aid of the Venetian art dealer Barozzi. WSP's purchase is noted in Elena Bassi, *Palazzi di Venezia: Admiranda urbis Venetae* (Venice: La Stamperia di Venezia, 1978), 94, 96, and Adriano Mariuz, *Giandomenico Tiepolo* (Venice: Alfieri, 1971), 146.

85. Henri de Régnier, *L'Altana ou la vie vénitiénne 1899–1924*, 2 vols. (Paris: Mercure de France, 1928), 2:145.

86. EP to AB, 19 May 1901, NAfr 17554:3.

87. Gastone Vio, *I Quaderni della Parrocchia di Santa Maria del Rosario (vulgo Gesuati) Venezia. L'organo della Chiesa parrochiale: da don Pietro Nacchini ai Bazzani* (Venice: private printing, 1982), 12.

88. WSP to AB, undated [January 1901], NAfr 17554:11; LMLV-F, 25 January 1901.

89. RM is making a highly insulting pun: in French, the word *cucul* means "silly" or "goofy."

90. Fonds Montesquiou, NAfr 15115:47.

91. Excerpt from Théophile Gautier, *Affinités secrètes*, in his *Émaux et camées* (Paris: Charpentier, 1872), copied into RM's papers, ibid.

92. Charles Bordes to EP, 18 March 1901, APEP.

93. LMLV-F, 19 April 1901, 2.

94. *La Vie parisienne*, 27 April 1901.

95. Camille de Polignac to EP, 12 September 1897, APEP.

96. Jeanne (Jane) Hatto (1879–1958) made her debut at the Opéra in 1899. She gave the first performance of Ravel's *Shéhérazade* in 1904. Vocally powerful, she enjoyed a long and successful career singing the great dramatic soprano roles. In later years she was the mistress of automobile industrialist Louis Renault.

97. "Bloc-Notes parisien: Une bonne oeuvre et une belle oeuvre, la Société Philanthropique et le prince Edmond de Polignac," *Le Gaulois*, 10 May 1901, 1.

98. Willy, "Lettre de l'Ouvreuse," *L'Écho de Paris*, 19 May 1901.

99. Joly, "Les Oeuvres du Prince Edmond de Polignac au Conservatoire," *Le Figaro*, 17 May 1901, 1. See also, "Au Conservatoire," *Le Matin*, 17 May 1901; X.-Marcel Boulestin, *Le Courrier Musical* (1 June 1901): 127.

100. Letters of congratulations to EP after the concert of his works written by, among others, AB, Camille Chevillard, Reynaldo Hahn, Maurice Lobre, and ANo, are housed in the APEP.

101. MP to EP, undated [20 May 1901], APEP.

102. Ibid.

103. René Lara, "Notre Page musicale," and EP, *Chanson de Barberine* (musical score), "Supplément littéraire," *Le Figaro*, 19 May 1901.

104. Isadora Duncan, *My Life* (New York: Liveright, 1995), 60.

105. Ibid, 62.

106. Ibid.

107. Ibid.

108. Ibid., 63.

109. Ibid.

110. LMLV-F, 19 May 1901, 2.

111. Duncan, *My Life*, 63.

112. WSP to AB, NAfr 17554:13–14.

113. LMLV-F, 24 May 1901, 2.

114. WSP to AB, NAfr 17554:13–14.

115. LMLV-F, 29 May 1901, 2.

116. AB [Jules Vontade], "Le Coeur innombrable," *Le Figaro*, 9 May 1901, 5. According to Mignot-Ogliastri, *Anna de Noailles*, 137, the volume inspired over thirty reviews in all of the important newspapers and literary journals.

117. Painter, *Marcel Proust*, 1:288–289; LMLV-F, 21 June 1901, 2.

118. Léon Daudet, 19 June 1901, *Souvenirs*, 641.

119. *Le Figaro*, 12 June 1901, 1; LMLV-F, 25 June 1901, 2.

120. LMLV-F, 27 June 1901, 2.

121. EP to WSP, undated [8 July 1900], FSP.

122. MP to Jeanne Proust, 31 August 1901, in Proust, *Correspondance*, 2:445.

123. AB to EP, undated [18 May 1901], APEP; EP to AB, 19 May 1901, NAfr 17554:3.

124. MP to Lucien Daudet, 13 July 1901, in Proust, *Correspondance*, 2:437.

125. MP to Jeanne Proust, 31 August 1901, ibid, note 622.

126. Ibid.

127. Ibid.

128. Eugène d'Harcourt, "Un Prince musicien," *Le Figaro*, 9 August 1901, 1.

129. HCC to AB, undated [22 August 1901], NAfr 17473:151–52.

130. ANo to AB, 9 August 1901, NAfr 17513:74.

131. HCC to AB, undated [22 August 1901], NAfr 17473:152.

132. GF to WSP, undated [late August 1901], FSP. In a subsequent letter dated September 1901, FSP, Fauré writes "I have just received the notification that the dear Prince left me, *with the most affectionate mention,* the sum of ten thousand francs."

133. LMLV-F, 14 August 1901, 2.

Chapter 7

1. MP to Jeanne Proust, in *Correspondance de Marcel Proust*, ed. Philip Kolb, 20 vols. (Paris: Plon, 1970–93), 2:444.

2. Ibid.

3. Ibid.

4. Edmond White, *Marcel Proust* (New York: Viking, 1999), 75.

5. Jean Lorrain, *Monsieur de Phocas* (Paris: Table ronde, 1992), 124.

6. Ibid., 122.

7. Ibid.

8. WSP to AB, 14 September 1901, NAfr 17554:8.

9. WSP to AB, 20 October 1901, NAfr 17554:20–21.

10. WSP to AB, undated [early 1902], NAfr 17554:31–32.

11. ANo to AB, 24 December 1901, NAfr 17514:10.

12. WSP, "Memoirs of the Late Princesse Edmond de Polignac," *Horizon* 12, no. 68 (August 1945): 132.

13. Léon Vallas, *Claude Debussy: His Life and Works*, trans. Maire and Grace O'Brien (New York: Dover, 1973), 122–25.

14. Jann Pasler, "*Pelléas* and Power: Forces behind the Reception of Debussy's Opera," *19ᵗʰ Century Music* 10, no. 3 (Spring 1987): 243–64.

15. WSP, "Memoirs," 128.

16. Eugène d' Harcourt, "La Reprise de *Pelléas et Mélisande,*" *Le Figaro,* 31 October 1902. For more about the critical reaction to *Pelléas,* see Pasler, "*Pelléas* and Power."

17. WSP, "Memoirs," 128.

18. WSP to AB, 8 April 1902, NAfr 17554:33.

19. Comtesse Élisabeth Greffulhe to WSP, October 1902, private collection.

20. Ibid.

21. The Salle Humbert-des-Romans, a nineteenth-century structure designed by Hector Guimard, was formerly located at 60 rue St-Didier, north of the Trocadéro. It was demolished in 1905. Its grand organ, with three keyboards and forty stops, was given to the Church of St-Vincent-de-Paul in the Paris suburb of Clichy.

22. Denys Cochin to WSP, undated [15 May 1903], FSP. Cochin (1851–1922), as Paris Deputy from 1893–1919, was a champion of educational reform and freedom of religious congregation under Waldeck-Rousseau and Combes.

23. LMLV-F, 14 May 1903.

24. WSP to AB, 18 August 1902, NAfr 17554:35.

25. WSP, "Memoirs," 116.

26. Henry David Thoreau, *Walden, or Life in the Woods* (New York: Signet, 1960), 92.

27. Comte Melchior de Polignac, unpublished *Souvenirs de famille* (1906), APEP.

28. WSP to AB, undated [December 1903], private collection.

29. Unpublished memoirs of Princesse Henri de Polignac, narrated to Anne de Lacretelle, 22, APEP.

30. Comte Melchior de Polignac, unpublished *Souvenirs de famille* (1906), APEP.

31. WSP to AB, 11 March 1903, NAfr 17554:52.

32. Ibid.

33. WSP to AB, 6 May 1903, NAfr 17554:59.

34. LMLV-F, 12 May and 26 May 1903.

35. LMLV-F, 3 June 1903.

36. MP to Antoine Bibesco, undated [6, 7, or 8 January 1903], in Proust, *Correspondance,* 3:209, n. 112.

37. MP [Horatio], "Le Salon de la Princesse Edmond de Polignac, " *Le Figaro,* 6 September 1903, 3.

38. Ibid.

39. Ibid.

40. MP to Ano, 15 January 1904, in Proust, *Correspondance,* 4:38.

41. WSP to AB, 3 December 1903, NAfr 17554:57.

42. WSP to AB, undated, NAfr 17554:62.

43. The French word *moralement,* literally "morally," is used as an American might use the word "psychologically."

44. WSP to AB, undated [December 1903], private collection.

45. Ibid.

46. Nesta Macdonald, in a letter to Ruth Brandon, dated 31 December 1976, relates this story, told by a neighbor and gambling partner of Mme. Sohège in Le Touquet at the turn of the century.

47. LMLV-F, 14 May 1904, 2.

48. Madame Sohège's will, dated 9 May 1904, is in the possession of the Singer heirs.

49. Fredrika Blair, *Isadora: Portrait of the Artist as a Woman* (New York: McGraw-Hill, 1986), 197.

50. I am extremely grateful to John R. A. Wilson of Torquay, Devon, biographer of Paris Singer and historian of the former Singer estate, now known as Oldway House, for providing me with fascinating information about its architectural history.

51. Achille Duchesne, the leading French landscape architect of the period, is best known for the design of Blenheim Palace's famous water garden.

52. HCC to AB, 12 September 1904, NAfr 17475:561–62.

53. HCC to AB, undated [May 1903], NAfr 17474:255.

54. Ethel Smyth to an unnamed correspondent, as quoted in Christopher St. John, *Ethel Smyth* (London: Longmans, Green, 1959), 124.

55. Ethel Smyth to AB, 11 March 1906, NAfr 17527:53.

56. St. John, *Ethel Smyth*, 124.

57. Ethel Smyth, *Der Wald* (Leipzig: Schott, 1902), BMFP.

58. ANo to AB, Wednesday [16 December] 1903, NAfr 17514:181.

59. ANo to AB, 10 December 1903, NAfr 17514:177.

60. HCC to AB, 16 September 1904, NAfr 17475:565.

61. Ethel Smyth to WSP, 1904, private collection.

62. Baron Adolph de Meyer-Watson (1868–1949); Baroness Olga de Meyer, née Caracciolo (1871–1931).

63. De Meyer was photographer for *Vogue* and *Vanity Fair* from 1913 to 1921 and chief photographer and Paris correspondent for *Harper's Bazaar* between 1921 and 1932. In addition to his photographs of fashionable women, de Meyer also left an important legacy as a dance photographer, especially his photographs of Nijinsky and the Ballets Russes.

64. Philippe Jullian, biographical essay in Adolf de Meyer, *De Meyer*, ed. Robert Brandau (New York: Knopf, 1976), 18, 27–29.

65. Ibid.

66. Ethel Smyth to AB, undated [late 1906], NAfr 17527:75–76.

67. Romaine Brooks (1874–1970).

68. Meryle Secrest, *Between Me and Life* (New York: MacDonald and Janes, 1974), 214.

69. Ibid.

70. Antoine Bertrand, *Les Curiosités esthétiques de Robert de Montesquiou* (Geneva: Droz, 1996), 418.

71. Robert de Montesquiou, "Cambrioleurs d'âmes (catalogue Romaine Brooks)," in *Têtes d'expression* (Paris: Émile-Paul, 1912), 137–38.

72. Excerpt from the memoirs of Romaine Brooks, entitled *No Pleasant Memories,* as quoted in Secrest, *Between Me and Life,* 215. Brooks's original manuscript is housed in the National Museum of American Art, The Smithsonian Institute, Washington, D. C.

73. A photocopy of Romaine Brooks's portrait of WSP, from an unspecified early twentieth-century exhibition catalogue, was kindly communicated to me by William Singer.

74. LMLV-F, 25 January 1907, 7 May 1908, 3 April 1909.

75. Romaine Brooks, as quoted in Secrest, *Between Me and Life*, 215.

76. LMLV-F, 25 January 1907, 6 May 1908, 3 April 1909.

77. LMLV-F, 2 February 1905.

78. Ibid.

79. LMLV-F, 16 February 1905.

80. Ibid.

81. *Le Figaro*, ibid., reports the performance of "les nouvelles oeuvres de Debussy." Viñes gave the first public performances of *Masques* and *L'Ile joyeuse* at the Société Nationale de Musique three days later, on 18 February, so it seems reasonable to assume that these works figured among those played at the Polignac salon.

82. Meg de Saint-Marceaux (MBSM) noted in her diary on 28 March 1905 (forthcoming in an edition by Myriam Chimènes [Paris: Éditions Fayard]), "Performance of works by Polignac [in WSP's salon]. A fancy crowd and music that's not as bad as I might have thought." LMLV-F mentions performances of EP's works in WSP's salon in its columns of 2 February 1905, 23 January 1906, 14 February 1906, and 3 April 1906. Comtesse René de Béarn featured EP's music in her salon in June 1905 (LMLV-F, 9 June 1905, 2). Additionally, a performance on 11 March 1906 of EP's *Les Adieux de Deidamia* took took place under the auspices of the Société Artistique des amateurs at the Salle d'Horticulture (LMLV-F, 5 and 12 March 1906).

83. GF, "'Échos de l'Orient judaïque' du Prince de Polignac," *Le Figaro*, 19 April 1905.

84. Francis Steegmuller, *Cocteau: A Biography* (Boston: Little, Brown, 1970), 67.

85. A portion of GA's lengthy correspondence with the Comtesse Greffulhe (1904–10) is contained in the NYPL-GAP103.

86. *Sur les Lagunes (Lamento)* is written on Théophile Gautier's famous poem (incipit: "Ma belle amie est morte"), previously set by Berlioz.

87. WSP to GA, 25 June 1905, FGA-AN, AP409/35.

88. WSP to GA, 1 August 1905, FGA-AN, AP409/35.

89. These works include *L'Abeille, Respect à la vieillesse,* and *Hirondelles.*

90. Octave Maus (1856–1919) was a Belgian composer, musicologist, and critic; a *mécène* of the avant-garde, he founded the influential weekly arts journal, *L'Art moderne.*

91. Letters concerning the "Fondation Edmond de Polignac," as well as a draft of its charter, are in the FGA-AN, AP409/35.

92. WSP to Raymond Poincaré, 20 December 1905, NAfr 16012:118.

93. "Your friend M. Cruppi is going to ruin us because of the inheritance." WSP to AB, 5 January 1905, NAfr 17554:75. Jean Cruppi (1855–1933) was a left-wing Parisian politician and a member of the Chamber of Deputies; he would go on to hold posts in the Ministries of Education, Commerce and Industry, Foreign Affairs, and Justice.

94. The case lasted for at least two years. On 18 May 1906, WSP wrote to Raymond Poincaré that she had just heard of the "happy results" of Poincaré's prosecution (NAfr 16012:125), but on 23 December 1907 Washington Singer wrote to his sister "What a slow lot these French lawyers are. When will they get on the Sohège case?" (private collection).

95. WSP to Raymond Poincaré, 24 December 1905, NAfr 16012:123.

96. WSP to Raymond Poincaré, 4 January 1906, NAfr 16012:121.

97. Ruth Brandon, *Singer and the Sewing Machine: A Capitalist Romance* (New York: Kodansha Globe, 1996), 198.

98. In his responding letter, William A. Singer thanks Winnaretta for her "very kind letter of the 13th inst." The letter has been lost.

99. Twenty-five pounds sterling was worth about $125 in 1905 dollars, or $1300 in 2002 dollars.

100. William A. Singer to WSP, 22 July 1905, text communicated by Ruth Brandon.

101. William A. Singer to WSP, 4 January 1906, August 1906, text communicated by Ruth Brandon.

102. Sir Francis Rose, *Saying Life* (London: Cassell, 1961), 357.

103. According to Jane Hamilton, librarian at Agnew's, London, extant stock books indicate that WSP purchased Whistler's *Three Figures: Pink and Grey* and *Nocturne in Green in Gold* on 14 June 1905 through intermediaries. The total purchase price for the two paintings was £2500. See also Andrew Wilton et al., *The Age of Rossetti, Burne-Jones and Watts: Symbolism in Britain 1860–1910* (London: Tate Gallery, 1997), 117–18.

104. The provenance of all but the last Monet canvas is a bit mysterious. In the Wildenstein *catalogue raisonée* of Monet's works, WSP is listed as the owner only of *Dindons* (Daniel Wildenstein, *Monet ou le triomphe de l'Impressionisme*, 4 vols. [Cologne: Taschen, 1996], 2:271, #727). Although no mention of her ownership of the other three paintings is made in Wildenstein's listings of provenance, they were incontestably in WSP's possession at the time that she drew up her will by 1938, at which time she bequeaths the canvasses to various individuals.

105. Provenance information kindly supplied by Christie's of London.

106. WSP to AB, 28 March 1906, NAfr 17554:101.

107. LMLV-F, 20 April 1906, 2.

108. Vallas, *Claude Debussy,* 150–51.

109. For a fuller discussion of Roussel's role in the "Scholist-Debussyist" conflict, see Jann Pasler, "Race, Orientalism, and Distinction in the Wake of the Yellow Peril," in *Western Music and Its Others,* ed. Georgina Born (Berkeley: University of California Press, 2000), 86–118.

110. Vallas, *Claude Debussy,* 150–51.

111. Armande de Polignac's article on the orchestra, entitled "Pensées d'ailleurs," appeared in *Le Mercure musical* 1, no. 4 (1 July 1905). Debussy, in a letter to Louis Laloy (13 September 1905), dismissed Armande's writings as "charming idiocies," but added, "Her ideas on the orchestra are touching and her views on music in general disarmingly individual" (Claude Debussy, *Letters,* ed. François Lesure and Roger Nichols, trans. Roger Nichols [Cambridge, Mass.: Harvard University Press, 1987], 160).

112. *Le Figaro,* "Notre Page musicale" and "Supplément littéraire," 1 December 1906.

113. Hedwige de Polignac, *Les Polignac* (Paris: Fasquelle, 1960), 254.

114. LMLV-F, 12 December 1905, 2.

115. MBSM, excerpt from an unpublished diary entry dated 10 December 1905, forthcoming in an edition by Myriam Chimènes (Paris: Éditions Fayard). Saint-

Marceaux was not very impressed with the pianist: "Selva plays very well but very boringly. It's impeccable and boring [*impeccable et assomant*]."

116. Andrew Thomson, *Vincent d'Indy and His World* (Oxford: Clarendon Press, 1996), 159.

117. LMLV-F, 12 December 1905, 2.

118. LMLV-F, 19 December 1905, 2.

119. Printed program, "Soiree du 14 Janvier 1906," FGA-AN 409 AP 35; LMLV-F, 23 January 1906.

120. The three trios for violin, cello, and piano performed were Roussel's Trio, Op. 2 (1902), Castéra's Trio in D Major, Op. 5 (1905), and Coindreau's Trio in D Minor, Op. 8 (1904). A score of Castéra's *Trio en ré* in the BMFP bears a dedication, "à Madame la Princesse Edmond de Polignac, hommage respectueux et dévoué, René de Castéra Nov. 1905," BMFP. A score of Roussel's *Trio en Mi-bémol majeure, Op. 2* in the BMFP bears a dedication "à Madame la Princesse Edmond de Polignac, en hommage très respectueux, Albert Roussel."

121. Albert Roussel to WSP, 31 January 1906, FSP.

122. MBSM-DD, excerpt from an unpublished diary entry, 28 January 1906, forthcoming in an edition by Myriam Chimènes (Paris: Éditions Fayard).

123. Printed program in FGA-AN, AP409/35. A handwritten written note gives the details of the "Programme de Mlle. Thomasset," the singer in the Ravel and the Balakirev.

124. In 1906, Isaac Albéniz was a member of the Schola Cantorum's piano faculty.

125. Printed program, "11 February 1906," FGA-AN, AP409/35; LMLV-F.

126. Several printed programs of early 1906 Polignac soirées are in FGA-AN 409–AP 35.

127. Typed "programme de Madame Wanda Landowska," dated 19 February 1906, FGA-AN 409–AP 35.

128. GA to WSP, 3 March 1906, FGA-AN AP409/35.

129. Henri Rabaud (1873–1949) went on to become conductor of the Opéra and the Opéra-comique. In letters between WSP and Astruc, 21 February 1906 and 5 March 1906, FGA-AN AP409/35, the possibility of a performance of Rabaud's Trio for Flute, Violin and Piano is discussed. Astruc calls the work "très particulièrement interéssante" (21 February).

130. Sévérac's opera, *Le Coeur de moulin,* was performed in WSP's salon on 27 May 1906.

131. WSP to AB, 26 March 1906, NAfr 17554:101–02.

132. Percy Grainger to Alfhild de Luce, 26 February 1906, in Grainger, *The Far Side of Humanness: Letters,* ed. Kay Dreyfus (St. Louis: Magnamusic-Baton, 1985), 56.

133. Grainger's dedicated scores are in the BMFP.

134. Jacques-Émile Blanche, *La Pêche aux souvenirs* (Paris: Flammarion, 1949), 405.

135. Ibid; see also Claude Mignot-Ogliastri, *Anna de Noailles, une amie de la Princesse Edmond de Polignac* (Paris: Fondation Singer-Polignac and Méridiens-Klincksieck, 1986), 218.

136. LMLV-F, 13 April 1907, 2.

137. Hahn's *Le Bal de Béatrice d'Este* was first performed in Madeleine Lemaire's

salon on 12 April 1905. MP mistakenly credited WSP with having hosted the premiere of this work; his error was subsequently carried forward in citations about the piece.

138. LMLV-F, 13 April 1907, 2.

139. MP to Reynaldo Hahn, 11 April 1907, in Proust, *Correspondance,* 7:139.

140. Ibid.

141. MP to Reynaldo Hahn, 1 July 1907, in Proust, *Correspondance,* 7:211–12.

142. This information comes from the unpublished memoirs of Baron Adolph (Gayne) de Meyer, "Exceptional People and the Photographer" (1944), 28–36. The de Meyer memoirs are part of the Baron Adolph de Meyer Estate, owned by the G. Ray Hawkins Gallery, Los Angeles. Excerpts making mention of WSP were communicated to me by Alexandra Anderson-Spivy, who, with G. Ray Hawkins, is the author of a forthcoming biography of Adolph and Olga de Meyer.

143. HCC to AB, 19 August 1907, NAfr 17476:260. HCC refers to Olga de Meyer only to "la personne."

144. HCC to ANo, quoted in Mignot, *Anna de Noailles,* 233.

145. ANo to WSP, undated [1907], FSP.

146. Isadora Duncan to Gordon Craig, September 1912, Craig-Duncan collection, NYPL, communicated by Kurth. Prince Francis of Teck was the brother of the Princess of Wales, the future Queen Mary of England.

147. *Écho de Paris,* 5 September 1907, 2.

Chapter 8

1. Filippo Tommaso Marinetti, "Le Manifesto de Futurisme," *Le Figaro,* 20 February 1909. Marinetti (1876–1944), an Italian writer and poet, the first spokeman for the international Futurist movement, became a supporter of Fascism after World War I, and joined Mussolini's Italian Academy.

2. Filippo Tommaso Marinetti, *Opere,* vols. 3–4 (Milan: Mondadori, 1969), 281.

3. Lynn Garafola, *Diaghilev's Ballets Russes* (New York: Oxford University Press, 1989), 273–301; Richard Taruskin, *Defining Russia Musically* (Princeton, N.J.: Princeton University Press, 1997), 182.

4. Richard Taruskin, *Stravinsky and the Russian Traditions: A Biography of the Works through "Mavra,"* 2 vols. (Berkeley and Los Angeles: University of California Press, 1996), 1:423–29.

5. Ibid., 445.

6. Ibid., 439.

7. Boris Kochno, *Diaghilev and the Ballets Russes,* trans. Adrienne Foulke (New York: Harper and Row, 1970), 4.

8. "Le Vernissage à l'exposition russe," *Le Figaro,* 16 October 1906, 5.

9. Robert Brussel, "Concert de l'Exposition de l'Art Russe," *Le Figaro,* 7 November 1906, 3.

10. Garafola, *Diaghilev's Ballets Russes,* 274.

11. Ibid.

12. Ibid.

13. *Le Libre Parole,* 10 May 1907, cited in Anne de Cossé-Brissac, *La Comtesse Greffulhe* (Paris: Perrin, 1991), 210.

14. Comte Greffulhe to his wife Élisabeth Greffulhe, May 1907, in Cossé-Brissac, *La Comtesse Greffulhe.*

15. Comtesse Greffulhe draft letter, 6 October 1906, NYPL-GAP103:12.

16. Russian soprano Félia Litvinne (1863–1936) was an ample woman with a large but nonetheless limpid and flexible voice. A Wagnerian soprano, she was equally fluent in the French and Russian repertoires, and switched languages freely throughout a performance depending on the tongue of the colleague with whom she was singing.

17. Vladimir Kastorsky (1871–1948).

18. LMLV-F, 29 May 1907, 2 and 13 May 1908, 2.

19. Comtesse Greffulhe draft letter, undated [May 1907], NYPL-GAP 104:1.

20. A score of Selva's *Les Ancêtres du Lys*, published under the auspices of the Schola's Édition Mutuelle and given as a gift to WSP, bears the dedication: "A Madame la Princesse Edmond de Polignac en vive reconnaissance et en très respectueuse affection, Blanche Selva, 24 Novembre 1907," BMFP.

21. According to legend, after Albéniz finished composing the first book of *Iberia*, he was depressed that no one would ever play the suite because of its difficulty. Just as he was set to destroy the manuscript, Selva managed to learn the whole book in a few days and played it for Albéniz completely from memory. It was only then that Albéniz completed the next three books.

22. Michel Raux Deledicque, *Albéniz, su vida inquieta y ardorosa* (Buenos Aires: Ediciones Peuser, 1950), 396. After the performance at the Polignac salon on 2 January 1908, Selva gave the first public performance of Books I and IV of Albéniz's *Iberia* five weeks later, on 8 February 1908, under the auspices of the SNM.

23. LMLV-F, 12 and 13 April 1908.

24. Princesse Marthe Bibesco, *Le Confesseur et les poètes* (Paris: Grasset, 1970), 72; Bibesco, "Jean Cocteau et son étoile" (1963), quoted in Frederick Brown, *An Impersonation of Angels* (New York: Viking Press, 1968), 46.

25. Jean Cocteau, *My Contemporaries* (London: Owen, 1967), 20.

26. The *feuilles de location* (seating charts) for the Ballets Russes's 1908 performances of *Boris Godunov* are located in AN, AJ[13] 1292. These charts indicate that WSP attended the opera on 19 and 21 May 1908, sitting in a box that she had purchased in the dress circle; her neighbors in the dress circle included the financiers Rothschild, Edwards, Bloch-Levallois, and Cahen d'Anvers, the Grand-Duke Paul and his Russian contingent, and the President of the French Republic.

27. 1908 Program of *Boris Godunov,* NYPL-GAP 123.

28. Garafola, *Diaghilev's Ballets Russes,* 283–84.

29. Ibid, 275–76.

30. Astruc narrates the story of the genesis of the Ballets Russes in a document entitled "Historique de la Saison Russe," dated 19 November 1909, an excerpt of a "Rapport confidentiel sur la Saison Russe," presented to Baron Fredericks, the Minister of the Russian Imperial Court. NYPL-GAP 25:17.

31. LMLV-F, 4 June 1908, 2. Although dubbed a "réception restreinte" (small reception), the news article lists the names of over one hundred guests.

32. Edmond Jaloux, *Les Saisons littéraires* (Paris: Plon, 1950), 2:50–51. Jaloux (1878–1949) was a novelist, literary critic, and historian.

33. *Le Figaro,* 4 June 1908, 2.

34. Ibid.

35. Jaloux, *Les Saisons littéraires,* 2:50–51.

36. Serge Lifar, *Serge Diaghilev: His Life, His Work, His Legend: An Intimate Biography* (New York: G. P. Putnam's Sons, 1940), 127.

37. Michael de Cossart, *The Food of Love: Princesse Edmond de Polignac (1865–1943) and Her Salon* (London: Hamish Hamilton, 1978), 102.

38. See, for example, Garafola in *Diaghilev's Ballets Russes*; she quotes Cossart verbatim on p. 186.

39. The dedication to EP is noted in Jory Bennett's list of Ethel Smyth's works in *The Memoirs of Ethel Smyth,* ed. Ronald Crichton (New York: Viking, 1987), 264. Ethel Smyth writes in her memoir *What Happened Next* (London: Longmans, Green, 1940), 260, that after no offers for another production of *The Wreckers* were forthcoming after the opera's premiere, WSP offered to contact the directors of the Théâtre de la Monnaie in Brussels to promote Smyth's work.

40. HCC to AB, 12 November 1906, NAfr 17476:80.

41. Robert Brussel, "Les Concerts," *Le Figaro,* 6 June 1908.

42. Ethel Smyth to AB, 4 September 1908, NAfr 17527:157.

43. Ethel Smyth to AB, undated [September 1908], NAfr 17527:172.

44. The address embossed on Ethel Smyth's stationery was actually "One Oak, Trimbly."

45. WSP to AB, 29 December 1908, NAfr 17554:132.

46. On 11 February 1909, Adela Maddison wrote to Frederick Delius, "Madame de Polignac was here for *Elektra*." In Frederick Delius, *Delius: A Life in Letters 1862–1934,* ed. Lionel Carley (London: Scolar Press in association with the Delius Trust, 1983), 2:14, n. 3.

47. LMLV-F, 9 January 1909, 2.

48. Ibid.

49. "Le Gala russe," *Le Figaro,* 19 May 1909; Kochno, *Diaghilev,* 85.

50. Garafola, *Diaghilev's Ballets Russes,* 39–42.

51. Isadora Duncan, *My Life* (New York: Liveright, 1995), 165.

52. Alva Johnson, *The Legendary Mizners* (New York: Farrar, Straus and Giroux, 1953), 40–43.

53. Ibid.

54. Ibid., 168, 170.

55. Paris Singer to WSP, undated, private collection.

56. List of the "capital guarantee committee," NYPL-GAP 43.

57. GA's "Confidential Report on the Russian Season," NYPL-GAP 25, would excoriate Diaghilev and his business and financial practices.

58. Garafola, *Diaghilev's Ballets Russes,* 174.

59. Comtesse Anna de Noailles, "Adieux aux Ballets Russes," in a special issue of *La Revue musicale* entitled "Les Ballets Russes de Serge Diaghilew," 1 December 1930, 384–91.

60. "Courrier des théâtres," *Le Figaro,* 19, 20, 21 May 1909.

61. Operatic bass Feodor Chaliapin (1873–1938) was the best-known singer-actor of his time. His interpretation of the title role in Musorgsky's *Boris Godunov* was his most famous. His other dramatic roles included Phillip II in Verdi's *Don Carlo* and the title role in Boito's *Mefistofele*; his comic roles included Don Basilio in *Il Barbiere di Siviglia* and Leporello in *Don Giovanni*.

62. Biographical sketch of Ida Rubinstein, NYPL-GAP 110:2.

63. "Un Monsieur de l'Orchestre," "La Soiree: La saison russe," *Le Figaro,* 5

June 1909. The original "Monsieur de l'Orchestre" was satirical critic Alfred Mortier; after his death, the title was appropriate by an unidentified author.

64. Brown, *An Impersonation of Angels,* 81–82.

65. Robert Brussel, "Les Théâtres: *Ballets Russes,*" *Le Figaro,* 8 June 1911; Taruskin, *Stravinsky and the Russian Traditions,* 1:551.

66. Calvocoressi, as quoted in Taruskin, *Stravinsky and the Russian Traditions,* 1:551, and Stephen Walsh, *Stravinsky: A Creative Spring: Russia and France, 1882–1934* (New York: Knopf, 1999), 131.

67. LMLV-F, 9 June 1909, 2. Some dance historians such as Buckle and Lifar have asserted that WSP's "Pink and White Ball" was given in honor of Isadora Duncan.

68. HCC to AB, 20 June 1909, NAfr 17477:12–14.

69. Ibid.

70. HCC to AB, 20 June 1909, NAfr 17477:12.

71. WSP to AB, 26 June 1909, NAfr 17554:139.

72. HCC to AB, 22 June 1909, NAfr 17477:15–16.

73. Ethel Smyth to AB, 16 October [1906 or 1907], NAfr 17527:71–72.

74. LMLV-F, 21 January 1910, 2.

75. Édouard Colonne (1838–1910) was the founder in 1873 of the "Concerts de l'Association Artistique," which came to be known as the Concerts Colonne. Colonne was a great champion of the music of Berlioz as well as members of the young French school. The organization bearing his name continued its support of contemporary composers into the twentieth century.

76. WSP owned a large number of scores of Debussy's *Trois Chansons de Charles d'Orléans,* and the work was performed often in her salon. The scores, housed of the BMFP, bear the names of the chorus members who sang the work in the *atelier* in 1910.

77. Debussy to WSP, 17 February 1910, FSP. The original date of the Debussy performance in WSP's salon was 6 February 1910. Because of the composer's illness, the soiree was cancelled and rescheduled for 23 February (LMLV-F, 1 and 6 February 1910). That performance did take place, but Debussy, still ill, did not participate.

78. LMLV-F, 24 February 1910, 2. Désiré Inghelbrecht (1880–1965) conducted Debussy's *Le Martyre de Saint-Sébastien* the following year, and went on to become an eminent conductor at the Opéra and the Opéra-Comique.

79. Charles Koechlin, *Gabriel Fauré* (London: Dennis Dobson Ltd., 1945), 93.

80. LMLV-F, 21 January 1910, 2.

81. Fauré's *La Chanson d'Eve,* Op. 95, was given its first performance by soprano Jeanne Raunay, the work's dedicatee, with the composer at the piano.

82. Reynaldo Hahn, *Thèmes variés* (Paris: Jadin, 1946), 138.

83. The date of Adela Maddison's move to Berlin is not certain, but she was living there by mid-December 1904, when she dined with Isadora Duncan and Duncan's lover Gordon Craig at the dancer's apartment. After supper Maddison entertained the couple with piano music by Fauré. Information kindly communicated by Peter Kurth.

84. WSP to AB, undated, NAfr 17554:53.

85. Ibid. The award of the Palmes Académiques was established in 1808 by Napoleon. It is the highest award that can be given to a scholar of French culture,

education, or the arts. The award was, and still is, given to a large number of French citizens, but rarely to foreign nationals.

86. Ibid.

87. WSP to AB, undated [1910], NAfr 17554:54. This letter refers to Winnaretta's attendance of the first performance of Maddison's *Der Talisman.*

88. RM, "Le Pavé rouge: Quelques réflexions sur l'Oeuvre' de M. Sargent," in *Altesses sérénissimes* (Paris: Société d'Édition et de Publications, Librairie Félix Juven, 1907), 83–114.

89. ANo as quoted in Ferdinand Bac, *Intimités de la Troisième République* (Paris: Hachette, 1935), 110–11, reprinted in Claude Mignot-Ogliastri, *Anna de Noailles, une amie de la Princesse Edmond de Polignac* (Paris: Fondation Singer-Polignac and Méridiens-Klincksieck, 1986), 285. ANo apparently did not care for Brooks's portrait of her, made in 1910. The artist had depicted the poet with a strangely simplified face, wild hair, an overly long neck, and overly anxious eyes. "I'd rather enter posterity smiling," was Noailles's comment to Brooks.

90. For her portrait of Madame Legrand, Romaine Brooks situated the model in one of her favorite haunts, the racetrack. The canvas, *Madame Legrand aux courses,* was purchased by RM, who in fact detested the woman, calling her a "hard-up Gioconda."

91. RM, "Cambrioleurs d'âmes," in *Têtes d'expression* (Paris: Émile-Paul, 1912), 127–42.

92. MBSM, unpublished diary entry, 20 May 1910, forthcoming in an edition by Myriam Chimènes (Paris: Éditions Fayard).

93. WSP to AB, NAfr 17554:145–61. From 24 August 1909 through 10 November 1910, WSP mentions the project of translating AB's articles in eight separate letters.

94. Vineta Colby, *The Singular Anomaly: Women Novelists of the Nineteenth Century* (New York: New York University Press, 1970), 237.

95. WSP to AB, 10 November 1910, NAfr 17554: 160–61.

96. Ibid.

97. WSP to AB, 8 December 1910, NAfr 17554:164.

Chapter 9

1. JC as quoted in Francis Steegmuller, *Cocteau: A Biography* (Boston: Little, Brown, 1970), 82; the same story, with slight variations, is recounted in Frederick Brown, *An Impersonation of Angels* (New York: Viking Press, 1968), 90.

2. Michel Calvocoressi, *La Mercure de France,* quoted in Richard Taruskin, *Stravinsky and the Russian Traditions: A Biography of the Works through "Mavra,"* 2 vols. (Berkeley and Los Angeles: University of California Press, 1996), 1:551, n.170.

3. Lynn Garafola, *Diaghilev's Ballets Russes* (New York: Oxford University Press, 1989), 288.

4. Diaghilev as quoted in Stephen Walsh, *Stravinsky, a Creative Spring: Russia and France, 1882–1934* (New York: Knopf, 1999), 127.

5. Walsh, *Stravinsky,* 143.

6. WSP, "Memoirs of the Late Princesse Edmond de Polignac," *Horizon* 12, no. 68 (August 1945): 133.

7. Jean Desbordes, "Grandes Dames de Paris: La princesse E. de Polignac ou le génie des Arts," *Paris-Midi*, 16 October 1934.

8. "Princesse Edmond de Polignac" calling card, undated [1910, PSS] confirms Igor Stravinsky's presence at a dinner given by Mrs. Fellowes; on another card she thanks him for "these precious tickets." The tickets may have been for the Paris debut of *Fireworks*, performed on 26 November 1910 at the Salle Gaveau.

9. "Princesse Edmond de Polignac" visiting card sent to IS from the Villa Borghese, Rome, undated [1911], PSS.

10. Arthur Gold and Robert Fizdale, *Misia: The Life of Misia Sert* (New York: Knopf, 1980), 141.

11. A letter from WSP to GA, AN AP409/35, invites Astruc to a *vernissage* of Sert's work to take place on Sunday, 19 February [1911].

12. The murals of José-Maria Sert (1875–1945) were commissioned by, among others, New York's Hotel Waldorf Astoria, Rockefeller Center, the Hispanic Society, and the Palace of Justice in Barcelona.

13. Armande de Polignac, speech "Homage" (1944), APEP.

14. The Abbé Mugnier (1853–1944) had at one time been the curate of Sainte-Clothilde. As erudite in literary subjects as in ecclesiastical matters, Mugnier spent a good deal of time acting as a private chaplain to many society figures. He was frequently seen at the salons and dinner tables of both aristocrats and artists, and some years later published his journal, a lively account of his *mondain* activities.

15. Jean Cocteau, *Portraits-Souvenirs 1900–1914* (Paris: Grasset, 1935), 213.

16. Jean Cocteau, *My Contemporaries* (London: Owen, 1967), 20.

17. Cocteau, *Portraits-Souvenirs,* 213.

18. Cocteau, *My Contemporaries,* 20.

19. Jean Taricat and Martine Villars, *Le Logement à bon marché: Chronique, Paris 1850–1930* (Boulogne: Apogée, 1982), 110.

20. Comte Paul-Gabriel d'Haussonville (1843–1924), a lawyer, essayist, and historian, was the Parisian representative of the Comte de Paris and editor of the arts magazine *La Revue des deux mondes.*

21. Ruth Brandon, *Singer and the Sewing Machine: A Capitalist Romance* (New York: Kodansha Globe, 1996), 195.

22. Comte Paul-Gabriel d'Haussonville, "Logis de pauvres, pauvres logis," *La Revue française politique et littéraire* (1896): 408.

23. Biographical information on Georges Vaudoyer (1877–1947) was kindly communicated by architectural historian Barry Bergdoll.

24. H. de Fels, "Les Maisons ouvrières de la Fondation Polignac-Singer," *La Revue française politique et littéraire* (1896): 407–8. See also Taricat and Villars, *Le Logement à bon marché,* 53, 116–17; Gaston Lefol, *Grandes Constructions à loyers économiques,* Bibliothèque documentaire de l'architecte (Paris: Massin, ca. 1920), 8–9, plates 23–27; and A. Richardière, "Une Maison ouvrière," *L'Architecte* (January 1913): 1–2.

25. C. Lucas, as cited in Taricet and Villars, *Le Logement à bon marché,* 116.

26. H.de Fels, "Les Maisons ouvrières de la Fondation Polignac-Singer," *La Revue française politique et littéraire* (1896): 407–8.

27. LMLV-F, 11 June 1911.

28. Robert Brussel, *Le Figaro,* 17 June 1911, 5.

29. Ibid.

30. Taruskin, *Stravinsky and the Russian Traditions*, 1:302–3.

31. Sir Ronald Storrs, *Orientations* (London: Nicholson and Watson, 1943), 116–17.

32. "Si on me coupait en deux, une moitié dirait du mal de l'autre; mais si on me recollait, je ne m'en voudrais pas." EP cited in Storrs, *Orientations*, 117.

33. *The London Times*, 29 September 1911, 6.

34. LMLV-F, 6 October 1911, 2.

35. Minutes of the Academic Committee, RSL, 23 November 1911, 52–53, RSL Archives, London.

36. WSP to Percy Ames, 28 November 1911, Cambridge University Library, Royal Society of Literature Archive, E5 (Correspondence with Fellows), Polignac file.

37. WSP to AB, undated [1911], NAfr 17554:172.

38. WSP to HCC, 8 January 1912, NAfr 17554:171

39. ANo's datebook (Archives Princesse Eugénie de Brancovan, communicated by Mignot-Ogliastri) indicates meetings with WSP on 13, 16, and 22 February 1912.

40. David Mitchell, *Queen Christabel* (London: MacDonald and Jane's, 1977), 181.

41. Ibid., 189.

42. French women were not given the vote until 1944, when General de Gaulle granted suffrage.

43. Mitchell, *Queen Christabel*, 207.

44. Annie Kenney, *Memories of a Militant* (London: Butler and Tanner, 1924), 176.

45. Ethel Smyth to WSP, 13 April 1912, NAfr 17527:316.

46. *Laggard Dawn* was published in 1911, along with *March of the Women*, in a group of choral works entitled *Songs of Sunrise*. The publisher was Breitkopf and Härtel, Leipzig.

47. Édouard Branly to WSP, seven letters dated 20 May 1912 through 31 December 1917, FSP. The annual stipend of four thousand francs in 1912 currency would equal roughly $75,000 in 2002 currency.

48. "L'Incident Marconi-Branly," *Le Figaro*, 18 May 1912.

49. WSP to AB, 20 May 1912, NAfr 17554:179.

50. LMLV-F, 18 February 1912, 3.

51. LMLV-F, 25 February 1912, 3. Edith Wharton attended at least one other gathering in the Polignac salon, on 22 December 1912 (LMLV-F, 24 December 1912).

52. Comtesse Jane d'Oilliamson, daughter of EP's eldest brother, Prince Alphonse de Polignac, had known Wharton since 1885; her translations of the writer's short stories were published in *La Revue des deux mondes* in 1907–8 (R. W. B. Lewis, *Edith Wharton: A Biography* [New York: Fromm, 1985], 197–98; *The Letters of Edith Wharton*, ed. R. W. B. Lewis and Nancy Lewis [New York: Collier, 1988], 137–38).

53. LMLV-F, 12 March 1912, 3.

54. WSP, "Memoirs," 140.

55. Igor Stravinsky and Robert Craft, *Memories and Commentaries* (Berkeley: University of California Press, 1981), 77.

56. "Échos de Paris," *Journal des débats*, 12 May 1911, 2.

57. Alexander Benois and Prince Peter Lieven cited in Steegmuller, *Cocteau,* 76.

58. Garafola, *Diaghilev's Ballets Russes,* 53, 121; Boris Kochno, *Diaghilev and the Ballets Russes,* trans. Adrienne Foulke (New York: Harper and Row, 1970), 80–81.

59. WSP to AB, 20 May 1912, NAfr 17554:179.

60. Debussy's letter of 10 October 1895 to an unidentified "Cher Monsieur" is in the archives of the FSP. It is reprinted in Roger Nichols, *The Life of Debussy* (Cambridge: Cambridge University Press, 1998), 83–84. Although Nichols and other scholars claim that the letter was addressed to Colette's husband Willy, the somewhat formal tone of the letter suggests that it may have been written to EP.

61. Ibid.

62. Charles Koechlin, unpublished journal, 11 June 1912, as quoted in the source notes of Michael de Cossart.

63. Reynaldo Hahn to WSP, 2 January, n.d. [1915–18], FSP.

64. Lord Douglas's quote communicated by Philip Errington, Archivist, The John Masefield Society; Barrie's 1912 presentation speech to the RSL communicated by the RSL Office in London.

65. WSP to Percy Ames, 12 September 1912, Cambridge University Library, Royal Society of Literature Archive, E5 (Correspondence with Fellows), Polignac file.

66. Letter from Charles Duff, grandson of Lady Ripon, to the author, October 2001.

67. Lewis, *Edith Wharton,* 321.

68. The Palazzo Venier dei Leoni was bought by Peggy Guggenheim in 1924; it now houses the Guggenheim Museum.

69. WSP, "Memoirs," 131.

70. WSP to IS, 20 November 1912, PSS.

71. Walsh, *Stravinsky,* 186–87.

72. WSP to IS, 20 November 1912, PSS.

73. WSP to AB, 22 October 1912, NAfr 17554:183–84.

74. WSP, "Memoirs," 134.

75. Ibid.

76. WSP to IS, 20 November 1912, PSS.

77. WSP to IS, 4 December 1912, ibid.

78. WSP to IS, 6 December 1912, ibid.

79. IS to WSP, unpublished letter, 11 December 1912, collection of Eric van Lauwe, Paris. Although the commission work eventually metamorphosed into the musical farce *Renard,* Stravinsky did in fact use this exact orchestration for the piano concerto that he did eventually write, the *Capriccio* of 1929.

80. WSP to IS, 12 December 1912, PSS.

81. The librettist Goloubeff may or may not have been related to Natalia de Goloubeff, the lover of d'Annunzio's, who followed the poet to Paris in 1912.

82. Armande de Polignac's ballet *La Source lointaine* was listed by Albert Soubies in the *Almanach des spectacles,* December 1912, 106–7. Actress Stacia Napierkowska (1886–1945), who "danced" *La Source lointaine,* was a frequent performer at the Opéra Comique; she is best known as the star of a 1915 silent "horror" movie, *Les Vampires,* directed by Louis Feuillade.

83. Ravel, writing for *Comoedia illustré*, as quoted in Arbie Orenstein, *Maurice Ravel: Lettres, écrits, entretiens* (Paris: Flammarion, 1989), 305.

84. Loïe Fuller (1862–1928).

85. Richard Nelson Current and Marcia Ewing Current, *Loïe Fuller: Goddess of Light* (Boston: Northeastern University Press, 1997), 147.

86. Ibid, 209.

87. Isadora Duncan, *My Life* (New York: Liveright, 1995), 188.

88. WSP to Madame Raymond Poincaré, 18 January 1913, NAfr 16022:219.

89. WSP to AB, undated [1912], NAfr 17532:181. In the same letter, WSP told AB that, in earlier years when she used to frequent his Montmartre café, Bruant, a notorious misogynist, had called her "Camel" whenever she walked in the door.

90. Maurice Paléologue, 9 March 1913, *Journal, 1913–1914* (Paris: Plon, 1947), 72–73.

91. Ibid.

92. Ibid. This is one of two poems entitled' *Femmes damnées* from Baudelaire's collection *Les Fleurs du mal*.

93. Jacques-Émile Blanche, private diary entry of 9 January 1913, quoted in Cocteau and ANo, *Correspondance*, 158.

94. Olga Popovitch, ed., *Catalogue des peintures du Musée des beaux-arts de Rouen* (Paris: Arts et métiers graphiques, 1967), 14.

95. Richard Buckle, *Diaghilev* (London: Weidenfeld and Nicolson, 1979), 172.

96. Musée du Petit Palais (Paris, France). *Ingres. [Exposition au] Petit Palais, Paris, 27 octobre 1967–29 janvier 1968*. Ministère d'État Affaires Culturelles, Ville de Paris (Paris: Réunion des Musées nationaux, 1967), 188–89.

97. WSP bequeathed the Pannini canvasses to the Musée du Louvre, Paris; the transfer was made in 1944.

98. Denis's paintings and Bourdelle's frescoes were modeled on choreographic poses by Isadora Duncan.

99. Garafola, *Diaghilev's Ballets Russes*, 297.

100. Marquise Guy de Polignac, DD, 3 April 1913, APEP.

101. Walsh, *Stravinsky*, 197.

102. Ibid., 195.

103. WSP to IS, 7 April 1913, PSS.

104. *The New York Times*, 22 April 1913.

105. Peter Kurth, *Isadora: A Sensational Life* (New York: Little, Brown, 2001), 300.

106. On 23 May 1913, Frederick Delius wrote to his wife Jelka, "I went to see the Princess," in *Delius: A Life in Letters 1862–1934*, ed. Lionel Carley, 2 vols. (London: Scolar Press in association with the Delius Trust, 1983–88), 2:106.

107. As long ago as February 1909, Adela Maddison had written to Delius, "[Madame de Polignac] wanted to do something of yours chez elle." On 14 April 1909 Maddison wrote to Jelka Delius, "Madame de Polignac is longing to see you both." In *Delius: A Life in Letters*, 2:14, n. 3.

108. Ronald Crichton, *"Pénélope," New Grove Dictionary of Opera*, ed. Stanley Sadie (London: Macmillan, 1992), 3:943–44.

109. Kochno, *Diaghilev*, 84.

110. Comte Melchior de Polignac, PD, 16 May 1913, APEP.

111. Marquise Guy de Polignac, DD, 5 June 1913, APEP.

112. WSP, "Memoirs," 133.

113. Marquise Guy de Polignac, who was in attendance that night, noted in her daily diary (16 June 1913, APEP), "Extreme heat, 33° [centigrade, or 90° Fahrenheit] in the shade."

114. LMLV-F, 17 June 1913, 3.

115. Paléologue, *Journal, 1913–1914*, 156.

116. Marquise Guy de Polignac, DD, 23 June 1913, APEP.

117. Cecil Roberts, *The Growing Boy* (London: Hodder and Stoughton, 1967), 39–40.

118. LMLV-F, 9 June 1913, 2. The plucky hostess, Princesse Amadée de Broglie, had apparently just learned these steps herself. On 29 May, the Marquise Guy de Polignac noted in her daily diary (APEP), "Tonight I went to the Agénor de Gramont's ball, where for the first time I danced the Tango and the One-Step. Mme. Moore and Mme. la Pcesse Amédée de Broglie danced [them too] even though they're not young!"

119. Darius Milhaud, *My Happy Life*, trans. Donald Evans and Christopher Palmer (London, New York: Marion Boyars, 1994), 52–53.

120. WSP to Percy Ames, 2 July 1913; James Stephens to Percy Ames, 22 October 1913, Cambridge University Library, Royal Society of Literature Archive, E5 (Correspondence with Fellows), Polignac file.

121. James Stephens, three-page commentary on winning the Polignac Prize, Special Collections and Archives, Kent State University (Ohio) Library. Used by permission of The Society of Authors (London).

122. James Stephens to Stephen McKenna, 12 January 1914, Special Collections and Archives, Kent State University (Ohio) Library. Used by permission of The Society of Authors (London).

123. Christopher Hassall, *Edward Marsh: Patron of the Arts* (London: Longmans, 1959), 294.

124. Letter from GA to the subscribers of the Société Gabriel Astruc, 30 April 1913, NYPL-GAP 96:20.

125. Garafola, *Diaghilev's Ballets Russes*, 297–98.

126. GA to MP, in MP, *Correspondance*, 12:385–86; reprinted in William C. Carter, *Marcel Proust: A Life* (New Haven, Conn.: Yale University Press, 2000), 559.

127. Marquise Guy de Polignac, DD, 15 November 1913, APEP.

128. Ibid.

129. Gabriel-Louis Pringué, *Portraits et fantômes* (Monaco: R. Solar, 1951), 235.

130. Ibid.

131. Although forgotten today, Alexandre Georges (1850–1938) was a respected composer of vocal music. His opera *Miarka* was presented by the Paris Opéra in 1905, and his *mélodies* were a staple of salon programs.

132. LMLV-F, 19 February 1914, 3.

133. LMLV-F, 28 March 1914, 3. There may have been some sly humor at work on Winnaretta's part in engaging the two sopranos, Vallin and Féart, only a few weeks apart. Both were renowned as interpreters of Debussy's music (Féart was a noted Mélisande; Vallin had sung *La Damoiselle élue*); both had been engaged for the world premiere of the composer's *Le Martyre de Saint Sébastien* at the Théâtre

du Châtelet in 1911—Féart as prima donna, and the (then) newcomer Vallin as her understudy. Rehearsals apparently went well until the morning of the dress rehearsal, when the director informed Féart that she would have to sing her role from a cat-walk high above the stage. Féart, every inch a diva, had refused to "sing up there," and had left the theater in a huff. Vallin sang the dress rehearsal, attended mostly by critics, and the first public performance on 22 May 1911. The critics, who couldn't see who was singing, wrote laudatory reviews, declaring that Mademoiselle Féart "hadn't sounded so good in years" (Stoullig, writing for the *Annales du théâtre et de la musique*, 1911, 391, commented on Féart's "divinely pure voice"). After that, Féart, not to be outdone by the younger soprano, was obliged to "sing up there."

134. Walsh, *Stravinsky*, 231–32.

135. LMLV-F, 12 March 1914, 3; 10 April 1914, 3.

136. ANo to WSP, 1 May 1914, as quoted in Mignot-Ogliastri, *Anna de Noailles*, 282.

137. Current and Current, *Loïe Fuller*, 209–11.

138. Fuller as quoted in ibid., 211.

139. Henri Quittard, "Courrier des théâtres: Loïe Fuller au Châtelet," *Le Figaro*, 11 May 1914, 6.

140. Henri Quittard, "Courrier des théâtres: Les concerts," *Le Figaro*, 9 May 1914, 5.

141. Ibid.

142. Ibid.; *The London Daily Mail* (Paris edition), 25 May 1914 (clipping, NYPL).

143. Henry Prunières, "Chroniques et notes: Ballet *Urashima* par Armande de Polignac," *La Revue musicale* 7, no. 4 (1 February 1926): 147–48.

144. Kurth, *Isadora*, 311–12.

145. WSP to her niece Winnaretta Singer, 25 May, 1914, Archives of Mrs. Gerald Selous, WSP's great-grand-niece.

146. "La Vie de Paris: La saison," *Le Figaro*, 8 May 1914, 1.

147. "Courrier musicale," *Le Figaro*, 5 May 1914, 6. The International Music Society (Internationale Musik-Gesellschaft) was created in Germany in 1899. The society was reconstituted in 1903 and organized by country into various branches; the founders of the French branch were Louis Laloy and Jules Écorcheville. Problems of language and dissension among the branches during the 1914 Paris conference spurred on the creation, in the same year, of the Société française de musicologie.

148. Jules Écorcheville (1862–1915), president of the French branch of the International Music Society, contributed important studies of Jean-Baptiste Lully and French lute music to French musicology. He was killed at the front in 1915.

149. Photocopy of a program of the conference procedings and concerts for the International Music Society, 1–10 June 1914, communicated by Jann Pasler.

150. Brian Rees, *Camille Saint-Saëns: A Life* (London: Chatto and Windus, 1999), 408.

151. André Schaeffner, "Cinquantenaire de la Société française de musicologie (allocution du 26 janvier 1967)," *Revue de musicologie* 53/2 (1967): 103–9.

152. LMLV-F, 28 June 1914, 2.

153. Ralph Hodgson won the Polignac Prize for two poems, "The Bull" and "The Song of Honour." In delivering the prize to his colleague, former Polignac Prize laureat John Masefield described the poems as "remarkable works, in that they take one to a world of delight and strangeness, with a sustained lyric swiftness

rare in modern poetry." From "Fourth Award of the Edmond de Polignac Prize," *Academic Committee of the Royal Society of Literature: Addresses of Reception*, 27 November 1914 (London: Humphrey Milford [Oxford University Press], 1915, 41–43.

154. From Ralph Hodgson, "The Bull" (1913). Used by permission of the Bryn Mawr College Library.

Chapter 10

1. Lynn Garafola, *Diaghilev's Ballets Russes* (New York: Oxford University Press, 1989), 303–6. Much of the financial backing for Diaghilev's London seasons was provided by Thomas Beecham's father, Sir Joseph Beecham.

2. John Bird, *Percy Grainger* (London: Faber and Faber, 1982), 151.

3. Ibid.

4. ANo to WSP, undated [between October and December 1914], FSP.

5. ANo to WSP, 2 August 1914, FSP. Emphasis in original.

6. WSP to Sir Ronald Storrs, 26 September 1914, Storrs Papers, Yale University Library (microfilm), Reel 4, Box II/3.

7. ANo to WSP, 8 August 1914, FSP.

8. ANo to WSP, 2 August 1914, FSP.

9. ANo to WSP, undated [October 1914], FSP.

10. Ibid.; Claude Mignot-Ogliastri, *Anna de Noailles, une amie de la Princesse Edmond de Polignac* (Paris: Fondation Singer-Polignac and Méridiens-Klincksieck, 1986), 292.

11. Ibid.

12. LMLV-F, 15 November 1914.

13. LMLV-F, 25 August 1914; *The London Times*, 25 August 1914.

14. WSP to Sir Ronald Storrs, 26 September 1914, Storrs Papers, Yale University Library (microfilm), Reel 4, Box II/3.

15. WSP to IS, 26 March 1916, PSS.

16. LMLV-F, 18 March 1916.

17. WSP to Marie Curie, 15 March 1915, BNF-Mss, MF 2663:95.

18. WSP to Marie Curie, 30 July 1915, BNF-Mss, MF 2664:11.

19. Adam Zamoyski, *Paderewski* (New York: Atheneum, 1982), 148.

20. Joseph Reinach (1856–1921), a cabinet member under Gambetta, then Secretary of the League of Patriots, was one of the first of Winnaretta's friends to be convinced of the falsity of the celebrated *bordereau* that had sealed Dreyfus's unmerited fate as a traitor. In 1911 he completed a seven-volume book on the *History of the Dreyfus Affair*.

21. WSP to Joseph Reinach, 9 and 12 November 1915, and an undated letter [December 1915], NAfr 24894:23–27.

22. LMLV-F, 5 December 1915, 3.

23. Elsa Maxwell, *I Married the World* (London: The Quality Book Club, 1956), 111.

24. Edward Gosse to Percy Ames, 18 August 1915, Cambridge University Library, Royal Society of Literature Archive, E5 (Correspondence with Fellows), Polignac file. Gosse did not care for WSP; he told Ames that "the fact that she is not an Englishwoman, but a French-American . . . makes her difficult to deal with."

25. Percy Ames to WSP, 10 December 1914; Percy Ames to W. B. Yeats, 27 January 1915, Cambridge University Library, Royal Society of Literature Archive, E5 (Correspondence with Fellows), Polignac file.

26. WSP to Percy Ames, 8 September 1915, undated [August 1916], Cambridge University Library, Royal Society of Literature Archive, E5 (Correspondence with Fellows), Polignac file.

27. Jacques Rouché to WSP, 1 November 1914, FSP. In his letter, Rouché asked WSP for a "subscription" of 25,000 francs.

28. "Au Jour le jour: Le retour de l'Opéra," *Le Figaro,* 9 December 1915, 1.

29. LMLV-F, 27 July 1915.

30. Norbert Dufourcq, "Eugène Gigout (1844–1925)," *L'Orgue cahiers et mémoires* 1, no. 27 (1982): 13. I am grateful to Dr. Carolyn Shuster for bringing this article to my attention.

31. Christian Goubault, *Claude Debussy* (Paris: Librairie Honoré Champion, 1986), 208.

32. Paul Morand, *Journal d'un Attaché d'Ambassade* (Paris: Gallimard, 1996), 24 December 1916, 121. Paul Morand (1888–1949), in addition to his work as attaché in the French diplomatic service, was the author of some of the best short novels in the French language. An inveterate traveler, he wrote numerous diaries and travel journals. He married the Roumanian Princesse Soutzo.

33. Morand, *Journal,* 14 October 1916, 37.

34. Ibid., 4 December 1916, 98.

35. MP would soon immortalize Madame Legrand as Madame Leroi.

36. Morand, *Journal,* 29 September 1916, 21.

37. MP to Lucien Daudet, undated [May 1916], *Correspondance de Marcel Proust,* ed. Philip Kolb, 20 vols. (Paris: Plon, 1970–93), 15:106. MP also accompanied WSP to visit Hahn's sister Maria, now Madame Raymond de Madrazo.

38. Morand, *Journal,* 16 December 1916, 103–4.

39. Even though Georges Vaudoyer was best known as a architect of public housing works, he also built luxury houses for wealthy clients throughout his career. He had built a house in Jouy-en-Josas for Meg de Saint-Marceaux in 1905; it was presumably through Saint-Marceaux that WSP made his acquaintance.

40. Born into a Napoleonic military family of limited means, Violette Ney d'Elchingen (1876–1936) had married the wealthy Napoleonic prince Eugène Murat. Although ugly and obese, the Princesse Murat enjoyed an estimable standing in society because of her natural elegance and sophisticated knowledge of literature and music. Author Maurice Rostand, in his *Confessions d'un demi-siècle* (Paris: Jeune Parque, 1948), wrote of her unusual ability to combine both "the Bohemian and the princely" in her milieu (15).

41. Prince Jean-Louis de Faucigny-Lucinge, *Un Gentilhomme cosmopolite* (Paris: Perrin, 1990), 59.

42. Gertrude Stein, *The Autobiography of Alice B. Toklas* (New York : Vintage Books, 1960), 102; Erik Satie, *Correspondance presque complète,* ed. Ornella Volta (Paris: Fayard, 2000), 277, 1029.

43. Comte Gilles de Gastines, grandson of Comtesse Isaure de Miramon, letter to the author, 1 September 1999.

44. ANo to Isaure de Miramon, undated [1916 or 1917], family archives of Comte Gilles de Gastines.

45. Morand, *Journal*, 25 August 1917, 328.

46. Stephen Walsh, *Stravinsky: A Creative Spring: Russia and France, 1882–1934* (New York: Knopf, 1999), 260. *The Firebird* was performed in Geneva in December 1915, first conducted by Stravinsky's great friend Ernest Ansermet, and subsequently by the composer himself.

47. Ibid.

48. The modernism of *Renard* and *Les Noces* has been examined at length in Richard Taruskin, *Stravinsky and the Russian Traditions: A Biography of the Works through "Mavra,"* 2 vols. (Berkeley and Los Angeles: University of California Press, 1996), 2:1237–92 (for *Renard*) and 2:1319–1422 (for *Les Noces*).

49. Walsh, *Stravinsky*, 1:236, 252; Garafola, *Diaghilev's Ballets Russes*, 78–81.

50. Taruskin, *Stravinsky*, 2:1246–53.

51. Ibid.

52. Afanasyev as quoted in Taruskin, *Stravinsky*, 2:1237.

53. In January 1915 IS met a Hungarian cimbalomist, Aladár Rácz, in a Geneva restaurant; it was this meeting that inspired the inclusion of the cimbalom in the orchestra of *Renard*. Walsh, *Stravinsky*, 248; Taruskin, *Stravinsky*, 2:1238–39, note 6.

54. "Le Courrier musical," *Le Figaro*, 10 December 1915, 31 December 1915.

55. In Igor Stravinsky, *An Autobiography* (New York: The Norton Library, 1962), 60, Stravinsky erroneously cites this January 1916 meeting as the first occasion that the commission from the Princesse de Polignac was discussed. The error has been corrected in Walsh's recent biography.

56. WSP to Prince Argutinsky, 4 January 1916, PSS. In this particular instance, the Princesse stipulates that the currency in question is Swiss francs. According to Stravinsky biographer Stephen Walsh, the French and the Swiss franc were roughly equal in value in 1916.

57. WSP to IS, 12 January 1916, PSS.

58. WSP to IS, telegram, 31 January 1916, PSS.

59. WSP, "Memoirs of the Late Princesse Edmond de Polignac," *Horizon* 12, no. 68 (August 1945): 135.

60. WSP to IS, 26 February 1916, PSS.

61. Although the *Scherzo fantastique* was conceived as a musical representation of *The Life of the Bees*, Stravinsky ultimately denied its programmatic origins. This led, in 1917, after the work's performance at the Opéra, to a prolonged contretemps with the author of the book, Maurice Maeterlinck, who was furious at not being asked for authorization to use his book as the libretto of a ballet. By this point Stravinsky was denying that that the music had ever had anything to do with bees in general, and Maeterlinck's work in particular.

62. Walsh, *Stravinsky*, 108.

63. Ibid., 183.

64. Ibid., 108.

65. Richard Taruskin, "Stravinsky's Angle," *Journal of the American Musicological Society* 38, no. 1 (Spring 1985): 139.

66. WSP to IS, telegrams of 24 and 30 October, 6 and 26 November, 9 and 19 December 1916; Rouché to Stravinsky, 16 October 1916; Stravinsky to Rouché, undated [24 October 1916], PSS.

67. WSP to IS, 26 March 1916, PSS.

68. IS to WSP, 12 October 1916, PSS.

69. IS to WSP, 12 October 1916, PSS.

70. WSP to IS, 2 July 1916, PSS.

71. IS to WSP, 11 July 1916 (rough draft), PSS.

72. Ibid.

73. Walsh, *Stravinsky,* 266–67.

74. The manuscript of Stravinsky's *Renard* is housed in the BMFP.

75. WSP to IS, 25 October 1916, PSS.

76. Afanasyev, from *A Book about Stravinsky,* as quoted in Taruskin, *Stravinsky,* 2:1237.

77. WSP to IS, 2 September 1916; Bankverein Suisse to IS, 8 September 1916; IS to Bankverein Suisse (rough draft), undated [September 1916], PSS.

78. Vera Stravinsky and Robert Craft, *Stravinsky in Pictures and Documents* (New York: Simon and Schuster, 1978), 138; François Lesure, ed., *Igor Stravinsky: La carrière européenne,* exhibition catalogue, "Festival d'Automne à Paris," 14 October–30 November 1980, Musée d'Art Moderne de la Ville de Paris (Paris: Presses de l'Imprimerie Union, 1980), 47.

79. C. F. Ramuz had previously translated IS's *Pribaoutki* and *Berceuse du chat;* in 1918 he would pen the text to the composer's *L'Histoire du soldat.*

80. C. F. Ramuz to IS, 20 July 1916, PSS.

81. IS to WSP, 5 October 1916, PSS. In Stravinky's *Selected Correspondence,* ed. Robert Craft, 3 vols. (New York: Knopf, 1982–1985), 3:20, n. 11, Craft mistakenly prints the amount as one thousand francs.

82. WSP to IS, 25 October 1916, PSS. Ramuz acknowledged receipt of the check on a card dated 12 November, [1916].

83. Walsh, *Stravinsky,* 271.

84. IS to an unnamed "Madame" (presumably Princesse Violette Murat), rough draft written by Ramuz, undated [late 1916], PSS.

85. Ibid.

86. Murat to an unnamed female correspondent, presumably Madame Igor Stravinsky, undated [March 1917], PSS.

87. Ibid. Murat wrote, "I have asked M. Stravinsky not to say that I was involved with getting anything engraved. I especially don't want my name to be mentioned."

88. Stravinsky and Craft, *Conversations,* 110.

89. WSP, in a letter to MF, 16 November 1918 (AMF), specified that Falla would have at his disposal "an orchestra of sixteen musicians." The number of players probably corresponded to a budgetary restriction, as opposed to referring to a pre-formed ensemble.

90. Satie, *Correspondance,* 1031–32.

91. Ibid., 727–28.

92. WSP, "Memoirs," 137. Translation of Chabrier's response, which appears in French in the *Horizon* article, is by the author.

93. Ibid., 138.

94. WSP, "Memoirs," 137.

95. See Satie's letter to Alexis Rouart of 4 October 1917, cited in Satie, *Correspondance,* 309. As with IS, WSP's agreement with Satie also stipulated that she would retain control over the work for a period of five years. A similar arrange-

ment was made in 1918 with MF for *El Retablo de Maese Pedro.*

96. Ibid., 138.

97. Morand, *Journal,* 6 October 1916, 28–29. Stravinsky, apparently, had no such negative feelings about Satie. He had apparently been so "enthusiastic" about *Parade* that he told Misia Sert that "he thought of combining this project with the new work that was commissioned from him by Polignac [*Renard*] to make a short and perfect evening" (Arthur Gold and Robert Fizdale, *Misia: The Life of Misia Sert* [New York: Knopf, 1980], 188).

98. ES to Valentine Gross, 6 January 1917, in Satie, *Correspondance,* 273.

99. ES to Valentine Gross, 18 January 1917, ibid., 277–78.

100. *Le Figaro,* 11 January 1917.

101. WSP to Madame Poincaré, 25 November and 28 November 1916, NAfr 16022:222, 223.

102. "Courrier des théâtres," *Le Figaro,* 27 December 1916, 4 January 1917.

103. WSP to IS, undated [December 1916], PSS.

104. "Courrier des théâtres," *Le Figaro,* 9 January 1917.

105. Ibid., 10 January 1917.

106. Ibid., 4 January 1917.

107. Henri Quittard, "Courrier des théâtres," *Le Figaro,* 20 January 1917.

108. LMLV-F, 21 January 1917.

109. *New York Times,* 3 March 1917, 3. More details about the background of the indictment can be found in *The London Times,* 25 October, 3 December, and 8 December 1916.

110. The exact title of the case is *The King v. The General Commissioners for the Purposes of Income Tax Acts for the District of Kensington: Ex parte Princess Edmond De Polignac* [1917].

111. *The London Times,* 8 December 1916.

112. *The London Times,* 19 April 1916. The court claimed that WSP's income from her Singer holdings had been £30,700 in 1908, peaking at £73,300 in 1913, declining in 1916 to £38,700.

113. Ibid., 26 April, and 4 May 1917; *The New York Times,* 26 April 1917, 7.

114. *New York Times,* 25 July 1917, 7.

115. WSP sold the King's Row House shortly after the conclusion of her trial. Years later the house would become the residence of British movie director Carol Reed. A letter from Gordon Stewart of the British attorney general's office to Lord Derby (private collection), indicates that the warrant for WSP's arrest was formally withdrawn only in December 1920.

116. Helen Radnor to AB, 28 March 1917, NAfr 17554:450.

117. WSP to AB, 19 May 1917, NAfr 17554:194–95.

118. Morand, *Journal,* 14 May 1917, 237. Morand does not name the pianist who performed at the soiree.

119. Alan A. Gillmor, *Erik Satie* (Boston: Twayne, 1988), 197.

120. Francis Poulenc, *My Friends and Myself,* trans. James Harding (London: Dennis Dobson, 1978), 68.

121. Steegmuller, *Cocteau: A Biography* (Boston: Little, Brown, 1970), 185–86.

122. Blaise Cendrars to ES, May 1917, in Satie, *Correspondance,* 289.

123. Volta, in ibid., 132.

124. ES to Jean Poueigh, 30 May 1917, in ibid., 289.

125. Gillmor, *Erik Satie,* 109.

126. ES to JC, 21 July 1917, APEP, reprinted in Satie, *Correspondance,* 292. Although he did not identify WSP by name, ES noted that he had written "two polite and friendly letters . . . to two good Women (Jouy and Versailles)." The second woman may have been Violette Murat, who had a country house in Jouy-en-Josas.

127. Morand, *Journal,* 1 December 1917, 436. In a letter from JC to his mother (Cocteau, *Lettres à sa mère,* 316–17), Cocteau makes reference to giving Satie's file to a "prince de Polignac," but this is surely an orthographical error.

128. ES to JC, 16 August 1917, in Satie, *Correspondance,* 297.

129. Morand, *Journal,* 1 September 1917, 337.

130. ES to Valentine Gross, 9 September 1917, in Satie, *Correspondance,* 305.

131. ES to Alexis Rouart, 4 October 1917, in ibid., 309.

132. Satie's autographed version of *Parade* (Rouart-Lerolle, 1917), dated 6 November 1917, is in the BMFP. The composer's little note is reprinted in Satie, *Correspondance,* 312.

133. Morand, *Journal,* 17 November 1917, 424.

134. Morand, *Journal,* 19 September 1917, 357.

135. Juliette Meerowitch had played *Parade* in its four-hand version with Satie, at the first performance of the work on 6 June 1917. She died at the age of 24 at the beginning of 1920. Satie dedicated his *Sonatine bureaucratique* to her.

136. Morand, *Journal,* 11 November 1917, 417. WSP's first letter to NB, 6 November 1917 (NLa 94:193), inquires about the possibility of NB's participation in an "organ gathering" (*séance d'orgue*) in the rue Cortambert *atelier.*

137. Morand, *Journal,* 23 November 1917.

138. Ibid.

139. McBrien, *Cole Porter,* 57–59.

140. Valentine Hugo, "Le Socrate que j'ai connu," *La Revue musicale* 214 (June 1952): 143.

141. ES to JC, undated [March 1918], APEP, reprinted in Satie, *Correspondance,* 322, 741.

142. ES to Henry Prunières, 3 April 1918, in Satie, *Correspondance,* 325.

143. Volta, introduction to 1918 correspondence, in ibid., 317.

144. Gillmor, *Erik Satie,* 219.

145. WSP to NB, NLa 95:194. WSP had already left Paris by 20 March 1918, on which date she telegraphed NB to offer her sympathies on the death of her sister, the composer Lili Boulanger.

146. WSP, "Memoirs," 128, 135. WSP was in St-Jean-de-Luz from mid-March to mid-November 1918. Her assertion on p. 135 that she "spent the last years of the 1914 war at St-Jean-de-Luz" is an error: either she mistakenly substituted the word "years" for "months," or her interviewer, Cyril Connelly, misquoted her.

147. Roger Nichols, *The Life of Debussy* (Cambridge: Cambridge University Press, 1998), 259.

148. WSP, "Memoirs," 135.

149. FP to Ricardo Viñes, 3 September 1918, in Francis Poulenc, *Correspondance, 1910–1963,* ed. Myriam Chimènes (Paris: Fayard, 1994), 64–65.

150. ES to JC, 7 April 1918, in Satie, *Correspondance,* 326. On 1 December Satie wrote to Henri-Pierre Roché that he had given several performances of *Socrate* before his artist friends (*Correspondance,* 348).

151. ANo to WSP, undated [21 May 1918], Archives Princesse Eugénie de Brancovan, reprinted in Mignot-Ogliastri, *Anna de Noailles,* 306. ANo's unpublished poem is housed in the Bibliothèque Jacques Doucet, MS 8.434.

152. Typewritten transcripts of two letters from MP to WSP, undated [both from September 1918], are housed in the FSP; the originals have not surfaced. These letters, which shall be referred to in subsequent citations as Letter 1 and Letter 2, are reprinted in Proust, *Correspondance,* 17:350–54 and 358–60, respectively.

153. MP to Paul Morand, 6 and 16 December 1917, in Proust, *Correspondance,* 16:344–45 and 363–64, respectively.

154. MP to WSP, mid-September 1918, Letter 2, FSP.

155. MP to WSP, early September 1918, Letter 1, FSP.

156. MP to WSP, Letter 2, FSP. Emphasis in original.

157. WSP's fear of a public perception of a homosexual relationship between EP and MP is part of the Singer family lore. Alain Ollivier first relayed this story to me in 1993; it has been recounted to me, with variations, several times by various other family members.

158. ES to WSP, 10 October 1918, FSP, reprinted in Satie, *Correspondance,* 340–41.

159. ES to JC, 21 October 1918, APEP, reprinted in Satie, *Correspondance,* 342.

160. Frederick Brown, *An Impersonation of Angels* (New York: Viking Press, 1968), 124–25.

161. WSP to MF, 25 October 1918, AMF.

162. The manuscript of Armande de Polignac's *La Recherche de la vérité* is in the BMFP. It is dedicated to WSP.

163. WSP to MF, 25 October 1918, AMF.

164. WSP, "Memoirs," 135.

165. WSP to MF, 25 October 1918, AMF. As with the Stravinsky commission, WSP would have absolute performance rights over the work for four years, but that would not preclude the possibility of having the work performed in public venues; additionally the work could be published at any time.

166. WSP to MF, 16 November 1918, 14 December 1918, AMF.

167. MF to WSP, 9 December 1918, FSP.

168. WSP to MF, 16 December 1918, AMF.

169. MF to WSP, rough draft of contract for *El Retablo* in Falla's hand, 9 January 1919, AMF. According to its terms, the composer was obligated to complete the work by 1 July 1919. Unlike in the Stravinsky and Satie cases, Winnaretta would pay for the work in three installments: the first, for one thousand francs, to be sent upon signing of the contract, the second, for an equal amount, to be paid on 1 April 1919, and the third, for two thousand francs, to be paid upon completion of the work and delivery of the orchestral score and piano-vocal reduction. Winnaretta would hold the "absolute right of theatrical execution" for four years, although Falla would reserve the right to have the work performed in concert version.

170. Marquise Guy de Polignac noted on 19 January and 16 February 1919 in her daily diary (APEP) that her daughter Diane de Polignac went "to hear music at Winnie's house."

171. On 23 January 1919, JC wrote to Georges Auric, "They're giving *Socrate* (piano-vocal version) at the Princesse [de Polignac]'s house with children's choir. The idea seemed detestable to Satie when *I* had it, but he just had it himself and she

is enthusiastic—that's the essential thing." In Georges Auric and Jean Cocteau, *Correspondance,* ed. Pierre Caizergues (Montpellier: Centre d'étude du 20ᵉ siècle, Université Paul-Valéry, 1999), 53–54.

172. Abbé Mugnier, *Journal de l'Abbé Mugnier (1879–1939)* (Paris: Mercure de France, 1985), 8 February 1919, 350.

173. See note 172. Although no printed program has surfaced, the proximity of this date to the aborted 7 February soiree suggests 16 February as the logical date for the first performance of *Socrate* in the Polignac salon.

174. Even though WSP had given permission for a May 1919 performance of *Socrate* by celebrated actor Pierre Bertin, in connection with a Larionov-Goncharova exhibition, Satie subsequently used the Princesse's proprietary rights to the work as a excuse to block the project, on the pretext was that Bertin's interpretation would violate certain "contractual agreements" stipulating the use of four sopranos for the performance. See Satie, *Correspondance,* letters to Bertin and Madame Bertin of 16 April 1919 (361, 978), 14 May 1919 (366, 689), 21 May 1919 (368, 978), 14 June 1919 (370, 979).

175. Poulenc, *My Friends and Myself,* 69–70.

176. Maurice Sachs, *Au Temps du Boeuf sur le Toit* (Paris: Nouvelle Revue Critique, 1948), 29–30.

177. David Mitchell, *Queen Christabel* (London: MacDonald and Jane's, 1977), 234.

178. Maxwell, *I Married the World,* 107–9. Maxwell lists Lady Ripon as having been on the guest list, but Gladys Ripon had died on 27 October 1917.

179. Marquise Guy de Polignac, DD, 14 December 1919, APEP.

180. LMLV-F, 28 January and 1 February 1920. The Czech Quartet was the former Bohemian Quartet, renamed in 1918. Its personnel consisted of Karel Hoffman and Josef Suk, violins; Jiri Hérold, viola; and Ladislaw Zelenka, cello.

181. Marcel Dupré, "Concerts," BNF-Mus, Rés. VmF ms58:6. Information transmitted by Dr. Carolyn Shuster-Fournier.

182. WSP to MF, 3 June 1919, AMF. Paris was already filled with dignitaries and visitors who had come in connection with the Versailles Treaty. "I'm putting a room at your disposal," wrote WSP to the composer, "in case you encounter some difficulties in finding a place to stay, for Paris is very full at this moment."

183. WSP, "Memoirs," 135–36.

184. Ibid.

185. On 21 November 1919 Satie wrote to the Comte de Beaumont that "the Princesse has kindly given me her authorization." In Satie, *Correspondance,* 382, 670.

186. The orchestral parts of *Socrate,* in the hand of a copyist, are today housed in the BMFP.

187. ES to Comtesse Étienne de Beaumont, 25 May 1920, in Satie, *Correspondance,* 407.

188. IS to Misia Sert, 24 July 1916, in Gold and Fizdale, *Misia,* 175–76.

189. Stravinsky and Craft, *Conversations,* 110–11.

190. This story was first told to me by Duc Élie Decazes in November 1993; it has been retold by various other family members with slight variations.

191. Roger Shattuck, *The Banquet Years* (London: Faber and Faber, 1958), 160. Satie was more hurt by the reaction to *Socrate* than he let on. To Belgian new music champion Paul Collaer, who in May 1920 gave a talk "in defense of Erik Satie's *Socrate,*"

he wrote, "That my music was poorly accepted didn't astonish me, but I was surprised to see the audience *laugh* at Plato's text" (Satie, *Correspondance,* 406, 756).

192. ES to Comtesse Étienne de Beaumont, 21 May 1920, in Satie, *Correspondance,* 407, 676.

193. Marya Freund (1876–1966) was a great interpreter of modern music. She was known especially as an interpreter of the music of Arnold Schoenberg, and in 1922 gave the first Paris performance of that composer's *Pierrot Lunaire.*

194. ES to Comte Étienne de Beaumont, 11 June 1920, in Satie, *Correspondance,* 411–12.

195. Volta in Satie, *Correspondance,* 1047. In his presentation of *Socrate,* before the first performance in WSP's salon, Satie declared that "In writing this work I wanted to add nothing to the beauty of the Dialogues of Plato. It is only an act of piety, the reverie of an artist, a humble homage. The aesthetic of the work I pledge to clarity; simplicity accompanies it, directs it, that is all: I desire nothing else." This autography of this speech is reproduced in facsimile in Ornella Volta, *L'Ymagier d'Erik Satie* (Paris: Van der Velde, 1979), 64.

196. Georges Auric, "Une Oeuvre nouvelle de Satie," *Littérature* 2 (April 1919): 23–24; Henri Collet, "Erik Satie," *L'Esprit nouveau* 2 (1920): 145–48.

197. Even though WSP never commissioned a work from Georges Auric, she admired him immensely. JC wrote to the composer on 23 January 1919, "What do you know, the Princesse likes you—all she ever talks about is you, she's asking for a [date] for a 'rambling Sunday' [to be] spent with her etc. etc." In Auric/Cocteau, *Correspondance,* 53–54.

198. Eventually, MP would cast Pierre as the Comte de Nassau in *A la Recherche du temps perdu.*

199. Marquise Guy de Polignac, DD, 1 February 1920, APEP. The Lamoureux Orchestra also performed a *Fantasy on Airs from Anjou* by Guillaume Lekeu, arias by Gluck sung by Jeanne Raunay, and the Tchaikovsky Piano Concerto, performed by Slominski.

200. Marquise Guy de Polignac, DD, 19 and 21 February 1920, APEP.

201. Marquise Guy de Polignac, DD, 20 March 1920; *Le Figaro,* 20 March 1920.

202. Comte Gilles de Gastines, INT, 24 July 1998; WSP to JP, 1925, APEP.

203. Comte Gilles de Gastines, INT, 24 July 1998.

204. LMLV-F, 8 July 1920.

205. LMLV-F, 28 July 1920.

206. WSP to AB, undated [summer 1920], NAfr 17554:198.

207. Marquise Guy de Polignac-DD, 20 and 24 August 1920, APEP.

208. Marquise Guy de Polignac-DD, 12 and 14 September 1920, APEP.

209. WSP to JP, Palais de Monaco, 18 January 1924, APEP.

210. MF to WSP, 30 November 1920, AMF.

211. WSP to MF, 9 December 1920, AMF.

Chapter 11

1. WSP to AB, 16 May 1922, NAfr 17554:199.

2. George D. Painter, *Marcel Proust: A Biography,* 2 vols. (New York: Vintage Books, 1978), 2:343.

3. James Lees-Milne, *Diaries: 1942–1945* (*Ancestral Voices; Prophesying Peace*) (London: John Murray, 1995), 245. WSP told Lees-Milne that the party's host, the Duke of Marlborough, who had no idea who Proust was, was indignant that some-one should have come to his house in such informal attire.

4. MP to Paul Morand, 16 June 1921, in *Correspondance de Marcel Proust,* ed. Philip Kolb, 20 vols. (Paris: Plon, 1970–93), 20:343.

5. See Lynn Garafola, *Diaghilev's Ballets Russes* (New York: Oxford University Press, 1989), chapter 4, about Cocteau's role of negotiator "between Left Bank art and Right Bank ideology."

6. WSP wrote to JC on 19 March 1919 to thank him for having sent a copy of his "book on music" (Jean Cocteau Papers, Harry Ransom Humanities Research Center, University of Texas at Austin).

7. Ibid.

8. Jean Wiéner, *Allegro Appassionato* (Paris: Pierre Belfond, 1978), 45.

9. Ibid.

10. Laurence Benaïm, *Marie-Laure de Noailles: La vicomtesse du bizarre* (Paris: Grasset, 2001), 122–25.

11. The most recent biography of Natalie Barney is Suzanne Rodriguez's *Wild Heart: A Life, Natalie Clifford Barney's Journey from Victorian America to Belle Époque Paris* (New York: Ecco, 2002).

12. Painter, *Marcel Proust,* 2:329.

13. Phillipe Jullian, *Robert de Montesquiou: A Fin-de-Siècle Prince,* trans. John Haylock and Francis King (London: Secker and Warburg, 1967), 131.

14. Claude Mignot-Ogliastri, *Anna de Noailles, une amie de la Princesse Edmond de Polignac* (Paris: Fondation Singer-Polignac and Méridiens-Klincksieck, 1986), 328.

15. The first issue of *La Revue musicale* under the editorship of Henry Prunières was launched on 1 November 1920.

16. Doda Conrad, *Dodascalies* (Arles: Actes Sud, 1998), 124.

17. Antonio Banès, "'Parade' aux Ballets Russes," *Le Figaro,* 26 December 1920.

18. IS to Maurice Ravel, 11 November 1912, collection of Eric van Lauwe.

19. Garafola, *Diaghilev's Ballets Russes,* 213–14.

20. Ibid., 218–19.

21. Ibid., 223.

22. The dedicated score of *Renard* is in the BMFP.

23. Tristan Tzara, "What We Are Doing in Europe," *Vanity Fair,* September 1922, 67.

24. Ibid.

25. Daniel Albright, *Untwisting the Serpent: Modernism in Music, Literature, and Other Arts* (Chicago: University of Chicago Press, 2000), 37–38.

26. WSP to IS, 16 June 1922, PSS.

27. IS to WSP, 18 July 1922, FSP.

28. William McBrien, *Cole Porter: A Biography* (New York. Knopf, 1998), 74–75.

29. Calvin Tompkins, *Living Well is the Best Revenge* (New York: Viking Press, 1962), 39.

30. Paul Thévanez to IS, 2 December 1919, PSS. The Swiss composer Paul Thévanez (1891–1921) was a pupil of Jean-Jacques Dalcroze, and, at that time, the lover of JC.

31. IS to WSP, 18 July 1922, FSP.

32. Albert Roussel to WSP, 22 May 1923, text communicated by Dr. Nicole Labelle.

33. Castelnuovo-Tedesco, unpublished autobiography, 175–76.

34. The score of Castelnuovo-Tedesco's *Cipressi* for piano in the BMFP bears the dedication "To Mme la Princesse de Polignac as a souvenir of Mario Castelnuovo-Tedesco, Florence, 4 September 1922."

35. In a letter to one of her personnel in Paris dated 30 August 1922, WSP asks that a round-trip ticket between Paris and Venice be bought and delivered to Tailleferre "around 7 September." The letter is in a private collection.

36. Duc Armand de Polignac to WSP, 18 July and 1 August 1922, APEP.

37. Maurice Barrès to WSP, 14 September 1922, FSP.

38. Prince Edmond de Polignac, INT, 23 January 2000.

39. Garafola, *Diaghilev's Ballets Russes,* 237–38; Arthur Gold and Robert Fizdale, *Misia: The Life of Misia Sert* (New York: Knopf, 1980), 245.

40. MF to WSP, 10 January 1923, FSP.

41. WSP to MF, 25 April 1923 and MF to WSP, 31 May 1923 (rough draft), both in AMF.

42. WSP to MF, 24 January 1923, AMF.

43. MF to WSP, 20 February 1923, FSP. The word *illusion* is used in the Spanish sense, meaning enthusiasm, hope, or commitment.

44. This "music budget" is mentioned numerous times in WSP's correspondence with composers. Unfortunately, there is no accurate data about the actual amount of money set aside for the commission of new compositions.

45. Manuel Infante's *Ritmo,* from his *Danses andalouses* bears the date April 1921.

46. A manuscript of *Le Marchand d'oiseaux* is housed in the BMFP.

47. Michael de Cossart, *The Food of Love: Princesse Edmond de Polignac (1865–1943) and Her Salon* (London: Hamish Hamilton, 1978), 151, 159.

48. Mario Castelnuovo-Tedesco, "Una Vita di musica," unpublished manuscript, 175–76, Mario Castelnuovo-Tedesco Archives, Nashville; this excerpt kindly communicated by Dr. Pietro Castelnuovo-Tedesco.

49. WSP's manuscript collection, currently housed in the BMFP, contains only the first two movements of the *Alt Wien* triptych, *Alt Wien* and *Nachtmusik.* The manuscript of the third movement, *Momento Mori* does not appear to have ever been given to its dedicatee.

50. Castelnuovo-Tedesco, "Una Vita di musica," 176.

51. Léon-Paul Fargue (1876–1947).

52. WSP, "Memoirs of the Late Princesse Edmond de Polignac," *Horizon* 12, no. 68 (August 1945), 138–39.

53. Ibid., 139.

54. Paul Valéry (1871–1945). The works that brought the poet to fame include *Le Jeune Pataque, Le Cimetière marin,* and *Ébauche d'un serpent.* Years later Valéry wrote two "melodramas," *Amphion* and *Sémiramis,* set to music, in 1931 and 1934 respectively, by Arthur Honegger.

55. Satie's *Socrate* was performed at the Théâtre des Champs-Élysées on 4 January 1923 by soprano Suzanne Balguérie, conducted by André Caplet, under the auspices of the Concerts Wiéner. WSP loaned Satie her set of orchestral parts for the

occasion (Erik Satie, *Correspondance presque complète,* ed. Ornella Volta [Paris: Fayard, 2000], 117, 1042). The performance was considered by many to be, in the words of Henry Prunières (*La Revue musicale,* 1 October 1924), "the one and only time" that the work was performed "in really satisfying manner."

56. WSP to Paul Valéry, undated [mid-January 1923], BNF-Mss, MF 2800:248.

57. Ibid., 27 January 1923, 238.

58. Paul Léautaud, *Journal littéraire,* vols. 4–5 (Paris: Mercure de France, 1957–58), 47.

59. Pozzi, diary entries of 2 and 19 May 1923, in Catherine Pozzi, *Journal, 1913–1934* (Paris: Seghers, 1990), 263 and 267.

60. Ibid., 20 July 1924, 311.

61. Ibid., 18 June 1923, 271–72.

62. Duchesse Edmée de La Rochefoucauld, *Images de Paul Valéry* (Strasbourg: Le Roux, 1949), 12.

63. Stephen Walsh, *Stravinsky: A Creative Spring: Russia and France, 1882–1934* (New York: Knopf, 1999), 365.

64. NB as quoted in Bruno Monsaingeon, *Mademoiselle,* trans. Robyn Marsack (Manchester: Carcanet, 1985), 92.

65. Serge Lifar, *Serge Diaghilev: His Life, His Work, His Legend: An Intimate Biography* (New York: G. P. Putnam's Sons, 1940), 259; see also Serge Lifar, "Misia," *Nouvelle Revue des deux mondes,* February 1975, 619.

66. Walsh, *Stravinsky,* 366.

67. Ibid., 366–67.

68. Calvin Tomkins, *Living Well Is the Best Revenge* (New York: Viking Press, 1962), 31.

69. Ibid., 32.

70. Ibid.

71. Michael Christoforidis, "From Folksong to Plainchant: Musical Borrowings and the Transformation of Manuel de Falla's Nationalism in the 1920s," in *Manuel de Falla,* ed. Nancy Harper (Lanham, Md.: Scarecrow, 2002).

72. Igor Stravinsky and Robert Craft, *Memories and Commentaries* (Berkeley: University of California Press, 1981), 80.

73. In *Manuel de Falla* (Philadelphia: Chilton Book Company, 1968), 119, Falla scholar Suzanne Demarquez claims that "the Princess spent her enormous fortune to enhance her private reputation rather than to be the patroness of the arts she claimed to be." Rubinstein described WSP "as the stingiest woman I ever met in my whole life" (*My Many Years,* 134).

74. Francis Poulenc, *My Friends and Myself,* trans. James Harding (London: Dennis Dobson, 1978), 45–47.

75. Boris de Schloezer, "Chroniques et notes: 'El Retablo' de Manuel de Falla (Concert Wiéner)," *La Revue musicale* 5, no. 2 (1 December 1924): 171–72.

76. MF to WSP, 15 March 1925, AMF.

77. JP to WSP, 22 July 1923, private collection.

78. In all, Poulenc dedicated fourteen songs and two piano works to Marie-Blanche de Polignac; many of the manuscripts of these works are housed in the BMFP.

79. Rubinstein, *My Many Years,* 131.

80. WSP to JP, 23 October 1923, APEP.

81. In an undated letter [1923–28] in the Serge Diaghilev Correspondence, folder 27/7, Dance Collection, NYPL, Cole Porter invites Serge Diaghilev to a dinner in Venice, enumerating Lifar, Rieti, Kochno among the guests; Porter adds "we have invited Tante Winnie, and I think that she'll be coming." The NYPL suggests a date of 1929, but WSP was not in Venice in 1929 until after Diaghilev's death on 19 August of that year.

82. Robert Orledge, "Cole Porter's Ballet 'Within the Quota,'" *Yale University Library Gazette* 50, no.1 (1975): 20; McBrien, *Cole Porter,* 88–91.

83. Gerald Tyrwhitt, Lord Berners (1883–1950).

84. Mark Amory, *Lord Berners: The Last Eccentric* (London: Pimlico, 1999), 80–81.

85. Rubinstein, *My Many Years,* 134.

86. Prince Jean-Louis de Faucigny-Lucinge, *Un Gentilhomme cosmopolite* (Paris: Perrin, 1990), 142.

87. This story has been recounted in various versions, with the jilted spouse identified by Phillipe Jullian (in his biographical essay in Adolf de Meyer, *De Meyer,* ed. Robert Brandau [New York: Knopf, 1976], 32) as Baron Adolf de Meyer, and by Faucigny-Lucinge (*Un Gentilhomme cosmopolite,* 146) as the husband of English socialite Ruby Peto.

88. The complicated but loving marriage of Vita Sackville-West and Harold Nicolson is the subject of a biography by their son, Nigel Nicolson, *Portrait of a Marriage* (London: Weidenfeld and Nicolson, 1973).

89. Trefusis, *Don't Look Round* (London: Hutchinson, 1952), 77.

90. WSP to Violet Trefusis, Violet Trefusis Papers, Yale University Library, Gen MSS 427:22.

91. Violet Trefusis, *Don't Look Round,* 78–79; Philippe Jullian and John Phillips, *Violet Trefusis: A Biography* (San Diego: Harcourt, Brace, 1976), 69; Henrietta Sharpe, *A Solitary Woman: A Life of Violet Trefusis* (London: Constable, 1981), 86–87.

92. The manuscript of Germaine Tailleferre's *Concerto pour piano,* housed in the BMFP, is inscribed "Bourdj-Polignac, Bouzareah 1924, Germaine Tailleferre"; it was presented to its dedicatee a year later with the dedication "to the Princesse Edmond de Polignac, with all my admiration, with all my affection, G. T. 1925."

93. Calvin Coolidge, "The Classics for America," 7 July 1921, transcribed and annotated by Dr. William Harris, 2001, <*http://www.calvin coolidge.org/pages/history/-speeches/asvp/21_07_07.html.*> Coolidge had given the speech while he was still Vice-President of the American Classical League, University of Pennsylvania.

94. Ibid.

95. WSP to JP, 18 January 1924, APEP. A portion of this letter appears at the end of Chapter Ten.

96. WSP, "Memoirs," 121.

97. GF to WSP, 12 January 1924, FSP.

98. Claude Francis and Fernande Gontier, *Creating Colette,* 2 vols. (South Royalton, Vt.: Steerforth, 1998–99), 2:75, 113.

99. Photograph album, Violet Trefusis Papers, Yale University Library, Gen MSS 427:116–17.

100. IS, *Autobiography,* 113.

101. WSP to IS, 7 April 1924, PSS.

102. Photocopy of printed program of the 14 May 1924 soiree in the Polignac salon in Wiéner, *Allegro appassionato*, 56.

103. Faucigny-Lucinge, *Un Gentilhomme cosmopolite*, 100.

104. LMLV-F, 26 May 1924. The first public performance of IS's Piano Concerto took place at the Opéra on 22 May, to great acclaim.

105. Boris de Schloezer, "Chroniques et notes: Concerto de Strawinsky," *La Revue musicale* 5, no. 9 (1 July 1924): 61–62.

106. Ibid.

107. The manuscript of Germaine Tailleferre's *Concerto pour piano* is housed in the BMFP.

108. LMLV-F, 2 July 1924.

109. Rubinstein, *My Many Years*, 282–83.

110. LMLV-F, 8 June 1924.

111. Volta, preface to the letters of 1924, in Satie, *Correspondance*, 579.

112. WSP to Marya Freund, 13 September 1924, archives of the author.

113. Calvin Coolidge, "Les Études classiques en Amérique," translated by WSP, *La Revue de Paris*, 1 August 1924, 481–90.

114. President Calvin Coolidge to WSP, 15 September 1924, FSP. The President wrote, on White House letterhead, "I wish to express to you my appreciation of your interest in my views on this subject, and my gratitude for the work you have done in translating it and publishing it."

115. WSP to IS, 20 September 1924, PSS.

116. WSP to MF, 14 October 1924, AMF.

117. WSP makes reference to Edgar Allan Poe's 1839 short story, *The Man That Was Used Up*.

118. Olga Robilant, later the Duchesse de Cadaval, was one of WSP's closest Venetian friends. A great music lover, she and her mother Clémentine lived in the Palazzo Mocenico, one of Venice's most beautiful dwellings.

119. WSP to MBP, 15 October [1924], APEP. WSP makes reference to Poulenc's ballet *Les Biches*.

120. Jim Samson, *The Music of Szymanowski* (New York: Taplinger, 1981), 188.

121. Karol Szymanowski to WSP, 29 December 1924, FSP.

122. Karol Szymanowski to Jan Smetelin, in Szymanowski and Smeterlin, *Correspondence*, trans. and ed. B. M. Maciejewski and Felix Aprahamian (London: Allegro Press, 1969), 32.

123. Rubinstein quoted in Harvey Sachs, *Rubinstein: A Life* (New York: Grove Press, 1995), 194.

124. Wiéner, *Allegro appassionato*, 57.

125. Schloezer, "Chroniques et notes: Concerto pour piano, de Jean Wiéner (Pasdeloup)," *La Revue musicale* 6, no. 2 (1 December 1924): 150–51. Russian-born Boris de Schloezer (1881–1969) was a philosopher and one of the most influential music writers and critics of his era. In addition to biographies of Scriabin, Stravinsky, and J. S. Bach, Schloezer was the author of *Problèmes de la musique moderne* (1959), a work on the fundamental tenets of aesthetics.

126. Schloezer, "Darius Milhaud," *La Revue musicale* 6, no. 5 (1 March 1925): 252–76.

127. Madeleine Milhaud, INT, Paris, 11 July 1992.

128. The manuscript of Darius Milhaud's opera *Les Malheurs d'Orphée* is housed in the BMFP.

129. MBP-PD, March 1933, APEP.

130. Great-grandson of Victor Hugo and nephew of Madame Ménard-Dorian (Carriès's patron), Jean Hugo (1894–1984) was a talented artist, illustrator, and scenic designer. After his 1929 divorce from the artist Valentine Gross (Satie's friend), Hugo married the beautiful Duchesse Maria de Gramont, née Ruspoli. A close friend of Les Six and of Jean and Marie-Blanche de Polignac, Hugo was an habitual summer guest at Kerbastic.

131. Paul Collaer, "Les Malheurs d'Orphée," *La Revue musicale* 6, no. 8 (1 June 1926): 313–14.

132. A performance of the two-piano version, played by Tailleferre and Wiéner, had taken place under the auspices of the Concerts Wiéner on 25 January 1925. The concerto was given its first public performance with orchestra under Koussevitzky's baton at the Opéra on 30 May 1925, with the composer at the piano.

133. Schloezer, "Chroniques et notes: Concerto de piano, par Germaine Tailleferre," *La Revue musicale* 6, no. 9 (1 July 1925): 62–63.

134. Marie-Rose Clouzot, *Souvenirs à deux voix de Maxime Jacob à Dom Clément Jacob* (Toulouse: Privat, 1969), 116.

135. WSP to MF, 22 March 1925, AMF.

136. Ibid.

137. LMLV-F, 4 and 9 April 1925.

138. WSP to MF, 11 May 1925, AMF.

139. MBP-PD, 13 May 1925, APEP.

140. MBP-PD, 28 May 1925, APEP.

141. WSP to IS, 14 May 1925, PSS; LMLV-F, 8 June 1925. WSP apparently paid IS a hefty sum to perform his work in her salon; a week later, the composer wrote to her, "I would like to come to your house one day, and play my sonata for you in the most absolute intimacy" (16 June 1925, FSP).

142. MBP-PD, 9 June 1925, APEP.

143. Serge Prokofiev, diary entry of 14 May 1920, in his *Dnevnik, 1907–1933* (Paris: sprkfv, 2002), 102.

144. Unpublished correspondence concerning Prokofiev's first performance in the Polignac salon from WSP to Serge Prokofiev (10 April 1925, 14 and 16 May 1925, 9 June 1925), from Prokofiev to WSP (17 April 1925, 15 May 1925), and from Prokofiev's agent Paul Boquel to the composer (30 May 1925, 13 June 1925), is housed in the Serge Prokofiev Archive, Goldsmiths College, London.

145. Serge Prokofiev, diary entries of 20 and 21 June 1925, in his *Dnevnik, 1907–1933,* trans. Sandra Kurvida, 330.

146. Arthur Rubinstein, *My Many Years* (New York: Knopf, 1980), 191–92.

147. Volta, preface to the letters of 1925, in Satie, *Correspondance,* 642.

148. WSP, "Memoirs," 138.

149. Poulenc, *My Friends and Myself,* 66.

150. MBP-PD, 6 and 7 June 1925, APEP.

151. WSP to MBP, 1 and 24 September 1925, APEP.

152. Rubinstein, *My Many Years,* 232–33.

153. Henry Prunières, "Chroniques et notes: Le Troisième Festival de la S.I.M.C. à Venise (3–8 Septembre 1925)," *La Revue musicale* 6, no. 12 (1 October 1925): 258.

154. Ibid.

155. Gian-Carlo Malipiero, *Strawinsky* (Venice: Cavallino, 1945), 13.

Chapter 12

1. Peter Kurth, *Isadora: A Sensational Life* (New York: Little, Brown, 2001), 359.

2. Palm Beach "scrapbook," Addison Mizner archives, Society of the Four Arts Library, Palm Beach, FL; MBP-PD, 26 January 1926, APEP.

3. LMLV-F, 7 December 1925.

4. Philippe Jullian and John Phillips, *Violet Trefusis: A Biography* (San Diego: Harcourt, Brace, 1976), 70.

5. MBP-PD, 26 January 1926, APEP.

6. Ibid., 27 January 1926.

7. Sir Oswald Mosley was the leader of the British Union of Fascists. During World War II he was imprisoned, deemed a "danger to the state."

8. Sir Oswald Mosley, *My Life* (London: Thomas Nelson, 1968), 204.

9. Ibid. The Everglades Club was not the only Palm Beach hotel to use classical music as a means of drawing a more elegant clientele: the Alba Hotel instituted a series of concerts during the same period, inaugurated by the renowned violinist Albert Spalding and a German *Lieder* singer, Madame Rethberg (MBP-PD, 1 February 1926, APEP).

10. MBP-PD, 28 January 1926, APEP. The name of the quartet is not noted, but MBP identifies the first violinist as Otto Karr.

11. Ibid.

12. MBP-PD, 29 January 1926, APEP.

13. MBP-PD, 29, 30 and 31 January 1926, APEP.

14. Trefusis's biographers, Philippe Jullian and John Phillips, assert that writer Rebecca West "ran into Violet Trefusis in Washington with the Princess as they were on the way to the White House" (Jullian and Phillips, *Violet Trefusis*, 69–70). Violet's presence during WSP's meeting with President Coolidge is not substantiated by French embassy records.

15. WSP to French Ambassador Henri Béranger, 8 February 1926, French Embassy Archives, Nantes.

16. Letters from the French Embassy to WSP, 13 and 23 February 1926, French Embassy Archives, Nantes. As the second of these two letters confirms a meeting between the president and WSP on 25 February, it is possible that there may have been two separate meetings, or that the first date was cancelled and scheduled for later in the month.

17. "Inauguration de la Cité de Refuge," *Le Temps*, 8 December 1933.

18. Brian Brace Taylor, *Le Corbusier: The City of Refuge, 1929–33* (Chicago: University of Chicago, 1987), 7.

19. WSP to LC, 26 July 1926, FLC, J2–17–37.

20. Gilles Ragot and Mathilde Dion, *Le Corbusier en France: Réalisations et projets* (Paris: Electra Moniteur, 1987), 156.

21. The commemorative plaque of the Palais de la Femme, 98 rue de Charonne, Paris, lists the Princesse de Polignac third on its list of "founders." She was one of the few French contributors, other than banks and companies; most of the other individual contributors were British and American *mécènes*.

22. Albin Peyron to LC, 12 July 1926, FLC, J2–17;93.

23. Taylor, *Le Corbusier*, 17.

24. Subscription card of the Princesse de Polignac for *L'Esprit nouveau,* FLC, A1–19–273.

25. WSP to LC, undated [May 1926], FLC, J2–17–27.

26. Le Corbusier, *Vers une Architecture* (Paris : Éditions G. Crès, 1923), 175. The crucial importance of the Golden Section formula, also set forth in the same work, would only retrospectively come to be seen as a major organizational method in the works of contemporary composers such as Debussy, Bartók, and others.

27. Le Corbusier, quoted in Jacques Guiton, ed., *The Ideas of Le Corbusier on Architecture and Urban Planning,* trans. Margaret Guiton (New York: G. Braziller, 1981), 64.

28. Taylor, *Le Corbusier,* 20.

29. WSP to LC, 16 June 1926, FLC, J2–17– 33.

30. Albin Peyron to LC, 12 July 1926, FLC, J2–17–93.

31. WSP to LC, 16 June 1926, FLC, J2–17–33. WSP obtained Le Corbusier's address from her nephew Comte Charles de Polignac, who was at that time considering engaging LC to build a home for him in Neuilly, a wealthy suburb of Paris (Charles de Polignac to LC, undated [1926], FLC, A1–5–148).

32. WSP to LC, 6 June 1926, FLC, J2–17–32.

33. WSP to LC, 16 June 1926, FLC, J2–17–33.

34. LC to WSP, 23 July 1926, FLC, J2–17–35.

35. LC to WSP, 27 September 1926, J2–17–41.

36. IS to WSP, 14 August 1926, PSS.

37. Ibid.

38. WSP to IS, 29 August 1926, PSS.

39. Ibid.

40. Virgil Thomson, *Virgil Thomson* (New York: Da Capo Press, 1966), 96.

41. Ibid., 97.

42. Ibid.

43. Paléologue in Edmond Faral and Roger Heim, *Les Heures de musique à la Fondation Singer-Polignac* (Paris: Fondation Singer-Polignac, 1966), 69.

44. Paléologue to WSP, 1 June 1927, FSP.

45. MBP-PD, 3 December 1926, APEP.

46. Ibid., 6 December 1926.

47. LMLV-F reports on 25 January 1927 that WSP gave a *matinée musicale* "yesterday"; the report regrettably gives no details of the program; Catherine Pozzi refers to the *matinées* of 31 January and 7 February 1927 in her *Journal, 1913–1934* (Paris: Seghers, 1990), 358, 360–61.

48. Pozzi, *Journal,* 358.

49. Ibid., 360–61.

50. Claude Mignot-Ogliastri, *Anna de Noailles, une amie de la Princesse Edmond de Polignac* (Paris: Fondation Singer-Polignac and Méridiens-Klincksieck, 1986), 370.

51. Ibid., 374.

52. See, for example, remarks made by Duff Cooper to his wife Diana in Duff Cooper and Diana Cooper, *A Durable Fire: The Letters of Duff and Diana Cooper (1913–1950),* ed. Artemis Cooper (London: Collins, 1983), 251.

53. Prince Edmond de Polignac, "Souvenirs de ma tante, la princesse Edmond" (September 1998), APEP.

54. Ibid.

55. Ibid.

56. IS to JC, 11 October 1925, PSS.

57. Igor Stravinsky, *An Autobiography* (New York: The Norton Library, 1962), 132.

58. André Aron was a Paris lawyer engaged by Stravinsky to handle the business aspects of some of his artistic projects.

59. JC to IS, 7 January 1927, PSS.

60. Ibid.

61. Ibid.

62. WSP quoted in JC's letter to IS, ibid.

63. WSP to JC, 2 April 1927, PSS.

64. IS to JC, undated [March 1927], PSS.

65. JC to IS, undated [March 1927], PSS.

66. IS to JC, undated [March 1927], PSS.

67. According to Vera Sudeikina's diaries (PSS), IS completed *Oedipus Rex* on 14 March 1927, and rehearsed the work in WSP's *atelier* on 17 March 1927. A telegram from WSP to IS, dated 15 March 1927 (PSS), confirms this rehearsal.

68. WSP to IS, 20 March 1927, PSS.

69. IS to WSP, 23 March 1927, FSP; a rough draft of the same letter is in PSS.

70. Ibid.

71. Richard Buckle, *Diaghilev* (London: Weidenfeld and Nicolson, 1979), 412.

72. Axel Madsen, *Chanel: A Woman of Her Own* (New York: Henry Holt, 1990), 113; Paul Morand, *L'Allure de Chanel* (Paris: Hermann, 1976), 84.

73. JC to IS, 2 April 1927, PSS.

74. WSP to JC, 2 April 1927, sent jointly with a letter from Cocteau to IS, 5 April 1927, PSS.

75. Stephen Walsh, *Stravinsky: A Creative Spring: Russia and France, 1882–1934* (New York: Knopf, 1999), 444–45.

76. Stravinsky, *Autobiography,* 132.

77. Eric Walter White, *Stravinsky: The Composer and His Works* (Berkeley: University of California Press, 1966), 70.

78. Stephen Walsh has communicated to me the text of an unpublished postcard (in Russian) from IS to Diaghilev, dated 21 April 1927 (original in the Kochno Archive, Paris): "I have just received a sweet letter from Mme de Polignac. . . . As you see, she is still in Paris. . . . The sum of 65 thousand gives us the possibility of augmenting the chorus somewhat, which on mature reflection is extremely necessary. . . . For God's sake hurry with this question, if only to [rally the singers]. . . . There are only 45 days left!!! I embrace you, I Stravinsky."

79. Igor Stravinsky and Robert Craft, *Conversations with Igor Stravinsky* (Garden City, N.Y.: Doubleday, 1959), 111.

80. MBP-PD, undated entry [June 1927], APEP.

81. MBP-PD, 22 April 1927, APEP.

82. Prince Edmond de Polignac, "Souvenirs de ma tante, la princesse Edmond" (September 1998), APEP.

83. A telegram from WSP to MF, dated Marseille, 23 April 1927 (AMF), announces her arrival in Granada on "the 27th."

84. Prince Edmond de Polignac, "Souvenirs de ma tante, la princesse Edmond" (September 1998), APEP.

85. Ibid.

86. A card commemorating the Lindbergh flight, with the text "New York-Paris l'Atlantique survolé, 20–21 Mai 1927 (33 heures, 28 minutes) par le Capitaine Charles Lindbergh, Lyautry," and signed by Lindbergh, among the Polignac archives, FSP.

87. On 10 May 1929, Vera Stravinsky wrote in her datebook (PSS) "Oedipus finished this morning." In *Dearest Babushkin: Selected Diaries of Vera and Igor Stravinsky,* ed. Robert Craft (New York: Thames and Hudson, 1985), Vera Stravinsky mistakenly identifies the date as 19 May.

88. Vera Stravinsky's datebook, PSS, notes "Tuesday 17, Oedipus choir"; WSP to IS, 19 May 1927, PSS.

89. Igor Stravinsky and Robert Craft, *Dialogues and a Diary* (Garden City, N.Y.: Doubleday, 1963), 7.

90. LMLV-F, 28 May 1927, 2. Although a printed program in PSS indicates that IS was the solitary pianist for the *avant-première* of Oedipus Rex in WSP's salon, Prokofiev wrote in his diary that night after the event, "I [was] helping Stravinsky. The chorus was sometimes a little off. It was hard to tell, being busy" (diary entry in his *Dnevnik, 1907–1933,* 563.) This substantiates the recollection of conductor Otto Klemperer (quoted by Peter Heyworth, *Conversations with Klemperer* [London: Gollancz, 1973], 60) who remembered Prokofiev playing a second piano part.

91. MBP-PD, undated entry [May 1927], APEP.

92. Stravinsky, *Autobiography,* 133; Walsh, *Stravinsky,* 446–47. The performance of Stravinsky's Oedipus Rex had been preceded by Gerald Berners's *The Triumph of Neptune* and Henri Sauguet's *La Chatte.*

93. Walsh, *Stravinsky,* 448.

94. Janet Flanner, *Paris Was Yesterday: 1925–1939* (New York: Viking Press, 1972), 25.

95. Doda Conrad, *Dodascalies* (Arles: Actes Sud, 1998), 87–88.

96. Henry Prunières, "Chroniques et notes: Vladimir Horowitz—Concert," *La Revue musicale* 7, no. 6 (1 April 1926): 69–70.

97. Harold Schonberg, *Horowitz: His Life and Music* (New York: Simon and Schuster, 1992), 87.

98. MBP-PD, undated entry [June 1927],APEP.

99. Horowitz to WSP, 17 June 1927, FSP.

100. WSP to MF, undated [spring 1927], AMF. Falla's Harpsichord Concerto had received its first performance by Wanda Landowska, the work's dedicatee, in Barcelona on 5 November 1926. Its Paris debut took place as part of an "All-Falla" program performed under the auspices of the Concerts Straram, with the composer as soloist, at the Salle Pleyel on 14 May 1927.

101. MBP-PD, undated entry [June 1927], APEP.

102. LC to Peyron, 1 March 1928, FLC, J2–17:117.

103. François Dupré to Peyron, 13 December 1926, FLC, J2–17:53;WSP to LC, 9 January 1927, FLC, J2–17:58. In subsequent renovations of the Palais du Peuple much of Le Corbusier's original design has been eradicated, but the memorial plaque is still affixed to the building, in the interior courtyard of 29 rue des Cordelières in the 13th *arrondissement.*

104. A letter from WSP to MBP (15 July 1927, APEP) is written on letterhead from "La Tour de Saint Loup, Saint Loup de Vaud, Seine et Marne."

105. Bruno Maderna (1920–1973).

106. Raymond Fearn, *Bruno Maderna* (Chur and London: Harwood, 1990), 1–2.

107. WSP to Serge Prokofiev, 29 November 1927, Serge Prokofiev Archive, Goldsmiths College, London.

108. Jérôme Spycket, *Clara Haskil* (Lausanne: Payot, 1975), 95.

109. LMLV-F, 12 May 1903, reports a performance by Enesco of Fauré's A-Major Violin Sonata in the Polignac salon, accompanied by the composer.

110. Spycket, *Clara Haskil,* 48.

111. Ibid., 95.

112. Ibid.

113. Ibid., 96.

114. WSP to JP, 29 February 1928, APEP.

115. WSP to Raymond Poincaré, 14 December 1927, NAfr 16012:126. In this letter, WSP recalls a recent conversation during a lunch with Poincaré and Paléologue; presumably she proposed the presidency of the new foundation to him at that time.

116. WSP to Raymond Poincaré, undated [1928], private collection.

117. Comte André de Fouquières, *Cinquante Ans de panache* (Paris: Horay, 1951), 172.

118. Annette Tapert and Diana Edkins, *The Power of Style: The Women Who Defined the Art of Living Well* (New York: Crown, 1994), 143.

119. WSP, "Notes sur la musique," *Vogue* (Paris edition), June 1928, 31.

120. Abbé Mugnier to WSP, 14 November 1928, FSP.

121. Ibid. During the 1920s the Cavaillé-Coll organ was moved from the upper balcony of the *atelier* down to the ground floor.

122. Buckle, *Diaghilev,* 508.

123. Igor Markevitch, *Être et avoir été* (Paris: Gallimard, 1980), 488.

124. Soon after the founding of the Orchestre Symphonique de Paris, Pierre Monteux, whose reputation as a conductor eclipsed those of Cortot, Ansermet, and Fourestier, assumed the mantle of leadership, becoming the group's music director and principal conductor.

125. Walsh, *Stravinsky,* 478–79.

126. "Les Concerts," *Le Figaro,* 23 November 1928, 6, and 10 December 1928, 6.

127. Robert Brussel, "L'Orchestre Symphonique de Paris," *Le Figaro,* 22 October 1928, 4.

128. WSP to JP, undated [9 April 1928]; MBP-PD, 4 January 1929, APEP; LMLV-F, 11 December 1928, 2. On 19 September 1927, while in the south of France, Duncan was strangled when her scarf was caught in the rear wheel of a convertible car.

129. *Vogue,* January 1929.

130. WSP to JP, 16 April 1929, APEP.

131. "Deux Précieux Appareils scientifiques ont été offerts au Collège de France," undated press clipping in a scrapbook, archives of Mrs. Gerald Selous, née Leeds; WSP to JP, 16 March 1929, APEP; Joseph Bédier to WSP, 2 June 1929, FSP.

132. WSP to JP, 16 April 1929, APEP.

133. The 1929 version of *Renard* marked Serge Lifar's début as choreographer with the Ballets Russes.

134. WSP to IS, 4 April 1929, PSS.

135. Ibid.

136. IS to WSP, 8 April 1929, PSS.

137. Ibid.

138. LMLV-F, 22 May 1929

139. Taylor, *Le Corbusier,* 2, 7; Ragot and Dion, *Le Corbusier en France,* 156.

140. Ibid.

141. Prince Edmond de Polignac, INT, January 1998, January 1999.

142. Ibid.

143. LMLV-F, 30 May 1929.

144. Ibid.

145. MBP-PD, undated entry [June 1929], APEP.

146. Ibid.; LMLV-F, 17 May 1928.

147. Violet Trefusis, *Don't Look Round* (London: Hutchinson, 1952), 99.

148. *The Times,* London, 15 July 1929, 11.

149. Ibid.

150. *The Times,* London, 1 August 1929, 17.

151. WSP to JP, undated [July 1929], APEP.

152. Ibid.

153. Nicolas Nabokov, *Old Friends and New Music* (London: Hamish Hamilton, 1951), 126. According to Nabokov, Hindemith was reluctant to write a ballet, and tried to convince Diaghilev to give the commission to Bohuslav Martinu instead. The issue became moot with Diaghilev's death the following month, in August 1929.

154. Markevitch, *Être et avoir été,* 164.

155. Nabokov, *Old Friends and New Music,* 126.

156. Lifar, quoted in John Drummond, *Speaking of Diaghilev* (London: Faber and Faber, 1997), 287.

157. MBP, private diary entry, August-September 1929, APEP.

158. Solange d'Ayen (1898–1976), née Labriffe, the Duchesse de Noailles, was one of WSP's closest friends among the younger members of the aristocracy.

159. Rubinstein enjoyed a long and fruitful musical collaboration with the violinist Paul Kochanski, who died of cancer in 1934, when he was forty-seven.

160. MBP-PD, August-September 1929, APEP.

161. Lifar, quoted in Drummond, *Speaking of Diaghilev,* 287.

162. WSP to PP, 1 November 1931, NAfr 18718:287.

Chapter 13

1. Jean-Michel Frank (1895–1941) was the most influential decorator of the *tout-Paris* in the 1930s and 1940s. He first introduced his signature style—spare, rectilinear furnishings and details—in his decoration of the home of Charles and Marie-Laure de Noailles on the place des États-Unis.

2. WSP to MBP, 15 August 1930, APEP; LMLV-F, 16 and 31 October 1930; WSP to Princesse Marthe Bibesco, 2 November 1930, Marthe Bibesco Papers, Harry Ransom Humanities Research Center, University of Texas at Austin.

3. Brian Brace Taylor, *Le Corbusier: The City of Refuge, 1929–33* (Chicago: University of Chicago Press, 1987), 17; *En Avant!,* 5 July 1930, 1.

4. Claude Francis and Fernande Gontier, *Creating Colette,* 2 vols. (South Royalton, Vt.: Steerforth, 1998–99), 2:148–49.

5. Colette, *Lettres à ses pairs* (Paris: Flammarion, 1973), 100.

6. WSP to Olga Rudge, 21 October 1930, ORP2–YCAL 54/1675.

7. Ibid., 21 and 30 October 1930. Olga Rudge to Ezra Pound, 2 November 1930, ORP1–YCAL 54/235, reprinted in Anne Conover, *Olga Rudge and Ezra Pound* (New Haven, Conn.; London: Yale University Press, 2001), 97.

8. WSP to Olga Rudge, two letters [undated, autumn 1931], ORP2–YCAL 54/1676.

9. WSP to Ezra Pound, undated, Ezra Pound Papers/ YCAL 43/1731; Olga Rudge, private diary, August–September 1934, ORP4/ YCAL 54/2675.

10. MBP, speech, "Homage" (1944), APEP.

11. *Le Figaro*, 9 May 1930.

12. *Le Figaro*, 14 January 1930.

13. Previously unpublished letter by Olga Rudge to Ezra Pound, ORP1–YCAL 54/263. This and all previously unpublished letters from Olga Rudge are copyright ©2003 by Mary de Rachewiltz and are used by permission of Mary de Rachewiltz.

14. Giorgio Levi, speech, "Homage" (1944), APEP.

15. Jérôme Spycket, *Nadia Boulanger* (Lausanne: Payot, 1987), 96–97.

16. "Les Concerts: L'Orchestre Poulet," *Le Figaro*, 17 November 1931; Olga Rudge to Ezra Pound, 21 November 1931, ORP1–YCAL 54/279.

17. Igor Markevitch, *Être et avoir été* (Paris: Gallimard, 1980), 222–23.

18. Colette refers to artist Luc-Albert Moreau and his wife, Hélène Jourdan-Morhange, both close friends of Ravel.

19. Francis Carco (1886–1958), a prolific realist writer, poet, and journalist between the two world wars (author of over one hundred works), took his characters from his adopted milieus of Pigalle, Clichy, and Montmartre. He was accepted into the Académie Goncourt after the success of his "Jésus La Caille."

20. Colette, *Lettres à ses pairs*, 346–47.

21. Élisabeth de Gramont, "Une Passion malheureuse," *La Revue de Paris* 19 (1 October 1931): 592–618.

22. Reynaldo Hahn's Piano Concerto (1930) received its first performance at the Théâtre des Champs-Élysées on 4 February 1931, with Magda Tagliaferro as soloist. The premiere was part of a grand gala concert given to benefit the "Charity for the Aged Musician," a retirement fund for older musicians. WSP and MBP were contributing members of the association. See *Le Gaulois*, 4 and 5 February 1931.

23. Vincent d'Indy to WSP, 27 November 1930, FSP.

24. Julien Green, *Journal 1928–1958* (Paris: Plon, 1961), 25 December 1930.

25. Laurence Benaïm, *Marie-Laure de Noailles: La vicomtesse du bizarre* (Paris: Grasset, 2001), 240–45.

26. The Dupuy family published more than a dozen periodicals devoted to world news, travel, sports, cinema, agriculture, gossip, science, children's comics, and weekend events.

27. Georges Sadoul, "Champagne et journaux d'enfants," *Commune* [date unknown], 1526–29.

28. "Matinée musicale chez la Princesse Edmond de Polignac," *Excelsior*, 1 July 1933.

29. "Les Concerts," *Le Figaro*, 10 June 1930.

30. Markevitch, *Être et avoir été*, 164.

31. Georges Mussy, "Les Concerts," *Le Figaro*, 19 December 1930.

32. WSP to IM, 13 December 1930, Fonds Markévitch, BNF-Mus.

33. Markevitch, *Être et avoir été*, 222–23.

34. WSP to Markevitch, 7 February 1931, Fonds Markévitch, BNF-Mus. WSP's contract with Markevitch required that the piano concerto should be dedicated to WSP, and that a manuscript of the full score and the piano reduction be given to her. The author's rights would belong to the composer, and the work could be sold to a publisher. The work's first performance should take place in the Polignac salon, with orchestral parts supplied by the composer, and it could not be performed for six months after that without WSP's permission.

35. Ibid.

36. WSP to IM, 1 April 1931, Fonds Markévitch, BNF-Mus.

37. IM to NB, 3 April 1931, APEP.

38. LMLV-F, 14 January 1931. The official nomination, in the Archives of the Grande Chancellerie de la Légion d'Honneur, Paris, includes the following itemization of WSP's charitable work: "In 1930 [she] gave 1,800,000 francs for the creation of the Cité de Refuge under the control of the Salvation Army; constructed with her own funds a housing project for workers; made a gift to the Université de Paris which will arrange to create a travel scholarship to permit a student to spend two months in Greece; gave an enormous sum to the Palais de la Femme, rue de Charonne, and had a pavilion constructed as a homeless shelter, rue des Cordelières."

39. WSP to Paul Valéry, 22 January 1931, BNF-Mss, MF 2800:246.

40. Claude Mignot-Ogliastri, *Anna de Noailles, une amie de la Princesse Edmond de Polignac* (Paris: Fondation Singer-Polignac and Méridiens-Klincksieck, 1986), 381.

41. ANo-Db, 7 May 1931, archives of Princesse Eugénie de Brancovan, communicated by Mignot-Ogliastri.

42. Previously unpublished letter by Olga Rudge to Ezra Pound, Monday [15 June 1931], ORP1–YCAL 54/263; Green, *Journal,* 22 June 1931, 35. WSP had loaned out Manet's *La Lecture* once before, for a London exhibition of "French Contemporary Decorative Art" that was to take place in 1914. According to a letter to WSP from the Galerie Bernheime Jeune, Paris, 27 June 1914 (private collection), the painting was valued for insurance purposes in 1914 at 30,000 francs.

43. Hindemith's Concerto would receive a second Paris performance later that year, on 28 October 1931, in a series of concerts sponsored by wealthy American patron Elizabeth Sprague Coolidge.

44. In 1894, Pleyel and Co. had invented a harp without pedals, having a set of white strings on the left for the natural notes and a set of black strings on the right for the sharps and flats.

45. This concert provides the only documentary evidence of a work of Strauss being performed in the Polignac salon.

46. Green, *Journal,* undated [early April 1931], 37.

47. LMLV-F, 2 April 1931.

48. Estimate from Georges Marie, administrator of the Orchestre Symphonique de Paris, for costs associated with a performance of Markevitch's *Partita* and a Brahms quintet (concert, rehearsals, instrument rental, and transportation, etc.), dated 12 May 1931, APEP.

49. The members of the École d'Arcueil included, besides Sauguet, Henri Cliquet-Pleyel, Roger Désormière, and Maxime Jacob.

50. FP to Comtesse Charles de Polignac, Thursday [13 August 1931], Fonds Colette, NAfr 18718:334; Francis Poulenc, *Correspondance, 1910–1963,* ed. Myriam Chimènes (Paris: Fayard, 1994), 343–44.

51. WSP to FP, 24 August 1931, in Poulenc, *Correspondance,* 344–45.

52. WSP to FP, 16 September 1931, ibid., 346 ; 1 October 1931, ibid., 346–47; Poulenc to Comtesse Charles de Polignac, Saturday [October 1931], NAfr 18718:336; Poulenc, *Correspondance,* 347–48.

53. WSP to FP, 1 October 1931, in Poulenc, *Correspondance,* 347–47.

54. WSP to Olga Rudge, 19 September 1931, ORP2–YCAL 54/1675; four un-dated letters [October 1931], ORP2–YCAL 54/1677.

55. WSP to Olga Rudge, 21 October 1931, ORP2–YCAL 54/1675.

56. Two previously unpublished letters by Olga Rudge to Ezra Pound, 24 July 1931, ORP1–YCAL 54/260. Pound's works, including an opera based on the writ-ings of François Villon, had been presented in concert in Paris during the 1920s.

57. WSP to Olga Rudge, 21 October 1931, ORP2–YCAL 54/1675.

58. Even though WSP had told Rudge in October 1930 that she could pay her "right away" for the summer rental of her house (21 October 1931, ORP2–YCAL 54/1675), she still hadn't paid the rent as of 19 November 1931 (previously unpub-lished letter by Olga Rudge to Ezra Pound, 19 November 1931, ORP1–YCAL 54/279).

59. WSP to Olga Rudge, undated [late November–early December 1931], ORP2–YCAL 54/1675.

60. MBP-PD, 11 December 1931, APEP.

61. Previously unpublished letter by Olga Rudge to Ezra Pound, 19 November 1931, ORP1–YCAL 54/279.

62. Ibid., 21 November 1931; ANo-Db [20 November 1931], archives of Princesse Eugénie de Brancovan, communicated by Mignot-Ogliastri.

63. MBP-PD, 25 November 1931, APEP.

64. WSP to FP, 1 October 1931, 25 November 1931, 4 December 1931, in Poulenc, *Correspondance,* 346–47.

65. ANo-Db [1 December 1931], archives of Princesse Eugénie de Brancovan, communicated by Mignot-Ogliastri; MBP-PD, 1 December 1931, APEP; LMLV-F, 4 December 1931.

66. ANo-Db [10 December 1931], archives of Princesse Eugénie de Brancovan, communicated by Mignot-Ogliastri.; LMLV-F, 4 December 1931. This advance notice of WSP's 11 December 1931 soiree, which mentions that "an orchestra of wind instruments would be heard," probably refers to Paris's eminent 'Ensemble d'Instruments à Vent,' which had performed frequently in WSP's salon.

67. Green, 11 December 1931, *Journal,* 60.

68. FP to Marie-Laure de Noailles, Saturday [12 December 1931], in Poulenc, *Correspondance,* 355.

69. WSP to FP, 19 December 1931, Archives Poulenc, communicated by Myriam Chimènes.

70. WSP refers (with an erroneous title) to Poulenc's 1918 song *Toréador,* on a text by Jean Cocteau, a work she particularly liked. In 1933 Poulenc would give the Princesse an autographed copy, with the inscription "with all my excuses, dear Princesse, for this 'Venice street,' barely conforming to that of your beautiful pal-ace, very faithfully, F. Poulenc 1933" (APEP).

71. WSP to FP, 4 December 1931, Archives Poulenc, communicated by Myriam Chimènes.

72. WSP to FP, 14 and 19 December 1931, ibid.

73. FP to Nora Auric, 12 January 1932, in Poulenc, *Correspondance*, 360–61.

74. The first public performance of Ravel's G-Major Piano Concerto was given by Marguerite Long, with Ravel conducting the Orchestre Lamoureux, at the Salle Pleyel on 14 January 1932. Poulenc was a new convert to the value of Ravel's music, which he had previously found cold and cerebral. His opinion changed when he heard the older composer's two piano concertos, written at approximately the same time that Poulenc was completing WSP's commission; he described the G-Major Concerto as "marvelous, stuffed with music with the verve of a 30–year-old musician" (Benjamin Ivry, *Maurice Ravel: A Life* [New York: Welcome Rain, 2000], 121–22).

75. Ernest Ansermet to WSP, 3 February 1931, FSP.

76. IS to WSP, 24 December 1931, FSP.

77. WSP to IS, 28 December 1931, PSS.

78. Georges Marie to IS, 29 December 1931, ibid.

79. IS to Georges Marie, 31 December 1931, PSS.

80. WSP to IS, 28 December 1931, PSS.

81. Myriam Chimènes, in Poulenc, *Correspondance*, 350, n.1, 351, n.1.

82. Publicity flyer for concerts by Katherine Heyman, pianist, January–February 1932, ORP1–YCAL 54/295.

83. Michel Duchesneau, *L'Avant-Garde musicale à Paris de 1871 à 1939* (Sprimont, Belgium: Pierre Mardaga, 1997), 133–42. Founded by Pierre-Octave Ferroud, Le Triton was governed by a large committee comprised exclusively of composers, including Florent Schmitt, Hindemith, Bartók, Casella, Schoenberg, and Stravinsky. They were among the few new music organizations in Paris that regularly presented first performances of works by German and Eastern European composers such as Martinu, Beck, and Bartók.

84. Yvonne de Casa Fuerte (1895–1984). Her husband, the Marquis Illan de Casa Fuerte, was one of Le Corbusier's most important private clients.

85. Duchesneau, *L'Avant-Garde musicale*, 123–32.

86. The other members of the founding committee of the Sérénade were MBP, Charles and Marie-Laure de Noailles, Comtesse Anne-Jules de Noailles, née Hélène de Wendel (ANo's daughter-in-law), Coco Chanel, Comte Étienne de Beaumont, David Weill, and Paul Goldschmidt.

87. In a previously unpublished letter to Ezra Pound, 22 February 1932, Olga Rudge noted among the audience members "[Natalie] Barney, the Clermont-Tonnerres, the Lancets, the Polignac tribe, minus Princesse, Picasso, Lifar etc. etc." ORP1–YCAL 54/304.

88. FP to Marie-Laure de Noailles, 14 February 1932, in Poulenc, *Correspondance*, 363.

89. Sonia Galperine, secretary of WSP, to IM, 12 January 1932, Fonds Markévitch, BNF-Mus.

90. Sonia Galperine to IM, 15 January 1932, ibid.

91. FP to Marie-Laure de Noailles, 14 February 1932, in Poulenc, *Correspondance*, 363.

92. WSP to IM, 21 May 1932, Fonds Markévitch, BNF-Mus.

93. WSP to FP, 12 April 1932, Archives Poulenc, communicated by Myriam Chimènes.

94. According to ANo-Db (Archives Princesse Eugénie de Brancovan, communi-

cated by Mignot-Ogliastri), ANo attended dinners at WSP's house on 5 and 17 January, and was present for the "Piano Fridays" on 15 January and 5 and 12 February 1932. The correspondence of MBP, APEP, mentions an additional soiree in the studio on 29 January 1932.

95. FP to Marie-Laure de Noailles, 14 February 1932, in Poulenc, *Correspondance,* 362–63.

96. Ibid.

97. Visiting card from MBP with a reminder of an appointment on 15 January 1932, ORP2–YCAL 54/1677; Sonia Galperine to Olga Rudge, 3 February 1932; WSP to Rudge, undated [10 February 1932], both items in ORP2–YCAL 54/1677

98. WSP to Olga Rudge, undated [6 February 1932], ibid.

99. Visiting card from the Princesse Edmond de Polignac, undated [February 1932], ibid.

100. Previously unpublished letter from Olga Rudge to Ezra Pound, undated [February 1932], ORP1–YCAL 54/301.

101. Ibid., 17 January 1932, ORP1–YCAL 54/295. The private showing of Cocteau's film *Le Sang d'un poète* took place on 20 January 1932; Rudge reported to Pound, "Cocteau film to me most beautiful."

102. WSP to Olga Rudge, undated [6 February 1932], ORP2–YCAL 54/1675. The Kolisch Quartet was known especially for its performances of contemporary string quartet repertoire. They gave first performances of, among others, the Arnold Schoenberg quartets. In an interview with Caroline Crawford (25 October 1989), Felix Khuner, the group's second violinist, recalled, "I would say that the best performances [of contemporary music] were played when we knew it was totally lost. Totally unwanted. I remember once we played the Lyric Suite in a private concert in Paris, and we knew it would be totally lost on the audience. We just did it because the hostess for some reason wanted it. It was the best performance we ever played! It was totally lost on everybody." *(http://www.khuner.com/history/)*

103. WSP to IM, 3 May 1932, Fonds Markévitch, BNF-Mus.

104. WSP to Comtesse Charles de Polignac, 15 May 1932, NAfr 18718:288–89. Menuhin's collaborative pianist for the 11 May recital was Arthur Balsam.

105. LMLV-F, 25 May 1932.

106. Mignot-Ogliastri, *Anna de Noailles,* 381.

107. ANo, autograph dedication to WSP inscribed in copy No. 1 of the first edition of *Exactitudes* (1930), APEP.

108. WSP to IM, 20 May 1932, Fonds Markévitch, BNF-Mus.

109. WSP to IM, 21 May 1932, ibid.

110. Previously unpublished letter from Olga Rudge to Ezra Pound, 30 May 1932, ORP1–YCAL 54/318. Markevitch would turn twenty in July 1932.

111. MBP-PD, 2 June 1932, APEP.

112. Markevitch, *Être et avoir été,* 227–28.

113. MBP-PD, 12 June 1932, APEP.

114. Henri Sauguet, *La Musique, ma Vie* (Paris: Librairie Séguer, 1990), 302.

115. Henry Prunières, "Chroniques et notes: 'Sérénade': Oeuvres de Berg, Sauguet, Poulenc, Milhaud," *La Revue musicale* 14, no. 134 (March 1933): 211–12.

116. MBP-PD, 15 June 1932, APEP.

117. *The Times of London,* 25 and 27 June 1932; *Le Figaro,* 25 June 1932.

118. Arthur Rubinstein, *My Many Years* (New York: Knopf, 1980), 322.

Rubinstein wrote, "The only person who did not give us anything was Princess Winnie de Polignac, but she invited us to spend a few weeks in Venice at her palazzo."

119. MBP-PD, September 1932, APEP.

120. Francis Poulenc, *My Friends and Myself,* trans. James Harding (London: Dennis Dobson, 1978), 90–91.

121. Ibid., 88–89.

122. Elsa Maxwell, *I Married the World* (London: The Quality Book Club, 1956), 14.

123. FP to Marie-Laure de Noailles, 10 August 1932, in Poulenc, *Correspondance,* 372.

124. WSP, "Memoirs of the Late Princesse Edmond de Polignac," *Horizon* 12, no. 68 (August 1945): 136.

125. WSP to Manuel de Falla, 5 October 1932, AMF.

126. Henry Prunières, "Le Festival de Venise," *La Revue musicale* (November 1932): 312–17.

127. The gamelan is a Southeast Asian musical ensemble. Indonesian and Malaysian gamelans include gongs, gong-chimes, metallophones, and drums; Javanese and Balinese gamelans include zither-like instruments, reed instruments, and bamboo rattles.

128. Claude Rostand, *Francis Poulenc: Entretiens avec Claude Rostand* (Paris: Julliard, 1954), 82.

129. MBP-PD, September 1932, APEP.

130. MF to WSP, 15 March 1925 (rough draft), AMF.

131. WSP to MF, 21 January 1928, AMF.

132. Jaime Pahissa et al., *Vida y obra de Manuel de Falla,* 2nd ed. (Ricordi: Buenos Aires, 1956), 132–33.

133. Falla, "Two extracts From *El Retablo de Maese Pedro,*" ms, BMFP.

134. WSP to Olga Rudge, 24 October 1932, ORP2–YCAL 54/1675.

135. WSP to Comtesse Charles de Polignac, undated [mid-October 1932], ibid., 292–93.

136. WSP to Comtesse Charles de Polignac, 3 October 1932, NAfr 18718:290–91.

137. "Les Concerts," *Le Figaro,* 28 December 1932; Suzanne Demarquez, "'Ouverture' de Germaine Tailleferre (OSP)," *La Revue musicale* 14, no. 133 (February 1933): 133.

138. WSP to IM, 5 October 1932, Fonds Markévitch, BNF-Mus.

139. WSP to IM, 14 and 17 November 1932, ibid. Although WSP does not mention outright a fee of ten thousand francs for Markevitch's new work, she refers to "installments" of twenty-five hundred francs to be paid on 1 December 1932, 1 January and 1 February 1933. As keeping with past practice, the final payment would presumably have been reserved until delivery of the manuscript.

140. IM to NB, 2 February 1933, NLa 83.

141. Henry Prunières, "Chroniques et notes: Oeuvres de Kurt Weill," *La Revue musicale* 14, no. 132 (January 1933): 45–47.

142. Kurt Weill to Lotte Lenya, 27 January 1930, in Kurt Weill and Lotte Lenya, *Speak Low (When You Speak Love),* ed. and trans. Lys Symonette and Kim H. Kowalke (Berkeley: University of California Press, 1996), 59.

143. According to Virgil Thomson (Virgil Thomson [New York: Da Capo Press,

1966], 225), the performance of *Mahagonny* was a forty-minute version of the complete opera created specially for Paris.

144. Kurt Weill to Universal Editions (Alfred Kalmus), 26 August 1932, KWF, reprinted in *Kurt Weill: Briefwechsel mit der Universal Edition,* ed. Nils Grosch (Stuttgart: J.B. Metzler, 2002), 411.

145. Weill and Lenya, *Speak Low,* 71.

146. Universal Editions (Alfred Kalmus) to Kurt Weill, 29 October 1932, KWF, reprinted in *Kurt Weill: Briefwechsel,* 416. Although the letter indicates that there was some question of WSP being asked to finance a Paris revival of *Threepenny Opera,* the project apparently never came to pass.

147. Kurt Weill to Alfred Kalmus, Universal Editions, 7 December 1932, KWF, reprinted in *Kurt Weill: Briefwechsel,* 417.

148. Weill mentions to Lenya in a letter of 29 November 1932 that "La Polignac has already paid me 5,000 francs" (*Speak Low,* 105). As WSP customarily paid one-quarter of the commission price at the time that the agreement was signed, it can reasonably be assumed that the total payment would have been twenty thousand francs.

149. "L'Homme du jour," feature article on Kurt Weill and *Mahagonny* from an unknown newspaper, early December 1932, in a scrapbook in the APEP.

150. Henry Prunières, "Chronique et notes: Oeuvres de Kurt Weill," *La Revue musicale* 14, no. 132 (January 1933): 45–47.

151. On 12 April 1932, *Le Figaro* ran a front-page article by François Coty, "The Financiers Who Rule the World"; two other articles in the same issue addressed "The Legitimate Anxiety of Pacifistic Jews" and "Exiles and the Insolence of Terrorist Jews." On 16 April a third article appeared, "The Dynasty That Is Rising Up in Israel."

152. Stan Golestan, "Les Concerts," *Le Figaro,* 19 December 1932.

Chapter 14

1. Samuel Dushkin had provided IS with technical assistance during the composition of Stravinsky's Violin Concerto; he subsequently played the premiere performances of the work in 1931.

2. Stephen Walsh, *Stravinsky: A Creative Spring: Russia and France, 1882–1934* (New York: Knopf, 1999), 511.

3. WSP to IM, 14 November 1932, Fonds Markévitch, BNF-Mus.

4. IM to NB, undated [November 1932], APEP.

5. NB-Db, October–December 1932, BNF-Mus, VmF ms 98/ 4–5.

6. For further insight into the history of women contestants for the Prix de Rome, see Annegret Fauser, "*La Guerre en dentelles*: Women and the Prix de Rome in French Cultural Politics," *Journal of the American Musicological Society* 51, no. 1 (Spring 1998): 83–129.

7. "Les Concerts," *Le Figaro,* 10 January 1908.

8. Printed program, PSS, with a note in Stravinsky's hand: "Nos concerts-duos avec Duschkin le 7 & 8 dec 1932 à Paris 1.) chez la Princesse de Polignac et 2.) à la Salle Pleyel."

9. WSP to IS, telegrams, 22 November 1932, PSS.

10. Valfleury, LMLV-F, 9 December 1932.

11. "Courrier des théâtres," *Le Figaro,* 7 December 1932; Henry Prunières, "Chroniques et notes: Concert Igor Stravinsky," *La Revue musicale* 14, no. 133 (February 1933): 129.

12. NB, Db, 14 December 1932, ibid; WSP to NB, 15 December 1932, NLa 94:196b.

13. MBP-PD, 23 February 1933, APEP.

14. Ibid.

15. WSP to NB, 23 December 1932, NLa 94:196c.

16. Poulenc had enclosed a note with the manuscript, dated 31 December 1932: "Dear Princesse, upon returning to Paris I finally found the first proofs of the Concerto [waiting for me]. I hasten to send you the manuscript, now free [to give to you]. Excuse the engravers who left a few dirty marks, and the musician who had wanted to do even better. See you this evening, and accept, dear Princesse, my respectful and grateful affection. Francis" (APEP, reprinted in Francis Poulenc, *Correspondance, 1910–1963,* ed. Myriam Chimènes [Paris: Fayard, 1994], 379).

17. NB-Db, January–March 1933, BNF-Mus, VmF ms 99/1. A complimentary ticket for the 22 January 1933 concert of the SMI , left for WSP by NB, is in the APEP.

18. WSP to NB, 6 January 1933, NLa 94:196.

19. Georges Marie to IS, 19 January and 8 February 1933, PSS.

20. WSP to IS, 9 January 1933, PSS.

21. WSP to IS, 5 February 1933, ibid.

22. IS to WSP, undated [mid-February 1933], NLa 94:200.

23. WSP to NB, 15 February 1933, NLa 94, 197–98.

24. NB to IS, 25 February 1933, PSS.

25. IS to NB, rough draft of telegram text, 27 February 1933, PSS. A second, slightly different rough draft concludes "Moreover, have written several times."

26. Georges Marie to IS, 28 February 1933, PSS; MBP-PD, undated entry [March 1933], APEP.

27. Georges Marie to WSP, 4 March 1933, NLa 94:202.

28. Colette to PP, undated [late February 1933], NAfr 18718:7. A *galette* is a round, flat cake made out of puff pastry; ambrosia is hot Beaujolais wine spiced with cinnamon, lemon, and sugar.

29. WSP to NB, undated [probably 5 March 1933], NLa 94:202; NB-Db, 4 March 1933, BNF-Mus, VmF ms 99/ 1. There are no scores of Frescobaldi or Buxtehude in the BMFP.

30. WSP to NB, 15 February 1933, NLa 94, 197–98, and undated [5 March 1933], NLa 94:202.

31. NB-Db, 25 February 1933, BNF-Mus, VmF ms 99/ 1.

32. WSP to NB, undated [5 March 1933], NLa 94:202.

33. MBP-PD, undated entry [March 1933], APEP.

34. "Markevitch massacred his *Partita,*" noted MBP in her diary, ibid.

35. Henry Prunières, "Chroniques et notes: Concert des oeuvres dédiées à la Princesse Edmond de Polignac," *La Revue musicale* 14, no. 135 (April 1933): 283–84.

36. Princesse Audrey Illinska, née Emery, was an American-born heiress and the wife of the handsome but borderline mentally impaired Grand-Duke Dimitri, who had been the co-assassin of Rasputin and the lover of Coco Chanel.

37. WSP, "Memoirs of the Late Princesse Edmond de Polignac," *Horizon* 12, no. 68 (August 1945): 178; MBP-PD, March 1933, APEP.

38. WSP, "Memoirs," 178.

39. British writer Rosamond Lehmann, in correspondence with James Lees-Milne, wrote that Trefusis, "so destructive, so egomaniac, and so idiotic," had made "an attempt on my virtue," and that she "was rescued from her clutches by Winnie de Polignac. . . . I never saw Violet Trefusis again." James Lees-Milne papers, Yale University Library, Gen Mss 476, folders 457 and 458, and by permission of the Society of Authors (London).

40. WSP to PP, 28 March 1933, NAfr 18718:331.

41. Virginia Woolf, in a letter to Vita Sackville-West, late December 1932, relates that Violet Trefusis had just sent her a "vast" bunch of lilacs, perhaps in an attempt to make both WSP and Sackville-West jealous. "No," Woolf assured Sackville-West, "I'm not spending the New Year between her and Mme. de Polignac. I wave the banner of chastity." In *The Letters of Virginia Woolf,* ed. Nigel Nicolson (New York: Harcourt, Brace, Jovanovitch, 1979–80), 5:147–48.

42. Philippe Jullian and John Phillips, *Violet Trefusis: A Biography* (San Diego: Harcourt, Brace, 1976), 69; Henrietta Sharpe, *A Solitary Woman: A Life of Violet Trefusis* (London: Constable, 1981), 85–86.

43. MBP-PD, undated entry [Spring 1933], APEP.

44. Ibid. Markevitch's ballet *Rebus* and Françaix's orchestrations of Boccherini arias were performed by the Ballets Russes in their 1933 season. MBP described new productions of the Ballets Russes de Monte Carlo, now under the direction of Comte Étienne de Beaumont, as "execrable."

45. WSP to NB, 14 April 1933, NLa 94:206; MBP-PD, undated entry [April 1933], APEP.

46. MBP, ibid.

47. Claude Mignot-Ogliastri, *Anna de Noailles, une amie de la Princesse Edmond de Polignac* (Paris: Fondation Singer-Polignac and Méridiens-Klincksieck, 1986), 381.

48. NB-Db, 3 May 1933, BNF-Mus, VmF ms 99/2.

49. Jeanice Brooks, "Nadia Boulanger and the Salon of the Princesse de Polignac," in *Journal of the American Musicological Society* 46, no. 3 (Fall 1993): 415–68. The article explores the professional ramifications of NB's friendship with WSP on her career as a pedagogue and conductor.

50. NB as quoted in Bruno Monsaingeon, *Mademoiselle,* trans. Robyn Marsack (Manchester: Carcanet, 1985), 92.

51. François Olivier to NB, 21 March 1933, NLa 91:315.

52. WSP to François Olivier, 22 March 1933, NLa 91:314b; François Olivier to NB, 22 March 1933, ibid., 314.

53. NB-Db, 22 March 1933, BNF-Mus, VmF ms 99/2.

54. WSP to NB, 15 February 1933, NLa 94:197.

55. MBP-PD, undated entry [May 1933], APEP.

56. NB-Db, May and June 1933, BNF-Mus, VmF ms 99/2. In addition to WSP's attendance of Wednesday cantata classes (3, 10, 17, 24, and 31 May, 7 and 14 June), NB's datebook notes meetings and/or meals with WSP on 6 May, 13 May (Jouy), 3 June, and 9 June 1933.

57. NB-Db, 30 April 1933, ibid; WSP to IM, 5 May 1933, Fonds Markévitch, BNF-Mus.

58. In a datebook (Collection Sauguet, Paris; information communicated by Bruno Berenguer), Henri Sauguet noted that the program in honor of Anna de Noailles performed in the Polignac salon on 23 May 1933 also included the Paris premiere of Gavriil Popov's Septet (later renamed *Chamber Symphony*). The following evening, 24 May 1933, the Sérénade's seventh concert at the Salle Gaveau included performances of Satie's *Socrate*, sung by Mme. F. Holnay, voice, conducted by Roger Désormière; the rest of the program consisted of Nabokov's *Fanfare* (first performance), Popov's Septet, Rieti's *Tableaux de cinéma,* and Milhaud's *La Mort du tyran, poème dansé.* It is possible, therefore, that the program in the Polignac salon was, in effect, a dress rehearsal for the Sérénade concert, but whether the works by Nabokov, Rieti, and Milhaud were also performed on that occasion cannot be ascertained.

59. NB-Db, 23 May 1933, ibid; MBP-Db, 23 May 1933, APEP. The singer for the *Socrate* performance is not identified by either woman.

60. WSP to IM, 5 January 1933, Fonds Markévitch, BNF-Mus.

61. WSP to IM, 19 May 1933, ibid. One week later, after meeting with Markevitch on 26 May, WSP wrote to the composer that the arrangements for the participation of the OSP for the performance of *Hymnes* had been confirmed with Georges Marie, and that she would be paying the OSP's fee of sixty-five hundred francs. Presumably the manuscript had been handed over to WSP that afternoon, for her note indicated that she was sending Markevitch a check for fifteen hundred francs (WSP to IM, 26 May 1933, ibid.).

62. Editors' note in Kurt Weill and Lotte Lenya, *Speak Low (When You Speak Love),* ed. and trans. Lys Symonette and Kim H. Kowalke (Berkeley: University of California Press, 1996), 79.

63. During his six weeks in Paris in May–June 1933, Arnold Schoenberg renounced his Christian faith and returned to Judaism.

64. An undated card from WSP in the Archives of the Arnold Schönberg Center announces that "The Princesse de Polignac will be at home, Friday, 9 June [1933], at 10:15."

65. NB-Db, 9 June 1933, BNF-Mus, VmF ms 99/2; MBP-Db, 9 June 1933, APEP.

66. FP to IM, undated letter [late May 1933], in Poulenc, *Correspondance,* 387. The first public performance of Markevitch's *Hymnes* was presented under the auspices of *La Revue musicale;* the composer's *L'Envol d'Icare* was presented on the same program. The concert was an enormous success: Milhaud called *L'Envol d'Icare* "a milestone in the development of music"; the renown brought to Markevitch by the event resulted in his being called by many "the second Igor" (Igor Markevitch, *Être et avoir été* [Paris: Gallimard, 1980], 111).

67. WSP to IM, 9 May 1933, Fonds Markévitch, BNF-Mus.

68. NB-Db, 10, 13, and 14 June 1933, BNF-Mus, VmF ms 99/2.

69. The manuscript of Nabokov's *Job* is dated "Kolbsheim, 31. III. 33," APEP. There is no dedication inscribed.

70. Maria Modrakowska (1896–1965) was a multifaceted musician and Polish woman of letters. A scientist as well as pianist and singer, she had come to Paris in 1931 specifically to study the Bach cantatas with NB and French song literature with Claire Croiza. She is the dedicatee of the eighth of Poulenc's *Huit Chansons populaires polonaises.*

71. Brooks, in an appendix to "Nadia Boulanger," mistakenly identifies this concert as having taken place in 1934.

72. NB-Db, 17 June 1933, BNF-Mus, VmF ms 99/2.

73. The manuscript of Vivaldi's D-Minor Organ Concerto, arranged by Nadia Boulanger, is in the BMFP.

74. MBP-PD, undated entry [June 1933], APEP.

75. David Schiff, *The Music of Elliott Carter* (New York: Da Capo Press, 1985), 215.

76. Printed program of 30 June 1933 concert in WSP's salon, APEP; MBP-PD, undated entry [June 1933], APEP.

77. "Matinée musicale chez la Princesse Edmond de Polignac," *Excelsior*, 1 July 1933, 1.

78. LMLV-F, 1 July 1933.

79. Colette to WSP, undated [June 1933], private collection.

80. WSP to PP, 17 July 1933, NAfr 18718:293.

81. NB-Db, 3–10 July 1933, BNF-Mus, VmF ms 99/3. The entries mention social events that included, among others, David Ponsonby, the Marquise de Chomondeley, Audrey Parr, Lord Berners, Francis Poulenc, and Jacques Février.

82. NB, as quoted in Monsaingeon, *Mademoiselle*, 91.

83. David Ponsonby to NB, 10 July 1933, NLa 94:379.

84. WSP to PP, 17 July 1933, NAfr 18718:293.

85. Jérôme Spycket, *Nadia Boulanger* (Lausanne: Payot, 1987), 121.

86. IM to WSP, 26 December 1933, FSP.

87. WSP to IM, 17 July 1933, Fonds Markévitch, BNF-Mus.

88. IM to NB, 22 July 1933, NLa 83.

89. WSP to NB, 13 October 1933, NLa 94:214.

90. NB-Db, 17–22 and 30 July, 6, 7, 10, and 11 August 1933, BNF-Mus, VmF ms 99/3.

91. NB-Db, 22 July 1933, ibid.; Jean Françaix to NB, 10 July 1933, NLa 71, 64. The Pasquier brothers were the preeminent string trio of the period. NB's datebook also mentions the presence of a "Horodjski" at the gathering, following the name of Schubert; this may have been a misspelled reference to the pianist Mieczyslaw Horszowski.

92. WSP to NB, 28 July 1933, NLa 94:210.

93. NB-Db, 6 August 1933, BNF-Mus, VmF ms 99/3.

94. WSP to NB, 14 August 1933, NLa 94:212.

95. WSP to PP, 12 September 1933, NAfr 18718:295.

96. Marguerite Long de Marliave to WSP, undated [September 1933], FSP.

97. WSP to Olga Rudge, 6 and 15 September 1933, ORP2–YCAL54, 1676.

98. Previously unpublished letter from Olga Rudge to Ezra Pound, 21 September 1933, ORP1–YCAL 54/358. Emphasis in original.

99. Anne Conover, *Olga Rudge & Ezra Pound* (New Haven: Yale University Press, 2001), 116.

100. WSP to FP, 24 September 1933, Archives Poulenc, communicated by Mryiam Chimènes.

101. NB-Db, 4 September 1933, BNF-Mus, VmF ms 99/3.

102. WSP to NB, 23 October 1933, NLa 94, 217–18 and 219; this last piece is a detailed estimate of the changes to the organ and the estimate for the work, which came to a total of 11,500 francs.

103. WSP to NB, 13 October 1933, NLa 94:214.

104. WSP to NB, 3 November 1933, NLa 94:221.

105. NB, as quoted in Montsaingeon, *Mademoiselle,* 99.

106. WSP to PP, undated [late October 1933], NAfr 18718:323.

107. Glenn Plaskin, *Horowitz* (New York: Quill, 1983), 163. Plaskin gives the official date of the engagement of Horowitz to Wanda Toscanini as 8 October 1933. They married in December 1933.

108. WSP to NB, 23 October 1933, NLa 94:217.

109. WSP to PP, undated [23–25 October 1933], NAfr 18718:324.

110. Alfredo Casella to WSP, 27 October 1933, NLa 94:199b.

111. WSP to NB, 3 November 1933, NLa 94:221.

112. WSP to Olga Rudge, 9 November [1933], ORP2–YCAL 54/1676.

113. WSP to Ezra Pound, undated [November 1933], Ezra Pound Papers, YCAL 43/1731, reprinted in Conover, *Olga Rudge & Ezra Pound,* 116. Pound took WSP's comment about not having time to dress as a hint that she didn't want to be invited to dinner afterwards (previously unpublished letter from Pound to Rudge, 11 November 1933, ORP1, YCAL 54/353).

114. Ezra Pound to WSP, previously unpublished photocopy of an unsigned typed letter, undated [presumably 11 November 1933], YCAL 53/350.

115. Ibid. For the performance of a Corelli trio sonata, Rudge and Münch were joined by violinist-conductor Luigi Sansone and cellist Marco Ottone.

116. Previously unpublished letter from Ezra Pound to WSP, 30 November 1933, Ezra Pound Papers, YCAL 43/1731.

117. Commissioner Albin Peyron to WSP, 24 February 1933, private collection.

118. Brian Brace Taylor, *Le Corbusier: The City of Refuge, 1929–33* (Chicago: University of Chicago Press, 1987), ix–x.

119. Le Corbusier to WSP, 4 December 1934, FLC, J2/5.

120. Ibid.

121. The Cité de Refuge, at the corner of rue Cantagrel and rue Chevaleret, in the southeast quadrant of the 13ᵗʰ *arrondissement,* still functions as a shelter operated by the Salvation Army.

122. Henri Sauguet to WSP, 11 December 1933, NLa 94:225.

123. Kurt Weill to Lotte Lenya, 8 December 1933, in Weill and Lenya, *Speak Low,* 105–7. In an earlier letter dated 29 November 1933, ibid., 104–5, Weill wrote that "La Polignac has already paid me 5000 francs." Presumably the second payment brought the total to an amount approximating 7000 francs.

124. Kurt Weill to WSP, 15 December 1933, FSP.

125. The manuscript of Kurt Weill's Symphony No. 2 is housed in the BMFP.

126. LMLV-F, 16 December 1933; Ezra Pound to Olga Rudge, "care of Madame la Princesse de Polignac," 11 December 1933, Ezra Pound Papers Addition, YCAL 53/364.

127. MBP-Db, 16 December 1933, and MBP-PD, 1934, APEP. The Sérénade program also included works by Sauguet, Prokofiev, Hindemith (the premiere of his Trio for Viola, Saxophone, and Piano), Poulenc's Sextet in its revised version, and the premiere of Milhaud's Suite for Ondes Martenot, played by Martenot and Jacques Février.

128. A manuscript of Georges Auric's *Alphabet* is housed in the BMFP; dated 31 December 1933, it is dedicated to Marie-Blanche de Polignac "in memory of her admirable performance the other night."

129. MBP-PD, 1934, APEP. MBP wrote modestly about her success at the Sérénade. "Nadia and Francis, and everyone, I should say, complimented me. In any case, even if my voice was small (I knew well that it was nothing remarkable in terms of beauty, strength, or range), what I did was simple and musical." APEP.

130. Guy de Pourtalès, "Musique: Nouveautés," press clipping from an unnamed newspaper, in a scrapbook in the APEP.

131. WSP to NB, undated [mid-December 1933], NLa 94:224.

132. MBP-PD, "January 1934," APEP. Her appreciation of NB's sparing use of rubato recalls NB's own remark on Toscanini, cited on p. 000.

133. Typed program of WSP's salon concert, 8 January 1934, APEP; "Réceptions," *Excelsior,* 11 January 1934.

134. Printed program of WSP's salon concert, 21 January 1934, APEP; "Réceptions," *Excelsior,* 22 January 1934.

135. *The Times of London,* 12 February 1934.

136. WSP to NB, 16 February 1934, NLa 94:229–30.

137. Kurt Weill to Lotte Lenya, 20 February 1934, in Weill and Lenya, *Speak Low,* 111–12.

138. Ibid., 26 February 1934, ibid., 113–14.

139. On 24 May 1934, Kurt Weill wrote to Lotta Lenya "Tomorrow [Friday, 25 May 1934] I'm invited to La Polignac's," making no mention of money (*Speak Low,* 128–29).

140. Cecil Blunt was born Blumenthal; his Jewish birth created a formidable obstacle when he sought to marry the niece of a pope. The solution was found to abbreviate Blumenthal to Blunt, and the pope gave Blumenthal the title of Conte Pecci-Blunt. This did not ameliorate all the couple's problems, however: Mimi Pecci was obliged to see Mussolini to ask for his permission to marry her daughter to an Italian prince.

141. WSP to NB, 27 February 1934, NLa 94:232; Giorgio Levi to WSP, undated [late February 1934], ibid., 233. Levi had written that "Markevitch's *Psaumes* made a great impression on me—an extraordinarily interesting and troubling work. Françaix's Trio is pleasing and elegant."

142. MBP-PD, undated entry [1933], APEP. MBP refers to Comtesse Marie d'Agoult, Franz Lizst's wife, and their daughter Cosima, who became Richard Wagner's second wife. Both women had left their husbands for these musicians and lived with them out of wedlock; both bore the composers' illegitimate children.

143. MBP-PD, 1934, APEP.

144. IM to NB, 13 March 1934, NLa 83:111.

145. WSP to NB, 3 March 1934, NLa 94:237.

146. WSP to Olga Rudge, ORP2–YCAL 54/1676.

147. Stravinsky, in Vera Stravinsky and Robert Craft, *Stravinsky in Pictures and Documents* (New York: Simon and Schuster, 1978), 299, claimed that a runthrough of *Persephone* took place in WSP's studio; he recalled "groaning [the choruses] at the piano," while Gide bridled at the unorthodox setting of his text. However, Walsh, in *Stravinsky,* 532, asserts that the composer recalled the location incorrectly, and that it in fact took place but in Ida Rubinstein's apartment in the place des États-Unis.

148. WSP to NB, 4 May 1934, NLa 94:239.

149. MBP-PD, 1934, APEP.

150. Igor Stravinsky, *An Autobiography* (New York: The Norton Library, 1962), 173; Walsh, *Stravinsky*, 535–36; Robert Brussel, "Les Ballets Ida Rubinstein," *Le Figaro*, 2 May 1934. Brussel wrote that "The music that M. Stravinsky has written is neither the best nor the worst that he has composed, but it reveals, in its harshness, in its obvious impoverishment, in its contempt for charm, an incontestable grandeur."

151. WSP to IS, 13 May 1934, PSS.

152. According to Cossart's source notes, Doda Conrad spoke to him in a 1975 interview about a performance of *Pierrot Lunaire* that was to take place with Freund and Scherchen in WSP's studio. In *Dodascalies* (Arles: Actes Sud, 1998), 124–26, however, Conrad writes that Henry Gouïn was to have hosted the performance.

153. Conrad, *Dodascalies*, 124–26.

154. Jean Roger-Ducasse (1873–1954), composer and educator, was a pupil of Fauré's and the 1902 Prix de Rome winner. Joaquin Nin (1879–1949), Spanish composer, pianist, and musicologist, studied at the Schola Cantorum, where in 1906 he was appointed professor of piano. Nin did important work in the field of Spanish musicology.

155. LMLV-F, 17 May 1934. Among his other colleagues from Les Six, Honegger had been the most successful (up to this point) in establishing an international reputation as a modernist composer; he was also one of the first French composers to follow the revolutionary example of Ravel in creating a new style of prosody in the setting of French texts.

156. Printed program of WSP's 17 May 1934 salon concert, APEP.

157. Julien Green, *Journal 1928–1958* (Paris: Plon, 1961), 17 May 1934, 165.

158. MBP-PD, 1934, APEP.

159. Maurice Paléologue to WSP, 19 May 1934, NLa 94:244.

160. Printed program of NB's concert at the École Normale de Musique, 13 February 1934, APEP.

161. Brooks, "Nadia Boulanger," 433–34.

162. Ibid.

163. Ibid., 436.

164. MBP-PD, 1934, APEP.

165. Marcelle de Manziarly to MBP, 14 August 1934, APEP. The following year, Marcelle de Manziarly wrote a song cycle for solo voice, *Trois Fables de La Fontaine*, specifically for MBP. This work and the *Trois Duos* are housed in the BMFP. The two works were performed as part of an all-Manziarly concert at the Revue musicale, 14 June 1935, performed by MBP, Irène Kédroff, and the Quintette Instrumental de Paris (printed program, APEP).

166. Ibid.

167. Printed program of NB's concert at the École Normale de Musique, 14 June 1934, APEP.

168. The manuscripts by Françaix and Schulé, and a photocopy of the manuscript of the Manziarly, are housed in the BMFP.

169. MBP-PD, undated entry, 1934, APEP.

170. MBP-PD, undated entry, 1934, APEP.

171. Brooks, "Nadia Boulanger," 434–36. On the manuscript of Françaix's *Trois Duos* (BMFP), MBP noted the following performances of the work: "École Normale Juin 1934, Cercle Interallié, 3 Décembre 1934, chez tante Winnie [17] Janvier 1935."

172. Brooks, "Nadia Boulanger," 434–36.

173. Printed program of WSP's concert in Jouy-en-Josas, 17 June 1934, APEP.

174. MBP-PD, undated entry, 1934, APEP.

175. WSP to PP, 12 September 1933, NAfr 18718:295.

176. WSP to MBP, 13 July 1934, APEP.

177. WSP to MBP, 13 July 1934, and to JP and MBP, 2 August 1934, APEP.

178. WSP to MBP, undated [late November 1934], APEP.

179. WSP to NB, 21 September 1934, NLa 94:251–54.

180. Olga Rudge, private diary, August–September 1934, ORP4/ YCAL 54/2675; reprinted in Conover, *Olga Rudge & Ezra Pound*, 115–17.

181. Conover, *Olga Rudge & Ezra Pound*, 117.

182. LMLV-F, 20 September 1934; Olga Rudge-PD, August–September 1934, ORP4/ YCAL 54/2675, reprinted in *Olga Rudge & Ezra Pound*, 119.

183. Leone Sinigaglia (1868–1944), Italian modernist composer. He had a second claim to fame: he climbed the Matterhorn in 1890.

184. Henri Büsser (1872–1973), French conductor and composer in the nineteenth-century tradition. His output included nine operas. From 1931 he was professor of composition at the Conservatoire, where his students included Henri Dutilleux and Marcel Landowski. Büsser made an extended study of the history of the organ in French music.

185. WSP to NB, 22 September 1934, NLa 94:250.

186. Guido Bianchini, speech, "Homage" (1944), APEP.

187. On 22 September 1934, WSP wrote to JP and MBP (APEP), that she was going to Cortina on "Wednesday," that is, 26 September 1934.

188. Ibid.

189. WSP to MBP, 9 October 1934, APEP.

190. Olga Rudge, private diary, August–September 1934, ORP4/ YCAL 54/2675; reprinted in Conver, *Olga Rudge & Ezra Pound*, 119.

191. WSP to NB, 22 September 1934, APEP. WSP's remark about Strauss's opera is her only extant written commentary on the composer's work.

192. Ibid.

193. Duc Élie Decazes, INT, 24 August 1994.

194. "Le Dollar américain," *Le Figaro,* 17 November 1933.

195. "M. Roosevelt et ses ennemis," *Le Figaro,* 22 December 1933.

196. WSP to NB, 21 September 1934, NLa 94:253.

197. WSP to FP, 16 September 1934, in Poulenc, *Correspondance,* 397–98.

198. Ibid.

199. NB to FP, September 1934, in Poulenc, *Correspondance,* 398. NB's use of the word "drawbacks" (*défauts*) is interesting. In a letter to the author, 7 February 2002, Cavaillé-Coll organ expert Dr. Carolyn Shuster-Fournier surmises that the limitations alluded to by NB are perhaps of an aesthetic nature, referring to the lack of certain neoclassical stops (mutation stops) that appeared in house organs at the beginning of the twentieth century. According to Shuster-Fournier, WSP's organ was a symphonic instrument that contained several solo reed stops, but no mutation stops.

200. WSP to NB, 23 September 1934, NLa 94:255–56.

201. WSP to NB, 6 October 1934, NLa 94:257–58; WSP to PP, 11 October 1934, NAfr 18718:301. WSP wrote to PP that "Jean Françaix is writing a work for

me, and wants to see my organ. Would you please telephone Nadia to tell her that he can go to see the organ whenever he pleases."

202. WSP to NB, 6 October 1934, NLa 94:257.

203. WSP to PP, 28 October 1934, NAfr 18718:304.

204. Kurt Weill to Lotte Lenya, undated [10 October 1934], in Weill and Lenya, *Speak Low,* 145.

205. Kurt Weill to Maurice Abravanel, 21 January 1935, Weill and Lenya, *Speak Low,* 145, n. 2.

206. Kurt Weill to Lotte Lenya, 10 October 1934, Weill and Lenya, in *Speak Low,* 145. On the eve of the premiere, Weill wrote, "Walter does [the Symphony] marvelously and everyone is really enthusiastic, especially the entire orchestra! . . . The people here are absolutely crazy about me—interviews, etc."

207. Henri Monnet, "Une Symphonie de Kurt Weil [*sic*] à Amsterdam," *Marianne,* 14 November 1934.

208. WSP to NB, 21 September 1934, NLa 94:251.

Chapter 15

1. News clipping from *Vendémiaire,* signed "Snob," reprinted in Jeanice Brooks, "Nadia Boulanger and the Salon of the Princesse de Polignac," in *Journal of the American Musicological Society* 46, no. 3 (Fall 1993): 437.

2. Writer and journalist Jean Desbordes was Jean Cocteau's next great love after the death of Raymond Radiguet in 1923. An unexceptional writer and a fellow opium-smoker, Desbordes remained with Cocteau until marrying his pharmacist in 1937. Active in the Resistance during World War II, he was tortured and killed by the Nazis in 1944.

3. Jean Desbordes, "Grandes Dames de Paris," *Paris-Midi,* 16 October 1934.

4. WSP, quoted in Desbordes, "Grandes Dames de Paris."

5. Typed program of WSP's salon concert, 17 January 1935, APEP; LMLV-F, 21 January 1935; "News of Americans in Europe," *New York Herald,* 19 January 1935.

6. WSP to NB, 18 January 1935, NLa 94, 266. The Boulanger Ensemble repeated its performance of the Schütz *Auferstehungs-Historie* at the Salle Gaveau in March 1935.

7. WSP to Ezra Pound, undated [late January or early February 1935], Ezra Pound Papers Addition, YCAL 14/350.

8. Previously unpublished letter from Ezra Pound to WSP, undated [March 1935], Ezra Pound Papers, YCAL 43/1731. Pound calls Bartók's opera *The Wonderful Mandarin.*

9. Clifford Curzon (1907–1982) was one of the greatest British pianists of the twentieth century. He was a specialist in the repertoire of Mozart, Beethoven, Schubert, Brahms, and Schumann.

10. WSP to PP, 8 February 1935, NAfr 18718:333; printed program of WSP's salon program, 28 February 1935, APEP.

11. Ibid.

12. LMLV-F, 25 January 1935, 2.

13. Pericles Argyropoulos to WSP, 13 February 1935, private collection.

14. WSP to NB, 15 March 1935, NLa 94:268; WSP to MBP, 12 March 1935, APEP.

15. NB to WSP, undated [between 16 and 19 March 1935], FSP.

16. WSP to NB, 28 March 1935, NLa 94:273.

17. Hugues Cuénod, as quoted in Jérôme Spycket, *Nadia Boulanger* (Lausanne: Payot, 1987), 102.

18. Doda Conrad, *Grandeur et mystère d'un mythe: Souvenirs de quarante-quatre ans d'amitié avec Nadia Boulanger* (Paris: Buchet Chastel, 1995), 62–66.

19. Invitation card to WSP's exhibition of paintings at the Galeries Jean Charpentier, 31 May–15 June 1935, illustrated by Christian Bérard, Archives of the Palace of Monaco.

20. LMLV-F, 2 June 1935, 2.

21. LMLV-F, 19 June 1935; MBP also notes the 24 June 1935 soiree in her datebook, APEP. Regrettably, neither source gives any further details of the concert.

22. LMLV-F, 24 June and 1 July 1935.

23. WSP to NB, 2 August 1935, NLa 94:280.

24. WSP to NB, 28 October 1935, NLa 94:289.

25. MBP, datebook entries of 3, 9, and 13 November 1935, APEP.

26. Printed program of two first performances in one afternoon of the Concerto for Two Pianos, on 21 November 1935, sponsored by the Université des Annales, PSS.

27. WSP to IS, 30 October and 22 November 1935, PSS.

28. WSP to Clive Bell, 7 November 1935, Charleston Papers, King's College Library, Cambridge, UK.

29. Virginia Woolf to Ethel Smyth, 4 December 1935, *The Letters of Virginia Woolf*, ed. Nigel Nicolson (New York: Harcourt, Brace, Jovanovitch, 1979–80), 5:446–47; Woolf to Clive Bell, 4 December 1935, in ibid., 5:451.

30. MBP-Db, 8 December 1935, APEP; WSP to NB, undated [December 1935], NLa 94:291.

31. WSP to NB, ibid.

32. Ibid.

33. The manuscript of Igor Markevitch's *Hymnes,* formerly among WSP's collection of musical autographs, is now housed in the BNF-Mus, Ms 19594. It is signed "IM 1933," and bears the following dedication: "This work, composed in 1933, at the request of Madame the Princesse Edmond de Polignac, is dedicated to her as testimony of my respectful gratitude."

34. Aaron Copland had studied composition with Nadia Boulanger during the period 1921–24; the other American students in his class included Roy Harris, Walter Piston, and Virgil Thomson.

35. Typed program of WSP's salon concert, 7 February 1936, APEP.

36. Typed program of WSP's salon concert, 13 February 1936, APEP.

37. Gioconda de Vito (1907–1994) was, as a young artist, a protégée of Mussolini, who put aside a large sum of money to help her buy a Stradivarius violin. Throughout her life Vito enjoyed a successful career, with numerous engagements and recordings. She married her British record producer in 1949, and settled in England, where she concertized frequently, while continuing to tour continental Europe.

38. Typed program of WSP's salon concert, 22 February 1936, APEP.

39. WSP to NB, 29 February 1936, NLa 94, 293.

40. Paul Makanowitzky to NB, undated [1936], NLa 82:383–84.

41. Typed program of WSP's salon concert, 18 March 1936, APEP.

42. Maurice Goudeket, *Close to Colette: An Intimate Portrait of a Woman of Genius* (New York: Farrar, Straus and Cudahy, New York, 1957), 141.

43. MBP-PD, 26 March 1936, APEP.

44. Claude Francis and Fernande Gontier, *Creating Colette,* 2 vols. (South Royalton, Vt.: Steerforth, 1998–99), 2:167.

45. Ibid., 2:113.

46. LMLV-F, 5 April 1936.

47. Goudeket, *Close to Colette,* 117.

48. The autograph of Colette's speech is housed at the FSP.

49. "Bienfaisance," *Le Figaro,* 1 May 1936; typed program of WSP's salon concert, 15 May 1936, APEP.

50. Doda Conrad, INT, 26 July 1991. During the 1935–36 BBC series Conrad sang recitals featuring the music of Schubert, Fauré, and Ravel.

51. Ibid.; Conrad, *Grandeur et mystère,* 74–75; Brooks, "Nadia Boulanger," 439.

52. WSP had been in London since at least 3 June 1936; on that date she wrote to Francis Poulenc to finalize their contractual arrangement for the commission of an organ concerto. "We are in agreement. . . Upon my return, I hope to have the joy of seeing you and talking with you again about our plans." In Francis Poulenc, *Correspondance, 1910–1963,* ed. Myriam Chimènes (Paris: Fayard, 1994), 415, n. 1.

53. Harold Nicolson to Vita Sackville-West, 11 June 1936, in *Vita and Harold: The Letters of Vita Sackville-West and Harold Nicolson,* ed. Nigel Nicolson (New York: G. P. Putnam's Sons, 1992), 282–83.

54. NB-Db, 3 and 7 July 1936, VmF ms 100/3.

55. Doda Conrad, INT, 26 July 1991; Doda Conrad, *Dodascalies* (Arles: Actes Sud, 1998), 145.<notes>56. WSP to NB, 26 July 1936, ibid.

57. Marchioness Sibyl Chomolondeley to MBP, 12 July 1936, APEP.

58. WSP to Doda Conrad, 18 July 1936, "Londres 1936" file, FINLB.

59. Marchioness Sibyl Chomolondeley to MBP, 12 July 1936, APEP.

60. WSP to NB, 26 July 1936, "Londres 1936" file, FINLB.

61. Athos Romanos to WSP, 3 August 1936, with an attached copy of a letter from Michel Vlasto to Romanos, 31 July 1936; both letters, private collection.

62. WSP to NB, 7 August 1936, NLa 94:296; WSP to PP, 8 August 1936, NAfr 18718:312.

63. WSP to NB, 26 July 1936, "Londres 1936" file, FINLB.

64. Hugues Cuénod, INT, 18 July 1992.

65. Letter from Hugues Cuénod to the author, 18 November 1992.

66. WSP to PP, 17 September 1936, NAfr 18718:313; Princesse Henri (Diane) de Polignac to Prince Louis de Polignac, 5 October 1936, APEP.

67. WSP to NB, 4 and 29 September and 1 October 1936, "Londres 1936" file, FINLB; WSP to NB, 28 August and 19 October 1936, NLa 94:296, 297; WSP to PP, 17 September 1936, NAfr 18718:313.

68. WSP to NB, 7 October 1936, "Londres 1936" file, FINLB.

69. Henry Prunières to WSP, 15 September 1936, NLa 94:180.

70. WSP to NB, 17 September 1936, ibid., NLa 94:182–83.

71. Henry Prunières to WSP, 14 October 1936, NLa 94:184.

72. Glenn Plaskin, *Horowitz* (New York: Quill, 1983), 180–82.

73. WSP to MBP, 12 October 1936, APEP.

74. MBP-PD, "Londres," 10 November [1938], APEP.

75. Invitation card for the "at home" hosted by Mrs. Robert Mayer, 19 November [1936], APEP.

76. Brooks, "Nadia Boulanger," 444, n. 70.

77. Doda Conrad, INT, 26 July 1991; Conrad, *Dodascalies*, 79–80; Conrad, *Grandeur et mystère*, 82–83.

78. MBP-PD, "Londres," 10 November [1938], APEP.

79. "A French Princess in London," in the "Londoner's Diary" column, *The Evening Standard*, 17 November 1936; Seymour Leslie, "Music by Night," *Vogue* (London), 11 November 1936, 92–93, 140. The latter article includes a picture of WSP taken at the 1935 Paris exhibition of her paintings.

80. Invitation card for WSP's "at home" matinee, 22 November 1936, and typed program for the evening soiree performed by the Nadia Boulanger Ensemble at Lady Cunard's, also 22 November 1936, APEP.

81. Conrad, *Grandeur et mystère*, 84.

82. Lennox Berkeley's *Dithyrambe and Hymn* received its Paris premiere at the Cercle Interallié on 15 December 1936. Typed program, APEP.

83. Brooks, "Nadia Boulanger," 443.

84. Review in *The Morning Post* (London), as quoted in Brooks, "Nadia Boulanger," 443.

85. Virginia Woolf, 25 November 1936, in *Diary of Virginia Woolf 1936–1941*, ed. Anne Olivier Bell (New York: Harcourt, Brace, Jovanovitch, 1984), 5:36–37.

86. Ibid., 27 November 1936, 37; Woolf to Ethel Smyth, 29 November 1936, in Woolf, *Letters*, 6:88.

87. Virginia Woolf to Dorothy Bussy, 15 December 1936, in Woolf, *Letters*, 6:100.

88. MBP-PD, "Londres," 10 November [1938], APEP.

89. Conrad, *Dodascalies*, 138.

90. Conrad, *Grandeur et mystère*, 88–92.

91. NB-Db, 11 February–13 March 1937, VmF ms101/1; MBP-Db, MBP-PD, 14, 17, 20 and 22 February 1937, APEP.

92. The recording of Monteverdi madrigals conducted by NB is available today on the Koch label, #9994.

93. WSP to NB, 7 January 1937, NLa 94:300; Colette to PP, 31 December 1936, NAfr 18718:11.

94. Colette to WSP, December 1936, FSP.

95. LMLV-F, 3 February 1937; WSP to NB, 8 February 1937, NLa 94:302; LMLV-F, 10 February 1937; WSP to NB, 10 February 1937, NLa 94:304; MBP-PD, 12 February 1937, APEP.

96. WSP to NB, 10 February 1937, NLa 94:304.

97. MBP-PD, 15 February 1937, APEP. The work in question is Brahms's Op. 52, No. 1.

98. Typed program of WSP's salon concert, 19 February 1937, APEP.

99. MBP-PD, 19 February 1937, APEP.

100. Rosamond Lehmann (1901–1982) was one of the best-loved and most successful British novelists of the 1930s and 1940s. Her works, which frequently drew on music for inspiration, include *A Note on Music* (1930), *Invitation to a Waltz* (1932), and *The Weather in the Streets* (1936). See Selina Hastings's recent biography, *Rosamond Lehmann: A Life* (London: Chatto and Windus, 2002).

101. Rosamond Lehmann to her brother John Lehmann, 24 February 1937, John Lehmann Papers, C0746, no. 31, Princeton University Library. Used by permission of The Society of Authors (London) and Princeton University Library.

102. Ibid.

103. NB-Db, 23 February 1937, VmF ms101/1.

104. MBP-PD, 23 February 1937, APEP.

105. Igor Markevitch, *Être et avoir été* (Paris: Gallimard, 1980), 283; Laurence Benaïm, *Marie Laure de Noailles: La vicomtesse du bizarre* (Paris: Grasset, 2001), 277, 295. According to Benaïm, Marie-Laure de Noailles first received the "d'Agoult" nickname from dancer Serge Lifar.

106. The bejeweled "circus feather" headband had been one of the sartorial trademarks of Anna de Noailles; in addition to having earned the disapprobation of the aristocracy because of her social behavior, Marie-Laure de Noailles was excoriated for having "usurped" her more famous cousin's "plume" (Benaïm, *Marie-Laure de Noailles*, 295).

107. MBP-PD, 23 February 1937, APEP.

108. Markevitch, *Être et avoir été*, 141. Markevitch's venemous description of Marie-Laure de Noailles's character was used as well for Violet Trefusis and Vita Sackville-West.

109. Igor Markevitch eventually became a well-known and highly respected conductor.

110. IM to WSP, 22 February 1937, FSP.

111. WSP to IM, first draft of an undated letter [later February 1937], FSP.

112. Eugène Bigot, who conducted the Orchestra of the Concerts Lamoureux in the Polignac salon that evening, enjoyed a successful conducting career in the years 1930–50; his numerous recordings include concerto collaborations with Fournier, Ricci, and Landowska, as well as productions by the Brussels Opera.

113. Program of concert in WSP's music room, 12 March 1937, APEP. The claim on the printed program that this was the first performance of Sauguet's Piano Concerto is incorrect. David L. Austin, in *Henri Sauguet: A Bio-Bibliography* (New York: Greenwood Press, 1991), 33, indicates that the first performance in the Polignac salon actually took place in a two-piano version, with Clara Haskil and the composer at the pianos.

114. Brooks, "Nadia Boulanger," 445.

115. MBP-PD, 21 May 1937, APEP.

116. MBP-PD, June 1937, APEP.

117. Ibid. A third album, a recording of the Brahms *Liebeslieder Waltzes* for vocal quartet and piano four hands, with NB and Dinu Lipatti, was subsequently released. It is available today on the EMI Classics label, #566425.

118. WSP to IS, 17 August 1937, PSS.

119. NB-Db, 4 and 24 September 1937, VmF ms101/3.

120. Gérard Baüer (1888–1967) was one of France's most eminent arts journalists. A writer for *L'Aurore* and *l'Écho de Paris*, he adopted the Proustian pen name "Guermantes" when he joined the staff of *Le Figaro* in 1935. A member of the Académie Goncourt, Baüer was also the winner of the Literary Grand Prize of the City of Paris.

121. Gérard Baüer, "Les Mots et leur usage," *Le Figaro*, 18 July 1966, 1.

122. Mary, Princesse Boris de Rachewiltz, *Discretions* (London: Faber and Faber, 1971), 102.

123. WSP to NB, 6 October 1937, NLa 94:308–9.

124. Anne Conover, *Olga Rudge & Ezra Pound* (New Haven, Conn.: Yale University Press, 2001), 126–28, 130.

125. Joseph Brodsky, *Watermark* (New York: Farrar, Straus and Giroux, 1993), 93–94.

126. WSP to Contessa Wally di Castelbarco, née Toscanini, 2 October 1937, The Vladimir and Wanda Toscanini Horowitz Papers, MSS 55, Irving S. Gilmore Music Library, Yale University. WSP wrote similar impressions of this concert to NB on 6 October 1937, NLa 94:308–9.

127. MBP-Db, 9, 10, and 12 November 1937, APEP.

128. WSP to NB, 6 October 1937, NLa 94:308–9.

129. LMLV-F, 18 October 1937.

130. Brooks, "Nadia Boulanger," 444–45.

131. Sir Anthony Chaplin (1906–1982).

132. MBP-PD, undated entry [London, 1937], APEP.

133. MBP-PD, "Londres," 10 Novembre [1938] APEP.

134. Alvilde Chaplin, née Bridges, later Mrs. James Lees-Milne (1909–1994). In the latter half of her life she was a well-known author of books on English country houses and gardens.

135. MBP-PD, "Londres," 10 November [1938], APEP.

136. MBP-PD, 3 November 1937, APEP.

137. Brooks, "Nadia Boulanger," 444.

138. WSP to NB, 23 September 1934, NLa 94:255–56.

139. Jean Françaix to NB, 27 October 1937, NLa 71:105.

140. Jean Françaix to NB, 10 November 1937, NLa 71:107.

141. Jean Françaix to NB, 6 December 1937, NLa 71:111.

142. Jean Françaix to NB, 8 January 1938, NLa 71:114.

143. WSP's name appears on a list of "subscribers" for the publication of La Chartreuse de Parme, December 1937, Sauguet Archives.

144. WSP to Ezra Pound, 17 January 1938; Ezra Pound to WSP, 18 January 1938 and undated [18–21 January 1938]; WSP to Ezra Pound, 22 January 1938, Ezra Pound Papers, YCAL 43/1731.

145. Edmond Faral and Roger Heim, *Les Heures de musique à la Fondation Singer-Polignac* (Paris: Fondation Singer-Polignac, 1966), 12.

146. Duc Élie Decazes, INT, 24 August 1994.

147. MBP-PD, "Amsterdam," 10 April [1938], APEP.

148. Ibid. Willem Mengelberg (1871–1951), one of the great conductors of the first part of the twentieth century, assumed the directorship of the Concertgebouw Orchestra in 1899. In addition to giving over three hundred world premieres of new compositions during his tenure, he also gave an annual performance of J. S. Bach's *St. Matthew Passion,* a tradition that lasted for over forty years.

149. MBP-PD, "Amsterdam," 10 April [1938], APEP.

150. WSP to NB, 20 April 1938, NLa 94:310.

151. MBP-Db and MBP-PD, 17 May 1938, APEP.

152. FP to MBP, undated [30 April 1936], APEP, reprinted in Poulenc, *Correspondance,* 414–15.

153. FP to MBP, 14 August 1936, APEP, reprinted in Poulenc, *Correspondance,* 419–20.

154. WSP to FP, 24 May 1938, in Poulenc, *Correspondance,* 462–63.

155. FP to WSP, undated [25 or 26 May 1938], in the Fonds Boulanger, NLa 95, 96–97.

156. WSP to FP, 27 May 1938 in Poulenc, *Correspondance,* 464, n. 4.

157. Jean Françaix to NB, 31 May 1938, NLa 71:116.

158. MBP-PD, 5 June 1938, APEP.

159. Robert and Mildred Woods Bliss were step-brother and sister through the second marriages of their parents. The *Dumbarton Oaks Concerto,* named for the Blisses' magnificent Washington, D.C., estate, was commissioned in honor of the couple's thirtieth wedding anniversary; it received its premiere on 8 May 1938. See Jeanice Brooks, "Mildred Bliss Tells Nadia Boulanger to Think of Herself for Once," in *Cultivating Music in America: Women Patrons and Activists since 1860,* ed. Ralph P. Locke and Cyrilla Barr (Berkeley: University of California Press, 1997), 209–13.

160. Stravinsky conducted the first public performance of the *Dumbarton Oaks Concerto* at the Salle Gaveau under the auspices of the Sérénade on 8 June 1938. The program also included the Concertino for String Quartet and *L'Histoire du soldat.*

161. MBP-PD, 6 June 1938, APEP.

162. MBP-PD, 12 June 1938, APEP.

163. Conrad, *Dodascalies,* 152–53.

164. MBP-PD, 14 June 1938, APEP.

165. Conrad, *Dodascalies,* 152–53. According to Conrad, the unnamed performers in the various concerts of the Société Schubert (1937–40) included, besides himself, Marya Freund, Pierre Bernac, Yvonne Gouverné, Erich-Itor Kahn, and Dinu Lipatti.

166. Typed program of WSP's salon concert, 30 June 1938, APEP.

167. Brooks, "Nadia Boulanger," 463.

168. Robert Brussel, "Charles Munch au Conservatoire," *Le Figaro,* 19 December 1938. Brussel wrote a complimentary, if not overly enthusiastic, review of *Le Diable boîteux*: "One finds its construction light and often humorous, its ideas fine and gracious. . . It seems however, monotonous and overlong because of too many niceties."

169. Jean Françaix to NB, 2 July 1938, NLa 71:119.

170. MBP-PD, "La Saison de Kerbastic 1938," APEP.

171. FP to MBP, undated [10 August 1938], APEP, reprinted in Poulenc, *Correspondance,* 465–66.

172. Pericles Argyropoulos to WSP, 13 February 1935, private collection; Athos Romanos to WSP, 3 August 1936, private collection.

173. MBP-PD, 25 August 1938, APEP.

174. MBP-PD, 25 and 31 August 1938, APEP.

175. WSP to NB, 12 September 1938, NLa 94:311. WSP is making a thinly veiled reference to Bach Cantata 82, *Ich Habe Genug.*

176. Ibid. The manuscript of Poulenc's Organ Concerto, signed and dated 1938, bears the following autograph inscription: "Dedicated very respectfully to the Princesse Edmond de Polignac by her loyal musician Francis Poulenc October 1938." BMFP.

177. Jérôme Spycket, *Clara Haskil* (Lausanne: Payot, 1975), 113.

178. Doda Conrad, INT, 24 July 1991, 10 August 1994; Conrad, *Grandeur et mystère*, 121, 125.

179. MBP, private diary entitled "Londres," 10 November [1938], APEP.

180. WSP to NB, undated [28 November 1938], NLa 94:316.

181. WSP to NB, 10 December 1938, NLa 94:318; WSP to NB, 15 December 1938, NLa 94:320; WSP to FP, 10 December 1938, in Poulenc, *Correspondance*, 472.

182. Doda Conrad, INT, 24 July 1991, 10 August 1994.

183. A manuscript of Poulenc's *Trois Poèmes de Louise de Vilmorin*, in the hand of a copyist, is housed in the BMFP.

184. The first public performance of the Poulenc Organ Concerto took place on 21 June 1939, with Roger Désormière and the OSP. It received an ambivalent reception in the press. See Robert Brussel, "Concerts," *Le Figaro*, 25 June 1939; and Norbert Dufourcq, "Chroniques et notes: Concerto en sol mineur, pour orgue, orchestre à cordes et timbales par Francis Poulenc (La Sérénade, 1re audition, 21 juin [1939]," *La Revue musicale* 20, no. 193 [August-November 1939]: 107–8).

185. FP to NB, undated [July 1939], NLa 95:98–99.

186. MBP-PD, 22 December 1938, APEP.

187. WSP to NB, 6 February 1939, NLa 94:321–22.

188. Virginia Woolf, diary entry of 4 December 1937, in Woolf, *Diary*, 5:120.

189. Virginia Woolf, diary entry of 29 January 1939, ibid., 5:202; Virginia Woolf to Ethel Smyth, 6 February 1939, in Woolf, *Letters*, 6:315.

190. Woolf to Jacques-Émile Blanche, 5 October 1938, in Woolf, *Letters*, 6:282.

191. In her "Memoirs of the Late Princesse Edmond de Polignac," *Horizon* 12, no. 68 (August 1945), WSP recalled the Beethoven String Quartet performance taking place on her fourteenth—not her thirteenth—birthday.

192. WSP to Virginia Woolf, 24 February 1939, The Monk's House Papers, University of Sussex Library (U.K.). The *Poems as Prose* are Baudelaire's *Petites Poèmes en prose*. The "Pléiade," a sixteenth-century French literary group, sought to prove that the French language was as important and beautiful as Greek or Latin; its members included du Bellay and Ronsard.

193. WSP's name appears on a list of individuals who attended the *générale* of Sauguet's *La Chartreuse de Parme* on 9 March 1939. She subsequently sent the composer a card, expressing her "admiration for the beautiful work that I got to know a bit at the piano. I retain a very great impression of it. It seems completely in the spirit and the 'ambience' of Stendahl." Both the list and the card are conserved in the Sauguet Archives, Paris.

194. MBP-PD, 21 March 1939, APEP.

195. MBP-PD, 22 March 1939, APEP.

196. Card, "In Memorium Raissa Boulanger, Lili Boulanger," FSP; WSP to NB, 16 April 1939, NLa 94:324.

197. MBP-PD, 24 May 1939, APEP.

198. MBP-PD, 27 May 1939, APEP.

199. "Les Indiscrétions de Saint-Loup: Les mystères de l'atelier," *L'Ordre*, 27 May 1939.

200. MBP-PD, 13 June 1939, APEP.

201. MBP-PD, 19 June 1939, APEP.

202. MBP-PD, 22 June 1939, APEP.

203. WSP to NB, 29 June 1939, NLa 94:326.

204. "News of Americans in Europe," *New York Herald-Tribune,* 5 July 1939.

Chapter 16

1. *Procès verbale* of 1 April 1940 affirming WSP's promotion to the grade of Officer of the Legion of Honor, Archives of the Grande Chancellerie of the Légion d'Honneur, Paris.

2. Ibid.

3. Prince Edmond de Polignac, "Souvenirs de ma tante, la princesse Edmond" (September 1998), APFK.

4. WSP to MBP, 25 August 1939, APFK. WSP quotes Lord Alfred Tennyson's poem "Break, Break, Break."

5. WSP to FP, 17 September 1939, in Francis Poulenc, *Correspondance, 1910–1963,* ed. Myriam Chimènes (Paris: Fayard, 1994), 481; WSP to Bruno Maderna, 17 September 1939, PSS.

6. WSP to MBP, 23 September 1939, APFK.

7. WSP to MBP, 12 October 1939, APFK.

8. WSP to NB, 8 October 1939, NLa 94:330–31.

9. Colette to WSP, undated [late 1939], as quoted in Joanna Richardson, *Colette* (New York: Franklin Watts, 1984), 177–78.

10. WSP to MBP, 12 October 1939, APFK.

11. WSP to MBP, 26 January 1940, APFK.

12. WSP to NB, 29 November 1939, NLa 94:332–33.

13. WSP to NB, 17 December 1939, NLa 94:334.

14. Alvilde Chaplin to NB, 12 March [1941], NLa 94: 93–5. Because she referred to WSP in her letters as "Tante Winnie," Chaplin was mistakenly catalogued as "Alvilda de Polignac" in the Fonds Boulanger of the BNF-Mus.

15. Prince Jean-Louis de Faucigny-Lucinge, *Un Gentilhomme cosmopolite* (Paris: Perrin, 1990), 100–101.

16. WSP to Daisy Singer Dugardin, telegram, 4 June 1940, private collection.

17. WSP to NB, 12 November 1940, NLa 94:345, 346.

18. Duc Élie Decazes interviewed by Cossart, source notes.

19. WSP to NB, 21 January 1941, NLa 94:348–51.

20. Colonel Jacques Balsan was a French aviator; in 1921 he married the American-born Duchesse of Marlborough, née Consuelo Vanderbilt, who divorced the British aristocrat in 1920. The Balsans emigrated to the United States at the outbreak of war. In 1942 Jacques Balsan wrote to President Roosevelt, asking if it might be possible to "form an American Legion in the American army," so that it would be possible for the numerous foreigners living in the United States to serve their host nation (FDR Library, 19 March 1942).

21. WSP to NB, 21 January 1941, NLa 94:348–51.

22. Mildred Woods Bliss to NB, 17 March 1941, NLa 56:254–56.

23. Ruth Reynolds, "Women Wealth: Isaac Singer, an Habitual Lover," *The [New York] Sunday News,* 15 March 1942, 64.

24. Alvilde Chaplin to NB, 12 March [1941], NLa 94:93–95.

25. WSP to Daisy Dugardin, 16 December 1941, private collection.

26. Ibid.; WSP to NB, 4 November 1942, NLa 94:357–58. The original type-

written manuscript of the WSP's memoirs, with corrections in her hand, is housed in the APFK.

27. Michael de Cossart, *The Food of Love: Princesse Edmond de Polignac (1865–1943) and Her Salon* (London: Hamish Hamilton, 1978), 217; Alvilde Lees-Milne interviewed by Cossart, source notes. Raymond Mortimer was a noted British journalist. Between the World Wars he wrote a regular column, "The London Letter," for *The Dial,* a prestigious journal of art and culture; he subsequently wrote for *The New Statesman.*

28. WSP to Violet Trefusis, 12 April [1942], Yale University Library, Violet Trefusis Papers, Gen Mss 427/22.

29. Ibid.

30. WSP to NB, 10 July 1942, NLa 94:355.

31. Cossart, *The Food of Love,* 216; Cossart, source notes.

32. WSP to NB, 4 November 1942, NLa 94:357–58.

33. Ibid.

34. Ethel Smyth, quoted by WSP to NB, ibid.

35. Howard Hollis, *The Best of Both Worlds: A Life of Sir William McKie* (Melbourne: Sir William McKie Memorial Trust, 1991), 60–62.

36. WSP to NB, 10 July 1942, NLa 94:355.

37. WSP to Daisy Dugardin, 11 July 1942, private collection.

38. The Britten-Pears Library, which houses the Benjamin Britten Archives, contains a letter written to Benjamin Britten on WSP's behalf, but not in her hand, sent from 64 avenue Foch and dated, "Paris, 23 October" [no year]. The sender thanks Britten for the "lovely time spent on Sunday night," and includes a typewritten list of compositions commissioned by and dedicated to WSP. Britten refers to his meeting with Polignac in a letter to Elizabeth Mayer, 8 December 1943, in *Letters From a Life: The Selected Letters and Diaries of Benjamin Britten 1913–1976,* vol. 2 [1939–45], ed. Donald Mitchell (London: Faber and Faber, 1998), 1177, n.7.

39. WSP to NB, 21 January 1941, NLa 94:348–51.

40. WSP to NB, 4 November 1942, NLa 94:357–58.

41. Stephen Spender (1909–1995), poet, novelist, and critic, was one of England's greatest twentieth-century writers. His autobiography, *World within World* (1951), is a re-creation of much of the political and social atmosphere of the 1930s. Spender was knighted in 1983.

42. James Lees-Milne, *Diaries: 1942–1945 (Ancestral Voices*; *Prophesying Peace)* (London: John Murray, 1995), 144–45.

43. Ibid., 176.

44. Lees-Milne, *Diaries,* 190–91.

45. Frederick Singer to NB, 14 October 1943, NLa 105:250. Frederick Singer was Franklin's son.

46. Sir Henry Channon, *Chips: The Diaries of Sir Henry Channon* (London: Weidenfeld and Nicolson, 1967), 376–77.

47. Lees-Milne, *Diaries,* 238.

48. Ibid., 245.

49. Edward Marsh, *A Number of People* (London: Harper, 1939), 269, 270.

50. Alvilde Lees-Milne interviewed by Cossart, source notes; Lees-Milne, *Diaries,* 247.

51. Comtesse Jean (Nelly) de Vogüé, INT, 19 July 1992.

52. Printed program of the Requiem Mass celebrated for WSP, 1 December 1943, private collection; the musical program was reprinted in *The Times of London*, 2 December 1943, 7.

53. Rosamond Lehmann, "Princess de Polignac," *The Times of London*, 6 December 1943, 6.

54. *The Times of London*, 2 December 1943, 7.

55. Alvilde Chaplin, "Princess de Polignac, A Further Tribute," *The Times of London*, 8 December 1943, 7.

Postlude

1. Lennox Berkeley to NB, 24 January 1944, Nla 53:245.

2. Gérard Baüer, "Une Initiatrice de la musique contemporaine," *Le Figaro*, 2 December 1944.

3. Armande de Polignac (Comtesse de Chabannes), speech, "Homage" (1944), APFK.

4. NB to IS, 7 and 14 November 1964, PSS.

5. IS to NB, telegram, undated [17 November 1964], NLa 105; a copy of the text is in PSS.

6. Bernard Gavoty, "A la mémoire de la Princesse de Polignac," *Le Figaro*, 9 December 1965.

Bibliography

Archives, Private Collections, and Special Collections

Archives de la Grande Chancellerie de la Légion d'Honneur, Paris
Archives Départementales de la Nièvre, Nevers (ADLN)
    Fonds Jean Carriès
Archives Madame Claude Baugnies
Archives Nationales, Paris (AN)
    Dossiers "Concours d'Opéra 1867–69"
    Dossiers Conservatoire de Paris
    Dossiers Opéra de Paris (Ballets Russes 1908–29)
    Fonds Gabriel Astruc
Archives of the Author
    Doda Conrad papers
Archives Prince Edmond de Polignac (APEP)
    Papiers Comtesse de Chabannes de La Palice, née Princesse Armande de Polignac
    Papiers Comtesse Guillaume d'Oilliamson, née Princesse Jane de Polignac
    Papiers Prince Camille de Polignac
    Papiers Prince Edmond de Polignac (I)
    Papiers Prince Edmond de Polignac (II)
    Papiers Princesse Edmond de Polignac, née Winnaretta Singer
    Papiers Marquis Guy de Polignac
    Papiers Marquise Guy de Polignac, née Louise Pommery
    Papiers Princesse Henri de Polignac
    Papiers Comte Jean de Polignac
    Papiers Comtesse Jean de Polignac, née Marguerite de Pietro
    Papiers Prince Jules de Polignac
    Papiers Princesse Jules de Polignac, née Charlotte-Maria Parkyns
    Papiers Prince Ludovic de Polignac
    Papiers Comte Melchior de Polignac
Archives Saint-Marceaux, Paris (ASM)
    Papiers Marguerite de Saint-Marceaux
Archivo Manuel de Falla (AMF), Grenada
    Manuel de Falla papers
Beinecke Library, Yale University, New Haven, Connecticut
    Ralph Hodgson Papers
    James Lees-Milne Papers
    Ezra Pound Papers
    Olga Rudge Papers
    James Stephens Papers
    Sir Ronald Storrs Papers
    Violet Trefusis Papers
Bibliothèque du Musée du Petit Palais, Paris
    Documentation concerning "La Porte de Parsifal" by Jean Carriès
Bibliothèque Musicale, Famille Polignac (BMFP)

Bibliothèque Nationale de France, Département des manuscrits (BNF-Mss)
    Fonds Augustine Bulteau
    Fonds Princesse Alexandre de Caraman-Chimay
    Fonds Colette
    Fonds Marie Curie
    Fonds Comte Robert de Montesquiou
    Fonds Comtesse Anna de Noailles
    Fonds Raymond Poincaré
    Fonds Joseph Reinach
    Fonds Paul Valéry
Bibliothèque Nationale de Paris, Département de la musique (BNF-Mus)
    Fonds Nadia Boulanger
    Fonds Gabriel Fauré
    Fonds Igor Markevitch
    Programmes imprimés
The Britten-Pears Library, UK
    Benjamin Britten Correspondence
Cambridge University Library, Cambridge, UK
    Royal Society of Literature Papers
Centre des archives diplomatiques de l'Ambassade de France, Nantes
    French Embassy (Washington) archives
Fondation Internationale Nadia et Lili Boulanger, Paris (FINLB)
    Fonds Nadia Boulanger
Fondation Le Corbusier, Paris (FLC)
    Correspondance Jeanneret (Le Corbusier)
Fondation Singer-Polignac, Paris (FSP)
    Papiers Winnaretta Singer, Princesse Edmond de Polignac (ex-Archives Alain
      Ollivier)
Glasgow University Library, UK
    Whistler Archive (Revillon Papers)
Goldsmiths College, University of London, UK
    The Serge Prokofiev Archive
Grande Chancellerie de la Légion d'Honneur, Paris
    Archives
Kent State University Libraries, Ohio
    James Stephens Papers
King's College Library, Cambridge, UK
    Charleston Papers (Clive Bell Papers)
The National Gallery, London, Archives Department
    Administrative file, "Wartime Storage of Pictures"
New York Public Library, Dance Collection
    Gabriel Astruc Papers
    Serge Diaghilev Papers
    Isadora Duncan Papers
Princeton University Library, Princeton, New Jersey
    John Lehmann Papers
Harry Ransom Humanities Research Center, University of Texas at Austin
    Princesse Marthe Bibesco Papers
    Jean Cocteau Papers

Royal Society of Literature, London
    Archives
Paul Sacher Foundation, Basel
    Bruno Maderna correspondence
    Igor Stravinsky correspondence
Henri Sauguet collection, Paris
Arnold Schoenberg Center, Vienna
    Arnold Schoenberg Correspondence
Society of the Four Arts Library, Palm Beach, Florida
    Addison Mizner Archives
State Historical Society of Wisconsin, Madison WI (SHSW)
    Singer Sewing Machine Company Archives
University of Sussex Library, UK
    The Monk's House Papers (Virginia Woolf)
Kurt Weill Foundation for Music, New York
    Kurt Weill Correspondence
Westchester County Archives, New York
    Proceedings of the Isaac M. Singer estate trial
Yale University Music Library, New Haven, Connecticut
    Vladimir Horowitz and Wanda Toscanini-Horowitz Papers

Books, Articles, and Dissertations

In order to avoid visual clutter, a number of newspaper articles cited in the notes, especially those consulted as clippings in the family scrapbooks, are not repeated here.

"A Duke's Funeral." *The New York World,* 7 September 1887.
"A French Princess in London." In "Londoner's Diary," *The Evening Standard* (London), 17 November 1936.
Albright, Daniel. *Untwisting the Serpent: Modernism in Music, Literature, and Other Arts.* Chicago: University of Chicago Press, 2000.
Alexandre, Arsène. *Jean Carriès, imagier et potier: Étude d'une oeuvre et d'une vie.* Paris: Librairies-Imprimeries Réunies, 1895.
Amory, Mark. *Lord Berners: The Last Eccentric.* London: Pimlico, 1999.
Astruc, Gabriel. *Le Pavillon des fantômes.* Paris: Belfond, 1978.
Auric, Georges. "Une Oeuvre nouvelle de Satie." *Littérature* 2 (April 1919).
Auric, Georges, and Jean Cocteau. *Correspondance.* Edited by Pierre Caizergues. Montpellier: Centre d'étude du 20ᵉ siècle, Université Paul-Valéry, 1999.
Austin, David L. *Henri Sauguet: A Bio-Bibliography.* New York: Greenwood Press, 1991.
Bac, Ferdinand. *Intimités de la Troisième République.* Paris: Hachette, 1935.
Barrès, Maurice. *L'Oeuvre de Maurice Barrès.* Vol. 20. Paris: Au Club de l'Honnête Homme, 1965–68.
———. *Scènes et doctrines du nationalisme.* Paris: Félix Guven, 1902.
Bassi, Elena. *Palazzi di Venezia: Admiranda urbis Venetae* (Venice: La Stamperia di Venezia, 1978).
Bathori, Jane. "Erik Satie," *Les Lettres françaises,* May–June 1966, 21–22.
Baüer, Gérard. "Une Initiatrice de la musique contemporaine." *Le Figaro,* 2 December 1944.

———— [Guermantes]. "Les Mots et leur usage." *Le Figaro*, 18 July 1966.

Beauchamp, Louis de. *L'Hôtel de la Princesse Edmond de Polignac*. Paris: Fondation Singer-Polignac, 1983.

————. "La Princesse Edmond de Polignac, Marcel Proust et la Musique." In *Bulletin de la Société des Amis de Marcel Proust* 35 (May 1985).

Bell, Quentin. *Virginia Woolf: A Biography 1912–1941*. New York: Harcourt, Brace, Jovanovitch, 1972.

Bellanger, Patrice. *Jean-Joseph Carriès, 1855–1894*. Paris: Galerie Patrice Bellanger, 1997.

Benaïm, Laurence. *Marie-Laure de Noailles: La vicomtesse du bizarre*. Paris: Grasset, 2001.

Bendehan, Daniel. *Reynaldo Hahn, su vida et su obra*. Caracas: C. A. Tabacalera Nacional, 1973.

Beauchamp, Comte Louis de. *L'Hôtel de la Princesse Edmond de Polignac*. Paris: Fondation Singer-Polignac, 1983.

Berenguer, Bruno, Denise Bouchet-Kervella, and Pauline Girard, eds. *Henri Sauguet et la scène*. Paris: Séguier, 2001.

Bergdoll, Barry. *Les Vaudoyer: Une dynastie d'architectes*. Exhibition catalogue, Musée d'Orsay, Paris. Paris: Réunion des Musées nationaux, 1991.

Bertrand, Antoine. *Les Curiosités esthétiques de Robert de Montesquiou*. Geneva: Droz, 1996.

Beucler, André. *The Last of the Bohemians: Twenty Years with Léon-Paul Fargue*. Translated by Geoffrey Sainsbury. New York: Sloan, 1954.

Bibesco, Princesse Marthe. *Le Confesseur et les poètes*. Paris: Grasset, 1970.

Bibliothèque Nationale (France). *Helleu [Exposition, 16 mai–15 juin 1957]*. Catalogue by Jean Adhémar. Paris, 1957.

Billy, André. *L'Epoque 1900*. Paris: J. Tallandier, 1951.

Bird, John. *Percy Grainger*. London: Faber and Faber, 1982.

Blair, Fredrika. *Isadora: Portrait of the Artist as a Woman*. New York: McGraw-Hill, 1986.

Blanche, Jacques-Émile. *Nouvelles Lettres à Andre Gide (1891–1925)*. Edited by Georges Paul Collet. Geneva: Droz, 1982.

————. *La Pêche aux souvenirs*. Paris: Flammarion, 1949.

Blanchet, Christian, and Bertrand Daud. *Statue of Liberty: The First Hundred Years*. Translated by Bernard A. Weisberger. New York: American Heritage, 1985.

"Bloc-Notes parisien: Une bonne oeuvre et une belle oeuvre, la Société Philanthropique et le Prince Edmond de Polignac." *Le Gaulois*, 10 May 1901, 1.

Brandon, Ruth. *The Dollar Princesses: Sagas of Upward Mobility 1870–1914*. New York: Knopf, 1980.

————. *Singer and the Sewing Machine: A Capitalist Romance*. New York: Kodansha Globe, 1996. First published London: Barrie and Jenkins, 1977.

Brett, Philip. "Music, Essentialism, and the Closet." In *Queering the Pitch: The New Gay and Lesbian Musicology*, edited by Philip Brett, Elizabeth Wood, and Gary C. Thomas., 235–46. New York: Routledge, 1994.

Bril, France-Yvonne. *Henri Sauguet*. Paris: Seghers, 1967.

Britten, Benjamin. *Letters from a Life: The Selected Letters and Diaries of Benjamin Britten 1913–1976*. Vol. 2 (1939–45). Edited by Donald Mitchell.

London: Faber and Faber, 1998.

Brodsky, Joseph. *Watermark*. New York: Farrar, Straus and Giroux, 1993.

Brody, Elaine. *Paris: The Musical Kaleidescope 1870–1925*. London: Robson Books, 1988.

Brooks, Jeanice. "Mildred Bliss Tells Nadia Boulanger to Think of Herself for Once." In *Cultivating Music in America: Women Patrons and Activists since 1860*, edited by Ralph P. Locke and Cyrilla Barr. Berkeley: University of California Press, 1997.

———. "Nadia Boulanger and the Salon of the Princesse de Polignac." In *Journal of the American Musicological Society* 46, no. 3 (Fall 1993): 415–68.

Brown, Frederick. *An Impersonation of Angels*. New York: Viking Press, 1968.

Bruyr, José. "Germaine Tailleferre." *Musica*, March 1957, 29–33.

Brussel, Robert. "Les Ballets Ida Rubinstein." *Le Figaro*, 2 May 1934.

———. "Charles Munch au Conservatoire." *Le Figaro*, 19 December 1938.

———. "Concert de l'Exposition de l'Art Russe." *Le Figaro*, 7 November 1906, 3.

———. "Les Concerts." *Le Figaro*, 6 June 1908.

———. "Les Concerts." *Le Figaro*, 25 June 1939.

———. *Le Figaro*, 17 June 1911, 5.

———. "L'Orchestre symphonique de Paris." *Le Figaro*, 22 October 1928, 4.

———. "Les Théâtres: *Ballets Russes*." *Le Figaro*, 8 June 1911.

Buckland, Sidney, and Myriam Chimènes, editors. *Francis Poulenc: Music, Art, and Literature*. Aldershot: Ashgate, 1999.

Buckle, Richard. *Diaghilev*. London: Weidenfeld and Nicolson, 1979.

Bulteau, Augustine [Jules Vontade]. "Le Coeur innombrable." *Le Figaro*, 9 May 1901, 5.

Caballero, Carlo. Review of *French Cultural Politics and Music: From the Dreyfus Affair to the First World War*, by Jane F. Fulcher. *Journal of the American Musicological Society* 55, no. 3 (Fall 2002): 563–78.

Campodonico, Luis. *Falla*. Paris: Le Seuil, 1959.

Carassus, Emilien. *Le Snobisme et les lettres françaises de Paul Bourget à Marcel Proust, 1884–1914*. Paris: A. Colin, 1966.

Carley, Lionel. *Frederick Delius: A Life in Letters 1862–1908*. 2 vols. London: Scolar Press, 1983.

Carter, William C. *Marcel Proust: A Life*. New Haven, Conn: Yale University Press, 2000.

Castellane, Boni de. *Mémoires*. Paris: Perrin, 1986.

Cattaui, Georges. *Marcel Proust*. Paris: Julliard, 1952.

Channon, Sir Henry. *Chips: The Diaries of Sir Henry Channon*. London: Weidenfeld and Nicolson, 1967.

Chastenet, Jacques. *Histoire de la Troisième République*. Vol. 3: *La République triomphante, 1893–1906*. Paris: Hachette, 1955.

Chimènes, Myriam. "La Musique dans les salons de la Belle Époque aux années Cinquante." In *Musique et Musiciens au Faubourg St-Germain*, edited by Jean Gallois, 89–101. Paris: Délégation à l'Action Artistique de la Ville de Paris, 1996.

———. "La Princesse Edmond de Polignac et la création musicale," In *La Musique et le Pouvoir*, edited by Hugues Dufort and Joël-Marie Fauquet. Paris: Aux Amateurs de Livres, 1987.

Christoforidis, Michael. "Aspects of the Creative Process in Manuel de Falla's *El*

Retablo de Maese Pedro and *Concerto.*" Ph.D. dissertation, University of Melbourne, 1997.

———. "From Folksong to Plainchant: Musical Borrowings and the Transformation of Manuel de Falla's Nationalism in the 1920s." In *Manuel de Falla,* edited by Nancy Harper. Lanham, Md.: Scarecrow, 2002.

Clouzot, Marie-Rose. *Souvenirs à deux voix de Maxime Jacob à Dom Clément Jacob.* Toulouse: Privat, 1969.

Cocteau, Jean. *The Journals of Jean Cocteau.* London: Museum Press, 1965.

———. *Lettres à sa mère.* Edited by Pierre Caizergues. Paris: Gallimard, 1989.

———. *My Contemporaries.* London: Owen, 1967.

———. *Portraits-Souvenir 1900–1914.* Paris: Grasset, 1935.

Cocteau, Jean, and Anna de Noailles. *Correspondance.* Edited by Claude Mignot-Ogliastri. Paris: Gallimard, 1989.

Cohen, Harriet. *A Bundle of Time.* London: Faber and Faber, 1969.

Colby, Vineta. *The Singular Anomaly: Women Novelists of the Nineteenth Century.* New York: New York University Press, 1970.

Colette. *Journal à rebours.* Paris: Fayard, 1941.

———. *Lettres à ses pairs.* Paris: Flammarion, 1973.

Collaer, Paul. "Chroniques et Notes: Les Malheurs d'Orphée." *La Revue musicale* 7, no. 8 (1 June 1926): 313–14.

———. *Darius Milhaud.* Translated and edited by Jane Hohfeld Galante. San Francisco: San Francisco Press, 1988.

Collet, Henri. "Erik Satie," *L'Esprit nouveau* 2 (1920).

Conover, Anne. *Olga Rudge & Ezra Pound.* New Haven, Conn.: Yale University Press, 2001.

Conrad, Doda. *Dodascalies.* Arles: Actes Sud, 1998.

———. *Grandeur et mystère d'un mythe: Souvenirs de quarante-quatre ans d'amitié avec Nadia Boulanger.* Paris: Buchet Chastel, 1995.

Coolidge, Calvin. "The Classics for America," 7 July 1921. Transcribed and annotated by Dr. William Harris, 2001 *http://www.calvincoolidge.org/pages/history/speeches/asvp/21_07_07.html*

———. "Les Études classiques en Amérique." Translated by Princesse Edmond de Polignac, *La Revue de Paris* 4, no.15 (1 August 1924): 481–89.

Cooper, Duff, and Diana Cooper. *A Durable Fire: The Letters of Duff and Diana Cooper (1913–1950).* Edited by Artemis Cooper. London: Collins, 1983.

Cossart, Michael de. *The Food of Love: Princesse Edmond de Polignac (1865–1943) and Her Salon.* London: Hamish Hamilton, 1978.

——— [Catherine van Casselaer]. *Lot's Wife: Lesbian Paris, 1890–1914.* Liverpool: Janus Press, 1986.

Cossé-Brissac, Anne de. *La Comtesse Greffulhe.* Paris: Perrin, 1991.

Crawford, Caroline. "Felix Khuner: 1906–1991, a Violinist's Journey: Interview History." *http://www.khuner.com/history.*

Cuneo-Laurent, Linda. "The Performer as Catalyst: The Role of the Singer Jane Bathori (1877–1970)." Ph.D. dissertation, New York University, 1982.

Current, Richard Nelson, and Marcia Ewing Current. *Loïe Fuller: Goddess of Light.* Boston: Northeastern University Press, 1997.

Daudet, Léon. *Souvenirs littéraires.* Paris: B. Gasset, 1968.

Dean, Winton. *George Bizet: His Life and Work.* London: Dent, 1975.

Deathridge, John, Martin Geck, and Egon Voss, eds. *Wagner Werk-Verzeichnis [WWV]: Verzeichnis der musikalischen Werke Richard Wagners und ihrer Quellen: erarbeitet im Rahmen der Richard Wagner-Gesamtausgabe.* Redaktionelle Mitarbeit, Isolde Vetter. Mainz, New York: Schott, 1986.

Debussy, Claude. *Lettres.* Edited by François Lesure. Paris: Hermann, 1980. Published in English as *Letters.* Selected and edited by François Lesure and Roger Nichols. Translated by Roger Nichols. Cambridge, Mass.: Harvard University Press, 1987.

Delahaye, Michel. "Marguerite de Saint-Marceaux (1850–1930)." In *Une Famille d'artistes en 1900: Les Saint-Marceaux.* Paris: Éditions de la Réunion des Musées nationaux, 1992.

Deledicque, Michel Raux. *Albéniz, su vida inquieta y ardorosa.* Buenos Aires: Ediciones Peuser, 1950.

Delius, Frederick. *Delius: A Life in Letters 1862–1934.* Edited by Lionel Carley. 2 vols. London: Scolar Press in association with the Delius Trust, 1983–88.

Demarquez, Suzanne. "Chroniques et Notes: Ouverture de Germaine Tailleferre." *La Revue musicale* 14, no. 133 (February 1933): 133.

———. *Manuel de Falla.* Philadelphia: Chilton Book Company, 1968.

De Meyer, Adolf. *De Meyer.* Edited by Robert Brandau, biographical essay by Philippe Jullian. New York: Knopf, 1976.

Desaymard, Joseph. *Chabrier d'après ses lettres.* Paris: Roches, 1934.

Desbordes, Jean. "Grandes Dames de Paris: La princesse E. de Polignac ou le génie des Arts." *Paris-Midi,* 16 October 1934.

Drummond, John. *Speaking of Diaghilev.* London: Faber and Faber, 1997.

Duchesneau, Michel. *L'Avant-Garde musicale à Paris de 1871 à 1939.* Sprimont, Belgium: Pierre Mardaga, 1997.

Duchin, Jessica. *Gabriel Fauré.* London: Phaedon, 2000.

Dufourcq, Norbert. "Chroniques et notes: Concerto en sol mineur, pour orgue, orchestre à cordes et timbales par Francis Poulenc (La Sérénade, 1re audition, 21 juin [1939]," *La Revue musicale* 20, no. 193 [August-November 1939]: 107–8).

———. "Eugène Gigout (1844–1925)." *L'Orgue Cahiers et Mémoires* 1, no. 27 (1982): 13.

Dujardin, Marie. "Marcel Proust à Venise." *Le Figaro,* 10 October 1931.

Duncan, Isadora. *My Life.* New York: Liveright, 1995.

Ebrecht, Ronald, ed. *Maurice Duruflé, 1902–1986: The Last Impressionist.* Lanham, Md.: Scarecrow Press, 2002.

Edel, Leon. *Henry James: A Life.* New York: Harper and Row, 1985.

Edwards, Allen. *Flawed Woods and Stubborn Sounds: A Conversation with Elliott Carter.* New York: W. W. Norton, 1971.

"Étincelle." "Mondanités." *Le Figaro,* 17 May 1888, 1.

Faral, Edmond, and Roger Heim. *Les Heures de musique à la Fondation Singer-Polignac.* Paris: Fondation Singer-Polignac, 1966.

Faucigny-Lucinge, Prince Jean-Louis de. *Un Gentilhomme cosmopolite.* Paris: Perrin, 1990.

Fauquet, Joël-Marie, and Antoine Hennion. *La Grandeur de Bach: L'amour de la musique en France au XIXe siècle.* Paris: Fayard, 2000.

Fauré, Gabriel. "Les Concerts: *Échos de l'Orient judaïque* du Prince Edmond de Polignac." *Le Figaro,* 19 April 1905, 5.

———. *Correspondance.* Edited by Jean Michel Nectoux. Paris: Flammarion, 1980.

Translated into English by J. A. Underwood as *Gabriel Faure: His Life through His Letters.* New York: Marion Boyars, 1984.

———. *Lettres intimes.* Edited by Philippe Fauré-Fremiet. Paris: Grasset, 1951.

———. "Souvenirs." *La Revue musicale,* Numéro speciale: Gabriel Fauré, 1924.

Fauser, Annegret. "La Guerre en dentelles: Women and the Prix de Rome in French Cultural Politics." *Journal of the American Musicological Society* 51, no. 1 (Spring 1998): 83–129.

Fearn, Raymond. *Bruno Maderna.* Chur and London: Harwood, 1990.

Fels, H. de. "Les Maisons Ouvrières de la Fondation Polignac-Singer." *La Revue française politique et littéraire,* 1896.

Flanner, Janet. *Paris Was Yesterday, 1925–1939.* New York: Viking Press, 1972.

Fouquier, Baron Michel. *Jours heureux d'autrefois.* Paris: Albin Michel, 1941.

Fouquières, Comte André de. *Cinquante Ans de panache.* Paris: Horay, 1951.

———. *Mon Paris et ses parisiens.* Vols. 1, 3, and 5. Paris: Horay, 1953–59.

Francis, Claude, and Fernande Gontier. *Creating Colette.* 2 vols. South Royalton, Vt.: Steerforth, 1998–99.

Fulcher, Jane F. *French Cultural Politics and Music: From the Dreyfus Affair to the First World War.* New York: Oxford University Press, 1999.

Gallois, Jean, and Isabelle Brétandeau. *Ernest Chausson, choix et présentation des écrits inédits.* Monaco: Éditions du Rocher, 1999.

Garafola, Lynn. *Diaghilev's Ballets Russes.* New York: Oxford University Press, 1989.

Garafola, Lynn, and Nancy Baer. *The Ballets Russes and Its World.* New Haven, Conn.: Yale University Press, 1999.

Gauthier-Villars, Henry [Willy]. "Lettre de l'Ouvreuse." *L'Écho de Paris,* 19 May 1901.

Gavoty, Bernard [Clarendon]. "A la Mémoire de la Princesse de Polignac." *Le Figaro,* December 9, 1965.

———. *Reynaldo Hahn, le musicien de la Belle Epoque.* Paris: Éditions Buchet Chastel, 1976.

———. *Louis Vierne, la vie et l'oeuvre.* Paris: Albin Michel, 1943.

Gerhard, Anselm. *The Urbanization of Opera: Music Theater in Paris in the Nineteenth Century.* Translated by Mary Whitall. Chicago: University of Chicago Press, 1998.

Gillmor, Alan A. *Erik Satie.* Boston: Twayne, 1988.

Gold, Arthur, and Robert Fizdale. *Misia: The Life of Misia Sert.* New York: Knopf, 1980.

Goncourt, Edmond and Jules de. *Journal.* Vol. 20. Monaco: Imprimerie Nationale, 1956.

Goubault, Christian. *Claude Debussy.* Paris: Librairie Honoré Champion, 1986.

Goudeket, Maurice. *Close to Colette: An Intimate Portrait of a Woman of Genius.* New York: Farrar, Straus and Cudahy, 1957.

"Graceful as a Bride." *New York Herald,* 16 December 1893.

Grainger, Percy. *The Far Side of Humanness.* Letters. Edited by Kay Dreyfus. St. Louis: Magnamusic-Baton, Inc., 1985.

Gramont, Élisabeth de. "Un Grand Poète." *Oeuvres Libres,* Nouvelle Série No. 8 (1946).

———. "Une Passion Malheureuse." *La Revue de Paris* 19 (1 October 1931): 592–618.

Green, Julien. *Journal 1928–1958*. Paris: Plon, 1961.

Guiton, Jacques, ed. *The Ideas of Le Corbusier on Architecture and Urban Planning*. Translated by Margaret Guiton. New York: G. Braziller, 1981.

Gumplowicz, Philippe. *Les Travaux d'Orphée, 150 ans de vie musicale amateur en France, Harmonies, chorales, fanfares*. Paris: Aubier, 1987.

Gunn, Peter. *Vernon Lee. Violet Paget, 1856–1935*. London: Oxford University Press, 1964.

Hahn, Reynaldo. *Thèmes variés*. Paris: Jadin, 1946.

Hall, Richard. "Princesse Winnie." *Opera News* 34, nos. 9–10 (27 December 1969–3 January 1970).

Harcourt, Eugène d'. "Un prince musicien." *Le Figaro*, 9 August 1901.

———. "La Reprise de *Pelléas et Mélisande*." *Le Figaro*, 31 October 1902.

Hassall, Christopher. *Edward Marsh: Patron of the Arts*. London: Longmans, 1959.

Hastings, Selina. *Rosamond Lehmann*. London: Chatto and Windus, 2002.

Hauert, Roger, and Bernard Gavoty. *Clara Haskil*. Geneva: René Kistler, 1962.

Haussonville, Comte Paul-Gabriel. "Logis de Pauvres, Pauvres Logis." *La Revue française politique et littéraire*, 1896.

Helleu, Paul. *Catalogue des pointes-sèches d'Helleu*. Paris: Lemercier, 1897.

Hermant, Abel. *Souvenirs de la vie mondaine*. Paris: Hachette, 1935.

Heyworth, Peter, ed. *Conversations with Klemperer*. London: Gollancz, 1973.

Hill, William H., Arthur F. Hill, and Alfred E. Hill. *Antonio Stradivari: His Life and Work, 1644–1737*. New York: Dover, 1963.

———. *The Violin Makers of the Guarneri Family (1626–1762): Their Life and Work*. London: Holland Press, 1965.

Hollis, Howard. *The Best of Both Worlds: A Life of Sir William McKie*. Melbourne: Sir William McKie Memorial Trust, 1991.

Huebner, Steven. *French Opera at the Fin de Siècle: Wagnerism, Nationalism, and Style*. New York: Oxford University Press, 1999.

Hugo, Valentine. "Le Socrate que j'ai connu." *La Revue musicale* 214 (June 1952): 139–45.

Indy, Vincent d', et al. *Le Schola Cantorum: Son histoire depuis sa fondation jusqu'en 1925*. Paris: Librairie Bloud and Gay, 1927.

Ivry, Benjamin. *Maurice Ravel: A Life*. New York: Welcome Rain, 2000.

Jaloux, Edmond. *Les Saisons littéraires*. Vol. 2. Paris: Plon, 1950.

James, Burnett. *Ravel: His Life and Times*. New York: Hippocrene Books, 1983.

Jean-Aubrey, G. "*El Retablo* by Manuel de Falla." *The Chesterian*, New Series no. 34 (October 1923): 37–46.

Johnson, Alva. *The Legendary Mizners*. New York: Farrar, Straus and Giroux, 1953.

Joly, Charles. "Les Oeuvres du Prince Edmond de Polignac au Conservatoire." *Le Figaro*, 17 May 1901, 1.

Jullian, Philippe. *Dreamers of Decadence*. London: Pall Mall, 1971.

———. *Robert de Montesquiou : A Fin-de-Siècle Prince*. Translated by John Haylock and Francis King. London: Secker and Warburg, 1967.

Jullian, Philippe, and John Phillips. *Violet Trefusis: A Biography*. San Diego: Harcourt, Brace, 1976.

Kenney, Annie. *Memories of a Militant*. London: Butler and Tanner, 1924.

Kochno, Boris. *Diaghilev and the Ballets Russes*. Translated by Adrienne Foulke. New York: Harper and Row, 1970.

Koechlin, Charles. "Erik Satie." *La Revue musicale* 5, no. 5 (1 March 1924): 193–207.
———. *Gabriel Fauré*. London: Dennis Dobson Ltd., 1945.
Kurth, Peter. *Isadora: A Sensational Life*. New York: Little, Brown, 2001.
Laloy, Louis. *La Musique retrouvée*. Paris: Plon, 1928.
Landowska, Wanda. *Landowska on Music*. New York: Stein and Day, 1964.
La Rochefoucauld, Duchesse Edmée de. *Images de Paul Valéry*. Strasbourg: Le Roux, 1949.
Lavignac, Albert. *Voyage artistique à Bayreuth*. Paris: Delagrave, 1897.
Léautaud, Paul. *Journal Littéraire*. Vols. 4–5. Paris: Mercure de France, 1957–58.
Le Corbusier. *Vers une Architecture*. Paris: Éditions G. Crès, 1923.
Lees-Milne, James. *Diaries: 1942–1945 (Ancestral Voices; Prophesying Peace)*. London: John Murray, 1995.
Lefol, Gaston. *Grandes Constructions à loyers économiques*. Bibliothèque documentaire de l'architecture. Paris: Massin, ca. 1920.
Lemaître, Georges. *Four French Novelists*. Port Washington, N.Y.: Kennikat Press, 1969.
"Les Compositeurs français en France." *Le Figaro*, 10 April 1890.
Leslie, Seymour. "Music by Night." *Vogue* (London), 11 November 1936, 92–93, 140.
Lesure, François. *Catalogue de l'oeuvre de Claude Debussy*. Geneva: Minkoff, 1977.
———. *Igor Stravinsky: La carrière européenne*. Exhibition catalogue. "Festival d'Automne à Paris," 14 October–30 November 1980, Musée d'Art Moderne de la Ville de Paris. Paris: Presses de l'Imprimerie Union, 1980.
Lewis, R. W. B. *Edith Wharton: A Biography*. New York: Fromm, 1985.
Lifar, Serge. *Ma Vie: From Kiev to Kiev*. Translated by James Holman Mason. Cleveland: World Publishing Company, 1970.
———. "Misia." *La Nouvelle revue des deux mondes*, March 1975.
———. *Serge Diaghilev: His Life, His Work, His Legend: An Intimate Biography*. New York: G. P. Putnam's Sons, 1940.
Lipatti, Anna. *Dinu Lipatti: La douleur de ma vie*. Geneva: Perret-Gentil, 1967
Locke, Ralph. P. "Cutthroats and Casbah Dancers, Muezzins and Timeless Sands: Musical Images of the Middle East." *Nineteenth-Century Music* 22, no. 11 (Summer 1998): 20–53.
Lorrain, Jean. *Monsieur de Phocas*. Introduction by Thibaut d'Anthonay. Paris: Table ronde, 1992.
Madsen, Axel. *Chanel: A Woman of Her Own*. New York: Henry Holt, 1990.
Malipiero, Gian-Carlo. *Strawinsky*. Venice: Cavallino, 1945.
Marinetti, F. T. "Le Manifesto de Futurisme." *Le Figaro*, 20 February 1909.
Mariuz, Adriano. *Giandomenico Tiepolo*. Venice: Alfieri, 1971.
Markevitch, Igor. *Être et avoir été*. Paris: Gallimard, 1980.
———. *Point d'orgue: Entretiens avec Claude Rostand*. Paris: Julliard, 1959.
Marsh, Edward. *A Number of People*. London: Harper, 1939.
Marsh, Edward, and Christopher Hassall. *Ambrosia and Small Beer*. London: Longmans, 1964.
Maurois, André. *Le Monde de Marcel Proust*. Paris: Hachette, 1960.
Maxwell, Elsa. *I Married the World*. London: The Quality Book Club, 1956.
McBrien, William. *Cole Porter: A Biography*. New York: Knopf, 1998.
Mignot-Ogliastri, Claude. *Anna de Noailles, une amie de la Princesse Edmond de Polignac*. Paris: Fondation Singer-Polignac and Méridiens-Klincksieck, 1986.
Milhaud, Darius. *My Happy Life*. Translated from the French by Donald Evans and Christopher Palmer. London; New York: Marion Boyars, 1994.

Mitchell, David. *Queen Christabel*. London: MacDonald and Jane's, 1977.

Monnet, Henri. "Une Symphonie de Kurt Weill à Amsterdam." *Marianne,* 14 November 1934.

Monsaingeon, Bruno. *Mademoiselle*. Translated by Robyn Marsack. Manchester: Carcanet, 1985.

Montesquiou, Robert de. "Cambrioleurs d'âmes (catalogue Romaine Brooks)." In *Têtes d'expression*. Paris: Émile-Paul, 1912, 127–42.

———. *Le Chef des odeurs suaves*. Paris: Georges Richard, 1893.

———. *Paul Helleu, peintre et graveur*. Paris: H. Floury, 1913.

———. "Le Pavé rouge: Quelques réflexions sur l'"Oeuvre' de M. Sargent." In *Altesses sérénissimes,* 83–114. Paris: Société d'Édition et de Publications, Librairie Félix Juven, 1907.

———. *Quarante bergères*. 3rd series, no. 20. Paris: private printing, undated.

Morand, Paul. *L'Allure de Chanel*. Paris: Hermann, 1976.

———. *Journal d'un Attaché d'Ambassade*. Paris: Gallimard, 1996.

Morton, Brian N. *Americans in Paris*. Ann Arbor, Mich.: Olivia and Hill Press, 1984.

Morton, Frederic. *The Rothschilds: A Family Portrait*. New York: Atheneum, 1962.

Mosley, Sir Oswald. *My Life*. London: Thomas Nelson, 1968.

Mugnier, Abbé. *Journal de l'Abbé Mugnier (1879–1939)*. Paris: Mercure de France, 1985.

Munhall, Edgar. *Whistler and Montesquiou*. New York: The Frick Collection, 1995.

Musée du Petit Palais (Paris, France). *Ingres. [Exposition au] Petit Palais. Paris, 27 octobre 1967–29 janvier 1968. Ministère d'État Affaires Culturelles, Ville de Paris*. Paris: Réunion des Musées nationaux, 1967.

Mussy, Georges. "Les Concerts." *Le Figaro,* 19 December 1930.

Myers, Rollo. *Emmanuel Chabrier and His Circle*. London: J. M. Dent, 1969.

———. *Erik Satie*. London: Dennis Dobson, 1948.

Nabokov, Nicolas. *Old Friends and New Music*. London: Hamish Hamilton, 1951.

Nattiez, Jean-Jacques. *Proust musicien*. Paris: Christian Bourgeois, 1999.

Nectoux, Jean-Michel. "Gabriel Fauré." *Le Monde de la musique,* no. 142 (March 1991): 64–70.

———. *Gabriel Fauré: Les voix du clair-obscur*. Paris: Flammarion, 1990.

———. "Le Salon de Marguerite de Saint-Marceaux." In *Une Famille d'artistes en 1900: Les Saint-Marceaux*. Exhibition catalogue, Musée d'Orsay, 62–92. Paris: Éditions de la Réunion des Musées nationaux, 1992.

"News of Americans in Europe." *The New York Herald,* 19 January 1935.

Nichols, Roger. *The Life of Debussy*. Cambridge: Cambridge University Press, 1998.

Nicolson, Nigel. *Portrait of a Marriage*. London: Weidenfeld and Nicolson, 1973.

Nijinsky, Vaslav. *The Diary of Vaslav Nijinsky*. Edited by Romola Nijinsky. Berkeley: University of California Press, 1936.

Noailles, Comtesse Anna de. "Adieux aux Ballets Russes." *La Revue musicale*. Special issue, "Les Ballets Russes de Serge Diaghilew" (1 December 1930): 384–91.

Oleggini, Léon. *Connaissance de Stravinsky*. Lausanne: Foetisch, 1952.

Olson, Stanley. *John Singer Sargent: His Portrait*. London: Barrie & Jenkins, 1989.

Orenstein, Arbie. *Maurice Ravel: Lettres, écrits, entretiens*. Paris: Flammarion, 1989.

———. *Ravel: Man and Musician*. New York: Dover, 1991.

———. *The Ravel Reader.* New York: Columbia University Press, 1990.

Orledge, Robert. "Cole Porter's Ballet 'Within the Quota.'" *Yale University Library Gazette* 50, no.1 (1975).

———. *Gabriel Fauré.* London: Eulenberg, 1979.

———. *Satie the Composer.* Cambridge: Cambridge University Press, 1990.

Ormond, Richard, and Elaine Kilmurray. *John Singer Sargent: The Early Portraits.* Vol. 1 of *Complete Paintings.* New Haven: Yale University Press, 1998.

Pahissa, Jaime et al. *Poesía. Número Monográfico Dedicado A Manuel de Falla.* Edited by Jorge de Persia, nos. 36 and 37 (1991).

———. *Vida y obra de Manuel de Falla.* 2nd edition. Ricordi: Buenos Aires, 1956.

Painter, George D. *Marcel Proust: A Biography.* 2 vols. New York: Vintage Books, 1978.

Paléologue, Maurice. *Journal, 1913–1914.* Paris: Plon, 1947.

Pasler, Jann. "The Ironies of Gender, or Virility and Politics in the Music of Augusta Holmès." *Women and Music* 2 (1998): 1–25.

———. "*Pelléas* and Power: Forces behind the Reception of Debussy's Opera." *Nineteenth-Century Music* 10, no. 3 (Spring 1987): 243–64.

———. "Race, Orientalism, and Distinction in the Wake of the Yellow Peril." In *Western Music and Its Others,* edited by Georgina Born, 86–118. Berkeley: University of California Press, 2000.

Perlemuter, Vlado, and Hélène Jourdan-Morhange, *Ravel according to Ravel.* Translated by Frances Tanner. Edited by Harold Taylor. White Plains, N.Y.: Pro/Am Resources, 1988.

Plaskin, Glenn. *Horowitz.* New York: Quill, 1983.

Polignac, Armande de. "Pensées d'ailleurs." *Le Mercure musical* 1, no. 4 (1 July 1905).

Polignac, Duc Jean-Héracle de. *La Maison de Polignac: Étude d'une évolution sociale de la noblesse.* Le Puy: Éditions Jeanne d'Arc, 1975.

Polignac, Hedwige de. *Les Polignac.* Paris: Fasquelle, 1960.

Polignac, Prince Louis de, ed.. *Hommage à Marie-Blanche, Comtesse Jean de Polignac.* Monaco: Jaspard, Polus, et Cie, 1965.

Polignac, Princesse Edmond de. *Lettres, 1888–1938.* Paris: Fondation Singer-Polignac, 1998.

———. "Memoirs of the Late Princesse Edmond de Polignac." *Horizon* 12, no. 68 (August 1945): 110–40.

———. "Mes Amis musiciens." *La Revue de Paris* 71 (August/September 1964): 97–105.

Popovitch, Olga, editor. *Catalogue des peintures du Musée des beaux-arts de Rouen.* Paris: Arts et Métiers graphiques, 1967.

Porcile, François. "Solfèges." In *Entre Deux Guerres: La création française 1919–1939* , edited by Olivier Barrot and Pascal Ory, 343–62. Paris: François Bourin, 1990.

Pottier, Edmond. "Les Salons de 1892." *Gazette des beaux-arts* (July 1892): 38–39.

Poulenc, Francis. *Correspondance, 1910–1963.* Edited by Myriam Chimènes. Paris: Fayard, 1994.

———. *Emmanuel Chabrier.* Paris: La Palatine, 1961.

———. *My Friends and Myself.* Translated by James Harding. London: Dennis Dobson, 1978.

Pound, Ezra. *The Letters of Ezra Pound, 1907–1941.* New York: Harcourt, Brace, 1950.

————. *Pound/Joyce: The Letters of Ezra Pound to James Joyce.* London: Faber and Faber, 1967.

Pozzi, Catherine. *Journal, 1913–1934.* Paris: Seghers, 1990.

Pringué, Gabriel-Louis. *Portraits et fantômes.* Monaco: R. Solar, 1951.

————. *Trente Ans de diners en ville.* Paris: Revue Adam, 1948.

Prokofiev, Sergei. *Dnevnik, 1907–1933.* Paris: sprkfv, 2002.

Proust, Marcel. *Autour de soixante lettres de Marcel Proust, par Lucien Daudet. Cahiers Marcel Proust No. 5.* Paris: Gallimard, 1929.

————. *Correspondance de Marcel Proust.* Edited by Philip Kolb. 20 vols. Paris: Plon, 1970–93.

————. "Le Salon de la Comtesse Aimery de La Rochefoucauld." *Cahiers Marcel Proust No. 3, Textes retrouvés.* Edited by Philip Kolb. Paris: Gallimard, 1971.

———— [Horatio]. "La Comtesse de Guerne," *Le Figaro,* 7 May 1905.

———— [Horatio], "Le Salon de la Princesse Edmond de Polignac: Musique d'aujourd'hui; échos d'autrefois." *Le Figaro,* 6 September 1903.

Prunières, Henry. "Chroniques et Notes: Ballet *Urashima* par Armande de Polignac."*La Revue musicale* 7, no. 4 (1 February 1926): 147–48.

————. "Chroniques et Notes: Concert des oeuvres dediées à la Princesse Edmond de Polignac." *La Revue musicale* 14, no. 135 (April 1933): 283–84.

————. "Chroniques et Notes: Concert Igor Stravinsky." *La Revue musicale* 14, no. 133 (February 1933): 129.

————. "Chroniques et Notes: Le Festival de Venise." *La Revue musicale* 14, no. 130 (November 1932): 312–17.

————. "Chroniques et Notes: Oeuvres de Kurt Weill." *La Revue musicale* 14, no. 132 (January 1933): 45–47.

————."Chroniques et Notes: 'Serenade': Oeuvres de Berg, Sauguet, Poulenc, Milhaud." *La Revue musicale* 14, no. 134 (March 1933): 211–12.

————. "Chroniques et Notes: Le Troisième Festival de La S.I.M.C. à Venise (3–8 September 1925)." *La Revue musicale* 6, no. 11 (1 October 1925): 252–59.

————. "Chroniques et Notes: Vladimir Horowitz—Concert." *La Revue musicale* 7, no. 6 (1 April 1926): 69–70.

Quennell, Peter. "Review: *The Food of Love* by Michael de Cossart." *The Financial Times of London,* 30 March 1978.

Quittard, Henri. "Courrier des Théâtres: Les Concerts." *Le Figaro,* 9 May 1914.

————. "Courrier des Théâtres: Loïe Fuller au Châtelet." *Le Figaro,* 11 May 1914.

————. "Théâtre du Châtelet, *La Pisanelle* ou *La Mort parfumée.*" *Le Figaro,* 13 June 1913.

Rachewiltz, Mary, Princesse Boris de. *Discretions.* London: Faber and Faber, 1971.

Radnor, Helen, Countess Dowager of. *From a Great-Grandmother's Armchair.* London: Marshall Press, 1927.

Ragot, Gilles, and Mathilde Dion. *Le Corbusier en France: Réalisations et projets.* Paris: Electra Moniteur, 1987.

Rees, Brian. *Camille Saint-Saëns: A Life.* London: Chatto and Windus, 1999.

Régnier, Henri de. *L'Altana ou la vie vénitienne 1899–1924.* Vol. 2. Paris: Mercure de France, 1928.

Richardière, A. "Une Maison ouvrière." *L'Architecture,* January 1913, 1–2.

Roberts, Cecil. *The Bright Twenties.* London: Hodder and Stoughton, 1970.

———. *The Growing Boy.* London: Hodder and Stoughton, 1967.

Robin-Harmel, Pierre. *Prince Jules de Polignac, Ministre de Charles X (1780–1847).* Paris: Aubanel Père, 1950.

Robinson, Harlow. *Sergei Prokofiev.* New York: Viking, 1987.

Rodriguez; Suzanne. *Wild Heart: A Life—Natalie Clifford Barney's Journey from Victorian American to Belle Époque Paris.* New York: Harper Collins/Ecco, 2002.

Rogers, W. G. *Ladies Bountiful.* New York: Harcourt, Brace, 1968.

Rorem, Ned. *Knowing When to Stop.* New York: Simon and Schuster, 1994.

———. "Notes on Weill." *Opera News,* 21 January 1984, 12–24.

Rose, Sir Francis. *Saying Life.* London: Cassell, 1961.

Rostand, Claude. *Francis Poulenc: Entretiens avec Claude Rostand.* Paris: Julliard, 1954.

Rostand, Maurice. *Confessions d'un demi-siècle.* Paris: Jeune Parque, 1948.

Rubinstein, Arthur. *My Many Years.* New York: Knopf, 1980.

———. *My Young Years.* New York: Knopf, 1973.

Rumbold, Sir Horace. *Recollections of a Diplomatist.* 2 vols. London: Arnold, 1903.

Ruppel, K. H. "Die Prinzessin Edmond de Polignac." *Melos* 34 (June 1967): 198–203. Also published as "Musikalische Avantgarde im feudalen Salon: Die Prinzessin Edmond de Polignac und ihr Pariser Kreis." *Suddeutsche Zeitung* 296 (22–23 December 1979): 79.

Sachs, Harvey. *Rubinstein: A Life.* New York: Grove Press, 1995.

Sachs, Maurice. *Au Temps du Boeuf sur le Toit.* Paris: Nouvelle Revue Critique, 1948.

———. *La Décade de l'illusion.* Paris: Gallimard, 1950.

Sackville-West, Vita, and Harold Nicolson. *Vita and Harold: The Letters of Vita Sackville-West and Harold Nicolson.* Edited by Nigel Nicolson. New York: G. P. Putnam's Sons, 1992.

"Saint-Loup." "Les Mystères de l'atelier ou une heure de musique chez la princesse Edmond de Polignac." *L'Ordre,* 27 May 1939.

St. John, Christopher. *Ethel Smyth.* London: Longmans, Green, 1959.

Samson, Jim. *The Music of Szymanowski.* New York: Taplinger, 1981.

Sanders, Ronald. *The Days Grow Short: The Life and Music of Kurt Weill.* New York: Holt, Rinehart and Winston, 1980.

Satie, Erik. *Correspondance presque complète.* Edited by Ornella Volta. Paris: Fayard, 2000.

Sauguet, Henri. *La Musique, ma Vie.* Paris: Librairie Séguer, 1990.

Schaeffner, André. "Cinquantenaire de la Société française de musicologie (allocution du 26 janvier 1967)." *Revue de musicologie* 53, no. 2 (1967): 103–9.

Schebra, Jürgen. *Kurt Weill in Texten, Bildern und Dokumenten.* Leipzig: Deutscher Verlag für Musik, 1990.

Schiff, David. *The Music of Elliott Carter.* New York: Da Capo Press, 1985.

Schloezer, Boris de. "Chroniques et Notes: Concerto de Piano, par Germaine Tailleferre." *La Revue musicale* 6, no. 9 (1 July 1925): 62–63.

———. "Chroniques et Notes: Concerto de Stravinsky." *La Revue musicale* 5, no. 9 (1 July 1924): 61–62.

———. "Chroniques et Notes: Concerto pour piano, de Jean Wiéner (Pasdeloup)." *La Revue musicale* 6, no. 2 (1 December 1924): 150–51.

———. "Chroniques et Notes: 'El Retablo' de Manuel de Falla (Concert Wiéner)." *La Revue musicale* 5, no. 2 (1 December 1924): 171–72.

———. "Darius Milhaud." *La Revue musicale* 6, no. 5 (1 March 1925): 252–76.

Schonberg, Harold. *Horowitz: His Life and Music.* New York: Simon and Schuster, 1992.

Secrest, Meryle. *Between Me and Life.* New York: MacDonald and Janes, 1974.

Servières, Georges. "Musique." *La Revue indépendante* 23, no. 66 (April 1892): 130–31.

Sharpe, Henrietta. *A Solitary Woman: A Life of Violet Trefusis.* London: Constable, 1981.

Shattuck, Roger. *The Banquet Years.* London: Faber and Faber, 1958.

Shuster-Fournier, Carolyn. "Les Orgues Cavaié-Coll au salon, au théâtre et au concert." Ph.D. diss., Université François-Rabelais de Tours, 1991.

———. "Les Orgues de salon d'Aristide Cavaillé-Coll." *L'Orgue, cahiers et mémoires* 57–58 (1997): 93–99.

Simier, Amélie. "Jean-Joseph Carriès, sculpteur-potier au coeur du symbolisme." In *Paris 1900 dans les collections du Petit Palais—Musée des Beaux-Arts de la Ville de Paris.* Exhibition catalogue, Musée d'Ixelles (Belgium), 112–16. Brussels: Marot, 2002.

"Singer and His Families." *The New York World,* 2 September 1887.

Siohan, Robert. *Stravinsky.* Translated by Eric Walter White. New York: Grossman, 1970.

Smyth, Ethyl. *As Time Went On. . . .* London: Longmans, Green, 1936.

———. *The Memoirs of Ethel Smyth.* Abridged and introduced by Ronald Crichton. With a list of works by Jory Bennett. New York: Viking, 1987.

———. *What Happened Next.* London: Longman, Green, 1940.

Souhami, Diana. *Mrs. Keppel and Her Daughter.* New York: St. Martin's Press, 1996.

Spycket, Jérôme. *Clara Haskil.* Lausanne: Payot, 1975.

———. *Nadia Boulanger.* Lausanne: Payot, 1987.

Steegmuller, Francis. *Cocteau: A Biography.* Boston: Little, Brown, 1970.

Stein, Gertrude. *The Autobiography of Alice B. Toklas.* New York: Vintage Books, 1960.

Storrs, Sir Ronald. *Orientations.* London: Nicholson and Watson, 1943.

Stravinsky, Igor. *An Autobiography.* New York: The Norton Library, 1962.

———. *Selected Correspondence.* Edited by Robert Craft. 3 vols. New York: Knopf, 1982–85.

Stravinsky, Igor, and Robert Craft. *Conversations with Igor Stravinsky.* Garden City, N.Y.: Doubleday, 1959.

———. *Dialogues and a Diary.* Garden City, N.Y.: Doubleday, 1963.

———. *Expositions and Developments.* Garden City, N.Y.: Doubleday, 1962.

———. *Memories and Commentaries.* Berkeley: University of California Press, 1981.

Stravinsky, Vera. *Dearest Bubushkin: Selected Diaries of Vera and Igor Stravinsky.* Edited by Robert Craft. New York: Thames and Hudson, 1985.

Stravinsky, Vera, and Robert Craft. *Stravinsky in Pictures and Documents.* New York: Simon and Schuster, 1978.

Szymanowski, Karol, and Jan Smeterlin. *Correspondence.* Translated and edited by B. M. Maciejewski and Felix Aprahamian. London: Allegro Press, 1969.

Tadié, Jean-Yves. *Marcel Proust: A Life*. Translated by Euen Cameron. New York: Viking, 2000.

Tapert, Annette, and Diana Edkins. *The Power of Style: The Women Who Defined the Art of Living Well*. New York: Crown, 1994.

Tardif, Cécile. "Fauré and the Salons." In *Regarding Fauré*, edited and translated by Tom Gordon, 1–14. Newark, N.J.: Gordon and Breach, 1999.

———. "Les Salons de musique à Paris sous la Troisième République." Masters' thesis, Université de Montréal, 1994.

Taricat, Jean, and Martine Villars. *Le Logement à bon marché: Chronique, Paris 1850–1930*. Boulogne: Apogée, 1928.

Taruskin, Richard. *Defining Russia Musically*. Princeton, N.J.: Princeton University Press, 1997.

———. *Stravinsky and the Russian Traditions: A Biography of the Works through "Mavra."* 2 vols. Berkeley and Los Angeles: University of California Press, 1996.

———. "Stravinsky's Angle." *Journal of the American Musicological Society* 38, no. 1 (Spring 1985): 72–142.

Tzara, Tristan, "What We Are Doing in Europe." *Vanity Fair* (September 1922), 67.

Taylor, Brian Brace. *Le Corbusier: The City of Refuge, 1929–33*. Chicago: University of Chicago Press, 1987.

Thomson, Andrew. *Vincent d'Indy and His World*. Oxford: Clarendon Press, 1996.

Thomson, Virgil. *Virgil Thomson*. New York: Da Capo Press, 1966.

Thoreau, Henry David. *Walden, or Life in the Woods*. New York: Signet, 1960.

———. "Walden, ou la vie dans les bois." Translated by Winnaretta Singer, *La Renaissance latine* 2, no. 12 (15 December 1903): 577–98, and 3, no. 1 (15 January 1904): 133–46.

Tomkins, Calvin. *Living Well Is the Best Revenge*. New York: Viking Press, 1962.

Trefusis, Violet. *Don't Look Round*. London: Hutchinson, 1952.

Trend, John. *Manuel de Falla and Spanish Music*. New York: Knopf, 1934.

Tuchman, Barbara W. *The Proud Tower: A Portrait of the World before the War, 1890–1914*. New York: Macmillan, 1966.

Vallas, Léon. *Claude Debussy: His Life and Works*. Translated by Maire and Grace O'Brien. New York: Dover, 1973.

Vaudoyer, Jean-Louis. "P.-J. Toulet et Madame Bulteau." *La Revue de Paris* 3, no. 12 (15 June 1924): 800–809.

Vio, Gastone. *I Quaderni della Parrocchia di Santa Maria del Rosario (vulgo Gesuati) Venezia. L'organo della Chiesa parrochiale: da don Pietro Nacchini ai Bazzani*. Venice: private printing, 1982.

Volta, Ornella. *Satie Seen through His Letters*. Translated by Michael Bullock. New York: Marion Boyars, 1989.

———. *L'Ymagier d'Erik Satie*. Paris: Van der Velde, 1979.

Wagner, Richard. *My Life*. Translated by Andrew Gray, edited by Mary Whittall. New York: Da Capo Press, 1992.

———. *Wagner Werk-Verzeichnis [WWV]: Verzeichnis der musikalischen Werke Richard Wagners und ihrer Quellen: erarbeitet im Rahmen der Richard Wagner-Gesamtausgabe*. Edited by John Deathridge, Martin Geck, Egon Voss; redaktionelle Mitarbeit, Isolde Vetter. Mainz, New York: Schott, 1986.

Wagstaff, John. *André Messager: A Bio-Bibliography*. New York: Greenwood Press, 1991.

Walsh, Stephen. *Stravinsky: A Creative Spring: Russia and France, 1882–1934.* New York: Knopf, 1999.

Weill, Kurt, and Lotte Lenya. *Speak Low (When You Speak Love).* Edited and translated by Lys Symonette and Kim H. Kowalke. Berkeley: University of California Press, 1996.

Wentworth, Michael. *James Tissot.* Oxford: Clarendon Press, 1984.

Wharton, Edith. *The Letters of Edith Wharton.* Edited by R. W. B. Lewis and Nancy Lewis. New York: Collier, 1988.

White, Edmund. *Marcel Proust.* New York: Viking, 1999.

White, Eric Walter. *Stravinsky: The Composer and His Works.* Berkeley: University of California Press, 1966.

———. *Stravinsky's Sacrifice to Apollo.* London: Hogarth, 1930.

Wickes, George. *The Life and Loves of Natalie Barney.* New York: G. P. Putnam's Sons, 1976.

Wiéner, Jean. *Allegro Appassionato.* Paris: Pierre Belfond, 1978.

Wildenstein, Daniel. *Monet ou le triomphe de l'Impressionisme.* 4 vols. Cologne: Taschen, 1996.

Wilton, Andrew, and Robert Upstone, eds. *The Age of Rossetti, Burne-Jones and Watts: Symbolism in Britain 1860–1910.* London: Tate Gallery, 1997.

Wood, Christopher. *Tissot.* London: Weidenfeld and Nicolson, 1986.

Wood, Elizabeth. "Sapphonics." In *Queering the Pitch: The New Gay and Lesbian Musicology,* edited by Philip Brett, Elizabeth Wood, and Gary C. Thomas, 27–66. New York: Routledge, 1994.

Woolf, Virginia. *Diary of Virginia Woolf.* Vol. 5: *1936–1941.* Edited by Anne Olivier Bell. New York: Harcourt, Brace Jovanovitch, 1984.

———. *The Letters of Virginia Woolf.* Vols. 5 and 6. Edited by Nigel Nicolson. New York: Harcourt, Brace, Jovanovitch, 1979–80.

Yriarte, Charles. "Beaux Arts: Troisième Exposition des Femmes Artistes." *Le Figaro,* 16 January 1895, 2.

Zamoyski, Adam. *Paderewski.* New York: Atheneum, 1982.

Index

The index below treats the main text of the book, not the appendices or notes. Appendix B serves as an index of the guests who attended the musical events listed in Appendix A.

Music's Modern Muse:
A Life of Winnaretta Singer, Princesse de Polignac

The American-born Winnaretta Singer (1865–1943) was a millionaire at the age of eighteen, due to her inheriting a substantial part of the Singer Sewing Machine fortune. Living in Paris, she quickly became active in musical life there, holding the premier avant-garde musical salon in her home from 1888 to 1939. Her 1893 marriage to Prince Edmond de Polignac, an amateur composer, brought her into contact with the most elite strata of French society.

After Edmond's death in 1901, she used her fortune to benefit the arts, sciences, and letters. Her most significant contribution was in the musical domain: in addition to subsidizing individual artists (Boulanger, Haskil, Rubinstein, Horowitz) and organizations (the Ballets Russes, l'Opéra de Paris, l'Orchestre Symphonique de Paris), she made a lifelong project of commissioning new musical works from composers, many of them un-known and struggling, to be performed in her salon. The list of works created as a result is long and extraordinary, and includes works by Stravinsky, Satie, Falla, and Poulenc. In addition, her salon was a gathering place for luminaries of French culture, among them Proust, Cocteau, Diaghilev, and Colette. Many of Proust's memorable evocations of salon culture were born during his attendance of concerts in the Polignac music room.

In addition to playing piano and organ, Singer-Polignac enjoyed some success as a painter: a number of her canvases were accepted for annual exhibitions of the Académie des Beaux-Arts. She supported the work of several women composers, including Ethel Smyth and Adela Maddison, using her influence to have their operas mounted in major European the-aters. After her death her legacy of enlightened generosity was carried on through the work of the Fondation Singer-Polignac.

Sylvia Kahan brings to life this passionate and powerful lover of the arts, whose influence on the twentieth-century world of music and litera-ture remains incalculable.

Sylvia Kahan, a pianist and scholar, is on the faculties of the City University of New York's Graduate Center and College of Staten Island. At the latter, she serves as Chair of the Department of Performing and Creative Arts.

Praise for *Music's Modern Muse*:

"As a frequenter in the 1950s of the last vestiges of the Proustian milieu depicted in *Music's Modern Muse,* I can vouch for the authenticity and scope of Sylvia Kahan's very readable portrait."
  —Ned Rorem, Pulitzer Prize–winning composer and author

"Sylvia Kahan's book gives a real sense of the birth of modern French music, and of what it must have felt like to be Winnie—to know everyone and to exercise a unique and autocratic power."
  —Ruth Brandon, author of *Singer and the Sewing Machine: A Capitalist Romance*

"*Music's Modern Muse* is an extraordinarily lively, richly detailed biography of one of the Belle Époque's most important musical patrons."
  —Jann Pasler, Professor of Music, University of California at San Diego

"Kahan's book is essential reading for anyone with an interest in French music from Gounod to Poulenc."
  —Steven Huebner, Professor of Musicology, McGill University